Criminal Litigation

Criminal Litigation

MARTIN HANNIBAL

LISA MOUNTFORD

OXFORD
UNIVERSITY PRESS

OXFORD
UNIVERSITY PRESS

Great Clarendon Street, Oxford, OX2 6DP,
United Kingdom

Oxford University Press is a department of the University of Oxford.
It furthers the University's objective of excellence in research, scholarship,
and education by publishing worldwide. Oxford is a registered trade mark of
Oxford University Press in the UK and in certain other countries

© Martin Hannibal and Lisa Mountford 2019

The moral rights of the authors have been asserted

Twelfth edition 2016
Thirteenth edition 2017
Fourteenth edition 2018

Impression: 1

Public sector information reproduced under Open Government Licence v3.0
(http://www.nationalarchives.gov.uk/doc/open-government-licence/open-government-licence.htm)

Published in the United States of America by Oxford University Press
198 Madison Avenue, New York, NY 10016, United States of America

British Library Cataloguing in Publication Data
Data available

ISBN 978–0–19–883854–8

Printed in Great Britain by
Bell & Bain Ltd., Glasgow

CONTENTS

Guided tour of the book   xiv
Guided tour of the online resources   xvi
Online resources contents   xviii
Foreword   xix
Preface   xx
Acknowledgements   xxii
Table of cases   xxiii
Table of legislation and other instruments   xxvii

Part I	**INTRODUCTION TO CRIMINAL LITIGATION**	**1**

1	**Introduction**	**3**
1.1	Introduction	4
1.2	Philosophy of *Criminal Litigation*	5
1.3	Online resources	6
1.4	Research sources	7
1.5	Classifying criminal offences	8
1.6	Personnel and organisations within the criminal justice system	9
1.7	The criminal courts and personnel	10
1.8	The European Convention on Human Rights 1950 (ECHR 1950)	13
1.9	Criminal Procedure Rules (Crim PR) 2015	15
1.10	Professional conduct—an introduction	17

2	**An Introduction to the Law of Criminal Evidence and Advocacy**	**33**
2.1	Introduction	33
2.2	The purpose of the law of criminal evidence	34
2.3	Facts in issue	34
2.4	Core concepts	34
2.5	Procedure for deciding the admissibility of disputed evidence	36
2.6	Assessing the evidence—the prosecuting solicitor's role	36
2.7	Assessing the evidence—the defence solicitor's role	37
2.8	Types of evidence	37
2.9	Clarifying the evidential issues	38
2.10	Concluding remarks on criminal evidence	39
2.11	Advocacy	39

Part II	**INVESTIGATION AND THE DECISION TO CHARGE**	**45**

3	**The Powers to Stop, Search and Arrest**	**47**
3.1	Introduction	47
3.2	Stop and search before arrest	48
3.3	Stop and search at common law	48
3.4	Statutory powers to stop and search in a public place before arrest	48
3.5	Specific powers to stop and search before arrest	50
3.6	The consequences of an unlawful stop and search	50
3.7	Powers of arrest	51
3.8	Street bail	56
3.9	Searching the suspect's person and/or property upon arrest	56
3.10	The European Convention on Human Rights 1950	60

4	**Detention and Interrogation**	**63**
4.1	Introduction	64
4.2	Interviewing a volunteer at the police station or elsewhere	65
4.3	Action immediately following arrest	66
4.4	The role of the custody officer	66
4.5	Detention without charge (following arrest)	69
4.6	Reviewing a suspect's detention	70
4.7	The suspect's right to intimation and/or legal advice	72
4.8	Other rights and safeguards enjoyed by the suspect whilst in detention	75
4.9	The treatment of vulnerable suspects and the provision of an appropriate adult (AA)	75
4.10	Interviewing the suspect	77
4.11	The requirement to caution	78
4.12	What constitutes a fair interview?	79
4.13	How should an interview be recorded?	80
4.14	Charging a suspect	80
4.15	Concluding remarks	84

5	**The Right to Silence at the Police Station**	**87**
5.1	Introduction	87
5.2	What are the risks associated with s. 34 CJPOA 1994?	88
5.3	Drawing inferences from a failure to account under ss. 36 and 37 CJPOA 1994	92
5.4	The practical aspects associated with remaining silent	94

6	**Challenging Unlawfully and Unfairly Obtained Evidence**	**98**
6.1	Introduction	98
6.2	What is unlawfully or unfairly obtained evidence?	99
6.3	What is a confession?	99
6.4	A suspect's rights at the police station	100
6.5	Challenging the admissibility of a confession under ss. 76 and 78 PACE 1984	101
6.6	The procedure for determining the admissibility of a confession	104
6.7	Editing a confession	104
6.8	Evidence obtained in consequence of an inadmissible confession	104
6.9	Challenging the admissibility of other non-confession prosecution evidence	105
6.10	Common law discretion	105
6.11	Discretion under s. 78 PACE 1984	105
6.12	Abuse of process	108
6.13	Illegally/unfairly obtained evidence—practical considerations	108

7	**Obtaining Identification Evidence**	**113**
7.1	Introduction	113
7.2	The dangers of eye-witness identification	114
7.3	How is eye-witness identification obtained?	114
7.4	Distinguishing between known and unknown suspects	114
7.5	When must an identification procedure be held?	115
7.6	Is a formal identification procedure a mandatory requirement?	117
7.7	The formal identification procedures	119
7.8	The consequences of failing to comply with Code D	120
7.9	Recognition by police officers from photographic and CCTV images	121
7.10	Voice identification	121
7.11	Dock identifications	121
7.12	Forensic identification procedures	122
7.13	Dna evidence	124
7.14	Facial mapping	124
7.15	The practical issues associated with identification evidence	125

8   **The Decision to Prosecute and the Prosecution's Duties
of Disclosure of Evidence**   **128**

8.1   Introduction   129
8.2   Statutory charging under the CJA 2003   130
8.3   CPS prosecuting policies   135
8.4   The threshold test   136
8.5   The selection of charges—section 6, Code for Crown Prosecutors   137
8.6   Alternatives to prosecution   138
8.7   The defence solicitor influencing the decision to charge   140
8.8   Pre-trial disclosure of evidence—an introduction   141
8.9   Used and unused material   143
8.10 Disclosure obligations on the police   143
8.11 The CPS obligation to disclose 'used' material—'IDPC'
      (Initial Details of the Prosecution Case)   145
8.12 CPS obligations to disclose unused material (Crim PR, Part 15)   146
8.13 Disclosing information held by third parties   148
8.14 Withholding relevant evidence   148
8.15 Further information on disclosure   149

Part III   FROM CHARGE TO TRIAL   **157**

9   **Funding of Criminal Defence Services and
First Appearance Process**   **159**

9.1   Introduction   160
9.2   Legal aid—a human right?   160
9.3   Legal aid agency   160
9.4   Pre-charge advice and assistance   161
9.5   Funded representation in court   161
9.6   Representation orders   162
9.7   The interests of justice test (CRM14)   162
9.8   Means testing (CRM15)   166
9.9   The means test as applied to cases tried in the magistrates' court   166
9.10 The means test in cases triable on indictment   169
9.11 What work can be done under a representation order?   171
9.12 Disbursements   171
9.13 Acquitted defendants and Defendants' Costs Order   172
9.14 Wasted costs   172
9.15 First appearance before the magistrates' court in summary-only
      and either-way offences   172
9.16 Preparing for the first appearance before the magistrates' court   175

10 **The Law and Practice Relating to Court Bail**   **181**

10.1 Introduction   181
10.2 What is bail?   182
10.3 A right to bail?   182
10.4 Section 25 CJPOA 1994   183
10.5 Grounds for refusing bail   183
10.6 Grounds for denying bail for an indictable imprisonable offence
      (Sch. 1 Part 1 para. 2 BA 1976)   183
10.7 Substantiating the grounds for opposing bail—the statutory factors
      (Sch. 1 Para. 9 BA 1976)   186
10.8 Grounds for denying bail for a summary-only imprisonable offence
      (Sch. 1 Part 1A)   187
10.9 Grounds for denying bail for a non-imprisonable offence (Sch. 1 Part II)   187

10.10	Bail conditions	188
10.11	Bail in practice	190
10.12	Procedure at a contested bail hearing	192
10.13	Remand periods	193
10.14	How many bail applications can be made?	194
10.15	Where bail is refused	194
10.16	Appeal by the prosecution	195
10.17	Reconsidering bail	195
10.18	Varying bail conditions	195
10.19	Where an accused fails to surrender to bail	196
10.20	Bail granted by the Crown Court	196
10.21	Bail and the High Court	197
10.22	Human rights and bail	197
10.23	Bail—the practical considerations	197

11	**Prosecuting an Either-Way Offence**	**203**
11.1	Introduction	203
11.2	Plea before venue	204
11.3	The allocation hearing—ss.17–20 MCA 1980	205
11.4	The reasons for electing trial in the magistrates' court or in the Crown Court	210
11.5	The special procedure in criminal damage cases	212
11.6	Special rules relating to certain either-way offences	212
11.7	Sending an either-way offence to the Crown Court	212
11.8	Post-allocation matters where case is to be sent to the Crown Court	214
11.9	Application for dismissal of the either-way offence sent to the Crown Court	215
11.10	Changing the allocation decision	216

12	**Prosecuting Summary Offences**	**220**
12.1	Introduction	220
12.2	Commencing a prosecution in the magistrates' court	221
12.3	Pleading guilty by post	222
12.4	Defendant unaware of court proceedings	222
12.5	Joinder of offences and defendants in the information	222
12.6	The early stages of a summary-only/either-way offence	224
12.7	Preparing for trial (defence perspective)	226
12.8	Preparing for trial (prosecution perspective)	229
12.9	Rights of audience before magistrates' court and terms of address	230
12.10	Failure of the defendant to attend trial	230
12.11	The procedure at a summary trial on a not guilty plea	230

13	**Crown Court Proceedings Pre-Trial**	**242**
13.1	Introduction	243
13.2	The Digital Case System (DCS)	243
13.3	The defendant's first court appearance for an indictable-only offence—s. 51 Crime and Disorder Act 1998	244
13.4	Better Case Management (BCM)	245
13.5	The Plea and Trial Preparation Hearing (PTPH)	246
13.6	Crown Court bail	249
13.7	Preparatory steps in the early stages of an indictable-only offence	249
13.8	Disclosing 'used' material in indictable-only cases	249
13.9	Disclosing 'unused' material—CPIA 1996	250
13.10	What if the pre-trial disclosure of evidence reveals a weak prosecution case?	255
13.11	Preparatory hearings	255
13.12	Preparing for trial	256

14	**Trial Before the Crown Court**	**273**
14.1	Introduction	274

14.2	The indictment	274
14.3	Supporting the advocate at trial	277
14.4	Last-minute checklist	277
14.5	First day of the trial	278
14.6	Plea bargaining	278
14.7	Arraignment and pleas	279
14.8	During the trial	280
14.9	The course of trial on indictment—Crim PR, Part 25.9	281
14.10	The course of trial—Presenting evidence—Crim PR, Part 25.11	282
14.11	Defence submission of no case to answer	284
14.12	The defence case	284
14.13	The closing speeches	285
14.14	The summing-up and directing the jury—Crim PR, Part 25.14	285
14.15	The verdict	287
14.16	The procedure after the jury's decision—Crim PR, Part 25.16	288
14.17	Acquitted defendants	288
14.18	The prosecution's right of appeal	288
14.19	Judge-only trials on indictment	289

Part iv PROVING THE CASE—THE RULES OF CRIMINAL EVIDENCE

Part iv PROVING THE CASE—THE RULES OF CRIMINAL EVIDENCE — **291**

15	**The Burden of Proof**	**293**
15.1	Introduction	293
15.2	The legal burden of proof—the general rule	293
15.3	Exceptions to woolmington—reverse burden clauses	294
15.4	The standard of proof required to discharge the legal burden	295
15.5	The evidential burden	295
15.6	Discharging the legal and evidential burdens of proof—an example	296
15.7	Challenges to reverse burden clauses under Article 6 European Convention on Human Rights 1950 (ECHR 1950)	296
15.8	Formal admissions—s. 10 CJA 1967	297
15.9	Burdens of proof—practical considerations	298

16	**Witness Evidence**	**300**
16.1	Introduction	300
16.2	Dealing with witnesses before testifying	301
16.3	Witness evidence—the preliminary issues	301
16.4	Testifying under a special measures direction	304
16.5	Types of special measures	305
16.6	The practical issues of witness evidence	308
16.7	Taking the oath or affirming	309
16.8	Examination-in-chief	309
16.9	Cross-examination	313
16.10	Cross-examining the witness on his physical or mental disability	317
16.11	Re-examination	318
16.12	Cross-examining the complainant in a sexual offence	318

17	**Corroboration, the '*Turnbull* Guidelines' and Opinion Evidence**	**323**
17.1	Introduction	323
17.2	What is meant by corroboration?	324
17.3	Corroboration required as a matter of law	324
17.4	Corroboration and the exercise of judicial discretion	324
17.5	The requirements of corroborative evidence	326
17.6	The '*Turnbull* Guidelines'	326
17.7	Opinion evidence	330

17.8	Facts personally perceived by the witness	330
17.9	Expert witnesses	330
17.10	Expert evidence—practical considerations	333

18	**Hearsay Evidence**	**337**
18.1	Introduction	337
18.2	Hearsay evidence—the general rule	338
18.3	Identifying hearsay evidence	338
18.4	The statutory exceptions to the hearsay rule	341
18.5	Hearsay evidence under the CJA 2003	341
18.6	The unavailable witness—s. 116 (first-hand hearsay)	342
18.7	Business documents—s. 117	344
18.8	Hearsay admissible under the preserved common law rules—s. 118 CJA 2003	345
18.9	Admitting hearsay by agreement—s. 114(1)(c) CJA 2003	347
18.10	The 'safety-valve'—s. 114(1)(d) and s. 121 CJA 2003	347
18.11	Miscellaneous hearsay provisions	349
18.12	Important safeguards when admitting hearsay evidence	349
18.13	Procedure for admitting hearsay evidence—Crim PR, Part 20	351
18.14	Hearsay evidence and the ECHR 1950	351
18.15	Hearsay evidence—trial considerations	353

19	**Character Evidence and the Accused as a Witness at Trial**	**355**
19.1	Introduction	355
19.2	The accused as a competent defence witness	356
19.3	The course of the defendant's evidence	356
19.4	Adverse inferences from the defendant's silence at trial—s. 35 CJPOA 1994	357
19.5	Disclosing evidence of the defendant's character	359
19.6	Admitting evidence of the defendant's bad character	361
19.7	Gateways to admission	362
19.8	Bad character admitted between co-defendants—s. 101(1)(e) CJA 2003	371
19.9	Bad character to correct a false impression given by the defendant—s. 101(1)(f) CJA 2003	374
19.10	Bad character admitted under s. 101(1)(g) CJA 2003	375
19.11	The practice and procedure for admitting evidence of a defendant's bad character	377
19.12	Relevance and use that can be made of bad character adduced under s. 101 and the importance of the direction to the jury	378
19.13	Miscellaneous matters	379

20	**Private Privilege**	**382**
20.1	Introduction	382
20.2	Legal professional privilege in criminal cases	383
20.3	The rationale for legal professional privilege	384
20.4	Legal professional privilege and the courts	384
20.5	Waiving/losing legal professional privilege	385
20.6	Powers of search and legal professional privilege	386
20.7	The privilege against self-incrimination	386

Part V	**POST-CONVICTION: SENTENCING AND APPEALS**	**389**

21	**Sentencing Procedure and the General Principles of Sentencing**	**391**
21.1	Introduction	391
21.2	New developments—warning	392
21.3	The role of the CPS on sentence	392
21.4	The procedure on sentencing	393
21.5	Hierarchy of sentences	394

21.6   Sentencing aims   395
21.7   The basis of sentencing under the CJA 2003   395
21.8   Sentencing Council for England and Wales   396
21.9   Sentencing guidelines in the Crown Court   399
21.10   How does the defence solicitor assess the seriousness of an offence?   399
21.11   Magistrates' Court Sentencing Guidelines (MCSGs 2017)   399
21.12   Personal offender mitigation   400
21.13   Discount for timely guilty pleas   400
21.14   What constrains sentencing?   401
21.15   The Crown Court's sentencing powers   402
21.16   What informs the process of sentencing?   403
21.17   Victim impact statements   404
21.18   Taking other offences into consideration   404

22   Specific Types of Sentence and the Plea in Mitigation   409
22.1   Introduction   410
22.2   When can a discretionary custodial sentence be imposed?   410
22.3   Custody between the ages of 18 and 21   411
22.4   Length of custodial sentence   411
22.5   Suspended sentence of imprisonment   414
22.6   Concluding remarks on discretionary custodial sentences
         with reference to SC guidelines   414
22.7   Fixed-length sentences   415
22.8   Sentencing dangerous offenders   415
22.9   Community sentences   419
22.10   Community sentences under the CJA 2003   420
22.11   The requirements   421
22.12   Guilty plea credit/time spent on remand and community orders   423
22.13   Enforcement of community orders under the CJA 2003—Sch. 8   424
22.14   Deferring sentence—ss. 1 and 2 PCC(S)A 2000   424
22.15   Fines   424
22.16   Compensation orders   426
22.17   Conditional discharge   427
22.18   Absolute discharge   428
22.19   Bind over   428
22.20   Ancillary orders   429
22.21   The plea in mitigation   431
22.22   Structuring a plea in mitigation   432
22.23   Advocacy and the plea in mitigation   435
22.24   Professional conduct   436

23   Appeals   442
23.1   Introduction   442
23.2   Reopening a case—s. 142 MCA 1980   443
23.3   Appeal to the Crown Court—s. 108 MCA 1980 (Crim PR, Part 34)   443
23.4   Appeal by way of case stated—s. 111 MCA 1980 and s. 28 Senior
         Courts Act 1981 (Crim PR, Part 35)   444
23.5   Judicial review   445
23.6   Appeal from the Crown Court (Crim PR, Parts 36 and 39)   446
23.7   Appeal against sentence from the Crown Court (Crim PR, Part 39)   448
23.8   Appeal to the Supreme Court (Crim PR, Part 43)   449
23.9   Attorney General's references (Crim PR, Part 41)   449
23.10   Criminal cases review commission   449
23.11   Does the prosecution enjoy a right to appeal?   450

Part VI	**YOUTH JUSTICE**	**453**
24	**Youth Justice—Introduction**	**455**
24.1	Introduction	455
24.2	The terminology of youth justice	457
24.3	The youth justice organisations	458
24.4	The statutory aims of the youth justice system	459
24.5	Parental responsibility	459
24.6	Police station detention and the young person	459
24.7	Dealing with a young client—a defence perspective	461
24.8	Preventing juvenile offending	462
24.9	The decision to prosecute	464
24.10	The procedure upon charge	465
24.11	Funding the young person's right to legal representation	465
25	**Prosecuting Young Offenders**	**467**
25.1	Introduction	467
25.2	The young person's first court appearance	468
25.3	Where will the young person be tried?	471
25.4	Safeguarding the young person's right to a fair trial in the Crown Court	478
25.5	Trial of a young person in the adult magistrates' court	479
25.6	Proceedings in the youth court	480
26	**Sentencing Young Offenders**	**483**
26.1	Introduction	484
26.2	Sentencing procedure in the youth court	486
26.3	Deferring sentence—s. 1 PCC(S)A 2000	486
26.4	Referral order—ss. 16 and 17 PCC(S)A 2000 and paras. 6.19–6.22 Sentencing Children and Young People—Definitive Guideline (2017)	487
26.5	Fine—Part vi PCC(S)A 2000 and paras. 6.17–6.18 Sentencing Children and Young People—Definitive Guideline (2017)	488
26.6	Conditional discharge—s. 12 PCC(S)A 2000 and para. 6.14 Sentencing Children and Young People—Definitive Guideline (2017)	489
26.7	Absolute discharge—s. 12 PCC(S)A 2000 and para. 6.13 Sentencing Children and Young People—Definitive Guideline (2017)	489
26.8	Reparation order—ss. 73–75 PCC(S)A 2000 and paras. 6.15–6.16 Sentencing Children and Young People—Definitive Guideline (2017)	489
26.9	Youth rehabilitation order (YRO)—s. 1 CJIA 2008 and paras. 6.23–6.41 Sentencing Children and Young People—Definitive Guideline (2017)	490
26.10	Detention and training order—ss. 100–107 PCC(S)A 2000 and paras. 6.50–6.53 Sentencing Children and Young People—Definitive Guideline (2017)	493
26.11	Endorsement or disqualification of the young offender's driving licence/record	494
26.12	Compensation order—ss. 130–135 PCC(S)A 2000	494
26.13	Parenting orders—ss. 8–10 CDA 1998 and para. 3.3 Sentencing Children and Young People—Definitive Guideline (2017)	495
26.14	Parental bind over—s. 150(1) PCC(S)A 2000 and para. 3.3 Sentencing Children and Young People—Definitive Guideline (2017)	495
26.15	Criminal Behaviour Order (CBO) and an Anti-Social Behaviour Injunction (ASBI)	495
26.16	Victim surcharge	496
26.17	Sentencing the young offender in the adult magistrates' court	496
26.18	Sentencing the young offender in the Crown Court	496
26.19	Sentencing a 'dangerous' young offender	497
26.20	Crossing a significant age threshold between commission of an offence and sentence	498

APPENDIX 1: Additional Chapters   500

APPENDIX 2: Extracts from *R v Lenny Wise*   501

APPENDIX 3: Extracts from Magistrates' Court Sentencing Guidelines   583

Index   611

GUIDED TOUR OF THE BOOK

Criminal Litigation by Hannibal and Mountford is a pedagogically rich text which has been designed to facilitate your learning and understanding of criminal litigation. This 'Guided Tour of the Book' will explain how to make the most of the text by illustrating each of the features used by the authors to explain the practical aspects of the criminal litigation process.

WITHIN EACH CHAPTER

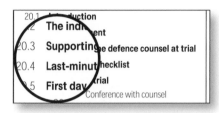

CHAPTER CONTENTS

A detailed contents list at the start of each chapter enables you to anticipate what will be covered and identify what the main topics of the chapter will be. Use this feature to also gain an understanding of how the topics fit together in the wider subject area.

EXAMPLES

Look for the example icon to find relevant, practical examples of how the law has been or could be applied in common situations. These examples bring the subject to life and allow you to examine how principles, rules and statutes work in practice.

'LOOKING AHEAD' BOXES

These boxes are used to highlight areas where the law may change. Potential reforms are considered, ensuring that once you go into practice, you're already aware of the changes on the horizon.

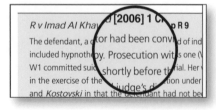

CASE OUTLINES

These case outlines give you an awareness of relevant case law in the subject area. Use these explanations to point you towards the most relevant case reports in your law library or to better inform your knowledge of how the law has been applied in court.

CASE STUDIES

Throughout the book, the authors refer to fictional case studies, which provide a practical focus on the law and procedures described in the text. The documentation for these case studies appears in the online resources. See the 'Guided Tour of the Online Resources' at page xvi for more information.

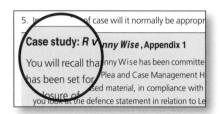

ONLINE RESOURCES ICON

Wherever this icon appears in the margin, more information is available in the online resources which accompany this manual. This may be video footage, case study documentation or links to other useful websites or guidance. See the 'Guided Tour of the Online Resources' at page xvi for more information.

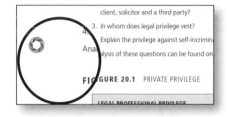

END OF CHAPTER FEATURES

KEY POINTS SUMMARY

The key points covered are summarised in a user-friendly list at the end of each chapter. Look to these summaries to help you consolidate your learning or to check your knowledge at revision time.

SELF-TEST QUESTIONS

These questions allow you to test yourself on particular areas of the law in preparation for your exams or to assess your learning throughout the duration of the course. Use these questions to highlight areas where you might need to improve your understanding by rereading the text or asking your lecturer. You will find the answers provided as a printable document in the online resources.

FIGURES

Flowcharts, shaded boxes or example forms provide a visual representation of what has been described within the chapter.

GUIDED TOUR OF THE ONLINE RESOURCES

Online resources are developed to provide students and lecturers with ready-to-use teaching and learning resources. They are free of charge, designed to complement the text and offer additional materials which are well suited to electronic delivery.

All these resources can be downloaded and are fully custom- isable allowing them to be incorporated into your institution's existing virtual learning environment. Turn to page xviii for a full list of the contents of the online resources to accompany this book.

All the resources on the site are freely accessible to all. Simply visit the site at www.oxfordtextbooks.co.uk/orc/crimlit18_19/.

CASE STUDY DOCUMENTATION

The fictional case studies in the book are accompanied by all of the documentation you would expect to see in reality. This allows you to see what a solicitor's file might typically contain and prepares you for what to expect when you go into practice.

LINKS TO LEGISLATION, RULES, AND OTHER DOCUMENTATION

This part of the website provides links to useful information which is freely accessible elsewhere on the internet. Use this resource to find relevant guidelines, statutes, codes of practice and other documentation quickly and easily.

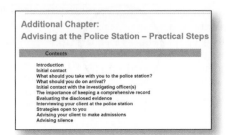

ADDITIONAL CHAPTER: ADVISING AT THE POLICE STATION—PRACTICAL STEPS

For students who are interested in pursuing police station accreditation as a qualification, we have included an additional online chapter which explores the practice and dynamics of police station practice. To reflect the increasing importance of bad character evidence, we include a comprehensive case law compendium on bad character.

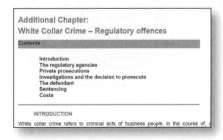

ADDITIONAL CHAPTER: WHITE COLLAR CRIME—REGULATORY OFFENCES

For students whose course has a City focus, corporate crime will be an important topic. An online chapter on regulatory crime written by two leading barristers in this area, Nicholas Yeo and Sarah Le Fevre, enables you to get to grips with an aspect of criminal law which is key for City lawyers.

ADDITIONAL CHAPTER: SENTENCING IN ROAD TRAFFIC CASES

For students with an interest in the particular sentencing considerations that apply to road traffic cases, this specialised chapter further develops the general sentencing practices explored in Chapters 21 and 22, in consideration of an area that occupies a considerable amount of time in magistrates' courts.

INTERACTIVE CRIMINAL LITIGATION TRAIN

You will find an interactive timeline which will help you to see how the whole criminal litigation process fits together and the issues that you need to keep in mind at particular points. The timeline distinguishes between the three classifications of offences (summary-only, either-way and indictable-only).

ANSWERS TO SELF-TEST QUESTIONS

Chapter-by-chapter answers to the self-test questions found in the manual are provided online as a downloadable and printable pdf.

LECTURER RESOURCES

VIDEO CLIPS

High-resolution video footage showing fictional criminal proceedings allows you to emphasise the practical application of what you describe in your teaching. Included on the site is video footage of:

- the case studies featured in the book;
- four 'free-standing' police station video scenario; and
- four 'free-standing' bad character applications.

(Selected, low-resolution video clips of the *R v Lenny Wise* case study are available to lecturers without a password.)

LINKS TO GUIDELINES AND CODES OF PRACTICE

Use this resource to easily find documents important for criminal litigators. Collected together in one place, this resource provides you with all the important documents to which you may want to refer your students.

ONLINE RESOURCES CONTENTS

STUDENT RESOURCES

○ **Bad character case compendium**

An account of a number of cases on bad character.

○ **Case study documentation**

Documentation in support of three of the fictional court scenario video case studies:

    Case study 1: *Regina v Lenny Wise*
    Case study 2: *Regina v William Hardy*
    Case study 3: *Regina v Roger Martin*

○ **Police station checklist**

To accompany Additional Chapter—Advising at the Police Station.

○ **Additional Chapter: Advising at the Police Station—Practical Steps**

Offers practical guidance on the legal representative called upon to advise a suspect at the police station.

○ **Additional Chapter: White Collar Crime—Regulatory Offences**

An additional chapter covering regulatory crime.

○ **Additional Chapter: Sentencing in Road Traffic Cases**

Leading on from the explanations of general sentencing practice in Chapters 21 and 22, this chapter examines the special sentencing considerations that apply to road traffic cases.

○ **Criminal litigation express train timeline**

An interactive timeline to help students put criminal litigation in context.

○ **Answers to self-test questions**

Freely accessible and printable answers to the self-test questions included in the book.

○ **Web-links**

Direct links to some useful websites relating to criminal litigation.

LECTURER RESOURCES

○ **Video case studies:**

    Case study 1: *Regina v Lenny Wise*
    Case study 2: *Regina v William Hardy*
    Case study 3: *Regina v Roger Martin*
    Case study 4: *Peter West role play*
    Case study 5: *Regina v Nicholas Jones*

FOREWORD

In my foreword to the first edition of this book I observed that the financial rewards available to the legal aid lawyer were poor in comparison to almost all other areas of law. Somewhat regrettably the passage of time has done nothing to correct this imbalance, and I suspect that the disparity in pay is greater now than it was back then.

Despite this fact, criminal law remains one of the most attractive careers that you could possible embark upon. At law school, when we speak of law we talk in terms of contract, tort, equity, and trusts etc. But in reality, law is in the main about one thing, people. How people interact with the State, and how they interact with each other.

We see disputes over who and how we can marry, whether very poorly children should live and whether very poorly adults should be allowed to die at a time of their choosing, and in criminal law we have the privilege of looking into the dark shadows of life.

On my first day at bar school a then Stipendiary Magistrate (Inigo Bing, who later went on to become a Circuit Judge) observed in a lecture that there were only three types of criminal, 'the mad, the bad and the sad'. Some years later I met him at a social event and opined that I thought he was incorrect. There was a fourth category, larger than the other three put together, the downright stupid.

It is the downright stupid that trouble me the most, it could be any one of us, at any point in time. If I am correct about that then it is surprising to find so many people disinterested in the criminal justice system, presumably as they believe it will never affect them.

The State has never been more powerful, surveillance techniques never more sophisticated, and the press never more willing at the slightest hint of an allegation to declare guilt. Our judiciary and institutions are under threat from two polarised extremes, yet at the heart of our democracy beats the rule of law.

Only if laws are equally and fairly applied do we have a right to demand punishment, because only then can we be satisfied of guilt. Any lesser standard takes us back to the dark days of English Law, being played out as I type this with inquests into pub bombings that happened some 45 years ago and a criminal trial into the Hillsborough disaster some 30 years ago. Undercover policing inquiries have yet to report, and there remain calls for inquiries into other issues of concern such as the treatment of Orgreave Miners.

Never in our history has the defence of the rule of law been more important. If you are up for the challenge then your days will be filled with laughter, sadness, despair, and the occasional ray of hope. You will live life, not just your own, but through the eyes of others.

This book will guide you in that journey, just as it has for thousands of students who came before you.

Andrew Keogh
March 2019

PREFACE

Our aim when we first conceived *Criminal Litigation* was to deliver a concise yet comprehensive text on all areas of criminal practice whilst at the same time providing a highly practical, innovative and contextual learning resource for students studying the compulsory Criminal Litigation element on the Legal Practice Course and/or an elective in Advanced Criminal Litigation. The text is now in its fourteenth edition and has proven to be an ideal source of reference for trainee and newly qualified solicitors, BPTC students, CPS prosecutors, associate prosecutors and caseworkers, legal executives, paralegals and for other criminal justice professionals.

The extremely positive feedback we have received from students, lecturers and practitioners about the earlier editions of *Criminal Litigation* have been very encouraging. We always welcome constructive comments from our readers about how the text or the extensive learning resources can be improved. Revisions are made with each published edition of the manual based on our readers' feedback. Your comments can be sent to us directly or through OUP.

An important part of the innovative approach *Criminal Litigation* adopts as a learning resource are the extensive online resources which includes specialist chapters on the practical aspects of advising a client at the police station and regulatory crime and fraud. A unique aspect of the online resources are the video clips of selected parts of the case studies that form the basis of ongoing exercises throughout the text. The video clips include a bad character application and sentencing hearing in the Crown Court, the practice of police station representation, a contested bail hearing and a sentencing hearing in a road traffic case. We hope that you find all the video clips a useful tool in adding to your knowledge and understanding of criminal litigation.

Criminal Litigation is divided into six sections:

Part I is an introduction to criminal litigation.

Part II considers the process of investigation up to the decision to charge, including relevant rules of criminal evidence.

Part III considers post-charge procedures up to and including trial.

Part IV considers the remaining rules of criminal evidence.

Part V considers the post-conviction matters of sentencing and appeals against conviction and/or sentence.

Part VI considers youth justice issues.

The pace of legislative change affecting the criminal justice system has been relentless in recent years. For practitioners, students and lecturers keeping up to date and in some instances ahead of the changes has been difficult! This edition incorporates all new developments since the publication of the previous edition.

Please be aware that as the rules of criminal litigation and evidence are always at the forefront of political controversy, public concern and legislative reform, any significant developments during the currency of this edition of the manual will be explained in the update section of the online resources.

The writing of *Criminal Litigation* and the production of the video case studies and online resources could not have been achieved without the cooperation and assistance of many friends and colleagues.

In relation to the video case studies of Lenny Wise/William Hardy and Roger Martin we say a special thank you to the following:

His Honour Paul Glenn
Milena Srdanovic (CPS lawyer)
Shaun Spencer (CPS lawyer)
Hayley Keegan (Defence lawyer)
Simon Leech (Defence lawyer)
Celia Laing (Defence lawyer)
Brian Baig (Staffordshire LPC student 2009–10)
Francis Chattie (Staffordshire LPC student 2009–10)
Alison Bailey (Legal adviser)
Sarah Murphy (Legal adviser)
Vicky Priestly (Legal adviser)
John Peel (CPS Associate prosecutor)
Jason Jamil (Staffordshire LPC student 2003–4)
Carol Hawthorne (Magistrate)
Dr Mike Carter (Magistrate)
Rev Christopher Dalton (Magistrate)
Prakash Samani (Magistrate)

For their contribution to the production of the Peter West Police Station Scenario, we would thank the following:

DC Keith Pagett (Staffordshire Police)
DS Angus Parker (Staffordshire Police)
Sgt Ian Cantrill (Staffordshire Police)
Lisa O'Shea (Accredited Police Station Representative with the Public Defender Service)
Peter Goold (Staffordshire LPC student 2004–5) who gave an outstanding and entirely convincing performance as Peter West, the suspect!
Each of these individuals very kindly gave up their time and volunteered their services for free thereby allowing us to bring our case studies to life.

Special thanks go to the camera crews involved in the filming of our various videos:

Ray Johnson (formerly Professor of Film Heritage and Documentary, Staffordshire University)
Darren Teale (Final year media student 2004)
Richard Edwards (Final year media student 2004)
Gary Robinson (Final year media student 2004)
Peter Robinson (formerly Senior Technician Staffordshire Law School)

We are indebted to Professor Ray Johnson for his tremendous help in directing the early films and undertaking the voice-over analysis. Special thanks also go to Darren Teale who undertook the filming and editing of *R v Lenny Wise* and *R v Roger Martin*. We are grateful to our dear friend and former colleague Peter Robinson (Staffordshire Law School's Senior IT Technician) for helping us to film our Police Station Scenario and for his very patient editing of the material. Peter has also directed and edited the revised William Hardy scenario and the Nick Jones bad character application.

Thanks are also due to the Chief Constable's Office of Staffordshire Police for allowing us to take over Uttoxeter Police Station in rural Staffordshire and for allowing us to use serving police officers.

We would like to thank Dr N. J. F. Smalldridge BA (Oxon), BM, MRC Psych for the time and effort he undertook in devising and writing a psychiatric report on behalf of our fictional defendant Lenny Wise.

We would like to single out Mike Benson for his immensely valuable comments and observa-tions and Sarah Murphy for her assistance. Thanks also to Robin Lichfield, partner and defence solicitor with Lichfield Reynolds Solicitors, North Staffordshire, Andrew Keogh, barris-ter and creator of the superb CrimeLine (http://www.crimeline.info/) and Claire Pickard, Legal Development Manager with the CPS, for answering all our questions! For the 15th edition, we extend our thanks to Leah Evan (Legal Advisor in North Staffordshire) and Callum Morris (our former student), Solicitor and HCA.

We thank the entire team at OUP past and present and specifically for this edition our editor Carlotta Fanton and OUP's IT specialists for their fantastic work in building and maintaining the online resources. Most of all we thank our families (Merryn, Matt, Nick, and Charlie Hannibal; Geoff and Joyce Hannibal; and Nick and Alexandra Mason) for their enduring patience!

This edition is dedicated to all those extremely committed and hard-working criminal defence practitioners who continue to uphold access to justice in the face of adversity. Acknowledgement is also due to our enthusiastic and hard-working students and former colleagues on the Staffordshire Law School Legal Practice Course.

Any errors or omissions are entirely ours.

The law is stated as at 30 March 2019.

Lisa Mountford
King' s College London and Keele University
Martin Hannibal
De Montfort Univeristy

ACKNOWLEDGEMENTS

The Crown Prosecution Service Press Releases and the Crown Prosecution Service logo are reproduced with the kind permission of the Crown Prosecution Service.

Criminal Procedure Rules forms are Crown Copyright and are reproduced by kind permission of the Ministry of Justice and the National Archives under the Open Govern-ment Licence (http://www.nationalarchives.gov.uk/doc/open-government-licence/).

The sentencing guidelines are Crown Copyright and are reproduced by kind permission of the Sentencing Council for England and Wales under the Open Government Licence. The guidelines are available online at http://sentencingcouncil.judiciary.gov.uk/guidelines/guidelines-to-download.htm.

Forms CRM14 and CRM1 are copyright of the Legal Aid Agency and are reproduced by kind permission of the Legal Aid Agency. Please note that the forms are current as at April 2018 but may be updated from time to time. The Legal Aid Agency's website at http://www.justice.gov.uk/about/laa holds the most up-to-date versions of all forms.

TABLE OF CASES

A (No. 2) [2002] 1 AC 45 . . . 16.12
Abdullah (1993) 97 Cr App R 99 . . . 6.5.1
Al-Khawaja [2006] 1 Cr App R 184 . . . 18.14
Al-Khawaja and Tahery v United Kingdom [2009] 1 EHRR 49 . . . 18.14
Al-Khawaja and Tahery v United Kingdom [2011] ECHR 2127 (Grand Chamber) . . . 18.14
Alexander, Re [2009] NIQB 20 . . . 3.7.5, 3.7.6
Alladice (1988) 87 Cr App R 380 . . . 6.5.3
Allen [1995] Crim LR 643 . . . 7.8.1
Anderson (1998), The Independent, 13 July 1998 . . . 14.11
Andrews [1987] AC 281 . . . 18.8.1
Argent [1997] 2 Cr App R 27 . . . 5.2.1, 5.4, Fig. 5.1
Aspinall [1999] 2 Cr App R 115; [1999] Crim LR 741 . . . 6.5.3, Fig. 6.1, App 2
Assim [1966] 2 QB 249 . . . 14.2.4
Associated Picture Houses Ltd v Wednesbury Corporation [1948] 1 KB 223 . . . 17.4
Attorney-General's Reference (No. 3 of 2000) [2001] 1 WLR 2060 . . . 6.11.3, 6.12, Fig. 6.1
Attorney-General's Reference (No. 4 of 2002); Sheldrake v DPP [2005] 1 AC 264 . . . 15.7.1
Attorney-General's Reference (No. 1 of 2004) [2004] 1 WLR 2111 . . . 15.7.1
Averill v United Kingdom (2001) 31 EHRR 36 . . . 5.2.6
Awoyemi and others [2016] 2 Cr App R 302 . . . 19.7.4, 19.7.5
Aziz [1995] 3 WLR 53 . . . 19.5.1

B v DPP [2008] EWHC 1655 (Admin) . . . 3.4.1
Bailey and Smith [1993] 3 All ER 365 . . . 6.11.1
Balabel v Air India [1988] 2 All ER 246 . . . 20.2.1
Ball [2005] EWCA Crim 2826 . . . 19.10.1
Barker [2010] EWCA Crim 4 . . . 16.3.2, 16.4.1
Barnaby v DPP [2015] EWHC 232 . . . 18.8.1
Barnes (1970) 55 Cr App R 100 . . . 14.7.1

Barnes v Chief Constable of Durham [1997] 2 Cr App R 505 . . . 7.11
Baskerville [1916] 2 KB 658 Fig. 17.1
Beckles [2005] 1 Cr App R 22 . . . 5.2.3
Bennett [2012] EWCA Crim 1509 . . . 18.12.3, 18.14
BH (a child) v Llandudno Youth Court [2014] EWHC 1833 (Admin) . . . 25.3.3
Blake (1989) 89 Cr App R 179 . . . 24.6.3
Brewster and Cromwell [2010] EWCA Crim 1194 . . . 16.9.4
Bristol [2007] EWCA Crim 3214 . . . 3.6
Britzman [1983] 1 WLR 350 . . . 19.10.1
Brown v Stott [2001] 2 WLR 817 . . . 20.7.3, Fig. 20.1
Brown (formerly Latham) [2015] EWCA Crim 1328 . . . 20.5
Brushett [2001] Crim LR 471 . . . 8.13
Burke (1986) 82 Cr App R 156 . . . 19.10.2
Burton (Stewart John) [2011] EWCA Crim 1990 . . . 18.10
Butler (1987) 84 Cr App R 12 . . . 19.7.5

C [2004] 2 WLR 335 . . . 8.14
Cadder v HM Advocate [2010] UKSC 43 . . . 4.7.3, 4.7.6
Camberwell Green Youth Court, ex p. D [2005] 2 Cr App R 1 . . . 16.5.2
Campbell [2007] 1 WLR 2798 . . . 19.7.5, 19.10.2, 19.12
Cape [1996] 1 Cr App R 191 . . . 17.6.5
Carp [2005] 1 WLR 3472 . . . 19.7.1, 19.12
Castillo [1996] 1 Cr App R 438 . . . 18.6.1
Chalkley [1998] 2 Cr App R 79 . . . 23.6.5
Cheema [1994] 1 WLR 147 . . . 17.4.1
Chief Constable of Norfolk v Clayton [1983] 2 AC 473 . . . 12.5
Chinn [2012] EWCA Crim 501 . . . 16.8.2
Chohan [2006] 1 Cr App R 3 . . . 19.7.4
Christie v Leachinsky [1947] AC 573 . . . 3.7.1

Claire [2012] EWCA Crim 1509 . . . 18.12.3, 18.14
Clare and Peach [1995] 2 Cr App R 333 . . . 7.14, 17.9.1
Clarke (Earl St John) [2013] EWCA Crim 162 . . . 17.9.1
Compton [2002] EWCA Crim 2835 . . . 5.3.1
Condron [1997] 1 WLR 827 . . . 5.2.1, 5.2.5, Fig. 5.1
Condron v United Kingdom (2001) 31 EHRR 1 . . . 4.7.3, 5.2.6
Consolidated Criminal Practice Directions [2013] EWCA Crim 1631 . . . 21.17, 25.4
Pt IV.43 . . . 6.4.1, 6.7
Cottrill [1997] Crim LR 56 . . . 20.5
Cowan, Gayle and Riccardi [1995] 4 All ER 939 . . . 19.4, Fig. 19.1
Cox [2007] EWCA Crim 3365 . . . 19.7.5
Cox and Railton [1884] 14 QBD 153 . . . 20.2
CPS v Picton [2006] EWHC 1108 (Admin) . . . 12.6.2
CPS v South East Surrey Youth Court and MG [2006] 1 WLR 2543 . . . 25.3.5
Craven [2001] 2 Cr App R 181 . . . 13.9.9
Criminal Practice Direction [2015] EWCA Crim 1567 . . . 1.9, 11.3.3, 12.6.1, 13.4
paras 3A.12–3A.20 . . . 13.5.2
para 3A.21 . . . 13.5.6
Pt 2 (paras 8A–10B) . . . 14.2
Cromwell [2010] EWCA Crim 1194 . . . 16.9.4
Crown Court at Inner London Sessions, ex p. Baines and Baines [1987] 3 All ER 1025 . . . 20.2.1

D [2005] EWCA Crim 2282 . . . 22.8
Davis [1998] Crim LR 659 . . . 18.3.1
Delaney [1988] 86 Cr App R 18 . . . 6.5.2
Derby Magistrates' Court, ex p. B [1996] AC 487 . . . 20.4, 20.6, Fig. 20.1
Dobson [2000] EWCA 1606 . . . 6.12
Doheny [1997] 1 Cr App R 369 . . . 7.13

Doran [2012] EWCA Crim 1509 . . . 18.12.3, 18.14

DPP, ex p. Lee [1999] 2 All ER 737; 2 Cr App R 304 . . . 8.10.2, 8.11.2, 8.15, 10.12

DPP v Chorley Justices [2006] EWHC 1795 (Admin) . . . 12.6.2

DPP v Hammerton [2009] EWHC 921 . . . 1.9

DPP v Merriman [1973] AC 584 . . . 14.2.2

Drummond [2002] 2 Cr App R 352 . . . 15.7.1

Duggan and Chohan [2006] 1 Cr App R 3 . . . 19.7.4

Easton [1995] 1 WLR 1348; [1995] 3 All ER 730 . . . 17.4, 17.4.1, 17.10, Fig. 17.1, 19.2.1

Edwards [2005] EWCA Crim 3244 . . . 19.8

Edwards [2006] 1 Cr App R 3 . . . 19.7.4

Elliott [2010] EWCA Crim 2378 . . . 19.7.5

Essa [2009] EWCA Crim 43 . . . 13.9.5

Farnham Justices, ex p. Gibson [1991] Crim LR 642 . . . 12.11

Finley [1993] Crim LR 50 Fig. 6.1

Flemming (1988) 86 Cr App R 32 . . . 6.6

Flynn [2008] 2 Cr App R 20 . . . 7.10

FNC [2015] EWCA Crim 1732 . . . 7.13

Forbes [2001] 1 AC 473 . . . 7.6, 7.8.1

Ford [2010] EWCA Crim 2250 . . . 18.10

Fox, Campbell and Hartley v United Kingdom [1990] 13 EHRR 157 . . . 3.10

Friend [1997] 2 Cr App R 231 . . . 19.4

Fulling [1987] QB 426 . . . 6.5.1, Fig. 6.2

Fysh [2006] 1 Cr App R 3 . . . 19.7.4

Galbraith [1981] 2 All ER 1060 . . . 14.11, 15.5.1, 15.6, Fig. 15.1

Gayle [1995] 4 All ER 939 . . . 19.4, Fig. 19.1

Ghosh [1982] 3 WLR 110 . . . 9.7.5

Gibson [1887] LR 18 QBD . . . 18.3

Gilmore [2005] 2 Cr App R 21 . . . 19.7.1, 19.7.5

Gleeson [2004] 1 Cr App R 29 . . . 1.10.6

Goldenberg (1988) 88 Cr App R

285 . . . 6.5.2

Gonez [1999] All ER (D) 674 . . . 14.9

Goodyear [2005] 3 All ER 117 . . . 14.6, 14.7.1

GR [2010] EWCA Crim 1928 . . . 13.9.6

Gray and Smith [2005] EWCA Crim 3244 . . . 19.8

H [2004] 2 WLR 335 . . . 8.14

H (Minors), Re (Sexual Abuse: Standard of Proof) [1996] 1 All ER 1 . . . 15.4, Fig. 15.1

Hamer [2010] EWCA Crim 2053 . . . 19.5.1

Hanson [2005] 2 Cr App R 21 . . . 19.7.1, 19.7.5, 19.8, 19.10.1, 19.13, Fig. 19.1

Harris [2003] EWCA 174 . . . 7.6

Hayward [2001] 3 WLR 125 . . . 14.8.6

Highton [2005] 1 WLR 3472 . . . 19.7.1, 19.10.2, 19.12, 19.13

Hoare [2005] 1 Cr App R 1 . . . 5.2.3

Hodges and Walker [2003] 2 Cr App R 247 . . . 17.9.1

Horncastle and Others [2009] EWCA Crim 964 . . . 18.6.1, 18.10, 18.14

Horncastle [2009] UKSC 14 . . . 18.14

Horsnell [2012] EWCA Crim 227 . . . 18.10

Howarth v Commissioner of Police for the Metropolis [2011] EWHC 2818 . . . 3.10

Howden-Simpson [1991] Crim LR 49 . . . 6.5.2

Howell [2005] 1 Cr App R 1 . . . 5.2.3, 5.2.4, 5.4, Fig. 5.1

Hunter and others [2015] EWCA Crim 631 . . . 19.5.1

Ibrahim v R [2012] EWCA Crim 1509 . . . 18.12.4

Ivey v Genting Casinos [2017] UKSC 67 . . . 9.7.5

J, S and M [2011] 1 Cr App R 5 . . . 14.19

Jeffries [1998] 2 Cr App R 79 . . . 23.6.5

Johnstone [2003] 2 Cr App R 33 . . . 15.7.1

Jones [2004] 1 Cr App R 5 . . . 17.4.1

Jones [2005] EWCA Crim 3115 . . . 21.15.2

Jones (Anthony William) [2003] 1 AC 1 . . . 14.8.6

Jonge [1999] 2 Cr App R (S) 1 . . . 22.16

Karia v DPP (2002) 166 JP 753 . . . 7.11

Keane [1994] 1 WLR 746 . . . 8.14

Kearley [1992] 2 AC 228 . . . 18.3

Kefford [2002] 2 Cr App R (S) 495 . . . 22.4, 22.21.2

Kefford [2002] 2 Cr App (S) R 106 . . . 22.2.2, 22.22

Kehoe [2008] EWCA Crim 819 . . . 22.8

Khan [1996] 3 All ER 298 . . . 6.11.1, 6.11.2, Fig. 6.1

Khan v United Kingdom (2001) 31 EHRR 45 . . . 6.11.1

Knight [2004] 1 Cr App R 9 . . . 5.2.3, 5.2.7, Fig. 5.1

Kostovski v Netherlands (1990) 12 EHRR 434 . . . 18.14

L v DPP [2002] 1 Cr App R 32 . . . 15.7.1

L [2012] EWCA Crim 1336 . . . 24.2.1

Lamaletie [2008] EWCA Crim 314 . . . 19.10.1

Lambert [2002] 2 AC 545 . . . 15.7, 15.7.1

Lang and Others [2005] EWCA Crim 2864; [2006] 1 WLR 2509 . . . 22.8, 25.3.5, 26.19.3

Latif and Shazard [1996] 1 WLR 104 . . . 6.11.3, 6.12

Lawson [2007] 1 WLR 1191 . . . 19.8

Lewis v Chief Constable of South Wales [1991] 1 All ER 206 . . . 3.7.10

Liverpool Juvenile Court, ex p. R [1987] 2 All ER 668 . . . 12.7.9

Looseley; Attorney-General's Reference (No. 3 of 2000) [2001] 1 WLR 2060 . . . 6.11.3, 6.12, Fig. 6.1

Luca v Italy (2003) 36 EHRR 46 . . . 18.14

Lucas [1981] QB 720 . . . 17.4.2, Fig. 17.1

M [2003] 2 Cr App R 21 . . . 18.14

M [2011] 1 Cr App R 5 . . . 14.19

M (Michael) [2007] Crim LR 637 . . . 19.7.5

McE and Others, In re [2009] UKHL 15 . . . 20.6

McEwan v DPP [2007] EWHC 740 . . . 18.10

McKenzie [2008] EWCA Crim 758 . . . 19.7.5

McLean [2005] EWCA Crim 3244 . . . 19.8

McNaghten's Case (1843) 10 Cl & F 200 . . . 15.3.1, Fig. 15.1

Maher v DPP [2006] EWHC 1271 (Admin) . . . 18.12.1

Major (Tara) [2010] EWCA Crim 3016 . . . 22.20.4

Makanjuola and Easton [1995] 1 WLR 1348; [1995] 3 All ER 730 . . . 17.4, 17.4.1, 17.10, Fig. 17.1, 19.2.1

Manchester Crown Court, ex p. R (Legal Professional Privilege) [1999] 1 WLR 832 . . . 20.2.1

Mason [1988] 1 WLR 139 . . . 6.5.3

Matthews [2004] QB 690 . . . 15.7.1

Maxwell [2011] 4 All ER 941 . . . 6.12

Mayers and Others [2008] EWCA Crim 1418 . . . 16.5.9

Metropolitan Police Commissioner, ex p. P [1995] TLR 305 . . . 8.6.1

Midmore [2017] EWCA Crim 533 . . . 18.3.2

Miles [2006] EWCA 256 . . . 21.18

Miller (1993) 97 Cr App R 99 . . . 6.5.1

Mills [2002] EWCA Crim 26 . . . 22.2.2

Mitchell [2017] Crim LR 310 . . . 19.7.5

Morse [1991] Crim LR 195 . . . 24.6.3

Murray v United Kingdom (1996) 22 EHRR 29 . . . 1.8.3, 4.7.3, 4.11, 5.2.1, 5.2.6

Myers [1998] AC 124 . . . 18.8.3

Newton (1982) 77 Cr App R 13 . . . 21.4.3, 21.18, Fig. 21.1, 22.16, 23.7

North Sefton Magistrates' Court, ex p. Marsh (1994) 16 Cr App R (S) 401 . . . 21.14.2

Northallerton Magistrates' Court, ex p. Dove [2000] 1 Cr App R (S) 136 . . . 22.20.1

Nottingham Justices, ex p. Davies [1981] 1 QB 38 . . . 10.14

O'Dowd [2009] EWCA Crim 905 . . . 19.7.5

O'Hara v Chief Constable, RUC [1997] AC 286 . . . 3.4.1, 3.7.6

O'Halloran v United Kingdom (2007) 47 EHRR 397 . . . 20.7.3

Ollerenshaw [1999] 1 Cr App R (S) 65 . . . 22.4

Olu [2010] EWCA Crim 2975 . . . 19.7.5

Omotoso [2018] EWCA Crim 1394 . . . 19.10.2

Otway [2011] EWCA Crim 3 . . . 7.14

Oyesiku (1971) 56 Cr App R 240 . . . 16.11

Paris, Abdullah and Miller (1993) 97 Cr App R 99 . . . 6.5.1

Peach [1995] 2 Cr App R 333 . . . 7.14, 17.9.1

Pendleton [2002] 1 WLR 72 . . . 23.6.5

Phillips [2012] 1 Cr App R 332 (25) . . . 19.8

Pickstone [2005] Cr App R 21 . . . 19.7.1, 19.7.5

Platt [2016] EWCA Crim 4 . . . 19.8

Plunkett [2013] EWCA 261 . . . 6.11.1

Practice Direction (Crime: Costs) [1991] 1 WLR 498 . . . 9.13, 12.11

Practice Direction (Criminal: Consolidated) [2002] 3 All ER 904 . . . 19.4, Fig. 19.1

Practice Direction (Submission of No Case) [1962] 1 WLR 227 . . . 12.11, Fig. 15.1

R (Anderson) v Secretary of State for the Home Department [2003] 1 Cr App R 32 . . . 1.8.3

R (B) v Brent Youth Court [2010] EWHC 1893 (Admin) . . . 10.14, 25.2.1

R (Bhatti) v Secretary of State for the Home Department, Lawtel 3/2/2010 . . . 3.9.8

R (D) v Manchester City Youth Court [2002] 1 Cr App R (S) 573 . . . 25.3.3

R (DPP) v Havering Magistrates' Court [2001] 2 Cr App R 2 . . . 1.8.3, 10.10.2

R (Grundy and Co Excavations Ltd and the Forestry Commission) v Halton Division Magistrates Court (2003) 167 JP 387 . . . 15.7.1

R (H) v DPP [2003] EWHC 133 . . . 7.6

R (H, A and O) v Southampton Youth Court [2005] 2 Cr App R (S) 30 . . . 25.3.3, 25.3.5

R (Kelly) v Warley Magistrates Court (the Law Society intervening) [2008] 1 Cr App R 14 . . . 1.10.6

R (on the application of P, G, and W (Respondents) v Secretary of State for the Home Department and another (Appellants) [2019] UKSC 3 . . . 24.8.1, 24.8.3

Railton [1884] 14 QBD 153 . . . 20.2

Raissi v Metropolitan Police Commissioner [2008] EWCA Civ 1237 . . . 3.7.6

Randall [2004] 1 Cr App R 26 . . . 19.8

Redknapp v Commissioner of the City of London Police and the City of London Magistrates' Court [2008] EWHC 1177 . . . 3.9.8

Renda [2005] EWCA Crim 2826 . . . 19.9

Revitt v DPP [2006] 1 WLR 3172 . . . 14.7.3

Riat, Doran, Wilson, Claire, Bennett [2012] EWCA Crim 1509 . . . 18.12.3, 18.12.4, 18.12.6, 18.14

Riccardi [1995] 4 All ER 939 . . . 19.4, Fig. 19.1

Rice v Connelly [1966] 2 All ER 64 . . . 3.3

Richardson [1971] 2 QB 484 . . . 16.2

RL v R [2008] 2 Cr App R 18 . . . 18.10

Roberts [1942] 1 All ER 187 . . . 16.8.3

Roberts [2000] Crim LR 183 . . . 7.10

Rowlands [2005] EWCA Crim 3244 . . . 19.8

Royston Lewis [2007] EWCA Crim 3030 . . . 19.10.2

Rutherford [1998] Crim LR 490 . . . 18.6.1

S [2011] 1 Cr App R 5 . . . 14.19

S and Marper v United Kingdom [2008] ECHR 1581 . . . 7.13.1

Salabiaku v France (1988) 13 EHRR 370 . . . 15.7.1

Salduz v Turkey (2008) 49 EHRR 19 . . . 4.7.3, 4.7.6

Samuel [1988] QB 615 . . . 6.5.3, Fig. 6.1

Sang [1980] AC 402 . . . 6.10, Fig. 6.1

Saunders v United Kingdom (1997) 23 EHRR 313 . . . 20.7.3

Schatschaschwili v Germany [2015] ECHR 1113 . . . 18.14

Seed [2007] 2 Cr App R (S) 69 . . . 22.2.2, 22.4, 22.22

Sellick and Sellick [2005] 1 WLR 3257 . . . 18.14

Selvey v DPP [1970] AC 304 . . . 19.10.1

Setz-Dempsey [1993] 98 Cr App R 23 . . . 18.6.1

Shannon [2001] 1 WLR 51 . . . 6.11.3

Shazard [1996] 1 WLR 104 . . . 6.11.3, 6.12

Smith [1993] 3 All ER 365 . . . 6.11.1

Smith [2005] EWCA Crim 3244 . . . 19.7.5, 19.8

Smith [2008] EWCA 1342 . . . 7.9

Smith (Grant Christopher) [2015] EWCA Crim 1482 . . . 21.9

Stafford Justices, ex p. Ross [1962] 1 WLR 456 . . . 1.7.3

Stafford v DPP [1974] AC 878 . . . 23.6.5

Stokes [2015] EWCA Crim 1911 . . . 19.9

Styles [2015] EWCA Crim 1619 . . . 19.5.1

Sully (2007) 151 SJLB 1564 . . . 19.7.5

T [2018] EWCA Crim 2464 . . . 26.19.3

T (D), unreported, 4 June 2009 . . . 18.6.1

T and V v United Kingdom (2000) 30 EHRR 121 . . . 1.8.3, 25.4

Thames Magistrates' Court, ex p. Polemis [1974] 1 WLR 1371 . . . 23.5

Thornton [1995] 1 Cr App R 578 . . . 17.6.5

Three Rivers District Council v Bank of England (No 6) [2004] UKHL 48 . . . 20.2.1, 20.3

Tibbs [2001] 2 Cr App R 309 . . . 13.9.6

Tompkins (1977) 67 Cr App R 181 . . . 20.5

TL [2018] EWCA Crim 1821) . . . 6.11.3

Toohey v Metropolitan Police Commissioner [1965] AC 595 . . . 16.10

Turnbull [1977] QB 224 . . . 7.2, 14.13, 17.6, 17.6.6, Fig. 17.1

Turner [1970] 2 QB 321 . . . 14.7.1

Turton [2018] EWCA Crim 2091 . . . 22.8

Twist [2011] 2 Cr App R 17 . . . 18.3.2

Underwood [2005] 1 Cr App R 178 . . . 21.4.3

Van Nguyen [2005] 1 WLR 3472 . . . 19.7.1, 19.12

Varley [1982] 2 All ER 519 . . . 19.8

Vasilou [2000] 4 Archbold News 1 . . . 8.12.2

Vye and Others (1993) 97 Cr App R 134 . . . 19.5.1, Fig. 19.1

W [2003] 2 Cr App R 29 . . . 18.8.1

Walker [2003] 2 Cr App R 247 . . . 17.9.1

Walsh (1990) 91 Cr App R 161 . . . 6.5.3, Fig. 6.1

Weir [2005] EWCA Crim 2866; [2006] 1 WLR 1885 . . . 16.9.4, 19.7.5

Williams (Michael) [2012] EWCA Crim 264 . . . 4.10.1

Williams (Oretto) [2012] EWCA Crim 2162 . . . 15.7.1

Wilson [2012] EWCA Crim 1509 . . . 18.12.3, 18.14

Woolmington v DPP [1935] AC 463 . . . 15.2, 15.3, 15.3.3, 15.9, Fig. 15.1

Xhabri [2005] EWCA Crim 3135 . . . 18.12.1

Z [2000] 3 WLR 117 . . . 19.7.5

Z [2009] 1 Cr App R 34 . . . 18.10

Zafran Akhtar Saleem [2007] EWCA Crim 1923 . . . 19.7.5

TABLE OF LEGISLATION AND OTHER INSTRUMENTS

Table of Statutes

Anti-social Behaviour, Crime and
Policing Act 2014 . . . 22.20.3

Bail Act 1976 . . . 1.8.3, 2.11.1,
2.11.2, 4.14.1, 4.14.4, 4.14.5,
8.4, 10.2, 10.3, 10.12, 10.18,
10.19, 10.23, Fig. 10.1, 13.5.6,
25.2.1, 25.6
s 3 . . . 10.10
s 3(a) . . . 10.18
s 3(b) . . . 10.18
s 3A . . . 4.14.1
s 4 . . . 10.3, 10.5, 10.11, Fig.
10.1
s 5 . . . 10.12.1
s 5(6A) . . . 10.20
s 5B . . . 10.17, 10.18
s 6(1) . . . 10.19
s 6(2) . . . 10.19
s 7 . . . 3.7.9, 10.6, 10.8, 10.9,
10.10.2
s 7(3) . . . 4.14.4
s 8 . . . 10.10
Sch 1
    Pt I . . . 10.5, 10.6, Fig. 10.1
        para 1A . . . 10.6
        para 2 . . . 4.14.4, 10.6,
            10.11, 25.2.1
        para 2(1) . . . 10.6, 10.7
        para 2(1)(a)–(c) . . . 10.6,
            10.11
        para 2(2ZA) . . . 10.6, 10.7
        para 2(3) . . . 10.6
        para 2(4) . . . 10.6
        para 2(5) . . . 10.6
        para 2(6) . . . 10.6
        para 2(6A–6C) . . . 10.6
        para 2(6ZA) . . . 10.6
        para 2(7) . . . 10.6
        para 2A . . . 10.6, 10.7
        para 6 . . . 10.6
        para 6A . . . 10.7
        para 6ZA . . . 10.6, 10.7
        para 9 . . . 4.14.4, 10.7,
            10.11, Fig. 10.1, 25.2.1
        para 9AA–9AB . . . 25.2.1
    Pt IA . . . 10.5, 10.8
        para 2 . . . 10.8
        para 3 . . . 10.8
        para 4 . . . 10.8
        para 5 . . . 10.8
        para 6 . . . 10.8
        para 7 . . . 10.8
        para 8 . . . 10.8
    Pt II . . . 10.5, 10.9
        para 2 . . . 10.9
        para 3 . . . 10.9
        para 4 . . . 10.9
        para 5 . . . 10.9
        para 6 . . . 10.9

    Pt IIA . . . 10.14, 13.6
Bail (Amendment) Act
1993 . . . 10.16
s 1 . . . 10.16

Children Act 1989 . . . 24.5
s 3(1) . . . 24.5
Children and Young Persons Act
1933
s 18(a) . . . 25.2
s 34A(1) . . . 25.4
s 39(1) . . . 25.4
s 44 . . . 24.11, 25.2.1
s 44(1) . . . 24.4
s 46(1)(a) . . . 25.2
s 107 . . . 25.2
Children and Young Persons Act
1963
s 18(a) . . . 25.2
s 46(1)(b) . . . 25.2
Companies Act 1985 . . . 20.7.3
Coroners and Justice Act
2009 . . . 16.5.2, 16.5.5
s 86 . . . 16.5.9
s 86(1) . . . 16.5.9
s 86(2)(a) . . . 16.5.9
s 86(2)(b) . . . 16.5.9
s 86(2)(d) . . . 16.5.9
s 86(4) . . . 16.5.9
s 87 . . . 16.5.9
s 88 . . . 16.5.9
s 88(2) . . . 16.5.9
s 88(3) . . . 16.5.9
s 88(4) . . . 16.5.9
s 88(5) . . . 16.5.9
s 90 . . . 16.5.9
s 114 . . . 10.6
s 115 . . . 10.6
s 122 . . . App 3
s 122(2) . . . App 3
s 125 . . . 21.8
s 125(1) . . . App 3
s 144 . . . 19.7.5
Courts Act 2003 . . . 12.7.9
s 28 . . . 1.7.3
s 45 . . . 12.6.2
s 65 . . . 1.7.2
s 66 . . . 1.7.5
Sch 3 . . . 6.6
Crime and Disorder Act 1998
ss 8–10 . . . 26.13
s 29 . . . App 3
s 37 . . . 24.11
s 37(1) . . . 24.1, 24.4, 25.2
s 37(2) . . . 24.4
s 50A(3) . . . 11.2
s 51 . . . 1.5.2, 1.5.3, 1.7.1,
8.11.2, Fig. 8.2, 10.6,
10.13.1, 10.20, 11.3.5, 11.6,
11.7, 11.7.2, 11.7.3, 11.8.3,

11.9, 13.1, 13.3, 13.3.1,
13.4.1, 13.8, 13.12.3,
Fig. 13.1, 14.2.1, 18.13, 25.5,
App 2
s 51(3) . . . 11.7.1, 13.3.1
s 51(3)(a) . . . 11.7.1, 13.3.1
s 51(3)(b) . . . 11.7.1, 13.3.1,
21.15
s 51(4) . . . 11.7.1, 13.3.1
s 51(5) . . . 11.7.2, 11.7.3,
13.3.2
s 51(7) . . . 13.3.3, 25.3.1,
25.3.6, 25.5, Fig. 25.1
s 51(8) . . . 25.3.1
s 51(11) . . . 11.7.1, 13.3.1
s 51A . . . 10.20, Fig. 25.1
s 51A(2) . . . 25.3.1
s 51A(3) . . . 25.3.1
s 51A(3)(b) . . . 25.3.1, 25.3.3,
25.3.5, Fig. 25.1
s 51A(3)(d) . . . 25.3.1, 25.3.4,
25.3.5, Fig. 25.1
s 51A(4) . . . 25.3.1, 25.3.3
s 51A(6) . . . 25.3.1
s 51E . . . 11.7.1, 13.3.1
s 57C . . . 9.15.1
s 57C(3) . . . 9.15.1
s 57C(4) . . . 9.15.1
s 57C(7) . . . 9.15.1
s 57D . . . 9.15.1
s 66B . . . 24.8.3
s 66ZA . . . 24.8.2
Sch 3 . . . 13.10.1, App 3
    para 1 . . . App 2
    para 2(1) . . . 11.9
    para 3 . . . 13.10.1
    paras 7–15 . . . 13.10.2
Sch 8
    para 5 . . . App 2
Crimes and Courts Act 2013
Sch 16 . . . 22.10
Criminal Appeal Act 1968
s 1 . . . 23.6
s 2(1) . . . 23.6.5
s 2(1)(a) . . . 23.6.5, 23.11,
Fig. 23.1
s 11(3) . . . 23.7
s 19 . . . 23.6.4
s 23 . . . 23.6.5
s 29 . . . 23.6.3
Criminal Appeal Act
1995 . . . 23.6.5, 23.10
s 9 . . . 23.10
s 11 . . . 23.10
s 13 . . . 23.10.1
s 15 . . . 23.10.1
ss 17–21 . . . 23.10.1
Criminal Damage
Act 1971
s 1 . . . 3.4.1, 11.5
s 1(1) . . . 11.3.5

Criminal Evidence Act
  1898 . . . 19.10.1
  s 1(1) . . . 19.2
  s 1(3)(ii) . . . 19.10.1
Criminal Justice Act 1967
  s 9 . . . 9.15.1, 12.3, 12.6.2,
    12.8, 12.11, 14.4, 14.4.1,
    14.10, 18.4.1, 18.5, 18.15,
    Fig. 18.1, 19.5.2, 25.6, App 2
  s 10 . . . 9.15.1, 12.6.2, 12.8,
    14.10, 15.8, App 2
Criminal Justice Act
  1988 . . . 18.4
  s 30 . . . 17.9.3, App 2
  s 36 . . . 23.9
  s 39 . . . 1.5.1
  s 139 . . . 3.4.1, 15.3.2, 15.7.1
  s 139(4) . . . 15.3.2
  s 154(2) . . . 10.14
Criminal Justice Act
  2003 . . . 4.14, 8.2, 8.12.5,
    Fig. 8.1, 9.7.5, 13.9.6, 13.9.7,
    16.9.4, 17.9.4, 18.2, 18.3.2,
    18.4, 18.6.1, 18.8, 18.10,
    18.11, 18.12, 18.12.6, 18.14,
    18.15, Fig. 18.1, 19.5.1, 19.6,
    19.6.1, 19.7.5, 19.8, 19.10.1,
    19.12, 19.13, 21.5, 21.6, 21.7,
    21.8, 22.4.2, 22.8, 22.9, 22.24,
    Fig. 22.2, 23.1, 23.11
  s 14 . . . 10.6, Fig. 10.1
  s 15 . . . 10.6, Fig. 10.1
  s 16 . . . 10.18
  s 19 . . . Fig. 10.1
  s 19(4) . . . 10.6
  s 23 . . . 8.6.2, Fig. 8.1
  s 23A . . . 8.6.3
  ss 24–27 . . . 8.6.2, Fig. 8.1
  s 29 . . . 12.2
  s 30 . . . App 2
  s 34 . . . 13.9.2
  ss 43–50 . . . 14.19
  s 51 . . . 16.5.11
  s 51(7) . . . 16.5.11
  s 57 . . . 23.11, Fig. 23.1
  s 58 . . . 14.18, 23.11, Fig. 23.1
  ss 59–60 . . . 23.11, Fig. 23.1
  s 61 . . . 23.11, Fig. 23.1
  s 62 . . . 23.11
  s 63 . . . 23.11
  s 66(3) . . . 21.7.2
  s 75(1) . . . 14.17.1
  s 76 . . . 14.17.1, 23.11,
    Fig. 23.1
  ss 77–80 . . . 14.17.1
  Pt 11 (ss 98–141) . . . 19.6
  s 98 . . . 16.9.4, Fig. 16.2,
    19.6.1, 19.7.4, Fig. 19.1
  s 98(a) . . . 19.6.1
  s 98(b) . . . 19.6.1
  s 99 . . . 19.6
  s 100 . . . 14.10.2, 16.9.2,
    16.9.4, 16.12, Fig. 16.2,
    19.10.1, 19.10.2
  s 100(1)(a) . . . 16.9.4, Fig. 16.2

s 100(1)(b) . . . 16.9.4
s 100(1)(c) . . . 16.9.4
s 100(3)(a)–(c) . . . 16.9.4
s 101 . . . 16.9.4, 19.12, 19.13,
  App 2
s 101(1) . . . 19.7, 19.11
s 101(1)(a) . . . 19.7.2, 19.7.3,
  Fig. 19.1
s 101(1)(b) . . . 19.5.1, 19.7.3,
  Fig. 19.1
s 101(1)(c) . . . 19.7.4, 19.13,
  Fig. 19.1
s 101(1)(d) . . . 19.7, 19.7.1,
  19.7.5, 19.8, 19.10.2, 19.13,
  Fig. 19.1, App 2
s 101(1)(e) . . . 19.8, 19.13,
  Fig. 19.1
s 101(1)(f) . . . 19.9, 19.13,
  Fig. 19.1
s 101(1)(g) . . . 16.9.4, Fig.
  16.2, 19.7, 19.7.1, 19.10,
  19.10.1, 19.10.2, 19.13,
  Fig. 19.1
s 101(2) . . . 19.7
s 101(3) . . . 19.7, 19.7.1,
  19.7.5, 19.9, 19.10.2, 19.11,
  19.13, Fig. 19.1
s 101(4) . . . 19.7, 19.7.1
s 102 . . . 19.7, 19.7.4, 19.13
s 103 . . . 19.7, 19.7.5, 19.13
s 103(1)(a) . . . 19.7.5
s 103(1)(b) . . . 19.7.5
s 103(2) . . . 19.7.5
s 103(3) . . . 19.7.5, Fig. 19.1
s 103(4)(a) . . . 19.7.5
s 103(4)(b) . . . 19.7.5
s 103(5) . . . 19.7.5
s 103(6) . . . 19.7.5
s 104 . . . 19.7, 19.8, 19.13
s 104(1) . . . 19.8
s 104(2) . . . 19.8
s 105 . . . 19.7, 19.9, 19.13
s 105(3) . . . 19.9
s 105(4) . . . 19.9
s 105(6) . . . 19.9
s 106 . . . 19.7, 19.10, 19.10.1,
  19.13
s 106(1) . . . 19.10
s 106(2)(b) . . . 19.10.1
s 107 . . . 19.13
s 108 . . . 19.13
s 110 . . . 19.11
s 112 . . . 19.6.1
s 114 . . . 14.4.1, 18.2, 18.5,
  18.15, Fig. 18.1
s 114(1) . . . 18.2
s 114(1)(a) . . . 18.5, Fig. 18.1
s 114(1)(b) . . . 18.5, Fig. 18.1
s 114(1)(c) . . . 18.5, 18.9,
  18.15, Fig. 18.1
s 114(1)(d) . . . 18.5, 18.10,
  18.15, Fig. 18.1
s 114(2) . . . Fig. 18.1
s 114(2)(a)–(i) . . . 18.10,
  18.12.1

s 115 . . . 18.3
s 115(2) . . . 18.3, 18.3.3
s 115(3) . . . 18.3, 18.3.2
s 116 . . . 18.3.4, 18.5, 18.6,
  18.6.1, 18.7.1, 18.10,
  18.12.2, Fig. 18.1
s 116(1) . . . 18.6
s 116(2) . . . 14.10, 18.7.1
s 116(2)(a) . . . 18.6, Fig. 18.1
s 116(2)(b) . . . 18.6, 18.6.1,
  18.7.1, Fig. 18.1
s 116(2)(c) . . . 18.6, Fig. 18.1
s 116(2)(d) . . . 18.6, 18.6.1,
  Fig. 18.1
s 116(2)(e) . . . 18.6, 18.6.1,
  18.10, Fig. 18.1
s 116(3) . . . 18.6.1
s 116(4) . . . 18.6.1
s 117 . . . 18.3.4, 18.5, 18.7,
  18.7.1, 18.8.2, 18.10,
  18.12.1, 18.15, Fig. 18.1
s 117(2) . . . 18.7, 18.12.2
s 117(2)(a) . . . 18.7
s 117(2)(b) . . . 18.7
s 117(2)(c) . . . 18.7
s 117(4) . . . 18.7.1
s 117(5) . . . 18.7.1
s 117(5)(b) . . . 18.7.1
s 117(7) . . . 18.7.1
s 118 . . . 18.2, 18.5, 18.8,
  18.10, Fig. 18.1
s 118(1) . . . 18.8.2
s 118(4) . . . 18.8.1
s 118(4)(a) . . . 18.8.1
s 118(5) . . . 18.8.3
s 119 . . . 18.11, 18.12.1,
  18.12.2
s 119(1) . . . 16.8.4, 16.9.3,
  Fig. 16.2
s 120 . . . 16.8.3, Fig. 16.2,
  18.11, 18.12.1, 18.12.2
s 120(2) . . . 16.8.3, 16.11,
  Fig. 16.2
s 120(3) . . . 16.8.2
s 120(4) . . . 16.8.3, 18.11
s 120(5) . . . 16.8.3, 18.11
s 120(6) . . . 16.8.3, 18.11
s 120(7) . . . 16.8.3, Fig. 16.2,
  18.11
s 121 . . . 18.10, 18.12.1
s 121(1)(b) . . . 18.12.1
s 121(1)(c) . . . 18.12.1
s 123 . . . 18.6, 18.12.2
s 124 . . . 18.12.3
s 125 . . . 18.12.4
s 126 . . . 18.12.5, 18.12.6,
  18.14
s 126(1) . . . 18.12.5
s 126(2) . . . 18.8.1, 18.12.6
s 129(1) . . . 18.3.4
s 129(2) . . . 18.3.4
s 137 . . . 16.5.5
s 139 . . . 16.8.2, Fig. 16.2
s 142 . . . 21.6, Fig. 21.2, 26.20
s 142(1) . . . 22.10.1

s 142A . . . 26.1.1
s 143 . . . 21.7.1, Fig. 21.2
s 143(1) . . . 21.7.1
s 143(2) . . . 21.7.1
s 143(3) . . . 21.7.1
s 144 . . . 21.7.1, 21.13, Fig.
  21.2, 22.4.3, 22.12, Fig. 22.1,
  26.10, App 3
s 145 . . . 21.7.1, Fig. 21.2
s 146 . . . 21.7.1, Fig. 21.2
s 148 . . . 22.9.1, 26.9
s 148(1) . . . Fig. 22.2
s 148(3) . . . 22.10.1, Fig. 22.2
s 150A . . . 22.9.1
s 152 . . . 22.24, 26.10
s 152(2) . . . 22.2, 22.2.1,
  Fig. 22.1
s 153 . . . 22.22, 26.10
s 153(2) . . . 22.4, 22.4.1,
  Fig. 22.1
s 156 . . . 21.16.1
s 161(2) . . . 22.2
s 162 . . . 22.15
s 162(1) . . . Fig. 22.2
s 164 . . . 22.15
s 164(2) . . . Fig. 22.2
s 174 . . . Fig. 21.2, App 3
s 174(1)(a) . . . 22.8
s 174(2) . . . Fig. 22.1
s 174(2)(b) . . . 21.13, 22.2
s 174(2)(d) . . . 22.4.3
s 174(4B) . . . 26.10
s 177 . . . 22.10, Fig. 22.2
s 177(2A) . . . 22.10
s 177(3) . . . 22.10
s 199 . . . 22.10, 22.11.1,
  Fig. 22.2
s 200A . . . 22.10, 22.11.2
s 200A(2) . . . 22.11.2
s 200A(3) . . . 22.11.2
s 200A(4) . . . 22.11.2
s 202 . . . 22.10, 22.11.3
s 203 . . . 22.10, 22.11.4
s 204 . . . 22.10, 22.11.5,
  Fig. 22.2
s 205 . . . 22.10, 22.11.6,
  Fig. 22.2
s 206 . . . 22.10, 22.11.7,
  Fig. 22.2
s 206(A) . . . 22.10
s 207 . . . 22.10, 22.11.8, App 3
s 208 . . . 22.11.9
s 209 . . . 22.10, Fig. 22.2,
  App 3
s 212 . . . 22.10, 22.11.10,
  App 3
s 212(A) . . . 22.10
s 214 . . . 22.10, 22.11.11
s 221 . . . Fig. 22.2
s 224 . . . 21.15.2, 22.4, 22.8,
  25.3.1, 25.6, 26.19, App 3
s 224A . . . 22.8
s 224A(3) . . . 22.8
s 224A(4) . . . 22.8
s 224A(5) . . . 22.8

s 224A(6) . . . 22.8
s 224A(7) . . . 22.8
s 224A(8) . . . 22.8
s 225 . . . 21.15.2, 22.4, 22.8,
  26.19
s 225(1) . . . 22.8
s 225(2) . . . 22.8
s 226 . . . 21.15.2, 22.4, 22.7,
  22.8, 25.3.1, 25.3.4, 25.5,
  Fig. 25.1, 26.19
s 226(1) . . . 26.19.1
s 226(2) . . . 26.19.1
s 226A . . . 22.8
s 226A(1) . . . 22.8
s 226A(2) . . . 22.8
s 226A(3) . . . 22.8
s 226A(5) . . . 22.8
s 226A(6) . . . 22.8
s 226A(7) . . . 22.8
s 226A(8) . . . 22.8
s 226A(9) . . . 22.8
s 226B . . . 26.19.2
s 226B(6) . . . 26.19.2
s 227 . . . 21.15.2, 22.4, 22.8,
  26.19
s 228 . . . 21.15.2, 22.4, 22.8,
  25.3.4, 26.19
s 229 . . . 21.15.2, 22.4, 22.8,
  26.19, 26.19.3
s 229(2) . . . 22.8
s 229(3) . . . 22.8
ss 237–239 . . . 22.4.2
s 240 . . . 22.4.2, Fig. 22.1, App
  3
s 240A . . . 22.4.4, App 3
s 240A(3) . . . 22.4.4
s 240ZA . . . 22.4.4
ss 241–268 . . . 22.4.2
s 256AA . . . 22.4.2
s 269 . . . 21.15.2, 26.18
ss 270–277 . . . 26.18
Sch 3 . . . 11.2, 13.10.1, App 2
Sch 5 . . . 14.17.1
Sch 8 . . . 22.13
  para 22 . . . App 3
Sch 12
  para 8 . . . 22.5
  para 11.1 . . . App 3
Sch 15 . . . 22.8, 25.3.4, 26.19
Sch 15B . . . 22.8
  Pt 1 . . . 22.8
Sch 23 . . . 22.14
Criminal Justice and Courts Act
2015
  s 17 . . . 8.6.1
  s 38 . . . 26.10
  s 41 . . . 24.8.2, 24.8.3
  s 43 . . . 26.4
  s 44 . . . 26.4
  s 48 . . . 12.2
Criminal Justice and Immigration Act 2008 . . . 22.8
  s 1 . . . 26.9
Criminal Justice and Police Act
2001

s 50 . . . 3.9.6
s 51 . . . 3.9.6
Criminal Justice and Public
Order Act 1994 . . . 5.1, 5.2.6,
  10.17, 13.9.5
  s 25 . . . 10.3, 10.4, Fig. 10.1
  s 34 . . . 1.8.3, 1.10.4, 4.11,
    4.14.3, 5.1, 5.2, 5.2.1, 5.2.6,
    5.2.7, 5.3, 5.3.1, 5.4, Fig. 5.1,
    9.7.5, 14.14, 17.5, 18.3.1
  s 34(1) . . . 5.2
  s 34(2) . . . 5.2
  s 34(2A) . . . 5.2.1, Fig. 5.1
  s 35 . . . 5.1, 14.14, 17.5, 19.1,
    19.2, 19.4, 19.4.1, 19.13,
    Fig. 19.1
  s 35(1) . . . 19.4
  s 35(2) . . . 19.4
  s 35(3) . . . 19.4
  s 35(4) . . . 19.4
  s 36 . . . 3.7.5, 4.11, 5.1, 5.3,
    5.3.1, 5.4, Fig. 5.1, 14.14,
    17.5
  s 36(2) . . . 5.3.1
  s 36(4A) . . . 5.3.1
  s 37 . . . 3.7.5, 4.11, 5.1, 5.3,
    5.3.1, 5.4, Fig. 5.1, 14.14,
    17.5
  s 37(2) . . . 5.3.1
  s 37(3A) . . . 5.3.1
  s 38 . . . 5.2.6
  s 38(3) . . . 5.3.1, 19.4, Fig. 19.1
  s 60 . . . 3.5
Criminal Law Act 1967
  s 3(1) . . . 3.7.7
Criminal Procedure Act 1865
  s 3 . . . 16.8.4, Fig. 16.2
  s 4 . . . 16.9.3, Fig. 16.2
  s 5 . . . 16.9.3
Criminal Procedure (Attendance
  of Witnesses) Act 1965 . . . 8.13
  ss 2–4 . . . 13.12.1
Criminal Procedure and Investigations Act 1996 . . . 8.8,
  8.10, 8.12, 8.12.1, 8.13, 8.15,
  Fig. 8.3, 11.4.2, 12.7.4, 13.9,
  13.9.9, 13.11.1, 13.12.3,
  17.9.3, App 2
  s 3 . . . 8.12.1, 8.12.2, 8.12.4,
    8.12.5, 8.15, Fig. 8.2, Fig.
    8.3, 9.16, 11.8.3, 12.7.5,
    12.7.6, 12.8, 13.8, 13.9.1,
    13.9.3, 13.9.7, Fig. 13.1,
    App 2
  s 5 . . . 8.12.4, Fig. 8.2, Fig. 8.3,
    11.8.3, 13.9.2, 13.9.3, 13.9.8,
    Fig. 13.1, App 2
  s 6 . . . Fig. 8.2, Fig. 8.3, 12.7.5,
    13.9.8, Fig. 13.1, App 2
  s 6A . . . 13.9.4, App 2
  s 6C . . . 8.12.4, Fig. 8.2, Fig.
    8.3, 11.8.3, 12.7.5, 13.9.2,
    13.9.4, Fig. 13.1, App 2
  s 6C(4) . . . 13.9.2
  s 6D . . . 17.9.4

s 6E . . . 13.9.6
s 7 . . . Fig. 8.3
s 7A . . . 8.12.5, Fig. 8.2, 12.7.5, 12.7.6, 13.9.7, Fig. 13.1
s 8 . . . 13.9.8, App 2
s 11 . . . Fig. 8.2, 13.9.2, 13.9.5, 13.9.6, 13.12.3, App 2
s 11(5) . . . 13.9.5
s 11(8) . . . 13.9.5
s 11(10) . . . 13.9.5
s 16 . . . 8.13
Pt II (ss 22–27) . . . App 2
s 23 . . . 8.8
s 26 . . . 8.8
ss 28–30 . . . 13.11
ss 31–34 . . . 13.11, 13.11.1
s 35 . . . 13.11, 13.11.1, 14.18, 23.11, Fig. 23.1
s 36 . . . 13.11, 13.11.1, 14.18, 23.11, Fig. 23.1
s 37 . . . 13.11, 13.11.1
s 38 . . . 13.11, 13.11.1
s 39 . . . 13.11.1
Sch 2 . . . 18.5
Criminal Procedure and Investigations Act 1996 Disclosure Code of Practice (CPIA 1996) revised 2015 . . . 8.8, 8.10, 8.12, App 2
para 3.5 . . . 8.10.1
para 5 . . . 8.10.1
para 5.4 . . . 8.10.1
para 6 . . . 8.10.2
Data Protection Act 1998 . . . App 2
Domestic Violence, Crime and Victims Act 2004
s 12 . . . 22.20.4
s 17 . . . 14.19
Drugs Act 2005
s 7 . . . 4.14.5
s 9 . . . 4.14.5

Education Act 1996 . . . 1.6.1
Equality Act 2010 . . . App 2

Family Law Act 1996
s 2 . . . 10.6, 10.8, 10.9
Firearms Act 1968 . . . Fig. 25.1
Firearms Act 1983
s 1(5) . . . 15.7.1
Fraud Act 2006
s 1 . . . 3.4.1

Harassment Act 1997 . . . 22.20.4
s 5(4) . . . 22.20.4
s 5(5) . . . 22.20.4
s 5(6) . . . 22.20.4
Health and Safety at Work Act 1974 . . . 1.6.1
Homicide Act 1957
s 2 . . . 15.3.2, Fig. 15.1
Human Rights Act 1998 . . . 1.8, 1.8.3, 8.1, 8.2.5, 15.7

s 1 . . . 1.8
s 2 . . . 1.8.1
s 3 . . . 1.8.1, 15.7
s 4 . . . 1.8.1
s 6 . . . 1.8.1
s 6(1) . . . 1.8.1
s 8 . . . 1.8.1
Sch 1 . . . *See* European Convention on Human Rights *under International Law*

Indictments Act 1915 . . . 14.2
s 5 . . . 14.2.5
s 5(3) . . . 14.2.3

Juries Act 1974
s 11 . . . 14.8.1
s 12(3) . . . 14.8.3
s 17 . . . 14.15.1
Justices of the Peace Act 1968
s 1(7) . . . 22.19

Legal Aid, Sentencing and Punishment of Offenders Act 2012 . . . 9.2, 9.13, 10.6, 14.17, 22.8, 24.8, App 2
s 84 . . . 26.9
s 91 . . . 25.2.2
s 91(6) . . . 25.2.2
ss 98–101 . . . 25.2.2
s 123 . . . 22.8, 26.19.2
s 124 . . . 26.19.2
s 125 . . . 26.19.2
Sch 11 . . . 10.6, 10.16
Licensing Act 2003 . . . 8.2.1

Magistrates' Courts Act 1980 [MCA 1980] . . . 1.7.1
s 1 . . . 3.7.1, 3.7.3
s 3(4) . . . App 3
s 5A(3)(a) . . . App 2
s 5B . . . App 2
s 11(1)(b) . . . 12.10
s 12 . . . 12.3
s 14 . . . 12.4
s 17 . . . 11.1, 11.3
s 17A . . . 11.2
s 18 . . . 11.1, 11.3
s 19 . . . 11.1, 11.3, 11.3.1, 11.3.2, 11.3.3, 11.10, Fig. 11.1, App 3
s 20 . . . 11.1, 11.3
s 21 . . . 11.1
s 22 . . . App 3
s 22A . . . App 3
s 24(1) . . . 25.3
s 24(1)(a) . . . 25.3.3
s 24A . . . 25.3.2
s 24A(6) . . . 25.3.2
s 25(2A) . . . 11.10
s 29 . . . 25.5
s 97 . . . 8.13, 20.4
s 97(2) . . . 12.7.8
s 101 . . . 15.3.3, Fig. 15.1

s 108 . . . 23.3, Fig. 23.1
s 111 . . . 1.7.6, 23.4, Fig. 23.1
s 111(1) . . . 23.4
s 111(2) . . . 23.4
s 113 . . . 23.4.1
s 123 . . . 12.5.1
s 127 . . . 4.2.1
s 127(1) . . . 12.2.1
s 128 . . . 10.12.1
s 128A . . . 10.13
s 133 . . . 21.14.1
s 133(1)–(2) . . . 21.14.1
s 142 . . . 23.1, 23.2, 23.11, Fig. 23.1
s 142(1) . . . 23.2
s 142(2) . . . 23.2
Mental Health Act 1983 . . . 19.3.1
Misuse of Drugs Act 1971 . . . 3.1, 3.5, 3.6, Fig. 10.1
s 5(2) . . . App 2
s 23 . . . Fig. 3.1
s 23(3) . . . 3.9.7
Modern Slavery Act 2015 . . . 8.3
Oaths Act 1978

s 1 . . . 16.7
s 5 . . . 16.7
Offences Against the Person Act 1861
s 18 . . . 11.7.3, 13.3.1, 21.8.1, 21.9, 25.3.4
s 20 . . . 19.7.5, 19.8, 21.8.1, 25.3.4
s 47 . . . 11.3.5, 19.7.5, 21.8.1, App 3
Offender Rehabilitation Act 2014 . . . 22.4.2
s 6 . . . 26.10

Perjury Act 1911
s 13 . . . 17.3
Police and Criminal Evidence Act 1984 . . . 2.1, 2.4.2, 3.1, 3.8, 4.1, 4.10, 4.15, 6.1, 6.2, 6.4, 6.5.2, 6.5.3, 6.13.2, 7.12.1, 7.13.1, 10.12.1, 19.10.1, 24.6.1, 24.6.3, App 2
s 1 . . . 3.4.1, 3.5, 3.10, Fig. 3.1
s 1(1) . . . 3.4.1
s 8 . . . 3.9.8, 20.6
s 10(1) . . . 20.2
s 10(1)(a) . . . 3.9.9, 20.2.1, Fig. 20.1
s 10(1)(b) . . . 20.2.2, Fig. 20.1
s 10(2) . . . 20.2
s 11 . . . 3.9.9
s 14 . . . 3.9.9
s 15 . . . 3.9.8
s 16 . . . 3.9.8
s 17 . . . 3.9.4
s 17(1)(b) . . . 3.9.6
s 18 . . . 3.7.5, 3.9.5, 3.9.6, Fig. 3.1, 4.3
s 18(2) . . . 3.9.5

s 18(5) . . . 3.9.5
s 19 . . . 3.9.6
s 24 . . . 3.7.4, 3.7.6, 3.10,
   Fig. 3.1, 4.2
s 24(1) . . . 3.7.1, 3.7.5
s 24(2) . . . 3.7.1, 3.7.5
s 24(3) . . . 3.7.1, 3.7.5
s 24(4) . . . 3.7.1, 3.7.5, 3.7.6
s 24(5) . . . 3.7.5, 3.7.6, Fig. 3.1
s 24(5)(e) . . . 3.7.5
s 24A . . . 3.7.1, 3.7.8, 3.10
s 24A(1) . . . 3.7.8
s 24A(2) . . . 3.7.8
s 24A(3)(a) . . . 3.7.8
s 24A(4) . . . 3.7.8
s 25(5) . . . 3.7.6
s 27 . . . 3.7.9
s 28 . . . 3.7.6, Fig. 3.1
s 30 . . . 3.7.6, 4.3
s 30A . . . 3.8, 4.3
s 30A(1A) . . . 3.8
s 30B . . . 3.8
s 30CA . . . 3.8
s 30CB . . . 3.8
s 32 . . . 3.9.3, 3.9.6, Fig. 3.1,
   4.3, App 2
s 32(1) . . . 3.9.2, 3.9.3
s 32(2)(b) . . . 3.9.3
s 32(4) . . . 3.9.2
Pt 4 (ss 34–52) . . . 4.5.1
s 34(2) . . . 4.5, 4.6.2
s 34(5) . . . 4.5
s 37 . . . 4.14.1
s 37(1) . . . 4.4.4
s 37(2) . . . 4.5, 4.5.2, 4.6.1
s 37(7) . . . 4.4.4, 4.14
s 37(7)(a) . . . 4.4.4, 4.14.1,
   4.14.2, 8.2.4, 8.4
s 37(7)(b) . . . 4.4.4
s 37(7)(c) . . . 4.4.4
s 37(7)(d) . . . 4.4.4
s 37(15) . . . 24.6.1
s 37A . . . 8.2
s 37B . . . 4.4.4, 8.2.4, Fig. 8.1
s 37B(4) . . . 8.2.4
s 37B(5) . . . 8.2.4
s 37C . . . 4.14.1
s 38 . . . 4.14.4, 4.15, 10.1,
   10.2, 10.3, 24.10
s 38(1) . . . 4.14.4
s 38(1)(c) . . . 4.14.4
s 38(6) . . . 24.10
s 39 . . . 4.4
s 40 . . . 4.6, 4.6.1, Fig. 4.1
s 41 . . . 4.5.2, Fig. 4.1
s 42 . . . 4.6.1, Fig. 4.1
s 42(1) . . . 4.5.3
s 42(6) . . . 4.5.3
s 42(10) . . . 4.5.3
s 43 . . . 4.5.4, 4.6.1, Fig. 4.1
s 44 . . . 4.5.4, 4.6.1, Fig. 4.1
s 45ZA(1) . . . 4.5.3
s 46(1) . . . 4.14.4
s 46A . . . 3.7.9
s 46A(1) . . . 4.14.1

s 46A(1A) . . . 4.14.1
s 47(1A) . . . 4.14.4
s 47(1)(e) . . . 4.14.1
s 47(6) . . . 4.6.1
s 47ZA–K . . . 4.14.2
s 54 . . . 3.9, 4.4.3
s 54A . . . 4.4.3
s 55 . . . 4.4.3
s 56 . . . 4.7.1, 4.7.2, Fig. 4.1,
   6.4, 24.6.4
s 56(1) . . . 4.7.1
s 56(2)–(5) . . . 4.7.2
s 58 . . . 4.7.3, Fig. 4.1, 5.2.1,
   5.2.6, 5.3.1, 6.4, 6.5.3,
   6.13.2,
   Fig. 6.2, 24.6.4, App 2
s 58(1) . . . 4.7.3
s 58(8) . . . 4.7.6, 4.11, 24.6.4
s 58(9) . . . 4.7.6
s 60B . . . 4.2.1
s 61 . . . 7.12.2, 7.15
s 61(2) . . . 7.12.2
s 61(3) . . . 7.12.2
s 61(4) . . . 7.12.2
s 61(6) . . . 7.12.2
s 61(6A) . . . 7.12.2
s 61A . . . 7.12.2
s 62 . . . 7.15, 17.5
s 62(4) . . . 7.12.4
s 62(10) . . . 7.12.4
s 63 . . . 7.12.3, 7.15
s 63(2) . . . 7.12.3
s 63(2A) . . . 7.12.3
s 63(3A) . . . 7.12.3
s 63(3B) . . . 7.12.3
s 63A . . . 3.7.9
s 63B . . . 4.14.5
s 64 . . . 7.13.1
s 64A(1) . . . 7.4.5
s 64A(2) . . . 7.4.5
s 65 . . . 7.12.3, 7.12.4, 24.6.4
s 67(11) . . . 4.1
s 76 . . . 3.6, 3.7.6, 4.1, 4.7,
   4.15, 6.1, 6.4, 6.5, 6.13.2,
   9.7.5, 13.10.1, 18.8.3, App 2
s 76(2) . . . 6.5, 6.5.2
s 76(2)(a) . . . 1.8.2, 4.10, 4.12.1,
   6.5, 6.5.1, 6.13.2, Fig. 6.2
s 76(2)(b) . . . 4.10, 6.5, 6.5.2,
   6.5.3, 6.13.2, Fig. 6.2, App 2
s 76(4) . . . 6.8
s 76(5) . . . 6.8
s 76(8) . . . 4.12.1, 6.5.1
s 76A . . . 18.8.3
s 78 . . . 2.4.2, 3.6, 3.7.6,
   3.7.10, 3.9.3, 4.1, 4.7, 4.10,
   4.15, 6.1, 6.4, 6.5, 6.5.3,
   6.10, 6.11, 6.11.1, 6.12,
   6.13.2, Fig. 6.1, Fig. 6.2, 7.6,
   7.8, 7.12.4, 7.15, Fig. 7.1,
   9.7.5, 13.10.1, 17.6, 18.3.2,
   18.8.1, 18.8.3, 18.12.6,
   18.14, Fig. 18.1, 19.7.1,
   19.7.5, 19.9, 19.11, 20.5,
   App 2

s 79 . . . 12.11, 14.12, 16.2,
   19.3, Fig. 19.1
s 80 . . . 16.3.3
s 80(3) . . . 16.3.3, Fig. 16.1
s 80(4) . . . 16.3.3
s 82(1) . . . 6.3, 6.13.2, Fig. 6.2
s 82(3) . . . 2.4.2, 6.10, 6.13.2,
   Fig. 6.1, 18.12.6, 19.9
Sch 2 . . . 3.7.1
Police and Criminal Evidence
   Act 1984 Codes of Prac-
   tice . . . 1.3, 2.1, 2.4.2, 3.1, 4.1,
   4.4.2, 4.10, 6.1, 6.2, 6.4, 6.5.2,
   6.5.3, 6.13.2, Fig. 6.1, 10.12.1,
   19.10.1
Code A . . . 3.1, 3.3, 3.4.1, 3.5,
   Fig. 3.1
para 1.1 . . . 3.4.1
paras 2.2–2.11 . . . 3.4.1
para 3.8 . . . 3.4.1
para 4.3 . . . 3.4.1
Annex A . . . 3.5
Code B . . . 3.1, 3.9, 3.9.8
Code C . . . 1.3, 3.7.5, 4.1,
   4.2.1, 4.4.2, 4.7.5, 4.9, 4.10,
   4.11, 4.12.1, 4.15, Fig. 4.1,
   6.4, 6.5.3, 6.11.1, 6.13.2,
   Fig. 6.1, Fig. 6.2, 9.7.5,
   24.6.2, 24.11, App 2
para 1.4 . . . 4.9
para 1.5 . . . 24.2, 24.6.1
para 1.7 . . . 24.6.3
para 1.7(b) . . . 4.9
para 1.7A . . . 24.6.3
para 1.7A . . . 4.9
para 1.13(d) . . . 4.9
Note 1B . . . 4.9
Note 1CA . . . 4.9
Note 1E . . . 4.9
Note 1GA . . . 4.9
para 2.1 . . . 4.4.1
para 2.4 . . . 4.4.1
para 2.4A . . . 4.4.1
para 3.1 . . . 4.4.2
para 3.5 . . . 4.4.2
paras 3.6–3.10 . . . 4.4.2, 24.6.2
para 3.12 . . . 4.4.2
para 3.12A . . . 4.4.2
para 3.13 . . . 24.6.2
para 3.15 . . . 4.9
para 3.17 . . . 4.9
para 3.21 . . . 4.2
para 3.21(a) . . . 4.2
para 3.21(b)(ii) . . . 4.2.1
para. 3.21A . . . 4.2.1
para. 3.21A(a)–(g) . . . 4.2.1
para. 3.22A . . . 4.2.1
para 5 . . . 4.7.1
para 6 . . . 4.7.3
para 6.1 . . . 4.7.5
para 6.4 . . . 4.7.5
para 6.5 . . . 4.9, 4.7.5
para 6.6 . . . 4.7.5, 4.12.4, 5.2.6
para 6.6(b) . . . 4.11
para 6.15 . . . 4.7.5

Note 6A . . . 4.7.5
Note 6D . . . 4.12.4
para 8 . . . 4.8
para 8.8 . . . 24.6.2
para 9 . . . 4.8
para 10.1 . . . 4.10.1
para 10.11 . . . Fig. 5.1
para 11 . . . 4.12.4
para 11.1 . . . 4.10.1
para 11.1A . . . 4.10.1, 5.2.1
para 11.2 . . . 4.7.5
para 11.5 . . . 4.9, 4.12.1,
    4.12.2
para 11.6 . . . 4.10.3
Note 11B . . . 4.12.4
Note 11ZA . . . 5.2.1
para 11.13 . . . 6.4.2
para 11.15 . . . 4.10.2
para 11.16 . . . 4.10.3
para 11.17 . . . 4.9, 4.12.5
para 12 . . . 4.8
para 12.2 . . . 4.8
para 12.3 . . . 4.10.2
para 12.4 . . . 4.12.3
para 12.8 . . . 4.8
para 13.1A . . . 4.8
paras 13.5–13.7 . . . 4.8
para 15.4 . . . 4.7.5
paras 15.9–15.11 . . . 4.6
para 16.4 . . . 4.7.5
para 16.5 . . . 4.7.5, 4.14.3
Note 16A . . . 4.14
para 17 . . . 4.14.5
Annex A . . . 4.4.3
para B.9 . . . 4.4.3
Annex B . . . 4.7.1, 4.7.2, 4.7.3,
    4.7.6
para A.3 . . . 4.7.6
para A.4 . . . 4.7.6
para A.6 . . . 4.7.6
Annex C . . . 5.2.1
Annex E . . . 4.9
Annex G . . . 4.10.1
Annex L . . . 4.4.3
Code D . . . 1.3, 6.2, Fig. 6.1,
    7.1, 7.2, 7.4, 7.5, 7.5.1, 7.6,
    7.7, 7.8, 7.8.1, 7.9, 7.10,
    7.15, Fig. 7.1, 9.7.5, 12.7.9,
    17.6, Fig. 17.1, App 2
para 2.3 . . . 7.6
para 3.1 . . . 7.3
para 3.1A(a) . . . 7.4.1
para 3.1A(b) . . . 7.4.1
para 3.2 . . . 7.4.2
para 3.3 . . . 7.4.3, Fig. 7.1
para 3.4 . . . 7.4.1, 7.4.4
para 3.5–3.10 . . . 7.5
para 3.12 . . . 7.5, 7.5.1, 7.6,
    Fig. 7.1
para 3.14 . . . 7.5.1
para 3.15 . . . 7.5.2
para 3.17 . . . 4.7.5, 7.5.2
para 3.23 . . . 7.5.2
para 3.35 . . . 7.9
para 3.36 . . . 7.9

para 3.36(a)–(k) . . . 7.9
para 3.37 . . . 7.9
paras 4.1–4.15 . . . 7.12.2
paras 5.12–5.18 . . . 7.4.5
para 6.2 . . . 7.12.4
para 6.3 . . . 4.7.5, 7.12.4
para 6.4 . . . 7.12.4
para 6.5 . . . 7.12.3
Annex A . . . 7.5.1, 7.7.1, 7.9,
    Fig. 7.1
Annex B . . . 7.5.1, 7.7.2, Fig.
    7.1
Annex C . . . 7.5.1, 7.7.3, Fig.
    7.1
Annex D . . . 7.5.1, 7.7.4, Fig.
    7.1
Annex E . . . 7.4.3, 7.9, Fig. 7.1
Code E . . . 4.2.1, 4.10, 6.4,
    6.4.1
para 2.1 . . . 6.4.1
para 2.3 . . . 6.4.1
para 3 . . . 6.4.1
para 3.1 . . . 6.13.2, 13.12.2
Code F . . . 4.2.1, 6.4.1
Code G . . . 3.7.5
para 1.2 . . . 3.7.5
para 1.3 . . . 3.7.4, 3.7.6
para 2.1 . . . 3.7.5
para 2.3A . . . 3.7.6
para 2.6 . . . 3.7.5
para 2.8 . . . 3.7.5, 3.7.6
Note 2G . . . 4.2
paras 3.1–3.7 . . . 3.7.6
para 4.1 . . . 3.7.6
Code H . . . 4.1
Police and Justice Act 2006
s 47 . . . 19.3.1
s 47(4) . . . 19.3.1
s 47(5) . . . 19.3.1
Policing and Crime Act
    2017 . . . 1.3
s 52 . . . 3.8
s 54 . . . 4.6.2, 4.14.2
s 76 . . . 4.12.3
Powers of Criminal Courts
(Sentencing) Act 2000
s 1 . . . 22.14, 26.3
s 2 . . . 22.14
s 3 . . . 11.2.1, 11.3.1, 11.4.2,
    12.11, 21.14.2, 21.14.3,
    App 3
s 3A . . . 11.3.5
s 3B . . . 25.3.2, 25.3.6, 26.18,
    App 3
s 3B(1) . . . 25.3.3, 25.5
s 3C . . . 25.3.5, 26.19
s 4 . . . 21.14.3
s 6 . . . 12.11, 21.14.2
s 8 . . . 26.18
s 12 . . . 22.17, 22.18, 26.6,
    26.7
s 16 . . . 26.4
s 17 . . . 26.4
Pt VI (ss 33–75) . . . 26.5
ss 73–75 . . . 26.8

s 78 . . . 21.14.1
s 89(1) . . . 22.3
s 90 . . . 26.18
s 91 . . . 25.3.1, 25.3.2, 25.3.3,
    25.5, 26.18
s 91(1)–(2) . . . 25.3.3
s 100 . . . 25.3.3
ss 100–107 . . . 26.10
s 101(8) . . . 26.10
s 103 . . . 26.10
s 110 . . . 21.15.2, 22.7
s 111 . . . 11.6, 21.15.2, 22.7,
    App 3
ss 126–129 . . . 22.15
s 130 . . . 22.16, Fig. 22.2,
    26.12
ss 131–135 . . . 26.12
s 143 . . . 22.20.2
s 145 . . . 22.20.2
s 150(1) . . . 26.14
s 155 . . . 21.15.1
Prevention of Crime Act 1953
s 1 . . . 3.4.1
Proceeds of Crime Act
    2002 . . . 22.20.2, Fig. 22.2
s 13 . . . App 3
Prosecution of Offences Act 1985
s 10 . . . 8.2.3
s 16 . . . 9.13, 12.11, 14.17
s 17 . . . 22.20.1
s 19 . . . 9.14
s 22 . . . 10.13.1
Protection of Freedom Act
    2012 . . . 7.13.1
Public Order Act 1986
s 3 . . . 13.3.1, App 3
s 4 . . . App 2
s 5 . . . 19.7.5

Regulation of Investigatory
    Powers Act 2000 . . . 6.11.1,
    6.11.2, 20.6
s 27 . . . 20.6
Rehabilitation of Offenders Act
    1974 . . . 1.10.1, 24.8.2
Road Traffic Act 1988
s 5(1)(a) . . . 20.7.3
s 41D . . . 3.7.6
s 143 . . . 15.3.3
s 172 . . . 20.7.2, 20.7.3
s 172(2) . . . 20.7.3
s 172(2)(a) . . . 20.7.2
s 172(3) . . . 20.7.2, 20.7.3
Road Traffic Regulation Act 1984
s 89 . . . 17.3
s 89(2) . . . 17.3

Senior Courts Act 1981 . . . 1.7.5
s 28 . . . 1.7.6, 23.4
s 48 . . . 23.3.2
s 79(3) . . . 23.3.2
s 81 . . . 10.15, 10.20, 23.6.4
Serious Organised Crime and
    Police Act 2005 . . . 3.1
s 8(2)–(4) . . . 3.9.8

s 73 . . . App 3
s 74 . . . App 3
Sexual Offences Act
2003 . . . 8.2.1, 19.7.5
s 1 . . . 25.3.4
s 3 . . . 25.3.3
s 8(1) . . . 25.3.3
s 8(3) . . . 25.3.3
Supreme Court Act 1981 *See*
Senior Courts Act 1981

Terrorism Act 2000 . . . 3.1, 4.1
s 11(1) . . . 15.7.1
Theft Act 1968 . . . 3.4.1, 21.15
s 1 . . . 1.5.2, 2.3, 3.4.1, 15.2,
App 3
s 8 . . . 1.5.3
s 8(1) . . . 15.6
s 9 . . . 3.4.1, App 3
s 9(1)(a) . . . App 2
s 9(1)(b) . . . App 2
s 12 . . . 3.4.1
s 31 . . . 20.7.2
Trade Descriptions Act
1968 . . . 1.6.1
Treason Act 1795
s 1 . . . 17.3

Youth Justice and Criminal Evidence Act 1999 . . . 16.5.11
s 16 . . . 16.4, 16.4.1, 16.4.2,
Fig. 16.1
s 17 . . . 16.4, 16.4.2, Fig. 16.1
s 17(2) . . . 16.4.2
s 19 . . . 16.3.2, 16.4.2, Fig.
16.1
s 19(2) . . . 16.4
s 21 . . . 16.4.1, 16.5.5
s 22A . . . 16.4.1, 16.5.5
s 23 . . . 16.5.1, Fig. 16.1
s 24 . . . 16.5.2, Fig. 16.1
s 25 . . . 16.5.3, Fig. 16.1
s 26 . . . 16.5.4, Fig. 16.1
s 27 . . . 16.5.5, Fig. 16.1,
25.3.6, App 3
s 28 . . . 16.5.6, Fig. 16.1,
25.3.6, App 3
s 29 . . . 16.5.7, Fig. 16.1
s 30 . . . 16.5.8, Fig. 16.1
s 33BA(2) . . . 19.3.1
s 33BA(2)(b) . . . 19.3.1
s 33BA(3) . . . 19.3.1
s 33BA(6) . . . 19.3.1
ss 34–36 . . . 9.7.9
s 38(4) . . . 19.10
s 41 . . . 16.12
s 42 . . . 16.12
s 43 . . . 16.12
s 53 . . . 16.3.2, 18.6, 19.2,
Fig. 19.1
s 53(1) . . . 16.3.1, Fig. 16.1,
19.2
s 53(3) . . . 16.3.1, Fig. 16.1
s 53(4) . . . 19.2.1, Fig. 19.1

s 53(5) . . . 19.2.1, Fig. 19.1
s 54 . . . 16.3.2, Fig. 16.1
s 54(3) . . . Fig. 16.1
s 55(2) . . . 16.3.1
s 56(1) . . . 16.3.1
s 58 . . . 4.11, 5.3.1

Table of Codes of Practice and Professional Conduct Rules

Code of Conduct (2018)
s 9 . . . 21.3
Code for Crown Prosecu-
tors . . . 2.6, 7.15, 8.1, 8.2,
8.2.5, 8.3, 8.15, Fig. 8.1, 15.9,
17.6.6, 24.8.2, 24.8.3, 24.9
s 2.4 . . . 14.9
s 3 . . . 8.2.4
s 4 . . . 8.2.3, 8.2.5
s 4.6 . . . 8.2.5
s 4.7 . . . 8.2.5
s 4.8 . . . 8.2.5
s 4.9 . . . 8.2.5
s 4.10 . . . 8.2.5
s 4.11 . . . 8.2.5
s 4.12 . . . 8.2.5
s 4.12(d) . . . 24.2
s 4.13 . . . 8.2.5
s 4.14 . . . 8.2.5
s 4.14(a)–(c) . . . 8.2.5
s 4.14(d) . . . 8.2.5, 24.9
s 4.14(e)–(g) . . . 8.2.5
s 5.1 . . . 8.4
s 5.2 . . . 8.4
s 5.3 . . . 8.4
s 5.4 . . . 8.4
ss 5.5–5.7 . . . 8.4
ss 5.8–5.10 . . . 8.4
s 5.11 . . . 8.4
s 6.1 . . . 8.5
s 7 . . . 8.6.2
s 7.1 . . . 8.6
s 9 . . . 21.4.3
Code of Practice for Adult
Conditional Cautions . . . 8.6.2
Code of Practice on the conduct of police interviews
(2010) . . . 13.9.2
Code of Practice for
Youth Conditional Cau-
tions . . . 24.8.3
CPS Victim's Code . . . 8.2.5

Disclosure Code of Prac-
tice (CPIA 1996) revised
2015 . . . *See* Criminal Procedure Investigations Act 1996
Discovery Code of Practice PACE
Codes of Practice . . . *See* Police
and Criminal Evidence Act
1984 Codes of Practice

Solicitors Code of Conduct
2007 . . . 1.10.5, 12.7.2

r 11 Note 15 . . . 1.10.5
Solicitors Code of Conduct
2019 . . . 1.10, 1.10.1, 1.10.2,
1.10.4, 9.16, 14.10, 8.1, 8.3,
12.7.2, 12.11
s 5 . . . 1.10.1
s 6 . . . 1.10.4, 1.10.5
s 7 . . . 1.10.1
ss 7.1–7.5 . . . 1.10.1
s 7.6 . . . 1.10.1
Principles . . . 1.10
Principle 1 . . . 1.10, 1.10.2,
1.10.3, 1.10.5, 12.6.2,
16.9.4, 22.24
Principle 2 . . . 1.10, 1.10.5,
16.9.4
Principle 3 . . . 1.10, 1.10.5
Principle 4 . . . 1.10, 1.10.5,
22.24
Principle 5 . . . 1.10, 1.10.5,
22.24
Principle 6 . . . 1.10, 1.10.4
Principle 7 . . . 1.10, 1.10.2,
1.10.3, 1.10.5, 1.10.6, 8.3,
9.2, 12.6.2
Streamlined Disclosure
Code . . . 8.8, 8.10.2

Table of International Legislation

European Convention on
Human Rights 1950 . . . 1.8,
1.8.1, 1.8.3, 3.10, 8.8, 10.22,
18.14, 20.1
Art 3 . . . 1.8.2, 25.4
Art 5 . . . 1.8.2, 1.8.3, 3.1,
3.7.5, 3.10, 10.1, 10.10.2,
10.22
Art 5(1) . . . 10.22
Art 5(1)(a) . . . 10.22
Art 5(1)(c) . . . 10.22
Art 6 . . . 1.8.2, 1.8.3, 1.9,
1.10.5, 2.2, 4.7.3, 5.2.6, 5.4,
6.1, 6.5.3, 6.11.1, 6.13.2,
10.10.2, 10.22, 13.9.5, 15.7,
Fig. 15.1, 16.5.2, 18.6.1,
18.8.1, 18.12, 18.12.3, 18.14,
18.15, Fig. 18.1, 20.7.2,
20.7.3, Fig. 20.1, 25.1, 25.2,
25.3.6, 25.4, App 2
Art 6(1) . . . 1.8.2, 8.8, 18.14
Art 6(2) . . . 1.8.2, 15.7, 15.7.1,
15.9, 20.7.3
Art 6(3) . . . 1.8.2, 1.8.3,
6.11.1
Art 6(3)(b) . . . 8.8
Art 6(3)(c) . . . 9.2
Art 6(3)(d) . . . 18.14
Art 8 . . . 1.8.2, 3.10, 6.11.1,
Fig. 6.1, 24.8.2
Art 10 . . . 3.10
Art 11 . . . 3.10
UN Convention on the Rights of
the Child 1989 . . . 24.9

Table of UK Statutory Instruments and EU Secondary Legislation

UK Statutory Instruments

Civil Procedure Rules 1998 (SI 1998/3132)
  Pt 54 . . . 1.7.6, 23.5, 23.5.1, Fig. 23.1
Crime and Disorder Act 1998 (Dismissal of Charges Sent) Rules 1998 (SI 1998/3048) . . . App 2
Crime and Disorder Act 1998 (Service of Prosecution Evidence) Regulations 2000 (SI 2000/3305) . . . App 2
Crime and Disorder Act 1998 (Service of Prosecution Evidence) Regulations 2005 (SI 2005/902) . . . 13.5.4
  reg. 2 . . . Fig. 8.2
Criminal Procedure and Investigations Act 1996 (Defence Disclosure Time Limits) Regulations 2011 . . . App 2
Criminal Procedure Rules 2011 (SI 2011/1709)
  Pt 27
    r 27.1 . . . App 2
Criminal Procedure Rules 2015 (SI 2015/1490) . . . 1.7.1, 1.7.5, 1.9, 8.1, 12.2, 12.6.1, 13.4, 13.4.1, 19.5.1, 19.7.5
  Pt 1 . . . 1.8.3, 1.9, 9.7.10, 9.15.1, 12.6.2, 25.2
    r 1.1 . . . 1.9
    r 1.2 . . . 1.9
  Pt 3 . . . 1.9, 6.13.1, 8.8, 9.16, 11.8.3, 12.6.2, 12.7, 12.11, 13.4.1, 13.9.6, 18.4.1, 25.2
    r 3.2 . . . 1.9, 12.6.2, 17.9.2
    r 3.2(2) . . . 12.6.2

r 3.2(3) . . . 12.6.2
r 3.3 . . . 1.9, 9.15.1, 12.6.2, 13.1, 19.7.5
r 3.5 . . . 12.6.2
r 3.5(3) . . . 13.4.1
r 3.5(6) . . . 1.9
r 3.9(7) . . . 13.5.6
r 3.14 . . . 13.11
r 3.21(4)(a) . . . 14.2.3
Pt 4 . . . 12.2
  r 4.6 . . . 13.2
Pt 7
  r 7.3 . . . 12.2, 12.5
  r 7.3(1) . . . 12.2
Pt 8 . . . Fig. 1.1, Fig. 1.2, 6.4.1, 8.11, 8.11.1, 8.11.2, 8.15, Fig. 8.2, Fig. 8.3, 9.15, 9.16, 11.2, 12.6, 12.7.4, 13.3, 13.12.2
  r 8 . . . 1.10.6
  r 8.2 . . . 8.11
  r 8.3 . . . 8.11
Pt 9 . . . 11.1, 11.2.1, 13.10.1
  r 9.2(6) . . . 11.7.2
  r 9.7(5)(a)(ii) . . . 13.4.1
  r 9.13 . . . 25.3.2
Pt 10 . . . 14.2
  r 10.2(2) . . . 14.2.2, 14.2.4
Pt 14 . . . 10.1
  r 14.8 . . . 10.15
  r 14.9 . . . 10.16
Pt 15 . . . 8.14
  r 15.4 . . . 14.9.1, App 2
Pt 16 . . . App 2
Pt 17 . . . 12.7.8
Pt 18 . . . 16.4, 16.5.10
Pt 19 . . . 12.7.3, 17.10, Fig. 17.1, App 2
  r 19.1(1) . . . 4.14.1
  r 19.2 . . . 17.9.2
  r 19.2(3)(c) . . . 17.9.2
  r 19.3 . . . 17.9.3
  r 19.4 . . . 17.9.3, 17.9.4
  r 19.6 . . . 17.9.4
  r 19.7 . . . 17.9.4

Pt 20 . . . 18.13, 18.15
Pt 21 . . . 19.11
  r 21.3 . . . 16.9.4
Pt 24 . . . 21.4.2
  r 24.3 . . . 12.11
  r 24.3(c) . . . 12.11
  r 24.8 . . . 12.3
  r 24.15 . . . 1.7.3
Pt 25 . . . 14.1, 21.4.2
  rr 25.6–25.8 . . . 14.8.1
  r 25.9 . . . 14.9, 14.9.1
  r 25.11 . . . 14.10
  r 25.14 . . . 14.14
  r 25.16 . . . 14.16
Pt 28 . . . 13.12.1
Pt 34 . . . 23.1, 23.3
  r 34.2 . . . 23.3.1
Pt 35 . . . 1.7.6, 23.1, 23.4
Pt 36 . . . 23.1, 23.6
Pt 37 . . . 14.18, 23.1, 23.11
Pt 38 . . . 23.1, 23.11
Pt 39 . . . 23.1, 23.6, 23.6.5, 23.7
Pt 40 . . . 23.1
Pt 41 . . . 23.1, 23.9
Pt 42 . . . 23.1
Pt 43 . . . 23.1, 23.8
Pt 44 . . . 23.1
Legal Aid, Sentencing and Punishment of Offenders Act 2012 (Criminal Legal Aid (General) Regulations) 2013(SI 2013/534) . . . 9.7

European Secondary Legislation

Directive 2010/64/EU (Right to Interpretation and Translation in Criminal Proceedings) . . . 4.8
Directive 2011/36/EU (Preventing and Combating Trafficking in Human Beings and Protecting the Victims) . . . 8.3

Part I

INTRODUCTION TO CRIMINAL LITIGATION

Part I equips the reader with important background information that will inform the substantive areas covered in later chapters.

Chapter 1 explains the aims of *Criminal Litigation* and its unique features. It introduces the key personnel and organisations in the criminal justice system and explains the importance of classifying criminal offences. It also addresses human rights and the rules of professional conduct in criminal cases.

Chapter 2 provides an introduction to criminal evidence and advocacy.

1 INTRODUCTION

1.1	**Introduction**	**4**
1.2	**Philosophy of *criminal litigation***	**5**
	1.2.1 Taking an integrated and practical approach	5
	1.2.2 Do I need to read all the chapters?	6
1.3	**Online resources**	**6**
1.4	**Research sources**	**7**
	1.4.1 Practitioner works	8
	1.4.2 Texts	8
	1.4.3 Journals	8
	1.4.4 Electronic research sources	8
1.5	**Classifying criminal offences**	**8**
	1.5.1 Summary-only offences	9
	1.5.2 Offences triable either way	9
	1.5.3 Indictable-only offences	9
1.6	**Personnel and organisations within the criminal justice system**	**9**
	1.6.1 Investigating and prosecuting organisations	9
	1.6.2 The Legal Aid Agency	10
	1.6.3 The Public Defender Service	10
1.7	**The criminal courts and personnel**	**10**
	1.7.1 Magistrates' court	10
	1.7.2 Magistrates	11
	1.7.3 The legal adviser	11
	1.7.4 Youth court	12
	1.7.5 The Crown Court	12
	1.7.6 The Administrative Court and the High Court	12
	1.7.7 The Court of Appeal (Criminal Division)	12
	1.7.8 The Supreme Court	13
1.8	**The European Convention on Human Rights 1950 (ECHR 1950)**	**13**
	1.8.1 How are the rights guaranteed under the Convention enforced in domestic law?	13
	1.8.2 Criminal litigation—the relevant Convention Articles	13
	1.8.3 The ECHR 1950 and the rules of criminal procedure and evidence	15
1.9	**Criminal Procedure Rules (Crim PR) 2015**	**15**
1.10	**Professional conduct—an introduction**	**17**
	1.10.1 The Solicitors Code of Conduct (2019)	18
	1.10.2 The 2019 Code and its application to criminal litigation	21
	1.10.3 Client care	22
	1.10.4 Conflict, confidentiality, and disclosure	22
	1.10.5 Dispute resolution and proceedings before courts, tribunals, and inquiries	24
	1.10.6 Professional conduct and the Criminal Procedure Rules	26

1.1 **INTRODUCTION**

> **CPS press release 20 December 2018: Man convicted of murdering woman in her home**
>
> *A man has been convicted of murdering a woman at her home in Crawley, after she was attacked on her 29th birthday.*
>
> *Lewes Crown Court heard that Zahid Naseem (48), from Amersham in Buckinghamshire (left), killed Christine Abbots at her flat in Highams Hill.*
>
> *The alarm was raised by friends after she failed to arrive at a celebration she had planned in London on the evening of her birthday on Friday 25 May.*
>
> *When police broke into the locked flat, Naseem was found lying motionless with self-harm type injuries to his wrist. A post mortem showed that Christine had been killed by a number of blows to her head during an attack a number of hours earlier.*
>
> *Jayne Cioffi, from the CPS, said: "The defendant's story changed over time, with him first claiming that he could not remember what had happened and refusing to accept any responsibility for Christine's death.*
>
> *"Faced with the sheer weight of forensic evidence against him, which clearly showed no-one else had been in the flat, Naseem then changed his story, claiming during his trial that he had killed Christine in self-defence.*
>
> *"The CPS was able to present a compelling case to the jury that Naseem was guilty of murder and that self-defence had not played any part in his actions that day.*
>
> *"Not only did Christine suffer multiple blows to the head, the defendant then failed to call 999 after the attack and for many hours afterwards, instead remaining in her flat until police broke in early the following morning.*
>
> *"Naseem then feigned unconsciousness when discovered, believing that would help him to evade justice. He was wrong."*

This case provides a dramatic snapshot of the work of those involved in the criminal justice system. The case, which took months to come to trial, required many hours of investigation by the police as well as painstaking file preparation and evaluation of the evidence by the Crown Prosecution Service (CPS). The defence team also spent many hours preparing the defendant's case for trial. As the trial date approached several ancillary criminal justice organisations became involved, including victim support, witness care, and Her Majesty's Court Service.

At the trial, the prosecution and defence advocates presented their parties' interpretation of the law to the facts of the case to the judge and jury. The judge summed the case up to the jury and the defendant's guilt or innocence was decided by the jury, which was made up of ordinary members of the public from wide and diverse backgrounds. At the conclusion of the case Naseem was given a life sentence with a minimum term of imprisonment of 19 years. The loss is even greater for the victims' family and friends, who are deprived forever of their loved one and left with only memories.

For those studying to be criminal lawyers and for those already in practice, the purpose of *Criminal Litigation* is to explain the legal, procedural and evidential rules governing how cases like those involving the Eyre family and thousands of other usually less serious cases are dealt with each year by the criminal justice system.

The text covers all the key aspects of the criminal litigation process. Whether you are studying criminal litigation as part of your LPC or BPTC or already work as a CPS lawyer, private practice solicitor, legal executive or paralegal, or have another professional involvement in the criminal justice system, we hope that you find the book an invaluable source of reference.

In this introductory chapter, we aim to:

* explain the philosophy of this book and its unique features;

- introduce the key personnel and organisations within the criminal justice system;
- introduce the Criminal Procedure Rules;
- explain the classification of offences according to their trial venue;
- provide a summary of the jurisdiction of the criminal courts;
- stress the importance of the pervasive issue of human rights; and
- highlight professional conduct considerations in the context of criminal litigation.

1.2 PHILOSOPHY OF *CRIMINAL LITIGATION*

Criminal Litigation provides an innovative approach to the study of criminal litigation and evidence and gives students and early-years practitioners a highly practical and comprehensive explanation of the key substantive, procedural and evidential issues that are encountered by both prosecution and defence lawyers in a criminal case. For those who wish to further their knowledge and understanding, there are also extensive learning resources that illustrate, through practice-based examples, diagrams, self-test exercises and case studies, the operation of the law in a very practical context.

1.2.1 TAKING AN INTEGRATED AND PRACTICAL APPROACH

Working as a criminal lawyer requires the practitioner to take an integrated and practical approach to their work. This approach is adopted in the manual. The integrated approach is reflected in our belief that students and practitioners should be aware that the rules of criminal procedure, criminal evidence, professional conduct and legal skills are not discrete elements, but are part of the integrated picture that is involved in representing a client in a criminal case.

The treatment of the rules of criminal evidence highlights this integrated approach. Both prosecutors and defence lawyers must understand that key evidential issues are relevant at all stages of a case including from when the CPS lawyer advises the police about the appropriate charge to the defence lawyer's earliest representation of a client at the police station or during the first interview in the office. Chapter 2 entitled: 'An Introduction to the Law of Criminal Evidence and Advocacy' provides an overview of criminal evidence and is designed to encourage you to think about evidence at the very outset, before aspects of criminal procedure and the substantive rules of evidence are covered in more detail later in *Criminal Litigation*.

The practical approach is achieved in different ways. We have attempted to explain the law and procedure in an accessible and reader-friendly style. The substantive content of each chapter is supplemented by practical examples and diagrams as well as self-test questions and answers. *Criminal Litigation* integrates three case studies throughout the book which are an essential part of our practical approach. The integrated case studies are:

Case study 1:   *R v Lenny Wise (not guilty plea in relation to an either-way offence of burglary)*

Case study 2:   *R v Roger Martin (guilty pleas in relation to summary-only offences of common assault and careless driving)*

Case study 3:   *R v William Hardy (guilty plea in relation to an indictable-only sexual offence)*

A selection of documentation supporting case study 1 is included in Appendix 2. The complete documentation to *R v Lenny Wise* and the other two case studies can be found in the case study section of the online resources. The case studies form the basis of ongoing exercises throughout the manual which are designed to give you the opportunity to apply your knowledge of criminal procedure and evidence in the context of a 'real' case. Keep the case studies in mind as you work through each stage of the criminal litigation process. Treat these fictional characters as your clients!

Key areas of practice and procedure in all our case studies have been filmed. The 'cases' were heard before a bench of serving lay magistrates (and in the matter of *R v William Hardy* before a Crown Court judge). All the participants in the video clips gave up their valuable time to assist us in making the films. The clips (all of which are held on the online resources) are learning aids that illustrate, in a practical way, aspects of criminal practice. We would ask you to make an allowance for the fact that some aspects of procedure have changed since filming was undertaken. We draw your attention to these changes where appropriate. The videos are not necessarily a depiction of how cases always proceed and they should not be regarded as definitive examples of how advocacy is conducted before a criminal court. Commentary is included on the clips. Transcripts of the principal submissions made by the advocates are included in the case study documentation.

1.2.2 DO I NEED TO READ ALL THE CHAPTERS?

LPC criminal litigation courses vary in length and substantive content. Whether you are a student embarking upon the vocational stage of your legal career or you work in criminal practice, *Criminal Litigation* aims to provide a practical and comprehensive explanation of the key principles of criminal procedure and evidence. In addition, this book includes several additional chapters located in its accompanying online resources which, if you are an LPC student, you are more likely to need in an advanced criminal litigation elective. It may therefore be unnecessary for you to read every chapter. Your course tutor will tell you which learning outcomes you need to achieve for this area of legal practice and so concentrate on those chapters and online materials that are relevant to your specific needs.

1.3 ONLINE RESOURCES

Our online resources can be accessed at www.oup.com/uk/crimlit19-20/. Features included are fully explained in the 'Guided Tour of the Online -Resources' at page xvi but it is helpful to introduce the resource here also. The website is divided into useful sections to help the individual reader and includes the following resources:

Section 1—password-protected lecturer resources: high-quality video clips bring to life the key procedural stages of *Criminal Litigation*'s case studies and are formatted for download through broadband, suitable for viewing on a computer or intranet. The clips include accompanying selective transcripts broadly based on the principal submissions made by the advocates. For those using *Criminal Litigation* as a core text on the LPC or BPTC there are also two further role-play scenarios available in the lecturer resource section.

Case study 4: *Peter West: Police Station Scenario.*

Case study 5: *R v Nicholas Jones: Bad character applications before a Crown Court judge.*

Case study 4 was filmed at an operational, rural police station.

Full instructions on the use that you might make of these two learning resources are included.

Section 2—open access lecturer resources: the video clips of the case scenarios are available for online browsing intended for lecturers to review the material available.

Section 3—student and practitioner resources: these are freely available resources and include answers to the self-test questions which can be found at the conclusion of most of the chapters; updates to cover recent developments in criminal litigation and criminal evidence; complete documentation supporting case studies 1, 2 and 3; and a comprehensive web-links section which will take you directly to resources such as the PACE Codes of Practice and the Magistrates' Court Sentencing Guidelines. It also includes an interactive timeline which will help you to see how the whole criminal litigation process fits together and the issues that you need to keep in mind at particular points. The timeline distinguishes between the three classifications of offences of summary-only, either-way and indictable-only.

Wherever you see this symbol there is a link to our online resources. In order to derive maximum benefit from this text you should make full use of the learning and information resources on our online resources.

The criminal justice system in England and Wales is rarely out of the news. These are challenging times for criminal lawyers with significant cuts to public funding in criminal defence cases as well as dealing with the effects of new legislation such as the Policing and Crime Act 2017, new criminal laws, frequent case law, and changes to sentencing. Revised versions of Codes C and D under the Police and Criminal Evidence Act 1984 (PACE 1984) were introduced in 2018 and 2017 respectively, and sentencing practice regularly changes with revised or new guidelines issued by the Sentencing Council and through the case law on sentencing.

Practitioners have also had to deal with the recommendations of the Leveson report published in January 2015 available at http://www.judiciary.gov.uk/publications/review-of-efficiency-in-criminal-proceedings-final-report/. Leveson's recommendations were intended to improve the efficiency of the criminal justice system and included:

- more efficient decision-making about charging decisions;
- more efficient use of streamlined disclosure;
- more robust decision-making about which cases are sent to the Crown Court;
- more robust and consistent case management by the courts;
- increased use of IT, including video-conference links from prisons to court;
- identification of a nominated person from the police/CPS and from the defence who has responsibility for the case.

On a practical level Leveson's legacy can be seen in the 'Transforming Summary Justice' (TSJ) (2015) initiative, and the introduction of the Plea Trial and Preparation Hearing (PTPH) before the Crown Court, which are covered in Chapters 9 and 13, respectively.

Finally, in early 2018 significant and it would seem systemic failings in the pre-trial disclosure duties that rest on the police and the CPS came to light across various media platforms, resulting in the collapse of a number of rape trials and a full-scale review of all live rape cases by the Metropolitan Police and the CPS. The well-publicised failings have rocked public confidence in the criminal justice system and will no doubt lead to changes in the way in which disclosure is made in the future. The law and practice on the pre-trial disclosure of evidence is explained in Chapters 8 and 13.

The update section of our online resources will highlight any significant changes during 2019–20 and also consider the way in which the changes are being applied in practice. Any reforms likely to be brought into force in the next 12 months are highlighted in the text by the feature entitled 'Looking Ahead'.

Students should be aware of these legislative changes, not only for learning and assessment purposes, but also because questions about recent legal developments are commonly asked at job interviews.

1.4 RESEARCH SOURCES

Legal research is a vital part of the work of a student and practitioner. While our online resources provide invaluable links to related websites from which you can access further useful information, we include here a summary of useful practitioner texts and practitioner journals.

1.4.1 **PRACTITIONER WORKS**

Blackstone's Criminal Practice

Also published by Oxford University Press, *Blackstone's Criminal Practice* is a leading work of reference for criminal practitioners. Annually updated and written in an accessible and user-friendly way, *Blackstone's* provides a detailed explanation of the main substantive criminal offences, the key stages of criminal procedure and the rules of criminal evidence.

Archbold Criminal Pleading and Practice

This well-established authoritative practitioner text is specifically directed to the practice and procedure of trials on indictment. *Archbold* now publishes a companion volume for proceedings in the magistrates' court.

Stone's Justices Manual

This is the most authoritative text for proceedings in the magistrates' court. *Stone's* is an indispensable source of reference for all criminal practitioners.

1.4.2 **TEXTS**

Defending Suspects at the Police Station (Ed Cape; published by the Legal Action Group)

This book offers a clear explanation covering all aspects of representing a client at the police station, including a detailed exposition of police powers and invaluable advice about the strategies to be adopted by the legal adviser.

The Golden Rules of Advocacy (Keith Evans; Oxford University Press)

An informative, short and entertaining book on developing or refining your advocacy skills.

1.4.3 **JOURNALS**

Journal articles can also provide information on current issues and recent developments in criminal procedure and evidence. The journals that might be of interest include the *Criminal Law Review* and the *Legal Action Group Magazine*. The Law Society Gazette will keep you up to date with developments in practice (see http://www.lawgazette.co.uk/).

1.4.4 **ELECTRONIC RESEARCH SOURCES**

 Electronic research sources from the key criminal justice organisations and an extensive set of web-links can be accessed via the web-links section from our online resources.

1.5 **CLASSIFYING CRIMINAL OFFENCES**

Whilst criminal offences can be classified in several ways, the most significant classification for criminal litigators determines whether the case will ultimately be dealt with in the magistrates' court or the Crown Court. An offence will either be:

- summary-only;
- triable either way; or
- indictable-only.

Always check the classification of an offence if you are not sure, whether in an assessment or in practice. The classification of all criminal offences can be researched in a practitioner work, such as *Blackstone's Criminal Practice*. The classification of the offence determines the procedural course the case will follow.

1.5.1 SUMMARY-ONLY OFFENCES

The least serious offences are known as summary-only offences and are dealt with summarily in the magistrates' court, whether or not the defendant pleads guilty or not guilty. Common assault (s. 39 Criminal Justice Act 1988) is a summary-only offence, as are a number of less serious motoring offences.

1.5.2 OFFENCES TRIABLE EITHER WAY

Either-way offences are middle-ranking offences in terms of seriousness and can be tried either summarily before a magistrates' court or on indictment before a judge and jury in the Crown Court. Theft (s. 1 Theft Act 1968) is an either-way offence. It is the defendant's indication of plea which determines where an either-way offence will be heard. If a defendant indicates a guilty plea, the case will remain in the magistrates' court and the court will proceed to sentence. The magistrates' court has the power to commit the defendant to be sentenced before the Crown Court upon conviction for an either-way offence where it considers its limited powers of sentence are insufficient.

If a defendant indicates a not guilty plea to an either-way offence, the magistrates' court will conduct an allocation hearing to decide whether to keep jurisdiction and try the case summarily or to decline jurisdiction and send the case to the Crown Court to be tried on indictment. If the magistrates' court declines jurisdiction, the accused has no choice and the case will be sent to the Crown Court, under s. 51 Crime and Disorder Act 1998, following the allocation hearing. If the magistrates' court accepts jurisdiction to try the either-way offence summarily, the accused has a choice: consent to summary trial or elect trial by jury on indictment before the Crown Court.

1.5.3 INDICTABLE-ONLY OFFENCES

The most serious crimes are known as indictable-only offences, which will be tried at the Crown Court before a judge and jury. The common law offence of murder and the statutory offence of robbery (s. 8 Theft Act 1968) are indictable-only offences. Whilst the defendant's case will be heard at the Crown Court, the prosecution of an indictable-only offence will commence in the magistrates' court. Following the defendant's initial appearance before a magistrates' court, the case is immediately sent to the Crown Court for trial under s. 51 Crime and Disorder Act 1998.

Where a defendant is charged with more than one offence with different trial venue classifications, the general rule is that the most serious offence will dictate the procedural course of the cases.

Figures 1.1, 1.2 and 1.3 at the end of this chapter illustrate the stages of a summary-only, either-way and indictable-only offence. Figure 1.4 provides an overview of the criminal litigation process.

1.6 PERSONNEL AND ORGANISATIONS WITHIN THE CRIMINAL JUSTICE SYSTEM

1.6.1 INVESTIGATING AND PROSECUTING ORGANISATIONS

The responsibility for investigating and prosecuting a criminal offence is shared between several organisations.

The vast majority of criminal investigations are conducted by the police. At the completion of the investigation, the matter is passed to the CPS which decides whether there is sufficient evidence to charge the suspect. The CPS, which is headed by the Director of Public Prosecutions (DPP), Max Hill QC, is divided into 13 areas with headquarters in London, York and Birmingham.

The conduct of most day-to-day prosecutions in the magistrates' court or the Crown Court will be dealt with either by a Senior Crown Prosecutor, Crown Prosecutor or an Associate Prosecutor. The former are legally qualified solicitors or barristers; the latter are not. An Associate Prosecutor's right to conduct a contested trial is restricted to non-imprisonable summary-only offences upon completion of designated training.

The CPS employs a number of administrative staff members known as caseworkers. A caseworker will assist CPS lawyers and Associate Prosecutors by preparing cases, attending court with counsel, liaising with witnesses and other criminal justice agencies as well as post-trial administration. Whilst the CPS clearly plays a dominant role in the prosecution of criminal offences, other public bodies also investigate and prosecute criminal offences in their specific areas of responsibility:

- the Serious Fraud Office investigates and prosecutes serious or complex fraud;
- the National Crime Agency (NCA) investigates serious and organised crime;
- the Health and Safety Executive (HSE) investigates and prosecutes criminal offences arising out of accidents in the workplace under the Health and Safety at Work Act 1974 (the Enforcement section of the HSE's website contains a lot of useful information);
- local authorities investigate and prosecute offences under the Trade Descriptions Act 1968, the Education Act 1996, environmental law cases and prosecutions relating to food and hygiene;
- the Environment Agency investigates and prosecutes environmental crime;
- the RSPCA brings private prosecutions for offences relating to the welfare of animals.

1.6.2 THE LEGAL AID AGENCY

A detailed examination of public funding of criminal defence services is considered in Chapter 9. The provision of public funding for legal services in England and Wales is overseen by the Legal Aid Agency (LAA). There are currently over 2,000 solicitors' firms which have contracts with the LAA to provide publicly funded criminal defence services. Public spending on criminal legal aid has regularly exceeded £1 billion every year. This has however been drastically reduced by government funding cuts.

1.6.3 THE PUBLIC DEFENDER SERVICE

The Public Defender Service (PDS) provides a limited alternative to a criminal client seeking advice and representation from a solicitor in private practice. Through the LSC, the PDS employs solicitors, legal executives and paralegals to provide advice, assistance and representation to clients. Currently there are PDS offices located in Darlington, Swansea, Pontypridd and Cheltenham.

1.7 THE CRIMINAL COURTS AND PERSONNEL

It is likely that you studied the hierarchy of the criminal courts during your academic studies. This section is intended to briefly remind you of the jurisdiction of each criminal court.

1.7.1 MAGISTRATES' COURT

Prosecutors and defence lawyers spend most of their time preparing for and appearing in cases listed in the magistrates' court. It is the workhorse of the criminal justice system. Virtually all criminal prosecutions commence in the magistrates' court. Over 90% of all criminal cases are dealt with in the magistrates' court, with the remaining cases heard in the Crown Court. There are 240 magistrates' courts throughout England and Wales. According to the Judicial and Court Statistics published by the Ministry for Justice, in the 12 months ending September 2018 approximately 1.12 million cases were heard in the magistrates' court. The practice and procedure in the magistrates' court is governed by the Magistrates' Courts Act 1980 (MCA 1980) and the Criminal Procedure Rules (2015).

The magistrates' court undertakes the following:

- deals with preliminary matters during the early stages of all prosecutions including:
  - application for an adjournment;
  - the defendant's bail status;
- tries summary offences (this includes an either-way offence which is to remain in the magistrates' court) and sentences defendants convicted of these offences;
- determines the allocation of an either-way offence for which the defendant has indicated a not guilty plea or has refused to give an indication;
- commits a defendant convicted of an either-way offence to the Crown Court for sentence where the magistrates consider their maximum sentencing powers to be insufficient;
- sends an either-way offence to the Crown Court which the magistrates' court has decided should be tried at the Crown Court or because the defendant has elected trial at the Crown Court;
- sends indictable-only offences to the Crown Court for trial under s. 51 Crime and Disorder Act 1998.

A magistrates' court can also issue warrants for arrest, removal to a place of safety, search of premises and seizure of property. If the police wish to detain a person for questioning beyond a period of 36 hours, they must get an order from the magistrates' court authorising this further period of detention without charge. The court also deals with fine enforcement and adjudicates on a number of civil law applications, including family law and licensing.

1.7.2 MAGISTRATES

A magistrate is either a justice of the peace or a District Judge or Deputy District Judge. Lay magistrates are unpaid, and whilst they are not required to hold any formal legal qualifications all magistrates undergo a period of induction and training. They are required to 'sit' for a prescribed number of days each year. There are approximately 21,500 active lay magistrates in England and Wales who normally try cases sitting as part of a bench of three.

Salaried District Judges are appointed from the rank of solicitors and barristers. A District Judge hears a case sitting alone and can exercise all the powers of a bench of lay magistrates. A District Judge may also exercise some of the powers of recorders who sit as judges in the Crown Court in certain cases (s. 65 Courts Act 2003). Deputy District Judges sit on a fee-paid basis in the magistrates' court for a minimum of 15 days a year. Generally, the jurisdiction of a Deputy District Judges is the same as a District Judge.

1.7.3 THE LEGAL ADVISER

When conducting a summary trial, lay magistrates will be assisted by a legal adviser who is usually a solicitor or a barrister. The law maintains a strict division of responsibilities between the magistrates and their legal adviser. The magistrates are the sole arbiters of law and fact. Section 28 Courts Act 2003 and Crim PR, Part 24.15 provide that the legal adviser will sit with lay magistrates to advise the bench on matters of law, evidence, human rights points and procedure. The legal adviser will also put the charge to the accused, take a note of the evidence in the case and help an unrepresented defendant present his case.

When the justices retire to consider their verdict, the legal adviser must only advise them on points of law and evidence and not on issues of fact (*Stafford Justices, ex p. Ross* [1962] 1 WLR 456).

1.7.4 YOUTH COURT

Generally, defendants who are under 18 should be dealt with in the youth court. All magistrates' courts have a youth court panel of specially trained magistrates who have been appointed because of their suitability for dealing with youth cases. The practice and procedure is more informal and less intimidating than in the adult court. A District Judge (who has undertaken the required training) may also sit alone in the youth court. The youth court is regarded as a specialist jurisdiction. For this reason, youth justice is dealt with separately in Chapters 24–26 of *Criminal Litigation*.

1.7.5 THE CROWN COURT

The Crown Court, which sits at approximately 75 different locations in England and Wales, deals with cases to be tried on indictment before a judge and jury. The practice and procedure in the Crown Court is now governed by the Senior Courts Act 1981 and the Criminal Procedure Rules (2015). In the year ended September 2018, 14,700 cases were tried before the Crown Court. This was the lowest caseload since 2000. The Crown Court exercises the following jurisdiction:

- tries either-way offences sent for trial at the Crown Court;
- tries indictable-only offences and any related offences;
- sentences offenders convicted before it and those who are committed for sentence by the magistrates' courts;
- hears an appeal against conviction and/or sentence arising out of a decision made by a magistrates' court or youth court.

Section 66 Courts Act 2003 enables a Crown Court judge to exercise the powers of a District Judge (magistrates' court).

The following types of judge preside over sittings of the Crown Court:

- High Court judges;
- circuit judges; and
- recorders and assistant recorders who are part-time judicial officers.

1.7.6 THE ADMINISTRATIVE COURT AND THE HIGH COURT

The Administrative Court has a limited jurisdiction in criminal matters. An action in judicial review can be commenced in the Administrative Court against a public body such as a court, the police or the CPS for exceeding or misusing their legal powers or for not following the correct procedures. Part 54 Civil Procedure Rules deals with judicial review actions.

The High Court hears appeals by case stated under s. 111 MCA 1980 arising from decisions taken in a magistrates' court and under s. 28 Senior Courts Act 1981 against a decision of the Crown Court. Both the prosecution and defence can appeal by way of case stated to the High Court. This method of appeal is appropriate where it is submitted that the magistrates' court or its legal adviser or the Crown Court has misinterpreted a point of law or evidence. The procedure is governed by Crim PR, Part 35.

1.7.7 THE COURT OF APPEAL (CRIMINAL DIVISION)

The Court of Appeal (Criminal Division) hears appeals against conviction and/or sentence from cases tried in the Crown Court. It also hears appeals or 'points of reference' from the Attorney General (AG) on points of law and sentences that are considered too lenient. The work of the Court of Appeal is presided over by the Lord Chief Justice. Cases are normally heard by the Lord Chief Justice sitting with two puisne judges or a Lord Justice of Appeal sitting with two ordinary judges.

The Court of Appeal additionally gives guidance on the procedures and practices of the criminal courts by issuing sentencing guidelines and practice directions.

1.7.8 **THE SUPREME COURT**

The judicial work of the Supreme Court (formerly the House of Lords) is presided over by the President of the Supreme Court. It is the final and the highest court in the criminal jurisdiction and hears appeals from the Court of Appeal (and occasionally from the Divisional Court) on points of law of public and constitutional importance. Leave to appeal is required.

1.8 **THE EUROPEAN CONVENTION ON HUMAN RIGHTS 1950 (ECHR 1950)**

The Human Rights Act 1998 (HRA 1998) provides the legal framework for using the ECHR 1950 in UK domestic law. Section 1 HRA 1998 formally incorporates ECHR law into UK domestic law which means that ECHR law can be cited in the criminal courts in support of the defendant's case.

1.8.1 **HOW ARE THE RIGHTS GUARANTEED UNDER THE CONVENTION ENFORCED IN DOMESTIC LAW?**

Section 3 HRA 1998 places an obligation on the criminal courts to interpret all legislation 'as far as possible' to comply with ECHR law. This is known as the interpretive obligation. In discharging the interpretive obligation to ensure compliance between Convention law and domestic law, s. 2 HRA 1998 requires courts to have regard to Convention law and to the decisions of the European Court of Human Rights (ECtHR). Therefore, when citing a relevant ECHR point in support of your legal argument you should research any ECtHR decisions on the point and any relevant domestic case law. Where it is not possible to give effect to the ECHR law in a case under the interpretive obligation, s. 4 HRA 1998 requires the superior courts (Court of Appeal and the Supreme Court) to make a declaration of incompatibility. It is then a matter for Parliament whether to amend the offending legislation.

In addition, s. 6 HRA 1998 places a duty on a public authority such as the police, the CPS and the courts, to discharge its legal duties in compliance with the ECHR 1950. Section 6(1) provides:

'It is unlawful for a public authority to act in a way which is incompatible with Convention rights.'

A range of remedies in the civil courts apply where a public authority acts in breach of its duties under s. 6 HRA 1998, including actions in tort and/or judicial review. Section 8 HRA 1998 requires that where a court finds that a public authority has acted unlawfully, it must grant a remedy that is 'just and appropriate'.

1.8.2 **CRIMINAL LITIGATION—THE RELEVANT CONVENTION ARTICLES**

Article 3—the prohibition of torture

'No one shall be subjected to torture or inhuman or degrading treatment or punishment.'

Thankfully this provision is unlikely to be invoked on a frequent basis, although it might be relevant when challenging the admissibility of a defendant's confession on the ground that it had been obtained by 'oppression' under s. 76(2)(a) Police and Criminal Evidence Act 1984. Article 3 will be relevant when arguing that the manner in which the police interrogated your client (e.g. by shouting or making threats to the suspect) breached Convention law.

Article 3 is an absolute right from which no derogation is permitted.

Article 5—the right to liberty and security

'1. Everyone has the right to liberty and security of person. No one shall be deprived of liberty save in the following cases and in accordance with a procedure prescribed by law:

(a) the lawful detention of a person after conviction by a competent court;

(b) the lawful arrest or detention of a person for non-compliance with the lawful order of a court . . .;

(c) the lawful arrest and detention of a person except for the purpose of bringing him before a court of competent legal authority on reasonable suspicion of having committed an offence or fleeing after having done so; . . .

2. Everyone who is arrested shall be informed promptly, in a language which he understands, of the reasons for his arrest and of any charge against him.

3. Everyone arrested or detained in accordance with paragraph 1c shall be entitled to trial within a reasonable time or to release pending trial. Release may be conditioned by guarantees to appear for trial.

4. Everyone who is deprived of his liberty by arrest or detention shall be entitled to take proceedings by which the lawfulness of his detention shall be decided speedily by a court.

5. Everyone who has been the victim of arrest or detention in contravention of the provisions of this article shall have an enforceable right to compensation.'

Article 5 is a qualified right allowing the state to derogate from it in defined circumstances.

Article 5 may be invoked where your client has been unlawfully arrested or otherwise detained by the police and may be relevant when challenging the decision of the police or the court to deny your client bail.

Article 6—the right to a fair trial

'1. In the determination of his civil rights and obligations, or of any criminal charge against him everyone is entitled to a fair and public hearing within a reasonable time by an independent and impartial tribunal established by law. Judgment shall be pronounced publicly but the press or public may be excluded in the interests of morals, public order or national security in a democratic society, where the interests of juveniles or the protection of private life of the parties so require, or to the extent strictly necessary in the opinion of the court in special circumstances where publicity would prejudice the interests of justice.

2. Everyone charged with a criminal offence shall be presumed innocent until proved guilty according to the law.

3. Everyone charged with a criminal offence has the following minimum rights:

(a) to be informed promptly, in a language which he understands and in detail of the nature and cause of the accusation against him;

(b) to have adequate time and facilities for the preparation of his defence;

(c) to defend himself in person or through legal assistance of his own choosing or, if he has not sufficient means to pay for legal assistance, to be given it free when the interests of justice so require;

(d) to examine or have examined witnesses against him and to obtain the attendance and examination of witnesses on his behalf under the same conditions as witnesses against him;

(e) to have the free assistance of an interpreter if he cannot understand or speak the language used in court.'

Article 6 is the most significant Convention right for criminal litigators and is relevant at all stages of a criminal case including:

• the defendant's right to have legal representation at the police station and at trial;

• the procedural and evidential rules adopted by the court at trial; and

• the principles applied when passing sentence.

The right to a fair trial in Article 6(1) is drafted in absolute terms. What constitutes a fair trial, however, is not defined. The presumption of innocence in Article 6(2) and the provisions of Article 6(3) are specified minimum general components of a fair trial. The jurisprudence of the ECtHR has implied a number of rights into Article 6, including the privilege against self-incrimination. In deciding the fair trial provisions under Article 6, it should be stressed that the ECtHR is not concerned with the guilt or innocence of the accused but rather whether the whole trial process was in accordance with Article 6.

It is open to a defence advocate to argue that the admissibility of a particular piece of evidence in a case will violate the defendant's right to a fair trial in accordance with Article 6.

Article 8—the right to respect for private and family life

'1. Everyone has the right to respect for his private and family life, his home and his correspondence.

2. There shall be no interference by public authority with the exercise of this right except such as is in accordance with the law and is necessary in a democratic society in the interests of national security, public safety or the economic well-being of the country, for the prevention of disorder or crime etc . . .'

Article 8 seeks to protect the individual from arbitrary interference by the state. It is, however, a qualified right and permits interference for the reasons stated above. Nonetheless, any interference must be authorised in accordance with the law and must be proportional. Article 8 may be cited by defendants to challenge the admissibility of evidence obtained in breach of the defendant's right to a fair trial under Article 6 (see Chapter 6).

1.8.3 THE ECHR 1950 AND THE RULES OF CRIMINAL PROCEDURE AND EVIDENCE

Whilst generally the practice and procedure of the English criminal trial satisfies the obligations laid down by the Convention, since the implementation of the HRA 1998 a number of important decisions have been made by the courts where Article 5 or Article 6 have been directly invoked. These decisions include:

* *R (DPP) v Havering Magistrates' Court* [2001] 2 Cr App R 2 confirmed that proceedings under the Bail Act 1976 were governed by Article 5;

* *T and V v UK* (2000) 30 EHRR 121 decided that the boys tried for the killing of James Bulger had not had a fair trial in the Crown Court under Article 6 because of their young age and also that the formality of the Crown Court procedures had prevented them from effective participation in the trial process;

* *R (Anderson) v Secretary of State for the Home Department* [2003] 1 Cr App R 32, the House of Lords decided that to comply with Article 6, where a prisoner was sentenced to life imprisonment, the decision as to how long the prisoner should serve in prison (known as the tariff) should be taken by a judge and not by the Home Secretary;

* *Murray v UK* (1996) 22 EHRR 29, the ECtHR held that adverse inferences could not be drawn from a suspect's silence at the police station where he had not been offered legal advice. UK domestic law was found to be in breach of Article 6(3) ECHR 1950. Section 34 Criminal Justice and Public Order Act 1994 had to be amended as a consequence.

These and other important decisions influenced by the ECHR 1950 are considered in more detail at appropriate places in the text. The recognition of a defendant's rights under Article 6 is specifically identified in Part 1 of the Criminal Procedure Rules as a component of the overriding objective of dealing with criminal cases justly.

1.9 CRIMINAL PROCEDURE RULES (CRIM PR) 2015

The Criminal Procedure Rules (Crim PR) first came into effect on 4 April 2005. The rules, which are regularly amended, provide a comprehensive criminal procedure code that governs the conduct of all criminal cases. Also in October 2015 new Criminal Practice Directions (Crim PD) made by the Lord Chief Justice came into force. A combined version of the Criminal Procedure

Rules and related Practice Directions are available at http://www.justice.gov.uk/procedure-rules/criminal/rulesmenu-2015. The web-links section of our online resources (Guidelines section) will also take you there. You will see references to the application of the Criminal Procedure Rules throughout this work.

The overriding objective of the Criminal Procedure Rules is stated in Part 1. It requires that all criminal cases must be dealt with justly. Part 1.1 defines this to include:

'(a) acquitting the innocent and convicting the guilty;

(b) dealing with the prosecution and the defence fairly;

(c) recognising the rights of a defendant, particularly those under Article 6 of the European Convention on Human Rights;

(d) respecting the interest of witnesses, victims and jurors and keeping them informed of the progress of the case;

(e) dealing with the case efficiently and expeditiously;

(f) ensuring that appropriate information is available to the court when bail and sentence are considered; and

(g) dealing with the case in ways that take into account:

   (i) the gravity of the offence alleged,

   (ii) the complexity of what is in issue,

   (iii) the severity of the consequences for the defendant and others affected, and

   (iv) the needs of other cases.'

Everyone involved in the criminal justice process must prepare and conduct cases in accordance with the overriding objective (Crim PR, Part 1.2).

To ensure that the overriding objective is achieved, courts are required to engage in robust and active management of cases (Part 3). Active case management is defined in Part 3.2 to include:

'(a) the early identification of the real issues;

(b) the early identification of the needs of witnesses;

(c) achieving certainty as to what must be done, by whom, and when, in particular by the early setting of a timetable for the progress of the case;

(d) monitoring the progress of the case and compliance with directions;

(e) ensuring that evidence, whether disputed or not, is presented in the shortest and clearest way;

(f) discouraging delay, dealing with as many aspects of the case as possible on the same occasion and avoiding unnecessary hearings;

(g) encouraging the participants to co-operate in the progression of the case; and

(h) making use of technology.'

Active case management involves courts giving directions to the parties that are appropriate to the needs of the case and are consistent with the overriding objective.

Crim PR, Part 3.3 imposes a duty on all parties to actively assist the court in fulfilling its duty under Part 3.2. A court can impose sanctions on parties for failing to comply with a rule or direction of the court (Part 3.5(6)). These might include a wasted costs order, the exclusion of evidence or the refusal of a request for an adjournment. In *DPP v Hammerton* [2009] EWHC 921, the High Court upheld a decision of a magistrates' court (taken in accordance with the overriding objective) to refuse to allow the CPS to substitute at a late stage and for no good reason, a less serious charge in place of the original charge.

The extent to which the defence solicitor's duties under Part 3 conflict with duties owed to a client in the conduct of a criminal case are considered at para. 1.10.7.

The case management responsibilities under Crim PR, Part 3 must now be read in conjunction with the principles enshrined in Stop Delaying Justice (SDJ) which applies to all cases that can be tried in the magistrates' court. SDJ is an initiative from the senior judiciary which aims to ensure that all contested trials in the magistrates' court are fully managed from the first hearing and disposed of at the second hearing. SDJ builds upon the improvements to the more efficient disposal of summary cases begun by the Criminal Justice—Simple, Speedy and Summary (CJ-SSS) and enhanced by the latest initiative, Transforming Summary Justice (TSJ). The practical effect of these initiatives on the conduct and management of summary cases is fully explained in Chapter 9.

The Criminal Procedure Rules are revised from time to time. Any significant developments will be brought to you in the update section of our online resources.

1.10 **PROFESSIONAL CONDUCT —AN INTRODUCTION**

The solicitors' rules of professional conduct, which are now part of the SRA's Standards and Regulations are an important pervasive area of legal practice that govern the solicitors' profession. A new regulatory framework for legal practice in England and Wales is due to come into force in 2019. We have therefore included the proposed SRA Principles and Code of Conduct for Solicitors, Registered European Lawyers (RELs), and Registered Foreign Lawyers (RFLs) on the basis that during the currency of this edition of *Criminal Litigation* that the more complex 2011 Code of Conduct will no longer be valid. If the final version of the SRA Principles and Code 2019 are materially different from the provisions highlighted in this chapter an updated version will be available on our online resources.

The 2019 Code provisions have separate rules and regulations for solicitors, RELs, and RFLs and for firms of solicitors. These have replaced the more detailed and prescriptive requirements of the 2011 Code which was around 30 pages long and described by the SRA as 'confusing and complicated'. Also, the 2011 Code only applied to individual solicitors, SRA regulated businesses and managers and employees of those firms. The 2019 provisions reflect the changing nature of legal practices and the solicitors' profession. In addition to practitioners from England and Wales, the Codes sets standards for the work of in-house lawyers, RELs, and RFLs.

The SRA intends that the 2019 provisions will ensure that practitioners and firms will continue to operate with a framework of competent and ethical practice and that every solicitor should be clear about their personal obligations and responsibility to maintain the highest professional standards. They are also intended to add clarity about the systems and controls that firms and regulated bodies should have in place to provide good legal services for the benefit of consumers and for the public. The 2019 Principles and Code can be accessed in full at https://www.sra.org.uk. We strongly suggest that all LPC students as well as practitioners are fully conversant with the new rules.

This section provides an interpretation of the obligations imposed on practitioners by the anticipated final version of the 2019 provisions when acting for a client in a criminal case.

The revised regulatory framework identifies seven mandatory all-pervasive *Principles*, which according to the SRA comprise the fundamental tenets of ethical behaviour that the SRA expects all those that they regulate to uphold. This *Principles* apply to solicitors, authorised firms, the firms' managers as well as their employees. The *Principles*, which are listed below, should be used as a starting point when a practitioner is faced with an ethical dilemma.

According to the *Principles*, a solicitor must act:

1. *in a way that upholds the constitutional principle of the rule of law; and the proper administration of justice;*
2. *in a way that upholds public confidence in the solicitors' profession and in legal services provided by authorised persons;*
3. *with independence;*
4. *with honesty;*
5. *with integrity;*
6. *in a way that encourages equality, diversity, and inclusion;*
7. *in the best interests of each client.*

Principle 2 is a new principle and has been included to set out clearly the expectations around maintaining public trust and confidence.

The Code for Solicitors describes the standards of professionalism that the SRA and the public expects of individuals (solicitors, in-house lawyers, RELs, and RFLs) authorised by the SRA to provide legal services.

The Code regulates the conduct and behaviour relating to legal practice and comprise a framework for ethical and competent practice which applies irrespective of the solicitor's role or the nature of their practice.

Under the Code, the solicitor must exercise their judgement in applying these standards to a range of situations encountered in their practice and should be taken into account when deciding on a particular course of action set against the background of the solicitor's role, their responsibilities and the nature of their clients, and their areas of practice. Every solicitor is personally accountable for their compliance with the Code—and with other regulatory requirements that apply to them.

The solicitor is reminded that a serious breach of the Code may result in the SRA taking regulatory action against them as result of a single breach or because their conduct or behaviour amounts to a persistent failure to comply with the Code. To add weight to these potentially punitive sanctions the solicitor should note that the Principles and Codes are underpinned by SRA's Enforcement Strategy.

1.10.1 THE SOLICITORS CODE OF CONDUCT (2019)

Selective parts of the draft 2017 Code of Conduct for Solicitors, RELs, and RFLs (2017) are provided as follow:

Maintaining trust and acting fairly

1.1 You do not unfairly discriminate by allowing your personal views to affect your professional relationship and the way in which you provide your services.

1.2 You do not abuse your position by taking unfair advantage of clients or others.

1.3 You perform all undertakings given by you and do so within a reasonable amount of time.

1.4 You do not mislead or attempt to mislead your clients, the court or others, either by your own acts or omissions or allowing or being complicit in the acts and omissions of others (including your client).

Dispute resolution and proceedings before courts, tribunals, and inquiries

2.1 You do not misuse or tamper with evidence or attempt to do so.

2.2 You do not seek to influence the substance of evidence, including generating false evidence or persuading witnesses to change their evidence.

2.3 You do not provide or offer to provide any benefit to witnesses dependent upon the nature of their evidence or the outcome of the case.

2.4 You only make assertions or put forward statements, representations, or submissions to the court or others which are properly arguable.

2.5 You do not place yourself in contempt of court, and you comply with court orders which place obligations on you.

2.6 You do not waste the court's time.

2.7 You draw the court's attention to relevant cases and statutory provisions, or procedural irregularities of which you are aware, and which are likely to have a material effect on the outcome of the proceedings.

Service and competence

3.1 You act only for clients on instructions from the client, or from someone properly authorised to provide instructions on their behalf. If you have reason to suspect that the instructions do not represent your client's wishes, you do not act unless you have satisfied yourself that they do. However, in circumstances where you have legal authority to act notwithstanding that is not possible to obtain or ascertain instructions of your client, then you are subject to the overriding obligation to protect your client's best interests.

3.2 You ensure that the service you provide to clients is competent and delivered in a timely manner.

3.3 You maintain your competence to carry out your role and keep your professional knowledge and skills up to date.

3.4 You consider and take account of your client's attributes, needs and circumstances.

3.5 Where you supervise or manage others providing legal services:

(a) you remain accountable for the work carried out through them; and

(b) you effectively supervise work being done for clients.

3.6 You ensure that the individuals you manage are competent to carry out their role, and keep their professional knowledge and skills, as well as understanding of their legal, ethical and regulatory obligations up to date.

Client money and assets

4.1 You properly account to clients for any financial benefit you receive as a result of their instructions, except where they have agreed otherwise.

4.2 You safeguard money and assets entrusted to you by clients and others.

4.3 You do not personally hold client money save as permitted under regulation 10.2(b)(vii) of the Authorisation of Individuals Regulations, unless you work in an authorised body, or an organisation of the kind prescribed under this rule on any terms that may be prescribed accordingly.

Section 5 deals with referrals, introductions, and businesses which is not considered here.

Conflict, confidentiality, and disclosure

6.1 You do not act if there is an own interest conflict or a significant risk of such a conflict.

6.2 You do not act in relation to a matter or a particular aspect of it if you have a conflict of interest or a significant risk of such a conflict in relation to that matter or aspect of it, unless:

(a) the clients have substantially common interest in relation to the matter or the aspect of it, as appropriate; or

(b) the clients are competing for the same objective,

and the conditions below are met, namely that—

(i) all the clients have given informed consent, given or evidenced in writing, to you acting;

(ii) where appropriate, you put in place effective safeguards to protect your clients' confidential information; and

(iii) you are satisfied that it is reasonable you to act for all the clients.

Confidentiality and disclosure

6.3 You keep the affairs of clients and former clients confidential unless disclosure is required or permitted by law or the client consents.

6.4 Where you are acting for client on a matter, you make the client aware of all information material to the matter of which you have knowledge, except when:

(a) the disclosure of the information is prohibited by legal restrictions imposed in the interests of national security or the prevention of crime;

(b) your client gives informed consent, given or evidenced in writing, to the information not been disclosed to them;

(c) you have reason to believe that serious physical or mental injury will be caused to your client or another if the information is disclosed; or

(d) information is contained in a privileged document that you have knowledge of only because it has been mistakenly disclosed.

6.5 You do not act for a client in a matter where that client has an interest adverse to the interest of another current client or a former client of yours or your business or employer for whom your business or employer holds confidential information which is material to that matter, unless:

(a) effective methods have been taken which result in there being no real risk of disclosure of the confidential information; or

(b) the current or former client whose information you or your business or employer holds has given informed consent, given or evidenced in writing, to you acting, including any measures taken to protect their information.

Section 7 imposes obligations of **Cooperation and accountability**. Practitioners are required to keep up to date with and follow the law and regulation governing the way in which they work (7.1). Practitioners must be able to justify their decisions and actions in order to demonstrate compliance with obligations under the SRA's regulatory arrangements as well as cooperating with the SRA, other regulators, ombudsman, and those bodies with the role overseeing and supervising the delivery of or investigating concerns in relation to legal services (7.2 and 7.3).

Practitioners are required to respond promptly to the SRA and provide full and accurate destinations, information and, documents in response to any request or requirement and ensure that relevant information held by them or by third parties carrying out functions on their behalf which are critical to the delivery of their legal services is available for inspection by the SRA (7.4).

No attempt should be made to prevent anyone from providing information to the SRA or any other regulatory or supervisory body. Practitioners must the SRA promptly if they are subject to any criminal charge, conviction or, caution subject to the Rehabilitation of Offenders Act 1974; or a relevant insolvency event occurred in relation to then and the information provided to the SRA by you or on your behalf, about you or your practice is or may be false, misleading, incomplete or inaccurate (7 .6).

When you are providing services to the public or a section of the public

Client identification

8.1 You identify who you are acting for in relation to any matter.

Complaints handling

8.2 You ensure that, as appropriate in the circumstances, you either establish and maintain, or participate in, a procedure for handling complaints in relation to the legal services you provide.

8.3 You ensure that clients are informed in writing at the time of engagement about:

(a) their right to complain to you about your services and your charges;

(b) how a complaint can be made and to whom; and

(c) any right they have to make a complaint to the Legal Ombudsman and when they can make any such complaint.

8.4 You ensure that when clients have made a complaint to you, if this has not been resolved to the client's satisfaction within 8 weeks following the making of a complaint they are informed, in writing:

(a) of any right that they have to complain to the Legal Ombudsman, the time frame for doing so and full details of how to contact the Legal Ombudsman; and

(b) if a complaint has been brought and your complaints procedure has been exhausted—

(i) that you cannot settle the complaint;

(ii) of the name and website address of an alternative dispute resolution (ADR) approved body which will be competent to deal with the complaint; and

(iii) whether you agree to use the scheme operated by that body.

8.5 You ensure that clients' complaints are dealt with promptly, fairly, and free of charge.

Client information and publicity

8.6 You give clients information in a way they can understand. You ensure that they are in a position to make informed decisions about the services they need, how their matter will be handled and the options available to them.

8.7 You ensure that clients receive the best possible information about how their matter will be priced and, both at the time of engagement and when appropriate as their matter progresses, about the likely overall cost of the matter and any costs incurred.

8.8 You ensure that any publicity you are responsible for in relation to your practice is accurate and not misleading, including that relating to your charges and the circumstances in which interest is payable by or to clients.

8.9 You do not make unsolicited approaches to members of the public, with the exception of current or former clients, in order to advertise legal services provided by you, or your business or employer.

8.10 You ensure that clients understand whether and how the services you provide regulated. This includes:

(a) explaining which activities will be carried out by you, as an authorised person;

(b) explaining which services provided by you, or your business or employer, and any separate business are regulated by an approved regulator; and

(c) ensuring that you do not represent any business or employer which is not authorised by the SRA, including any separate business, as being regulated by the SRA.

8.11 You ensure that clients understand the regulatory protections available to them

It is our view that the SRA Code of Conduct for Firms (2019) falls outside the scope of *Criminal Litigation* and therefore if you need to review the proposed Code's regulatory framework for firms and its accompanying consultation paper go to https://www.sra.org.uk/sra/consultations/code-conduct-consultation.

1.10.2 THE 2019 CODE AND ITS APPLICATION TO CRIMINAL LITIGATION

Criminal cases are conducted in an adversarial system of enquiry where the aim of each side is to win. *Principle 7* requires a defence solicitor to act in the best interests of her client. In an effort to win, the solicitor will need to be a partisan advocate for and on behalf of her client. However, as an officer of the court, a solicitor also serves the wider public interest in upholding the rule of law and the administration of justice (*Principle 1*). Serving the best interests of a client can sometimes bring a solicitor into conflict with her duty to the proper administration of justice. Where there is conflict between the Principles those Principles which safeguard the wider public interest (such as the rule of law, and public confidence in a trustworthy solicitors' profession and a safe and effective market to regulated legal services) take precedence over the individual client's interests. Practitioners are required to inform their client of the circumstances in which their duty to the Court and other professional obligations outweigh their duty to the client.

Professional conduct issues in relation to criminal clients are most likely to arise in the following contexts:

- duties to the client;
- duties to the court;
- confidentiality;
- conflict of interest;
- interviewing witnesses; and
- specific duties on advocates.

The following paragraphs provide an overview of your professional conduct obligations that apply to criminal practice.

1.10.3 CLIENT CARE

All of the SRA *Principles* are relevant to client care including, for example, *Principle 1* (to uphold the rule of law and the proper administration of justice) and *Principle 7* (to act in the best interests of each client).

Also, whilst s. 1 of the Code for Solicitors, RELs, and RFLs 'Maintaining trust and acting fairly' applies to all types of legal practice there are some specific provisions that should be considered by the criminal practitioner. Under para. 1.1, a solicitor should not unfairly discriminate by allowing their personal views to affect their professional relationship in the services they provide. Criminal practitioners are often asked how they can defend a suspect when they know that they are guilty or are charged with a particularly unpleasant crime. A common response is that a defendant is presumed to be innocent until they have either pleaded guilty or have been found guilty by a criminal court. Your professional conduct obligations also require you to represent your client to the best of your knowledge and ability without taking a personal or moral view on their culpability. Note also the requirements of para. 1.2 about not taking unfair advantage of your clients or others and para. 1.4, which requires you not to mislead or attempt to mislead your clients by your acts or omissions or by the acts or omissions of others. For example, a practitioner would be in breach of the Code if they advised a client to plead to guilty where the prosecution case against them does not disclose a *prima facie case*.

Specific client care obligations are dealt with in '**Client information and publicity**'. Paragraph 8.6 requires that you give the client information in a way that they can understand to ensure they can make informed decisions. As many of criminal clients will be represented under legal aid, para. 8.7 about how their matter will be priced and paid for will be less important than for other areas of legal practice—although the client's entitlement to legal aid must be discussed including advice about where they would be required to make a contribution under a representation order. Many of the requirements of this section will be dealt with in the client care letter and the agreement to act.

Principle 7, the requirement to act in the best interests of each client, will include discussing their entitlement to public funding and explaining to a client charged with a criminal offence that if he is convicted, he could be made to pay some or all of the prosecution's costs. Whilst no client should be advised to plead guilty if the prosecution case against him is not strong, a defence solicitor (when purporting to act in the best interests of his client) ought to explain the advantages of a timely guilty plea in terms of sentence (see Chapter 21).

1.10.4 CONFLICT, CONFIDENTIALITY, AND DISCLOSURE

All legal firms are required to have in place a system that enables conflicts of interests to be identified. *Principle 6* requires you to act in the best interests of your client. Section 6 of the Code deals with **conflict, confidentiality, and disclosure**. You need to carefully read this section and be aware of the obligations that are placed upon you as a criminal practitioner. The Code acknowledges that conflict, confidentiality, and disclosure commonly overlap.

Based on the attributed meanings in the 2011 Code a conflict can include 'own interest conflict', which is a conflict between you and your client, and 'client conflict', which is a conflict arising between one or more current clients. An 'own interest conflict' could arise because of a financial interest, personal or employment relationship you may have or because you or a member of your firm or family have been appointed to public office. Paragraphs 6.1 and 6.2 of the Code set out the general provisions dealing with conflict of interest and then provides several exceptions where a conflict may not apply. These exceptions include where your clients have an agreed common purpose, or are competing for the same objective, which, if attained by one client will make that objective unattainable to the other client.

When considering instructions from more than one client, the solicitor needs to ask: is there a conflict of interest between them or a significant risk of a conflict arising arise at some point in the future? A conflict of interest can commonly arise when the solicitor is called upon to represent two or more suspects at the police station who are being investigated for the same offence. A conflict may subsequently arise in a case where both clients plead not guilty but one of them later pleads guilty. The solicitor should be aware that even when two clients indicate that they will plead guilty, a conflict of interest could still arise when the solicitor comes to mitigate on their individual behalf.

Useful guidance on the practical application of the conflict rule is available in the Law Society Practice Note 'Conflicts of interests in criminal cases' which was published on 3 October 2013. The Practice Note can be accessed at http://www.lawsociety.org.uk/support-services/advice/practice-notes/conflict-of-interests-criminal/. (We assume that the Practice Note will support the 2017 Code.)

The Practice Note suggests that a conflict of interest can arise where it is in the best interests of client A:

'(a) to give evidence against client B;

(b) to make a statement incriminating client B;

(c) to implicate client B in a police interview;

(d) to provide prejudicial information regarding client B to an investigator;

(e) to cross-examine client B in such a manner as to call into question his or her credibility;

(f) to rely upon confidential information given by client B without his or her consent; or

(g) to adopt tactics in the course of the retainer which potentially or actually harm client B.'

The Practice Note cautions that if these obligations actually come into conflict when acting for two or more clients, the lawyer will have to cease to act for one and often both.

The obligation about actual or a significant risk of conflict can arise at an early stage in your involvement in a case at the police station. The Practice Note advises that in order to assess whether you can act for both clients it is important that you do not interview the clients together and that you get instructions which are as full as possible from the first client before any substantial contact with the second client. You should not allow the police to deter you from seeing the second client because they think there is a conflict—that decision must be yours.

Obvious indicators of a conflict would include clients having differing accounts of the important relevant circumstances of the alleged crime, or where one seems likely to change his or her plea. Less obvious indicators which may give rise to a significant risk of future conflict include situations where there is clear inequality between the co-defendants which might, for example, suggest that one client is acting under the influence of the other rather than on his or her own initiative. If you act for both, it may be difficult to raise and discuss these issues equally with them. By helping one, you might undermine the other. If you believe you are unable to do your best for one without prejudicing the other, you should only accept instructions from one. Should two or more clients decide to plead guilty, you need to consider at the outset whether you would be able to mitigate fully and freely on behalf of one client without harming the interests of the other. If one client is more criminally sophisticated than the other, it may be that the other client was led astray or pressurised into committing the crime and would want you to emphasise this in mitigation. If there is a significant risk of this happening, you should not accept instructions from either.

Where a conflict has arisen and you must decide whether you can continue to act for one client but not another, the Practice Note advises that you need to consider whether in the changed circumstances your duty to disclose all relevant information to the retained client will place you in breach of your duty of confidentiality to the other client. In practice you must decide whether you hold confidential information about the former client which is now relevant to the retained client. If you have this information, then you cannot act for either client.

From a public funding perspective, it is cheaper for the same solicitor to represent two clients than having different firms represent each client. However, the Practice Note clearly states that you should resist such pressure from whatever source (court or police station) if it would be unprofessional for you to act or to continue to act for both clients. If asked by the court why you cannot act for both defendants, you must not give information which would breach your duty of confidentiality to your client(s). This will normally mean that you can say no more than that it would be unprofessional for you to continue to act.

Confidentiality and disclosure are dealt with in paras. 6.3–6.5 of the Code. The protection of confidential information is a fundamental feature of your relationship with clients and that the duty continues after the end of the retainer and even after the death of the client. You therefore have a strict duty to keep your client's affairs confidential (para. 6.3) unless the client consents or the disclosure is required or permitted by law such as under the money-laundering reporting regulations or issues involving child protection or disclosure to the Legal Aid Agency in the case of a publicly funded client. Given the nature of criminal proceedings and the potential consequences for your client, confidentiality is particularly important to a client under suspicion of a criminal offence. The duty of confidentiality continues for all time unless the client agrees to waive confidentiality.

Communications between a solicitor and her client are additionally protected from disclosure even to the court by legal professional privilege. The privilege extends in criminal cases to communications passing between a solicitor and a third party, such as a barrister or expert witness, provided the communication was made in connection with actual or contemplated litigation. Legal professional privilege does not extend where a solicitor has been used in furtherance of a crime. In such a case the police can seize documents relevant to the investigation. The rules relating to legal professional privilege are considered further in Chapter 20.

Issues of confidentiality are likely to arise in criminal cases where professional embarrassment (see the solicitor's overriding duty to the court later) forces the solicitor to withdraw from a case. Solicitors cannot in these circumstances explain to a court why they are no longer acting.

The issue of confidentiality may also arise at the police station. When advising a suspect to remain silent, the legal adviser may be called upon to explain the reasons for this advice if s. 34 Criminal Justice and Public Order Act 1994 is invoked at trial. The legal adviser can only do this if the client consents to waive his legal professional privilege. The matter is considered further in Chapter 5.

You are under a duty when advising a client to make the client aware of all information material to the client's retainer (para. 8.6) and in a way they can understand. Therefore, a solicitor cannot continue to act for A and B where a conflict of interest arises between them. Can the solicitor continue to act for A but not B? The answer is yes, but only where the solicitor's duty of confidentiality to B is not put at risk. You cannot therefore continue to act for A in these circumstances.

1.10.5 DISPUTE RESOLUTION AND PROCEEDINGS BEFORE COURTS, TRIBUNALS, AND INQUIRIES

Principle 1 requires you to uphold the rule of law and the proper administration of justice. *Principle 2* requires you to ensure that your conduct upholds public confidence in the solicitors' profession and those delivering legal services. *Principles 3, 4, 5, and 6* require that you act with independence, and with honesty and integrity and in a way that encourages diversity and inclusion.

A solicitor is under a duty not to mislead the court including the requirement to draw to the court's attention relevant cases and statutory provisions or procedural irregularities that are likely to have a material effect on the outcome of the proceedings (para. 2.7). You should not tamper with evidence (para. 2.1) or seek to influence the substance of evidence including generating false evidence or persuading witnesses to change their evidence (para. 2.2).

As it is common for clients charged with criminal offences to lie or be economical with the truth, what should a solicitor do if she becomes aware that her client intends to lie to the police or to the court or has lied? What if the prosecution gives information to the court which the defence solicitor knows is incorrect? This could arise where a solicitor is satisfied that her client is adopting false particulars (name or address or date of birth) with the intention of deceiving a court by failing to disclose previous convictions to achieve a more favourable sentence or bail outcome. In such circumstances, the solicitor would need to explain to her client that she cannot allow such a course to be pursued and that unless her client is willing to correct the details or is willing to change his mind, the solicitor will have to withdraw from the case.

Paragraph 2.7 applies if the solicitor becomes aware that during the proceedings, they mistakenly mislead the court. In this situation the solicitor must, with the client's consent, immediately inform the court. If the client does not consent, the solicitor must cease to act. A solicitor may believe that the client is being untruthful. However, suspicion is not the same as knowledge. If a client was to admit to his solicitor, during ongoing proceedings, that he had misled the court or committed perjury, the solicitor must not act further unless the client agrees to disclose the truth.

Is a solicitor under a duty to correct an omission or mistake by the prosecution?

What if the prosecution gives information to the court which the solicitor knows is incorrect? For example, if on checking a client's list of previous convictions, the defence solicitor realises that it is incomplete by failing to show the client's most recent conviction. When the prosecutor hands in a copy of the defendant's previous convictions, is the solicitor under a duty to advise the court about the omission? The guidance to Rule 11 (Note 15) of the 2007 Code covered this dilemma and in the absence of specific guidance on this point under the 2017 Code this is helpful guidance about the action the solicitor might take. Note 15 to the 2007 Code provided that a solicitor acting for the defence is not under an obligation to correct information given to the court by the prosecution or any other party which the solicitor knows may allow the court to make an incorrect assumption provided the solicitor does not indicate agreement with that information. The position would of course be different if the defence solicitor was asked to confirm the list of previous convictions as being correct. The incorrect assumption made by the court may well assist the client; however, it could also be said that you would not be upholding the proper administration of justice (*Principle 1*) or acting with integrity and honesty (*Principles 4 and 5*). The sensible course to take would be to discuss the prosecution's omission with your client and gain his consent to correct the omission.

Where there has been a procedural irregularity in the case or a failure by the prosecution to draw the court's attention to relevant case law or to a statutory provision then to comply with *Principles 1, 4 and 5*, you should bring it to the court's attention. Apart from this, there is no wider obligation upon the defence to disclose to the court or the prosecution facts or witnesses that may be of assistance to the other side. Such disclosure would not be acting in the best interests of each client (*Principle 7*) and would be a breach of confidentiality in any event (*Section 6* of the Code).

Duties on the prosecutor

The prosecutor has a duty to act as a minister of justice and must never attempt to secure a conviction at all costs. The role of the CPS is considered in Chapter 8. The chapter explains in detail the onerous nature of the prosecutor's duty to make pre-trial disclosure of relevant material that undermines the case for the prosecution or assists the defence which is fundamental to a defendant's right to a fair trial under Article 6.

What action should a solicitor take where her client changes his version of events?

A commonly encountered professional conduct issue occurs where a client keeps changing his version of the facts in the case. There is no general duty upon a solicitor to enquire in every case whether the client is telling the truth. If a client makes inconsistent statements, this is not a ground for refusing to act. However, the solicitor would need to be wary and must cease to act where it is clear that the client is attempting to put forward false evidence as this will conflict with the solicitor's duty as an officer of the court as required by *Principle 1* and para. 2.2 of the Code. A solicitor should never suggest a defence to the client to fit the facts, nor must the solicitor fabricate a defence. This extends to taking witness statements as outlined in para. 2.3 which provides that you must not offer any benefit to a witness (financial or otherwise) and under para. 2.2, a solicitor should never put words into a witness's mouth,

What is the position where a client admits guilt but wants to plead not guilty?

This situation can arise at the police station as well as at court. Can the solicitor continue to act? An earlier version of the Code contained the following statement which we consider still to be valid at the time of writing:

> 'A solicitor who appears in court for the defence in a criminal case is under a duty to say on behalf of the client what the client should properly say for himself or herself if the client possessed the requisite skill and knowledge. The solicitor has a concurrent duty to ensure that the prosecution discharges the onus placed upon it to prove the guilt of the accused.'

In answer to the question posed above, a solicitor can continue to represent the client on a not guilty plea, as it is the solicitor's professional duty to require the prosecution to prove its case beyond reasonable doubt.

However, the solicitor must not do anything to positively assert his client's innocence under para. 1.4 of the Code. If at the close of the prosecution's case, the client has given evidence on oath or called witnesses to testify about the client's innocence (i.e. which expressly or by implication suggests someone other than the client committed the crime), the solicitor would be knowingly misleading the court. If the client persisted in this course of action, the solicitor would be required to withdraw from the case.

In those cases where a solicitor ceases to act, the solicitor's duty of confidentiality owed to the client under Section 6, precludes the solicitor from informing the court of the reason for the decision to withdraw.

What if a client has a defence but wishes to plead guilty?

A client may not wish to stand trial even though he has a defence to the allegation. It is the duty of the defence solicitor to point out such a defence. If the client insists on pleading guilty because it is more convenient to do so, the solicitor can continue to act for the client but the client should be warned when the solicitor is delivering a plea in mitigation on his behalf that the solicitor will not be able to rely on any facts that would constitute a defence. A solicitor should keep a file note of advice given and ask the client to sign a written statement confirming his wishes notwithstanding the advice given.

1.10.6 PROFESSIONAL CONDUCT AND THE CRIMINAL PROCEDURE RULES (CRIM PR)

A defence solicitor must always act in the best interests of her client (*Principle 7*). In a case where a solicitor is instructed by the client to plead not guilty, it is the duty of the defence solicitor to put the prosecution to proof of its case. In an attempt to frustrate the prosecution, the defence solicitor may feel that the client's best interests are served by playing a tactical game, perhaps by withholding certain information from the prosecution and the court. Such a tactical game could frustrate the obligation of the court to actively manage cases in accordance with Crim PR, Parts 1 and 3 (see para. 1.10). The effect of the case management powers given to the court under Crim PR, Part 3 and initiatives such as TSJ (see Chapter 9) have significantly increased the pressures on all those involved in the conduct of criminal cases as they are now much more accountable to the court for a failure to actively progress a case. In a situation where a solicitor perceives a conflict between his duty to act in the best interests of the client and the duty to promote the administration of justice by actively assisting the court's management of cases (*Principle 1*), which takes precedence?

In *R v Gleeson* [2004] 1 Cr App R 29, defence advocates were reminded that:

> 'A criminal trial is not a game under which a guilty defendant should be provided with a sporting chance. It is a search for truth in accordance with twin principles that the prosecution must prove its case and that a defendant is not obliged to inculpate himself, the object being to convict the guilty and acquit the innocent. Requiring a defendant to indicate in advance what he disputes about the prosecution case offends neither of those principles.'

The Practice Note makes it clear that defence solicitors must assist a court to conduct cases justly and expeditiously and be aware of the consequences of failing to do so. However, a court cannot, in the exercise of its case management powers, compel a defence solicitor to breach a professional conduct obligation owed to a client. Thus, for example, a court cannot compel a defence solicitor to represent two clients where the solicitor concludes that there is a significant risk of conflict between them, even though single representation might be more expeditious. Neither can a court require the defence solicitor to disclose privileged communications with her client (*R (Kelly) v Warley Magistrates Court (the Law Society intervening)* [2008] 1 Cr App R 14).

The Practice Note echoes an earlier version. Paragraph 2.5 of the draft Code makes it clear that you must comply with court orders and further requires that you must not place yourself in contempt of court. Paragraphs 2.5, 2.6, and 2.7 impose duties that you must observe including complying with court orders, not wasting the court's time and drawing the court's attention to relevant cases and statutory provisions, or procedural irregularities which are likely to have a material effect on the outcome of the proceedings.

KEY POINT SUMMARY

- Understand that criminal offences are classified as either summary-only, either-way or indictable-only and that the classification enables you to chart the procedural course of the case.

- Always research the classifications of the offence(s) you are dealing with: never guess.

- Know the jurisdiction of the criminal courts.

- Arguments based on Article 6 ECHR 1950 can arise in many situations in criminal procedure and evidence.

- The right to a fair trial in Article 6 comprises many rights, some of which are specifically defined in Article 6 while others are implied.

- Domestic courts must as far as possible interpret domestic law in accordance with Convention rights.

- In determining rights under the Convention, regard must be had to the jurisprudence of the ECtHR.

- Human rights issues and professional conduct are pervasive—they can arise at any time.

- Have a thorough working knowledge of the rules of professional conduct and know the typical instances where professional conduct dilemmas are likely to arise in the context of criminal litigation.

SELF-TEST QUESTIONS

1. We would like you to begin to familiarise yourself with our fictional clients, Lenny Wise, Roger Martin and William Hardy and the nature of the accusations that have been made against each of them. Documentation pertaining to the first case study can be found in Appendix 2 of this manual.

    The complete version of the documentation supporting *R v Lenny Wise* and the entire documentation supporting *R v Roger Martin* and *R v William Hardy* can be accessed from the student resource section of the online resources. Analysis of all self-test questions can be found in the online resources.

    (a) Case study 1: *R v Lenny Wise*

    Consider Document 6 (Lenny Wise's proof of evidence) and Documents 26(A)–(J) which comprise the nature of the prosecution's evidence against Lenny. What offence is Lenny charged with? What is the classification of this offence?

    (b) Case study 2: *R v Roger Martin*

    Consider Document 1 (Roger Martin's initial statement given to his solicitor) and Documents 9(A)–(F) which comprise the nature of the prosecution's evidence against Roger. What offences is Roger Martin charged with? What is the classification of the offences he faces?

    (c) Case study 3: *R v William Hardy*

    Consider Document 1 (William Hardy's initial statement given to his solicitor) and Documents 10(A)–(E) which comprise the nature of the prosecution's evidence against William. What offence is William Hardy charged with? What is the classification of the offence William is charged with?

2. How are the following offences classified according to place of trial? (You may have to do some legal research to discover the answer to some of the questions. A good place to start is *Blackstone's Criminal Practice*.)

    (a) Criminal damage where the value of the damaged property is less than £5,000, s. 1 Criminal Damage Act 1971.

    (b) Criminal damage where the value of the damaged property is more than £5,000.

    (c) Possession of a controlled drug, s. 5 Misuse of Drugs Act 1971.

    (d) Careless driving, s. 3 Road Traffic Act 1988.

    (e) Burglary, contrary to s. 9 Theft Act 1986.

    (f) Affray, contrary to s. 3 Public Order Act 1986.

    (g) Theft to the value of £50 contrary to s. 1 Theft Act 1968.

3. Explain what is meant by a summary-only offence.

4. Explain what is meant by an indictable-only offence.

5. In what circumstances would an allocation hearing be held?

6. Identify the overriding objective of the Criminal Procedure Rules.

7. Explain how Convention rights are incorporated into domestic law and how a defence solicitor might make use of such Convention rights.

8. What are the potential consequences of failing to spot and comply with an aspect of the Solicitors' Code of Conduct?

FIGURE 1.1 SUMMARY-ONLY OFFENCE

FIGURE 1.2 EITHER-WAY OFFENCE

FIGURE 1.3 INDICTABLE-ONLY OFFENCE

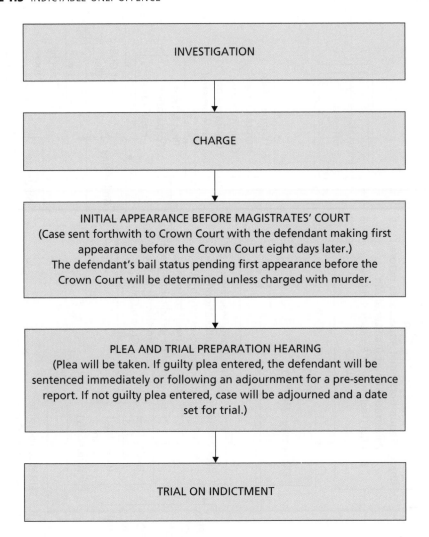

FIGURE 1.4 A FLOWCHART OF CRIMINAL PROCEDURE IN ENGLAND AND WALES

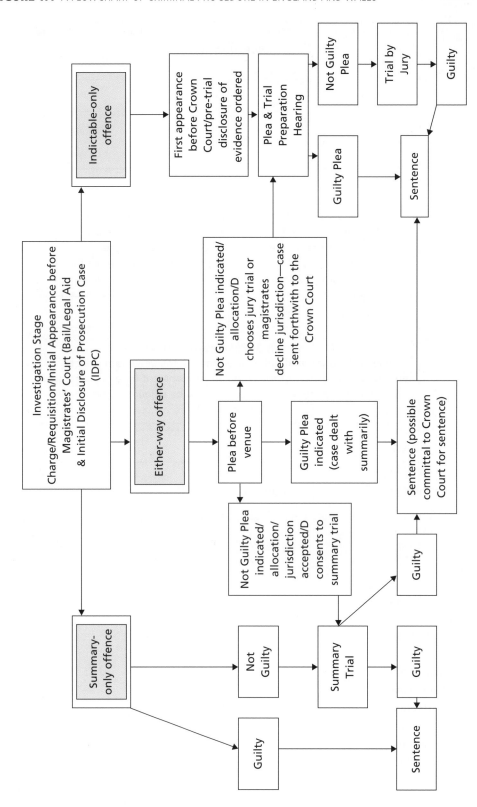

2 AN INTRODUCTION TO THE LAW OF CRIMINAL EVIDENCE AND ADVOCACY

2.1	**Introduction**	**33**
2.2	**The purpose of the law of criminal evidence**	**34**
2.3	**Facts in issue**	**34**
2.4	**Core concepts**	**34**
	2.4.1 Relevance	34
	2.4.2 Admissibility	35
	2.4.3 Weight	35
	2.4.4 Who decides questions of law and questions of fact?	36
2.5	**Procedure for deciding the admissibility of disputed evidence**	**36**
2.6	**Assessing the evidence—the prosecuting solicitor's role**	**36**
2.7	**Assessing the evidence—the defence solicitor's role**	**37**
2.8	**Types of evidence**	**37**
	2.8.1 Oral testimony	37
	2.8.2 Opinion evidence	37
	2.8.3 Documentary evidence	37
	2.8.4 Real evidence	38
	2.8.5 Direct and circumstantial evidence	38
2.9	**Clarifying the evidential issues**	**38**
2.10	**Concluding remarks on criminal evidence**	**39**
2.11	**Advocacy**	**39**
	2.11.1 Effective advocacy	39
	2.11.2 What makes an oral presentation persuasive?	40

2.1 INTRODUCTION

It is essential for both prosecutors and defence lawyers to have a good understanding of the rules of criminal evidence and to be able to apply the rules in a highly practical way to the issues in a case. The rules are relevant not only when preparing for trial and during the trial but are pervasively significant throughout the whole case. One of the aims of *Criminal Litigation* is to reflect the practical integration of the rules of criminal evidence with procedure. For example, the way in which the police gather evidence against an accused during the investigation may have important evidential consequences at trial if the substantive provisions of the Police and Criminal Evidence Act 1984 (PACE 1984) and the Codes of Practice are not complied with. The Crown Prosecution Service (CPS) lawyer needs to understand the rules of evidence to evaluate the strength of the evidence gathered by the police during the investigation to advise on the appropriate charge.

In preparing a client for the police interview the defence lawyer will need to apply his knowledge of the evidential rules to assess the strength of the prosecution evidence against his client to decide whether to advise silence.

Those of you in practice will already understand the importance of the rules of evidence to the work of a criminal lawyer. The challenge for law students is to recognise and apply the evidential rules in the practical context of real-life cases.

For those who require it this chapter provides a brief introduction to the main evidential rules which are considered further in later chapters. In particular, it addresses the following:

- the purpose of rules of evidence;
- the core concepts of relevance, admissibility and weight;
- the different types of evidence.

2.2 THE PURPOSE OF THE LAW OF CRIMINAL EVIDENCE

The law of evidence is the body of rules which prescribe the ways in which evidence can be presented in a criminal trial. The rules regulate how the prosecution proves its case to the court and, in exceptional situations, how the defendant might prove his innocence. Most importantly, the rules of evidence seek to ensure that the accused receives a fair trial—a right guaranteed under Article 6 European Convention on Human Rights 1950. The right to a fair trial may require a court to exercise its judicial discretion to exclude or prevent the admission of a piece of evidence where it may have been obtained illegally or unfairly.

2.3 FACTS IN ISSUE

Where the defendant pleads not guilty, the facts in issue identify what has to be proven by the prosecution for the defendant to be found guilty, or exceptionally what the defendant has to prove in order to establish his or her innocence. The facts in issue are determined by reference to the *actus reus* and the *mens rea* of the offence with which the defendant is charged. Your knowledge of substantive criminal law is assumed. The burden of proving the defendant's guilt beyond reasonable doubt rests, for the most part, on the prosecution. In discharging the burden of proof, both the defence and the prosecution will have researched the elements of the offence(s) charged as these will identify what needs to be proved in a case. In a charge of theft under s. 1 Theft Act 1968 the facts in issue are:

Actus reus	*mens rea*
Appropriates	Dishonestly
Property	Intention to permanently deprive
Belonging to another	

The prosecution must prove each element of the *actus reus* and the *mens rea* of the offence for the defendant to be found guilty. This may include disproving any defence relied on by the accused. This is known as discharging the legal burden of proof. The prosecution will discharge the legal burden of proof by putting evidence before the court in support of each fact in issue. Legal and evidential burdens of proof are considered in greater detail in Chapter 15.

2.4 CORE CONCEPTS

Criminal evidence has three core concepts: relevance, admissibility and weight.

2.4.1 RELEVANCE

For evidence to be put before the court, it must be relevant or probative of a fact in issue or to a collateral fact in the case. An example of a collateral fact is the competence of a witness to give evidence in the case. Evidence assumes logical relevance if it has a bearing on the facts in issue in a particular case or to collateral facts that are relevant to the facts in issue. For evidence to be relevant, there must be a logical relationship between the evidence tendered and the fact to be proved. All that is necessary for a piece of relevant evidence to be admitted at trial is that it should increase or diminish the probability of the existence of a fact in issue. There are no special rules to decide the question of relevance—it is a matter of common sense. For example, on a charge of the theft of a bottle of wine from a supermarket, it is not relevant for the prosecution to put forward evidence that the defendant drove to the supermarket in a car with defective lights or that the defendant has recently been divorced. It is relevant, however, for a prosecution witness to tell the court that he saw the accused put a bottle of wine under her coat and walk out of the supermarket without paying.

2.4.2 ADMISSIBILITY

For the court to receive evidence it not only has to be relevant to a fact in issue, it must also be admissible. Admissible evidence is evidence which, as a matter of law, can be received by the court. Evidence will be admissible unless it is excluded either under a mandatory rule of exclusion or in the exercise of the court's discretion to ensure the defendant enjoys a fair trial. There are few categories of evidence which are mandatorily excluded apart from the opinion evidence of a lay witness and the unlawful disclosure of evidence protected by legal professional privilege. Most evidence is excluded at a criminal trial under the exercise of judicial discretion to ensure a defendant's right to a fair trial.

The right to a fair trial embraces many facets. Sometimes the right will require the exclusion of evidence which the prosecution seeks to admit as part of its case because of the manner in which the evidence was obtained by the police. This could apply to confession evidence or identification evidence obtained in breach of the defendant's rights under the substantive provisions of PACE 1984 and/or the Codes of Practice. Prosecution evidence may also be excluded if its admission would prejudice a fair trial. By prejudice we mean the damaging effect the admission of a particular piece of evidence might have on the minds of the jury or magistrates. Relevance and admissibility are closely connected. Would a jury or magistrates attach too much significance to a particular piece of evidence compared to other evidence in a case which might raise a reasonable doubt about the defendant's guilt? Consider the prejudice that could be caused by the admission of the defendant's previous conviction for downloading indecent images of children at X's trial for sexual assault. The discretion to exclude prosecution evidence is contained in s. 78 PACE 1984 (unfairness) whilst a general exclusionary discretion is available under s. 82(3) PACE 1984 (probative value outweighed by prejudicial effect).

Where the admissibility of evidence is disputed, the decision to admit or exclude evidence rests with the judge in the Crown Court and with the magistrates or District Judge in the magistrates' court. A decision to admit disputed evidence which results in a conviction may provide grounds for an appeal against conviction. Equally, a decision to exclude a particular piece of evidence may have profound implications for the prosecution's ability to discharge its legal burden of proof beyond reasonable doubt.

2.4.3 WEIGHT

Even where evidence is relevant and admissible, this does not mean that the jury or magistrates will find the evidence convincing or persuasive. In many cases an assessment of the weight of evidence is made on the basis of a wide range of factors. For example, when assessing the cogency of a witness giving oral testimony to the court, the following factors will be significant:

- the magistrate's or juror's intuition based on his or her life experiences;
- the age, demeanour, credibility of the witness; and
- the witness's involvement in the events about which he is testifying.

Less weight is likely to be attached to the evidence of a biased witness than to the testimony of a witness who is perceived to be 'independent'. Similarly, jurors or magistrates may be sceptical about believing a witness who has previous convictions for dishonesty and may therefore not attribute as much weight to that witness's evidence as to a witness with good character. By comparison due to its exceptionally high reliability, DNA evidence is capable of carrying significant weight.

The weight to be attached to a particular piece of evidence is a matter for the jury in the Crown Court and the magistrates in summary proceedings. Advocates on either side may make representations about the weight to be attached to particular evidence in the case.

2.4.4 WHO DECIDES QUESTIONS OF LAW AND QUESTIONS OF FACT?

Questions arising in a trial will either be questions of law or questions of fact. In jury trials a strict division of responsibilities is applied between judge and jury: the trial judge determines all questions of law whilst the jury decides all questions of fact. Questions of law can include:

- issues of substantive criminal law;
- a witness's competence to give evidence;
- whether particular evidence should be admitted or excluded;
- whether to withdraw the case from the jury and direct an acquittal;
- the trial judge's directions when summing-up to the jury.

An important part of the trial judge's role is summing-up the case for the jury and directing the jury as to the relevant law. Judges are greatly assisted in this task by Part 1 of the Crown Court Compendium 2018 (see https://www.judiciary.uk/wp-content/uploads/2018/06/crown-court-compendium-pt1-jury-and-trial-management-and-summing-up-june-2018-1.pdf), which contains guidance on all aspects of criminal law and evidence and suggested directions to the jury.

Questions of fact for the jury to decide include:

- the credibility of a witness;
- the weight to be accorded to a piece of evidence;
- whether the prosecution has discharged its legal burden of proof and proved the defendant's guilt beyond reasonable doubt.

In the magistrates' court, the magistrates are the ultimate arbiters of both fact and law. Advice on the law, court procedure, and evidence is provided by the magistrates' legal adviser.

2.5 PROCEDURE FOR DECIDING THE ADMISSIBILITY OF DISPUTED EVIDENCE

Often a dispute about the admissibility of evidence is resolved at a pre-trial hearing. A binding ruling on a point of law may be given at this hearing based purely on legal argument. Sometimes, however, it is necessary for evidence to be adduced and for findings of fact to be made before the admissibility of a particular piece of evidence can be decided. Where this is necessary a *voir dire*, or trial within a trial, will need to be held during the course of the trial. The *voir dire* procedure works more effectively in the Crown Court because of the separation of functions between the judge and the jury as previously highlighted. If, after hearing the evidence and legal arguments, the trial judge decides that the disputed evidence must be excluded, the jury will never know about the existence of the disputed evidence.

2.6 ASSESSING THE EVIDENCE—THE PROSECUTING SOLICITOR'S ROLE

In deciding whether a prosecution should be commenced, the Code for Crown Prosecutors (see Chapter 8) requires the CPS lawyer to determine whether there is sufficient evidence to secure a conviction. In making this assessment, the CPS lawyer will be mindful of the rules of evidence. The CPS lawyer has no active investigative role and therefore must assess the evidence gathered by the police by considering the witness statements and items of real evidence which may have been subject to forensic analysis. The prosecutor now has direct access to witnesses but this is not routinely exercised. Based on the assessment of the evidence, the CPS lawyer might suggest to the police that further investigation is needed or will be satisfied that there is sufficient evidence to charge the suspect.

2.7 ASSESSING THE EVIDENCE—THE DEFENCE SOLICITOR'S ROLE

Irrespective of whether the defendant is to be tried summarily or on indictment, the rules relating to pre-trial disclosure of evidence mean the defence solicitor will know the evidence against his client before trial. In assessing the strength of the disclosed prosecution evidence, the defence advocate should apply the core concepts of relevance, admissibility and weight to make an initial assessment of whether the prosecution has a case against the defendant, to identify any prosecution evidence that might be challenged and to advise the client about plea. The defence lawyer should not advise a guilty plea unless the evidence against his client is relevant, admissible and persuasive.

2.8 TYPES OF EVIDENCE

Where evidence is relevant and admissible, it will be presented to the court in one of the following forms.

2.8.1 ORAL TESTIMONY

This is evidence given orally by a witness in court on factual matters within the witness's personal knowledge and experience. An example of a witness giving factual evidence would include the witness stating that: 'I saw the defendant break the car window and drive the car away at speed.' In a criminal trial, direct oral testimony is the preferred way for evidence to be put before the court and is likely to be the type of evidence that the court will find the most persuasive.

2.8.2 OPINION EVIDENCE

A 'lay' witness is called at a trial to give factual evidence based on the witness's personal knowledge and experience. The witness should not offer an opinion on what they saw or heard. The general rule is that where a witness gives opinion evidence, it will be inadmissible. It would not be possible for a witness to state: 'It's obvious that the defendant killed him.'

There are two exceptions to this general rule. First, an expert may give opinion evidence on a matter that goes beyond the ordinary competence of the court. A common form of expert evidence given at a criminal trial is the evidence of a forensic scientist or a medical expert. Expert evidence is considered in more detail in Chapter 17. Second, a lay person may state his or her opinion on a matter not requiring expertise as a way of conveying facts that they have personally perceived. A witness will be allowed to say that when she saw the accused 'he appeared to be drunk' or 'the car was speeding immediately before it hit the pedestrian'.

2.8.3 DOCUMENTARY EVIDENCE

Relevant and admissible evidence may be contained in a document. A witness statement is an example of documentary evidence. Other types of documentary evidence include:

* photographs;
* maps;

- plans;
- computer print-outs;
- business documents;
- expert reports.

2.8.4 REAL EVIDENCE

Real evidence are objects produced in court so the court may draw inferences from the condition and existence of the object. In a murder trial, a knife produced as the murder weapon, or the defendant's bloodstained clothing, would be examples of real evidence. In a public order offence, CCTV or mobile telephone footage of the incident would constitute real evidence.

2.8.5 DIRECT AND CIRCUMSTANTIAL EVIDENCE

In whatever form evidence is admitted, it will have either direct or circumstantial relevance. Direct evidence requires nothing more than the jury or magistrates accepting or rejecting the evidence that has been given. If X testifies that he saw Y walk up to Z, take out a knife and stab Z, this is direct evidence of the *actus reus* of murder. At his trial for murder, however, Y calls a witness who states she was with Y at the time of the alleged murder 30 miles away. If accepted, this constitutes direct evidence of alibi. Circumstantial evidence requires the court not only to accept the witness's account but also to draw an inference from the evidence. If X testifies that he saw Y running away from Z and that he observed that Y had bloodstains on his clothing, this would constitute circumstantial evidence linking Y to the murder of Z. Expert forensic evidence may suggest that the blood on Y's clothing matches that of the victim Z. Again, if the evidence is accepted by the court, it provides circumstantial evidence that Y was in close contact with the victim of the crime at the relevant time. A criminal case may be based entirely on circumstantial evidence. The trial of Ian Huntley (2003) for the murders of Holly Wells and Jessica Chapman and the trial of Steve Wright (2008) for the murders of five prostitutes in Ipswich are examples of two high-profile convictions based on circumstantial evidence.

2.9 CLARIFYING THE EVIDENTIAL ISSUES

In any contested criminal case there will be a number of evidential issues. It is important, however, not to lose sight of the 'big picture'. Advocates on each side need to make sense of the evidence and to develop a theory of the case which is supported by the evidence. In this way a coherent and focused case can be put before the jury or magistrates. The core issues in a case need to be distilled from the mass of detail and if the case is to be contested, a defence theory needs to be developed.

The defence theory is a clear and concise explanation of why the case should be resolved in the defendant's favour. In devising a plausible defence theory, the evidence that needs to be challenged and marshalled will become clear. On a charge of theft, for example, if the defendant denies a dishonest intent, the defence advocate will need to organise the evidence and develop an argument with this central issue in mind. Perhaps the defendant will challenge the prosecution's suggestion that he or she was responsible for the crime, on the basis of mistaken identification. If this is the defence theory of the case, the defence advocate should concentrate on challenging the prosecution's evidence of identification and present any evidence which supports the theory advanced by the defendant such as evidence of alibi. The development of a theory of the case helps both the prosecution and defence advocates decide the questions to be asked of a witness in both examination-in-chief and in cross-examination. This is why, in a contested case, it is important for both the prosecution and the defence to crystallise the facts in issue.

2.10 CONCLUDING REMARKS ON CRIMINAL EVIDENCE

This chapter has introduced some of the core concepts that apply in the context of criminal evidence. Later chapters will examine the evidential considerations that arise in the context of:

- a confession made to the police;
- obtaining evidence of eye-witness identification;
- a defendant exercising a right to silence at the police station;
- admitting hearsay evidence;
- admitting evidence of a defendant's bad character;
- the admissibility of opinion evidence;
- evidence of corroboration;
- the evidence of a child or mentally handicapped witness;
- the admissibility of illegally/unfairly obtained prosecution evidence.

The rules are significant at all stages of a criminal case, and a good understanding of the law and the ability to apply the principles in a practical way to the facts of the case are important for the successful criminal litigator. The rules of criminal evidence cannot be ignored—so in a determined and purposeful way, after carefully reading this introductory chapter, move on to the other chapters which deal with the evidential rules in practice.

2.11 ADVOCACY

Advocacy is the legal skill most often associated with criminal litigation. Put simply, advocacy is the art of communication. Having come this far you will hopefully have begun to develop your oral communication skills and an ability to put forward structured and coherent arguments. Those skills now need to be harnessed and applied in a different context.

The most common situations where a criminal advocate's oral presentation skills can be highly significant are at contested bail hearings, pleas in mitigation of sentence and, of course, in conducting trials. Unless you are already qualified, it will be some time before you undertake any of these independently, although non-legally qualified staff do have rights of audience before Crown Court judges in chambers and may therefore represent a defendant on a bail application following a magistrates' court refusal to grant bail. In this short section on advocacy we identify some of the key components of the art of persuasion.

2.11.1 EFFECTIVE ADVOCACY

Whether appearing for the prosecution or the defence, effective advocacy depends on:

- good preparation; and
- persuasive oral communication skills.

Good preparation presupposes a thorough knowledge of both the facts in the case and the relevant law. For example, when making or opposing a bail application, you would be expected to have a good working knowledge of the Bail Act 1976 and to apply the facts of the case to the law. The submission of a plea in mitigation presupposes a thorough knowledge of sentencing principles and practice.

Similarly, if you were to make an application to have evidence excluded at trial, your preparation would have alerted you to the relevant legal basis of your submission and the facts that you would need to prove in order to substantiate your submission.

Whilst knowledge and understanding of the relevant law and facts are important, you must also be able to present your legal argument in a structured, coherent and persuasive way.

2.11.2 WHAT MAKES AN ORAL PRESENTATION PERSUASIVE?

The following checklist is based on our experience of developing and assessing advocacy skills in various contexts. Whatever the context of your presentation, an awareness of what may be termed 'credibility factors' may help.

Eye contact

Eye contact greatly enhances an oral presentation. It shows you are confident enough to move away from a prepared script and enables you to assess and gauge the reaction your submission is having on your listener. If you want to get your message across you must engage your listener. Maintaining eye contact is an obvious way of helping to achieve this.

Posture

Do not slouch. Stand up straight with your head slightly elevated. Posture affects the resonance of your voice. Your posture should make you appear relaxed and confident.

Voice

Accents are not a problem, providing you are clear in your enunciation of words. The acoustics vary from courtroom to courtroom so you may need to explore your voice audibility levels. Avoid being too loud and aggressive, or too softly spoken. The latter does not inspire confidence. Deep breathing (from the diaphragm) can help your voice to resonate more, thereby making you more audible. If you think you have a monotone delivery, try to get some vocal variety into your voice. Try reading a children's story to a young relative: you will soon find out ways to make your delivery more interesting.

Pace

It is very important to correctly pace your submission. True advocacy is not about reading from a prepared script, as this will make it more likely that you will read too quickly and consequently your audience will be unable to follow your argument. Too slow a delivery can have a stultifying effect upon your audience. Experiment, and choose a pace that is suitable.

Pause

The pause is a simple but very effective persuasive device. Use it for dramatic effect. If you have a particularly telling point to advance, make the point and then . . . pause momentarily. Allow the point to be considered by your listener. Used in combination with voice inflection, the effect should resonate with your audience.

Distracting mannerisms

We all have them. You will be the best judge of your own distracting mannerisms. If you have the opportunity, why not record yourself making an oral submission. When you review your performance, ask yourself: does my body language detract from the message I am putting across? Are you fiddling with the loose change in your pocket or juggling a pen in your hands? Do you sway from side to side? Are you constantly touching your face or your hair? Look at the expression on your face. Is it the face of someone who feels relaxed and confident in the submission they are making? Do you look up and smile occasionally or are you frowning/perplexed/refusing to make eye contact? All of these mannerisms distract from the message you are trying to put across.

Structure

A persuasive argument will be delivered in a structured fashion. Devising a structure should help you to avoid unnecessary repetition. The simplest and most effective structure for any submission is for it to have a beginning, middle and end. Break up your submission into listener-friendly portions, for example:

> 'Ma'am, I have three points I would like to make this morning: My first point is this . . . . my second point is this . . . . my third and final point is this. . . . . In summary, Ma'am. . . . . '

Sometimes the nature of your submission will determine its structure. When preparing and delivering a submission on bail, for example, the Bail Act 1976 provides a logical structure within which to work.

Keep your submission concise. Cut down on the verbiage. Try to avoid reading out sections from statute and case law. Copy and highlight the relevant sections/passages and then hand them in for the bench/judge to read.

Brevity

You will soon come to realise that a court's time is very precious. With this in mind, always try to make your submission succinct. Developing a logical structure to your submission will assist. Try to avoid unnecessary repetition.

Persona

It is important when appearing as an advocate that you look confident—even if you do not feel confident! Dressing suitably and smartly helps an advocate to step into the role. It also helps to inspire confidence in you and conveys the correct impression to the court, your client and the public. First impressions really do count. Without being dramatic, your opening address needs to capture the court's attention. Consider carefully what sort of individual engages you on an intellectual level. The more open and interesting the advocate's personality, the more likely the audience will be attentive. Behavioural psychology has much to teach the aspiring advocate!

Be prepared to make appropriate concessions. Avoid being arrogant or patronising. Organise yourself and your notes so that your composure and professionalism come across.

Etiquette

You must be familiar with the etiquette of the court before which you are appearing. This includes dressing appropriately and properly addressing the court and your opponent.

A trainee defence solicitor does not have a right of audience before a magistrates' court or the Crown Court but can appear in a closed hearing before a Crown Court judge in chambers in connection with a bail application. Solicitors (and, subject to certain restrictions, Associate Prosecutors) have a right of audience before a magistrates' court. A solicitor has a limited right of audience before the Crown Court on an appeal against conviction and/or sentence where the solicitor represented the defendant in the magistrates' court. Some solicitors have a Higher Right of Audience qualification which enables them to exercise full rights of audience before the Crown Court. When appearing as a solicitor-advocate before a Crown Court, a solicitor must be appropriately robed in a black stuffed gown and winged collar.

The correct form of address before a judge of the Crown Court (which would include a circuit judge or recorder) is 'Your Honour . . . '. You should always defer to the court and be extremely courteous. With this in mind you will often hear the phrase: 'May it please Your Honour, I appear on behalf of the defendant in this matter.' 'Has Your Honour had the time to consider the pre-sentence report that has been prepared in connection with this matter? I am grateful for that indication.'

The correct form of address before a District Judge or Deputy District Judge sitting in a magistrates' court is 'Sir' or 'Madam'.

When addressing a bench of lay magistrates, the correct term of address is 'Your worships, or Sir/Madam and your colleagues . . .'.

Solicitors refer to a fellow solicitor as 'my friend for the prosecution' or 'my friend for the defence'. A barrister or counsel is referred to as being 'my learned friend'. It is customary to refer to the court's legal adviser as 'your learned legal adviser . . .'.

As an officer of the court, a solicitor should always be appropriately attired when appearing before a court. Where this does not require the solicitor to be duly robed, suitable attire will normally be a sombre-coloured suit.

Language

Persuasion is as much about your choice of language as anything else. Words can be very powerful tools with which to convey a message. Think carefully about your choice of words.

Can you find a more powerful adjective to advance the point you are making? Try to use language which includes your audience. For example, you might say: 'Let's examine together the circumstances in which the defendant's confession was obtained . . .'. Personalise the situation: 'Ma'am, I invite you to consider what you would have done in the same situation as my client . . .'.

Some people are natural advocates. They have charm and exude confidence. If they combine their natural ability with knowledge and application of the law, they are capable of making a persuasive submission even in the most hopeless of cases. Other individuals might initially be less comfortable in the spotlight which the art of advocacy demands. Advocacy skills can be developed with practice and reflection.

If you are accessing our online resources you will be able to see some examples of advocacy in our filmed case studies. *R v Lenny Wise* contains a fully contested application for bail. *R v Hardy* and *R v Martin* both comprise pleas in mitigation. The specifics of each of these submissions are considered in Chapter 10 (on bail) and the Chapters 21 and 26 (on sentencing). **The clips should be viewed as learning aids that illustrate, in a practical way, aspects of criminal practice. They should not be regarded as definitive examples of how advocacy might be conducted before a criminal court.**

KEY POINT SUMMARY

- Generally the prosecution bears the legal burden of proving a defendant's guilt beyond reasonable doubt. The elements of the offence charged determine what the prosecution needs to prove if it is to secure a conviction.

- To be admissible, evidence must be relevant to the facts in issue but not all relevant evidence is admissible.

- Evidence can be excluded under the mandatory rules of exclusion and/or through the exercise of judicial discretion in the interests of ensuring a fair trial.

- In the Crown Court, matters of relevance and admissibility of evidence are determined by the judge in the absence of the jury. Matters of fact are determined by the jury. There is no separation of function in the magistrates' court and so magistrates determine matters of fact and law.

- An accused is entitled to pre-trial disclosure of the evidence to be used against him, enabling his advocate to evaluate the strengths and weaknesses of the prosecution case.

- Where an accused chooses to plead guilty, the evidence against him is not tested in open court.

SELF-TEST QUESTIONS

Case Study: *R v Lenny Wise*

Consider Documents 6 and 26(A–Q) in Appendix 2. Given that we have yet to cover the rules of criminal evidence in detail, simply describe in very general terms the nature of the evidence that is said to link Lenny Wise to the burglary allegation. In doing so, can you identify any issues of evidence this scenario is likely to give rise to? In simplistic terms at this stage, consider how Lenny will challenge the nature of the evidence against him and, in doing so, start to formulate a theory of the defence case.

An analysis of all self-test questions can be found in the online resources.

FIGURE 2.1 AN OVERVIEW OF CRIMINAL EVIDENCE

PURPOSES OF THE LAW OF EVIDENCE

- The law of evidence regulates how the prosecution and, exceptionally, the defence prove their case to the court.

- The rules determine what evidence may be received and what evidential use can be made of that evidence, and in so doing they seek to ensure the defendant receives a fair trial.

- In the Crown Court, the judge determines the admissibility of disputed evidence in the absence of the jury.

- In a summary trial, issues relating to the admissibility of disputed evidence are resolved by the magistrates with legal advice provided by their legal adviser.

FACTS IN ISSUE

- The primary facts in issue are the *actus reus* and the *mens rea* of the offence charged and any defence raised by the accused.

- It is for the prosecution (or exceptionally the defence) to prove the facts that are in issue at a trial.

- The facts in issue can also include secondary facts which are relevant to the facts in issue such as the admissibility of a piece of evidence.

BASIC EVIDENTIAL RULES

- To be heard at trial, evidence must be:
  - relevant to a fact in issue; and
  - admissible (i.e. as a matter of law, the evidence can be put before the court).

- The weight to be afforded to a particular piece of evidence is a question of fact for the jury/magistrates.

TYPES OF ADMISSIBLE EVIDENCE

- Relevant and admissible evidence will be presented at trial as one of the following types:
  - oral testimony;
  - documentary evidence;
  - real evidence.

Part II

INVESTIGATION AND THE DECISION TO CHARGE

Part II deals with the investigation of criminal offences and the decision to charge.

In Chapter 3 we explain general and specific police powers of investigation and in Chapter 4 the process of detention and questioning. In Chapter 5 we explore the evidential rules and practical issues concerning the position of a suspect in the police interview. The rules of evidence for challenging 'tainted' prosecution evidence are considered in Chapter 6 and the admissibility of identification evidence in Chapter 7. Finally, the decision to charge a suspect or to offer alternatives to prosecution are considered in Chapter 8, which also examines the role of the Crown Prosecution Service (CPS) and its duties of pre-trial disclosure of evidence.

Part II is supplemented by a further chapter available online through the online resources which focuses on the practical steps that a legal adviser might take at the police station and explains the process of police station accreditation.

3 THE POWERS TO STOP, SEARCH AND ARREST

3.1	**Introduction**	**47**
3.2	**Stop and search before arrest**	**48**
3.3	**Stop and search at common law**	**48**
3.4	**Statutory powers to stop and search in a public place before arrest**	**48**
	3.4.1 The general power to stop and search—s. 1 PACE 1984	48
3.5	**Specific powers to stop and search before arrest**	**50**
3.6	**The consequences of an unlawful stop and search**	**50**
3.7	**Powers of arrest**	**51**
	3.7.1 What is an arrest?	51
	3.7.2 Arrest at common law	51
	3.7.3 Arrest with a warrant—s. 1 Magistrates' Courts Act 1980	51
	3.7.4 Statutory power of arrest—s. 24 PACE 1984 and Code G	51
	3.7.5 Arrest without a warrant by a constable	52
	3.7.6 The requirements for a lawful arrest under s. 24 PACE 1984	53
	3.7.7 The use of reasonable force	55
	3.7.8 Citizen's power of arrest—s. 24A PACE 1984	55
	3.7.9 Preserved powers of arrest	55
	3.7.10 Taking action against an 'unlawful' arrest	55
3.8	**Street bail**	**56**
3.9	**Searching the suspect's person and/or property upon arrest**	**56**
	3.9.1 Searching with the suspect's permission	56
	3.9.2 Search of an arrested person away from the police station—s. 32(1) PACE 1984	57
	3.9.3 Search at premises where the suspect has been arrested—s. 32 PACE 1984	57
	3.9.4 The power to enter and search—s. 17 PACE 1984	57
	3.9.5 Search of an arrested person's premises—s. 18 PACE 1984	58
	3.9.6 The power of seizure—s. 19 PACE 1984	58
	3.9.7 Preserved powers of entry	59
	3.9.8 Search warrants—s. 8 PACE 1984 (code B)	59
	3.9.9 Material that may not be seized	60
3.10	**The European Convention on Human Rights 1950**	**60**

3.1 INTRODUCTION

The police have extensive statutory powers to stop and search and to arrest a person in connection with the investigation of a criminal offence. Under the Police and Criminal Evidence Act 1984 (PACE 1984), the powers to stop and search and arrest are general powers, to be used in a wide range of situations. The police also have a vast array of specific powers to stop, search and arrest under various statutes, including the Terrorism Act 2000, the Misuse of Drugs Act 1971 and the Serious Organised Crime and Police Act 2005.

In this chapter we examine:

* powers of stop and search before arrest;

* powers of arrest under PACE 1984;

- powers to search a person and his property after arrest;
- the power to grant street bail; and
- the right to liberty under Article 5 European Convention on Human Rights (ECHR 1950).

Reference will be made throughout this chapter to PACE 1984 Code of Practice A which deals with police powers to stop and search, and Code B which governs the search and seizure of property. Both Codes can be accessed online from the Home Office. Our online resources include a link to the PACE 1984 Codes of Practice.

3.2 STOP AND SEARCH BEFORE ARREST

The primary purpose of stop and search is to enable an officer to allay or confirm his suspicion about a person being in possession of stolen or prohibited articles or drugs without arresting him. Stop and search is one of the most controversial aspects of police powers and consequently the law provides detailed guidance about the officer's conduct when questioning or searching a person in a public place before arrest.

3.3 STOP AND SEARCH AT COMMON LAW

At common law, an officer cannot stop or detain a person unless the person volunteers to cooperate with the officer (*Rice v Connelly* [1966] 2 All ER 64). Code A Notes for Guidance para. 1 recognises that an officer may speak to a person in the normal course of his duties without detaining him or exercising any compulsion over the person. The person being questioned has a civic but not a legal duty to assist the officer.

Unless the officer exercises a statutory power to stop and search or arrest, the person cannot be compelled to remain with the officer.

3.4 STATUTORY POWERS TO STOP AND SEARCH IN A PUBLIC PLACE BEFORE ARREST

The police have wide statutory powers to stop and search a person or his motor vehicle, which can be exercised either under a general power or under a specific stop and search power.

3.4.1 THE GENERAL POWER TO STOP AND SEARCH—S. 1 PACE 1984

Section 1 PACE 1984 (as supplemented by Code A) gives the police the general power to stop and search a person and/or his vehicle before arrest in a public place or a place to which the public have access, where the officer has reasonable grounds for suspecting the person is in possession of stolen or prohibited articles.

Code A para. 1.1 requires that stop and search must be used 'fairly, responsibly, with respect for those being searched and without unlawful discrimination'.

To be a lawful search under s. 1 PACE 1984, the following factors must be present.

(1) The stop and search must be in connection with stolen or prohibited articles
Stop and search under s. 1 PACE 1984 may be exercised to discover:

- stolen articles; or
- prohibited articles; or
- an article to be used for an offence under s. 139 Criminal Justice Act 1988 (possession of a bladed instrument); or
- a prohibited firework.

What are stolen articles?

'Stolen' articles have the same meaning as in the Theft Act 1968 and includes items arising from an offence of theft, burglary, robbery or criminal deception.

What are prohibited articles?

'Prohibited' articles include offensive weapons or articles made or adapted for use or intended use in an offence under the Theft Act 1968 and under s. 1 Criminal Damage Act 1971. The Theft Act 1968 offences include theft (s. 1), burglary (s. 9), taking a motor vehicle without consent (s. 12) or fraud (s. 1 Fraud Act 2006) and includes items such as a crowbar, car keys, a credit card or any relevant item provided the user has the necessary intent to commit an offence under the 1968 Act.

An offensive weapon, similar to s. 1 Prevention of Crime Act 1953, is an article made or adapted for use for causing injury to a person or intended for such use and includes articles that are offensive weapons in themselves such as knives and guns and everyday articles that have been made or adapted for use as an offensive weapon including, for example, a bottle that has been deliberately broken.

(2) The requirement for reasonable suspicion

Under s. 1 PACE 1984, reasonable suspicion will be present where:

- the officer has actual suspicion that the person is in possession of stolen or prohibited articles (the subjective test); and
- there are reasonable grounds for that suspicion (the objective test).

Detailed guidance on the meaning of reasonable suspicion is found in Code A paras. 2.2–2.11. Code A stipulates that reasonable suspicion:

- is determined on the facts of each case, including the time and the place the power was exercised and the suspect's behaviour, for example where the suspect is seen by the officer on the street late at night and appears to be hiding something;
- can never be determined on the basis of personal factors such as the person's race, ethnic background, religion, appearance or previous convictions;
- should normally be based on good, reliable and recent police intelligence.

For judicial guidance on the reasonable suspicion test, see *O'Hara v Chief Constable, RUC* [1997] AC 286, at para. 3.7.6.

(3) Where can the stop and search take place?

The officer may only stop and search in a 'public place or a place to which the public has access', s. 1(1) PACE 1984. This includes the street or in a park or in a cinema, which are places to which the public have access. The power under s. 1 PACE 1984 cannot be exercised inside the suspect's home or in any other dwelling without the occupier's consent but may be exercised in a garden or yard attached to a house where the officer reasonably believes that the suspect does not live at that address and is not on the land with the express or implied permission of the occupier.

(4) Additional rights under s. 1 PACE 1984 and Code A

- In accordance with Code A para. 3.8, the officer must explain that the person is being detained for the purpose of a search. In addition, the officer must tell the person his name (unless the officer thinks this will place him in danger in which case a warrant or identification number must be given) and the police station at which he is based, the legal search power that is being used, the object of the proposed search and the person's entitlement to a copy of the record of the search if they ask within three months of the date of the search. Code A requires a police officer in plain clothes who wishes to stop and search to produce a warrant card before exercising the power. A failure to do so will result in the search being unlawful as the officer would not be acting in the execution of his or her duty (see *B v DPP* [2008] EWHC 1655 (Admin)).

- The search must be conducted at or near the place where the suspect was first detained. Reasonable force may be used as a last resort.

- Generally, only the suspect's outer clothing should be searched—where the search requires the removal of more than the outer clothing it should be conducted in private (e.g. in a police van or nearby police station).

- The officer must make a record of the search at the time unless there are exceptional circumstances which would make this wholly impracticable. A copy of the record must be given immediately to the person. Alternatively, the person can be given an electronic receipt of the stop and search. The officer must explain how a full copy of the record can be obtained. The required contents of the written record are set out in Code A para. 4.3 and if they are arrested a record of the stop and search must form part of the person's custody record at the police station.

 Example

Consider the following illustration of a search conducted under s. 1 PACE 1984.

WPC Atherton is on uniform night patrol when she sees Danny walking through the town centre carrying a tool bag. There have been several burglaries in the locality in recent months. When the officer stops and questions Danny, she is exercising her powers under s. 1 PACE 1984. The officer will be acting lawfully if the following conditions are present:

- Danny has been stopped in a public place or a place to which the public has access;

- the officer had reasonable suspicion based on the recognised tests;

- the purpose of the stop and search was to discover whether Danny was in possession of stolen or prohibited articles or articles to be used in connection with an offence of criminal damage;

- the procedural requirements of Code A were complied with.

3.5 SPECIFIC POWERS TO STOP AND SEARCH BEFORE ARREST

There are statutory stop and search powers available to the police to use in specific situations. A summary of the main stop and search powers is contained in Annex A of Code A and includes the power to search for drugs (Misuse of Drugs Act 1971). In addition to the general power of stop and search under s. 1 PACE 1984, there is a further power to stop and search under s. 60 Criminal Justice and Public Order Act 1994 upon the authorisation of an inspector who reasonably believes that incidents involving serious violence may take place in the local area and it is expedient to give an authorisation to prevent their occurrence, or that dangerous instruments or offensive weapons are being carried or have been used in the local area. An officer can stop and search under this statutory power whether or not the officer has any grounds for suspecting that the person is carrying weapons or instruments on his person or in their vehicle. This power is regulated by Code A of the Codes of Practice.

3.6 THE CONSEQUENCES OF AN UNLAWFUL STOP AND SEARCH

If a suspect has been unlawfully stopped and searched, for example if the police officer cannot prove he or she had reasonable grounds to support the decision to stop and search, the admissibility of any resulting evidence may be challenged at trial by the defence under s. 78 PACE 1984 on the basis that the admission of the evidence would have 'an adverse effect on the fairness of the proceedings' or under s. 76 PACE 1984 if it comprises admissions of a self-incriminating nature (a confession). Both provisions are considered more fully in Chapter 6. An unlawful stop and search would provide a defence for a person suspected of obstructing/resisting or assaulting a police constable in the execution of his or her duty. In *R v Bristol* [2007] EWCA Crim 3214, B's conviction for obstructing a police constable in the execution of his duty was quashed as the officer, who was exercising a power to stop and search under the Misuse of Drugs Act 1971, had failed to give his name and police station when applying force to B's jaw in an attempt to get him to spit out a suspected ingestion of drugs.

3.7 POWERS OF ARREST

An arrest will occur during a criminal investigation where the police have the legal and factual grounds to justify depriving the suspect's liberty. The usual reason for arrest is to question the suspect about possible involvement in, or knowledge of, a criminal offence.

3.7.1 WHAT IS AN ARREST?

While there is no legal definition of 'arrest', *Christie v Leachinsky* [1947] AC 573 suggested that an arrest was 'the beginning of imprisonment'. On a factual basis, a person will be under arrest where the person is deprived of his or her liberty, usually, though not exclusively, by physical restraint, so that the person is not free to go where he or she pleases.

Common law and statutory powers of arrest exist in the following situations:

- at common law an officer can arrest the suspect for a breach of the peace;
- the execution of an arrest warrant obtained from a magistrate—s. 1 Magistrates' Courts Act 1980;
- arrest without a warrant by a police constable in connection with a criminal offence where the legal grounds under s. 24(1), (2) or (3) and s. 24(4) PACE 1984 apply;
- arrest without a warrant by a citizen in connection with an indictable offence where the legal grounds under s. 24A PACE 1984 apply;
- preserved powers of arrest in a limited range of offences listed in Sch. 2 PACE 1984.

3.7.2 ARREST AT COMMON LAW

The common law power of arrest applies in connection with an anticipated or an actual breach of the peace. The arrest may be made by a police officer or member of the public.

3.7.3 ARREST WITH A WARRANT—S. 1 MAGISTRATES' COURTS ACT 1980

Arrest under a warrant is now a less common method of detaining a suspect. Section 1 Magistrates' Courts Act 1980 states that a justice of the peace may issue an arrest warrant on the basis of written information substantiated on oath that a person has or is suspected of having committed an offence, and:

- the suspect is over the age of 18;
- the offence alleged is indictable or punishable with imprisonment; or
- the suspect's address cannot be sufficiently established for the service of a written charge/summons.

3.7.4 STATUTORY POWER OF ARREST—S. 24 PACE 1984 AND CODE G

There is a single, generic power of arrest for all offences contained in s. 24 PACE 1984, as amended. Code G para. 1.3 provides that the use of the statutory power of arrest must be fully justified and officers exercising the power should consider if the necessary objectives can be met by other, less intrusive means. It goes on to provide that the absence of justification for exercising the power of arrest may lead to challenges should the case proceed to court and could also lead to civil claims against police for unlawful arrest and false imprisonment.

3.7.5 ARREST WITHOUT A WARRANT BY A CONSTABLE

The main power of arrest without a warrant under s. 24(1)–(3) PACE 1984 is exercisable by a police officer in connection with any criminal offence. Under Code G para. 2.1 for there to be a lawful arrest, two key elements must be present:

- a person's involvement in or suspected involvement in or attempted involvement in the commission of an offence; and

- reasonable grounds for believing that the person's arrest is necessary.

Under s. 24(1) PACE 1984, an officer may arrest without a warrant:

'(a) anyone who is about to commit an offence; or

(b) anyone who is in the act of committing an offence; or

(c) anyone whom he has reasonable grounds for suspecting to be about to commit an offence; or

(d) anyone whom he has reasonable grounds for suspecting to be committing an offence.

(2) If a constable has reasonable grounds for suspecting that an offence has been committed, he may arrest without a warrant anyone whom he has reasonable grounds to suspect being guilty of it.

(3) If an offence has been committed a constable may arrest without a warrant—

(a) anyone who is guilty of the offence;

(b) anyone whom he has reasonable grounds for suspecting to be guilty of it.'

For the arrest to be lawful not only must one of the grounds in s. 24(1)–(3) PACE 1984 be made out, the officer must additionally prove that he or she had reasonable grounds for believing that an arrest was *necessary* (s. 24(4)) for one or more of the reasons listed in s. 24(5) PACE 1984.

The '*necessity*' conditions which are set out in s. 24(5) PACE 1984 and which are further defined in Code G include:

(a) *to enable the person's name to be ascertained where the constable does not know and cannot readily ascertain the person's name or has reasonable grounds for doubting the name given by the person is the person's real name* (this includes the situation where the person's name cannot be readily ascertained or the officer has grounds for doubting whether the name given by the person is, in fact, his real name);

(b) *to enable the person's address to be ascertained* (an officer might decide that a person's address cannot be readily ascertained if they fail or refuse to give it when asked, particularly after being warned that such a failure or refusal is likely to make their arrest necessary);

(c) *to prevent the person in question*:

  (i) causing physical injury to himself or another;

  (ii) suffering physical injury;

  (iii) causing loss or damage to property;

  (iv) committing an offence against public decency;

  (v) causing unlawful obstruction of the highway;

  (this might apply where the suspect has already used or threatened violence against others and it is thought likely that he may assault others if he is not arrested or where the suspect's behaviour and actions are believed likely to provoke, or have provoked, others to want to assault him unless he is arrested for his own protection);

(d) *to protect a child or vulnerable person from the person*;

(e) *to allow the prompt and effective investigation of the offence or of the conduct of the person* (this is the widest necessity ground and is the one that has given rise to a number of recent judicial review decisions. The prompt investigation of an offence can include the need to interview the suspect when the person's voluntary attendance is not considered to be a practicable alternative to arrest because it is thought that the suspect is unlikely to attend voluntarily for interview; or arrest would enable the special warning to be given under ss. 36 and 37 Criminal Justice and Public Order Act 1994 (see Chapter 5); or it is thought likely that they will steal or destroy evidence or threaten potential witnesses; or because there is a need to exercise a power of search under s. 18 PACE 1984; or when considering arrest in connection with an offence to which the statutory Class A drug-testing requirements in Code C apply, to enable testing when it is thought that drug misuse might have caused or contributed to the offence. See Chapter 4);

(f) *to prevent the prosecution for the offence being hindered by the disappearance of the person in question* (this may be used where there are grounds for believing that if the person is not arrested he will not attend court).

The arrest conditions give police officers operational discretion to decide whether an arrest is necessary by requiring the officer to examine and justify the reason(s) why a person should be taken to the police station for the custody officer to decide whether the person should be detained (see Code G para. 2.6). In deciding whether to make an arrest, the officer will consider the particular circumstances of the case including the victim's situation; the nature of the offence; the circumstances of the offender; and the needs of the investigation (Code G para. 2.8). Instead of arresting an individual, a police officer could charge by post, grant street bail (see later) or issue a fixed penalty notice.

The requirement for an arrest to be necessary has given rise to an ever-increasing body of case law, particularly in relation to s. 24(5)(e) PACE 1984 (see earlier). If a police officer cannot establish that it is necessary for him to arrest the individual concerned, the arrest and any continued detention is unlawful. No individual should be arrested simply because the power of arrest is available. Code G para. 1.2 provides that the exercise of the power of arrest has 'an obvious and significant interference with the right to liberty and security under Article 5 of the European Convention on Human Rights'. It warns police officers that the absence of justification for exercising a power of arrest may lead to challenges in court and claims against police for unlawful arrest and false imprisonment. In *Re Alexander* [2009] NIQB 20, it was held that an officer who does not apply his mind to alternatives short of arrest (e.g. inviting the suspect to attend the police station for interview on a voluntary basis) is open to challenge. Further detailed guidance on the necessity test and its practical application by police officers is provided in Code G.

3.7.6 **THE REQUIREMENTS FOR A LAWFUL ARREST UNDER S. 24 PACE 1984**

An arrest will only be lawful if made in accordance with s. 24 PACE and if the person is told they are under arrest (however obvious this might be) and the grounds for their arrest (s. 28 PACE 1984).

Whilst the arrested person must also be informed why the arrest was believed to be necessary for the purposes of s. 24(4) PACE 1984, a failure to inform does not make the arrest unlawful.

Where reasonable suspicion is a requirement under s. 24 PACE 1984, the reasonable grounds requirement is applied in accordance with the two-part test from the House of Lords case of *O'Hara v Chief Constable, RUC* [1997] AC 286:

- first, there must be actual suspicion on the part of the officer that an offence was at some stage of commission; and

- second, there must be reasonable grounds for that suspicion.

Code G para. 2.3A provides that:

'There must be some reasonable, objective grounds for the suspicion, based on known facts or information which are relevant to the likelihood the offence has been committed and the person liable to arrest committed it'.

(1) The first requirement involves a subjective assessment by the police officer, whilst the second requirement is assessed objectively. Whilst the threshold to satisfy the reasonable grounds test is low, it will not be satisfied where the arresting officer has been instructed by a superior officer to make an arrest or where the arresting officer believes that a superior officer probably did have information to justify an arrest but which the superior officer had not conveyed to the arresting officer (see *Raissi v Metropolitan Police Commissioner* [2008] EWCA Civ 1237).

(2) The arresting officer must also have reasonable grounds for believing that an arrest is necessary in accordance with s. 24(5) PACE 1984 (see para. 3.7.5).

(3) Having been arrested or as soon as reasonably practicable thereafter, the officer must caution the suspect, in accordance with Code G paras. 3.1–3.7, in the following terms:

> 'You do not have to say anything. But it may harm your defence if you do not mention when questioned something which you later rely on in court. Anything you do say may be given in evidence.'

The failure to caution does not render the arrest unlawful but it may provide grounds for excluding evidence under ss. 76 and 78 PACE 1984 (see Chapter 6). Having been arrested, the suspect must then be taken to a designated police station as soon as is reasonably practicable (s. 30 PACE 1984), unless granted street bail (see later).

Anything said by the arrested person at the time of his arrest must (along with the circumstances and reasons for arrest and the fact that the caution was given) be recorded in the arresting officer's notebook (Code G para. 4.1) which must be completed at the time of the arrest or as soon as practicable thereafter.

 Example

Consider the following scenario. Do you feel the arrest by PC Taylor was justified?

John is 30 but looks considerably younger. He drives an expensive Porsche. On 5 November at 18:30 hours, his car is pulled over by the road traffic police. John asks the police officer why he has been pulled over. The officer, PC Taylor, informs him that he wishes to check whether John is insured to drive such a powerful car. John assures PC Taylor that he is insured and that he does not wish to be delayed any further. John waits whilst the officer conducts a mobile check on his insurance details. The officer confirms there is no problem with the insurance. PC Taylor then asks John to get out of the car. When John asks why, PC Taylor replies that his colleague says he saw John using his mobile telephone whilst driving. John is incredulous and offers to show PC Taylor that his mobile telephone is in his jacket which is in the boot of his car. John informs PC Taylor that he is not prepared to be detained any longer and asks for PC Taylor's collar number. At this point, PC Taylor informs John that he is under arrest for driving whilst using a mobile telephone contrary to s. 41D Road Traffic Act 1988. In reply to being cautioned, John is recorded as having said: 'I have nothing to say. This has to be some kind of wind-up right?' John is granted police bail to attend the police station in seven days' time.

The arrest by PC Taylor is questionable on two grounds. The evidence suggests that John was pulled over because there were doubts about whether he was an insured driver. It is only when this is resolved in John's favour that it is suggested that John was driving whilst using a mobile telephone. This is denied by John. No attempt was made by PC Taylor to ascertain whether John was telling the truth about his mobile telephone being in his jacket pocket in the boot of his car (this is contrary to the requirements of Code G para. 2.3A). In the circumstances it is difficult to see how PC Taylor could have had reasonable grounds for suspecting that John has committed an offence. Even if PC Taylor had reasonable grounds, in what sense could the officer form the view that it was necessary to arrest John having regard to the offence and the needs of the investigation (s. 25(5) PACE 1984 and Code G para. 2.8)? PC Taylor had John's name and address. Having regard to the judgment in *R v Alexander* [2009] and to Code G para. 1.3, the actions of the police on this occasion appear to be wholly disproportionate. John might seek a judicial review of the actions of the police in this situation.

3.7.7 THE USE OF REASONABLE FORCE

Section 3(1) Criminal Law Act 1967 allows reasonable force to be used when making an arrest or when preventing a criminal offence. The 'reasonable force' test is decided by the magistrates or by the judge on the specific facts of each case.

3.7.8 CITIZEN'S POWER OF ARREST—S. 24A PACE 1984

Section 24A PACE 1984 permits a citizen to arrest a person in connection with an indictable offence (including an either-way offence).

Section 24A(1) PACE 1984 provides:

'A person other than a constable may arrest without a warrant—

(a) anyone who is in the act of committing an indictable offence; or

(b) anyone whom he has reasonable grounds for suspecting to be committing an indictable offence.'

Section 24A(2) PACE 1984 further provides that:

'Where an indictable offence has been committed a person other than a constable may arrest without a warrant—

(a) anyone who is guilty of the offence or

(b) anyone whom he has reasonable grounds for suspecting to be guilty of it.'

Section 24A(3)(a) PACE 1984 requires that *in addition* to satisfying one of the grounds mentioned in s. 24A(1)–(2) PACE 1984, the arrest will only be lawful if the citizen has reasonable grounds for believing that an arrest is necessary for one or more of the reasons listed in s. 24A(4) PACE 1984 *and* it appears to the person making the arrest that it is not reasonably practicable for a constable to make the arrest instead.

Section 24A(4) PACE 1984 defines the grounds to include:

(a) causing injury to himself or any other person;

(b) suffering physical injury;

(c) causing loss or damage to property;

(d) making off before a constable can assume responsibility for him.

3.7.9 PRESERVED POWERS OF ARREST

The following statutory powers of arrest are preserved:

- in connection with the taking of fingerprints at a police station (s. 27 PACE 1984);
- for taking samples in specified circumstances at a police station (s. 63A PACE 1984);
- for failing to surrender to police bail (s. 46A PACE 1984);
- where a person has broken or is likely to break a condition of bail (s. 7 Bail Act 1976).

3.7.10 TAKING ACTION AGAINST AN 'UNLAWFUL' ARREST

A failure to comply with the correct procedure renders the arrest unlawful—although an unlawful arrest can be remedied after the proper formalities have been complied with (*Lewis v Chief Constable of South Wales* [1991] 1 All ER 206). Where the police have made an unlawful arrest, the defence may challenge the admissibility of prosecution evidence obtained as a result of it. The defence could submit that admitting the prosecution evidence would have an 'adverse effect on the fairness of the proceeding'; s. 78 PACE 1984 (see Chapter 6 for consideration of the principles that apply to the exclusion of unlawfully obtained evidence).

Where a suspect has not been properly cautioned, an application can be made by the defence at trial to have any resulting evidence excluded. An unlawful arrest may be subject to judicial review and a claim for damages for false imprisonment.

3.8 STREET BAIL

The traditional position has been that PACE 1984 has required an arrested person to be taken to a designated police station as soon as possible. It was then a matter for the custody officer to decide whether to charge the suspect, or to detain the suspect without charge, or to release the suspect on police bail.

Section 30A PACE 1984 provides that where a suspect is arrested at the scene of the offence, he may be given 'street bail' without being taken to the police station. The suspect will be required to attend the police station to answer to bail at a later date unless he is informed otherwise. He must be given a written notice stating the offence for which he was arrested and the time and date at which he is required to attend the police station (s. 30B PACE 1984). Changes under s. 52 Policing and Crime Act 2017 (see para 4.14.2) have now established the presumption that, where a police officer decides that it is appropriate to release an arrested person rather than taking him to a police station, that release will be without bail unless the requirements under s. 30A(1A) PACE 1984 are met. These requirements are that the constable is satisfied that bail is proportionate and necessary in all the circumstances (having regard, in particular, to any bail conditions that would be imposed) and bail is authorised by an officer of at least the rank of inspector.

Conditions can be attached to the grant of 'street bail' for the purposes of securing surrender, preventing further offences, preventing interference with witnesses or obstruction of the administration of justice, or for the person's own protection. Common conditions that can be imposed include residence, exclusion from a particular place or non-contact with a particular individual. An inspector is prohibited from imposing the following conditions on a suspect released on street bail:

- surety;
- security;
- residence at a bail hostel.

The written notice issued to the suspect under s. 30B PACE 1984 must state clearly any conditions that are to be attached to the grant of police bail and give details about how the conditions can be varied. An application to vary conditions may be made to the custody officer at the police station at which the person is required to attend (s. 30CA PACE 1984) or a magistrates' court (s. 30CB PACE 1984). There is a power of arrest for failing to attend at a police station and for breaking any conditions imposed.

The grant of police bail is considered further in Chapter 4.

3.9 SEARCHING THE SUSPECT'S PERSON AND/OR PROPERTY UPON ARREST

Where the suspect has been arrested, the police have a wide range of legal powers to search any property or premises owned or occupied by the suspect for evidence relating to the offence(s) under investigation. The power of the custody officer under s. 54 PACE 1984, to search the suspect on arrival at the police station and to seize and retain property is addressed in Chapter 4 where the process of detention and questioning of suspects is considered. The power to take intimate and non-intimate samples is considered in Chapter 7.

PACE 1984 Code B deals with police powers to search premises and to seize and retain property found on premises and persons.

3.9.1 SEARCHING WITH THE SUSPECT'S PERMISSION

The detained person may agree to his home or business premises being searched. Where consent is not given, however, the police have a wide range of legal powers to carry out a lawful search.

3.9.2 **SEARCH OF AN ARRESTED PERSON AWAY FROM THE POLICE STATION—S. 32(1) PACE 1984**

Where the suspect has been arrested away from the police station, s. 32(1) PACE 1984 permits a constable to search an arrested person if the constable has reasonable grounds for believing that:

- the arrested person may present a danger to himself or others; or
- may have concealed on him anything which he might use to assist the arrested person in escape from lawful custody; or
- may have concealed on him anything which might be evidence relating to an offence.

Section 32(1) gives the police wide discretion in the way in which the power to search is exercised. It means that a police officer may search an arrested person for 'anything' on that person. In practice this means that the officer can search an arrested person for items which might be wholly unrelated to the reason why the initial arrest was made as the words 'relating to an offence' do not necessarily relate to the offence for which the arrest is made. These wide powers are limited to some extent as the officer must have reasonable grounds for believing that a search is necessary. Simply making a search at the time of arrest would be unlawful unless the officer could prove the necessary 'reasonable grounds' for this belief. A power to seize and retain items found is included.

A police officer may not require a person to remove any clothing in public other than an outer coat, jacket or gloves, although the search can include the search of a person's mouth (s. 32(4) PACE 1984).

3.9.3 **SEARCH AT PREMISES WHERE THE SUSPECT HAS BEEN ARRESTED—S. 32 PACE 1984**

Section 32(2)(b) PACE 1984 confers on a police officer the power to enter and search any premises where the suspect was at the time of his arrest or immediately before his arrest, for evidence relating to the offence for which the suspect is under arrest provided the offence is an indictable offence (which includes all offences triable either way) and the officer has reasonable grounds for believing that there is evidence relating to the offence for which the suspect has been arrested.

In every case where entry is made under s. 32 PACE 1984, it is a question of fact whether the officer considered that reasonable grounds existed for the officer's belief that evidence might be found as a result of the search.

Where the reasonableness of the officer's belief and/or the admissibility of any evidence discovered as a result of the search is disputed by the defence, the issue will be decided prior to trial or in a *voir dire* (trial within a trial). Evidence obtained as a result of an unlawful search remains admissible subject to the court's exclusionary discretion under s. 78 PACE 1984 (see Chapter 6).

Section 32(1) PACE 1984 confers the power to seize and retain any item for which a police officer is authorised to search.

3.9.4 **THE POWER TO ENTER AND SEARCH—S. 17 PACE 1984**

Section 17 PACE 1984 allows a police officer to enter and search any premises for the purposes of:

(a) executing a warrant of arrest;

(b) arresting a person for an indictable offence;

(c) arresting a person for a specified non-indictable offence;

(d) recapturing any person who is unlawfully at large; or

(e) saving life or limb or preventing serious damage to property.

The power under s. 17 PACE 1984 can only be exercised (with the exception of (e)) if the police officer has reasonable grounds for believing that the person being sought is on the premises.

3.9.5 **SEARCH OF AN ARRESTED PERSON'S PREMISES—S. 18 PACE 1984**

Section 18 PACE 1984 deals with searching any premises *occupied or controlled* by a person who is under arrest for an indictable offence (which includes all offences triable either way). A search is permitted if there are reasonable grounds for suspecting that there is evidence on the premises (other than items subject to legal privilege) that relate either to the indictable offence or some other connected or similar indictable offence and the written authority of an inspector is obtained. Prior authorisation is not required where the conditions under s. 18(5) PACE 1984 are met in that before the arrested person is taken to the police station, that person's presence at a place (other than a police station) is necessary for the effective investigation of the offence. Section 18(2) confers the power to seize and retain any item for which a police officer is authorised to search.

3.9.6 **THE POWER OF SEIZURE—S. 19 PACE 1984**

Section 19 provides that a constable who is lawfully on any premises has power to seize anything which is on the premises if the constable has reasonable grounds to believe that it has been obtained in consequence of the commission of an offence, or that it is evidence in relation to an offence and that it is necessary to seize it in order to prevent it from being concealed, lost, altered or destroyed.

The power of seizure does not extend to items that the constable has reasonable grounds to suspect are subject to legal privilege (see para. 3.9.9). An additional power of seizure has been granted to the police under ss. 50 and 51 Criminal Justice and Police Act 2001, which enables the police to remove material which cannot be practically examined on the premises with a view to determining whether it contains evidence capable of being seized or whether the material may be subject to excluded categories of material (see para. 3.9.9). The most obvious example of this would be a personal computer containing material that might disclose evidence of the commission of an offence or contain evidence relevant to an offence.

 Example

Police powers to search an arrested person and/or property under ss. 18 and 32 PACE 1984 can be confusing. Depending on the facts of the case, in some situations either s. 18 or s. 32 can be used. In other situations, only one of the statutory provisions may apply. Consider the following examples which illustrate the position.

Janice, who is the managing director of a small double-glazing firm, is arrested at work on suspicion of having committed fraud.

As Janice has been arrested, the police may search her office under s. 32 PACE 1984 because she has been arrested in connection with an indictable offence provided the officers have reasonable grounds for believing that there is evidence in Janice's office connecting her to the fraud offences.

The appropriate power of search is s. 32 PACE 1984 which permits the police to search premises where the arrested person was immediately before or at the time of his or her arrest.

The term 'where the suspect was at the time of arrest or immediately before arrest' is given a restrictive meaning as s. 32 could not be used if the police searched Janice's office six hours after her arrest. To be lawful under s. 32 PACE 1984, the search must be almost contemporaneous with the arrest.

Janice may also be the subject of a personal search under s. 32 PACE 1984 if the officer reasonably believes that Janice has concealed on her person anything which may present a danger to herself or others; or anything which she might use to assist her to escape or anything which might be evidence relating to an offence.

The police would have entered Janice's office under s. 17(1)(b) PACE 1984 to arrest her for an indictable offence.

The police may use s. 18 PACE 1984 to search Janice's home and a lock-up garage that she rents close to home. Section 18 applies in this situation provided the police have reasonable grounds for believing there is evidence on the properties that relates to an indictable offence or to other similar or connected offences and the search is authorised by an officer of at least the rank of inspector. The house and lock-up garage satisfy the requirement that the properties are occupied or controlled by Janice. Section 32 PACE 1984 does not apply here because Janice was not at home or in the garage at or immediately before the time of her arrest.

If Janice had been arrested at home, the police could have searched under s. 18 or s. 32 PACE 1984.

3.9.7 PRESERVED POWERS OF ENTRY

A number of statutes provide police officers with a power to search a suspect's premises to obtain evidence in relation to the investigation of a specific offence. Section 23(3) Misuse of Drugs Act 1971 allows the police to enter and search premises in connection with an investigation under the 1971 Act. A warrant to enter the premises must be obtained from a magistrate.

3.9.8 SEARCH WARRANTS—S. 8 PACE 1984 (CODE B)

The powers of search discussed so far give the police the power to search premises owned by the arrested person or to search the premises where the person was arrested. What can the police do where it is not possible or practicable to contact the person who could allow the police to enter premises to search for evidence in connection with an offence? In these circumstances, an officer of the rank of inspector or above can make a written application to a magistrate under s. 8 PACE 1984 for a warrant authorising a police officer to enter and search the premises specified in the application. Several other enactments permit an application for a search warrant for a wide range of offences.

To be granted a search warrant under s. 8 PACE 1984, the officer must satisfy the magistrate that there are reasonable grounds for believing that:

- an indictable offence has been committed (this includes an indictable-only offence and an offence triable either way); and
- there is material on the premises which is likely to be of substantial value to the investigation of the offence; and
- the material is likely to be relevant evidence; and
- the evidence does not include items subject to legal professional privilege, excluded material, or special procedure material; and
- it is not practicable to communicate with any person entitled to grant entry or, if it was, it is likely that the purpose of the search will be frustrated or seriously prejudiced.

Two types of warrant may be issued. First, a specific premises warrant authorises the police to search the address specified on the warrant. Alternatively, s. 8(2)–(4) Serious Organised Crime and Police Act 2005 provides for an all-premises warrant which covers all premises owned or occupied by the person named in the application but where it is not reasonably practicable to specify each of the premises at the time of the application. The warrant gives the police access to all premises occupied or controlled by the person whether they are specified on the application or not. The warrant can authorise the police making multiple visits on multiple occasions to the premises specified in the warrant—subject to the requirement that any second and subsequent visits must be authorised by an officer of at least the rank of inspector. The entry and search under the warrant must be completed within three months of issue.

Sections 15 and 16 PACE 1984 provide further safeguards against potential misuse of the warrant by the police under s. 8 PACE 1984. Any non-compliance with the statutory safeguards renders a search and entry of premises unlawful, see *Harry and Sandra Redknapp v Commissioner of the City of London Police and the City of London Magistrates' Court* [2008] EWHC 1177. In *R (Waqar Bhatti) v Secretary of State for the Home Department*, Lawtel 3/2/2010, the Divisional Court held that the practice of officers inserting by hand the address of the property to be searched on the copy of an all-premises warrant at the point of execution was unlawful and in breach of the procedural requirements. As the search was unlawful the items seized had to be returned.

3.9.9 MATERIAL THAT MAY NOT BE SEIZED

It is important to note that certain categories of 'material' cannot be seized by the police. These are items subject to legal professional privilege, 'excluded material' and 'special procedure material'.

(1) Items subject to legal professional privilege

These are defined by s. 10(1)(a) PACE 1984 and include any communication containing legal advice. The doctrine of legal professional privilege requires that any written and/or oral legal advice passing between a lawyer and client in connection with a case is privileged and cannot be divulged to a third party without the client's consent.

(2) 'Excluded' material

'Excluded material' is defined by s. 11 PACE 1984 and consists of personal records held in confidence by the person who created them. Personal records are defined as medical records, records of spiritual healing and files kept by social workers and probation officers about their clients.

(3) 'Special procedure material'

Section 14 PACE 1984 defines 'special procedure material' as material which has been acquired by a person in the course of his or her trade, business or profession or other occupation or office, who holds it subject to an express or implied undertaking to keep it confidential. It also extends to journalistic material unless it has been acquired in confidence, in which case it will be regarded as excluded material under s. 11 PACE 1984.

3.10 THE EUROPEAN CONVENTION ON HUMAN RIGHTS 1950

A person who has been stopped and searched and/or arrested is entitled to the protections under the Convention. The Articles that are most relevant to this area are Article 5 (the right to liberty and security of the person including the right not to be detained by the police without lawful authority), Article 8 (the right to privacy), Article 10 (freedom of expression) and Article 11 (freedom of assembly and association).

When exercising stop and search powers, the police will be required to show that:

- the power to stop and search was prescribed by law; and
- the power was exercised in pursuance of a legitimate aim; and
- the exercise of the power was proportionate to the aim to be achieved.

In deciding the lawfulness of a stop and search the court will often balance the competing interests of a suspect's right to be free to go about his lawful business against the wider obligations on the police to prevent crime of which the powers under s. 1 PACE 1984 are considered to be a highly effective provision. This balancing exercise is well illustrated by the decision in *Howarth v Commissioner of Police for the Metropolis* [2011] EWHC 2818 where the High Court decided that the power to stop and search the applicant was reasonable and proportionate for the legitimate purpose that existed on the facts of the case.

An arrest will satisfy the requirements of Article 5 ECHR 1950 where the person is brought before a competent legal authority such as a court either on reasonable suspicion of having committed an offence or to prevent that person from committing an offence or from escaping after having committed an offence (*Fox, Campbell and Hartley v UK* (1990) 13 EHRR 157).

The lawfulness of an arrest may also be judged according to whether:

- the legal authority for the arrest is precise and accessible; and
- is procedurally fair and not arbitrary; and
- proportionate to the aim of depriving a person of his or her liberty.

The test of reasonable suspicion will satisfy Article 5 provided that an objective observer would be satisfied that the suspect may have committed an offence (*Fox, Campbell and Hartley v UK* (1990) 13 EHRR 157).

KEY POINT SUMMARY

- Know the legal grounds that permit a person to be stopped and searched before arrest (s. 1 PACE 1984).
- Know the legal grounds under which a person can be arrested (ss. 24 and 24A PACE 1984).
- Have a good working knowledge of the law governing the powers to search the suspect and/or the suspect's property after arrest.
- If you represent the defendant, where appropriate, be prepared to challenge the legality of an arrest and/or search and any evidence obtained as a result. The challenge may be made to the police, the CPS or to the court at the defendant's trial.
- Be aware of the pervasive influence of the ECHR 1950 in relation to stop and search and arrest and cite ECHR case law to support your submissions.

SELF-TEST QUESTIONS

1. Where can you find guidance on the reasonable suspicion or belief test?
2. Which caution should be given to the suspect on arrest?
3. Where are the police powers to search a person and his property after arrest contained?
4. In what circumstances will the police apply to a magistrate for a warrant to be issued under s. 8 PACE 1984?
5. Police are called to a public order disturbance in town. By the time they arrive, the incident appears to be over. CCTV operators have provided a description of a male wearing a football top who appears to have been the instigator of the trouble and was waving some kind of bottle or weapon in his hand. One of the police officers notices a male wearing similar clothing walking towards a taxi rank. On approaching the male (Antonio), he runs off. He is apprehended within a matter of minutes. What powers do the police have in relation to Antonio?
6. A short, factual scenario based on the exercise of police powers appears at the end of Chapter 6 (scenario 1); although the focus of the question is based on the admissibility of unlawfully obtained evidence, you may wish to consider what aspects of police procedure relating to stop and search and arrest might be considered unlawful.

Analysis of all self-test questions can be found in our online resources.

FIGURE 3.1 POLICE POWERS OF STOP/SEARCH/SEIZURE AND ARREST

STOP AND SEARCH BEFORE ARREST
Section 1 PACE 1984 and Code A

- A person may be stopped and/or searched in a public place or in a place to which the public has access where the officer reasonably suspects the person is in possession of:

  – stolen articles; or

  – prohibited articles.

SEARCHING THE SUSPECT AFTER ARREST

- With the suspect's consent; or

- under s. 32 PACE 1984 where the officer:

  – has reasonable grounds for believing the suspect may present a danger to himself or others; or

  – has concealed anything on him he might use to escape from custody; or

  – has concealed on him evidence which might be related to an offence.

SEARCH OF PREMISES AFTER ARREST

- Search with the suspect's consent;

- search of premises at which the suspect is arrested, s. 32 PACE 1984 (applies to an indictable offence);

- search of premises owned/controlled by the suspect, s. 18 PACE 1984 (applies to an indictable offence and inspector's authorisation needed);

- preserved powers of entry and search, e.g. s. 23 Misuse of Drugs Act 1971.

POLICE OFFICER ARREST WITHOUT A WARRANT

- Section 24 PACE 1984 where a police officer has reasonable grounds for suspecting that the person:

  – is about to commit an offence; or

  – is committing an offence; or

  – has committed an offence; *and*

  – it is necessary to arrest the individual for any of the following reasons (s. 24(5)):

    • to enable the person's name to be ascertained where the constable does not know and cannot readily ascertain the person's name or has reasonable grounds for doubting the name given by the person is his real name; or

    • to enable the person's address to be ascertained;

    • to prevent the person in question:

      – causing physical injury to himself or another;

      – suffering physical injury;

      – causing loss or damage to property;

      – committing an offence against public decency; or

      – causing unlawful obstruction of the highway;

  – to protect a child or vulnerable person from the person; or

  – to allow the prompt and effective investigation of the offence or of the conduct of the person;

  – to prevent the prosecution for the offence from being hindered by the disappearance of the person in question.

CHECKLIST FOR A LAWFUL ARREST—S. 28 PACE 1984

- There must be a legal ground for the arrest, e.g. s. 24 PACE 1984.

- There must be the factual grounds for the arrest, e.g. reasonable grounds for believing that an offence has been committed.

- The person must be cautioned as follows:

  – 'You do not have to say anything. But it may harm your defence if you do not mention when questioned something which you later rely on in court. Anything you do say may be given in evidence.'

- The person must be informed of the reason for his arrest.

- The person should be taken to a designated police station as soon as is reasonably practicable.

4 DETENTION AND INTERROGATION

4.1	**Introduction**	**64**
4.2	**Interviewing a volunteer at the police station or elsewhere**	**65**
	4.2.1 Rights of a volunteer	65
4.3	**Action immediately following arrest**	**66**
4.4	**The role of the custody officer**	**66**
	4.4.1 The custody record	66
	4.4.2 Informing suspects of their rights	67
	4.4.3 Search on arrival at the police station—s. 54 PACE 1984	68
	4.4.4 Is there sufficient evidence to charge?	68
4.5	**Detention without charge (following arrest)**	**69**
	4.5.1 How long can a suspect be detained without charge?	69
	4.5.2 Initial detention period of 24 hours	69
	4.5.3 Detention beyond 24 hours?	69
	4.5.4 Detention beyond 36 hours—warrant of further detention	70
4.6	**Reviewing a suspect's detention**	**70**
	4.6.1 When must the reviews be conducted?	71
	4.6.2 Granting police bail pending further investigation	72
4.7	**The suspect's right to intimation and/or legal advice**	**72**
	4.7.1 The right to inform someone of the arrest—s. 56 PACE 1984	72
	4.7.2 Delaying the right to have someone informed of the arrest	72
	4.7.3 The suspect's right to legal advice—s. 58 PACE 1984	73
	4.7.4 Who pays for legal advice given at the police station?	73
	4.7.5 Providing access to legal advice	73
	4.7.6 Delaying the right to legal advice	74
4.8	**Other rights and safeguards enjoyed by the suspect whilst in detention**	**75**
4.9	**The treatment of vulnerable suspects and the provision of an appropriate adult (AA)**	**75**
4.10	**Interviewing the suspect**	**77**
	4.10.1 What constitutes an interview?	78
	4.10.2 Fitness to be interviewed	78
	4.10.3 When must an interview cease?	78
4.11	**The requirement to caution**	**78**
4.12	**What constitutes a fair interview?**	**79**
	4.12.1 Oppressive interviews	79
	4.12.2 Inducements to confess	79
	4.12.3 Physical conditions of the interview	79
	4.12.4 The legal adviser's role during the interview	80
	4.12.5 The appropriate adult's role in the interview	80
4.13	**How should an interview be recorded?**	**80**
4.14	**Charging a suspect**	**80**
	4.14.1 Pre-charge police bail where the police have referred the case to the CPS for a charging decision—s. 37(7)(a) bail	81
	4.14.2 Pre-charge bail in all other cases—release under investigation and time limits	81
	4.14.3 Questioning after charge	82
	4.14.4 Police bail after charge	82
	4.14.5 Drug testing at the police station (Code C para. 17)	84
4.15	**Concluding remarks**	**84**

4.1 **INTRODUCTION**

Following arrest (unless granted street bail), the suspect should be brought to a designated police station as soon as is reasonably practicable. The suspect is now the centre of the police investigation and the police will want to question the suspect and may undertake certain investigatory procedures including:

- taking fingerprints;
- taking a biometric sample or impression;
- taking photographs;
- requiring the suspect to participate in a formal identification procedure.

In this chapter, we consider the process of detention, questioning, and charge. The procedures for obtaining identification evidence (including biometric samples) are considered in Chapter 7.

A detailed legal framework for the treatment of suspects at the police station is provided by the Police and Criminal Evidence Act 1984 (PACE 1984) and the Codes of Practice, particularly the revised 2018 version of Code C. The provisions define the power(s) the police may exercise over a suspect but also provide a number of safeguards. A copy of Code C is accessible from the Home Office website—our online resources includes a link taking you to the most recent version of the Codes of Practice. The safeguards contained in PACE 1984 and its accompanying Codes of Practice exist to ensure the suspect enjoys fair treatment while in detention and also to promote investigative integrity by the police, ensuring the quality and reliability of evidence obtained at the police station. Evidence obtained at the police station in breach of PACE 1984 and Code C is vulnerable to challenge, and a defence lawyer might seek to exclude any resulting evidence under s. 78 PACE 1984 and under s. 76 PACE 1984, in the case of a confession (see Chapter 6). Section 67(11) PACE 1984 allows the Codes of Practice to be admissible in evidence if relevant to a matter to be decided by a court.

It is the legal adviser's duty at the police station to advance and protect his client's rights. To do this, the legal adviser needs a detailed knowledge of PACE 1984 and the Codes of Practice to challenge the police if they breach the letter and/or the spirit of the suspect's legal rights.

Be aware that there are more extensive powers governing the detention and interrogation of persons suspected of involvement in terrorist activities. These provisions which are found in the Terrorism Act 2000 and Code H are outside the scope of this work. More details can be found in *Blackstone's Criminal Practice*.

In the password-protected lecturer resources section in our online resources, we offer a 'stand alone' video case study/role play, entitled the 'Peter West Police Station Scenario', with supporting documentation. The video is divided into different sections covering the investigation of an offence of rape. It explores all aspects of a suspect's detention at the police station, including the legal adviser's role and illustrates many of the points covered in this chapter. (**In the freely available online resources accompanying this book, you will find an Additional Chapter entitled 'Advising at the Police Station—Practical Steps' which comprehensively explores the practical nature of the defence solicitor's role at the police station, taking into account everything that is covered in this chapter and in the succeeding chapters which address some of the important rules of evidence that can arise out of the process of investigation.**)

In this chapter, we explain the process of detention and charge including the following:

- the custody officer's role;
- the importance of the custody record;
- the circumstances in which a suspect can be detained without charge;

- the length of time a suspect can be kept in custody;
- the obligation to review the suspect's detention;
- the suspect's right to have someone informed of his arrest;
- the suspect's right to legal advice;
- the suspect's basic rights in custody;
- specific safeguards in relation to vulnerable suspects;
- the conduct of an interview; and
- the decision to charge and withhold bail.

We begin by mentioning those who voluntarily attend at the police station.

4.2 INTERVIEWING A VOLUNTEER AT THE POLICE STATION OR ELSEWHERE

The police have faced significant budgetary cuts in recent years. Detaining a suspect in custody is expensive. An increasingly common way for the police to interview a person suspected of involvement in a criminal offence is to invite them to attend the police station as a volunteer without formally arresting them. It has been reported that some of these 'voluntary interviews' have occurred in the home and, in some instances, at their place of work. A volunteer answering questions at the police station was always known euphemistically as 'helping the police with their enquiries'. It is easy for a suspect to fall into a false sense of security in this situation and to believe that a legal advisor is not required. For an illustration of the potential dangers of self-incrimination whilst being interviewed as a 'volunteer' having declined legal advice, see the must publicised 'crime' of the unwitting Nicole Bailey who was convicted of theft after keeping a £20 note she found in a shop even though the police initially told her 'not to worry' about speaking to them and that they wanted 'a chat' (see http://www.bbc.co.uk/news/uk-england-stoke-staffordshire-39129975).

A volunteer is entitled to leave police custody at any time as they are not under arrest and no custody record will be opened (Code C para. 2.1(a)).

If the volunteer decides to leave and the police have not asked all relevant questions, they may arrest the volunteer under s. 24 PACE to 'ensure a prompt and effective investigation takes place (Code G, Note 2G—see Chapter 3). When arrested the status of a volunteer changes to that of a detainee and a custody record will be opened (Code C para. 2.1(a)).

4.2.1 RIGHTS OF A VOLUNTEER

The legal safeguards afforded to volunteers who agree to be interviewed by the police have been strengthened under the 2018 version of Code C.

If an arrest is not necessary and the volunteer is to be interviewed under caution (with a view to obtaining evidence against them), Code C para. 3.21(b) requires the interviewing officer to explain that the volunteer is not under arrest, is free to leave and what their rights, entitlements and safeguards are in accordance with Code C para. 3.21(A), see below. Code C para. 3.21(b) also imposes a duty on the interviewing officer to ascertain whether the volunteer is a juvenile or is vulnerable, and is therefore entitled to have the services of an appropriate adult.

Code C para3.21(b)–(ii) stipulates as follows: '*the suspect must not be asked to give their informed consent to be interviewed until after they have been informed of the rights, entitlements and safeguards that apply to voluntary interviews. These are set out in para. 3.21A and the interviewer is responsible for ensuring that the suspect is so informed and for explaining these rights, entitlements and safeguards.*'

Code C para. 3.21(A) contains significant safeguards for those under suspicion who are attending an interview as a volunteer. It must be explained to the suspect that the purpose of the voluntary interview is to question them to obtain evidence about their involvement or suspected involvement in the offence(s) described when they were cautioned and told that they were not under arrest. The interviewer must ensure the following rights, articulated at Code C para. 3.21(A) (a)–(g) are explained before informed consent to be interviewed as a volunteer is given:

- their right to information about the offence(s) in question by providing sufficient information to enable them to understand the nature of any such offence(s) and why they are suspected of committing it;

- their right to obtain free and independent legal advice and if declined to record why;

- their right to an appropriate adult if the interviewer determines they are a juvenile or vulnerable;

- their right to an interpreter in appropriate cases; and

- that the interview must be recorded in accordance with the requirements of Codes E and F.

Code C para. 3.22(A) provides: 'Before asking the suspect any questions about their involvement in the offence they are suspected of committing, the interviewing officer must ask them to confirm that they agree to the interview proceeding. This confirmation shall be recorded in the interview record . . .'

'After the police have interviewed a suspect voluntarily, they may inform the volunteer that they will be 'reported for summons.' The suspect can expect to receive a 'postal requisition' (summons to attend court) in the post. In other instances, the volunteer will leave the interview with no clear outcome. There is a six-month time limit for the prosecution of a summary-only offence (s. 127 Magistrates' Court Act 1980). Section 60B PACE makes provision for a person who is interviewed as a volunteer to be notified in writing that they are not to be prosecuted where the police have taken such a decision.

4.3 **ACTION IMMEDIATELY FOLLOWING ARREST**

Unless 'street bail' is granted under s. 30A PACE 1984 (see para. 3.8), s. 30 PACE 1984 requires an **arrested person** to be taken to a designated police station as soon as practicable after arrest. A designated police station is equipped with the appropriate facilities for dealing with a suspect in detention. The rules permit the arrested person's arrival at a police station or release on 'street bail' to be delayed if the suspect's presence is required elsewhere to assist the police with their investigation. This might include a search of the arrested person under s. 32 PACE 1984 and/or entry and search of premises under s. 32 or s. 18 PACE 1984.

After arriving at the police station, the suspect must be taken to the custody suite for 'booking-in' as soon as practicable. This will be carried out by the custody officer on duty.

4.4 **THE ROLE OF THE CUSTODY OFFICER**

The custody officer plays an essential role in ensuring that the suspect's legal rights at the police station are complied with (s. 39 PACE 1984). The officer should always remain independent and impartial of the criminal investigation and should not question the suspect about his involvement in the alleged offence. The custody officer is responsible for taking important decisions in relation to the suspect, including whether the suspect should be detained or released and, in conjunction with the Crown Prosecution Service (CPS), whether the suspect should be charged.

4.4.1 **THE CUSTODY RECORD**

The custody officer is also responsible for compiling the suspect's custody record. A custody record must be opened as soon as is reasonably practicable for each person brought to a police station (Code C para. 2.1). The suspect's legal adviser and/or appropriate adult have a right of access to the custody record 'at any time while the person is detained' (Code C para. 2.4). When a detained person leaves the police station, he is entitled to a copy of the custody record upon request (Code C para. 2.4A).

The custody record has important evidential value to both the prosecution and defence by providing a detailed record of all aspects of the suspect's detention. (We have included extracts from the custody record in relation to our case study *R v Lenny Wise* in Appendix 2. The complete documentation, including the full custody record, can be accessed on our online resources.)

The custody record will include details of:

- the suspect's arrest;
- the reason for the suspect's detention;
- authorisation of search procedures or continued detention;
- risk assessment and provision of an appropriate adult if appropriate;
- requests for legal advice/medical advice;
- details of the review(s) of the suspect's detention;
- details of meals and refreshments; and
- any complaints made by the suspect.

One of the first tasks the legal adviser should undertake at the police station is to carefully scrutinise their client's custody records to ensure that the client's legal rights have been complied with by the police.

Where questions about the admissibility of evidence obtained during the investigation arise, the custody record may be put in evidence at trial. For this reason, the legal adviser should ensure that any representations that he or she makes regarding their client's detention are recorded in the custody record.

4.4.2 **INFORMING SUSPECTS OF THEIR RIGHTS**

On arrival at the police station, Code C para. 3.1 requires the custody officer to explain to the suspect, that the suspect has the following rights which may be exercised at any stage:

- the right to have someone informed of their arrest;
- the right to consult in private with a solicitor, such advice being free and independent;
- the right to consult the Codes of Practice;
- if applicable, their right to an interpreter.

The detainee must also be given a written notice, setting out:

(i) their rights under paras. 3.1, 3.12, and 3.12A;

(ii) the arrangements for obtaining legal advice;

(iii) their right to a copy of the custody record;

(iv) their right to remain silent as set out in the caution;

(v) their right to have access to materials and documents which are essential to effectively challenging the lawfulness of their arrest and detention for any offence and (as the case may be) any further offences for which they are arrested whilst in custody;

(vi) the maximum period for which they may be kept in police detention without being charged, when detention must be reviewed and when release is required.

(vii) their right to medical assistance in accordance with Code C; and

(viii) their right, if they are prosecuted, to have access to the evidence in the case before their trial.

The custody officer, as required by Code C para. 3.5 shall ask the suspect whether they:

- want legal advice;
- want to inform someone of their arrest; and ask the detainee to sign the custody record to confirm their decisions in respect of these rights.

Furthermore, and importantly, custody officer shall determine whether the detainee is or might be, in need of medical treatment or attention, is a juvenile and/or vulnerable and therefore requires an appropriate adult, requires help to check documentation or an interpreter.

The custody officer must also undertake a risk assessment in accordance with Code C paras. 3.6–3.10 to ascertain the level of risk in relation to the detainee. The risk assessment should identify mental health issues; vulnerabilities; language difficulties; risk of self-harm and risk to others and may trigger access to health care evaluation and/or access to an appropriate adult or regular monitoring (see 4.9 below). Risk assessment is an ongoing process and assessments must always be subject to review if the circumstances change.

4.4.3 SEARCH ON ARRIVAL AT THE POLICE STATION—S. 54 PACE 1984

The custody officer must record a suspect's property when brought into custody (s. 54 PACE 1984). Property and clothing may be seized and retained if they could cause injury or damage to persons or property or could be used to assist an escape from lawful custody. Strip searches and intimate searches require special justification (see Code C Annex A). A strip search involves the removal of more than outer clothing which includes socks and shoes (Code C Annex A, B.9) and may only be undertaken in two situations. First, where the custody officer thinks it is necessary to remove an article which the detained person is not allowed to keep whilst in detention and the officer reasonably considers the detainee might have concealed such an article or, second, for the purposes of a search under s. 54A PACE 1984. Under s. 54A PACE 1984 a search or examination may be authorised by an officer of the rank of inspector or above for the purpose of ascertaining whether a detained person has any mark (e.g. a tattoo) that would tend to identify him as a person involved in the commission of an offence. Authorisation may only be given if the detained person refuses to consent to the examination/search or it is not reasonably practicable to seek the person's consent where the officer has reasonable grounds for suspecting that the detained person is not the person he claims to be or he refuses to confirm his identity. Any identifying marks may be photographed with or without consent.

An intimate search of a body orifice (other than the mouth) can only be carried out in accordance with s. 55 PACE 1984 and Code C Annex A.

Annex L of Code C makes provision for establishing the gender of a person when a search is conducted.

4.4.4 IS THERE SUFFICIENT EVIDENCE TO CHARGE?

Following the suspect's arrival at the police station and having completed the necessary formalities, the custody officer must decide whether there is sufficient evidence to charge the suspect with the offence for which he has been arrested (s. 37(1) PACE 1984).

If the custody officer concludes that **there is sufficient evidence to charge**, s. 37(7) PACE 1984 requires that the suspect must either be:

- released without charge and on bail (with or without conditions) or kept in police detention for the purpose of enabling the CPS to make a charging decision under s. 37B (s. 37(7)(a)); or

- released without charge and without bail unless the pre-conditions for bail are satisfied to allow for enquiries to continue (s. 37(7)(b)); or
- released without charge and on bail if the pre-conditions for bail are satisfied (bail may be conditional) (s. 37(7)(c)); or
- charged (s. 37(7)(d)).

Police bail and the decision to charge are further considered at para. 4.14.

4.5 DETENTION WITHOUT CHARGE (FOLLOWING ARREST)

Under s. 37(2) PACE 1984, if the custody officer determines that there is **insufficient evidence to charge**, the suspect shall be released without bail unless the pre-conditions for bail are satisfied or on bail if those pre-conditions are satisfied (conditional or otherwise), unless the custody officer has reasonable grounds for believing that the suspect's detention without charge is necessary:

- to secure or preserve evidence relating to an offence for which the suspect is under arrest; or
- to obtain such evidence by questioning the suspect.

The reasons for continuing to detain the suspect without charge must be noted in the custody record. The grounds are easily made out in a case where the investigating officer needs to interview witnesses or the suspect, or to undertake personal searches.

Where the custody officer becomes aware that the detention grounds have ceased to exist, there is an obligation on the custody officer to release the suspect immediately and unconditionally (s. 34(2) PACE 1984), unless it appears that there is a need for further investigation in which case release can be on bail (s. 34(5) PACE 1984). Currently, no conditions can be attached to the grant of bail under s. 34 (5) PACE 1984 (see further at para. 4.6.2 which also defines pre-conditions of bail).

4.5.1 HOW LONG CAN A SUSPECT BE DETAINED WITHOUT CHARGE?

There are strict time limits on how long a suspect can be detained at a police station without charge. Unauthorised detention beyond the permitted time limits is unlawful. **Detention time limits generally begin to run from the time of the suspect's arrival at the police station** This is referred to as the 'relevant' time, which must be noted in the custody record. Under Part 4 of PACE 1984 a suspect can be detained without charge for a maximum period of 96 hours subject to the safeguards explained below. (Longer periods of detention without charge apply to suspects arrested in connection with terrorism offences.)

4.5.2 INITIAL DETENTION PERIOD OF 24 HOURS

The general position is that the suspect can be detained at the police station without charge for 24 hours from the 'relevant' time (s. 41 PACE 1984) providing the detention grounds in s. 37(2) PACE 1984 are met.

At the end of the 24-hour period the suspect must either be charged or released unconditionally or on bail.

4.5.3 DETENTION BEYOND 24 HOURS?

The basic 24 hours of detention without charge can be extended up to 36 hours from the 'relevant' time for an indictable offence (which includes either-way offences) where the provisions of s. 42(1) PACE 1984 apply. These are that:

- a senior officer of at least the rank of superintendent authorises the suspect's continued detention; and
- the officer has reasonable grounds for believing that it is necessary to detain the suspect without charge to secure or preserve evidence or to obtain evidence by questioning the suspect; and
- the investigation is being conducted diligently and expeditiously.

An important safeguard is that before deciding whether to authorise the person's continued detention the officer must give the suspect or her solicitor an opportunity to make representations about the detention, s. 42(6). The representations can be made orally or in writing.

Where these conditions apply, the suspect can be detained for an additional period of up to 12 hours, making a total of 36 hours from the time of arrival at the police station. The reasons for extending the suspect's detention must be noted on the custody record. Continued detention is easily justified where investigating officers wish to interview or re-interview a suspect or to undertake an intimate search or to arrange an identification procedure. At the end of the 36-hour period the suspect must either be charged or released unconditionally or on bail unless detention without charge is further extended (s. 42(10) PACE 1984). Section 45ZA(1) PACE 1984 enables these functions to be performed by an officer who is at a different location to where the suspect is held but has access to the use of live link, provided certain safeguards (including advice from a solicitor and the consent of the suspect) are met.

4.5.4 DETENTION BEYOND 36 HOURS—WARRANT OF FURTHER DETENTION

Where the police wish to detain the suspect without charge beyond 36 hours, an application under s. 43 PACE 1984 must be made to the magistrates' court for a warrant of further detention. The application may now be made in court or through a live link. A court will grant a warrant if satisfied that there are reasonable grounds for believing that further detention is justified beyond 36 hours. An application for continued detention beyond 36 hours can only be made in relation to an indictable offence (which includes either-way offences). The police must make an application on oath supported by their reasons for seeking the warrant. In so doing, the police will need to explain the circumstances of the suspect's arrest, what investigatory steps have been undertaken so far and what further enquiries are needed.

The suspect has the right to be present at the hearing and to be legally represented. In practice, the application for a warrant of further detention is invariably granted by the magistrates.

Where the police persuade the court that the suspect should be detained for a further period without charge, the court may authorise detention for a further period of up to 36 hours making a total of 72 hours from his arrival at the designated police station—the 'relevant' time.

At the end of 72 hours, where the police wish to continue holding the suspect without charge, a further application for an extension of the warrant of further detention must be made to the magistrates' court. Provided the court is again satisfied that there are reasonable grounds for believing that the further detention is justified, it can extend detention for a further 24 hours, making a total of 96 hours from the time of the suspect's arrival at the police station.

At the end of 96 hours, the suspect must either be charged or released unconditionally or on police bail (s. 44 PACE 1984).

4.6 REVIEWING A SUSPECT'S DETENTION

Section 40 PACE 1984 requires the police to carry out periodic reviews of the suspect's detention, the details of which must be recorded in the custody record. The review is to ensure the suspect's continued detention is lawful.

Where the suspect has not been charged, the review of the suspect's detention must be carried out by an officer of at least the rank of inspector who has not been directly involved in the investigation. This officer is known as the 'review officer'. Under s. 40 PACE 1984 and

Code C paras. 15.9–15.11, the review can be carried out in person or by telephone or through a live link (a telephone review is not permitted where facilities for review using a live link exist and it is practicable to use them, see para.15.9B). The suspect can make representations about his continued detention.

Where the suspect has been arrested and charged, the review can be carried out by the custody officer.

4.6.1 **WHEN MUST THE REVIEWS BE CONDUCTED?**

The first review of detention must be made no later than six hours **after the detention was first authorised** by the custody officer and thereafter every nine hours to ensure that the reasons for detaining the suspect's detention continue to apply. Please see Table 4.1 for more guidance.

TABLE 4.1 BRIEF SUMMARY OF DETENTION TIME LIMITS

BRIEF SUMMARY OF DETENTION TIME LIMITS		
Time	**Relevant officer**	**Requirements/Reasons**
10am: Suspect arrives at police station (detention clock begins to tick)	Custody officer	Custody record opened
10.15am: Detention without charge authorised (review clock begins to tick)	Custody officer	Reasonable grounds for believing that detention is necessary to secure or preserve evidence or to obtain evidence by questioning (s. 37(2) PACE 1984)
4.15pm: First review deadline	Inspector not involved in the case	First review of detention no later than six hours after detention first authorised (s. 40 PACE 1984) Thereafter, at nine-hourly intervals
1.15am: Second review deadline	Inspector not involved in the case	Second review of continued detention
10am: 24 hours (maximum duration for a summary-only offence)	Superintendent	Continued detention beyond 24 hours (s. 42 PACE 1984) for an indictable offence if there are reasonable grounds for believing that detention is necessary to secure or preserve evidence or to obtain evidence by questioning
10.15am: Third review deadline	Inspector not involved in the case	Reviews of continued detention will continue at nine-hourly intervals
10pm: 36 hours	Magistrates' court	(S. 43 PACE 1984) Warrant of further detention must be sought to continue to detain beyond 36 hours—same conditions must be present when further detention was authorised after 24 hours
72 hours	Magistrates' court	Extension of warrant of further detention must be sought
96 hours	Custody officer	(S. 44 PACE 1984) Charge or release as maximum period in detention has been reached

NB: at any time during the detention process, the suspect can be released on bail (with or without conditions) to attend the police station at a later date. The detention clock freezes at this point and resumes ticking once police bail is answered (s. 47(6) PACE 1984).

The legal adviser should ensure the suspect's detention is lawful at all times. The custody record should help to determine this. If the detention ground under s. 37(2) PACE 1984 no longer exists or never existed or if a detention review was not carried out, the suspect's continued detention is unlawful.

4.6.2 GRANTING POLICE BAIL PENDING FURTHER INVESTIGATION

As outlined at para. 4.5, where the custody officer believes that the detention grounds no longer apply, the custody officer must release the suspect immediately and unconditionally from custody (s. 34(2) PACE 1984), unless it appears that there is a need for further investigation by the police. In this situation s.54 Policing and Crime Act 2017 creates the presumption that the suspect will be released without bail unless the custody officer believes that release on bail is necessary and proportionate to the case. For a further explanation of pre-charge bail see para. 4.14.2 below.

4.7 THE SUSPECT'S RIGHT TO INTIMATION AND/OR LEGAL ADVICE

The importance of a suspect's rights at the police station cannot be overstated. Where incriminating admissions or inferences from silence have been obtained in breach of these rights, exclusion of this evidence can be sought under ss. 76 and 78 PACE 1984 (see Chapter 6).

4.7.1 THE RIGHT TO INFORM SOMEONE OF THE ARREST—S. 56 PACE 1984

Section 56(1) PACE 1984 provides that where a person has been arrested and held in custody, that person is entitled, as soon as is reasonably practicable, to have a friend, relative or some other person who is likely to be interested in that person's welfare informed of the arrest. For some suspects, especially those inexperienced at dealing with the police, the right of intimation under s. 56 PACE 1984 is important.

Guidance on the right is contained in Code C para. 5 supplemented by Annex B.

Contact can extend to the suspect speaking on the telephone to a specified individual (although this is unlikely to be a private call) and writing to the person concerned (although this correspondence is likely to be read). At the custody officer's discretion, the suspect can be visited at the police station by the specified individual.

4.7.2 DELAYING THE RIGHT TO HAVE SOMEONE INFORMED OF THE ARREST

The suspect's general right to inform someone of his arrest may be delayed where the grounds in s. 56(2)–(5) PACE 1984 Code C Annex B are made out.

Section 56 provides that:

- the suspect must have been arrested in connection with an indictable offence (this includes an either-way offence); and

- an officer of at least the rank of inspector authorises the delay on the basis that the officer has reasonable grounds for believing that telling the suspect's relative, friend or other person likely to take an interest in the suspect's welfare of the arrest will:

  - lead to interference with or harm to evidence connected with an indictable offence; or

  - lead to interference with or physical injury to other persons; or

  - lead to the alerting of other persons suspected of having committed such an offence but not yet arrested for it; or

  - hinder the recovery of any property obtained as a result of such an offence.

The authorisation for the delay may be given to the suspect orally or in writing. The reason for the delay must be noted in the custody record and, if justified, may not exceed 36 hours from the time the suspect arrived at the designated police station.

4.7.3 THE SUSPECT'S RIGHT TO LEGAL ADVICE—S. 58 PACE 1984

The general right to legal advice under s. 58 PACE 1984 (supplemented by Code C para. 6 and Annex B) is one of the most important protections against the abuse of the suspect's legal rights by the police. Section 58(1) PACE 1984 provides that a person arrested and held in custody in a police station or other premises shall be entitled, if he so requests, to consult a solicitor privately at any time. The importance of ensuring a suspect has access to legal advice while in police detention has been repeatedly emphasised by the European Court of Human Rights: *Murray v UK* (1996) 22 EHRR 29 and *Condron v UK* (2001) 31 EHRR 1. Indeed, the right to a fair trial under Article 6 European Convention on Human Rights 1950 normally requires that a suspect has access to a lawyer at the initial stages of a police investigation (*Salduz v Turkey* (2008) 49 EHRR 19, applied in *Cadder v HM Advocate* [2010] UKSC 43).

Legal advice at the police station may be provided by a solicitor or by a legal executive/ trainee/paralegal/clerk who is either accredited by the Solicitors Regulation Authority under the Police Station Representatives Accreditation Scheme (PSRAS) or is registered as a probationary police station representative whilst undertaking the process of accreditation in accordance with the PSRAS. The scheme is explained in more detail in the Additional Chapter: 'Advising at the Police Station—Practical Steps' available in the online resources, which comprehensively addresses the role of the legal adviser at the police station taking into account everything covered in Part II of the manual.

4.7.4 WHO PAYS FOR LEGAL ADVICE GIVEN AT THE POLICE STATION?

Unless the suspect chooses to pay and to be privately represented by their own solicitor, the Police Station Advice and Assistance Scheme administered by the Legal Aid Agency entitles a suspect to publicly funded free legal advice. All requests for publicly funded police station representation must be made through the Defence Solicitor Call Centre (DSCC). The DSCC will then determine whether legal advice should be limited to telephone advice or whether a solicitor should attend the police station in person. Legal advice will be restricted to telephone advice provided by a DSCC adviser if the suspect is:

• detained for a non-imprisonable offence;

• arrested on a bench warrant for failing to appear in court and is being held for production before a court;

• arrested on suspicion of driving with excess alcohol, failure to provide a specimen, driving while unfit;

• detained in relation to breach of police or court bail conditions.

Attendance in connection with these cases may be justified if an interview or identification procedure is going to take place, the client requires an appropriate adult or interpreter, is unable to communicate over the telephone or is complaining of serious maltreatment.

4.7.5 PROVIDING ACCESS TO LEGAL ADVICE

Code C places strict obligations on the police to ensure access to legal advice including:

• All detainees must be informed of the right to consult and communicate with a solicitor in private and at any time, free of charge (Code C para. 6.1).

• Nothing must be said or done by the police with the intention of dissuading a detainee from obtaining legal advice (Code C para. 6.4).

• Any request for legal advice must be noted in the custody record.

• If the detainee declines to speak to a solicitor in person, it should be explained to the detainee that he has a right to speak with that person on the telephone and if the detainee continues to waive this right, the custody officer should ask the detainee why and the reasons should be recorded on to the custody record (Code C para. 6.5).

- When a solicitor arrives at the police station to see the suspect, the suspect must be informed of the solicitor's arrival and asked if he would like to see the solicitor even where legal advice was earlier declined (Code C para. 6.15).

- A detainee who wants legal advice may not be interviewed until the detainee receives advice unless the circumstances listed in Code C para. 6.6 apply.

- Where the suspect has access to legal advice, the suspect must be allowed to have his solicitor present for the interview.

- If the solicitor is travelling to the police station an interview should not normally start until the solicitor arrives (Note 6A).

- Where the suspect requests legal advice during an interview, there should be no further questioning until the suspect has spoken to the legal adviser (Code C para. 6.6).

The police are also required to remind the suspect about the right to legal advice at the following stages of detention:

- immediately before the commencement or recommencement of any interview at the police station (Code C para. 11.2);

- before a review of detention takes place (Code C para. 15.4);

- after the suspect has been charged, if a police officer wishes to draw the suspect's attention to any written or oral statements made by any other person (Code C para. 16.4);

- after the suspect has been charged, if further questions are to be put to the suspect about the offence (Code C para. 16.5);

- prior to an identification parade, group identification or video identification being held (Code D para. 3.17);

- prior to the taking of an intimate body sample (Code D para. 6.3).

4.7.6 DELAYING THE RIGHT TO LEGAL ADVICE

The suspect's general right to legal advice may be delayed where the grounds under s. 58(8) PACE 1984 (supplemented by Code C Annex B) apply. The decision to delay the right to legal advice in an individual case is a serious step and must be justified by the police, as it can have significant implications for the admissibility of evidence obtained from a suspect (*Salduz v Turkey* (2008) 49 EHRR 19, applied in *Cadder v HM Advocate* [2010] UKSC 43). The evidential rules that govern the admissibility of confession evidence are covered in Chapter 6. The grounds for delaying the right to legal advice under s. 58(8) PACE 1984 and Code C Annex B are as follows:

- the suspect has been arrested in connection with an indictable offence; and

- an officer of at least the rank of superintendent authorises the delay on the ground that the officer has reasonable grounds for believing that if the suspect was permitted to exercise his right to receive legal advice it will:

  - lead to interference with or harm to evidence connected with an indictable offence or interference with or physical injury to other persons; or

  - lead to the alerting of other persons suspected of having committed such an offence but not yet arrested for it; or

  - hinder the recovery of any property obtained as a result of such an offence.

The reason for the delay must be noted in the custody record and, if justified, may not exceed 36 hours from the time the suspect arrived at the designated police station. The suspect must be informed of the reason for the delay (s. 58(9) PACE 1984). If the grounds for delaying access to legal advice cease to apply, the suspect must be asked whether he wants to see his legal adviser (Code C Annex B, A.6).

The police may not delay access to a particular solicitor on the grounds that the solicitor may advise the suspect not to answer questions or that the solicitor was initially asked to attend the station by someone else (Code C Annex B, A.4).

If the authorising officer concludes that any of the risks identified here apply to the solicitor requested, the detainee must be allowed to choose another legal adviser (Code C Annex B, A.3). Where access to legal advice is delayed, inferences from a suspect's decision to remain silent cannot be drawn (see para. 4.11).

4.8 OTHER RIGHTS AND SAFEGUARDS ENJOYED BY THE SUSPECT WHILST IN DETENTION

Code C paras. 8–9 and 12 recognise that a suspect is entitled to certain fundamental rights while detained at the police station. They include:

- A right to an adequately heated, cleaned and ventilated cell; access to toilet facilities.

- At least two light meals and one main meal in any 24-hour period, taking account of special dietary requirements, and regular refreshments.

- A requirement that a detainee receives appropriate clinical attention as soon as reasonably practicable if the person appears to be suffering from physical illness, is injured, appears to need clinical attention or appears to be suffering from a mental disorder. If a detainee requests medical attention, a health-care professional must be called. If a detainee needs to take prescribed medication, an appropriate health-care professional must be called, and in some instances may be the only person who can administer the medication.

- The requirement that in any 24-hour period the suspect must be allowed at least eight hours' continuous rest, preferably at night and free from questioning (Code C para. 12.2).

- Breaks during the interview should occur at normal meal times, and short breaks should be held approximately every two hours (Code C para. 12.8).

- The right to an interpreter if the suspect is deaf or has speech difficulties (Code C paras. 13.5–13.7).

- The right to an interpreter for a suspect who does not understand English in compliance with the EU Directive on Interpreters and Translation. The Directive requires that interpretation and translation facilities must be provided so that the suspect can communicate effectively with police officers, interviewers, solicitors and appropriate adults in the same way as a suspect fully able to speak and understand English (Code C para. 13.1A).

4.9 THE TREATMENT OF VULNERABLE SUSPECTS AND THE PROVISION OF AN APPROPRIATE ADULT (AA)

A key right in protecting the vulnerable suspect is access to an appropriate adult. A suspect who is or appears to be under the age of 18 (termed juveniles for these purposes) is also entitled to the services of an appropriate adult. Aspects of criminal procedure specifically relevant to young people (those under the age of 18) are considered in Chapters 24 to 26.

Code C 2018 has strengthened the provision for the identification and treatment of vulnerable suspects. The risk assessment which the custody officer must undertake at the beginning of the suspect's detention (see para. 4.4.2 above) should identify those detainees who might be 'vulnerable'. (The investigating officer is under a similar duty where the person has not been arrested or detained.)

Code C para. 1.13(d) now defines the term, 'vulnerable' to include: any person who because of their mental health condition or mental health disorder

(i) *may have difficulty understanding or communicating effectively about the full implications for them of any procedures and processes connected with:*

- *their arrest and detention; or (as the case may be)*
- *their voluntary attendance at a police station; or their presence elsewhere (see para. 3.21) for the purpose of a voluntary interview; and*
- *the exercise of their rights and entitlements.*

(ii) *does not appear to understand the significance of what they are told, of questions they are asked or of their replies:*

(iii) *appears to be particularly prone to:*

- *becoming confused and unclear about their position;*
- *providing unreliable, misleading, or incriminating information without knowing or wishing to do so;*
- *accepting or acting om suggestions from others without consciously knowing or wishing to do; or*
- *readily agreeing to suggestions or proposals without any protest or question.*

There is now a requirement that all proactive steps to be taken to identify vulnerability. Code C para. 1.4 stipulates that if at any time an officer has any reason to suspect that a person of any age may be vulnerable then, in the absence of clear evidence to dispel that suspicion, that person shall be treated as vulnerable. The officer should then make all reasonable enquiries to ascertain whether any of the factors stated in Code C Para 1.13(d) applies to the person. These factors include becoming confused and unclear about their position or readily agreeing to suggestions or proposals without any protest or question. Examples of relevant information that may be available are identified in Notes for Guidance 1GA and include:

- the behaviour of the adult or juvenile;
- the mental health and capacity of the adult or juvenile;
- what the adult or juvenile says about themselves;
- information from relatives and friends of the adult or juvenile;
- information from police officers and staff and from police records;
- information from health and social care (including liaison and diversion services) and other professionals who know, or have had previous contact with, the individual and may be able to contribute to assessing their need for help and support from an appropriate adult.

Notes for Guidance 1GC clarifies that a person who is under the influence of drink and/ or drugs, should not be treated as vulnerable and requiring an appropriate adult for the purpose of para. 1.4 unless other information indicates that any of the factors described in para. 1.13(d) may apply to that person. When the person has recovered from the effects of drink and/or drugs, they should be re-assessed in accordance with para. 1.4.

The custody officer must inform an appropriate adult as soon as possible about the detention and request the appropriate adult to attend the police station as soon as practicable (Code C para. 3.15).

Code C para. 1.7(b) identifies who can act as the appropriate adult (AA). The AA for a vulnerable suspect or detainee can be a relative, guardian, or other person responsible for their care or custody who must be independent of the police. A person should not be an AA if they are:

- suspected of involvement in the offence;
- the victim;
- a witness;
- involved in the investigation; or
- received admissions prior to attending to act as the appropriate adult (Code C, Notes for Guidance 1B).

Code C para. 1.7A, now makes clear the role of the AA:

The role of the appropriate adult is to safeguard the rights, entitlements and welfare of juveniles and vulnerable persons . . . . For this reason, the appropriate adult is expected, amongst other things, to:

- *support, advise, and assist them when, in accordance with this Code or any other Code of Practice, they are given or asked to provide information or participate in any procedure;*
- *observe whether the police are acting properly and fairly to respect their rights and entitlements, and inform an officer of the rank of inspector or above if they consider that they are not;*
- *assist them to communicate with the police whilst respecting their right to say nothing unless they want to as set out in the terms of the caution . . .);*
- *help them to understand their rights and ensure that those rights are protected and respected (see paras. 3.15, 3.17, 6.5A, and 11.17).*

Annex E to Code C provides a detailed summary of the important provisions in relation to vulnerable detainees.

The right of access to an appropriate adult is additional to the right to legal advice. Code C para. 11.5 stipulates that in the case of a young person or mentally vulnerable person, no interview should be undertaken in the absence of the appropriate adult. Code C para. 1, Notes for Guidance 1E states that a detainee should always be given an opportunity, when an appropriate adult is called to the police station, to consult privately with a solicitor in the appropriate adult's absence if they want. An appropriate adult is not subject to legal privilege.

4.10 INTERVIEWING THE SUSPECT

The police investigation will involve questioning the suspect after arrest or as a volunteer and interviewing other witnesses to gather sufficient evidence to charge the suspect or to exclude the suspect from the investigation. Interviewing a person suspected of committing the crime is the centrepiece of most police investigations. Even for those experienced at dealing with the police, the police interview can be very intimidating. The intimidating environment may lead some suspects to admitting to crimes they have not committed, or being susceptible to a particular line of police questioning, bullying or inducements. For these reasons, the substantive provisions of PACE 1984 and Codes C and E closely regulate the conduct of police interviews.

A suspect's legal rights whilst in custody under the substantive provisions of PACE 1984 and the Codes of Practice exist to ensure the reliability and fairness of evidence resulting from the suspect's detention. The admissibility of evidence obtained in the police interview, particularly confession evidence, is vulnerable to challenge under s. 76(2)(a) or (b) and s. 78 PACE where it has been obtained in breach (accidental or otherwise) of PACE 1984 and the Codes of Practice (see Chapter 6).

4.10.1 WHAT CONSTITUTES AN INTERVIEW?

Code C para. 11.1A defines an interview as:

> 'the questioning of a person regarding his involvement in a criminal offence where there are grounds to suspect him of such an offence or offences which, by virtue of paragraph 10.1 of Code C must be carried out under caution.'

All interviews must be carried out at a police station except in the limited circumstances in Code C para. 11.1 where delay in conducting an interview would:

(a) lead to interference with or harm to evidence connected with an offence; interference with or physical harm to other people or serious loss of or damage or damage to property; or

(b) lead to alerting other people suspected of committing an offence but not yet arrested for it; or

(c) hinder the recovery of property obtained in consequence of the commission of an offence.

The effect of Code C para. 11.1A is to permit an informal conversation between an investigating officer and a suspect, provided it does not relate to the offence under investigation. This covers such matters as verifying someone's identity but would not cover a prolonged conversation to encourage the suspect to make admissions to be used in evidence (see *R v Williams (Michael)* [2012] EWCA Crim 264).

4.10.2 FITNESS TO BE INTERVIEWED

Before any interview the custody officer must assess whether the detainee is fit to be interviewed (Code C para. 12.3). This is particularly appropriate to a detainee who is drunk or under the influence of an illicit substance. In some instances, the custody officer will need to consult an appropriate health-care professional to determine the suspect's fitness to be interviewed. Consult Annex G of Code C for a summary. As previously indicated, vulnerable suspects have the right to have an appropriate adult present during the interview (Code C para. 11.15).

4.10.3 WHEN MUST AN INTERVIEW CEASE?

Code C para. 11.6 provides that an interview should cease when the officer in charge of the investigation:

- is satisfied all the questions considered relevant to obtaining accurate and reliable information about the offence have been put to the suspect, including allowing the suspect an opportunity to give an innocent explanation and asking questions to test this;

- has taken account of any other available evidence; and

- the officer in charge of the investigation, or in the case of a detained person, the custody officer, reasonably believes that there is sufficient evidence to provide a realistic prospect of conviction.

4.11 THE REQUIREMENT TO CAUTION

At the beginning of the interview the suspect must be cautioned. Where the interview recommences after a break, the investigating officer must remind the suspect that he remains under caution and, where the officer considers it to be appropriate, the caution should be read to the suspect again.

The suspect can be cautioned in one of two ways depending whether an adverse inference may be drawn from the suspect's silence under ss. 34, 36, and 37 Criminal Justice and Public Order Act 1994 (see Chapter 5).

Where an adverse inference may be drawn at trial from the suspect's silence at the police station, the caution should be given as follows:

'You do not have to say anything. But it may harm your defence if you do not mention when questioned something which you later rely on in court. Anything you do say may be given in evidence.'

This caution will be appropriate where the suspect has been offered and/or received legal advice.

Under Code C the police are required to administer an alternative caution where:

- a person's right to legal advice has been delayed under s. 58(8) PACE 1984; or

- a superintendent authorises an interview to proceed under Code C para. 6.6(b) before the suspect has been given an opportunity to receive legal advice; or

- the suspect is to be interviewed after charge.

The alternative caution reads:

'You do not have to say anything. But anything you do say may be given in evidence.'

The alternative caution was introduced to comply with the European Court of Human Rights decision in *Murray v UK* (1996) 22 EHRR 29 and is given statutory effect in s. 58 Youth Justice and Criminal Evidence Act 1999.

4.12 WHAT CONSTITUTES A FAIR INTERVIEW?

4.12.1 OPPRESSIVE INTERVIEWS

It is an essential requirement of fairness that when interviewing a suspect about his involvement in an offence, the police do not abuse their position of trust by conducting the interview in an 'oppressive' manner. This requirement is recognised by Code C para. 11.5, which provides:

'No police officer may try to obtain answers to questions or to elicit a statement by the use of oppression.'

'Oppression' is not defined in Code C, but is partially defined by s. 76(8) PACE 1984, to mean torture, inhuman or degrading treatment and the use or threat of violence. Section 76(2)(a) PACE 1984 requires the court to exclude a confession that has been obtained through oppression and is considered further in Chapter 6.

4.12.2 INDUCEMENTS TO CONFESS

Code C para. 11.5 makes it clear that no interviewer shall indicate, except to answer a direct question, what action will be taken by the police if the person being questioned answers questions, makes a statement or refuses to do either.

4.12.3 PHYSICAL CONDITIONS OF THE INTERVIEW

An interview should take place in a room which is properly heated, lit and ventilated (Code C para. 12.4). There is no limit to the number of officers who may be present during the interview, but the officer in charge must identify them to the suspect and should be aware of the possibility that the presence of too many officers might be seen as oppressive. Provision (s. 76 Policing and Crime Act 2017) has recently been made for an audio-recorded interview in accordance with PACE to be carried out remotely by an investigating officer from a location other than where the suspect has been detained via live link technology.

4.12.4 THE LEGAL ADVISER'S ROLE DURING THE INTERVIEW

Apart from a restricted number of exceptions, a suspect who has requested legal advice may not be interviewed or continue to be interviewed until the suspect has met with his legal adviser (Code C para. 6.6).

Code C Notes for Guidance para. 6D acknowledges the nature of the legal adviser's role in the interview:

> 'The solicitor's only role in the police station is to protect and advance the legal rights of his client. On occasions this may require the solicitor to give advice which has the effect of his client avoiding giving evidence which strengthens a prosecution case. The solicitor may intervene in order to seek clarification, challenge an improper question to their client or the manner in which it is put, advise their client not to reply to particular questions or if they wish to give their client further legal advice.'

The practical aspects of the legal adviser's role at the police station are considered in a separate Additional Chapter in the online resources entitled 'Advising at the Police Station—Practical Steps'.

Code C para. 11 Notes for Guidance 11B reminds investigators that they should pursue all reasonable lines of enquiry, whether these point towards or away from the suspect when deciding what questions should be asked.

4.12.5 THE APPROPRIATE ADULT'S ROLE IN THE INTERVIEW

Code C para. 11.17 provides that if an appropriate adult is present in an interview they must be told:

- that they are not expected to act simply as an observer; and
- that the purpose of their presence is to:
- advise the person being interviewed;
- observe whether the interview is being conducted properly and fairly; and
- facilitate communication with the person being interviewed.

4.13 HOW SHOULD AN INTERVIEW BE RECORDED?

An interview is recorded in many different ways depending on the technology at the police station where the suspect is being detained. An explanation of the recording requirements for interviews is provided in para. 6.4.1.

4.14 CHARGING A SUSPECT

Under the statutory charging scheme introduced by the Criminal Justice Act 2003 (CJA 2003) charging decisions are divided between the CPS and the police. As an alternative to charging, the custody officer or CPS lawyer may decide to divert an individual from prosecution by offering a caution instead. A caution is an alternative to a prosecution and Code C Notes for Guidance para. 16A requires the custody officer to take account of alternatives to prosecution. The charging process and the availability of diversionary schemes are considered more fully in Chapter 8.

As explained at para. 4.4.4, as soon as there is sufficient evidence to charge a suspect, s. 37(7) PACE 1984 requires the custody officer to charge or release the suspect. The decision to charge will be made either by the custody officer or by the CPS, in accordance with the statutory charging regime under the CJA 2003 and the DPP's Guidance on Charging (see Chapter 8).

4.14.1 PRE-CHARGE POLICE BAIL WHERE THE POLICE HAVE REFERRED THE CASE TO THE CPS FOR A CHARGING DECISION—S. 37(7)(A) **BAIL**

Where the custody officer has determined that **there is sufficient evidence to charge** but the final decision to charge is to be taken by the CPS, the suspect can either be detained in custody or released on unconditional or conditional bail under s. 37(7)(a) PACE 1984, pending a decision to charge. The suspect is under a duty to surrender to police bail at the appointed time unless notified in writing by the custody officer that his attendance is not required.

Section 46A(1) PACE 1984 confers a power of arrest for failure to surrender to pre-charge police bail. A power of arrest exercised in these circumstances can result in a hastening of a decision to charge with the original offence for which pre-charge bail was granted (s. 37(C) PACE 1984) and would not assist a defendant's application for bail to a court.

Conditions can be attached to the grant of pre-charge bail under s. 37 PACE 1984 if it is necessary to prevent that person from failing to surrender to custody, or committing an offence while on bail, or interfering with witnesses or otherwise obstructing the course of justice and/or for his own welfare (s. 3A Bail Act 1976). Any condition may be imposed that could be imposed by the court when granting court bail under the Bail Act 1976 other than a condition that the person resides at a bail hostel—provided the conditions are proportionate. (Court bail is explained in Chapter 10.)

Section 46A(1A) PACE 1984 gives the police the power of arrest where there are reasonable grounds to believe that the person has broken pre-charge bail conditions. A person who has been made subject to bail conditions may apply to the same or another custody officer serving at the same police station for the conditions to be varied. The person may alternatively or in addition apply to a magistrates' court for variation (s. 47(1)(e) PACE 1984 and see Crim PR, r. 19.1(1)).

4.14.2 PRE-CHARGE BAIL IN ALL OTHER CASES—RELEASE UNDER INVESTIGATION AND TIME LIMITS

Pre-charge bail in all other cases was significantly reformed by s. 54 Policing and Crime Act 2017 (inserting s. 47ZA–K into PACE 1984). The main change is that where the case is **still under investigation and has not yet been referred to the CPS for a charging decision (s. 37(7)(a))**, there is a presumption that a suspect will simply be 'released under investigation' (RUI). Only where bail is felt to be '**necessary and proportionate**' will the suspect be released on bail but this is subject to a 28-time limit with extensions requiring the approval of a senior police officer and thereafter a magistrate (see below).

Release under investigation not on bail

Where a suspect is released under investigation, there is no time limit imposed upon the police as to when a decision is required. A suspect can therefore be released under investigation for a very long time with little or no indication of where they stand. The reason for this significant shift on pre-charge bail was the well-founded criticism that far too many individuals were being subject to bail conditions for prolonged periods of time (two years or more in some cases), only to find, at the conclusion of the investigation, that they were not to be charged.

Following a Freedom of Information request to the 43 police forces in England and Wales (to which 12 responded), the BBC reported on 30 March 2018 that in a three-month period between April–June 2017, the number of suspects bailed following arrest had fallen by two-thirds since the time limit restrictions came into force. The figures included 1,692 people arrested for violent crimes, 768 rape suspects, and 31 questioned on suspicion of murder and are of concern. In its February 2019 report, Her Majesty's Inspectorate of Constabulary and

Fire and Rescue Services found that the number of people being released on bail for domestic abuse crimes had dropped by 65% because of the changes. This is a cause of concern. This aspect of pre-charge bail is likely to be reviewed in the future.

Practitioners are reporting an increasing reluctance on the part of the police to arrest a suspect preferring to interview the person as a 'volunteer' (see para. 4.2 earlier). A voluntary interview negates the need for an arrest and bail can only ever be given to a suspect who has been arrested. This change has also contributed to the increasing use of postal requisitions (charging individuals by post) instead of charging them at the police station. A person who is voluntarily interviewed and subsequently charged by postal requisition must attend court on the date notified to answer the allegation against them. The requisition process is explained in Chapter 12. The written charge/postal requisition procedure is now also used increasingly for serious offences.

Release under investigation but on bail

Release on bail pending further investigation can only be imposed where it is 'necessary and proportionate' in all the circumstances. This provision has implications for the grant of street bail (see Chapter 3, para. 3.8), as arrest is now much more likely to be followed by a RUI. Where the 'necessary and proportionate' criteria is met, a 28-day period of pre-charge bail can be granted by an inspector, with a further extension to three months in total by a superintendent. This is called the 'Applicable Bail Period' (APB). Any further periods on bail after this time must be granted by a magistrates' court. There are extended time periods for complex fraud investigations.

4.14.3 QUESTIONING AFTER CHARGE

On charging or informing the suspect that he might be prosecuted for an offence, no further questions may be asked of the suspect except in the circumstances provided for in Code C para. 16.5. They include where an interview is necessary:

- to prevent harm or loss to some other person, or the public; or
- to clear up an ambiguity in a previous answer or statement; or
- in the interests of justice for the officer to ask the question(s) and for the suspect to comment on information concerning the offence which has come to light since the suspect was charged, or informed that he might be prosecuted.

Before an interview starts, detainees must be cautioned that they do not have to say anything, but that anything they do say may be given in evidence. The adverse inference provision under s. 34 Criminal Justice and Public Order Act 1994 (see Chapter 5) has no application in this situation.

4.14.4 POLICE BAIL AFTER CHARGE

Once the defendant has been charged the decision whether to remand or release him pending his first appearance before a magistrates' court is made by the custody officer. Section 38 PACE 1984 requires the custody officer to have regard to the same considerations as those which a court is required to consider when taking a decision under the Bail Act 1976. Bail as a substantive topic in its own right is considered in detail in Chapter 10. A custody officer can refuse bail if one or more of the grounds under s. 38(1) PACE 1984 apply. They include:

- The suspect's name or address cannot be ascertained, or the custody officer has reasonable grounds for doubting whether a name or address furnished by the suspect is that person's real name or address.
- The custody officer has reasonable grounds for believing that the person arrested will fail to attend court to answer bail.

- In the case of a person arrested for an imprisonable offence, the custody officer has reasonable grounds for believing that the detention of the person arrested is necessary to prevent that person from committing an offence.

- In the case of a person arrested for a non-imprisonable offence, the custody officer has reasonable grounds for believing that the detention of the person arrested is necessary to prevent physical injury to any other person or causing loss or damage to property.

- The custody officer has reasonable grounds for believing that the detention of the person arrested is necessary to prevent that person from interfering with the administration of justice or with the investigation of offences or a particular offence.

- The custody officer has reasonable grounds for believing that the detention of the person arrested is necessary for that person's own protection.

These grounds are the same as those applied by a court under Sch. 1 Part 1 para. 2 Bail Act 1976 (see Chapter 10). In determining whether the accused is likely to abscond, commit further offences or interfere with the course of justice, the custody officer will have regard to the factors set out in Sch. 1 Part 1 para. 9 Bail Act 1976, including:

- the defendant's bail record;

- the nature of the offence;

- the defendant's community ties;

- the defendant's criminal record.

A person charged with murder cannot be granted bail by the custody officer (s. 38(1)(c) PACE 1984).

Where bail has been denied to a defendant in custody under s. 38(1) PACE 1984, he must appear before a magistrates' court as soon as is practicable (s. 46(1) PACE 1984). In practice, the defendant will be produced before the remand court the next day unless the next day is a Sunday or is Christmas Day or Good Friday.

Post-charge release on police bail

Instead of remanding a defendant into custody pending his first appearance before a court, the custody officer may release the defendant on unconditional or conditional bail pending his first appearance before a magistrates' court. A failure to answer police bail without reasonable excuse in these circumstances is an offence under the Bail Act 1976 and carries a power of arrest.

Under s. 47(1A) PACE 1984 the custody officer may impose conditions to post-charge police bail in much the same way as a court. These include conditions of residence, reporting to a police station, the imposition of a curfew, prohibiting contact with a particular individual or access to a particular place. A custody officer may not, however, impose a condition requiring the defendant to reside in a bail hostel. Conditions may only be imposed where the custody officer considers them to be necessary to ensure the defendant surrenders to custody, does not commit an offence while on bail or interfere with witnesses or obstruct the course of justice. Conditions may also be imposed for the defendant's own protection or welfare. A failure by an accused to abide by the conditions of post-charge police bail will result in the accused being arrested and brought before a magistrates' court (s. 7(3) Bail Act 1976). A proven failure to abide by such conditions would be a significant factor in determining whether the accused should be remanded into custody throughout the rest of the proceedings. The accused may apply to the same or another custody officer serving at the same police station or a magistrates' court to vary post-charge bail conditions (see para. 4.14.1).

The legal adviser at the police station may make representations to the custody officer where it is proposed to remand the defendant in custody pending his first appearance before a magistrates' court, or as to the appropriateness of bail conditions whether they be imposed post- or pre-charge.

4.14.5 **DRUG TESTING AT THE POLICE STATION (CODE C PARA. 17)**

Section 63B PACE 1984, as amended by s. 7 Drugs Act 2005, gives the police the power to demand a urine sample or non-intimate sample (saliva) from a suspect aged 18 and over upon arrest or after charge (this power extends to individuals over the age of 14 in order to test for the presence of a Class A drug at police stations where arrangements are in place). The power to take a sample arises in relation to certain 'trigger offences' or for any offence where an inspector, or above, has reasonable grounds to suspect that misuse of a Class A drug caused or contributed to the offence. Additionally, s. 9 Drugs Act 2005 gives the police the power to require a person who has tested positive to undergo an initial assessment to see if the person has a propensity to misuse Class A drugs and would be suitable for treatment. A failure to give a sample or to consent to undergo an initial assessment or follow-up treatment results in the commission of an offence. Where the test shows the presence of a Class A drug and the person concerned refuses to consent to an initial assessment or to follow-up treatment, the information will be passed on to a court which must take it into account when making a bail decision under the Bail Act 1976 (see Chapter 10, para. 10.6). The testing procedure is currently operational in several police force areas.

4.15 **CONCLUDING REMARKS**

This chapter and Chapter 3 have explained the procedures relevant to arrest, search, detention and processing of the suspect. Knowledge and understanding of the procedures is vital to those who prosecute and defend. For the purpose of deciding whether to charge or to prove the case at trial, prosecutors will want to be sure that the police have gathered the evidence lawfully. In evaluating the evidence that has been disclosed by the prosecution and prior to advising on plea, the defence practitioner will know that the prosecution's case is weaker if the admissibility of evidence can be challenged on the basis that it was obtained unlawfully.

KEY POINT SUMMARY

- Be aware of the custody officer's extensive duties and responsibilities.

- Understand the suspect's right to legal advice and to have someone informed of his or his arrest at the police station and the circumstances in which the exercise of these rights can justifiably be delayed.

- Understand the suspect's rights at a voluntary interview

- Understand that the safeguards contained in PACE 1984 and in Code C not only seek to protect the suspect while in custody but that they also seek to promote the integrity of the investigative process so as to ensure the reliability of evidence obtained in consequence.

- Understand the importance of the custody record in evidential terms as it contains everything relevant to a suspect's detention at the police station, including the justifications for the decisions taken.

- Be aware of custody detention time limits and the obligation to charge or release when there is sufficient evidence etc.

- Know the definition of a vulnerable suspect and the additional rights that such a suspect enjoys.

- Know which caution should be administered in which situation.

- Understand that evidence obtained as part of the investigation into a criminal offence in breach of PACE/Code C is vulnerable to challenge under s. 78 PACE 1984 and/or s. 76 PACE 1984. Under s. 78 PACE 1984 such evidence can be excluded in the exercise of the court's discretion to ensure the defendant enjoys a right to a fair trial.

- Know the circumstances in which conditions can be imposed on the granting of police bail, both pre-charge and post-charge.

- Know the grounds upon which a custody officer can refuse police bail post-charge (s. 38 PACE 1984).

SELF-TEST QUESTIONS

The self-test questions that support this chapter are located at the conclusion of Chapter 6, which considers the admissibility of confession evidence. Chapter 6 also includes analysis of the admissibility of the confession in our case study, *R v Lenny Wise.*

FIGURE 4.1   MAXIMUM PERIODS OF DETENTION WITHOUT CHARGE AT THE POLICE STATION

Summary-only offence: 24 hours maximum, after which defendant must be released (unconditionally or on police bail) or charged, s. 41 PACE 1984.

Indictable offence (which includes an either-way offence): 24 hours unless a superintendent or above authorises detention for further 12 hours (24 + 12 = 36 hours) where the officer has reasonable grounds for believing that:

- the detention is necessary to secure or preserve evidence; or
- to obtain such evidence by questioning the suspect; and
- the investigation is being conducted diligently and expeditiously, s. 42 PACE 1984.

Detention beyond 36 hours

- Section 43 PACE 1984 permits detention without charge beyond 36 hours.
- Police must apply to a magistrates' court for a warrant of further detention where:

    - the detention is necessary to secure or preserve evidence; or to obtain such evidence by questioning the suspect; and
    - the offence is an indictable offence; and
    - the investigation is being conducted diligently and expeditiously.

A warrant may authorise detention for a further 36 hours (24 + 12 + 36 = 72 hours).
The police may apply for a further warrant of detention for 24 hours (24 + 12 + 36 + 24 = 96 hours).
At the end of 96 hours, the suspect must either be released on police bail or unconditionally, or charged (s. 44 PACE).

SUMMARY OF RIGHTS WHILE IN CUSTODY

- Right to legal advice in private (s. 58 PACE 1984);
- right to have someone informed of your arrest (s. 56 PACE 1984);
- continual review of detention (s. 40 PACE 1984);
- right to an appropriate adult if you are vulnerable (Code C);
- right to medical advice (Code C);
- right to basic human rights (food/sleep/refreshments) (Code C).

5 THE RIGHT TO SILENCE AT THE POLICE STATION

5.1	**Introduction**	**87**
5.2	**What are the risks associated with s. 34 CJPOA 1994?**	**88**
	5.2.1 The conditions for drawing adverse inferences under s. 34 CJPOA 1994	88
	5.2.2 What is meant by an adverse inference?	89
	5.2.3 Remaining silent on legal advice	90
	5.2.4 Remaining silent on legal advice after *R v Howell*	91
	5.2.5 Advising silence and legal professional privilege	91
	5.2.6 Silence and the right to a fair trial	91
	5.2.7 Submitting a prepared statement to the police	92
5.3	**Drawing inferences from a failure to account under ss. 36 and 37 CJPOA 1994**	**92**
	5.3.1 What is the evidential effect of ss. 36 and 37 CJPOA 1994?	93
5.4	**The practical aspects associated with remaining silent**	**94**

5.1 INTRODUCTION

An important part of the defence solicitor's role at the police station is to advise the suspect about what he should do in the police interview. The interview is a crucial stage in the police investigation of a criminal offence and will often result in evidence being obtained against the suspect which can be used by the prosecution at any later trial. Evidence obtained in the police interview commonly comprises lies or inconsistencies told by the suspect about his involvement in the offence. Alternatively the suspect may admit his involvement in the offence(s), or may refuse to answer police questions but at trial put forward a defence, and adverse inferences may be drawn against his silence at the police station. Whilst a suspect enjoys the right to silence at the police station and cannot be compelled to answer police questions or otherwise respond to the allegations that have been made against him, under the Criminal Justice and Public Order Act (CJPOA) 1994, the suspect no longer enjoys a completely unfettered right to silence at the police station. Adverse inference arising from silence can be drawn under the following sections:

- s. 34 CJPOA 1994 (failure to mention facts in interview or upon being charged which are subsequently relied on by the defendant in his defence at trial);
- s. 36 (failure to account for an object, substance or mark at the time of arrest);
- s. 37 (failure to account for presence at a particular place upon arrest).

In preparing a suspect to be interviewed by the police, the defence representative may advise her client to:

- admit guilt; or
- answer questions and perhaps advance a defence to the allegations made; or
- exercise the right to remain silent (which may include putting forward a prepared statement).

When advising silence, the legal adviser will always be aware that this can have evidential repercussions if the client is subsequently charged. A legal adviser must therefore fully understand the law relating to the right to silence, if silence is to be advised. **(For a** detailed exploration of the defence solicitor's role at the police station please refer to our Additional Chapter in the online resources entitled 'Advising at the Police Station—Practical Steps'.)

The purpose of this chapter is to explain the substantive law governing a defendant's silence at the police station under ss. 34, 36 and 37 CJPOA 1994.

The evidential implications of an accused not giving evidence in his defence under s. 35 CJPOA 1994 are explained in Chapter 19.

5.2 WHAT ARE THE RISKS ASSOCIATED WITH S. 34 CJPOA 1994?

Section 34 provides:

> '(1) Where, in any proceedings against a person for an offence, evidence is given that the accused—
>
> (a) at any time before he was charged with the offence, on being questioned under caution by a constable trying to discover whether or by whom the offence had been committed, failed to mention any fact relied on in his defence in those proceedings; or
>
> (b) on being charged with the offence or officially informed that he might be prosecuted for it, failed to mention any such fact, being a fact which in the circumstances existing at the time the accused could reasonably have been expected to mention when so questioned, charged or informed, as the case may be . . .
>
> (2) . . .
>
> (c) the court, in determining whether there is a case to answer; and
>
> (d) the court or jury, in determining whether the accused is guilty of the offence charged, may draw such inferences from the failure as appear proper.'

Section 34 encourages an accused who has a defence to the allegation made against him to disclose that defence at the first, reasonable opportunity—in the police interview or on being informed that he is to be charged or when charged. If the accused remains silent but at trial chooses to rely on a fact in his defence, adverse inferences may be drawn against the accused's silence if the jury or magistrates consider that the accused could reasonably have mentioned the fact at the police station. The evidential effect of s. 34 is to undermine the accused's defence at trial.

A defendant does not need to remain completely silent in interview for s. 34 to be triggered. It is the defendant's failure to mention *any fact* which he subsequently relies on in his defence that may trigger s. 34. If a defendant puts forward facts or an explanation at the police station but then departs from that version at trial or advances new facts, the defendant is still at risk of an adverse inference.

5.2.1 THE CONDITIONS FOR DRAWING ADVERSE INFERENCES UNDER S. 34 CJPOA 1994

Adverse inferences may only be drawn from 'silence' where the following conditions are satisfied:

(1) the defendant was offered access to a legal adviser at the police station under s. 58 Police and Criminal Evidence Act 1984 (PACE 1984); and

(2) whilst being interviewed under caution or on being informed that he was to be charged or on being charged, the defendant failed to mention a fact which he later relied on for his defence; and

(3) the court concludes that the defendant 'could reasonably have been expected to mention' the fact that he later relies on for his defence.

If all these conditions are satisfied, the court may draw such inferences as appear proper. We will now consider each of these conditions in more detail.

(1) The police must have offered the defendant access to a legal adviser under s. 58 PACE 1984

Under s. 34(2A) CJPOA 1994 adverse inferences cannot be drawn where access to a legal adviser has been delayed, see *Murray v UK* (1996) 22 EHRR 29 at para. 5.2.6. Where the right to legal advice has been delayed (see Chapter 4, para. 4.7.6) and adverse inferences cannot be drawn, the defendant should be cautioned (see Chapter 4, para. 4.11) at the outset of the interview in this way: 'You do not have to say anything, but anything you do say may be given in evidence' (Code C Annex C).

(2) Whilst being interviewed under caution or on being informed that he is to be charged or on being charged the defendant failed to mention a fact which he later relies on for his defence

For adverse inferences to be drawn whilst being interviewed, the failure to mention facts must occur during questioning by the police to discover whether an offence has been committed and the identity of the person who committed it. The defendant must have been cautioned in this way: 'You do not have to say anything. But it may harm your defence if you do not mention when questioned something you later rely on in court. Anything you do say may be given in evidence.'

(3) The jury or magistrates conclude that the defendant 'could reasonably have been expected to mention' the fact that he later relies on for his defence

'Reasonableness' is a question of fact for the jury or magistrates to decide, see *R v Condron* [1997] 1 WLR 827; *R v Argent* [1997] 2 Cr App R 27. At trial, to prevent adverse inferences from being drawn, the defendant may well have to explain his reasons for remaining silent from the witness box and, if necessary, call the legal adviser who advised him at the police station to give evidence to explain the reasons for advising silence. This will almost certainly require an accused to waive legal professional privilege (see para. 5.2.5). It will then be a matter for the jury or magistrates to decide whether it was reasonable in the circumstances for the defendant to have remained silent.

What amounts to 'reasonable' will depend on the particular circumstances of each case.

In *R v Argent* [1997] 2 Cr App R 27, the Court of Appeal identified the following non-exhaustive factors to decide the reasonableness test including:

- the time of day;
- the defendant's age and state of mind;
- the defendant's experience of dealing with the police;
- whether the police have made 'sufficient' disclosure of the evidence against the defendant, Code C para. 11.1A. (The disclosure must be 'sufficient' for the person to understand the nature of any offence—but does not require the disclosure of details which might prejudice the police investigation, see also Note 11ZA Code C.)

The court or jury must consider these factors subjectively from the defendant's perspective at the time of detention at the police station. If the court or jury concludes that 'in all the circumstances existing at the time' at the police station, it was not reasonable for the defendant to have remained silent for the reason(s) given, adverse inferences may be drawn.

5.2.2 **WHAT IS MEANT BY AN ADVERSE INFERENCE?**

The jury or magistrates do not have to draw an adverse inference if they consider that it is not 'proper' to do so. If they choose to draw adverse inferences, they may conclude that the defendant remained silent because:

- the defendant had no answer to the allegations being made against him; or

- none of the defendant's answers would have stood up to critical examination by the police; or
- the defendant has subsequently made up a defence to fit the facts as disclosed by the prosecution.

5.2.3 **REMAINING SILENT ON LEGAL ADVICE**

Can adverse inferences be drawn where the accused remained silent on legal advice? The answer is yes. A defendant is not insulated from having an adverse inference drawn against him because he remained silent on legal advice.

For adverse inferences not to be drawn, the court must be persuaded that the defendant's reliance on legal advice to remain silent was 'reasonable' and 'genuine'. This point has been made clear in numerous Court of Appeal decisions including: *R v Howell* [2005] 1 Cr App R 1; *R v Hoare* [2005] 1 Cr App R 1; *R v Knight* [2004] 1 Cr App R 9; and *R v Beckles* [2005] 1 Cr App R 22. In *Howell*, Lord Justice Laws observed:

> 'We do not consider . . . that once it is shown that the advice (of whatever quality) has genuinely been relied on as the reason for the suspect's remaining silent, adverse comment is thereby disallowed. The premise of such a position is that in such circumstances it is in principle not reasonable to expect the suspect to mention the facts in question. We do not believe that is so. What is reasonable depends on all the circumstances.'

In *Hoare,* Lord Justice Auld observed:

> '. . . even where a solicitor has in good faith advised silence and a defendant has genuinely relied on it in the sense that he accepted it and believed that he was entitled to follow it, a jury may still draw an adverse inference if it is sure that the true reason for his silence is that he had no or no satisfactory explanation consistent with innocence to give . . . Legal entitlement is one thing. An accused's reason for exercising it is another . . . The question in the end, which is for the jury, is whether regardless of advice, genuinely given and genuinely accepted, an accused has remained silent not because of that advice but because he had no or no satisfactory explanation to give.'

It is helpful to consider the facts in *R v Howell*.

> ### *R v Howell* [2005] 1 Cr App R 1
>
> Howell was suspected of involvement in a serious assault on his flatmate. He told his solicitor, as he would later tell the jury, that he had acted in self-defence when he stabbed his flatmate. His solicitor asked the investigating officers if the victim of the attack had made a written statement. The victim had not made a written statement but had given the investigating officers a detailed verbal account, including the specific allegation that the defendant had attacked him with a knife. The defendant had indicated to his solicitor that the victim might withdraw his allegation. Consequently the solicitor advised him to make no comment in interview. No evidence was forthcoming from the solicitor as to the reasons for his advice. The defendant was asked in cross-examination, why, if he was an innocent man, he had not taken the opportunity of putting forward his version of events at the police station. The defendant gave as his reason for not answering questions the fact that he had simply followed his solicitor's advice. In his summing-up the trial judge instructed the jury to consider whether the defendant had been right to act upon the advice of his solicitor.
>
> On the facts of *Howell*, the Court of Appeal concluded that the absence of a written complaint from the victim, especially as adequate oral disclosure had been given, and the belief that the complainant might not pursue a prosecution were not 'good reasons' for remaining silent. This was not a case where it would have been difficult for the defendant to recall events. The defendant had been there in the flat. He must have known whether he acted in self-defence or not. In the circumstances it had been permissible for the jury to draw an adverse inference on the basis that it had been reasonable to expect the defendant to mention such facts, notwithstanding the advice of his solicitor.

5.2.4 REMAINING SILENT ON LEGAL ADVICE AFTER *R v HOWELL*

In *Howell*, the Court of Appeal talked of the important responsibility defence solicitors have when giving advice at police stations:

> 'there must always be soundly based objective reasons for silence, sufficiently cogent and telling to weigh in the balance against the clear public interest in an account being given to the suspect by the police. Solicitors bearing the important responsibility of giving advice to suspects at police stations must always bear that in mind.'

The Court of Appeal further observed that:

> 'The kind of circumstance which may most likely justify silence will be such matters as the suspect's condition (ill-health, in particular mental disability; confusion; intoxication; shock, and so forth—of course we are not laying down an authoritative list), or his inability genuinely to recollect events without reference to documents which are not to hand, or communication with other persons who may be able to assist his recollection.'

Howell and the other cases cited have to be considered by the legal adviser when giving advice to remain silent at the police station, especially in an investigation where the suspect is indicating that he may have a defence to put forward or an explanation to offer. Notwithstanding the fact that legal advice might be genuinely given and received, it will be for the jury or magistrates to determine whether it was reasonable in all the circumstances for the defendant to have mentioned the fact he now seeks to rely on. This may well require the legal adviser to explain the basis for her advice (see waiver of legal professional privilege, below). If the advice was based purely on tactical considerations, the defendant clearly risks having an adverse inference drawn against him.

5.2.5 ADVISING SILENCE AND LEGAL PROFESSIONAL PRIVILEGE

Communications between solicitor and client are protected from disclosure by legal professional privilege. The privilege belongs to the client and, as such, only the client may choose to waive it. In *R v Condron* [1997] 1 WLR 827, the Court of Appeal observed that for the defendant to simply assert in the witness box, 'I chose not to answer questions on the advice of my solicitor', would be unlikely to impress the jury. If sufficient weight is to be given to the defendant's reasons for not mentioning relevant facts, more explanation would almost certainly have to be given. In order to achieve this, the defendant may need to waive legal professional privilege in order to explain the basis on which his solicitor's advice was given. Having waived privilege, the defendant can be cross-examined on how much he told his solicitor at the relevant time. If the legal adviser is also called, the legal adviser can be asked whether there were any other reasons for the advice, in order to explore whether the advice may have been given for tactical reasons. Where a legal advisor is in danger of being called to give evidence of fact, the defendant needs to be represented by someone else in the firm.

5.2.6 SILENCE AND THE RIGHT TO A FAIR TRIAL

The right to silence is an implied right under Article 6. Its importance was acknowledged in *Murray v UK* (1996) 22 EHRR 29:

> 'Although not specifically mentioned in Article 6 of the Convention, there can be no doubt that the right to remain silent under police questioning and the privilege against self-incrimination are generally recognised international standards which lie at the heart of the notion of a fair procedure under Article 6. By providing the accused with protection against improper compulsion by the authorities, these immunities contribute to avoiding miscarriages of justice and to securing the aims of Article 6.'

Is the decision to draw adverse inference compatible with Article 6 European Convention on Human Rights 1950? The short answer is yes—provided a number of safeguards contained in the Judicial Studies Board (JSB) specimen direction on s. 34 are met. These include:

(a) Under s. 38 CJPOA 1994, adverse inferences cannot be the sole reason for finding a defendant guilty. This is supported by *Murray v UK* (1996) 22 EHRR 29, in which the European Court of Human Rights (ECtHR) held that to base a conviction solely or mainly on a defendant's silence would contravene Article 6.

(b) Adverse inferences may not be drawn where the police have delayed a detainee's access to a solicitor under s. 58 PACE 1984 and Code C para. 6.6. This amendment to the CJPOA 1994 was enacted to take account of decisions of the ECtHR in *Murray v UK* (1996) 22 EHRR 29, *Condron v UK* (2001) 31 EHRR 1 and *Averill v UK* (2001) 31 EHRR 36, which have consistently stressed the fundamental importance of access to a solicitor at the police station.

(c) An adverse inference may only be drawn when, having listened to any explanation put forward by the defendant for his failure to mention facts and being satisfied that a sufficiently strong case against the defendant is made out, the jury or magistrates conclude that the only sensible explanation for his silence is that the defendant had no answer to the prosecution's case at the time or none that would stand up to scrutiny.

(d) The jury or magistrates should regard an adverse inference as providing additional support only in a situation where the prosecution's case, apart from the defendant's silence, is so strong as to call for an answer from the accused.

5.2.7 SUBMITTING A PREPARED STATEMENT TO THE POLICE

An alternative to advising silence in interview is to put forward an accused's denial and/or his defence to the allegations against him in a written statement, which will then be read by the legal adviser to the police during the interview. This approach prevents a s. 34 CJPOA 1994 inference being drawn against a defendant at a subsequent trial, provided the facts disclosed in the written statement are consistent with the defence case at trial.

The prepared statement must be carefully drafted, as omitting a fact that is later relied on at trial or any departure from the statement at trial would leave the defendant vulnerable to an adverse inference under s. 34 CJPOA 1994. In *R v Knight* [2004] 1 Cr App R 9, the Court of Appeal held that, provided the defendant mentioned in his prepared statement all the facts he later relied on in court, adverse inferences would not be drawn, as this practice satisfied the purpose of s. 34, that is, the early disclosure of the suspect's account.

5.3 DRAWING INFERENCES FROM A FAILURE TO ACCOUNT UNDER SS. 36 AND 37 CJPOA 1994

While most judicial attention has been focused on the application of s. 34 CJPOA 1994, the potential for adverse inferences being drawn from the defendant's silence under ss. 36 and/or 37 should not be forgotten.

Adverse inferences may also be drawn where a suspect fails to account for an object, substance or mark found on the suspect's person (s. 36 CJPOA 1994) and/or from the suspect's failure to account for his presence at a particular place (s. 37 CJPOA 1994).

As with s. 34, a competent criminal defence lawyer will have a good understanding of the ambit of ss. 36 and 37 and be prepared to apply this knowledge in support of her client's case. Consider each section.

Section 36

'(1) Where—

(a) a person is arrested by a constable, and there is—

(i) on his person; or

(ii) in or on his clothing or footwear; or

(iii) otherwise in his possession; or

(iv) in any place in which he is at the time of his arrest,

any object, substance or mark, or there is any mark on any such object; and

(b) that or another constable investigating the case reasonably believes that the presence of the object, substance or mark may be attributable to the participation of the person arrested in the commission of an offence specified by the constable; and

(c) the constable informs the person arrested that he so believes, and requests him to account for the presence of the object, substance or mark; and

(d) the person fails or refuses to do so, then . . .

(2) . . .

(c) the court, in determining whether there is a case to answer; and

(d) the court and the jury, in determining whether the accused is guilty of the offence charged, may draw such inferences from the failure or refusal as appear proper.

(3) Subsections (1) and (2) above apply to the condition of clothing or footwear as they apply to a substance or mark thereon.

(4) Subsections (1) and (2) above do not apply unless the accused was told in ordinary language by the constable when making the request mentioned in subsection (1)(c) above what the effect of this section would be if he failed or refused to comply with the request.'

Section 37

'(1) Where—

(a) a person arrested by a constable was found by him at a place at or about the time the offence for which he was arrested is alleged to have been committed; and

(b) that or another constable investigating the offence reasonably believes that the presence of the person at that place and at that time may be attributable to his participation in the commission of the offence; and

(c) the constable informs the person that he so believes, and requests him to account for that presence; and

(d) the person fails or refuses to do so, then if, in any proceedings against the person for the offence, evidence of those matters is given . . .

(2) . . .

(c) the court, in determining whether there is a case to answer; and

(d) the court or the jury, in determining whether the accused is guilty of the offence charged, may draw such inferences from the failure or refusal as appear proper.

(3) Subsections (1) and (2) do not apply unless the accused was told in ordinary language by the constable when making the request mentioned in subsection (1)(c) above what the effect of this section would be if he failed or refused to comply with the request.'

5.3.1 WHAT IS THE EVIDENTIAL EFFECT OF SS. 36 AND 37 CJPOA 1994?

An adverse inference may only be drawn under s. 36 or s. 37 in accordance with the precise wording in the sections. Most importantly the suspect must be properly cautioned. A failure to properly caution the suspect about the evidential consequences of not providing an account under either s. 36 or s. 37 means that an adverse inference cannot be drawn, and the defendant's replies should be edited out of the transcript of the interview that is put before the court.

The evidential effect of an inference drawn under either section is to strengthen the prosecution's case, irrespective of any defence subsequently advanced by the defendant in court. The safeguard under s. 38(3) CJPOA 1994 applies, in that no one will have a case to answer, or be convicted of an offence, based solely on an inference drawn from a failure or refusal as prescribed in s. 36(2) and s. 37(2). Also, in accordance with s. 58 Youth Justice and Criminal Evidence Act 1999, an adverse inference under s. 36(4A) and s. 37(3A) CJPOA 1994 cannot be drawn where access to a solicitor has been delayed under s. 58 PACE 1984.

Unlike s. 34, very few cases have gone to appeal on ss. 36 and 37, although for further reference see *R v Compton* [2002] EWCA Crim 2835 in which the Court of Appeal considered the operation of s. 36 CJPOA 1994.

Consider the following examples of ss. 36 and 37.

 Example 1

Andrew is implicated in a recent offence of assault. On his arrest, he has visible bruising on his face. Andrew tells you he has no knowledge of the incident alleged. Andrew will be asked to account in interview for the bruising visible on his face. A failure under caution to offer some explanation for the bruising may lead to an adverse inference being drawn under s. 36.

 Example 2

The police are investigating an attempted arson offence at a school. Tracey is arrested on the school playing fields shortly after the alarm was raised. Tracey denies any involvement in the matter. In interview, Tracey is bound to be asked to account for her presence on the school fields. A failure under caution to offer an explanation may result in an adverse inference being drawn under s. 37. If it later transpires that Tracey's jeans disclose traces of petrol, she can expect to be asked in interview to account for its presence in accordance with s. 36.

5.4 THE PRACTICAL ASPECTS ASSOCIATED WITH REMAINING SILENT

It will be apparent from all that has been said that the practical operation and effect of s. 34 CJPOA 1994 is complex. The law under ss. 36 and 37 CJPOA 1994 is much clearer. The practical issues associated with advising silence is a matter for the defence. For the prosecution the issue of adverse inferences will arise at the defendant's trial. In the case preparation, a prosecutor will have identified the possibility of adverse inferences being drawn where a defendant 'unreasonably' fails to mention a fact he is now relying on at trial or fails to account for objects etc. found on his person or fails to account for his presence at a particular place.

For the defence, the issue of adverse inferences potentially arises at the police station and at trial. The challenges for effective police station representation should not be overestimated. Advising clients at the police station makes demands on the police station advisers' powers of analysis, negotiation and advocacy as well as their legal knowledge and nerve!

A key question for the legal adviser at the police station is whether to advise a client to answer questions or to put forward a written statement or to remain silent. Relevant considerations in this regard include the strength or otherwise of the evidence the police claim to have, the client's instructions to the legal adviser and the client's ability to deal with the intense psychological pressure of the police interview. Do not forget that where silence is advised there should be a sound, objective reason for the advice (*R v Howell*).

Anticipating questions likely to form the basis of an inference under s. 36 or s. 37 must also be considered. Good practice requires that the custody record should be carefully checked to see what has been seized from the suspect or his property and what searches have been undertaken and whether final or preliminary results are available. The defence lawyer may need to ask the client some searching questions about the state of the evidence against him and prepare him for the sort of questioning that could form the basis of an adverse inference.

A more detailed explanation of the practical issues involved in representing a client at the police station can be found in our Additional Chapter available in the online resources entitled 'Advising at the Police Station—Practical Steps'. This chapter is written exclusively from the defence perspective.

As with the prosecution, good case preparation will alert the defence to the possibility of adverse inferences being drawn at trial. The advocate will know the conditions that need to be satisfied under ss. 34, 36 and 37 CJPOA 1994 and will be prepared to argue against adverse inferences being drawn.

For a summary of the precise conditions that a jury or magistrates must find before an adverse inference properly be made (i.e. in accordance with Article 6), consider sections 17.1 and 17.2 of the Crown Court Compendium (CCC). The CCC seeks to ensure that all Crown Court judges adopt a consistent approach to the application of the rules relating to criminal law, evidence and procedure when summing-up to the jury and can be accessed at https://www.judiciary.uk/wp-content/uploads/2018/06/crown-court-compendium-pt1-jury-and-trial-management-and-summing-up-june-2018-1.pdf.

KEY POINT SUMMARY

- If a defendant advances facts in support of his defence at trial which he failed to mention in interview, the defendant may have an adverse inference drawn against him if the court considers it was reasonable, at the time, for the defendant to have advanced the particular facts.

- The reasonableness of a defendant's decision depends upon a number of factors (some of them are canvassed in *R v Argent*).

- Adverse inferences may still be drawn where the defendant's decision to remain silent was based on legal advice given at the time—it is still a matter for the jury/magistrates.

- An inference can only be drawn by a jury/magistrates if, having worked through the specified safeguards in the JSB's specimen directions, the jury/magistrates conclude the defendant remained silent because the defendant had no answer to the allegations, or none that he was prepared to have subjected to critical scrutiny.

- A conviction cannot be based solely upon an adverse inference.

- An adverse inference may not be drawn where the court concludes the accused genuinely and reasonably relied on legal advice.

- Defence legal advisers must consider whether there are sound objective reasons for advising silence.

- Where a defendant relies on legal advice as the reason for seeking to avoid an adverse inference, the defendant must expect to waive legal professional privilege.

- Where an adverse inference is drawn, it is a contributing evidential component of the prosecution's case and a conviction cannot be based wholly or mainly on the fact of silence.

SELF-TEST QUESTIONS

Consider the following short scenarios and decide whether s. 34, 36 or 37 is engaged.

Scenario 1

Karl is being questioned on suspicion of manslaughter. He refuses to answer questions put by the police. At his trial Karl gives evidence to the effect that he acted in self-defence.

Scenario 2

Shania is arrested on suspicion of murder. During her interview she puts forward a defence of loss of self-control. At trial she gives evidence consistent both with loss of self-control and self-defence.

Scenario 3

Jason is arrested on suspicion of attempted rape. The victim of the attack retaliated, scratching her assailant's face. In interview Jason is cautioned and asked to account for scratch marks that can be seen on his face. Jason chooses not to reply. In fact, he remains silent throughout the interview. Giving evidence at his trial, Jason states he has been mistakenly identified in that he has an alibi.

Scenario 4

Following a burglary, Rio is arrested a few hours later. It is clear that the burglar exited the property along a muddy track and over a wall topped with metal spikes. In interview Rio advances a defence of alibi. In the course of the interview he is cautioned and asked to account for a tear on the sleeve of his jacket and mud on his shoes. Rio is unable to offer any explanation for either.

Scenario 5

Jane is arrested on a Sunday evening on suspicion of criminal damage. She is found by a police officer near to a field where genetically modified maize is under cultivation. Several crops have been uprooted. When questioned under caution about the alleged offence, Jane is asked to account for her presence near to the field. Jane refuses to reply. She also refuses to give evidence at her trial.

Scenario 6

Carley is arrested on suspicion of being in possession of a controlled drug with intent to supply. She admits to being in possession, but denies intent to supply. Her solicitor believes that she is unfit to be interviewed by the police due to drug withdrawal symptoms. The police doctor disagrees. Carley takes the advice of her solicitor and chooses not to answer questions during the interview. She is charged with possession with intent to supply. At trial she will give evidence denying intent to supply. Does she have anything to fear from her failure to answer questions at the police station?

 An analysis of all self-test questions can be found in our online resources in the Answers to the Self-Test Questions.

FIGURE 5.1 DRAWING ADVERSE INFERENCES FROM SILENCE

ADVERSE INFERENCES: S. 34 CJPOA 1994

- Section 34 CJPOA 1994 does not abolish the right to silence.

- Section 34 CJPOA 1994 applies where a defendant:

  - is questioned under caution; or on being charged; or

  - fails to mention a fact that he later relies on in his defence.

- An adverse inference may only be drawn where:

  - the defendant has been offered legal advice, s. 34(2A) CJPOA 1994; and

  - the court considers it would have been reasonable for the defendant to have mentioned the fact; see *R v Condron*; *R v Argent*.

- The reasonableness test includes the defendant's:

  - age and experience of dealing with the police;

  - mental capacity;

  - state of health; and whether legal advice was given.

- It is a matter for the jury/magistrates as to whether an adverse inference should be drawn having regard to any reason advanced by the defendant in evidence.

- In a jury trial, the judge must direct the jury in accordance with the Crown Court Compendium guidance, including:

  - conviction cannot be based wholly or mainly on a failure to mention;

  - the court must consider the reason for the defendant remaining silent;

  - an adverse inference may only be drawn if the jury concludes that the real reason for the defendant's failure was that he had no answer to the allegation, or none that would withstand critical scrutiny.

- A court may not draw an adverse inference where the defendant reasonably and genuinely relied on legal advice; see *R v Howell*.

- A solicitor advising silence at the police station must make his client fully aware of the risks.

- A prepared statement containing all the defence facts may prevent adverse inferences from being drawn; see *R v Knight*.

ADVERSE INFERENCES: S. 36 CJPOA 1994

- Adverse inferences may be drawn where, after arrest, the defendant refuses to account for any object, substance or mark on his person; or in his clothing; or otherwise in his possession; and

- the officer has a reasonable belief that the object etc. may be attributable to his participation in the offence; and

- the possible effect of his failure or refusal to account for the object was explained to the defendant, Code C para. 10.11.

ADVERSE INFERENCES: S. 37 CJPOA 1994

- Adverse inferences may be drawn where, after arrest, the defendant refuses to account for his presence at a particular place; and

- the officer has a reasonable belief that his presence may be attributable to his participation in the offence; and

- the possible effect of his failure or refusal to account for his presence was explained to the defendant, Code C para. 10.11.

6 CHALLENGING UNLAWFULLY AND UNFAIRLY OBTAINED EVIDENCE

6.1	**Introduction**	**98**
6.2	**What is unlawfully or unfairly obtained evidence?**	**99**
6.3	**What is a confession?**	**99**
6.4	**A suspect's rights at the police station**	**100**
	6.4.1 Recording requirements for interviews	100
	6.4.2 'Off the record' comments	101
6.5	**Challenging the admissibility of a confession under ss. 76 and 78 PACE 1984**	**101**
	6.5.1 Oppression—s. 76(2)(a) PACE 1984	101
	6.5.2 Unreliability—s. 76(2)(b) PACE 1984	102
	6.5.3 Unfairness—s. 78 PACE 1984	103
6.6	**The procedure for determining the admissibility of a confession**	**104**
6.7	**Editing a confession**	**104**
6.8	**Evidence obtained in consequence of an inadmissible confession**	**104**
6.9	**Challenging the admissibility of other non-confession prosecution evidence**	**105**
6.10	**Common law discretion**	**105**
6.11	**Discretion under s. 78 PACE 1984**	**105**
	6.11.1 Use of trickery or deception by the police	105
	6.11.2 Unauthorised surveillance methods	107
	6.11.3 Entrapment	107
6.12	**Abuse of process**	**108**
6.13	**Illegally/unfairly obtained evidence—practical considerations**	**108**
	6.13.1 Illegally/unfairly obtained evidence from the prosecution perspective	108
	6.13.2 Illegally/unfairly obtained evidence from the defence perspective	109

6.1 INTRODUCTION

The purpose of the police investigation into a criminal offence is to secure sufficient evidence to charge a person(s) suspected of committing the offence(s) and to take the matter to trial. It should be remembered that for both prosecution and defence, whilst the rules of evidence are applied primarily at trial, they also underpin the construction of the whole case. The manner in which the police obtain evidence during the investigation may have implications for the admissibility of evidence at any later trial. Therefore, working in partnership with the Crown Prosecution Service (CPS), the police will be aware that the chances of a conviction will be greatly enhanced by presenting admissible evidence to the court which has been obtained in a lawful, fair and reliable way. On the other hand, the defence will carefully scrutinise the prosecution case and should challenge the admissibility of any evidence obtained in breach of the substantive provisions of the Police and Criminal Evidence Act 1984 (PACE 1984), the Codes of Practice and other investigatory powers. Challenges to prosecution evidence by the defence can be made at a pre-trial hearing or at the trial itself.

With this in mind, both prosecution and defence will be aware that a defendant enjoys the right to a fair trial both in domestic law and under Article 6 European Convention on Human Rights 1950 (ECHR 1950). You should remember, however, that Article 6 has broad application and is not solely concerned with unlawfully obtained evidence, as Article 6 applies to the 'fairness' of the trial process as a whole. To ensure the defendant's right to a fair trial is not prejudiced by being convicted on unlawfully or unfairly obtained evidence, the courts have powers to exclude any prosecution evidence where the admission of the evidence would prejudice a fair trial.

This chapter examines the court's powers to exclude unlawfully or unfairly obtained prosecution evidence by examining the position in relation to:

- confession evidence:
  - excluded under ss. 76 and 78 PACE 1984;
- other prosecution evidence excluded:
  - at common law; and
  - under s. 78 PACE 1984; and
  - as an abuse of process.

Challenging the admissibility of identification evidence is considered in Chapter 7.

First, however, how may the police obtain evidence against an accused in an unlawful or unfair way?

6.2 WHAT IS UNLAWFULLY OR UNFAIRLY OBTAINED EVIDENCE?

Unlawfully or unfairly obtained evidence can be described as any prosecution evidence which has been obtained in a 'questionable' manner and includes:

- a confession obtained in breach of the safeguards under PACE 1984 and the Codes of Practice;
- evidence obtained as a result of an unlawful search of a person or his or her property;
- evidence obtained by entrapment;
- identification evidence obtained in breach of Code D PACE Codes of Practice;
- evidence obtained by an unlawful search or by unlawful surveillance;
- evidence (including confession evidence) obtained by deception or trickery;
- evidence obtained in violation of legal professional privilege (unless specifically authorised by statute).

Whilst 'underhand' investigation methods can yield highly relevant evidence of a suspect's guilt, it poses a dilemma for the court because to exclude such evidence may mean a guilty defendant walking free, but to admit the evidence would be to condone unlawful activities by the police as well as potentially prejudicing the defendant's right to a fair trial. Unlawfully obtained evidence remains admissible subject to the exercise of judicial discretion to exclude it. How do the courts apply these exclusionary powers? We will first consider this question in the context of confession evidence.

6.3 WHAT IS A CONFESSION?

A confession is defined by s. 82(1) PACE 1984 as:

'Any statement wholly or partly adverse to the person who made it, whether made to a person in authority or not and whether made in words or otherwise.'

The definition of a confession is extremely wide and covers any statement made by the accused on which the prosecution relies in support of its case. In some situations, a suspect may fully admit his involvement in an offence by stating 'OK officer. It was me. I robbed the old lady in the High Street.' In other situations, the suspect's response may be more ambiguous by admitting to only partial involvement in a crime.

To be admissible against the defendant, a confession does not have to be made to a person in authority, for example a police officer. It is also possible to secure a conviction on confession evidence alone. A well-known example is Michael Stone's conviction for the double fatal hammer attack on Lin and Megan Russell in 1996 which was based on a confession he was alleged to have made in earshot of a convicted, serving prisoner while on remand awaiting trial.

The prosecution is fully aware of the high probative value that attaches to a confession and therefore the police are well versed in the psychology of interrogation techniques as the entire interview process is geared to persuading the suspect to talk. By talking, the suspect is more likely to say something of a revealing, incriminating or contradictory nature, especially over the course of several interviews.

Conversely legal advisers at the police station must always be vigilant about how they advise clients to answer questions in the police interview to avoid their clients making incriminating statements.

6.4 A SUSPECT'S RIGHTS AT THE POLICE STATION

Crucially relevant to the admissibility of confession evidence are the safeguards contained in PACE 1984 and the Codes of Practice, including ss. 56 and 58 PACE 1984 Codes C and E. Many of these safeguards were considered in Chapter 4. Whilst a breach of PACE 1984 and/ or the Codes will not automatically persuade the court to exclude the defendant's confession, substantial breaches of a suspect's legal rights by the police provide evidence for the defence advocate to argue the confession should be excluded under ss. 76 and/or 78 PACE 1984. A causal link must always be established between the alleged breach and the resulting confession. In challenging the confession's admissibility, the custody officer's role and the evidential significance of the custody record will be highly relevant.

6.4.1 RECORDING REQUIREMENTS FOR INTERVIEWS

The recording requirements for interviews are of practical importance in providing an accurate account of what took place and assist the police and the suspect as they protect the police from accusations that they have 'verballed' the suspect (i.e. they have attributed comments to the suspect which the suspect denies making). Any departure from normal practice in recording the interview immediately compromises the integrity of the investigating officers and may form the basis of a challenge to exclude disputed evidence of incriminating admissions. The relevant PACE Codes are E and F (2018).

An interview in relation to a summary-only or indictable offence (including an offence triable either way) must be audio-recorded (Code E para. 2.1). There are limited exceptions to this under Code E 2.3, where a written record must then be made. Interviews should be recorded with the full knowledge of the person being interviewed and are recorded on two audio-tapes unless recorded via a secure digital network (see Code E para. 3). One is a working copy, with the other (master copy) being sealed at the completion of the interview. A transcript of the interview is produced from the working tape and must be a 'balanced' version of the interview. The tape and the transcript must record where the interview took place, the identity of the people present, the time the interview commenced, the time of any breaks and the time the interview finished. The transcripts of interviews in our case studies (*R v Lenny Wise*; *R v Roger Martin*; and *R v William Hardy*) can be located in the case studies section of our online resources. Appendix 2 includes the transcript of interview in relation to *R v Lenny Wise*.

A written summary of the audio-recorded interview will be sent to the defence as part of the prosecution's obligation to provide initial details of the prosecution case under Crim PR, Part 8 (see Chapter 8). The defence has the right to have a copy of the tape to check the accuracy of the summary prepared by the prosecution. If the defence agrees that the summary served by the prosecution is accurate, the written summary will be part of the evidence in the case. If the defence does not agree with the summary, the tape will be transcribed in full for use at the trial. If necessary, the tape will be played in full at the trial. (Consolidated Criminal Practice Direction, Part IV.43).

PACE Code F provides for the visual recording of interviews with a suspect. There is no statutory requirement on police officers to visually record interviews, but the requirements and safeguards of Code F must be applied if visual recording is used.

6.4.2 'OFF THE RECORD' COMMENTS

It is not unusual for a suspect to make unsolicited comments off the record outside the formal interview which may be relevant to the police investigation. Code C para. 11.13 requires the police to keep a written record of any unsolicited comments, which should be signed and dated. The suspect should be given the opportunity to read the record and to sign it as being an accurate record of what was said.

6.5 CHALLENGING THE ADMISSIBILITY OF A CONFESSION UNDER SS. 76 AND 78 PACE 1984

Section 76(2) provides two grounds under which a confession can be excluded—oppression and unreliability:

> 'If, in any proceedings where the prosecution proposes to give in evidence a confession made by an accused person, it is represented to the court that the confession was or may have been obtained—
>
> (a) by oppression of the person who made it; or
>
> (b) in consequence of anything said or done which was likely, in the circumstances existing at the time, to render unreliable any confession which might be made by him in consequence thereof,
>
> the court shall not allow the confession to be given in evidence against him except in so far as the prosecution proves to the court beyond reasonable doubt that the confession (notwithstanding that it may be true) was not obtained as aforesaid.'

Where the defence (or the court) raise the issue of the confession's admissibility the prosecution has the legal burden of proving that the confession was not obtained through oppression (s. 76(2)(a)) and/or is not unreliable (s. 76(2)(b) PACE 1984). If the prosecution cannot prove beyond reasonable doubt that the confession has not been obtained by oppression or is not unreliable, it must be excluded notwithstanding that it may be true.

Each provision will now be considered in turn.

6.5.1 OPPRESSION—S. 76(2)(A) PACE 1984

Oppression is partially defined in s. 76(8) to include torture, inhuman or degrading treatment, and the use or threat of violence (whether or not amounting to torture).

In the leading case of *R v Fulling* [1987] QB 426, the Court of Appeal stated that oppression should be defined by its dictionary definition as being 'the exercise of authority or power in a burdensome, harsh or wrongful manner; unjust or cruel treatment of subjects, inferiors, etc; the imposition of unreasonable or unjust burdens'.

Fulling establishes that for conduct to amount to oppression within the meaning of s. 76(8) there must be deliberate misconduct by the police. Oppression is a question of degree. What is oppressive to one suspect may not be oppressive to another. Therefore, the accused's personal characteristics including his mental strengths and weaknesses are relevant.

'Oppressive' conduct was found to have occurred in *R v Paris, Abdullah and Miller* (1993) 97 Cr App R 99, in which the defendants appealed against their conviction for murder. During the investigation, M was interviewed a total of 13 hours over five days. A solicitor was not present during the first two interviews and M consistently denied his involvement in the crime during the first seven interviews. During interviews eight and nine, M accepted that he was present at the crime scene. He was then pressed to say who had stabbed the victim. M finally confessed that he had. Having denied his involvement over 36 times on tape, he later agreed with the officer's suggestion that he may have been under the influence of drugs and stabbed the victim without knowing what he was doing. He finally admitted: 'I just stabbed, not stabbed her . . . just thumped her in the face I mean.'

6.5.2 UNRELIABILITY—S. 76(2)(B) PACE 1984

The key issue under s. 76(2)(b) is whether the confession was obtained in circumstances that renders it unreliable. The 'unreliability' ground is much wider than the 'oppression' ground.

In applying the 'unreliability' test, s. 76(2)(b) requires the court to consider 'anything said or done to the accused . . . in the circumstances existing at the time'. Therefore, the court must examine all the relevant circumstances of the accused's detention and interrogation and take account of what was said or done to the accused.

As well as the suspect's subjective characteristics, breaches of PACE 1984 and the Codes of Practice will be relevant to excluding a confession on the ground of unreliability. Although a breach will not render a confession automatically inadmissible, the safeguards under PACE 1984 and the Codes exist to ensure the reliability of a confession by protecting the suspect's basic rights.

Bad faith by the police is largely irrelevant to a s. 76(2)(b) submission. What is important is the effect any breach had on the particular suspect at the time. A failure by the police to identify a particular vulnerability due to a medical condition or substance abuse and to make an appropriate provision may provide grounds for the court to exclude a confession under this section. Inducements from the police to encourage the suspect to confess, such as the promise of bail or a lesser charge, are also relevant considerations. For s. 76(2)(b) PACE 1984 to apply, there must be a proven causal link between what was said and done at the police station and the resulting confession.

***R v Delaney* (1988) 86 Cr App R 18: failure to secure legal representation for a vulnerable suspect**

The defendant was convicted of the indecent assault of a three-year-old girl. The only evidence against him was his confession. He had been interviewed at length, having declined the services of a solicitor. Although he was 17 he had an IQ of only 80 and was educationally subnormal. There was evidence from an educational psychologist, which, if accepted, established the defendant as a vulnerable suspect. The interview had been conducted on a sympathetic basis with the officers being at pains to minimise the seriousness of the defendant's position. On several occasions during the interview, reference was made to the defendant's need for treatment rather than punishment. Given the nature of the questioning on such a vulnerable suspect, who was not legally represented, the risk of it producing a false confession was too high and the confession was excluded.

***R v Howden-Simpson* [1991] Crim LR 49: inducement to confess**

The appellant was an organist and choirmaster. His duties included paying junior choir members for their services at weddings. He failed to pay the money to the choristers and was charged with theft. His confession was excluded under s. 76(2) PACE 1984 because of an inducement to confess. The investigating officers had indicated that they would proceed on two non-payment charges only if he admitted the theft. If he did not admit the two charges they would interview every chorister not paid and make a separate charge for each. In the circumstances the Court of Appeal decided the confession should have been excluded under s. 76(2)(b) PACE 1984. The position the appellant was placed in by the officers rendered his confession unreliable.

The following illustrate the case-by-case approach to assessing admissibility under s. 76(2)(b).

A confession will not be excluded where the suspect's conduct created the unreliable circumstances (a so-called self-induced confession). In *R v Goldenberg* (1988) 88 Cr App R 285, it was held that s. 76(2)(b) does not apply where what was said or done was induced by the accused where he admitted the offence out of a desperate desire to obtain bail, as he was suffering from drug withdrawal. It was not possible in these circumstances to establish a causal link between anything said or done to the accused and the resulting confession.

6.5.3 UNFAIRNESS—S. 78 PACE 1984

The wider application of s. 78 PACE 1984 will also be considered later in the chapter in relation to unlawfully obtained prosecution evidence other than confessions. The judicial discretion under s. 78 provides:

'In any proceedings the court may refuse to allow evidence on which the prosecution proposes to rely to be given if it appears to the court that, having regard to all the circumstances, including the circumstances in which the evidence was obtained, the admission of the evidence would have such an adverse effect on the fairness of the proceedings that the court ought not to admit it.'

Section 78 PACE 1984 might be applied to incriminating admissions that have been obtained as a result of unfair conduct by the police, including:

- failing to secure access to a solicitor;
- failing to properly record an interview;
- failing to provide safeguards in relation to a vulnerable suspect;
- deceiving a suspect into making a confession or offering inducements;
- acting in deliberate breach of Code C.

An illustration of the application of s. 78 PACE 1984 is provided by *R v Mason* [1988] 1 WLR 139. The defendant (M) was in custody on suspicion of having petrol-bombed the car of his ex-girlfriend's father. M and his solicitor were told (untruthfully) by two police officers that M's fingerprints had been found on pieces of glass from the petrol bombs that had shattered near the car. As a result of this deception, and perceiving his position to be hopeless, M confessed, which led to his conviction for arson which the Court of Appeal later quashed. It appears from the judgment that the deception practised on the solicitor (an officer of the court) was particularly objectionable, and that the trial judge ought to have exercised his discretion to exclude the confession, as its admission had had an adverse effect on the fairness of the proceedings.

There is an overlap between the type of factors justifying exclusion under s. 76(2)(b) and under s. 78 PACE 1984 including any breaches of PACE 1984 and the Codes of Practice, although a breach of Code C does not guarantee that the confession will be automatically excluded under s. 78 PACE 1984. There must also be a causal connection between the breach of the suspect's legal rights and the resulting confession otherwise there is no unfairness (*R v Alladice* (1988) 87 Cr App R 380).

The importance that the Court of Appeal attaches to a suspect's access to a solicitor at the police station under s. 58 PACE 1984 has been underlined in a number of cases including *R v Samuel* [1988] QB 615 and *R v Walsh* (1990) 91 Cr App R 161. In *Walsh* access to a solicitor had been wrongfully denied and the interview was not contemporaneously recorded. W confessed to robbery. The judge admitted the confession into evidence. The Court of Appeal quashed the conviction concluding that if there had been 'significant and substantial breaches of section 58, then prima facie the standards of fairness set by Parliament have not been met'.

Another helpful illustration of the application of s. 78 PACE 1984 to a confession is provided by *R v Aspinall* [1999] Crim LR 741. A, a schizophrenic, was convicted on drug charges. At the police station two police surgeons had pronounced him fit for interview. When asked by the officers whether he wanted to see a solicitor, A had replied: 'No I want to get home to my missus and kids.' A was interviewed without a solicitor or an appropriate adult. The trial judge rejected a s. 78 submission, concluding that A had been lucid at the time of interview.

In allowing his appeal and quashing the conviction, the Court of Appeal held that A had been unable to assess what was in his best interests. According to A's consultant psychiatrist A had been tired and stressed whilst at the police station which resulted in him lacking assertiveness when dealing with the police. The absence of an appropriate adult (a specific requirement under Code C for a vulnerable person) rendered the confession unfair. The Court of Appeal concluded there had been a breach of Article 6 caused by the delay in access to legal advice as the duty solicitor had been otherwise engaged at the relevant time.

6.6 THE PROCEDURE FOR DETERMINING THE ADMISSIBILITY OF A CONFESSION

The procedure to challenge the admissibility of a confession is through a trial within a trial, otherwise known as a *voir dire*. Where the confession's admissibility is raised at trial, the issue will be resolved in the absence of the jury. A *voir dire* can, however, be conducted at a pre-trial hearing at which a binding ruling can be made. Schedule. 3 Courts Act 2003 permits binding rulings to be made at a pre-trial hearing in summary proceedings.

A *voir dire* need only be held where it is represented that the confession was obtained by oppression or is unreliable. This will normally involve a mixed question of law and fact. If an accused denies making a confession, that is, maintains his signature has been forged or denies words attributed to him, then this becomes a factual matter only and should be dealt with by the jury/magistrates (*R v Flemming* (1988) 86 Cr App R 32).

At either the pre-trial stage or at trial, the judge when conducting a *voir dire* will hear evidence about how the confession was obtained and will hear legal argument from both sides.

In discharging its legal burden to prove the confession's admissibility, the prosecution will usually call the interviewing officers and custody officer(s) to give evidence and will submit the custody record into evidence. The prosecution evidence will be cross-examined by the defence. The defendant may testify at the hearing and expert evidence may be heard. The judge will consider the evidence, apply the law and decide whether the confession should be admitted in evidence. If it is excluded, the jury will never know about the confession. If ruled admissible, the accused is still entitled to repeat his allegations about how the confession was obtained in an attempt to persuade the jury that the confession carries little evidential weight.

6.7 EDITING A CONFESSION

If a confession contains other inadmissible evidence, for example hearsay, or discloses the accused's previous convictions, the defence should seek to have the offending material edited out before it is put before the court. The rules regarding the evidence of tape-recorded interviews are contained in the Consolidated Practice Direction, Part IV.43. The defence is required to notify the prosecution of whether the transcript of the tape-recorded interview is acceptable. If not, the rules require both parties to try to resolve any disputed issues as it will save valuable time at trial if an edited transcript can be agreed.

6.8 EVIDENCE OBTAINED IN CONSEQUENCE OF AN INADMISSIBLE CONFESSION

If a confession is ruled inadmissible, it does not mean that evidence obtained as a result of the confession must also be excluded. Section 76(4) and (5) PACE 1984 permit other incriminating evidence discovered as a result of an inadmissible confession to be introduced provided no reference is made to the confession. Where the incriminating evidence cannot be adduced without referring to the inadmissible confession, neither the confession nor the facts discovered will be admissible.

6.9 CHALLENGING THE ADMISSIBILITY OF OTHER NON-CONFESSION PROSECUTION EVIDENCE

Where the defence or the court submit that 'other' prosecution evidence was obtained in an unfair or unlawful way, the evidence may be excluded by the court under the common law discretion or on the ground of unfairness or as an abuse of process.

6.10 COMMON LAW DISCRETION

The criminal courts have always retained the common law power to exclude evidence capable of prejudicing a fair trial. This discretion is specifically preserved by s. 82(3) PACE 1984. If the prejudicial effect of the evidence sought to be adduced by the prosecution exceeds its probative value, the evidence must be excluded. This requires a careful balancing exercise to be undertaken by the trial judge or magistrates.

Prosecuting lawyers have long relied on the narrow approach adopted by the common law to exclude illegally or unlawfully obtained evidence. Provided the evidence is relevant and reliable, its admission is not generally regarded as prejudicing the defendant's right to a fair trial. The discretion will certainly not be used to discipline the police about the way in which prosecution evidence was obtained. The limited application of the common law is illustrated by Lord Diplock in the leading case of *R v Sang* [1980] AC 402 (a case where the defendant argued he had been entrapped by prosecution authorities):

'(1) A trial judge in a criminal trial has always a discretion to refuse to admit evidence if in his opinion its prejudicial effect outweighs its probative value.

(2) Save with regard to admissions and confessions and generally with regard to evidence obtained from the accused after commission of the offence, he has no discretion to refuse to admit relevant admissible evidence on the ground that it was obtained by improper or unfair means. The court is not concerned with how it was obtained.'

Whilst the absence of significant case law under s. 82(3) PACE 1984 indicates that it is not commonly invoked, defence lawyers should be prepared to cite the section when challenging the manner in which the police obtained evidence against the accused. It is common to base the defence argument not only under s. 82(3) PACE 1984 but also under the wider discretion in s. 78 PACE 1984.

6.11 DISCRETION UNDER S. 78 PACE 1984

As previously explained, s. 78 PACE 1984 gives the court discretion to exclude any prosecution evidence where the admission of the evidence would have an adverse effect on the fairness of the proceedings. Although the fairness of the proceedings is not defined, the court is invited by the wording in the section to have regard to all the circumstances in which the evidence was obtained.

Consider the following examples illustrating the practical application of s. 78.

6.11.1 USE OF TRICKERY OR DECEPTION BY THE POLICE

R v Bailey and Smith [1993] 3 All ER 365

The accused were arrested in connection with an armed robbery. Both were legally represented and remained silent. They were charged and brought before a magistrates' court where they were remanded into police custody for the purposes of attending an identification parade. Although the questioning of suspects after charge is prohibited under Code C, the investigating officers put the defendants in the same cell, in an attempt to obtain further useful evidence by falsely telling the defendants that they must share a cell because of an uncooperative custody officer. The cell was bugged. The defendants believed the police even though their solicitor had warned them that the bugging of police cells was not uncommon. While together in the cell, they made incriminating admissions which were used in evidence against them. The Court of Appeal held the trial judge had rightly admitted the evidence.

More recently in *R v Plunkett* [2013] EWCA 261 the defendants were arrested on suspicion of aggravated burglary. On three occasions as the suspects were being transported to the police station in a police van their conversations were covertly recorded by the police. During the journeys the suspects made incriminating admissions. In the police interviews the defendants remained silent following legal advice. At trial, evidence of the covert recordings was admitted and the defendants were convicted. On appeal the Court of Appeal upheld the trial judge's ruling that the covert recordings should not have been excluded under s. 78 PACE 1984 and the defendants' right to a fair trial under Article 6(3) ECHR 1950 had not been infringed. There had been no misrepresentation, misconduct or entrapment by the police nor had the confidentiality between the appellants and their lawyer been breached.

Prosecution evidence (including incriminating admissions obtained outside a formal police interview) may be excluded under s. 78 PACE 1984 where the police obtained the evidence through trickery or deception. As *R v Bailey and Smith* illustrates, when exercising its discretion under s. 78 PACE 1984, the court is less concerned with the nature of the police conduct in breaching a defendant's legal rights than the reliability of the evidence that was obtained as a result of the trickery or deception.

R v Khan [1996] 3 All ER 298

Khan was suspected of drug smuggling. To obtain evidence against him, investigating officers attached a listening device to a property visited by Khan, of which neither Khan nor the flat's owner had any knowledge. Whilst Home Office Guidelines existed regarding the use of covert surveillance, there was no statutory authorisation for the use of such devices at the time, although the officers had sought and obtained permission of the chief constable. As a result of the operation, the police obtained a tape recording that proved Khan was involved in importing heroin.

At Khan's trial the prosecution sought to admit the tape recording in evidence whilst accepting that there was no statutory authority for using the device and that placing it on the property without the owner's permission constituted a civil trespass. Khan conceded that the tape was authentic and that it was his voice which could be heard. On appeal it was argued on Khan's behalf that the evidence had been obtained in violation of Article 8, guaranteeing a right of privacy, and that the trial judge should have excluded the tape-recorded conversations in the exercise of his discretion either at common law or under s. 78 PACE 1984.

Notwithstanding there may have been a violation of Article 8, the House of Lords concluded that the evidence was rightly admitted at common law and under s. 78. The evidence was especially relevant and could not be said to have adversely affected the fairness of the proceedings.

Khan subsequently took his case to the European Court of Human Rights (ECtHR), in *Khan v UK* (2001) 31 EHRR 45. Whilst finding the UK to be in violation of Article 8, the ECtHR determined that the evidence against the applicant was reliable and had not been obtained by inducements. There had been no violation of Article 6 as the applicant had enjoyed a fair trial because s. 78 PACE 1984 had afforded Khan the opportunity to challenge the admissibility of the prosecution evidence in court.

As a result of this decision, the use of covert/intrusive surveillance for investigatory purposes was placed on a statutory footing with the enactment of RIPA 2000 and its accompanying Code of Practice.

Further consideration of the provisions under RIPA fall outside the scope of this text, see *Blackstone's Criminal Practice* for more detailed guidance.

6.11.2 UNAUTHORISED SURVEILLANCE METHODS

The increasing sophistication of surveillance technology allows the police to obtain evidence in many covert ways. Such surveillance operations must be authorised under the Regulation of Investigatory Powers Act 2000 (RIPA 2000). Where such surveillance methods are unauthorised or where the police act in breach of the criminal and/or the civil law, should the evidence be admitted? Consider the case of *R v Khan* which pre-dates RIPA 2000.

6.11.3 ENTRAPMENT

Entrapment is conduct by a law enforcement agent inducing a person to commit an offence that the person would otherwise have been unlikely to commit.

Entrapment often involves an agent provocateur, such as an undercover police officer. Evidence obtained in this way can be challenged at common law or under s. 78 PACE 1984 or as an abuse of process subject to the proviso that entrapment is not a defence in English criminal law.

The law governing the admissibility of evidence obtained by entrapment continues to evolve (see recent cases of *R v TL* [2018] EWCA Crim 1821 and *R v Syed* (Haroon Ali) [2018] EWCA 2809. An important statement of the principles which takes account of Convention law on the issue (see *Teixeira de Castro v Portugal* (1998) 28 EHRR 242) was provided by the House of Lords in the following case which combined two appeals.

R v Loosely; Attorney-General's Reference (No. 3 of 2000) [2001] 1 WLR 2060

In Loosely's case, an undercover officer posed as a prospective buyer of drugs. His actions were part of an authorised surveillance in the Guildford area, which had seen a rise in the supply of heroin. The focus of suspicion fell on a particular public house in which the undercover officer had been given the defendant's contact number as a possible source of supply. On contacting the defendant, the officer asked if he could 'sort us a couple of bags'. The defendant responded willingly to the request and immediately arranged to take the undercover officer to a place where he was able to obtain the drugs.

In the *Attorney-General's Reference*, undercover officers offered the defendant contraband cigarettes. After a lengthy conversation about the cigarettes, one of the officers asked the defendant if he could 'sort him some brown'. It was only after numerous conversations, much persuasion and the offer of further contraband cigarettes, that the defendant eventually obtained a quantity of heroin for the officers. On handing the drug over to the undercover officers, the defendant was recorded as saying: 'I am not really into heroin myself.' In interview he maintained he had nothing to do with heroin and had only supplied the officers because of their requests and as a favour for the contraband cigarettes.

The House of Lords concluded that in entrapment cases the application to have the evidence excluded is in practice an application to stay the proceedings for an abuse of process since the evidence obtained through the use of entrapment usually forms the entire basis of the prosecution's case. If the evidence of entrapment was to be excluded the prosecution case would collapse. For this reason, an abuse of process application was the appropriate remedy. Accordingly, the relevant test to be applied in English law was that set out in *R v Latif and Shazard* [1996] 1 WLR 104: namely, where the conduct of the prosecuting authorities had been so shameful and unworthy as to constitute an affront to the public conscience the case should be stopped as an abuse of process. It is conduct so seriously improper as to bring the administration of justice into disrepute.

On the facts, the House of Lords concluded that Loosely's appeal should be dismissed. His arrest had come about as a result of legitimate concern in the rising supply of hard drugs in the Guildford area and from one public house in particular. As Loosely expressed himself keen to arrange a supply, the undercover officer had not needed to undertake any persuasion, and therefore his actions clearly fell within the bounds of acceptable conduct. In relation to the *Attorney-General's Reference*, the House of Lords concluded it would not interfere with the trial judge's exercise of discretion. The defendant in that case had come under considerable and sustained pressure by officers to supply them with a Class A drug and could be said to have been induced to commit the offence based on the continued supply of contraband cigarettes to him.

'Entrapment' is not confined to state agencies and extends to private entrapment (*R v Shannon* [2001] 1 WLR 51 and *R v TL* [2018] EWCA Crim 1821).

6.12 **ABUSE OF PROCESS**

In addition to the discretion to exclude evidence at common law and under s. 78 PACE 1984, the criminal courts have an inherent jurisdiction to stay proceedings for abuse of process. This would be a very serious step for a court to take as its effect is to bring the trial to an end. In *R v Maxwell* [2011] 4 All ER 941, Lord Dyson summarised the two categories of cases in which the court has the power to stay proceedings for abuse of process as (i) where it would be impossible to give the accused a fair trial, and (ii) where it offends the court's sense of propriety and justice to try the accused in the particular circumstances of the case. Where a stay is ordered the court believes that either the defendant cannot enjoy a fair trial or, as a result of the actions of the prosecuting authorities, it is not fair to try the accused.

An abuse of process submission would be appropriate in the following circumstances where:

- there has been considerable delay by the prosecution in bringing charges; or
- adverse pre-trial publicity makes a fair trial impossible;
- there is a later prosecution where a previous trial was halted;
- it is decided to commence a prosecution in circumstances where the prosecution agreed an alternative course of action, that is, to caution (see *R v Dobson* [2000] EWCA 1606);
- the prosecution has lost or failed to secure evidence relevant to the crime which might have assisted the defendant;
- the prosecution has withheld relevant evidence; or
- where evidence has been obtained by entrapment (see *R v Loosely* discussed above).

Where proceedings are stayed because of the unlawful activities of the prosecuting authorities, the court is effectively stating that such activities will not be tolerated and cannot be condoned. The exercise of discretion under abuse of process is therefore wider than the discretion exercised under s. 78 PACE 1984. However, the type of misconduct involved for an abuse of process application to succeed must be such that it would be an affront to public conscience for the proceedings to continue or for the conviction to stand (*R v Latif* [1996] 1 WLR 104).

6.13 **ILLEGALLY/UNFAIRLY OBTAINED EVIDENCE—PRACTICAL CONSIDERATIONS**

Prosecutors and defence lawyers are aware from the case law that the courts appear to adopt a more proactive approach to excluding confession and identification evidence than to other 'tainted' prosecution evidence. This dual approach will be taken into account by both sides when preparing their case for trial.

6.13.1 **ILLEGALLY/UNFAIRLY OBTAINED EVIDENCE FROM THE PROSECUTION PERSPECTIVE**

For both prosecution and defence, the most important part of successful representation in court is case preparation. For cases to be tried in the Crown Court, the prosecutor is alerted from the defence statement, disclosed under the pre-trial disclosure of evidence rules (see Chapter 13), of any potential defence challenges to the admissibility of prosecution evidence. In summary cases where a defence statement is not mandatory, the defence is required, by Crim PR, Part 3, to assist the court in identifying the issues that are in dispute in a contested case. In anticipating any challenges the prosecutor will be prepared through diligent research of the relevant case law to argue against excluding any evidence either at pre-trial hearing or in the *voir dire* at trial.

6.13.2 **ILLEGALLY/UNFAIRLY OBTAINED EVIDENCE FROM THE DEFENCE PERSPECTIVE**

Under the pre-trial disclosure of evidence rules in both summary and indictable proceedings the prosecution will have made full disclosure of the case against the accused. The disclosed evidence should be looked at critically by the defence team and whilst the courts tend to adopt a relatively restrictive approach to their exclusionary powers, the defence advocate should argue against admitting 'tainted' evidence. Therefore, the current law in relation to the exercise of judicial discretion under s. 76 and s. 78 in relation to confessions, and s. 78 and/or s. 82(3) PACE 1984 in relation to other prosecution evidence, should not inhibit a defence advocate from making an application to have unlawfully obtained evidence excluded. Defence advocates should also be aware of the potential for making an abuse of process application where appropriate and the pervasive influence of Article 6 ECHR 1950.

For a practical exercise to challenge the admissibility of prosecution evidence, consider the following self-test questions.

KEY POINT SUMMARY

- A confession is widely defined and covers any incriminating admissions made by an accused.

- Breaches of PACE 1984 and the Codes of Practice are important in determining the admissibility of confession evidence where such evidence is disputed—although a breach will not automatically lead to a confession being excluded.

- 'Oppression' (s. 76(2)(a)) is narrowly defined and will invariably involve some deliberate misconduct on the part of the police.

- 'Unreliability' (s. 76(2)(b)) has a much wider application. It does not require bad faith on the part of the police and the defendant's mental state will be a relevant consideration.

- If a confession is admissible under s. 76 PACE 1984, it may still be excluded under s. 78 PACE 1984 if its admission would have an adverse affect on the fairness of the case.

- Every accused enjoys the right to a fair trial including the right to challenge any evidence that might be said to have been obtained unlawfully or in a dubious manner.

- The power to exclude evidence in the interests of securing a fair trial exists at common law and under s. 78 PACE 1984—both are exercised on a discretionary basis.

- Section 78 PACE 1984 has largely superseded the common law which is now found in s. 82(3) PACE 1984.

- Section 78 PACE 1984 applies to all types of prosecution evidence, including prosecution evidence that has been obtained unlawfully.

SELF-TEST QUESTIONS

A reminder of Code C safeguards

Exercise 1

In order to refresh your memory in this regard, see if you can answer the following short questions.

1. At what stages does the suspect have to be cautioned? Would a confession that has been obtained following a failure to properly caution an individual be admissible?

2. On arrival at the police station what rights should be explained to the suspect by the custody officer?

3. What initial assessment must the custody officer undertake in relation to each suspect and who might be said to constitute a vulnerable suspect?

4. The right of access to a solicitor is governed by the all-important s. 58 PACE 1984. In what circumstances may access to a solicitor be delayed? If access was delayed and a confession was obtained, would the confession be admissible?

5. Can the investigating officers begin to question a suspect when the suspect has requested a solicitor?

6. What are the maximum periods of detention and at what intervals should detention be reviewed? (Clearly, the longer an individual is detained in custody the more he or she may be tempted to confess in order to relieve the pressure of the situation.)

7. What basic human rights are suspects entitled to while in custody, including rest periods?

8. What actually constitutes an interview under Code C?

9. What is the procedure if the suspect appears to be unfit to be interviewed?

10. What safeguards apply as regards the conduct of an interview in relation to non-vulnerable and vulnerable suspects?

Exercise 2: *R v Lenny Wise*

Consider the Lenny Wise scenario.

We have begun the process of evaluating the evidence against Lenny Wise. You will see from Document 26E (included in Appendix 2) that Lenny makes a confession. What he states in his interview satisfies the statutory definition of a confession under s. 82(1) PACE. His interview is tape-recorded in accordance with the requirements of Code E para. 3.1. Having regard to Lenny's proof of evidence (Document 6) and the custody record (Document 9) consider the following questions:

• Do you feel you have grounds for challenging the admissibility of Lenny's confession in due course? If so, what will be the legal basis for your submissions?

• What arguments will you put forward in support of your submissions?

• Consider the manner in which the confession was obtained. Can you point to any specific breaches of Code C?

• How will the admissibility of Lenny's confession be resolved and what evidence will need to be adduced and challenged in this regard?

Exercise 3

Ranjit Singh will state as follows:

'Shortly before midnight last night I was driving home in my mother's Ford Escort Cabriolet, registration number R457 KYE. I had just parked the car and was removing my sports bag from the boot. It contained my squash equipment. I was wearing my black tracksuit trousers and hooded sweatshirt. I was searching for my mobile phone in the back of the car when two men approached me. One reached into the car and grabbed me by the arm. It was dark. I could not see what they were wearing. Fearing a racial attack, I just lashed out and hit one of them. I extricated myself and started to run. One of them shouted: "Stop we're police officers." I was grabbed in a matter of seconds. The other man began to search my bag and then me. The other searched my car. Finally, I heard one of them say, "Let's teach him a lesson." With that I was handcuffed. They emptied my pockets and removed my trousers, socks and shoes. They found a small quantity of cocaine tucked inside my sock. I was then arrested and subsequently charged with (a) possession of a controlled drug and (b) assaulting a police officer in the execution of his duty.'

Do you feel you can challenge the admissibility of the evidence in the case? If so, upon what grounds? Guidance on all the above questions can be found in our online resources.

FIGURE 6.1 UNLAWFULLY AND UNFAIRLY OBTAINED EVIDENCE

WHAT CONSTITUTES UNLAWFULLY OBTAINED EVIDENCE?

- Any evidence obtained unlawfully or in an underhand manner, which can include:
  - evidence obtained in breach of Codes of Practice under PACE;
  - evidence obtained through the use of an agent provocateur;
  - evidence obtained in breach of rights under PACE—unlawful arrest search/seizure;
  - evidence obtained in violation of Article 8—the right to privacy;
  - evidence obtained in violation of the privilege against self-incrimination.

COMMON LAW PRESERVED BY S. 82(3) PACE

- Illustrated in *R v Sang* and *R v Khan*;
- restrictive in its application;
- save for evidence of a self-incriminating nature obtained by means of trickery/deception after commission of offence, evidence obtained unlawfully or unfairly remains admissible if it is relevant and reliable;
- if the prejudicial effect of the evidence exceeds its probative value, the evidence will be excluded.

SECTION 78 PACE 1984

- Gives courts discretion to exclude *any* prosecution evidence, the admission of which would have an adverse effect on the fairness of the proceedings;
- application of s. 78 is pervasive and is not confined to unlawfully obtained evidence;
- used most successfully to exclude confession evidence obtained in breach of safeguards of PACE and Code C (*R v Aspinall*; *R v Walsh*; *R v Samuel*);
- also used to exclude identification evidence obtained in breach of safeguards under Code D (*R v Finley*)—see Chapter 7;
- less successfully used in relation to other types of evidence, i.e. unlawful arrest/search/seizure, unauthorised surveillance/underhand tactics where the evidence yielded is relevant, reliable and authentic (*R v Khan*);
- on the use of an agent provocateur see *R v Loosely* and the application of abuse of process;
- case law suggests that unless the reliability of the evidence is tainted by the illegality or unfairness, making it more difficult for the defendant to challenge the evidence, it is likely to be admitted.

FIGURE 6.2 CONFESSION EVIDENCE

- A confession is any statement wholly or partly adverse whether made to a person in authority or not: s. 82(1) PACE 1984.

- Procedure for challenging the admissibility of confession evidence is a *voir dire* (trial within a trial).

- The admissibility of a confession may be challenged on the basis of:

OPPRESSION

- The exercise of power in a burdensome, harsh or wrongful manner;

- S. 76(2)(a) PACE 1984: requires deliberate and serious misconduct on the part of the police;

- See *R v Fulling* for definition of oppression.

UNRELIABILITY

S. 76(2)(b) PACE 1984: in consequence of anything said or done which, at the time, was likely to render unreliable any confession made by the suspect:

- breaches of Code C safeguards highly relevant to this ground;

- can include failure to secure access to legal advice in breach of s. 58 PACE 1984;

- offering a suspect inducements to confess;

- errors or omissions on the part of the police need not be deliberate;

- burden of proving the absence of unreliability on prosecution.

UNFAIRNESS

S. 78 PACE 1984: the admission of the confession would have an adverse effect on the fairness of the proceedings:

- significant and substantial breaches of Code C highly relevant to this ground;

- failure to spot and deal with a vulnerable suspect;

- taking advantage of a vulnerable suspect;

- failing to properly record an interview;

- factors relevant to this ground overlap with s. 76(2)(b).

7.1	**Introduction**	**113**
7.2	**The dangers of eye-witness identification**	**114**
7.3	**How is eye-witness identification obtained?**	**114**
7.4	**Distinguishing between known and unknown suspects**	**114**
	7.4.1 What is a known suspect?	114
	7.4.2 Where the suspect is unknown	115
	7.4.3 Showing photographs to a witness	115
	7.4.4 Where the suspect is known and available	115
	7.4.5 Taking the suspect's photograph at the police station	115
7.5	**When must an identification procedure be held?**	**115**
	7.5.1 Types of identification procedures	116
	7.5.2 The suspect's rights at an identification procedure	117
7.6	**Is a formal identification procedure a mandatory requirement?**	**117**
7.7	**The formal identification procedures**	**119**
	7.7.1 Video identification (Annex A)	119
	7.7.2 Identification parade (Annex B)	119
	7.7.3 Group identification (Annex C)	120
	7.7.4 Confrontation by a witness (Annex D)	120
7.8	**The consequences of failing to comply with Code D**	**120**
	7.8.1 Directing the jury where there has been a breach of Code D	120
7.9	**Recognition by police officers from photographic and CCTV images**	**121**
7.10	**Voice identification**	**121**
7.11	**Dock identifications**	**121**
7.12	**Forensic identification procedures**	**122**
	7.12.1 Forensic evidence	122
	7.12.2 Fingerprints and footwear impressions	122
	7.12.3 Non-intimate sample	123
	7.12.4 Intimate sample	123
7.13	**Dna evidence**	**124**
	7.13.1 Retaining forensic samples	124
7.14	**Facial mapping**	**124**
7.15	**The practical issues associated with identification evidence**	**125**

7.1 INTRODUCTION

Proof of the defendant's presence at the crime scene through identification evidence can be presented at trial in a number of ways, including:

- visual identification of a suspect by an eye-witness;

- real evidence: CCTV surveillance has led to the increasing use of video and photographic stills at trials. This type of real evidence can give the court a direct view of the incident enabling the jury or the magistrates to decide whether the defendant is the person seen participating in the criminal activity captured on film;

- forensic evidence: identification may also be proved by the opinion of a forensic scientist establishing a connection between the defendant and the crime scene based on the scientific comparison of forensic samples, for example fingerprints or DNA discovered at the crime scene compared with evidence found on the defendant or otherwise in his possession.

In this chapter, we consider:

- the dangers of eye-witness identification;
- how identification evidence is obtained by the police during the police investigation;
- the pre-trial safeguards contained in the identification procedures under Code D;
- the admissibility of eye-witness evidence obtained in breach of Code D;
- obtaining fingerprints and intimate and non-intimate samples at the police station;
- identification evidence given by expert witnesses.

Numerous references will be made in this chapter to Code D which can be freely accessed from the Home Office website—our online resources provide a link to the full text of Code D.

7.2 THE DANGERS OF EYE-WITNESS IDENTIFICATION

Eye-witness identification has been proven to be inherently unreliable by psychological experiments and by miscarriages of justice. Identification is often made in difficult circumstances where, for example, a crime-related incident is over in a matter of seconds or minutes or in circumstances of heightened awareness where the witness is in fear. Safeguards are required to ensure identification evidence is gathered in a scrupulously fair manner and is treated with caution at trial. The principal safeguards are provided pre-trial by the Police and Criminal Evidence Act 1984 (PACE 1984) Code D and at trial by the *Turnbull* guidelines (*R v Turnbull* [1977] QB 224). The application of the *Turnbull* guidelines are considered in Chapter 17.

7.3 HOW IS EYE-WITNESS IDENTIFICATION OBTAINED?

Eye-witness identification may come about in many different ways. A witness to a crime will typically give an initial statement to the police including a description of the person or persons the witness believes were involved. Code D para. 3.1 requires the police to make a record of the suspect's description as first given by a potential witness and for the suspect or his legal adviser to be given a copy of the record.

On the basis of the information provided, the police may compile a photofit of a suspect they wish to speak to and circulate it to the media. In some instances, witnesses may be taken on a tour of the area in the immediate aftermath of a crime to see if they are able to spot the person(s) they think they saw involved in the offence. The police may show witnesses 'mug shots' of convicted offenders, or CCTV footage or photographic stills, to see if they can identify the culprit.

7.4 DISTINGUISHING BETWEEN KNOWN AND UNKNOWN SUSPECTS

For the purposes of identification procedures, Code D distinguishes between a known and an unknown suspect. The distinction is of considerable practical importance.

7.4.1 WHAT IS A KNOWN SUSPECT?

Code D paras. 3.1A(a) and (b) provide guidance about when a suspect is 'known' and 'available'. A suspect is known where there is sufficient information known to the police to justify the arrest of a particular person for suspected involvement in an offence. A suspect is available if he is immediately available or will be available within a reasonably short period of time and is willing to take part in an identification procedure. In this situation, Code D para. 3.4 provides the identification procedures that must be used are a video identification or an identification parade or a group identification as explained at para. 7.5.1 below.

7.4.2 WHERE THE SUSPECT IS UNKNOWN

Where the suspect is unknown, the police may take a witness to a particular neighbour-hood or place to see if the witness can identify the suspect. Code D para. 3.2 stipulates the safeguards the police need to consider when taking a witness around an area. A detailed record of all the circumstances must be kept and the police must not direct the witness's attention to a particular individual.

7.4.3 SHOWING PHOTOGRAPHS TO A WITNESS

If the suspect's identity is not known, the witness may be shown photographs subject to safeguards contained in Code D Annex E including:

- a requirement that the witness should be shown 12 photographs at a time which should be of a similar type;
- a witness must not be prompted or guided in his choice in any way;
- if a witness makes a positive identification from a set of photographs no other witness can be shown the set and each of the witnesses should be asked to attend a parade.

Once the police have a known suspect in mind they should proceed to an arrest and convene a formal identification procedure if required.

Code D para. 3.3 prevents a witness from being shown photographs if the suspect's identity is known to the police and the suspect is available to participate in an identification procedure. Showing photographs in advance of a formal identification procedure seriously compromises the integrity of the procedure and effectively renders the procedure irrelevant.

7.4.4 WHERE THE SUSPECT IS KNOWN AND AVAILABLE

Once a suspect is known and is available the police should proceed to a formal identification procedure where the circumstances prescribed by Code D para. 3.4 apply.

7.4.5 TAKING THE SUSPECT'S PHOTOGRAPH AT THE POLICE STATION

A person detained at the police station may be photographed with or without their consent under s. 64 A(1) PACE 1984 and Code D paras. 5.12–5.18. The police may require the person to remove any item or substance worn on or over the whole, or any part of their head or face. If the request is not complied with the police may use force to remove the item or substance, under s. 64A (2) PACE 1984. The police may also take a photograph without the person's consent by making a copy of an image of them taken at any time on a camera system installed anywhere in the police station. This is known as a covert image.

7.5 WHEN MUST AN IDENTIFICATION PROCEDURE BE HELD?

Where an eye-witness purports to identify a suspect at the crime scene and the suspect denies being the person the witness is alleged to have seen, Code D imposes a virtually mandatory requirement on the police to convene an identification procedure to confirm or disprove the witness's identification.

Code D para. 3.12 provides:

'If before any identification procedure set out in paragraphs 3.5 to 3.10 has been held

(a)   an eye-witness has identified a suspect or purported to have identified them; or

(b)   there is an eye-witness available who expresses an ability to identify the suspect; or

(c)   there is a reasonable chance of an eye-witness being able to identify the suspect,

and the eye-witness in (a) to (c) has not been given an opportunity to identify the suspect in any of the procedures set out in paragraphs 3.5 to 3.10, then an identification procedure shall be held if the suspect disputes being the person the eye-witness claims to have seen on a previous occasion (see paragraph 3.0), unless:

(i)   it is not practicable to hold any such procedure; or

(ii)   any such procedure would serve no useful purpose in proving or disproving whether the suspect was involved in committing the offence, for example:

   • where the suspect admits being at the scene of the crime and gives an account of what took place and the eye-witness does not see anything which contradicts that; or

   • when it is not disputed that the suspect is already known to the eye-witness who claims to recognise them when seeing them commit the crime.'

Also para. 3.12 provides that an eye-witness identification procedure may also be held if the officer in charge of the investigation, after consultation with the identification officer, considers it would be useful.

7.5.1   TYPES OF IDENTIFICATION PROCEDURES

In order to test the witness's ability to identify a suspect and to safeguard against mistaken identity, the police use a number of formal identification procedures, which are governed by Code D and its Annexes A–D.

The annexes to Code D provide the following procedures:

• Annex A: video identification.

• Annex B: identification parades.

• Annex C: group identification.

• Annex D: confrontation with an eye-witness.

In the hierarchy of identification procedures, the video identification is the preferred choice. It is easier to organise and is less intimidating for witnesses. Where an identification procedure is to be held in accordance with Code D para. 3.12, para. 3.14 provides that the suspect must be initially invited to take part in a video identification unless:

• this is not practicable; or

• an identification parade is more practicable and suitable; or

• the officer in charge of the investigation considers that a group identification is more suitable than the other forms of identification and the identification officer believes it is practicable to arrange.

The decision to adopt a particular procedure is taken by the officer in charge of identification procedures in consultation with the investigating officer. A suspect must be allowed to make representations about the procedure to be adopted, and before an option is offered the suspect must be reminded of his entitlement to free legal advice (Code D para. 3.14).

The conduct of the identification procedure is the responsibility of the identification officer who is at least the rank of inspector and is independent of the investigation.

7.5.2 **THE SUSPECT'S RIGHTS AT AN IDENTIFICATION PROCEDURE**

Some important rights must be explained to the suspect by the police before convening an identification procedure. They are set out in Code D para. 3.17 and include:

* the purpose of the procedure;
* the suspect's right to free legal advice and their right to have a solicitor or friend present;
* an explanation that the suspect does not have to consent or cooperate in a video identification, identification parade or group identification but that if the suspect does not consent, his refusal can be given in evidence against him in any subsequent trial and the police may proceed covertly without the suspect's consent or make other arrangements to test whether a witness can identify him;
* that if the suspect has significantly altered his appearance between being offered an identification procedure and the convening of the procedure, the identification officer may consider other forms of identification and the fact that the suspect significantly changed his appearance may be given in evidence to the court if the case comes to trial;
* whether, before the suspect's identity became known, the police showed the witness photographs and/or a computerised or artist's composite image.

The formal identification procedures regarded as the fairest to the suspect are the video parade and the identification parade because they provide the suspect with the best chance of not being selected, as he has some control in their composition.

A suspect who refuses the identification procedure in which the suspect is first invited to take part shall be asked to state their reason for refusing and may get advice from their solicitor or their appropriate adult. The solicitor or appropriate adult can make representations about why another procedure should be used. A record should be made of the reasons for the refusal and any representations made. The identification officer may then invite the suspect to take part in an alternative procedure which the officer considers suitable and practicable (Code D para 3.15), and make arrangements for the suspect's image to be captured covertly or for photographs to be used in the compilation of the video-identification procedure. The confrontation procedure is a procedure of last resort and may not be used unless all other options are impracticable (Code D para. 3.23).

7.6 **IS A FORMAL IDENTIFICATION PROCEDURE A MANDATORY REQUIREMENT?**

The issue of whether the police must convene an identification procedure has been heard in a number of appeals culminating in the House of Lords decision in *R v Forbes* [2001] 1 AC 473, which concerned an earlier version of Code D.

In *Forbes*, the victim was attacked and almost robbed at a cash-dispensing machine. The victim managed to get away and called the police. He was taken on a tour of the area and was able to point out his assailant. The appellant was arrested. He vigorously protested his innocence. No parade was convened as the police believed it would have been futile as a firm street identification had been made. The House of Lords held that a parade was a mandatory requirement save in exceptional cases where the eye-witness insists that he cannot identify the person responsible, or in a case of pure recognition of someone well known to the eye-witness.

Statutory effect has been given to the decision in *R v Forbes* in the 2017 edition of Code D. However, the question of whether an identification procedure is mandatory in all cases remains uncertain. The requirement to convene an identification procedure under Code D para. 3.12 is rebutted where, in all the circumstances, it would serve no useful purpose in proving or disproving whether the suspect was involved in the offence, including, for example, where the suspect is well known to the witness making the identification.

It will be apparent that Code D gives the police discretion to decide whether a suspect is well known to the witness and whether an identification procedure would therefore serve any useful purpose. A decision by the police not to convene an identification procedure should always be critically scrutinised by the defence lawyer as it provides a potential ground to seek the exclusion of the identification evidence on the ground of 'unfairness' under s. 78 PACE 1984. The failure to hold a formal procedure also means that the reliability of the identification was never tested before trial.

The issue of the mandatory requirement to convene a parade was central to the two cases mentioned here which concern earlier versions of Code D, although the decisions remain relevant to the current version of Code D.

R (H) v DPP [2003] EWHC 133

The victim (V) was 15. It was alleged that she had been assaulted by the defendant (D), a 16-year-old. The assault lasted several minutes. V had been assaulted on a previous occasion by D and had reported the matter to the police. D denied the assault and denied being present when the attack took place. No identification parade was held. At her summary trial, D's defence solicitor submitted there had been a breach of Code D para. 2.3 (under the previous Code D), and that consequently there was no evidence of identification.

V had known D for about 18 months and had been a credible witness. Finding D guilty, the magistrates concluded that the police were entitled to refuse to hold an identification parade as it would have been futile. Applying the dicta in *Forbes* (highlighted previously), the Divisional Court concurred with the magistrates' decision. The defendant had indicated she knew V and it was not suggested by the defendant or her legal representative at any time during her police interview that the question of recognition was an issue for her. In these circumstances this was a case of recognition and an identification parade would have served no useful purpose as V was bound to have identified D.

R v Harris [2003] EWCA 174

Two victims (A and B) were robbed of their mobile phones in the street by a group of youths. Both A and B claimed to recognise the appellant (C). They had previously been at school with C and knew him by his first name of Tristan. C had been in the year above them. A and B claimed to recognise C even though he was wearing a hooded top. A had recognised the boy's voice when he came over to him. It was accepted by A and B that they had not known C well at school and that they had not seen him since he had left. C denied any involvement and put forward an alibi. There was no other evidence to link him to the crime. Evidence was given from the school's headmaster, who confirmed that A and B would have been in attendance from 1998 until 2000 when C had left. There would have been 500 pupils in the school at the time and only one pupil at that time and since had the name of Tristan. No identification parade had been held and the defence submitted at trial that the identification evidence should have been excluded under s. 78 PACE 1984.

Although the defendant had not requested a parade, he had made it clear to the police that he denied involvement and that he did not know A or B. Was C well known to A and B, within the meaning of Code D? The Court of Appeal concluded he was not: neither A nor B had seen C for the past two years; C would have been 14 at the time; neither A, B or C had been in the same class; there had not been any direct contact between them. The Court of Appeal concluded that there was at least: 'a live possibility that one or both witnesses might not have picked out the appellant on an identification parade. In that event, the defence would have been able to rely at trial on such non-identification as adding weight to the defence of alibi.'

In quashing C's conviction, the Court of Appeal held that the trial judge's failure to properly direct the jury about the purpose of Code D and the effect of a breach, meant the defendant had not received a fair trial.

7.7 THE FORMAL IDENTIFICATION PROCEDURES

Whichever identification procedure the police use, the specific safeguards associated with each procedure are contained in the annexes supplementing Code D. We include here a summary of the main provisions.

7.7.1 VIDEO IDENTIFICATION (ANNEX A)

- A set of video images including the suspect and at least eight others is shown to the witness;
- where there are two suspects of similar appearance, at least 12 images should be shown to the witness;
- the eight other people should resemble the suspect in age, height, general appearance and position in life and should show the suspect and the other people in the same position or carrying out the same sequence of movements;
- steps must be taken to conceal any distinguishing features the suspect may have;
- the suspect's solicitor must be offered the opportunity to attend the identification suite when the video parade is compiled and when the compilation is subsequently shown to the eye-witness;
- witnesses must not be allowed to communicate with each other;
- the suspect or the suspect's solicitor/appropriate adult must be given the opportunity to see the complete set of images before it is shown to any witnesses. If the suspect has reasonable objections to the set of images or any of the participants, steps shall, if practicable, be taken to remove the grounds for objection;
- the witness sees all the images at least twice and be told that the person they saw on the earlier occasion may or may not appear in the images shown;
- the witness is asked whether the suspect is the person seen on a previous occasion;
- a record must be made of procedures and those involved and, in the absence of the suspect's solicitor, the viewing of the parade by a witness shall be video-recorded.

7.7.2 IDENTIFICATION PARADE (ANNEX B)

- The parade should consist of at least eight people in addition to the suspect who as far as possible should resemble the suspect in terms of appearance, age, etc.;
- the suspect must be told that he may object to the arrangements or to a participant and that he may obtain legal advice;
- witnesses attending the parade must not be allowed to communicate with each other about the case or overhear a witness who has already made an identification;
- witnesses must not be allowed to see any participant in advance of the parade or see or be reminded of any photographs or description of the suspect or be given any indication as to the suspect's identity;
- the suspect may choose his own position in the line;
- each witness should be brought into the identification suite one at a time and be told that the person they saw on an earlier occasion may or may not be present and if they cannot make a positive identification, they should say so;
- video recording or colour photograph shall normally be made of the parade;
- where the identification officer is satisfied that the witness has properly looked at each member of the parade, the officer will ask the witness whether the person the witness saw on the earlier relevant occasion is on the identification parade and, if so, indicate the number of the person concerned;

- if the witness wishes to hear any identification parade member speak or adopt any specified posture or move, the witness will first be asked whether the witness can identify on the basis of appearance alone and will be reminded that the participants in the parade have been chosen on the basis of their appearance alone.

7.7.3 GROUP IDENTIFICATION (ANNEX C)

- May be held with or without the suspect's consent;
- the witness sees the suspect amongst a group of other people, for example shopping centre, railway station;
- the chosen location should take into account the number of people present, general appearance of people;
- a colour photo or video should be taken at the scene immediately after identification;
- the suspect's solicitor or friend can be present.

7.7.4 CONFRONTATION BY A WITNESS (ANNEX D)

- Before the confrontation takes place, the witness must be told that the person they saw at the crime scene may, or may not, be the person they are about to confront and that if the witness is unsure about the person's identity, the witness should say so;
- the confrontation must take place in the presence of the suspect's solicitor and/or interpreter and/or friend unless this would cause unreasonable delay;
- the witness is asked: 'Is this the person you saw on the earlier occasion?';
- force may not be used to make the suspect's face visible to the witness;
- the confrontation may either be through a one-way screen or face-to-face with the suspect;
- the confrontation will usually be held at the police station in a normal room or one equipped with a screen permitting a witness to see the suspect without being seen.

7.8 THE CONSEQUENCES OF FAILING TO COMPLY WITH CODE D

The safeguards provided by Code D are important. If the police obtain identification evidence in breach of the safeguards, the defence advocate can apply to have the evidence excluded under s. 78 PACE 1984. The court's discretion to exclude illegally or unfairly obtained evidence is considered in Chapter 6.

Breach of Code D does not inevitably lead to identification evidence being excluded. It is for the court to decide whether the admission of the evidence in these circumstances would have such an adverse effect on the fairness of the trial, that it ought to be excluded. Decisions on identification evidence turn largely on their own facts. The more blatant the breach, the better the prospects are for exclusion.

7.8.1 DIRECTING THE JURY WHERE THERE HAS BEEN A BREACH OF CODE D

The Court of Appeal in *R v Allen* [1995] Crim LR 643 makes it clear that a trial judge must explain to the jury why identification evidence is being admitted in breach of Code D. Guidance has also been provided by the House of Lords in *R v Forbes* [2001] 1 AC 473. Where there has been a breach of the requirement for the police to convene an identification parade or video parade, a trial judge must explain to the jury that the purpose of the parade is to enable a suspect to test the reliability of a witness's identification. In cases where an identification/video parade has not been held contrary to Code D, the suspect loses the benefit of the safeguard a parade gives him. The jury must be directed to take account of this when assessing the case against the defendant. Additionally, even where an informal identification is followed up by a properly conducted parade from which the defendant is chosen, a warning should still be given to the jury. The judge must explain that although the prosecution case is strengthened by the identification, the jury should be aware of the possible risk that the witness might have identified, not the culprit who committed the crime, but the suspect identified by the witness on the earlier occasion.

7.9 RECOGNITION BY POLICE OFFICERS FROM PHOTOGRAPHIC AND CCTV IMAGES

An increasingly common type of identification evidence is derived from either moving or still images captured on CCTV. Police officers are frequently asked to view CCTV records in the hope that they might pick out someone they know or recognise from past experience. In *R v Smith* [2008] EWCA 1342, the Court of Appeal held that Code D did not apply to this situation as the police officer reviewing CCTV footage is not in the same position as a witness asked to identify someone committing a crime. Whilst according to *R v Smith*, Code D had no formal application to this type of identification, safeguards should still be applied to ensure fairness to the defendant, including an independent, contemporaneous record of the police officer's reactions to the CCTV recording which enables a court to assess the reliability of the police officer's assertion.

Code D now provides for the situation described in *R v Smith*. A new Part B has been inserted which applies to police officers asked to review CCTV and other visual media to see if they recognise anyone in the images. Code D paras. 3.35–3.37 identify several key safeguards that should be deployed in this situation, including the requirement that films, photographs and other images must be shown to officers on an individual basis to avoid any possibility of collusion. The showing of photographs or images shall as far as possible follow the principles for video identification if the suspect is known (Annex A), or identification by photographs if the suspect is not known (Annex E). A record must also be kept of the precise circumstances of the viewing, including what was communicated to the officer beforehand about the possible identity of a person(s) in the visual media and the confidence with which an identification is made (see Code D para. 3.36 (a)–(k)).

7.10 VOICE IDENTIFICATION

Code D does not apply to voice identification. Voice identification is fraught with more dangers than visual identification, and requires special caution. For two cases in which the defendant was identified by voice identification, see *R v Roberts* [2000] Crim LR 183 and *R v Flynn* [2008] 2 Cr App R 20. Home Office guidance on the use of voice identification is available.

7.11 DOCK IDENTIFICATIONS

Dock identifications occur where the victim or another witness testify on oath that the accused standing in the dock is the person they saw at the crime scene. Dock identifications are rare because they have little probative value as the identification of the accused in these circumstances is virtually inevitable and therefore highly prejudicial. Exceptionally a dock identification might be used where the defendant has resisted all other pre-trial identification methods. Even where this occurs, to ensure fairness the defendant should be asked to take a seat in the courtroom as opposed to standing alone in the dock to be formally identified. The principles governing the use of dock identifications were restated in *Barnes v Chief Constable of Durham* [1997] 2 Cr App R 505 and *Karia v DPP* (2002) 166 JP 753.

7.12 **FORENSIC IDENTIFICATION PROCEDURES**

7.12.1 **FORENSIC EVIDENCE**

Forensic evidence found at the crime scene may provide compelling circumstantial evidence linking the defendant to the offence. Forensic evidence can be available in several forms. The defendant may have left fingerprints, a sample of handwriting, footprints, ear prints, a dental impression or DNA. DNA can be extracted from blood, semen stains, saliva, sweat or body hairs found at or near the crime scene or on the victim. Alternatively, specimens from the crime scene, such as fragments of glass, pollen or foliage, may be present on the suspect's clothing or footwear.

The forensic science service plays an important role in collecting and analysing forensic evidence. DNA is extracted from the crime scene sample and a profile is obtained. The profile is forensically compared to DNA profiles kept on the national database or to a suspect's known sample and an opinion is reached about the DNA's probable source. If the expert's opinion is accepted by the court it can provide very strong circumstantial evidence of the defendant's presence at the scene and his consequent involvement in the crime.

The police are able to assist the forensic investigation by exercising powers under PACE 1984 to obtain intimate and non-intimate body samples from suspects to enable forensic comparison with samples found at the crime scene.

The suspect is a very important source of evidence and as part of the criminal investigation the police may wish to obtain a set of fingerprints or a sample from a suspect for forensic comparison with evidence linked with the commission of the crime.

7.12.2 **FINGERPRINTS AND FOOTWEAR IMPRESSIONS**

The power to obtain fingerprints and footwear impressions is contained in ss. 61 and 61A PACE 1984 and Code D paras. 4.1–4.21. These powers can be exercised by a constable. The power to take fingerprints is very wide and can be exercised in the following circumstances:

- s. 61(2) PACE 1984—with the suspect's written consent at the police station.
- s. 61(3) PACE 1984—without the suspect's consent where—
  - the suspect has been arrested and detained in connection with a recordable offence; and
  - the suspect has not had his fingerprints taken in the course of the investigation taken or if he has, a complete set was not taken or some or all of the fingerprints taken have proved unsuitable or of insufficient quality to allow satisfactory analysis, comparison, or matching.
- s. 61(4) PACE 1984—without consent where—
  - the detained person has been charged with or informed that he will be prosecuted for a recordable offence; and
  - he has not had his fingerprints taken in the course of the investigation; or
  - if he has, a complete set was not taken or some or all of the fingerprints taken have proved unsuitable or of insufficient quality to allow satisfactory analysis, comparison, or matching.
- s. 61(6) PACE 1984—from a person who has been convicted, cautioned, warned or reprimanded for a recordable offence if—
  - since their conviction, caution, warning or reprimand their fingerprints have not been taken; or
  - their fingerprints which have been taken since then do not constitute a complete set; or
  - some, or all, of the fingerprints are not of sufficient quality to allow satisfactory analysis, comparison or matching; and

– in either case, an officer of inspector rank or above is satisfied that taking the fingerprints is necessary to assist in the prevention or detection of crime and authorises the taking.

Section 61(6A) PACE 1984 allows a constable to take a person's fingerprints without consent prior to an arrest and away from the police station where:

- the officer reasonably suspects that the person is committing or attempting to commit an offence or has committed or has attempted to commit an offence; and

- the name of the person is unknown and cannot be readily ascertained by the officer; or

- the officer has reasonable grounds for doubting whether a name furnished by the person is that person's real name.

The power to take fingerprints other than at a police station using s. 61(6A) PACE 1984 is tied to the development and use of mobile digital fingerprint readers connected to the National Automated Fingerprint Identification System (NAFIS) by mobile communications technology and means the police can verify a person's identity at the crime scene in accordance with s. 61(6A) PACE 1984.

As with intimate and non-intimate samples (see below), fingerprint and footwear impressions may be used for a speculative search against forensic databases and the suspect should be warned of this fact.

7.12.3 NON-INTIMATE SAMPLE

A non-intimate sample is defined in s. 65 PACE 1984 to include a sample of hair other than pubic hair, a scraping from under a nail, a swab taken from a part of the body that would not qualify as an intimate sample, i.e. the mouth, a footprint, or bodily impression. Code D para. 6.5 provides that a non-intimate sample may be taken with consent under s. 63(2) PACE 1984 or, where consent is withheld, under the circumstances provided for by s. 63 PACE 1984. A non-intimate sample to be taken in the following circumstances:

- s. 63(2A) PACE 1984—where the suspect has been arrested and detained in connection with a recordable offence and no such sample has yet been taken or, if it has, it has proved unsuitable or insufficient. The power also covers a suspect who has been arrested but released on bail;

- s. 63(3A) PACE 1984—where the suspect has been charged with a recordable offence (whether in police custody or not) and no such sample has yet been taken or, if it has, it has proved unsuitable or insufficient;

- s. 63(3B) PACE 1984—following a conviction, caution, reprimand or warning if, since their conviction, caution, warning or reprimand, a non-intimate sample has not been taken from them or a sample which has been taken since then has proved to be unsuitable or insufficient and, in either case, an officer of inspector rank or above is satisfied that taking the fingerprints is necessary to assist in the prevention or detection of crime and authorises the taking.

7.12.4 INTIMATE SAMPLE

An intimate sample (also defined in s. 65 PACE 1984) includes a dental impression or a sample of blood, tissue fluid, urine, pubic hair or swabs taken from a person's genitals or body orifice other than the mouth. The taking of an intimate sample is also governed by Code D paras. 6.2–6.4.

Two important conditions apply before an intimate sample may be lawfully taken. First, the sample may only be taken when authorised by a police officer of at least the rank of inspector who has reasonable grounds for suspecting the person to be involved in a recordable offence and that the sample would confirm or disprove the suspect's involvement. Second, under s. 62(4) PACE 1984, the suspect's written consent must be obtained and the sample (other than urine) must be taken by a registered health-care professional or dentist. The failure to consent to provide an intimate sample without good reason can be used in evidence against the defendant at trial (s. 62(10) PACE 1984).

Evidence from samples obtained unlawfully remains admissible subject to the court's exclusionary discretion at common law and under s. 78 PACE 1984 (see Chapter 6).

7.13 DNA EVIDENCE

The UK has one of the most comprehensive DNA databases in the world. The forensic techniques involved in extracting an individual DNA profile and comparing it with other DNA samples have attracted considerable attention from scientists, lawyers and the media. The techniques, which were developed in the late 1980s, have grown increasingly sophisticated and reliable which has resulted in DNA evidence providing potentially compelling evidence. Every human being has a unique DNA make-up (apart from an identical twin). The profiling techniques enable a forensic scientist to compare two biological samples and to determine the likelihood that the two samples originated from the same source. DNA evidence is perceived as being particularly cogent evidence because of the statistical improbabilities that profiling produces. The process of extraction, extrapolation, interpretation and presentation of results is explained by Lord Justice Phillips in *R v Doheny* [1997] 1 Cr App R 369.

R v Doheny establishes the procedure the prosecution should follow in respect to the disclosure and presentation of DNA evidence. The defence may call their own expert witness to challenge the validity of the opinion provided by the prosecution's expert witness. Issues of sample degeneration, cross-contamination and deliberate planting of samples by prosecuting authorities can significantly diminish the probative value of the DNA evidence. Indeed, there may be a perfectly innocent explanation to account for a defendant's DNA being found at the crime scene. The ultimate evaluation of DNA evidence, as with other forensic opinion evidence, is a matter for the jury or magistrates. DNA technology today is approaching individualisation. When odds against a random match of one in 60 billion are quoted, DNA evidence all but positively identifies the person whose profile matches the crime stain obtained by the police.

For a recent illustration of the approach taken by the courts to the admission of evidence based on DNA profiling in the light of improved techniques of forensic analysis, please read the case of *R v FNC* [2015] EWCA Crim 1732.

7.13.1 RETAINING FORENSIC SAMPLES

The retention and use of a suspect's fingerprint/footwear impression and DNA samples has long been a controversial practice. Until the European Court of Human Rights (ECtHR) decision in *S and Marper v UK* [2008] ECHR 1581, s. 64 PACE 1984 (as amended) permitted the indefinite retention of DNA material even when taken from a suspect who was later acquitted or from someone who was never the subject of criminal proceedings. In *S and Marper* the ECtHR ruled that this practice constituted a disproportionate interference with the applicants' right to privacy under Article 8.

As a response to the *S and Marper* decision, the Protection of Freedoms Act 2012 amended the relevant provisions of PACE 1984 by creating a new statutory framework for dealing with the retention and use of fingerprints and DNA profiles in the following ways. A helpful summary of the key provisions can be found at https://www.gov.uk/government/publications/protection-of-freedoms-act-2012-dna-and-finger-print-provisions/protection-of-freedoms-act-2012-how-dna-and-fingerprint-evidence-is-protected-in-law.

7.14 FACIAL MAPPING

Evidence about a defendant's involvement can be provided by other expert testimony including experts in facial mapping techniques, 'walking gait analysis' (see *Otway* [2011] EWCA Crim 3) and voice recognition experts. The admissibility of expert opinion evidence is considered in Chapter 17. Facial mapping might be required in a case where still photographs or a video image have been taken of the suspect and a comparison with the suspect is available. Experts in photographic technologies and anatomical features can enhance picture quality and offer an opinion as to the likelihood of the defendant and the person pictured being one and the same. In *R v Clare and Peach* [1995] 2 Cr App R 333, a police officer who had viewed a video recording some 40 times with lengthy and studious consideration was permitted to give evidence on whether persons shown on the recording committing acts of violent disturbance inside a football ground were the accused.

7.15 THE PRACTICAL ISSUES ASSOCIATED WITH IDENTIFICATION EVIDENCE

Identification evidence, whether based on eye-witness testimony or obtained through forensic procedures, is a significant evidential component in many cases and most commonly tendered as part of the prosecution's case.

The prosecutor is aware that, provided the proper procedures were complied with during the investigation of the offence, identification evidence has high evidential value in proving the case against the defendant. Identification obtained through forensic procedures usually requires the prosecutor to work closely with an expert witness. As noted at para. 7.12.1, provided there is no contamination of the forensic samples and the legal grounds for obtaining the evidence were correctly applied, forensic evidence found at the crime scene can provide compelling circumstantial evidence linking the defendant to the offence.

For the prosecutor, provided the proper procedures under Code D were followed, eye-witness identification evidence has considerable probative value. The investigating officer's decision whether to convene an identification procedure requires careful consideration and may be a significant factor in the Crown Prosecutor's assessment of the reliability of the prosecution evidence in deciding whether the evidential test is satisfied under the Code for Crown Prosecutors (see Chapter 8, para. 8.2.5). Such important decisions illustrate the practical advantages of the close working relationship between the police and the Crown Prosecution Service (CPS) under the statutory charging scheme (see Chapter 8, para. 8.2), as a CPS lawyer either in person or by telephone through CPS Direct is available to advise the police on the practical evidential issues that arise during the police investigation. Finally, where the eye-witness identification is likely to be challenged at trial by the defence, the prosecutor must closely examine the circumstances in which the prosecution witness purported to have identified the accused at the crime scene to ensure the identification will satisfy the *Turnbull* guidelines (see Chapter 17, para. 17.6).

Just as prosecutors appreciate the potential probative value of identification evidence, defence lawyers are aware that identification evidence can be a weak link in a prosecution case where the proper procedures under Code D were not followed. The practical aspects of identification procedures are considered further in our additional chapter 'Advising at the Police Station—Practical Steps' available in the online resources.

KEY POINT SUMMARY

- Eye-witness identification is of huge practical importance in an investigation but is notoriously unreliable.

- To effectively advise on police procedures governing identification evidence, both the defence legal adviser and the duty prosecutor must have a thorough working knowledge of Code D and its Annexes.

- A failure by a suspect to cooperate in the conduct of an identification procedure or to provide an intimate sample can lead to adverse evidential inferences being drawn.

- Know the key safeguards which apply to the main identification procedures such as the video parade.

- Know when it is permissible to show photographs to an eye-witness in advance of a formal identification procedure and what safeguards apply in this regard.

- Understand that the admissibility of identification evidence obtained in breach of Code D is vulnerable to challenge under s. 78 PACE 1984, but that breach does not mean such exclusion will be automatic.

- Know when the police are justified in obtaining a sample from a suspect under ss. 61–63 PACE 1984.

SELF-TEST QUESTIONS

Consider our case study *R v Lenny Wise*.

You will recall Lenny has been charged in connection with a burglary at the home of an old-age pensioner. His defence is one of complete denial; however, he is linked to the crime by, *inter alia*, eye-witness identification. In discharging its legal burden of proof beyond reasonable doubt, the prosecution will be relying on evidence of identification in this case.

1. Assess the strength of the identification evidence against Lenny.

2. Consider how the evidence of identification in this case has actually materialised.

3. Can you point to any specific breaches of Code D in relation to the manner in which the evidence has been obtained and which would, in your view, enable the trial advocate to apply to have the evidence excluded under s. 78 PACE 1984 in the interests of ensuring a fair trial?

 An analysis of the self-test questions can be found in the online resources.

FIGURE 7.1 OBTAINING EVIDENCE OF IDENTIFICATION

Pre-trial safeguards under Code D—their purpose

- To ensure the quality and reliability of eye-witness identification, the detail of which can be found through:
  - video parade Annex A;
  - identification parade Annex B;
  - group parade Annex C;
  - confrontation Annex D;
  - showing photographs Annex E.

When can an eye-witness be shown photographs?

- When there is no known and available suspect in mind (Code D para. 3.3).

When must an identification procedure be convened?

- Where the suspect disputes being the person the witness claims to have seen, an identification procedure should be held unless:
  - it is not practicable; or
  - it would serve no useful purpose in proving or disproving the suspect was involved in the offence, Code D para. 3.12.

CHALLENGING THE ADMISSIBILITY OF EYE-WITNESS IDENTIFICATION

- Use s. 78 PACE 1984 on the basis that the admission of such evidence would have an adverse effect on the fairness of the proceedings.
- Relevant factors would be proven breaches of Code D, including:
  - failure to convene an identification procedure;
  - failure to properly record an identification procedure;
  - failure to disguise a prominent feature in the suspect's appearance;
  - allowing eye-witnesses contact with one another before a parade;
  - use of photographs in a case where the suspect was known;
  - a failure to properly conduct an identification procedure—see annexes to Code D;
  - failure to secure access to legal advice beforehand.

8 THE DECISION TO PROSECUTE AND THE PROSECUTION'S DUTIES OF DISCLOSURE OF EVIDENCE

8.1	**Introduction**	**129**
8.2	**Statutory charging under the CJA 2003**	**130**
	8.2.1 Offences where the police can charge the suspect	130
	8.2.2 The responsibility of the CPS to charge	131
	8.2.3 Charging decisions taken by the police	131
	8.2.4 Charging decisions taken by the Crown Prosecution Service	132
	8.2.5 The Full Code Test—section 4, Code for Crown Prosecutors	133
8.3	**CPS prosecuting policies**	**135**
8.4	**The threshold test**	**136**
8.5	**The selection of charges—section 6, Code for Crown Prosecutors**	**137**
8.6	**Alternatives to prosecution**	**138**
	8.6.1 Simple caution	138
	8.6.2 Conditional caution (CPS Code section 7)	139
	8.6.3 Conditions that can be attached	140
	8.6.4 Failing to comply with the conditional caution	140
8.7	**The defence solicitor influencing the decision to charge**	**140**
8.8	**Pre-trial disclosure of evidence—an introduction**	**141**
8.9	**Used and unused material**	**143**
8.10	**Disclosure obligations on the police**	**143**
	8.10.1 Keeping track of investigative material	143
	8.10.2 Disclosure schedules	144
8.11	**The CPS obligation to disclose 'used' material—'IDPC'** **(Initial Details of the Prosecution Case)**	**145**
	8.11.1 When must the CPS comply with Crim PR, Part 8?	145
	8.11.2 Initial disclosure of the prosecution case in indictable-only cases	146
8.12	**CPS obligations to disclose unused material (Crim PR, Part 15)**	**146**
	8.12.1 The specific disclosure duties on the CPS under the CPIA 1996	146
	8.12.2 Initial disclosure of unused material—s. 3 CPIA 1996	147
	8.12.3 Initial disclosure of unused material—time limits	147
	8.12.4 Defence disclosure	148
	8.12.5 Prosecutor's continuing duty	148
8.13	**Disclosing information held by third parties**	**148**
8.14	**Withholding relevant evidence**	**148**
8.15	**Further information on disclosure**	**149**

8.1 **INTRODUCTION**

CPS Press Release 14 February 2019

The Crown Prosecution Service has decided that no further action should be taken against a driver involved in a collision on the A149 at Sandringham.

Chris Long, Chief Crown Prosecutor for CPS East of England, said: 'The CPS has carefully reviewed material submitted by the police in relation to a traffic collision on the A149 on 17 January this year.'

'We took into account all of the circumstances in this case, including the level of culpability, the age of the driver and the surrender of the driving licence.'

'We have decided that it would not be in the public interest to prosecute.'

'All those involved in the collision have been informed and provided with a full explanation in writing.'

The decision was made after considering all the evidence submitted by the police and in accordance with the two stage test in the Code for Crown Prosecutors.

Any decision by the CPS does not imply any finding concerning guilt or criminal conduct; the CPS makes decisions only according to the test set out in the Code for Crown Prosecutors and it is applied in all decisions on whether or not to prosecute.

It is not the function of the CPS to decide whether a person is guilty of a criminal offence, but to make fair, independent and objective assessments about whether it is appropriate to present charges for the criminal court to consider. The CPS assessment of any case is not in any sense a finding of, or implication of, any guilt or criminal conduct. It is not a finding of fact, which can only be made by a court, but rather an assessment of what it might be possible to prove to a court, in accordance with the Code for Crown Prosecutors.

This assessment is based on the evidence available arising out of the police investigation and not on the evidence that is likely to be gathered by the defence, and likely to be used to test the prosecution evidence. The CPS charging decision is therefore necessarily an assessment on the basis of the evidence that is available to the CPS at the time the decision is made.

If the CPS finds that a case passes the evidential test, it then assesses public interest. This is based on a variety of factors, including the level of culpability, the harm done, the age of the suspect and whether a prosecution is a proportionate response in the circumstances. For a prosecution to take place, prosecutors must be satisfied that that the public interest is best served by a prosecution.

CPS prosecutors must also keep every case under review, so that they take account of any change in circumstances that occurs as the case develops, including what becomes known of the defence case. If appropriate, the CPS may change the charges or stop a case.

This chapter is divided into two parts. The first part explains the role of the Crown Prosecution Service (CPS) and the factors that are taken into account when deciding to charge a suspect or to divert him from prosecution. The second part of the chapter examines the very important obligations which are placed upon the CPS both at common law and under statute to serve pre-trial disclosure of evidence upon the defendant.

The CPS was set up in 1986 and is the main body which prosecutes criminal cases investigated by the police in England and Wales.

In 2009, the CPS published a Statement of Ethical Principles for the Public Prosecutor. The Statement can be accessed at https://www.cps.gov.uk/legal-guidance/ethical-principles-public-prosecutor-statement.

The principles require prosecutors to:

- act in accordance with the law in England and Wales in a way that is compatible with the Human Rights Act 1998;

- prepare and conduct cases in accordance with the Criminal Procedure Rules;

- at all times abide by the Code for Crown Prosecutors; and

- uphold the Code of Conduct set by professional regulators including the Solicitors Regulation Authority.

The statement sets out the professional conduct requirements generally expected of public prosecutors, which include the requirement for a prosecutor to be independent, fair and impartial. It further identifies specific professional conduct duties in the context of criminal proceedings. Most importantly, it reminds all public prosecutors of their 'duty to the court in question to act with independence in the interests of justice'. An important aspect of this duty is the requirement to endeavour to ensure that evidence which is favourable to the defendant or which undermines the prosecution case is disclosed as soon as reasonably practicable in accordance with the law.

Underpinning every charging decision is the Code for Crown Prosecutors. The most recent version of the Code came into force on 26 October 2018 and can be accessed via through the CPS website at https://www.cps.gov.uk/publication/code-crown-prosecutors.

For the suspect to be charged, the two elements of the Full Code Test must be satisfied. The Crown Prosecutor (or the police where they can charge) must be satisfied that:

- there is sufficient evidence to provide for a realistic prospect of conviction; and
- that it is in the public interest to prosecute.

8.2 STATUTORY CHARGING UNDER THE CJA 2003

Under the statutory charging procedure introduced by the Criminal Justice Act 2003 (CJA 2003) the decision to charge a suspect with a criminal offence rests, for the most part, with the CPS, although the police retain the right to charge in a range of circumstances outlined at para. 8.2.1. However mundane or high profile an investigation might be, the decision to charge is reached in each case by the CPS lawyer/police applying the Full Code Test under the Code for Crown Prosecutors to the evidence gathered as part of the investigative process. As the CPS press release at the outset of this chapter shows, a decision not to charge needs as much justification as a decision to charge. The driver concerned was the Duke of Edinburgh.

In a straightforward case, the suspect may be charged within a few hours after the commission of the alleged offence. The investigation of a more serious offence may take several days or weeks or even months. The CPS Victims' Right of Review Scheme (http://www.cps.gov.uk/legal-guidance/victims-right-review-scheme) gives victims a right to seek a review of a CPS decision not to prosecute or to discontinue or otherwise terminate all proceedings.

As part of statutory charging, the police liaise with their local CPS counterparts who provide charging advice based on the available evidence. Out-of-hours and weekend access to the CPS is provided by prosecuting lawyers who work from home for CPS Direct, which provides a telephone and IT-based service to the police.

Important guidance on the operation of the statutory charging scheme can be found in a CPS document entitled Director's Guide on Charging: Guidance to Police Officers and Crown Prosecutors issued by the Director of Public Prosecutions under s. 37A PACE 1984 (5th edn, May 2013). The guidance is accessible via the web-link section of our online resources and at https://www.cps.gov.uk/legal-guidance/charging-directors-guidance-2013-fifth-edition-may-2013-revised-arrangements.

8.2.1 OFFENCES WHERE THE POLICE CAN CHARGE THE SUSPECT

Under the Director of Public Prosecution's (DPP) Guidance on Charging (2013), the police may charge the suspect with any summary-only offence including an offence of criminal damage where the value of the damage or loss is less than £5,000 irrespective of anticipated plea; any offence of retail theft (shoplifting) or attempted retail theft irrespective of plea provided it is suitable for sentence in the magistrates' court; and any either-way offence anticipated as a guilty plea and suitable for sentence in a magistrates' court, provided it is not:

- a case requiring the DPP's consent to prosecute;
- a case involving a death;
- connected with terrorist activity or official secrets;
- classified as hate crime or domestic violence under CPS policies;
- an offence of violent disorder or affray;
- causing grievous bodily harm or wounding, or actual bodily harm;
- an offence committed under the Sexual Offences Act 2003 by or upon a person under 18;
- an offence under the Licensing Act 2003.

In any case where the custody officer is uncertain about whether the police or the CPS should charge, the duty prosecutor should be consulted.

8.2.2 THE RESPONSIBILITY OF THE CPS TO CHARGE

Except for the situations outlined at para. 8.2.1, where the police may decide to charge or divert from prosecution, the Crown Prosecutor must decide the charge in every other case including indictable-only offences and either-way offences not suitable for sentence in a magistrates' court or not anticipated as a guilty plea.

The DPP's guidance provides that a *guilty plea is anticipated* where either:

- the suspect has made a clear and unambiguous admission to the offence and has said nothing that could be used as a defence; or
- the suspect has made no admission but has not denied the offence or otherwise indicated it will be contested and the commission of the offence and identification of the offender can be established by reliable evidence or the suspect can be seen clearly committing the offence on a good quality visual recording.

A case may be considered suitable for sentence in a magistrates' court unless:

- the loss or damage relating to the charge is more than £5,000 or would exceed that sum if more than one offence is charged (or taken into consideration); or
- the overall circumstances of the offence are so serious that the court may decide that a sentence of more than six months' imprisonment justifies sending the case to the Crown Court; or
- the offence has been committed whilst the suspect was subject to a Crown Court order then in force.

8.2.3 CHARGING DECISIONS TAKEN BY THE POLICE

In deciding whether to charge, the custody officer applies the Full Code Test to the alleged offence. For a charge to be laid, the Full Code Test, which is found in section 4 of the Code for Crown Prosecutors (see para. 8.2.5), requires the custody officer to be satisfied that, first, 'there is sufficient evidence to achieve a realistic prospect of a conviction' and, second, that 'it is in the public interest for the suspect to be charged'. If both elements are satisfied the suspect can be charged.

After charge, the police pass the case file to the Crown Prosecutor, who, under section 4 of the Code for Crown Prosecutors, is under a duty to review the file to confirm that the defendant has been charged with the correct offence and that the evidential and public interest criteria under the Full Code Test are satisfied (s. 10 Prosecution of Offences Act 1985).

In practice the police make the charging decision in up to 80% of all cases although this figure is made up of a high volume of less serious offences. The CPS continue to be responsible for the charging decision in the most serious and complex cases.

Police-led prosecutions

There are also a limited number of cases where the police will prosecute the offence in court rather than the CPS. The prosecution of these offences are known as 'specified proceedings'. This new initiative is presently being tested in nine police areas. A key requirement for a prosecution to be a 'specified proceeding' is that the defendant pleads guilty to one of the offences listed below:

- criminal damage where the value of the property involved is no more than £5,000 (not including arson);
- shoplifting where the value of the stolen goods is worth £200 or less;
- careless or inconsiderate driving;
- failing to comply with a traffic direction;
- failing to stop, report an accident or give information or documents;
- consumption of alcohol in a designated public place;
- disorderly behaviour while drunk in a public place;
- being drunk in a highway, other public place or licensed premises;
- failing to give a sample for the purposes of testing for the presence of Class A drugs;
- failing to attend an assessment following testing for the presence of Class A drugs;
- trespassing or throwing stones on the railway;
- knowingly giving a false alarm of fire;
- behaviour likely to cause harassment, alarm or distress;
- contravention of a prohibition or failure to comply with a requirement imposed by or under fireworks regulations or making false statements;
- depositing and leaving litter.

The CPS continues to prosecute those offences where:

- the defendant pleads not guilty; or
- the defendant is under the age of 16; or
- the case commenced by the defendant being charged by a custody officer at a police station.

8.2.4 CHARGING DECISIONS TAKEN BY THE CROWN PROSECUTION SERVICE

Early advice about the charge at the police station enables the prosecutor to determine whether a simple or conditional caution (or a youth caution or a youth conditional caution for a young offender) can be offered as an alternative to prosecution or, if not, what the appropriate charge should be (see s. 3 of the Code for Crown Prosecutors). It is the prosecuting lawyer's duty to advise the investigating police officer about the evidence and what, if any charge, the evidence supports and whether further evidence is required. Whilst it is for the police to conduct an investigation, s.3.2 of the Code states prosecutors should advise the police and other investigators about possible reasonable lines of inquiry, evidential requirements, pre-charge procedures, disclosure management, and the overall investigation strategy. Section 3.3 of the Code further provides that whilst Prosecutors cannot direct the police or other investigators they must have regard to the impact of any failure to pursue an advised reasonable line of inquiry or to comply with a request for information, when deciding whether the application of the Full Code Test should be deferred or whether the test can be met at all.

Prosecutors must review every case they receive from the police or from other investigators. The review is a continuing process and prosecutors must take account of any change in circumstances that occur as the case develops (see s.3.6 of the Code).

In many cases where the Crown Prosecutor decides to charge, the suspect will previously have been released on bail under s. 37B Police and Criminal Evidence Act 1984 (PACE 1984). Under s. 37(7)(a) PACE 1984, conditions may be attached to bail pending a decision whether to charge (see Chapter 4, para. 4.14).

After the suspect has been bailed, an officer involved in the investigation of the offence will refer the case file (known as MG3 'Report to Crown Prosecutor for a Charging Decision') to the Crown Prosecutor for a decision.

In deciding whether to charge, the Crown Prosecutor will apply the Full Code Test to decide whether the evidence discloses a realistic prospect of a conviction and if it is in the public interest for the suspect to be charged.

After applying the Full Code Test, the Crown Prosecutor will give the investigating officer written notice of his decision (s. 37B(4) PACE 1984). If the prosecutor decides that no charges shall be laid and no caution offered, the decision not to prosecute must be communicated in writing to the suspect by the custody officer (s. 37B(5) PACE 1984).

8.2.5 THE FULL CODE TEST—SECTION 4, CODE FOR CROWN PROSECUTORS

For the suspect to be charged, the two elements of the Full Code Test must be satisfied. The custody officer or the Crown Prosecutor must be satisfied that:

- there is sufficient evidence to provide for a realistic prospect of conviction; and

- that it is in the public interest to prosecute.

The Code is the basis for the prosecutor's work (and for the police when making charging decisions) to ensure that fair and consistent decisions are made about commencing and continuing with a prosecution. The most recent version of the Code came into force on 26 October 2018 and can be accessed via through the CPS website at https://www.cps.gov.uk/publication/code-crown-prosecutors.

Section 2.1 of the Code reaffirms the independence of the prosecutor as a central principle of the criminal justice system in a democratic society and s.2.10 states that prosecutors must apply the principles of the European Convention on Human Rights, in accordance with the Human Rights Act 1998, at each stage of a case.

In deciding whether to charge and what the appropriate charge should be, the Code will also be used in conjunction with other official documents including the DPP's Guidance on Charging (see para. 8.2) and any applicable prosecuting policies (see CPS website). A defence lawyer should have a good working knowledge of the Code and understand the way in which the local Crown Prosecutors and supporting staff apply its provisions. The CPS has an extremely informative website at http://www.cps.gov.uk/.

What is the evidential stage? (Code sections 4.6–4.8)

The evidence in the case should provide a realistic prospect of conviction against each suspect on each charge.

The prosecutor must consider what the defence case may be, and how it is likely to affect the prospects of a conviction. A case that does not pass the evidential stage must not proceed, no matter how serious or sensitive it may be.

The finding that there is a realistic prospect of conviction is based on the prosecutor's objective assessment of the evidence, including the impact of any defence, and any other information that the suspect puts forward or on which they might rely. It means that an objective, impartial and reasonable jury or bench of magistrates or judge hearing the case alone, properly directed and acting in accordance with the law, is more likely than not to convict the defendant of the charge alleged.

When deciding whether there is sufficient evidence to prosecute, prosecutors should ask themselves: 'Can the evidence be used in court?' Prosecutors should consider whether there is any question over the admissibility of certain evidence including the importance of that evidence in relation to the evidence as a whole.

'Is the evidence reliable?' This includes considering the accuracy and integrity of the evidence.

'Is the evidence credible?' Whether there are any reasons to doubt the credibility of the evidence.

'Is there any other material that might affect the sufficiency of the evidence?' Any examined and unexamined material in the possession of the police and any material that might be obtained through further reasonable lines of enquiry by the police must also be considered by the prosecutor. Based on these factors, if the evidential stage is satisfied, the prosecutor will then apply the factors under the 'public interest' stage.

The 'public interest' stage (Code sections 4.9–4.14)

In every case where there is sufficient evidence to justify a prosecution or to offer an out-of-court disposal, prosecutors must consider whether a prosecution is required in the public interest. It has never been the rule that a prosecution will automatically take place once the evidential stage is met. In some cases the prosecutor may be satisfied that the public interest can be properly served by offering the offender the opportunity to have the matter dealt with by an out-of-court disposal rather than being prosecuted.

When deciding the public interest, the prosecutor should consider each of the questions set out in s.4.14 (a)–(g) of the Code. These questions include:

(a) **How serious is the offence committed?** The more serious the offence, the more likely it is that a prosecution is required. When assessing the seriousness of an offence, the prosecutor should include in their consideration the suspect's culpability and the harm caused as identified at paragraphs (b) and (c) below.

(b) **What is the level of the suspect's culpability?** The greater the suspect's level of culpability, the more likely it is that a prosecution is required. Culpability is likely to be determined by the suspect's level of involvement, the extent to which the offending was premeditated or planned or whether the defendant has previous criminal convictions or out-of-court disposals or was on bail or subject to a court order at the time of the offence. Other factors include whether the offending was or is likely to be continued, repeated or escalated; the suspect's age and maturity. There is likely to be a lower level of culpability where the suspect was compelled, coerced, or exploited, particularly if he or she is the victim of crime that is linked to their offending. Prosecutors should also have regard to whether the suspect is or was at the time of the offence affected by any significant mental or physical illness or disability. In some circumstances this may make it less likely that a prosecution is required. However, prosecutors will also need to consider how serious the offence was, whether the suspect is likely to reoffend and the need to safeguard the public or those providing care to the public.

(c) **What were the circumstances of and the harm caused to the victim?** The circumstances of the victim are highly relevant. The greater the victim's vulnerability, the more likely it is that a prosecution is required. This includes where a position of trust or authority exists between the suspect and the victim or where the offences have been committed against a person who was at the time serving the public. A prosecution is also more likely if the offences are motivated by prejudice against a victim's ethnic or national origin, gender, disability, age, religion or belief, sexual orientation or gender identity etc. Prosecutors should also take into account the views expressed by the victim about the impact of the offences have had, including where appropriate, the views of the victim's family.

(d) **The suspect's age and maturity at the time of the offence is also a significant factor.** As the criminal justice system treats children and young people differently from adults, significant weight must be attached to the suspect's age if he or she is a child or a young person under 18. (See Chapter 24, para. 24.9 below for further guidance on this point). The interests and welfare of the child or young person must be considered including whether a prosecution is likely to have an adverse impact on their future prospects that is disproportionate to the seriousness of the offending. Regard must also be had to the principal aim of the youth justice system, which is to prevent offending by children and young people and to the UK's obligations arising under the United Nations 1989 Convention on the Rights of the Child. Prosecutors should also consider the suspect's maturity, as well as his or her chronological age, as young adults will continue to mature into their mid-20s. Although the younger the suspect, the less likely it is that a prosecution is required, even where the suspect is under 18 or lacks maturity, a prosecution is in the public interest where the offence committed is serious or the suspect's past record suggests there are no suitable alternative to prosecution or the absence of an admission means that out-of-court disposals are not available.

(e) **What is the impact on the community?** The greater the impact of the offending on the community, the more likely it is that a prosecution is required. The prevalence of an offence in a community may cause particular harm to that community, increasing the seriousness of the offending. A community is not restricted to communities defined by location and may relate to a group of people who share certain characteristics, experiences, or backgrounds such as an occupational group. Evidence of impact on the community may be obtained by a Community Impact Statement.

(f) **Is prosecution a proportionate response?** The prosecutor should also consider whether prosecution is proportionate to the likely outcome in the case by taking into account the cost to the CPS and the wider criminal justice system of any prosecution weighed against any likely penalty. A further consideration is whether the case can be prosecuted in accordance with the principles of effective case management. For example, in a case involving multiple suspects, a prosecution might be reserved for the main participants only to avoid excessively long and complex proceedings.

(g) **Do sources of information require protecting?** Special care should be taken when proceeding with a prosecution where information may be disclosed that could harm an ongoing criminal investigation(s), the UK's international relations, national security, or confidential sources of information. Where these factors are relevant it is essential that cases are kept under continuing review.

8.3 CPS PROSECUTING POLICIES

In addition to the Code for Crown Prosecutors, the CPS has published policies for prosecuting certain types of offences, including, for example, offences of domestic abuse. The policy document explains that while there is no statutory offence of domestic abuse, the term is used to describe a range of behaviour often used by one person to control and dominate another, with whom there is or has been a close or family relationship. An offence involving domestic abuse may arise out of the physical, sexual, psychological, emotional or financial abuse by one person against another. While most abuse is perpetrated by a male family member on a female, the policy recognises that abuse can also be inflicted on victims in same-sex relationships or the victims of abusive family members. The policy also recognises that members of certain minority ethnic groups, the disabled, lesbians and gay men may be reluctant to report abuse. Other factors which may prevent the reporting of domestic violence are religious, cultural or language barriers.

In June 2014 the then DPP, Alison Saunders, in conjunction with the Metropolitan Police published a new national rape action plan which contained a clear commitment to address the issues which commonly prevent rape cases from successfully progressing through the criminal justice system. Included in the action plan are steps to ensure the better application by the police, the CPS and the courts of the current law on consent and the requirement that the police and prosecutors should investigate more fully the steps taken by a suspect to ensure that the victim was consenting where consent is an issue in the case. New draft guidance to prosecutors on dealing with defendants with mental health disorder has recently been published and is subject to a public consultation period (https://www.cps.gov.uk/cps/news/new-guidance-prosecutors-mental-health-conditions-and-disorders).

The CPS works closely with other criminal justice agencies such as the police, Victim Support and Refuge. In deciding whether to prosecute, the safety of the victim, any children in the case and any other person involved are given priority—although in more serious cases a prosecution may continue even where the victim has requested that no further action should be taken against the alleged perpetrator. In deciding whether a domestic violence case should be prosecuted or continue, the CPS will again apply the 'public interest' and the 'evidential' tests to the facts of the particular case.

The CPS has prosecution policies on a wide range of offences including; assisted suicide, benefit fraud, and bribery. The CPS website also includes extensive legal guidance on a very wide range of criminal offences and criminal procedure as well as charging standards for a number of criminal offences.

An important recent example of CPS prosecuting policy is in relation to cases of human trafficking. The policy can be accessed at http://www.cps.gov.uk/publications/docs/policy_for_prosecuting_cases_of_human_trafficking.pdf. Human trafficking offences are increasingly becoming part of the caseload of both CPS prosecutors and defence solicitors.

UK domestic law is based on the European Directive on Preventing and Combating Trafficking in Human Beings and Protecting its Victims (2011/36/EU) which stated that human trafficking victims should not face prosecution or punishment for criminal activities, such as the use of false documents, cultivation of cannabis and importation of drugs, dishonesty offences, prostitution, and immigration offences that they have been compelled to commit as a direct consequence of being subject to trafficking. The Modern Slavery Act 2015 now creates defences for victims of slavery or trafficking victims who commit offences.

Defence representatives are likely to encounter suspects and defendants who may in fact be the victims of human trafficking, who are suspected or charged with offences listed above.

The Law Society has revised its Practice Note on this area and is essential reading for all criminal law practitioners. The Practice Note (which we assume will continue to apply when the 2019 Solicitors Code of Conduct is brought into force) is directly relevant to Principle 7, the duty to 'act in the best interests of each client'. The Practice Note outlines the duty of all practitioners (defence and prosecution) to enquire and, if necessary, investigate further any claim that an individual is a victim of trafficking. The Practice Note can be read at https://www.lawsociety.org.uk/support-services/advice/practice-notes/criminal-prosecutions-of-victims-of-trafficking/.

8.4 **THE THRESHOLD TEST**

As noted at para. 8.2.4, in many cases, the suspect may be bailed under s. 37(7)(a) PACE 1984 to allow the Crown Prosecutor to make a charging decision. However, there will be a limited number of cases where there are substantial grounds for the prosecution to object to the suspect being granted bail and the seriousness and circumstances of the case justifies an immediate charging decision. In these circumstances and where all of the five conditions outlined below are met, the suspect may be charged under the Threshold Test (ss. 5.1 and 5.2 of the Code).

The conditions to be applied by the prosecutor are as follows:

First condition—there are reasonable grounds to suspect that the person to be charged has committed the offence.

Prosecutors must be satisfied, on an objective assessment of the evidence, that there are reasonable grounds to suspect that the person to be charged has committed the offence. The assessment must consider the impact of any defence of information that the suspect is put forward or on which they might rely. In determining whether there are reasonable grounds to suspect, prosecutors must consider all of the material or information available. Prosecutors must be satisfied that the material to be relied on at this stage is capable of being: put into an admissible format to be presented in court; reliable; and credible (ss. 5.3 and 5.4 of the Code).

Second condition—further evidence can be obtained to provide a realistic prospect of conviction.

Prosecutors must be satisfied that there are reasonable grounds to believe that the continuing investigation will provide further evidence, within a reasonable period of time, so that when all the evidence is considered together, it is capable of establishing a realistic prospect of conviction under the Full Code Test. Amongst the factors to be taken into account the prosecutor must consider the nature, extent, and admissibility of any likely further evidence and the impact it will have on the case, the charge(s) that all the evidence will support, the reasons why the evidence is not already available and whether the delay in applying the Full Code Test is reasonable in all the circumstances (ss. 5.5–5.7 of the Code).

Third condition—the seriousness or the circumstances of the case justifies an immediate charging decision. The seriousness and the circumstances of the case should be assessed in relation to the alleged offending and should be linked to the level of risk created by granting bail (s. 5.8 of the Code).

Fourth condition—there are continuing substantial grounds to object to bail in accordance the Bail Act 1976 and in all the circumstances of the case it is proper to do so. This determination must be based on a proper risk assessment, which reveals that the suspect is not suitable to be bailed, even with substantial conditions. This will include for example, a dangerous suspect who poses a serious risk of harm to the public or to a particular person or a suspect who poses a serious risk of absconding or interfering with witnesses (s. 5.9 of the Code).

Fifth condition—it is in the public interest to charge the suspect.

Prosecutors must apply the public interest stage of the Full Code Test based on the information available at that time (s. 5.10 of the Code).

A decision to charge under the Threshold Test must be kept under review (s. 5.11 of the Code). The prosecutor should be proactive to secure from the police the identified outstanding evidence or other material in accordance with the agreed timetable. The evidence must be regularly assessed to ensure that the charge is to appropriate and that continued objection to bail is justified. The Full Code Test must be applied as soon as the anticipated further evidence or material is received and, in any event, in Crown Court cases, usually before the formal service of the prosecution case (s. 5.11 of the Code).

8.5 THE SELECTION OF CHARGES—SECTION 6, CODE FOR CROWN PROSECUTORS

Under section 6.1 of the Code, the Crown Prosecutor should select charges which:

- reflect the seriousness of the offence and the extent of the offending;
- give the court adequate powers to sentence and impose appropriate post-conviction orders;
- allow a confiscation order to be made in appropriate cases, where a defendant is benefit from criminal conduct; and
- enable the case to be presented in a clear and simple way.

Where there is a range of possible charges available (i.e. careless driving/dangerous driving, common assault/assault occasioning actual bodily harm) the CPS lawyer will review the available evidence against the CPS's Charging Practice for the particular offence (see the Legal Guidance section of the CPS website).

8.6 ALTERNATIVES TO PROSECUTION

Under section 7.1 of the Code, an out-of-court disposal may be given to an adult offender if this is considered to be an appropriate response to the offender and/or the seriousness and consequences of the offending. These alternatives to prosecution include community resolution; Cannabis or Khat warning; Penalty Notice for Disorder; an adult caution; and an adult conditional caution. According to the Ministry of Justice, for the year ending September 2018, 222,800 individuals received an out-of-court disposal. This total includes 21,800 receiving Penalty Notices for Disorder (PNDs) and 102,100 receiving Community Resolutions. A young person may be given a youth caution or a youth conditional caution (see Chapter 24). As the CPS Guidance on Cautioning and Diversion (available at https://www.cps.gov.uk/legal-guidance/cautioning-and-diversion) explains, there are a number of ways in which a suspect may be diverted from formal criminal proceedings.

8.6.1 SIMPLE CAUTION

According to the Ministry of Justice, 72,000 cautions (including both simple and conditional cautions) were administered for the year ending September 2018. Drug offences, theft, and violence against the person were the most common indictable offences for which an offender received a caution.

Generally the police retain the discretion to caution an adult offender in connection with all offences. However under s. 17 Criminal Justice and Courts Act 2015 an offender may only be given a simple caution for an indictable-only offence or a 'specified' either-way offence if there are exceptional circumstances relating to the person or the offence which justify it. The 'exceptional circumstances' test also extends to a number of either-way offences to be specified by order of the Secretary of State. Section 17 also provides that a simple caution cannot be given if two years before the commission of the offence the person has been convicted of, or cautioned for, a similar offence unless there are exceptional circumstances relating to the person, the current offence that has been admitted or the previous offence.

The decision to issue a simple caution must be made in accordance with the Director of Public Prosecution's Guidance (see earlier). The police may take advice from the CPS at any stage as to whether a simple caution might be appropriate. The main points are as follows.

A simple caution will be appropriate where:

- the evidence is sufficient to warrant a prosecution (i.e. there is a realistic prospect of conviction based on the Full Code Test);
- the offender admits her guilt;
- it is in the public interest for a simple caution to be administered (the views of any victim should be sought); and
- the offender agrees to such a disposal after being made aware that the caution may be cited in court if she offends in the future.

An important precondition for a simple caution is that the offender must unequivocally admit their guilt. The court may strike down a caution where no admission by the defendant has been obtained (see *Metropolitan Police Commissioner, ex p. P* [1995] TLR 305). A simple caution is formally administered at a police station by an officer of at least the rank of inspector. The offender will sign a form agreeing to the caution and that she admits her involvement in the offence.

The offender should be advised that while a simple caution does not constitute a conviction, records are kept and the caution may be cited in court if she later reoffends. A simple caution issued for a sexual offence will require registration on the Sex Offenders' Register and must be disclosed. A simple caution may also have to be disclosed for certain types of employment. It is also important to advise that a caution does not prevent the possibility of future prosecution. The CPS may still instigate proceedings at a later date even after the detainee has been formally cautioned although the defence could strongly argue that this constitutes an abuse of process (see Chapter 6).

While any adult may be cautioned, in practice a 'vulnerable' person is more likely to receive a simple caution than other offenders, depending on the nature of the offence alleged. Included in the category of a vulnerable person are:

- the elderly;
- the infirm;
- a detainee suffering from a mental condition or impairment;
- a detainee suffering from a physical disability;
- a detainee under severe emotional distress.

Whilst the simple caution is more suited to low-level offending behaviour, it can exceptionally be used to deal with more serious offences. The Association of Chief Police Officers (ACPO) has developed a Gravity Factors Matrix which assists the police to determine the seriousness of the offence and to consider the suitability of a simple caution. Each offence included in the gravity matrix is scaled between 1 and 5, with 1 being the least serious. The presence or absence of aggravating features influences the overall score. A score of 5 requires the offence to be prosecuted.

8.6.2 CONDITIONAL CAUTION (CPS CODE SECTION 7)

A conditional caution is a disposal available under ss. 23–27 CJA 2003 and is appropriate where the prosecutor considers that there is sufficient evidence for a prosecution but it is in the interests of the offender, the victim and the community to require the offender to comply with specified conditions aimed at rehabilitation, reparation and punishment. A factor in deciding whether a conditional caution is required, as opposed to a simple caution or prosecution, is whether the specified conditions will be an appropriate and effective way of dealing with an offender's behaviour, or making reparation for the effects of the offence on the victim and on the community.

Under s. 23 CJA 2003, a conditional caution is available where:

- the authorised person (usually a police officer or prosecutor) must have evidence that the offender committed an offence; and
- the authorised person decides there is sufficient evidence to charge the offender with the offence and that a conditional caution should be given to the offender in respect of the offence; and
- the offender must admit committing the offence to the authorised person; and
- the authorised person must explain the effect of the conditional caution and warn the offender that failure to comply with any aspect of the conditions may result in the prosecution of the offence; and
- the offender must sign a document containing the details of the offence, an admission of guilt, consent to be cautioned and details of the conditions attached to the caution.

A conditional caution can be given by either a police officer or by a Crown Prosecutor. Detailed guidance on conditional cautioning can be found in the Code of Practice for Adult Conditional Cautions (April 2013), which can be accessed at https://www.gov.uk/government/publications/code-of-practice-for-adult-conditional-cautions. The CPS legal guidance on conditional cautioning can be found at http://www.cps.gov.uk/publications/directors_ guidance/adult_conditional_cautions.html. A link in our online resources (web-links section: Guidelines) will take you there.

In addition to the requirements of s. 23 CJA 2003, as explained earlier, in deciding whether a conditional caution is appropriate, regard should be had to a range of factors, including the seriousness of the offence, the circumstances of the case, the views of the victim and the background, circumstances and previous offending history of the offender. Conditional cautions are a proportionate response to low-level offending, which allows the offender to make swift reparation to victims and communities.

8.6.3 CONDITIONS THAT CAN BE ATTACHED

The conditions attached to the caution must be:

- appropriate to the offence;
- achievable; and
- proportionate.

The conditions should have one or more of the following objectives which are aimed at the offender's rehabilitation, reparation and/or punishment. The rehabilitative element may require the offender to attend a drug or alcohol rehabilitation course or anger management classes. The reparative element might include repairing or making good any damage caused to property such as cleaning graffiti or simply apologising to the victim. A financial penalty is the only punitive element currently available and can include a fine or a compensation payment to the victim. The provisions of a financial penalty condition are set out in s. 23A CJA 2003.

8.6.4 FAILING TO COMPLY WITH THE CONDITIONAL CAUTION

If the suspect fails to comply with the conditions of the caution, she is liable to be prosecuted for the original offence as the public interest test will have been satisfied. The conditional caution, although not a conviction, forms part of the offender's record and may be cited in any subsequent criminal proceedings.

8.7 THE DEFENCE SOLICITOR INFLUENCING THE DECISION TO CHARGE

The direct access between the police and their local CPS counterparts means that custody officers will usually be acting on the advice of the Crown Prosecutor. It should still be possible, however, for the defence solicitor/legal adviser to influence the decision to charge where the evidence that links the suspect to the offence appears to be weak or unreliable. In this situation, the solicitor should persuade the custody officer to release his client unconditionally or on police bail. Even where the evidence discloses a case to answer, the defence solicitor could persuade the Crown Prosecutor through the custody officer, to deal with his client by an alternative disposal to a formal prosecution.

In many cases, and especially where the police have made a full disclosure of the evidence against the suspect, it will be clear that the Full Code Test is satisfied and the defence solicitor's latitude for negotiation is limited. In some situations it might be in a detainee's interest to be charged as soon as possible where, for example, he has been in police detention for a long time or where the defence solicitor considers that it would not be in his client's interests to be interviewed again by the police.

As with all representations made in connection with a client's detention at the police station, it is vital to ensure that the custody officer's or Crown Prosecutor's responses are accurately recorded on the custody record and in the defence solicitor's contemporaneous notes.

8.8 PRE-TRIAL DISCLOSURE OF EVIDENCE—AN INTRODUCTION

The right to the pre-trial disclosure of evidence is enshrined in the European Convention on Human Rights 1950 (ECHR 1950) as being fundamental to the right to a fair trial under Article 6(1). Article 6(3)(b) provides:

> 'Everyone charged with a criminal offence has the right to be informed promptly, in a language which he understands and in detail of the nature and cause of the accusation against him.'

At numerous stages in a criminal case the rules governing the pre-trial disclosure of evidence impose extensive obligations on the CPS which are critical to a defendant's right to a fair trial. Clearly a defendant cannot be expected to defend allegations made against her unless she is aware of the evidence that will be given in support of those allegations. It would be morally wrong for the prosecution to withhold evidence that weakens the prosecution case or assists the defence case. Although the aim in the adversarial system is to win, there are wider obligations on the prosecution to assist in the search for the truth and to ensure that a miscarriage of justice does not occur. The following account of the collapse of a rape case against student Liam Allan vividly demonstrates this:

> **'Police and prosecutors have apologised after a student's rape trial collapsed because an officer had failed to disclose key evidence'**
>
> *The case against Liam Allan, 22, was thrown out of court after it emerged a detective had not handed over text messages from the accuser's phone.*
>
> *Messages between the complainant in the case and others were only passed to the defence days before the trial collapsed at Croydon Crown Court.*
>
> *After a review, the Metropolitan Police and Crown Prosecution Service (CPS) said the mistake was not deemed deliberate and no officers or prosecutors have been disciplined over the case.*
>
> *But Mr Allan said he had concerns that certain messages in his case "were plucked specifically to go against me".*
>
> *In a joint statement, the Met Police and CPS said: "The disclosure problems in this case were caused by a combination of error, lack of challenge, and lack of knowledge."*
>
> *Mr Allan had been charged with 12 counts of rape and sexual assault before his trial was dropped in December.*
>
> *The case was thrown out after evidence on computer disk containing 40,000 messages revealed Mr Allan's accuser had pestered him for "casual sex".*
>
> *Mr Allan said he suffered "stress and anxiety" during his ordeal and wanted to return to a "normal life".*
>
> *Metropolitan Police Commander Richard Smith said he had met with Mr Allan to offer a 'personal apology".*
>
> *Claire Lindley, chief crown prosecutor for London South, said the case "highlighted some systemic and deep-rooted issues".*
>
> *She explained: "The prosecutors involved in this case did not sufficiently challenge the police about digital material," she said.*
>
> *"That meant that it took longer than was necessary to drop Mr Allan's case. For that, the CPS has offered an unreserved apology to him which I delivered to him in person yesterday."*

All rape and serious sexual assault cases in England and Wales—including 600 in London—are being re-viewed by the CPS to ensure evidence has been disclosed after a series of collapsed cases in recent weeks.

A rape case against Oxford University student Oliver Mears was dropped after fresh evidence—includ-ing a diary that supported his case—was passed to the CPS.'

(See https://news.sky.com/story/liam-allan-police-apologise-for-students-rape-trial-col-lapse-11228722.)

The fallout from this and other well publicised cases demonstrate there are systemic and worrying flaws in the pre-trial disclosure process in England and Wales (see https://www.bbc.co.uk/news/uk-42795058). A full review by the CPS of all rape cases was launched in early 2018. The results of the review were published in June 2018 (https://www.cps.gov.uk/cps/news/cps-publishes-outcome-sexual-offences-review). Of the 3637 cases reviewed, 47 were dropped for systemic disclosure failings. In November 2018, the Attorney General published a Review of the Efficiency and Effectiveness Disclosure of Disclosure in the Criminal Justice System available at https://www.gov.uk/government/publications/review-of-the-efficiency-and-effectiveness-of-disclosure-in-the-criminal-justice-system.

The Review announced a series of policy initiatives to strengthen the operation of the current statutory rules on disclosure and the culture within the prosecuting authorities about the importance of disclosure as an essential element of the defendant's right to a fair trial.

As well as supporting the defendant's right to a fair trial, the pre-trial disclosure of evi-dence greatly assists in the administration of justice by enabling the court and the parties to identify the issues that are likely to be disputed at trial. This is a key aspect of the court's case management duties under Crim PR, Part 3. There are also time-saving advantages in requir-ing pre-trial disclosure of evidence. On the basis of the disclosed evidence, a defendant may be advised to plead guilty at an early stage. Pre-trial disclosure may also lead to the evidence of some prosecution witnesses being agreed by the defence that it should be admitted at the defendant's trial in the form of a written statement. This arrangement relieves the need for the witness to attend court, which in turn, saves valuable time and expense at the trial.

A key piece of legislation that governs disclosure is the Criminal Procedure and Investi-gations Act 1996 (CPIA 1996). The Act, which imposes onerous disclosure duties upon the prosecution as well as duties on the defendant, is supplemented by a detailed Code of Prac-tice (2015) (Part II CPIA 1996 (s. 23)). The Code (which we refer to as the Disclosure Code) can be accessed via the web-links section of the online resources and at https://www.gov.uk/government/publications/criminal-procedure-and-investigations-act-code-of-practice.

In accordance with the Transforming Summary Justice (TSJ) initiative, a Streamlined Disclosure Code (SCD) is used in summary-only or either-way offences where, on a reasonable assessment of the case, the matter is likely to be dealt with in the magistrates' court. The Stream-lined Disclosure Code is available on the CPS website at http://www.gov.uk/legal-guidance-/streamlined-summary-disclosure.

Section 26 CPIA 1996 makes the Disclosure Code admissible in evidence where a breach of its provisions is relevant to a question in the proceedings. A failure to comply with the Code does not impose civil or criminal liability on the police.

Importantly however, a failure by the CPS to comply with its disclosure obligations clearly affects the fairness of the proceedings and may be the subject of a defence application to stay the proceedings for abuse of process (see Chapter 6).

In complying with its disclosure obligations, the CPS lawyer will apply the guidance provided in the Attorney General's Guidelines on Disclosure (December 2013). The im-portance of these guidelines cannot be underestimated. They can be accessed from our online resources, and at http://www.gov.uk/government/publications/attorney-generals-guide-lines-on-disclosure-2013.

A Judicial Protocol on the Disclosure of Unused Material in Criminal Cases was pub-lished in 2013 and can be accessed at http://www.judiciary.gov.uk/wp-content/uploads/JCO/Documents/Protocols/Disclosure+Protocol.pdf.

8.9 USED AND UNUSED MATERIAL

Central to an understanding of the disclosure rules is the distinction between 'used' and 'unused' material. These words are not defined by statute but are adopted by us as convenient labels to assist understanding.

'Used' material refers to evidence that will form part of the prosecution's case against the defendant and is the evidence to be used to prove the defendant's guilt at trial. The prosecution is under a duty to disclose its used evidence at an early stage in the case. Our case studies (*R v Lenny Wise*; *R v Roger Martin*; *R v William Hardy*) include examples of 'used material'.

'Unused' material is evidence collected during the investigation into the offence but which is not part of the prosecution's case against the accused at trial but which may assist the defence or undermine the case for the prosecution. The prosecution's duty to disclose 'unused' material arises at a later stage in the case.

As the CPS can only make disclosure of evidence to the defence based on the evidence gathered or generated as part of the police investigation, what disclosure obligations fall on the police?

8.10 DISCLOSURE OBLIGATIONS ON THE POLICE

The obligations upon the police to record, retain and reveal to the prosecutor material collected in the course of the criminal investigation are contained in the CPIA 1996 and the accompanying Disclosure Code.

8.10.1 KEEPING TRACK OF INVESTIGATIVE MATERIAL

The Disclosure Code (para. 5) requires the recording and retention of all relevant information and material gathered or generated during an investigation. A disclosure officer must be appointed to each investigation and may be a member of the investigation team. There is a requirement to record all types of information, including evidence obtained during the investigation (the record of searches of the suspect's person and/or property), evidence generated by the investigation (incriminating admissions and no comment interviews, etc.), and information received verbally. Paragraph 5.4 of the Code specifies the types of relevant material which should be routinely retained in a criminal case. It includes:

- crime reports;
- custody records;
- records of telephone calls, for example 999 calls;
- final versions of witness statements (and draft versions, where their content differs from the final version);
- interview records;
- communications between the police and experts such as forensic scientists, reports of work carried out by experts, and schedules of scientific material prepared by the expert for the investigator, for the purposes of criminal proceedings;
- information provided by an accused person which indicates an explanation for the offence with which that person has been charged;
- any material casting doubt on the reliability of a confession;
- any material casting doubt on the reliability of a witness;
- records of first description of a suspect by each potential witness who purports to identify or describe the suspect, whether or not the description differs from that of subsequent descriptions by that or other witnesses.

Where there is any doubt about the relevance of material gathered or generated, the investigator must retain it.

Paragraph 3.5 of the Disclosure Code states that:

'In conducting an investigation, the investigator should pursue all reasonable lines of enquiry, whether these point towards or away from a suspect. What is reasonable in each case will depend on the particular circumstances.'

8.10.2 **DISCLOSURE SCHEDULES**

Paragraph 6 of the Disclosure Code requires material that is relevant to the investigation and which the disclosure officer thinks will not form part of the prosecution case to be listed on a schedule (MG6C form) which will form part of the police file sent to the CPS.

The case management and disclosure procedure will then differ depending on whether the case is likely to be heard in the magistrates' court or in the Crown Court as a Streamlined Summary Disclosure procedure applies in the instances described below.

If the defendant is charged with a summary offence or an either-way offence that is likely to remain in the magistrates court the procedure to be followed will depend on whether it is anticipated that the defendant will plead guilty or not guilty. The acronym GAP stands for 'Anticipated Guilty Plea,' whilst NGAP stands for 'Not Guilty Anticipated Plea'.

In all summary cases where a not guilty plea is anticipated by the police and CPS, *and* the case is likely to remain in the magistrates' court, a Streamlined Disclosure Certificate (SDC) replaces the MG6 forms. The Streamlined Summary Disclosure process is fully explained on the CPS website at https://www.cps.gov.uk/legal-guidance/streamlined-summary-disclosure.

In the event of a GAP listing an SDC is not required. However, the common law duty to disclose material which may assist the defence at a bail hearing or in the early preparation of their case (*R v DPP, ex p. Lee* [1992] 2 Cr App R 304) continues to apply, and where there is such material the police must certify on the file submitted to the CPS (see Form 8.1).

If unexpectedly the accused pleads not guilty at the GAP first hearing, the disclosure officer must ensure that the SDC is prepared and submitted as soon as reasonably practicable after the not guilty plea.

If the accused is charged with a summary-only offence or an either-way offence that is likely to remain in the magistrates' court and the plea is likely to be not guilty (NGAP), the disclosure officer must prepare an SDC. A template copy of the SDC can be seen at the conclusion of this chapter (see Form 8.1). If there is no material or other evidence that is considered as undermining the prosecution case or assisting the defence the officer should complete the appropriate entry on the SDC. The SDC will be served on the defence, at or before first hearing, as part of the Initial Details of the Prosecution Case (IDPC)—see para. 8.11 below.

Crown Court

Where the accused is charged with an indictable-only offence or with an either-way offence that is likely to be tried on indictment the disclosure officer must ensure that a disclosure schedule on form MG6 is prepared.

Sensitive material and other evidence

Sensitive material and other evidence is material which the investigating officer believes would not be in the public interest to disclose in the case including evidence relating to national security or police informants, the location of surveillance positions and material relating to children.

For cases to be heard in the magistrates' court if there is any sensitive unused material to disclose the disclosure officer should complete a sensitive material schedule (form MG6D and MG6E) and attach it to the prosecution file.

For cases to be heard in the Crown Court any sensitive material or other evidence must be listed on a schedule of sensitive material or in cases of extreme sensitivity should be revealed to the prosecutor separately.

8.11 THE CPS OBLIGATION TO DISCLOSE 'USED' MATERIAL—'IDPC' (INITIAL DETAILS OF THE PROSECUTION CASE)

The CPS must disclose any 'used' material in a case that can be tried summarily before a magistrates' court in accordance with Crim PR, Part 8 and which are reproduced in part below:

'**Providing initial details of the prosecution case**

8.2—

(1) The prosecutor must serve initial details of the prosecution case on the court officer—

    (a) as soon as practicable; and

    (b) in any event, no later than the beginning of the day of the first hearing.

(2) Where a defendant requests those details, the prosecutor must serve them on the defendant—

    (a) as soon as practicable; and

    (b) in any event, no later than the beginning of the day of the first hearing.

(3) Where a defendant does not request those details, the prosecutor must make them available to the defendant at, or before, the beginning of the day of the first hearing.

Content of initial details

8.3 Initial details of the prosecution case must include—

    (a) where, immediately before the first hearing in the magistrates' court, the defendant was in police custody for the offence charged—

        (i) a summary of the circumstances of the offence, and

        (ii) the defendant's criminal record, if any;

    (b) where paragraph (a) does not apply—

        (i) a summary of the circumstances of the offence,

        (ii) any account given by the defendant in interview, whether contained in that summary or in another document,

        (iii) any written witness statement or exhibit that the prosecutor then has available and considers material to plea, or to the allocation of the case for trial, or to sentence,

        (iv) the defendant's criminal record, if any, and

        (v) any available statement of the effect of the offence on a victim, a victim's family or others.'

8.11.1 WHEN MUST THE CPS COMPLY WITH CRIM PR, PART 8?

The prosecution's obligations to provide IDPC must be given before the first hearing in the magistrates' court in connection with an either-way offence or summary offence for the hearing to be an 'effective' hearing. An effective first hearing requires that:

(a) a plea be taken;

(b) the appropriate trial venue is determined;

(c) the real issues are identified;

(d) the case (including sentence) can be concluded on the day or, if not, directions can be given so that it can be concluded at the next hearing or as soon as possible after that.

To ensure that the first hearing is effective an initiative known as CJ-SSS (Simple, Speedy, Summary, Criminal Justice) came into operation in all magistrates' courts in 2007. The practices reflected by CJ-SSS were supplemented by a further initiative, Stop Delaying Justice (SDJ), and most recently by TSJ which are fully explained in Chapter 9 later.

TSJ requires the CPS to serve sufficient disclosure of the prosecution's case on the accused as early as possible and at the latest by 9 am on the day of the first hearing to enable the defendant to enter a firm plea. In compliance with TSJ, the court will expect the defendant to enter or indicate a plea at the first hearing whether appearing in custody or not.

Where a not guilty plea is anticipated in preparation for the initial hearing of an offence which may be tried summarily, the CPS will serve the 'IDPC' on the defence. It will comprise the charge sheet (MG4); the police report (MG5), which includes a police officer's summary of the key evidence (including copies of any handwritten key witness statements); a Streamlined Forensic Report (if applicable); a summary of the defendant's interview and a list of non-key witness evidence; and what each non-key witness states and a list of the defendant's previous convictions (see Appendix 2 Document 2 for an illustration of IDPC in the context of our fictitious case study, *R v Lenny Wise*). If the case proceeds to summary trial or is sent to the Crown Court, the CPS file will be upgraded to take account of its more onerous disclosure duties in these circumstances.

As part of the wider reforms to make greater use of technology in the criminal justice system the CPS, which has traditionally complied with its disclosure obligations by serving hard copy documents, has and is moving towards the production and service of digital case files and the adoption of a single information management system. This includes the digital transfer of over 90% of files from the police to the CPS and the use of digital case files for traffic and shoplifting cases leading to the establishment of digital case files for all other offences by April 2015. Defence practitioners should be prepared for the digital service revolution.

8.11.2 INITIAL DISCLOSURE OF THE PROSECUTION CASE IN INDICTABLE-ONLY CASES

There are separate disclosure rules for offences that are triable only on indictment which apply once the offence has been sent to the Crown Court under s. 51 Crime and Disorder Act 1998 (CDA 1998). The rules are considered in Chapter 13. Although Crim PR, Part 8 has no application to an indictable-only offence, the CPS will normally serve available 'IDPC' at an early stage in an indictable-only case where a request is made and where fairness requires such disclosure. This is particularly important where the CPS has information that might affect a bail decision. (Indeed, it is part of the CPS common law duty of disclosure in accordance with as laid down in *R v DPP, ex p. Lee* [1992] 2 Cr App R 304.)

8.12 CPS OBLIGATIONS TO DISCLOSE UNUSED MATERIAL (CRIM PR, PART 15)

The CPIA 1996 and the Disclosure Code impose duties on the CPS lawyer to disclose unused evidence that will not form part of the prosecution case.

At what point does the obligation to disclose unused material arise?

- When an either-way offence is sent to the Crown Court, the disclosure provisions relating to 'unused material' arise at this stage.

- If an offence is to be tried summarily and a not guilty plea has been entered, an SDC dealing with 'unused' material will be served along with the IDPC at the first hearing or soon thereafter (see para. 8.10.2).

- For an offence triable only on indictment, unused material is included in the case sent bundle (see Chapter 13 which explains the procedural course of an offence triable only on indictment).

8.12.1 THE SPECIFIC DISCLOSURE DUTIES ON THE CPS UNDER THE CPIA 1996

Based on the disclosure schedules/SDC prepared by the disclosure officer in the case (see para. 8.10.2), the CPS lawyer must review the evidence on the file and decide whether any disclosure is required by s. 3 CPIA 1996.

8.12.2 INITIAL DISCLOSURE OF UNUSED MATERIAL—S. 3 CPIA 1996

'The prosecutor must—

(a) disclose to the accused any prosecution material which has not previously been disclosed to the accused and which might reasonably be considered capable of undermining the case for the prosecution against the accused or of assisting the case for the accused.'

In *R v Vasilou* [2000] 4 Archbold News 1, the Court of Appeal held this would include the disclosure of a prosecution witness's previous convictions.

The test to be applied under s. 3 CPIA 1996 is objective and requires the prosecutor to decide which evidence might reasonably undermine the prosecution case. Paragraph 5 of the revised December 2013 Attorney General's Guidelines on Disclosure states that prosecutors will only be expected to anticipate what material might undermine their case or strengthen the defence in the light of information available at the time of the disclosure decision, and they may take into account information revealed during questioning.

The Guidelines provide, at paras. 6–10, some assistance to Crown Prosecutors as to what might need to be disclosed in accordance with s. 3 CPIA 1996:

'6. In deciding whether material satisfies the disclosure test, consideration should be given amongst other things to:

a the use that might be made of it in cross-examination;

b its capacity to support submissions that could lead to:

(i) the exclusion of evidence;

(ii) a stay of proceedings, where the material is required to allow a proper application to be made;

(iii) a court or tribunal finding that any public authority had acted incompatibly with the accused's rights under the ECHR;

c its capacity to suggest an explanation or partial explanation of the accused's actions;

d the capacity of the material to have a bearing on scientific or medical evidence in the case.

7. It should also be borne in mind that while items of material viewed in isolation may not be reasonably considered to be capable of undermining the prosecution case or assisting the accused, several items together can have that effect.

8. Material relating to the accused's mental or physical health, intellectual capacity, or to any ill-treatment which the accused may have suffered when in the investigator's custody is likely to fall within the test for disclosure set out in (s. 3 CPIA 1996).

9. Disclosure must not be an open-ended trawl of unused material . . .

10. Disclosure should be conducted in a thinking manner and never be reduced to a box-ticking exercise; at all stages of the process, there should be consideration of why the CPIA disclosure regime requires a particular course of action and what should be done to achieve that.'

Disclosure under s. 3 CPIA 1996 is limited to information in the prosecutor's possession or evidence which the prosecutor has inspected. The prosecutor's disclosure duty depends on the efficiency and honesty of the disclosure officer who prepares the schedule. Disclosure can be made by either giving a copy of the material to the defence or allowing the defence to inspect it at a reasonable time and place.

If initial disclosure is not available, the CPS must provide a written statement to the defendant confirming this. Along with initial disclosure the CPS must also disclose a copy of the schedule of non-sensitive material prepared by the disclosure officer in the case.

8.12.3 INITIAL DISCLOSURE OF UNUSED MATERIAL—TIME LIMITS

In the case of a summary trial standard directions give the prosecution 28 days from the date of the defendant's not guilty plea to serve initial disclosure of unused material. In accordance with TSJ, the SDC will normally be served at or before first hearing, as part of the IDPC where a not guilty plea is anticipated.

For all cases that have been sent to the Crown Court for trial the process and time limits for the disclosure of unused material will be managed by the judge at the Plea and Trial Preparation Hearing (PTPH) before the Crown Court (see Chapter 13).

8.12.4 DEFENCE DISCLOSURE

The defence obligations to make pre-trial disclosure of evidence are considered in greater detail in Chapter 13. For all cases that are tried on indictment, the defendant must serve a defence statement on the prosecution under s. 5 CPIA 1996 once the CPS has complied or has purported to comply with its disclosure duties under s. 3 CPIA 1996. Defence statements are considered in detail in Chapter 13. The service of a defence statement is optional in a case that is to be tried summarily (see Chapter 12). In addition to serving a defence statement, the defendant must also give written notice of his intention to call defence witnesses (s. 6C CPIA 1996) irrespective of whether the case is to be tried summarily or on indictment (see Chapters 12 and 13).

8.12.5 PROSECUTOR'S CONTINUING DUTY

Section 7A CPIA 1996 (as amended by the CJA 2003) provides that after the prosecutor has complied with initial disclosure under s. 3 CPIA 1996 and before the accused is acquitted or convicted or the prosecutor decides not to proceed with the case (and, in particular, following the service of a defence statement), the prosecutor must keep under review whether there is any further prosecution material that might reasonably be considered capable of undermining the prosecution case against the accused or of assisting the defence case. Following the service of a defence statement if the prosecution concludes there is no further evidence to disclose, this should be communicated to the defendant.

A summary and flowchart depicting the various stages of the disclosure regime in relation to the **classification of criminal offences can be found at Figures 8.2 and 8.3**.

8.13 DISCLOSING INFORMATION HELD BY THIRD PARTIES

The CPIA 1996 does not apply to potentially relevant evidence in the possession of a third party such as a local authority, hospital, school, or a forensic science organisation but which is not directly involved in the case. The Attorney General's Guidelines (paras. 56–57) deal with third party disclosure.

If a third party will not voluntarily disclose information, either side may issue a witness summons under the Criminal Procedure (Attendance of Witnesses) Act 1965 (Crown Court) and s. 97 Magistrates' Courts Act 1980 (magistrates' court) requiring the third party to disclose the evidence. The third party may resist the application on the basis of public interest immunity in accordance with the procedure set out in s. 16 CPIA 1996 (*R v Brushett* [2001] Crim LR 471). The principles relating to public interest immunity are briefly discussed later.

8.14 WITHHOLDING RELEVANT EVIDENCE

Occasionally, the prosecution or a third party will resist the disclosure of otherwise relevant and admissible evidence on the basis that it is 'sensitive' and it is not in the wider public interest for it to be heard in the public domain of a criminal trial. Evidence covered by public interest immunity includes:

- documents and other material relating to national security;
- confidential information;
- the identity of police informants and undercover police officers;

- details of premises used for police surveillance; and

- information dealing with the welfare of children.

The defence advocate, however, may wish to see such evidence to evaluate it and perhaps challenge it. Where disclosure is opposed on this basis, the prosecution will claim the evidence is covered by Public Interest Immunity (PII).

While many aspects of disclosure are regulated by statute, the principles relating to PII remain governed by the common law. The procedural rules governing public interest immunity applications are contained in Crim PR, Part 15, which take account of the leading case on PII, which is the House of Lords decision in *R v C; R v H* [2004] 2 WLR 335.

The overriding principle which governs a judge's or magistrate's decision whether to order disclosure is based on ensuring an innocent defendant is not convicted. This principle is derived from the judgment of Lord Taylor CJ in *R v Keane* [1994] 1 WLR 746:

> 'If the disputed material may prove the accused's innocence or avoid a miscarriage of justice, then the balance comes down resoundingly in favour of disclosing it.'

8.15 FURTHER INFORMATION ON DISCLOSURE

For further detailed consideration of pre-trial disclosure of evidence, please refer to the CPS Disclosure Manual at http://www.cps.gov.uk/legal/d_to_g/disclosure_manual/index.html.

KEY POINT SUMMARY

- Understand the division of charging responsibilities between the police and the CPS.

- Know the procedures to be followed where the decision to charge is taken by the police or the CPS.

- Have a good working knowledge of the Full Code Test under the Code for Crown Prosecutors and an understanding of the ways in which the evidential and the public interest tests are applied in the decision to charge.

- Know when the Threshold Test applies.

- Understand the alternatives to prosecution and the applicable criteria for them.

- Understand that an accused is entitled to disclosure of the evidence the prosecution intends to rely on (*'used'* material) in discharging its burden of proof.

- The right to a fair trial is fundamentally underpinned by the rules on the disclosure of both 'used' and 'unused' material.

- Be able to give an account of IDPC rules under Crim PR, Part 8 (Initial Disclosure of Prosecution Case) and understand that whilst they do not apply to an indictable-only case, the CPS must comply with its common law obligations under *R v DPP ex p. Lee* [1999] 2 All ER 737 to disclose material that may assist the defence with the early preparation of their case or at a bail hearing.

- The obligation to serve IDPC arises at a very early stage before the first hearing where the case can be tried before the magistrates' court (see TSJ).

- Understand the test that the CPS lawyer must apply in discharging his or her 'unused' material disclosure duties under s. 3 CPIA 1996.

- Entitlement to disclosure of unused material under s. 3 CPIA 1996 only arises in a case to be tried summarily where a not guilty plea is indicated. SDC now applies to anticipated not guilty pleas in a case that must or might be tried summarily.

- The submission of a defence statement is voluntary in summary cases but mandatory in indictable cases (see Chapters 12 and 13).

- The prosecution is obliged to keep disclosure of unused material under constant review, particularly in the light of service of a defence statement.

- Where the prosecution seeks to withhold relevant/material evidence on the ground that it is sensitive, application must be made to a court to sanction the withholding of such material.

- Important detail as regards the operation and effect of the CPIA 1996 is contained in its accompanying Code of Practice and in the Attorney General's Guidelines on Disclosure (2013).

SELF-TEST QUESTIONS

Question 1

The following self-test questions are designed to test your understanding and application of the evidential and public interest tests applied by Crown Prosecutors. Before attempting the questions, consider the following example.

Wayne, aged 24, has been arrested on suspicion of assault occasioning actual bodily harm under s. 47 Offences Against the Person Act 1861. The offence occurred during Wayne's wedding reception, when Brian, the bride's brother, made insulting comments about Wayne. There are several witnesses to the offence who would be willing to testify in court. Wayne denies the offence and Brian has indicated to the CPS that he wishes further action to be taken against Wayne. Wayne has two convictions for violent disorder for separate offences outside a nightclub. Consider whether the evidential and public interest tests are satisfied as required by the Full Code Test under the Code for Crown Prosecutors.

Advice

In applying the Code for Crown Prosecutors to Wayne's case, it appears that the evidential test is satisfied as there are several witnesses to the offence who would be willing to testify in court. There is nothing to suggest that these witnesses would not give relevant and reliable testimony and that the *actus reus* and *mens rea* of the offence could be proven. In terms of the public interest test, there are factors in favour of continuing the prosecution, not least the use of violence and in his previous criminal conduct, Wayne appears to have a propensity to be violent. On the particular facts of the case, it is likely that Wayne will be charged and prosecuted.

By applying the Code for Crown Prosecutors, consider whether the 'evidential' test and the 'public interest' test are satisfied in the following cases. You might also consider whether there are alternative methods by which the potential defendant may be dealt with.

(a) Gerald, aged 75, has been charged with 14 counts of sexual assault arising out of his employment in a residential home for children. The alleged offences occurred between 1968 and 1973. The police have traced four victims of the offences who are willing to testify at Gerald's trial. Gerald, who has no criminal convictions, has recently been diagnosed with a serious heart complaint.

(b) Debbie, aged 35, is a single parent with three children. She has been arrested on suspicion of theft. It is alleged that she stole a pack of disposable nappies, a jar of coffee and a bottle of vodka from Cutcost Supermarket. Debbie is advised to make no comment in interview. The supermarket's policy is always to prosecute shoplifters. In support of the prosecution case, the store detective will testify at trial and there is a security video of the alleged offence. Debbie has no previous convictions apart from a conviction for careless driving. In a private discussion with her solicitor, Debbie discloses that she does not really know why she took the items and that she is recovering from a nervous breakdown having been in an abusive marriage which has recently ended in divorce.

(c) After Patrick, aged 14, tells his father, Frank, that he (Patrick) is in a gay relationship, Frank hits Patrick, causing him actual bodily harm. Patrick is attacked by his father on two further occasions. Frank also locks Patrick in his room preventing him from leaving the house to keep him away from his boyfriend. After a week, Patrick's mother, Marie, tells the police who intervene and arrest Frank. Patrick does not want any action to be taken against Frank. Frank has no previous convictions.

Question 2

The following scenario explores prosecution disclosure obligations. Try to attempt to answer the questions posed at the conclusion.

Barry (aged 28) is charged with rape contrary to s. 1 Sexual Offences Act 2003. His victim is Tina, aged 15. The attack is alleged to have occurred in some public toilets inside a park where Barry is employed as a park attendant. Tina reported the rape to staff at the care home where she resides some two days after it was alleged to have occurred. Tina is subjected to a full forensic examination which reveals visible bruising around her vagina.

Having identified Barry as being the man responsible, he is arrested. He too is subject to a full forensic examination. In interview Barry denies the offence, stating Tina approached him outside the public toilets in the park offering him sex in return for money. He refused her advances. She called him a paedophile and walked off.

The attack is said to have been witnessed by Leroy aged 15. He has given a statement to the police stating he witnessed a girl matching Tina's description emerge from some public toilets in the park in a state of distress claiming she had been raped. Kelly, a friend of Tina, has given a statement to the police claiming that Barry has asked Tina for sex on a number of occasions and became aggressive when Tina refused. Barry informs you that he has observed Tina in the company of males on numerous occasions while in the park and believes her to be sexually promiscuous. The allegations against him are a complete fabrication.

A defence witness has come forward who wishes to remain anonymous claiming that Tina is an attention seeker and that she has previously made a false accusation of rape against a male care-worker several months ago, having allegedly offered him sex. She later withdrew the allegation. Leroy is also a resident of the care home at which Tina resides and is very much under Tina's 'control'.

Chart the various stages of disclosure in this case by answering the following questions:

- What is the classification of the offence with which Barry is charged?

- Can you expect initial disclosure of the prosecution evidence and other material in this case, and if so, what do you anticipate you are likely to receive? (Think in terms of what the investigative process is likely to yield.)

- At what stage will the prosecution come under an obligation to disclose 'unused' material?

- Will the defence need to serve a defence statement in this case, and if so, what will the content of that statement comprise?

- Do you anticipate there may be material that the prosecution might not wish to disclose? If so, on what basis and how would the situation be resolved in procedural terms?

Analysis of questions 1 and 2 is provided in our online resources, where scenario 2 is further developed.

FIGURE 8.1 THE DECISION TO CHARGE

The decision to charge or to offer an alternative course is for the most part the responsibility of the CPS in conjunction with the custody officer under the CJA 2003 (s. 37B PACE).

The decision to charge is based on two tests contained within the CPS Code for Crown Prosecutors. The test comprises:

- evidential test—is there sufficient evidence to provide for a realistic prospect of conviction?

- public interest test—is it in the public interest that the defendant is prosecuted? (This requires the application of various factors listed in the Code.)

ALTERNATIVES TO PROSECUTION

Simple caution

- Defendant may be cautioned where:
  - the offence is not an indictable-only offence or a specified either-way offence (unless exceptional circumstances apply);
  - evidence is sufficient to have warranted prosecution;
  - defendant admits guilt; and
  - defendant agrees to be cautioned

Conditional cautions: ss. 23–27 Criminal Justice Act 2003

- Defendant may receive a conditional caution where:
  - defendant admits the offence to an authorised person; and
  - in the opinion of the prosecutor there is sufficient evidence to charge, and the public interest is satisfied by the offer of a conditional caution.
- The condition(s) attached to the caution must be:
  - proportionate to the offence;
  - achievable; and
  - appropriate.
- The condition(s) might require the defendant:
  - to attend drug/alcohol rehabilitation course;
  - to attend anger management course;
  - to make good damage to property; and
  - to pay a fine.

FIGURE 8.2 PRE-TRIAL DISCLOSURE OF EVIDENCE

SUMMARY-ONLY OFFENCES

- Prosecution will disclose used material—initial details of the prosecution case (IDPC).

- If defendant pleads not guilty, any 'unused' material which might reasonably be considered capable of undermining the case for the prosecution or of assisting the case for the accused must be disclosed, s. 3 CPIA 1996.

- Within 14 days of initial disclosure, defence may voluntarily serve a defence statement, s. 6 CPIA 1996 but must serve a defence witness statement, s. 6C CPIA 1996.

- Prosecution must serve any further 'unused' evidence which might reasonably be expected to assist the defence as disclosed in the defence statement under its continuing duty to review unused material, s. 7A CPIA 1996.

OFFENCES TRIABLE EITHER WAY

- Prosecution will make disclosure of IDPC against the accused under Crim PR, Part 8.

- The disclosure obligations on each party will then depend on whether the case is to be tried summarily or on indictment.

- If sent for trial to the Crown Court, initial disclosure of prosecution unused material should be served in accordance with s. 3 CPIA 1996, in accordance with time limits.

- If being tried before a magistrates' court as per summary offences above.

- If being tried on indictment, as per indictable offences below.

INDICTABLE-ONLY OFFENCES AND CASES TO BE TRIED ON INDICTMENT

- Evidence and other material which the prosecution intends to use at trial will be disclosed to the defence under reg. 2 Crime and Disorder Act 1998 (Service of Prosecution Evidence) Regulations 2005 within 70 or 50 days of the case being sent to the Crown Court for trial under s. 51 Crime and Disorder Act 1998.

- Any 'unused' material (initial disclosure), which might reasonably be considered capable of undermining the case for the prosecution or of assisting the case for the accused must be disclosed, s. 3 CPIA 1996, thereafter in accordance with time limits.

- Within 28 days of initial disclosure, defence must serve a defence statement, s. 5 CPIA 1996 (note the possible drawing of adverse inferences under s. 11 CPIA 1996). The defendant must also serve a defence witness statement, s. 6C CPIA 1996.

- Prosecution must serve any further 'unused' evidence which might reasonably be expected to assist the defence as disclosed in the defence statement under its continuing duty to review unused material, s. 7A CPIA 1996.

FIGURE 8.3 DISCLOSURE FLOWCHART

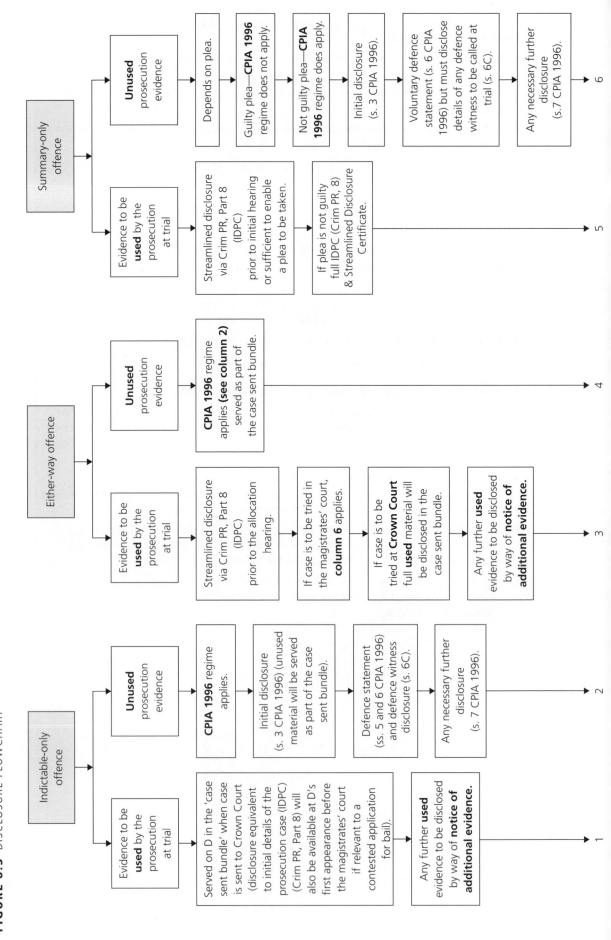

FORM 8.1 DECLARATION ON THE MG5/DIGITAL CASE FILE

Declaration on the MG5/Digital Case File (DCF)

1. **FOR USE IN GAP CASES AT 1ST HEARING WHERE THERE IS NOTHING TO DISCLOSE PURSUANT TO R v DPP *ex parte* LEE**

URN: **Defendant:** First Name Last Name

Reporting Officer's Certification
In accordance with Common Law I certify that to the best of my knowledge and belief there is no relevant unused material that might reasonably assist the defence with the early preparation of their case or at a bail hearing. Reporting Officer Name   SIGNATURE Date

Streamlined Disclosure Certificate – nothing to disclose

2. **FOR USE IN ALL NGAP CASES AT 1ST HEARING WHERE THERE IS NOTHING TO DISCLOSE**

URN: **Defendant:** First Name Last Name

SCHEDULE OF NON-SENSITIVE UNUSED MATERIAL – NOT FOR DISCLOSURE		
No.	Police use (Brief description of materials)	CPS use
1		Having applied the disclosure tests set out in the CPIA 1996, I am satisfied from the descriptions listed in this schedule that the items in question are clearly not disclosable.
2		
3		
4		
5		
6		
7		
8		
9		
10		
Disclosure Officer's Certification I certify – • that any relevant unused material has been recorded and retained in accordance with the CPIA 1996 Code of Practice (as amended), • that such material as is non-sensitive is shown on the schedule above, • and that to the best of my knowledge and belief there are no items shown in the schedule that might reasonably undermine the prosecution case, or, so far as it is apparent, assist the defence with the early preparation of their case or at a bail hearing. Disclosure Officer Name SIGNATURE:	CPS Prosecutor Name SIGNATURE:
Date	Date

Streamlined Disclosure Certificate – items to disclose

3. FOR USE IN ALL NGAP CASES AT 1ˢᵀ HEARING WHERE THERE ARE SOME ITEMS TO DISCLOSE

URN: **Defendant:** First Name Last Name

No.	SCHEDULE OF NON-SENSITIVE UNUSED MATERIAL		
	Police use	**CPS use**	
	(Brief description of materials including those falling under para.7.3 of the Code)	(Against each item insert **D** for disclose; **I** for inspect; **CND** for clearly not disclosable)	
1			
2			
3			
4			
5			
6			
7			
8			
9			
10			

Disclosure Officer's Certification	
Disclosure Officer's Certification I certify – <ul><li>that any relevant unused material has been recorded and retained in accordance with the CPIA 1996 Code of Practice (as amended)</li><li>that such material as is non-sensitive is shown on the schedule above,</li></ul> and that to the best of my knowledge and belief items… in the schedule might reasonably undermine the prosecution case, or assist the defence with the early preparation of their case or at a bail hearing, because…. Disclosure Officer Name SIGNATURE:	 CPS Prosecutor Name SIGNATURE:
Date	Date

Part III

FROM CHARGE TO TRIAL

Part III considers the procedural stages between charge/ requisition and a defendant having to appear in court to answer the allegations made against him.

In Chapter 9 we consider public funding of criminal proceedings and the early stages of the criminal litigation process.

Chapter 10 explains the court's role in granting and refusing bail.

Chapter 11 considers the special procedure in relation to an either-way offence.

In Chapter 12 we consider summary trials and the steps to be taken in preparing for a trial in the magistrates' court.

Finally, in Chapters 13 and 14 we explain the procedural stages of a trial on indictment in the Crown Court.

9.1	**Introduction**	**160**
9.2	**Legal aid—a human right?**	**160**
9.3	**Legal Aid Agency**	**160**
9.4	**Pre-charge advice and assistance**	**161**
	9.4.1 At the police station	161
	9.4.2 Pre-charge advice outside the police station	161
9.5	**Funded representation in court**	**161**
	9.5.1 Duty Solicitor Scheme	161
9.6	**Representation orders**	**162**
	9.6.1 Applying for a representation order	162
9.7	**The interests of justice test (CRM14)**	**162**
	9.7.1 Articulating the interests of justice test	163
	9.7.2 Loss of liberty	163
	9.7.3 Loss of livelihood	164
	9.7.4 Damage to reputation	164
	9.7.5 Substantial question of law	164
	9.7.6 Inadequate knowledge of english—physical or mental disability and cannot put case	165
	9.7.7 Tracing and interviewing of witnesses	165
	9.7.8 Expert cross-examination	165
	9.7.9 The interests of someone other than the defendant	165
	9.7.10 Any other reason	166
9.8	**Means testing (CRM15)**	**166**
9.9	**The means test as applied to cases tried in the magistrates' court**	**166**
	9.9.1 What counts as income?	167
	9.9.2 Is a partner's income included?	167
	9.9.3 Is capital taken into account?	168
	9.9.4 The full means test	168
	9.9.5 Payment for assisting a client to complete CRM14 and 15	168
	9.9.6 Hardship/eligibility review	169
	9.9.7 Right of appeal against a refusal of a representation order?	169
9.10	**The means test in cases triable on indictment**	**169**
	9.10.1 Provision for an either-way case sent to the Crown Court	170
	9.10.2 Provision in relation to a case which is committed for sentence	170
	9.10.3 Provision for an appeal against conviction and/or sentence to the Crown Court	170
	9.10.4 A summary of key differences between means testing in the magistrates' court and Crown Court	171

9.11 **What work can be done under a representation order?** 171

9.12 **Disbursements** 171

9.13 **Acquitted defendants and Defendants' Costs Order** 172

9.14 **Wasted costs** 172

9.15 **First appearance before the magistrates' court in summary-only and either-way offences** 172

    9.15.1 Case management of trial at first hearing 174

9.16 **Preparing for the first appearance before the magistrates' court** 175

9.1 INTRODUCTION

In this chapter we consider:

• the state funding of criminal defence work; and

• the early stages of a criminal case, including a defendant's first appearance before a magistrates' court and the steps a defence practitioner will take to prepare for this hearing.

9.2 LEGAL AID—A HUMAN RIGHT?

Every person charged with a criminal offence is entitled to defend himself in person or through legal assistance. Article 6(3)(c) European Convention on Human Rights 1950 enshrines this right and further stipulates that the entitlement to legal representation must be free where the person has insufficient means to pay and when the interests of justice require it.

A defendant faced with a criminal charge may pay privately for legal representation (but see para. 9.13 as there are implications for what may be recovered from public funds where the defendant is acquitted). The private funding of legal representation is relatively rare because apart from road traffic offences the vast majority of defendants who retain a defence solicitor have their legal expenses met by the state under the Legal Aid, Sentencing and Punishment of Offenders Act 2012 (LASPO 2012). It is part of defence solicitors' professional duty to consider the provision of state-funded assistance for their clients, Principle 7, Solicitors' Code of Conduct (2019).

The budget for the public funding of criminal defence services has been severely cut in recent years leading to a crisis in the criminal justice system which has been much documented in the press and on social media. In its 12 report on Criminal Legal Aid in July 2018, the Justice Select Committee recommended a comprehensive and independent review of criminal legal aid. A review of criminal legal aid was announced by the Ministry of Justice in December 2018 and will report in 2020.

The acute failings within the criminal justice system in the age of austerity and cuts have been exposed in the anonymous award-winning, best-selling, '*Stories of the Law and How it is Broken*' written by the Secret Barrister. We strongly recommend anyone who is passionate about criminal law practice to read this important work.

Approximately £1.2 billion is spent every year on criminal legal aid.

9.3 LEGAL AID AGENCY

The Legal Aid Agency (LAA) which is an executive agency working within the Ministry of Justice is responsible for administering criminal and civil legal aid.

Under the LAA Standard Crime Contract, which sets out the terms and conditions for firms selected to provide criminal legal aid services, all client files must be opened and maintained in a quality-assured way. Firms 'report' the work they have undertaken to the LAA and receive regular payments on that basis. Trainee solicitors, legal executives and paralegals working in franchised firms will be inducted into the procedures for opening and maintaining files to comply with LAA requirements. All of the CRM forms relating to the public funding of criminal defence services can be accessed from the LAA's website (http://www.gov.uk/government/organisations/legal-aid-agency). All files must contain a completed CRM1.

9.4 PRE-CHARGE ADVICE AND ASSISTANCE

9.4.1 AT THE POLICE STATION

Assistance at the police station is provided under the Police Station Advice and Assistance Scheme, which is explained in Chapter 4, para. 4.7.4.

9.4.2 PRE-CHARGE ADVICE OUTSIDE THE POLICE STATION

Reference should also be made to the pre-charge advice and assistance scheme. Funding under this scheme requires the defence practitioner to complete forms CRM1 and CRM2. The scheme is means-tested. Defendants receiving certain welfare benefits (including income-based job seeker's allowance and income support) qualify automatically in terms of their means. Assistance can only be provided under this scheme where the defence practitioner believes there is sufficient benefit to the client to justify the work being carried out. The scheme covers a client who seeks advice outside the police station in connection with a matter for which the client is under investigation but has not been charged. It also covers representation in connection with an investigation by a non-police body such as the Department for Work and Pensions.

9.5 FUNDED REPRESENTATION IN COURT

A defendant charged with a criminal offence who wishes to be represented by a solicitor in court must either:

- seek representation by the Court Duty Solicitor;
- apply to the court for a representation order; or
- pay privately.

9.5.1 DUTY SOLICITOR SCHEME

Representation at court by a duty solicitor is free and not subject to a means or merits test. However, a duty solicitor can only represent a defendant who is:

- in custody;
- charged or requisitioned in connection with an imprisonable offence;
- applying for bail (unless the defendant has used a duty solicitor for a previous application);
- at risk of imprisonment for failing to pay a fine or failing to obey a court order.

A duty solicitor *may not* represent someone in connection with:

- a trial;
- a hearing to send a case to the Crown Court;

- an application for bail (if that person has used a duty solicitor for a previous application); or

- a non-imprisonable offence (unless that person is in custody).

A duty solicitor is most likely to represent a defendant making a first appearance before a magistrates' court who wishes to plead guilty to a non-indictable-only offence(s) and be sentenced or who wishes to apply for bail, having been denied post-charge police bail. In this situation the defendant will appear before the magistrates' court in custody. If further representation beyond the limited scope of the duty solicitor scheme is required, the defendant must either represent himself or instruct a solicitor to appear for him under a representation order.

9.6 **REPRESENTATION ORDERS**

If a defendant requires publicly funded representation in court, the defendant must obtain a representation order. For both magistrates' court and Crown Court proceedings a defendant must satisfy a means test and the interests of justice (merits) test.

9.6.1 **APPLYING FOR A REPRESENTATION ORDER**

The relevant forms are:

- CRM14 eForm (Application for Legal Aid in Criminal Proceedings);
- CRM15 (Financial Statement for Legal Aid in Criminal Proceedings).

CRM14 eForm must be completed in all cases whether tried summarily or on indictment and contains the interests of justice test and the applicant's relevant personal information. The applicant **may** additionally be required to complete CRM15 (statement of financial means). A representation order application is processed administratively by the LAA. Ninety per cent of applications are determined within 48 hours, with priority applications (which include a defendant appearing in court in custody, having been denied police bail) being dealt with in a matter of hours. CRM14 eForm is completed and submitted electronically. The applicant is required to sign a declaration form which is to be kept on file which contains some important declarations and authorisations (see FORM 9.1 at the end of this chapter). The CRM14 eForm incorporates CRM15 and CRM15C (if required). To access the user guide for completing an online application, see https://www.gov.uk/guidance /legal-aid-crime-eform.

For a comprehensive explanation of criminal legal aid, consult the Criminal Legal Aid Manual available at https://www.gov.uk/government/publications/criminal-legal-aid-manual.

9.7 **THE INTERESTS OF JUSTICE TEST (CRM14)**

- The interests of justice (IoJ) test is automatically satisfied in a case where an accused is charged with an indictable-only offence which is sent to the Crown Court. The applicant needs only to tick the 'Indictable' box on the front page of CRM14 eForm for it to be processed on this basis.

- Where an accused is charged with a summary-only or either-way offence, a representation order will only be granted if the IoJ criteria are met.

- If an either-way offence fails the IoJ test but is subsequently sent to the Crown Court (see Chapter 11), the IoJ test is automatically satisfied by the sending.

- The IoJ test must be met where a convicted defendant seeks publicly funded representation to appeal against conviction and/or sentence before the Crown Court.

The Legal Aid, Sentencing and Punishment of Offenders Act 2012 (Criminal Legal Aid (General) Regulations 2013) provides that if any of the following grounds apply, the IoJ test is satisfied and a defendant is entitled to a representation order:

- **if proven the defendant is likely to lose his liberty or livelihood or suffer serious damage to his reputation;**
- **the case involves a substantial question of law;**
- **the defendant is under a mental or physical disability or has inadequate knowledge of English such that the defendant is unable to follow the proceedings or put his case;**
- **the defence involves the tracing and interviewing of witnesses or expert cross-examination of a prosecution witness;**
- **legal representation is desirable in the interests of someone other than the accused.**

9.7.1 ARTICULATING THE INTERESTS OF JUSTICE TEST

How does the defence practitioner articulate the IoJ test?

Take a look at CRM14 (see the completed copy in relation to the *Lenny Wise* case study in Appendix 2—this is not the eForm version). The interests of justice grounds are listed at Question 29 of the form. Defence practitioners should articulate as many of the grounds as possible, in sufficient detail to maximise the chances of a representation order being granted. A copy of the non e-version of CRM14 can be found on the LAA's website: https://www.gov.uk/government/publications/criminal-legal-aid-application-forms. Helpful guidance on completing CRM14 and CRM15 can also be found on this page. Detailed guidance on completing the interests of justice test can be accessed at https://www.gov.uk/government/uploads/system/uploads/attachment_data/file/314453/LAA-guidance-consideration-defence-representation-order-applications.pdf.

The articulation of the IoJ test will now be considered.

9.7.2 LOSS OF LIBERTY

Obviously the more serious the offence, the more likely the defendant could go to prison if convicted. There must be a real—as opposed to a theoretical—risk of imprisonment. Many offences carry a theoretical risk of imprisonment, for example theft. However, a first-time conviction for theft of a small sum of money would not result in imprisonment.

The defence practitioner should research the relevant sentencing guidelines for the offence charged by reference to the Magistrates' Court Sentencing Guidelines (MCSGs) (extracts from which are reproduced at Appendix 3). The MCSGs indicate the starting point and the range of sentences based on the type of conduct in the commission of the offence. If the sentencing guidelines suggest that a custodial sentence is the appropriate starting point upon conviction, the guidelines should be cited to support the loss of liberty ground. You should also list any aggravating features in the alleged commission of the offence (i.e. vulnerable victim or a theft in breach of trust etc.).

If the guidelines suggest a sentencing starting point of a community penalty, the defence practitioner needs to consider whether any aggravating features in the offence makes custody more likely. This would include where the defendant has previous convictions for a similar offence or the offence was committed whilst on bail in connection with other criminal matters. Full details of previous offending and the sentence imposed should be given. If a copy of the defendant's criminal record is available this should be included in the application. If the defendant is subject to a suspended sentence of imprisonment, the risk of a prison sentence on conviction for the new offence is more likely. Similarly, if the defendant is subject to an existing community order, conviction for the current offence may result in that order being revoked and the defendant being resentenced for the earlier offence. By definition, being charged with a serious either-way offence gives rise to a real risk of imprisonment upon conviction; being charged with a summary-only offence does not.

9.7.3 LOSS OF LIVELIHOOD

Does the defendant stand to lose his job if convicted? If so, this needs to be carefully and fully articulated. The likely loss of livelihood should be a direct consequence of the conviction or sentence. Articulation of this ground depends on the defendant's job and the nature of the offence. If a defendant is at risk of a custodial sentence, the chances of him losing his employment are likely to be high. The prospect of lost employment would be particularly high where, for example, the offence involves an allegation of theft from an employer or the offence is of a sexual or violent nature and the defendant's job includes contact with children and young people. Loss of livelihood normally refers to current livelihood. Arguably, a client training for a profession may be eligible to be included in this ground.

Road traffic offences may result in loss of livelihood through disqualification from driving upon conviction. However, some driving offences are minor in nature and, consequently, it may be difficult to obtain a representation order for minor driving offences. Assertions that mandatory disqualification from driving will result in a loss of livelihood will be examined critically. A right to representation would not normally be justified where a defendant seeks to avoid disqualification under the totting-up disqualification procedure having acquired 12 or more penalty points on his driving licence, or for a drink-driving offence. Where there is a strong argument for advancing special reasons for avoiding disqualification (see the Additional Chapter 'Sentencing in Road Traffic Cases' in the online resources), the interests of justice might be met.

9.7.4 DAMAGE TO REPUTATION

If convicted, is the defendant likely to suffer serious damage to his reputation? If so, this needs to be articulated. Examples might include a conviction for a sexual offence or a first-time conviction for dishonesty. If the defendant already has a previous conviction for a similar offence or has a conviction for a more serious offence, it will be difficult to argue that the defendant is likely to suffer damage to his or her reputation. A previous conviction of itself, however, does not preclude applying under this ground where, for example, the defendant has been convicted of a relatively minor offence, or a 'spent' conviction, but is now charged with a much more serious offence. The defendant's job and the precise nature of the offence are relevant when assessing loss of reputation.

9.7.5 SUBSTANTIAL QUESTION OF LAW

Does the applicant's case involve a substantial question of law? If it does, the defence practitioner should explain in detail what the point of law is. This includes a legal argument about the *actus reus* and *mens rea* elements of the offence, where, for example, a defendant is pleading not guilty to assault, submitting that she acted in self-defence or was intoxicated (where the crime is one of specific or ulterior intent) or lacked dishonest intent on a charge of theft in accordance with *R v Ghosh* [1982] 3 WLR 110 and *Ivey v Genting Casinos* [2017] UKSC 67. In this situation it is clearly in the interests of justice for the defendant to be legally represented.

A substantial question of law also covers challenging the admissibility of evidence including:

- arguments about whether it is appropriate to draw an adverse inference from an accused's silence at the police station under s. 34 Criminal Justice and Public Order Act 1994 (see Chapter 5);

- applying to have a confession excluded under ss. 76 and 78 Police and Criminal Evidence Act 1984 (PACE 1984) for breaches of Code C (see Chapter 6);

- applying to have identification evidence excluded under s. 78 PACE 1984 for breach of Code D (see Chapter 7);

- disputing the admissibility of hearsay evidence (see Chapter 18);

- disputing the admissibility of bad character evidence under the Criminal Justice Act 2003 (see Chapter 19).

The IoJ test requires the defence lawyer to explain precisely the point of law that applies to the applicant's case.

9.7.6 INADEQUATE KNOWLEDGE OF ENGLISH—PHYSICAL OR MENTAL DISABILITY AND CANNOT PUT CASE

This ground applies where the applicant has inadequate knowledge of English, or is unable to communicate (perhaps because of a speech impediment or lack of literacy), or suffers from a mental or physical disability. Clearly it is in the interests of justice for the defendant to be represented by a lawyer. Full details of the lack of knowledge of English or the disability must be given, for example: 'I have been diagnosed with clinical depression by my GP who has prescribed a tranquilliser', 'I speak Urdu and have a little knowledge of basic English but would be unable to understand the advance information or follow technical or legal phrases adequately.'

9.7.7 TRACING AND INTERVIEWING OF WITNESSES

If the accused's defence requires a witness to be traced and/or interviewed this should be explained and details provided. The reason for wanting to trace or interview a witness should be made clear, along with an indication of how the witness will assist the defendant's case. For example, a witness may provide the defendant with an alibi. Where a defence witness is known to the defendant, it is often better for the witness to be approached and interviewed by the legal representative in order to preserve the witness's independence. If a prosecution witness is to be interviewed on behalf of the defendant, this should also be undertaken by a lawyer, although it is unusual for a defence practitioner to interview a prosecution witness before the trial as this would raise professional conduct issues (see Chapter 1, para. 1.11.6). This ground under the IoJ test can also be used where the defence seeks to instruct an expert witness.

9.7.8 EXPERT CROSS-EXAMINATION

This ground is not confined to the cross-examination of an expert witness but can be used for any defendant who is pleading not guilty as this will trigger the need to cross-examine witnesses. The defence practitioner should explain why the defendant would have difficulty in personally cross-examining the witnesses. The witness might be, for example, an expert or a police officer or an eye-witness whose evidence is crucial or someone with a purpose of their own to serve. The cross-examination may raise points of law, which necessarily requires legal expertise.

9.7.9 THE INTERESTS OF SOMEONE OTHER THAN THE DEFENDANT

Is it in the interests of someone other than the defendant that the defendant should be represented by a solicitor?

This ground often causes confusion. The 'someone other' is largely restricted to those who are directly affected by the proceedings in their capacity as witnesses. It would clearly not be in the interests of justice if an accused charged with a sexual offence was to cross-examine the alleged victim in person. Similarly, in the case of a vulnerable prosecution witness, such as an elderly eye-witness to a burglary or a child witness. This also applies when the matter relate to a domestic abuse allegation. At no point would it be appropriate to cross examine in these circumstances. It would be argued that it is in the interests of justice for the accused to be represented by a solicitor rather than to allow the accused himself to cross-examine the witness. Indeed sections 34–36 Youth Justice and Criminal Evidence Act 1999 prohibit a defendant from personally cross-examining a complainant in specified sexual offence cases and this prohibition extends to personally cross-examining a child witness in relation to an offence of a sexual or violent nature.

9.7.10 ANY OTHER REASON

This final, catch-all ground could include the need to skilfully examine a defence witness or to carefully review the evidence in the case or to seek further disclosure from the prosecution. Perhaps even the overriding objective in Crim PR, Part 1, and specifically the need for cases to be dealt with expeditiously might be cited in support of 'any other reason'.

A defendant will be granted a representation order where the defendant's case satisfies one or more of the IoJ criteria as previously explained. Obviously it is more difficult to satisfy the test where the defendant is charged with a minor, summary-only offence and conversely the IoJ test is more easily satisfied in connection with a serious either-way offence. Remember that the IoJ test is automatically satisfied where the applicant is charged with an indictable-only offence.

9.8 MEANS TESTING (CRM15)

Means testing applies to representation orders in the Crown Court and in the magistrates' court. Some applicants are 'passported', which means they do not need to complete CRM15. 'Passported' applicants include those:

- under 18; and
- applicants in receipt of any of the following welfare benefits: Income Support, Income Based Jobseeker's Allowance, Guaranteed State Pension Credit, and Income-Based Employment Support Allowance.

In addition, applicants with an income of less than £12,475, who do not own a house and who do not have any savings/investments, are not required to complete CRM15.

Applicants must provide their National Insurance number if aged over 16, or proof of welfare benefits. The application cannot be processed without this information. All other applicants must complete the means test on CRM15 and, depending on the answers given on CRM 15, also complete CRM15C. The applicant's financial eligibility is determined administratively by the LAA. Criminal defence practitioners can give clients an indication as to whether they are likely to pass the means test by inputting their financial details on the LAA's Online Financial Eligibility Calculator, which can be accessed at http://www.justice. gov.uk/legal-aid/assess-your-clients-eligibility.

9.9 THE MEANS TEST AS APPLIED TO CASES TRIED IN THE MAGISTRATES' COURT

Means testing in magistrates' court proceedings is confined to an assessment of income alone. In contrast to Crown Court means testing, capital is not taken into account. The means testing scheme in the magistrates' court is said to be an 'in or out' scheme. The applicant either qualifies in terms of his means, in which case (subject to satisfying the IoJ test) he qualifies for a representation order, or he does not, in which case he is ineligible.

The magistrates' court means test comprises two elements: an initial assessment and a full means test. The initial assessment takes account of the applicant's gross annual income and adjusts it against the applicant's family unit size by applying a 'weighting' formula. Once the applicant's 'weighted' gross annual income figure is determined the applicant will either be:

- eligible; or
- ineligible; or
- a full means test will be required.

On current figures the thresholds are as follows:

- A 'weighted' gross annual income of less than £12,475: applicant passes the means test and need not complete CRM15.
- Greater than £22,325 and CRM15 will need to be completed: applicant fails the means test and cannot therefore be granted a representation order to cover proceedings in the magistrates' court.
- If the applicant's 'weighted' income falls between the lower and upper threshold, a full means test must be undertaken and CRM15 will need to be completed.

9.9.1 WHAT COUNTS AS INCOME?

Income for these purposes is total income from all sources, including wages, state benefits (unless specifically disregarded), maintenance payments, benefits in kind, income from savings and investments, rent and student loan payments. The calculation is based on income received in the 12-month period before the application. Disregarded state benefits for this purpose include:

- attendance allowance;
- severe disablement allowance;
- carer's allowance;
- disability living allowance;
- housing benefit;
- council tax benefit;
- any payment made out of a social fund.

The applicant must produce proof of income. This can include the most recent wage slip or, where self-employed, the most recent tax return or set of accounts. Proof of income can be waived for an employed or self-employed applicant who has been produced before a magistrates' court in police custody and who is subsequently remanded into custody by the magistrates' court and who therefore cannot get access to financial information. This must be indicated on CRM15.

For the purposes of the initial assessment, the applicant's gross annual income is 'weighted' by applying a mathematical formula which takes account of a partner and children living as dependants in the same household.

9.9.2 IS A PARTNER'S INCOME INCLUDED?

A partner's income is included in the assessment of means. A partner is defined as anyone (including a person of the same sex) with whom the applicant lives as a couple.

The applicant's partner is required to sign CRM14 and 15 where their means are aggregated. The requirement for a signature is waived if the applicant is remanded in custody by the court or the partner is indisposed in some way. The eForm is submitted without a signature. To prevent false statements from the applicant, the LAA requires the applicant and partner (if applicable) to sign a paper form declaration to confirm the accuracy of the information provided which must be retained on the client's file.

A partner's income will not be aggregated where the partner has a contrary interest including where the partner is:

- the alleged victim; or
- a prosecution witness; or
- both are defendants and there is a conflict between them.

9.9.3 IS CAPITAL TAKEN INTO ACCOUNT?

An applicant's capital assets are completely ignored for means testing in relation to magistrates' court proceedings.

9.9.4 THE FULL MEANS TEST

The purpose of the full means test is to calculate the applicant's annual disposable income. This is based on the applicant's gross annual income (not 'weighted' annual income). Where the applicant's annual disposable income currently exceeds £3,398, the applicant will be financially ineligible to receive public funding for proceedings in the magistrates' court.

In calculating the applicant's annual disposable income, deductions are made for:

- income tax and National Insurance contributions (for the applicant and partner if partner's income is aggregated);
- housing costs (i.e. rent/mortgage);
- childcare fees (excluding private education);
- maintenance to a former partner;
- an annual living allowance (calculated using a mathematical formula).

The calculations required for both the initial and full means test can be performed on the LAA's online financial calculator. You are reminded that it is the court which undertakes the means test to determine eligibility. For detailed guidance on all aspects of means testing for magistrates' court and Crown Court proceedings (see later) access: https://www.gov.uk/criminal-legal-aid-means-testing.

9.9.5 PAYMENT FOR ASSISTING A CLIENT TO COMPLETE CRM14 AND 15

A defendant who wishes to apply for a representation order will require assistance to complete CRM14 and 15 if applicable. Where a representation order is granted, the defence practitioner can claim 30 minutes' worth of assistance under the representation order. Where a representation order is refused because the applicant fails the means test, the solicitor can claim a fixed fee of £75 under the *early cover scheme* provided the applicant instructed his solicitor before the first hearing and his solicitor submitted his application for a representation order within five days of being instructed. Where a representation order is refused under the IoJ test, the solicitor can claim one hour's preparatory work under the *pre-order cover scheme*. The work typically covered under these post-charge schemes includes:

- taking a client's instructions;
- assisting the client to complete an application for a representation order;

- routine letters and telephone calls to the court and the Crown Prosecution Service (CPS).

9.9.6 HARDSHIP/ELIGIBILITY REVIEW

A hardship/eligibility review application may be submitted when:

- a defendant is refused legal aid because he fails the means test; or
- a defendant thinks he will fail the means test but has exceptional financial circumstances perhaps due to unusually high outgoings or because defence costs are likely to be unusually expensive.

To apply for a hardship/eligibility review, the applicant must complete CRM16.

9.9.7 RIGHT OF APPEAL AGAINST A REFUSAL OF A REPRESENTATION ORDER?

If the applicant fails the IoJ test, he has the right to submit a further application and thereafter a right of appeal to the magistrates' court.

If the applicant fails the means test there is no right of appeal. However, the applicant can ask for a reassessment of his means if his circumstances have changed or a recalculation if the applicant thinks that an error has been made.

9.10 THE MEANS TEST IN CASES TRIABLE ON INDICTMENT

A defendant charged with an indictable-only offence or charged with an either-way offence whose case is sent to the Crown Court will be means-tested to determine whether the defendant is eligible and, if so, how much the defendant will have to contribute towards the costs of his defence.

As already noted, there is a significant difference between the means testing scheme applicable to magistrates' court proceedings and the scheme in the Crown Court. In the magistrates' court, means testing is restricted solely to the applicant's income. The Crown Court scheme is *contributory* and is assessed against the applicant's *income, capital and equity*. This requires the applicant to provide additional information on CRM15/CRM15C relating to income and capital assets. There is no self-certification of income for employed or self-employed applicants who are remanded into custody by a court as there is for cases that are concluded in the magistrates' court. Whilst the application can be processed without proof of income, outgoings and capital, proof must be submitted within 14 days of the case being sent to the Crown Court. An additional fee is available to defence solicitors who assist defendants to obtain the required evidence where they have been remanded in custody. If supporting evidence of income is not provided, an 'income evidence sanction' will be applied which can increase the amount to be paid under a contribution notice to £900 per month or more, depending on income. If evidence of capital assets is not provided the rules permit removal of the £30,000 allowance with the result that a convicted offender may be asked to pay his costs in full.

Subject to the outcome of the means assessment in the Crown Court, some defendants may have to contribute to some or all of their defence legal costs under a *contribution notice/order*. The contribution may be from income, capital or a combination of each. Some applicants will be ineligible. Income thresholds now apply to the Crown Court following changes brought into effect on 27 January 2014.

A client whose annual household disposable income is £37,500 or more is ineligible for legal aid in Crown Court trials and must pay privately for legal representation. Applicants who are refused legal aid for a Crown Court trial because they have disposable income of over the £37,500 threshold may also submit a CRM16 to request an 'Eligibility Review'.

As in the magistrates' court, certain applicants automatically qualify in terms of their means. They include applicants under 18 and those in receipt of any of the following welfare benefits: Income Support, Income-Based Jobseeker's Allowance; Guaranteed State Pension Credit. Such applicants do not need to complete CRM15. An applicant whose annual household disposable income is between £3,399 and £37,499.99 will be subject to a contribution notice. Income-based contributions are set at 90% of disposable income (limited to a maximum contribution calculated according to the type of offence being tried) and are payable by six monthly instalments (five, if all instalment payments are paid on time). If the defendant is acquitted, all income-based payments made under a contribution notice will be refunded with interest.

The combined capital and equity threshold for Crown Court proceedings is £30,000. Any capital-based contributions under a contribution order are payable at the conclusion of the case if the applicant is convicted and his monthly contributions from income have not covered his defence costs in full.

Any applicant who is assessed as having to make a contribution towards his legal costs can submit a hardship review application and can ask for his contribution order to be reviewed and recalculated if he feels it has been computed in error or his circumstances have changed.

A Crown Court representation order will not be revoked or withdrawn for non-payment of a contribution order. However, there are enforcement measures available and non-payment will increase the overall cost liability.

9.10.1 PROVISION FOR AN EITHER-WAY CASE SENT TO THE CROWN COURT

When applying for a representation order to cover the proceedings before the magistrates' court, the applicant will need to complete CRM14 and (if applicable CRM15 including the property and capital aspect of the form). If the applicant failed the IoJ test initially but his case is subsequently sent to the Crown Court for trial, he will be passported through the IoJ test.

What happens to an applicant who is charged with an either-way offence who fails the means test in the magistrates' court but whose case is subsequently sent to the Crown Court? The applicant's means will be reassessed to calculate any contribution order/notice. The applicant's representation order will then cover proceedings from the date after the case has been sent to the Crown Court.

9.10.2 PROVISION IN RELATION TO A CASE WHICH IS COMMITTED FOR SENTENCE

A representation order granted in the magistrates' court will cover proceedings subsequently committed for sentence to the Crown Court.

Any applicant who failed to apply for funding in the magistrates' court may apply to cover the proceedings in connection with a committal for sentence. Such an applicant would automatically satisfy the IoJ test but would be subject to a means test based on income only. If the applicant applied for a representation order before the magistrates' court but failed the means test, the regulations stipulate that such an individual will be ineligible for publicly funded assistance upon committal for sentence in the Crown Court unless there has been a change in circumstances. The applicant can submit a hardship review application using form CRM16.

9.10.3 PROVISION FOR AN APPEAL AGAINST CONVICTION AND/OR SENTENCE TO THE CROWN COURT

Where an appeal is made to the Crown Court against conviction and/or sentence in summary proceedings a further CRM14 application is required. If the appellant was granted a representation order by the magistrates' court and his financial circumstances have not

TABLE 9.1 A SUMMARY OF KEY DIFFERENCES

Magistrates' court	Crown Court
Must meet the interests of justice test.	'Passported' through interests of justice test (except for appeals).
Income-only means test.	Income, capital and equity are means-tested.
Simple in/out test (if income means tested is failed, no representation order).	In/out income test and also contribution-based scheme if capital is above a certain level and/or income is within certain thresholds. If so, a representation order will still be granted subject to a contribution order/notice.
Representation order issued for eligible defendants.	Contribution order/notice issued alongside representation order.
Evidence of income required.	Evidence of income and capital required.
Self-certification of income for defendants remanded in custody.	No self-certification of income/capital for defendants remanded in custody.

changed and he indicates this on CRM14, he need not submit a further CRM15. The IoJ test will need to be satisfied where a convicted applicant seeks publicly funded representation on appeal before the Crown Court. Financial eligibility is based on the 'in or out' scheme that applies in the magistrates' court. However, where an applicant's income is above the threshold and the appeal is abandoned or the appeal is partly or wholly unsuccessful, the applicant will have to make a contribution ranging from £250 to £500.

9.10.4 A SUMMARY OF KEY DIFFERENCES BETWEEN MEANS TESTING IN THE MAGISTRATES' COURT AND CROWN COURT

Table 9.1 summarises the key differences between means testing in the magistrates' court and the Crown Court.

9.11 WHAT WORK CAN BE DONE UNDER A REPRESENTATION ORDER?

A representation order covers the entire proceedings in the magistrates' court including an application for bail before the Crown Court. It covers advice about a possible appeal to the Crown Court against conviction and/or sentence. For representation at an appeal, a further application for a representation order has to be made to either the magistrates' court or the Crown Court (see para. 9.10.3).

Where a representation order is granted to cover cases triable on indictment, the order will cover the costs of representation in the Crown Court and will extend to obtaining advice when appealing against conviction and/or sentence to the Court of Appeal.

9.12 DISBURSEMENTS

It may be necessary for the accused's lawyer to incur disbursements in preparing the defence case. This might include instructing an expert witness, an interpreter or enquiry agent or obtaining the transcript of an interview. Solicitors should always seek prior authorisation from the LAA to incur expenditure in excess of £100 using Form CRM4 eForm. It will be necessary to show that this course of action is in the client's best interests and that it is reasonable to incur the disbursement and that the amount to be incurred is reasonable. The defence practitioner should therefore ascertain in advance the amount of expenditure that will be needed. In the *R v Lenny Wise* case study (the complete version of which can be accessed in the online resources), as part of the case preparation, Lenny Wise's solicitor obtains the LAA's prior authorisation to obtain an expert report from Lenny's consultant psychiatrist.

9.13 ACQUITTED DEFENDANTS AND DEFENDANTS' COSTS ORDER

An acquitted defendant who has incurred expenditure in conducting his defence (which clearly applies to a privately funded acquitted defendant) is generally entitled to costs from central funds (Defendants' Costs Order) for such an amount as the court considers reasonably sufficient to compensate for costs incurred (s. 16 Prosecution of Offenders Act 1985 (POA 1985)). While such orders are at the court's discretion, they should normally be awarded unless it is felt that the accused brought suspicion on himself by his conduct and misled the prosecution into thinking the evidence against him was stronger than it was. Guidance can be found in *Practice Direction (Crime: Costs)* [1991] 1 WLR 498.

A legally aided acquitted defendant's costs will obviously be met under the representation order.

Provision in LASPO 2012 has seen the amount payable to a privately paying acquitted defendant out of central funds capped to legal aid rates for magistrates' court cases. In relation to Crown Court cases, an acquitted privately funded client will only be able to recover defence costs at legal aid rates, if a determination of financial ineligibility has been made because the applicant's annual disposable income exceeds £37,500. To ensure that a non-legally aided client can apply to recover legal costs in the event of an acquittal (albeit limited to legal aid rates), they must apply for a representation order, even if likely to be ineligible. No costs can be recovered where a client, who would have been eligible for legal aid with a contribution, chooses to pay privately, but is then acquitted. This change effectively compels some clients to accept legal aid with a contribution rather than paying privately.

The implications of recent changes to s. 16 POA 1985 has led the Law Society to issue a Practice Note: http://www.lawsociety.org.uk/advice/practice-notes/defence-costs-orders/. This Practice Note should be read by all criminal lawyers. It stipulates that a client must be advised of all the relevant funding options that are open to them and the advantages and disadvantages of each. The advice must be set out in a client care letter and must include information on the effect of s. 16 POA 1985. In relation to Crown Court proceedings, the Practice Note states at para. 2.5.

> 'You must advise your client to apply for legal aid, even if likely to be ineligible, to preserve their right to recover some of their legal costs, in the event they are acquitted or otherwise successful.'

9.14 WASTED COSTS

Where a defence solicitor or the CPS has wasted the court's time by an improper, unreasonable or negligent act or omission, s. 19 POA 1985 permits the court to make a wasted costs order.

9.15 FIRST APPEARANCE BEFORE THE MAGISTRATES' COURT IN SUMMARY-ONLY AND EITHER-WAY OFFENCES

This next section should be read in conjunction with the disclosure of evidence rules explained in Chapter 8.

Irrespective of the classification of the offence charged the defendant's first appearance will be before a magistrates' court—even in the case of an indictable-only offence. (The procedure at the first appearance in connection with an indictable-only offence is explained in Chapter 13.)

The procedure at the defendant's first court hearing in connection with a summary-only or an either-way offence will be required to comply with the requirements of several policy initiatives that have been introduced with the aim of making the criminal justice system more efficient. These initiatives are CJ-SSS (Simple, Speedy, Summary, Criminal Justice) and SDJ (Stop Delaying Justice) and most recently Transforming Summary Justice (TSJ) which was introduced in 2015.

Where an offence may be tried summarily, TSJ requires a magistrates' court to:

(a) take a plea from the accused at the first hearing; and

(b) where a not guilty plea is entered (and the case is to remain in the magistrates' court) to engage in robust case management in order to set a firm date for a summary trial to be held within six to eight weeks of the defendant's first court appearance.

TSJ adopts a near zero tolerance to adjournments in cases that can be tried summarily.

Building upon these reforms the defendant's first court appearance in connection with a summary offence will be governed by whether it is anticipated that the defendant will plead guilty or not guilty. On this basis under TSJ the defendant's first hearing in the magistrates' court will either be before a 'guilty anticipated plea' court (GAP) or a 'not guilty anticipated' court (NGAP).

TSJ aligns with the new Streamlined Disclosure Certificate (SDC) outlined in Chapter 8.

Guilty Anticipated Plea (GAP)

Where the defendant is expected to plead guilty at the first hearing the case will be listed within 14 days of being charged with the aim of dealing with the matter at one hearing. There is an expectation that the defendant will be sentenced on the day with no adjournment for the preparation of a pre-sentence report. If a pre-sentence is required it will be prepared by the Probation Service on the day or, if required, following an adjournment.

Prior to the GAP hearing the CPS will comply with its obligations under Crim PR, Part 8 by serving on the defence initial details of the prosecution case (IDPC) and written confirmation that the prosecution has complied with its common law duties of disclosures as a streamlined disclosure certification (SDC) is not required (see Chapter 8, para. 8.10.2).

If an unexpected not guilty plea is entered before a GAP hearing, the court will proceed to an allocation hearing if the offence is triable either-way (see Chapter 11) and/or the court will set a firm date for a summary trial.

Anticipated Not Guilty Plea (NGAP)

Anticipated not guilty plea cases will be listed for hearing 28 days after charge, allowing time for review and to prepare for the first hearing.

If the accused is charged with a summary offence or an either-way offence that is likely to remain in the magistrates' court and it is considered that they will plead not guilty, the disclosure officer must prepare an SDC as explained in Chapter 8, para. 8.10.2. The SDC will be served on the defence at or before the first hearing along with the IDPC.

If there is no material or other evidence that is considered as undermining the prosecution case or assisting the defence the officer should complete the appropriate entry on the streamlined disclosure certificate.

All NGAP cases are prepared with the expectation that the trial will take place on the day or if not, a definite trial date will be set.

If the defendant chooses to plead guilty at a NGAP hearing the magistrates' court will proceed to sentence immediately.

If a not guilty plea is entered and the offence is triable either-way, the magistrates' court will expect to proceed to the allocation hearing (see Chapter 11) and if the matter is to remain in the magistrates' court to be tried summarily, the court will want to fix a firm date for summary trial, as explained at para. 9.15.1. The magistrates' court will expect each party to be in possession of sufficient information (including witness availability) to enable the date to be fixed for a summary trial. Where the case is adjourned the defendant will either be released unconditionally or be remanded on bail or in custody.

Remand court

A defendant appearing for the first time before a magistrates' court in custody (having been denied bail by the police upon being charged (see Chapter 4, para. 4.14.3) will appear before the remand court of the magistrates' court. Such a court has a secure dock facility. The defendant on remand is still expected to enter a plea based on the available IDPC which will be handed to the defence at court.

For an excellent illustration of simple, speedy summary justice, consider the prosecution of Paul Mitchell. On Sunday 10 March 2019 Mitchell ran onto the pitch during the football match between Birmingham City and Aston Villa, and assaulted the Villa captain Jack Grealish. He was arrested for pitch invasion and assault, charged and denied police bail that same day. He appeared before Birmingham Magistrates' Court the next day, 11 March where he pleaded guilty and was imprisoned for 14 weeks and was given a 10-year football match banning order before his tearful family. (See https://www.independent.co.uk/sport/football/football-league/jack-grealish-attack-birmingham-city-fan-paul-mitchell-aston-villa-jail-a8817911.html.)

9.15.1 CASE MANAGEMENT OF TRIAL AT FIRST HEARING

A key part of the efficient case management under TSJ is the mandatory requirement for all magistrates' courts to use the trial preparation form, a copy of which can be found at the end of Chapter 12 (Form 12.1). This paragraph should be read in conjunction with Chapter 12, para. 12.6.2.

To assist the court to complete the trial preparation form, the defendant will be asked to explain why he is pleading not guilty and what aspects of the prosecution's case he disputes.

Both the defence and the prosecution will be expected to identify what is in issue between them (Crim PR, Part 3.3) and whether any point of law arises. If the defence fails or refuses to identify the real issues in dispute the defendant is unlikely to be allowed to advance at trial a defence he has not disclosed on the case management form. The court will want to know how many witnesses each side will be calling; whether any witness statements can be agreed and be read at court under s. 9 Criminal Justice Act 1967 (CJA 1967) (see Chapter 12, para. 12.6.2); whether any live witnesses are likely to need special measures (see Chapter 16); and whether hearsay (see Chapter 18) or bad character (see Chapter 19) applications are envisaged. When taking the parties through the trial preparation form, the court will actively enquire as to why it is necessary for a particular witness to attend and whether, in the light of the issues that are in dispute, the witness's evidence can be agreed and read to the court. The parties will be encouraged to draft appropriate admissions under s. 10 CJA 1967 (see Chapter 15, para 15.8) to avoid unnecessarily calling witnesses and to identify the core issues in the case. The case management aspect of TSJ is entirely consistent with the overriding objective in Crim PR, Part 1 that cases will be dealt with justly, efficiently and expeditiously taking into account the gravity of the offence alleged, the complexity of what is in issue, the severity of the consequences for the defendant and others affected and the needs of other cases. For consideration of the professional conduct obligations which are placed on criminal defence practitioners as a consequence of active case management by the courts see Chapter 1, para. 1.11.8.

'Virtual' courts

Section 57C CDA 1998 permits a magistrates' court to direct that a preliminary hearing before a court be conducted via live-link from a police station. The provisions apply both to defendants who are detained at the police station under s. 57C(3) CDA 1998 and to defendants who have been bailed to return to the police station for a live-link appearance in connection with the offence ('live-link bail') (s. 57C(4) CDA 1998). Section 57C(7) contains an express requirement for the defendant's consent to be given before the court makes a live-link direction. An accused answering to live-link bail is to be treated as having surrendered to custody of the court from the time when it makes a live-link direction in respect of him.

Section 57D CDA 1998 provides that where the accused attends a preliminary hearing over a live-link and is convicted in the course of it, and the court proposes to proceed immediately to sentence, the accused may continue to attend over the link provided that he or she agrees and the court is satisfied that it is not contrary to the interests of justice.

The LAA funds representation before a virtual court through the 'Advocacy Assistance Scheme' (CRM 3). This is a non-means tested, virtual court fixed fee simply to cover this hearing. If the matter proceeds to a second hearing a legal aid application has to be made in the usual way, otherwise the advocate will receive only the fixed fee.

The Law Society has issued a Practice Note on Virtual Courts accessible at http://www.lawsociety.org.uk/support-services-/advice/practice-notes/virtual-courts/ which explains what a defence practitioner should have regard to when advising a client whether to consent to appear via live-link from a police station.

9.16 PREPARING FOR THE FIRST APPEARANCE BEFORE THE MAGISTRATES' COURT

Typical steps to be undertaken in preparation for an accused's first appearance before a magistrates' court include:

- conducting an initial interview with the defendant (this interview may take place at the police station, in the solicitor's office or at court);
- opening a file;
- completing an application for a representation order;
- requesting IDPC from the CPS (if there is time before the first hearing);
- anticipating problems with bail.

Opening a file
Every publicly funded defence practitioner is required to open a file for each new client and to complete a standard CRM1 form. Every file has to be allocated a Unique File Number (UFN), a requirement under the General Criminal Contract. All fee-earning time spent on the matter must be recorded.

Initial interview
If the defendant has been charged and released on police bail or has received a requisition/summons, the defendant should be in possession of a summons/requisition or charge sheet which will enable the defence practitioner to check the precise nature of the allegations which her client is facing. The initial interview is important for extracting information whilst events are hopefully still fresh in the defendant's mind. The defence practitioner should obtain all the defendant's personal details as well as an accurate list of previous convictions and details of the defendant's financial circumstances.

During the first interview, the defence practitioner must discuss funding issues with her client. If representation in court is needed, a representation order should be applied for without delay. If the defendant is required to produce evidence of income in support of his application for a representation order, he must be instructed to produce this information without delay.

General advice about the likely progress of the case and the possible plea/sentence might be offered to the defendant at this stage. Unless the matter is very clear-cut, however, defence practitioners should wait until they are in possession of the prosecution's evidence (IDPC) before offering any firm advice as to plea.

At the conclusion of the initial interview, the defence practitioner will typically:

- submit an application for a representation order;
- write to her client confirming his instructions;
- request disclosure of the prosecution's case (IDPC);
- contact any potential defence witnesses with a view to taking a statement.

Each of these will now be briefly considered.

Submit an application for a representation order

The application for a representation order will be submitted electronically or sent to the appropriate office of the LAA.

Write to her client confirming her instructions

At an early stage the defence practitioner will send her client a client care letter in accordance with the SRA Code of Conduct 2019 (see Chapter 1) which should confirm her client's instructions and provide information about costs. It is customary for a file to hold a client's proof of evidence. A proof of evidence is a statement of the facts recounted at the client's initial interview. In due course (and especially where a not guilty plea is anticipated) the proof of evidence will be an important source of information to the advocate representing the defendant at trial. If an initial proof of evidence is drafted, the client should be given the opportunity to review its content, sign and date it (see Appendix 2, Document 6).

Request disclosure of the prosecution's 'used' material

The rules relating to the pre-trial disclosure of evidence against a defendant are of considerable importance and have been considered in greater detail in Chapter 8. Crim PR, Part 8 requires the CPS to serve initial details of the prosecution case (IDPC) on the accused in all cases that are triable summarily. In accordance with TSJ, where a guilty plea is anticipated, this will include a statement to the effect that the prosecution understands its common law duties of disclosure have been complied with. Where a not guilty plea is anticipated, IDPC will additionally include a Streamlined Disclosure Certificate (SDC) comprising any unused material which needs to be disclosed in accordance with the prosecutor's duty under s. 3 CPIA 1996. The CPS has moved to the digital service of evidence, although paper copies are still being served in custody cases. In indictable-only offences, further comprehensive disclosure is made later in the proceedings but, in accordance with the prosecution's common law duties of disclosure, it must disclose any evidence at this early state which would assist the defence with the early preparation of their case or at a bail hearing. Under TSJ, IDPC must be available on the defendant's first appearance before a magistrates' court.

The importance of obtaining IDPC in all but the most straightforward cases cannot be overstated. A defence practitioner cannot properly advise a client on his plea/venue for trial unless she is in possession of and has evaluated the IDPC.

The defendant will need to be taken through the IDPC and advised on plea. In accordance with TSJ, if the plea is not guilty, the magistrates' court will want to proceed to the allocation hearing in the case of an either-way offence and set a firm date for summary trial if required. If a not guilty plea is entered to an offence that can only be tried summarily, the defence must assist the court with its duties to actively manage cases under Crim PR, Part 3 and TSJ (see para. 9.15.1 for an account of what will be expected from the defence). Given the need for the case to be fully case managed for trial at the first hearing, this requires the defence practitioner to work fast and to have the necessary information about witness availability to hand (if possible) before the first hearing.

Approaching potential defence witnesses

If a not guilty plea is anticipated, potential defence witnesses should be approached as soon as possible whilst events are still fresh. Where required an enquiry agent may be used to track down a potential witness. Witness statements should be taken in the absence of the defendant and without the witness having seen any prosecution witness statements in advance. It is important to obtain the witness's honest, unrehearsed account of the events witnessed.

KEY POINT SUMMARY

- Be able to differentiate between the various funding schemes for the different criminal defence services that can be offered to a client.

- When articulating the interest of justice test for a representation order use as many aspects of the criteria as you can and articulate them fully and accurately.

- Understand the means testing process as it applies to cases in the magistrates' court and in the Crown Court. ·

- Understand the importance of keeping and maintaining accurate file notes and efficient time recording on LAA client files.

- The defence practitioner should use the initial interview with the client to take a detailed statement and to apply for public funding.

- Unless the offence is triable only on indictment understand that at the first hearing before the magistrates' court, the defendant will be expected to enter a plea and the magistrates' court will want to progress the case to the next stage (the allocation hearing if applicable and/or set a firm date for summary trial if necessary). A defendant should not be advised on plea unless the defence practitioner or duty solicitor has had the opportunity to consider IDPC served by the prosecution, which should be available in time for the first hearing.

SELF-TEST QUESTIONS

Case studies: *R v Roger Martin; R v William Hardy; R v Lenny Wise*

You are familiar with the issues in relation to *R v Roger Martin*, *R v Lenny Wise* and *R v William Hardy*. Having regard to each client's proof of evidence try to complete an application for a representation order on behalf of each of them. You will find a completed application for a representation order in Appendix 2 in so far as Lenny Wise is concerned. Roger Martin's and William Hardy's applications for a representation order can be found in the case study section of the online resources.

The complete version of all three case studies can be accessed in the online resources where you can see all the steps described in the second part of this chapter (including initial file notes and early correspondence) illustrated on the solicitor's file.

FIGURE 9.1 CRITERIA FOR APPLYING FOR A REPRESENTATION ORDER

FORM 9.1 APPLICANT'S DECLARATION FOR ONLINE SUBMISSIONS

 Legal Aid Agency

Criminal legal aid - Applicant's declaration for online submissions

Use this form where you are making an application using LAA Online.

PLEASE NOTE

Making a false declaration is an offence. If you are found doing so, you may be prosecuted, potentially leading to a fine and/or a prison sentence. The Legal Aid Agency has a zero tolerance approach to fraud and will look to prosecute where there is evidence of fraud.

Declaration by Applicant

USN: Full name:

National Insurance Number: Date of birth:

I apply for the right to representation for the purposes of criminal proceedings under the Legal Aid, Sentencing and Punishment of Offenders Act 2012.

I declare that my application will be made electronically by my legal representative.

I understand that if I have declared anything that is not true, or left anything out that:

• I may be prosecuted for fraud. I understand that if I am convicted, I may be sent to prison or pay a fine.

• My legal aid may be stopped and I may be asked to pay back my costs in full to the Legal Aid Agency (LAA).

• If my case is in the Crown Court, the LAA may change the amount of the contribution which I must pay.

I agree to tell the LAA or HM Courts & Tribunals Service (HMCTS) **immediately** if my income or capital or those of my partner, change. These changes include the sale of property, change of address, change in employment and change in capital.

Evidence I agree to provide, when asked, further details and evidence of my finances and those of my partner, to the LAA, its agents, or HMCTS, to help them decide whether an Order should be made and its terms.

Ending legal aid I understand that I must tell my solicitor and write to the court if I no longer want public representation. I understand that if I decline representation I may be liable for costs incurred to the date when my solicitor and the court receive my letter.

I authorise such enquiries as are considered necessary to enable the LAA, its agents, HMCTS, or my solicitor to find out my income and capital, and those of my partner. This includes my consent for parties such as my bank, building society, the Department for Work and Pensions, the Driver and Vehicle Licensing Agency or HM Revenue and Customs to provide information to assist the LAA, its agents or HMCTS with their enquiries.

I consent to the LAA or my solicitor **contacting my partner** for information and evidence about my partner's means. This includes circumstances where my partner is unable to sign or complete the form.

I understand that if the information which my partner provides is incorrect, or if my partner refuses to provide information, then: if my case is in the magistrates' court, my legal aid may be withdrawn or, if my case is in the Crown Court, I may be liable to sanctions. I understand that the sanctions may result in me paying, or paying more towards my legal costs, or paying my legal aid costs in full.

I understand that in Crown Court proceedings the information I have given in this form will be used to determine whether I am eligible for legal aid and, if so, whether I am liable to contribute to the costs of my defence under an Income contribution Order during my case or, if I am convicted, under a Final Contribution Order at the end of my case, or both.

I understand that if I am ordered to pay towards my legal aid under an Income Contribution Order, or if I am convicted and ordered to pay under a Final Contribution Order but fail to pay as the Order instructs me, interest may be charged or enforcement proceedings may be brought against me or both.

I understand that I may have to pay the costs of the enforcement proceedings in addition to the payments required under the Contribution Order, and the enforcement proceedings could result in a charge being placed on my home.

Declaration by Applicant continued

Data Sharing I agree that, if I am convicted, the information in this form will be used by HMCTS or a designated officer to determine the appropriate level of any financial penalty ordered against me, and for its collection and enforcement. I have read the **Fraud Notice**.

Signed: _____   Dated: _____

Full name (in block capitals): _____

Declaration by your (the applicant's) partner:

I declare that the information included in this application is a true statement of all my financial circumstances to the best of my knowledge and belief. I agree to the LAA and HMCTS, or my partner's solicitor, checking the information I have given, with the Department for Work and Pensions, HM Revenue and Customs or other people and organisations. I authorise those people and organisations to provide the information for which the LAA, HMCTS or my partner's solicitor may ask.

I understand that this application will be made electronically by the legal representative.

I have read the **Fraud Notice**.

Signed: _____   Dated: _____

Full name (in block capitals): _____

If your partner has not signed the declaration, please explain why:

Declaration by the legal representative:

I represent the applicant. I confirm that I am authorised to provide representation under a contract issued by the LAA ☐

I confirm that I have been instructed to provide representation by:

☐ a firm which holds a contract issued by the LAA

☐ a solicitor employed by the LAA in the Public Defender Service who is authorised to provide representation.

I confirm that I have gone through the questions on the Interests of Justice and financial assessment aspects of the application with the applicant.

I confirm that the applicant has not provided me with any information which contradicts the information provided in this declaration of financial circumstances and has given me no indication that information declared is incomplete or untrue.

Signed: _____

Full name (in block capitals): _____

Provider's LAA Account Number: _____

Fraud Notice

If false or inaccurate information is provided and fraud is identified, details will be passed to fraud prevention agencies to prevent fraud and money laundering.

Further details explaining how the information held by fraud prevention agencies may be used can be found in the 'Fair Processing Notice', available on the website at: www.justice.gov.uk/legal-aid/make-an-application

10 THE LAW AND PRACTICE RELATING TO COURT BAIL

10.1	**Introduction**	**181**
10.2	**What is bail?**	**182**
10.3	**A right to bail?**	**182**
10.4	**Section 25 CJPOA 1994**	**183**
10.5	**Grounds for refusing bail**	**183**
10.6	**Grounds for denying bail for an indictable imprisonable offence (Sch. 1 Part 1 para. 2 BA 1976)**	**183**
10.7	**Substantiating the grounds for opposing bail—the statutory factors (Sch. 1 para. 9 BA 1976)**	**186**
10.8	**Grounds for denying bail for a summary-only imprisonable offence (Sch. 1 Part 1A)**	**187**
10.9	**Grounds for denying bail for a non-imprisonable offence (Sch. 1 Part II)**	**187**
10.10	**Bail conditions**	**188**
	10.10.1 Surety/security	189
	10.10.2 Failing to comply with bail conditions	189
10.11	**Bail in practice**	**190**
10.12	**Procedure at a contested bail hearing**	**192**
	10.12.1 The court's decision—giving reasons	192
10.13	**Remand periods**	**193**
	10.13.1 Custody time limits	193
10.14	**How many bail applications can be made?**	**194**
10.15	**Where bail is refused**	**194**
10.16	**Appeal by the prosecution**	**195**
10.17	**Reconsidering bail**	**195**
10.18	**Varying bail conditions**	**195**
10.19	**Where an accused fails to surrender to bail**	**196**
10.20	**Bail granted by the Crown Court**	**196**
10.21	**Bail and the High Court**	**197**
10.22	**Human rights and bail**	**197**
10.23	**Bail—the practical considerations**	**197**

10.1 INTRODUCTION

Whenever a magistrates' court or Crown Court adjourns a case, the court must decide whether the defendant should be remanded on bail or remanded in custody during the adjournment period.

Bail may be granted by the police or by the court. In this chapter, we explain the practice and procedure of court bail. If you have read about police bail in Chapter 4, you will recognise that many of the principles that apply to police bail under s. 38 Police and Criminal Evidence Act 1984 (PACE 1984) (see Chapter 4, para. 4.14.2) also apply to court bail.

In this chapter we examine:

- the grounds upon which bail might be refused;
- the factors a court can have regard to when deciding whether bail should be granted;
- the procedure at a contested bail application;
- appeals against bail decisions;
- bail and Article 5 European Convention on Human Rights 1950 (ECHR 1950).

The practice and procedure governing court bail is contained in Crim PR, Part 14.

10.2 **WHAT IS BAIL?**

Bail is the release of the defendant subject to a duty to surrender to the court at a specified time and date. Bail may be granted to a defendant unconditionally or with conditions attached.

The provisions governing court bail are contained in the Bail Act 1976 (BA 1976). In many cases a defendant's bail status will be negotiated between the prosecution and the defence subject to the court giving consent. Where the prosecution opposes bail, a contested bail hearing will be held. Most bail hearings are conducted in magistrates' courts.

After being charged, where a defendant is refused police bail under s. 38 PACE 1984, the refusal is often an indication that bail will be opposed by the Crown Prosecution Service (CPS) when the defendant makes his first court appearance. For the court, the enquiry into bail requires a speculative exercise. Bail is essentially a question of trust. Can the court trust this defendant to be released back into the community on bail? Occasionally this trust can be abused, as in the case of ex-Metropolitan Police Inspector Gary Weddell who, in January 2008, was granted conditional bail on a charge of murdering his wife, and whilst on bail murdered his mother-in-law before killing himself.

10.3 **A RIGHT TO BAIL?**

Section 4 BA 1976 gives the defendant a prima facie right to bail (a presumption in favour of bail) when charged with a criminal offence irrespective of how serious the offence is. Where the prosecution seek to rebut this presumption by objecting to the defendant being granted bail, the court will invite both the prosecution and the defence to make submissions on the matter. In deciding whether the accused should be granted bail, the court will carefully consider whether the grounds for objecting to bail put forward by the prosecution and challenged by the defence are established by having regard to the statutory factors outlined at para. 10.6.

The presumption in favour of bail under s. 4 BA 1976 generally applies at all stages of the court proceedings from post-charge to immediately before conviction and continues to apply post-conviction where a court adjourns for the preparation of a pre-sentence report. Strictly speaking, s. 4 BA 1976 has no application:

- to police bail when the defendant is charged at the police station—s. 38 PACE 1984 (see Chapter 4);
- on summary conviction where the offender appeals against conviction or sentence;
- on summary conviction where the magistrates' court decides to commit the defendant to the Crown Court for sentence.

Although the presumption to bail does not apply in these situations, the court retains discretion to grant bail where the defendant appeals to the Crown Court and where the defendant is committed to the Crown Court for sentence. In deciding bail the magistrates will apply the criteria under the BA 1976.

The presumption in favour of bail puts the onus on the prosecution to show a good reason why bail should be withheld. The presumption in favour of bail is subject to s. 25 Criminal Justice and Public Order Act 1994 (CJPOA 1994).

10.4 SECTION 25 CJPOA 1994

Section 25 CJPOA 1994 provides that where the accused is charged with or convicted of murder, attempted murder, manslaughter, rape or attempted rape and has been previously convicted of any of these offences, the accused shall be granted bail only if a court is satisfied that there are exceptional circumstances which justify it. Section 25 CJPOA 1994 effectively creates a presumption against granting bail in these circumstances.

10.5 GROUNDS FOR REFUSING BAIL

Notwithstanding the general presumption to grant bail under s. 4 BA 1976, a court may withhold bail if one or more statutory grounds under the BA 1976 apply.

The BA 1976 draws a distinction between grounds for refusing bail in relation to:

* an indictable imprisonable offence (Sch. 1 Part 1 BA 1976);
* a summary-only imprisonable offence (Sch. 1 Part 1A BA 1976);
* a non-imprisonable offence (Sch. 1 Part II BA 1976).

10.6 GROUNDS FOR DENYING BAIL FOR AN INDICTABLE IMPRISONABLE OFFENCE (SCH. 1 PART 1 PARA. 2 BA 1976)

Where the accused is charged with an imprisonable offence triable on indictment (this includes an either-way offence), Sch. 1 Part 1 para. 2 BA 1976 provides for a number of instances where the accused need not be granted bail. Note, however, important changes to Sch. 1 Part 1 para. 2 detailed in the box below.

Important recent change restricting a court's power to withhold bail

Provisions under the Legal Aid, Sentencing and Punishment of Offenders Act 2012 (LASPO 2012) have inserted a new para. 1A into Sch. 1 Part 1 which restricts a court's powers to remand an adult defendant in custody prior to conviction where there is *no real prospect of the defendant receiving a custodial sentence* if convicted.

* The para. 1A restriction applies to the three main exceptions to bail outlined in para. 2(1) (failure to surrender/commission of further offences or interfering with witnesses etc.); para. 2A (refusal of bail where defendant appears to have committed an indictable or either-way offence whilst on bail); and para. 6 (refusal of bail where defendant has been arrested for breaking conditions of bail or failing to surrender to previously granted bail).
* Paragraph 1A does not, however, apply to a defendant who needs to be kept in custody for his own protection or where there is a risk of further offending that may take the form of domestic violence. The restriction only affects cases where the alleged offence, taken in combination with the relevant circumstances (e.g. the defendant's previous convictions) does not justify a custodial sentence. In such a case the CPS will not seek a remand in custody. In less clear-cut cases, the CPS may make representations against bail but invite the court to consider whether the no 'real prospect' restriction applies. The court is not expected to engage in a sentencing exercise in advance of trial but merely to form a view on the facts. If it is not clear to the court that there is no real prospect of custody, the restriction does not apply.

---

(1) Paragraph 2(1)

The accused need not be granted bail where the court is satisfied that there are *substantial grounds for believing* that, if released on bail (conditional or otherwise), the accused would:

> '(a) fail to surrender to custody, or
>
> (b) commit an offence while on bail, or
>
> (c) interfere with witnesses or otherwise obstruct the course of justice, whether in relation to himself or any other person.'

In practical terms, the first three substantive grounds set out in para. 2(1)(a)–(c) of Sch. 1 are the most important and account for 95% of refusals of bail. Given the frequency with which these grounds are commonly cited, we consider them in detail at para. 10.12.

(2) Paragraph 2(2ZA) (inserted by Sch. 11 LASPO 2012)

> 'The defendant need not be granted bail if the court is satisfied that there are substantial grounds for believing that the defendant, if released on bail (whether subject to conditions or not), would commit an offence while on bail by engaging in conduct that would, or would be likely to, cause—
>
> (a) physical or mental injury to an associated person; or
>
> (b) an associated person to fear physical or mental injury [an associated person is defined by s. 2 Family Law Act 1996].'

(3) Paragraph 2A

> '2A The defendant need not be granted bail if—
>
> (a) the offence is an indictable offence or an offence triable either way; and
>
> (b) it appears to the court that he was on bail in criminal proceedings on the date of the offence.'

Therefore, if X is presently on police bail in connection with an allegation of vehicle interference (summary-only) and is subsequently arrested and charged with burglary (either-way) as X was on police bail at the date of the alleged burglary offence, the court need not grant him bail in accordance with para. 2A.

There are currently two versions of para. 2A, both of which are in force. The original version of para. 2A is as already set out. It is prospectively repealed by s. 14 Criminal Justice Act 2003 (CJA 2003). The 'new' version, which was enacted under s. 14 CJA 2003, effectively creates a presumption against bail being granted by providing that bail *may not* be granted to a suspect aged over 18 who is already on bail on the date of the offence unless there is no significant risk of the defendant committing an offence whilst on bail. This provision came partially into force on 1 January 2007 but only in relation to offences carrying life imprisonment.

Therefore, if X is on bail for an alleged assault and is subsequently arrested and charged with robbery (an offence which carries a life sentence) the prosecutor should refer the court to the application of s. 14 CJA 2003.

(4) Paragraph 2(3)

> 'The defendant need not be granted bail if the court is satisfied that he should be kept in custody for his own protection or if he is a child or young person, for his own welfare.'

Defendants are likely to be remanded in custody for their own protection where they pose a danger to themselves (self-harm) or are charged with an offence that incites considerable public revulsion, for example child sexual abuse/paedophilia.

(5) Paragraph 2(4)

> 'The defendant need not be granted bail if he is already serving a custodial sentence.'

Obviously a defendant who is already serving a custodial sentence for another crime will not be granted bail in connection with new matters and should not apply for bail. The court should, however, ascertain the earliest date of release to ensure a defendant is not remanded in custody beyond that date.

(6) Paragraph 2(5)

> 'The defendant need not be granted bail where the court is satisfied that it has not been practicable to obtain sufficient information to take a decision in relation to bail.'

There may be cases where the police have charged a suspect but have insufficient details regarding the suspect's identity and address or his previous convictions. In this situation a court can refuse bail until information is available although it must be said that para. 5 is used sparingly in practice.

(7) Paragraph 2(6)

> 'Having been released on bail in connection with the same offence, the defendant has been arrested under s. 7 Bail Act 1976 (for absconding or breaking bail conditions).'

If a defendant is granted bail (whether by the court or the police) and fails to surrender to bail or breaks any bail conditions, the defendant can be arrested and held in custody (s. 7 BA 1976). If the failure to surrender is admitted or proved, the defendant commits the criminal offence of absconding. Where a breach of bail conditions is admitted or proved, this does not constitute an offence. However, in both situations, a court can choose to withhold bail under para. 6.

As with para. 2A, there are two versions of para. 6 currently in force. The original version is as already outlined. It is prospectively repealed by s. 15 CJA 2003. The 'new' version which was enacted under s. 15 CJA 2003 effectively creates a presumption against bail being granted in that it provides that bail *may not* be granted to a suspect aged over 18 who it appears, having been released on bail in connection with the proceedings, has failed to surrender to custody, unless the court is satisfied that there is no significant risk that if released on bail, the defendant would fail to surrender to custody. This provision came partially into force on 1 January 2007 but only in relation to offences carrying life imprisonment.

(8) Paragraph 2(6A–6C): positive drug testing at the police station

Bail *may not* be granted in the circumstances specified by s. 19(4) CJA 2003 (inserting paras. 6A–6C into Sch. 1 Part 1 BA 1976) unless the court is satisfied there is no significant risk of the accused committing an offence while on bail (whether subject to conditions or not). The relevant circumstances are that the accused must:

- be over 18;
- have tested positive for the presence of a Class A drug;
- be charged with a Class A-related drug offence or the court must have substantial grounds for believing that the misuse of a Class A drug caused or contributed to the offence with which the accused is charged; and
- refuses (a) to undergo an assessment of his dependency on or propensity to misuse drugs, or (b) having undergone such an assessment, and having had follow-up action proposed to address his dependency/propensity, refuses to undergo such follow-up action.

Where bail is granted under s. 6B, it must be subject to a condition that the defendant undergoes an initial assessment or participates in any follow-up treatment. The power of the police to take a drug sample at the police station and to require a defendant to undergo an initial assessment where he has tested positive is considered in Chapter 4, para. 4.14.3.

(9) Paragraph 2(6ZA): special provision in relation to murder cases

A special provision relating to bail in murder cases came into force on 1 February 2010 (s. 114 Coroners and Justice Act 2009 (C&JA 2009) inserting s. 6ZA into Sch. 1 Part 1 BA 1976).

Section 6ZA BA 1976 provides that a defendant who is charged with murder may not be granted bail unless the court is of the opinion that there is no significant risk that, if released on bail, the defendant would commit an offence that would be likely to cause physical or mental injury to another person.

Section 115 C&JA 2009 provides that a defendant who is charged with murder may not be granted bail except by a Crown Court judge. The power of a magistrates' court to consider bail in murder cases at any stage is therefore removed. A bail decision in a murder case must be made as soon as reasonably practicable, and in any event within 48 hours (excluding public holidays) beginning the day after the defendant's appearance in the magistrates' court. If necessary the defendant must be committed to the Crown Court whilst in custody to enable a bail decision to be made, whether he or she is at the same time sent for trial under s. 51 Crime and Disorder Act 1998 (see Chapter 13).

(10) Paragraph 2(7)

'Where the case has been adjourned for enquiries or a report, it appears to the court that it would be impracticable to complete the enquiries or make a report unless the accused is kept in custody.'

This ground applies where a defendant has been convicted of an offence or has pleaded guilty but there are concerns that the defendant may not cooperate with the Probation Service in the preparation of a pre-sentence report. A common example is where defendants are unable to offer a fixed address to which they can be bailed and contacted.

10.7 SUBSTANTIATING THE GROUNDS FOR OPPOSING BAIL—THE STATUTORY FACTORS (SCH. 1 PARA. 9 BA 1976)

Sch. 1 Part 1 para. 9 BA 1976 requires a court to have regard to a number of factors in determining whether the grounds for denying bail under paras. 2(1), 2A, 2ZA, 6A and 6ZA are made out. These include:

- the nature and the seriousness of the offence and the probable method of dealing with it;
- the defendant's character, record, associates and community ties;
- the defendant's bail record;
- the strength of the evidence against the defendant;
- if the court is satisfied that there are substantial grounds for believing that the defendant, if released on bail (whether subject to conditions or not), would commit an offence while on bail including the risk that the defendant may do so by engaging in conduct that would, or would be likely to cause, physical or mental injury to any person other than the defendant; and
- any other relevant factor.

Many of the factors in Sch. 1 Part 1 para. 9 are self-explanatory. In practice, the more serious the offence, the greater the risk of a custodial sentence being imposed and therefore the greater the risk the defendant will abscond. In completing the case file for the CPS, the police will provide details of the defendant's past criminal record and personal circumstances. The CPS will therefore be aware of the type of person the defendant is and whether the defendant has family, a job or other commitments in the area. Clearly the defendant's previous bail record will be of considerable importance to the court.

It is the interrelationship between the grounds for refusing bail and the applicable factors which determine the grant or refusal of bail. In para. 10.12 we consider bail in practice and illustrate the interrelationship between the grounds for refusing bail and the factors the court takes into account.

10.8 GROUNDS FOR DENYING BAIL FOR A SUMMARY-ONLY IMPRISONABLE OFFENCE (SCH. 1 PART 1A)

Bail can be refused in connection with a summary-only imprisonable offence under Sch. 1 Part 1A on one or more of the following grounds (note that paras. 2, 3 and 7 do not apply to an accused who is 18 and who has not been convicted in the case if it appears to the court that there is no real prospect of the defendant receiving a custodial sentence in the event of conviction):

- if, having been previously granted bail, the defendant has failed to surrender to custody and the court believes that, if released on bail, he would do so again (para. 2);

- if the defendant was on bail on the date of the offence and the court has substantial grounds to believe that, if released, he would commit an offence on bail (para. 3);

- there are substantial grounds for believing that, if released on bail, the defendant would commit an offence by engaging in conduct that would be likely to cause physical or mental injury to an associated person (as defined by s. 2 Family Law Act 1996) or cause an associated person to fear physical or mental injury (para. 4);

- the court is satisfied the defendant should be kept in custody for his own protection (para. 5);

- the defendant is already serving a custodial sentence (para. 6);

- having been released on bail in connection with the present offence, the defendant has been arrested for absconding or breaking bail conditions under s. 7 BA 1976 and there are substantial grounds for believing that the defendant, if released on bail (whether subject to conditions or not), would fail to surrender to custody, commit an offence on bail or interfere with witnesses or otherwise obstruct the course of justice (para. 7);

- lack of sufficient information (para. 8).

The provisions in relation to drug testing outlined at para. 10.6 apply to a defendant charged with a summary-only imprisonable offence.

10.9 GROUNDS FOR DENYING BAIL FOR A NON-IMPRISONABLE OFFENCE (SCH. 1 PART II)

Where the accused is charged with a non-imprisonable offence, Sch. 1 Part II BA 1976 provides that the accused need not be granted bail where:

- it appears to the court that, having been previously granted bail, the defendant has failed to surrender to custody and the court has substantial grounds to believe, in view of that failure, that if released on bail (whether subject to conditions or not) the defendant would fail to surrender (para. 2); or

- the court is satisfied that the accused should be kept in custody for his own welfare or protection (para. 3); or

- the defendant is already in custody in respect of any sentence (para. 4); or

- having been released on bail in connection with the present offence, the defendant has been arrested for absconding or breaking bail conditions under s. 7 BA 1976, there are substantial grounds for believing that the defendant, if released on bail (whether subject to conditions or not), would fail to surrender to custody, commit an offence on bail or interfere with witnesses, or otherwise obstruct the course of justice (para. 5); or

- having been released on bail in connection with the present offence, the defendant has been arrested for absconding or breaking bail conditions under s. 7 BA 1976, there are substantial grounds for believing that, if released on bail, the defendant would commit an offence by engaging in conduct that would be likely to cause physical or mental injury to an associated person (as defined by s. 2 Family Law Act 1996) or cause an associated person to fear physical or mental injury (para. 6).

10.10 BAIL CONDITIONS

A defendant may be granted conditional or unconditional bail. It is very common for the court to impose conditions under s. 3 BA 1976 on a defendant when granting bail. Common bail conditions include:

[handwritten annotation: → Can say they refer to this when deciding to give bail.]

- reporting to a police station (perhaps two or three times a week or even daily);
- living at a specified/alternative address (including a bail hostel);
- avoiding contact with prosecution witnesses;
- avoiding a particular area (this could require a defendant not to enter a particular building or area or go within a specified radius of it);

[handwritten annotation: he breached this condition]

- avoiding a particular activity (this could include a condition that the defendant does not visit licensed premises or sit in the front seat of any vehicle);
- imposing a curfew (requiring a defendant to remain at a specified address between certain hours—e.g. 8 pm to 7 am—it could also include a 'doorstep' condition or electronic tagging);
- requiring a surety (see later);
- surrendering a passport.

In accordance with s. 8 BA 1976, conditions may only be attached to bail where it is necessary to ensure either that a defendant:

- will surrender to custody;
- does not commit further offences;
- does not interfere with witnesses or obstruct the course of justice; or
- for the person's own protection; or
- in the case of a convicted offender, to ensure the accused is available to enable enquiries for the purposes of a report to be made to the court.

To reduce the risk of absconding, a court can impose a condition that the defendant reside at a specified address and/or report to a police station. A condition that the defendant surrenders his passport and/or provides a surety is also designed to reduce the risk of an accused failing to surrender.

Where a court is concerned that a defendant might commit further offences, it could impose a curfew where, for example, a defendant is accused of committing night-time burglaries.

A condition could also be imposed to prevent the accused from entering a specified place; for example, a supermarket from which he habitually steals merchandise. Where there is a risk of an accused committing further offences because of the accused's relationship with a particular victim, a condition could require that the accused resides at an alternative address and must not contact the injured party. These final two conditions are appropriate to prevent an accused from interfering with a witness or obstructing the course of justice.

The decision to impose one or more conditions must be a proportionate measure to reduce the risk(s) identified by the court. In negotiating bail with the CPS, the defence solicitor may need to offer or agree to certain conditions subject to his client's consent. The defence solicitor should discuss this with his client either at the police station or in the holding cell at court. Where an alternative address is likely to be needed, the defence solicitor may have to find alternative accommodation. If a bail hostel place is required, the defence solicitor will liaise with the Probation Service to see if a place is available and it is suitable for the defendant. This option would not be suitable, for example, for a mentally unstable or drug-dependent defendant.

Where a court grants bail to someone charged with murder in circumstances outlined at para. 10.6(8), then unless a satisfactory report on the defendant's mental condition has been obtained, the court must impose a condition requiring the defendant to undergo examination by two medical practitioners, including a psychiatrist.

Where the court grants bail in the circumstance outlined at para. 10.6(7), it must be subject to a condition requiring the defendant to undergo an initial drug assessment or to participate in follow-up treatment.

10.10.1 SURETY/SECURITY

A court may require a defendant to provide a suitable surety or sureties before granting bail. A surety is a person who promises to forfeit a sum of money fixed by the court (known as a recognisance) if the defendant fails to attend court as directed. It is the surety's solemn duty to ensure the defendant's future attendance at court. The amount of recognisance is determined by the court and depends on the surety's financial resources. If the defendant fails to answer his bail, any surety is liable to forfeit whole or part of the recognisance.

A surety must be a suitable person who will be required to attend court and give evidence on oath, confirming, amongst other things, his financial resources, his character and any previous convictions, and his relationship and proximity to the defendant. Such a condition can be imposed where the defendant is at risk of failing to surrender, perhaps because the defendant has links to a foreign jurisdiction.

A court can require a defendant to deposit a security before being released. This is rather like a bail bond. It requires the defendant or someone on his behalf to deposit a sum of money or other valuable security as a guarantee to ensure attendance. The sum can be forfeited if the defendant absconds.

10.10.2 FAILING TO COMPLY WITH BAIL CONDITIONS

If bail is granted subject to conditions, the importance of complying with the conditions will be explained to the defendant in court. The defence solicitor should remind his client of their importance.

A failure to abide by any condition of bail can lead to a defendant's arrest and reappearance before the court in custody (s. 7 BA 1976). A power of arrest is available where a police constable has reasonable grounds for believing that a person has broken, or is about to break, a bail condition. If the breach is proved or admitted, then although the defendant does not commit a further offence by breaking a bail condition, the court may decide the defendant has had his chance and should be remanded in custody for the duration of the proceedings (para. 10.6(7)). Alternatively, the court might impose more onerous conditions or give the defendant a stern warning about the importance of abiding by conditions of bail.

Having been arrested for suspected breach of bail conditions, s. 7 BA 1976 requires the defendant to be brought before a magistrate within 24 hours of arrest, excluding Sundays.

Where a breach of bail conditions is denied, the Divisional Court held in *R (DPP) v Havering Magistrates' Court* [2001] 2 Cr App R 2, that the breach proceedings fall within Article 5 ECHR 1950 and do not invoke the right to a fair trial provisions in Article 6. Although the proceedings do not constitute a trial, the need for the hearing to be adversarial with each side enjoying equality of arms, means the prosecution has to adduce some evidence of the breach (this can include hearsay evidence). In turn the defendant must have a full and fair opportunity to contest the allegation if he denies it.

10.11 **BAIL IN PRACTICE**

The most commonly cited reasons for opposing court bail are contained in Sch. 1 para. 2(1)(a)–(c), namely that there is a substantial risk that if released on bail the defendant will:

- abscond; or

- commit further offences; or

- interfere with witnesses and obstruct the course of justice.

These grounds are further strengthened in the circumstances outlined at para. 10.6.

On a daily basis magistrates' courts hear arguments based on these grounds. It is not enough for the prosecution to suggest that the defendant might abscond, or might commit further offences, there must be *substantial grounds* for the belief.

Here, we provide some typical arguments put forward by the CPS when opposing bail on the grounds set out in Sch. 1 para. 2. You will see how the statutory factors listed in para. 9 (see para. 10.7) are used to substantiate the prosecution's grounds for opposing bail. We further consider how the defence advocate might counter the prosecution's objections.

 Examples

The risk of absconding from the prosecution perspective

Why can the defendant not be trusted to remain in the local area? What incentive does the defendant have to abscond? Perhaps the defendant is charged with a serious offence and risks a substantial sentence of imprisonment if convicted or is currently subject to a suspended sentence of imprisonment. Even if a prison sentence for the new offence is not a certainty, a further conviction would put the defendant in breach of a suspended prison sentence and may provide the incentive to abscond. Perhaps the defendant has previous convictions for failing to surrender. If the defendant has poor community ties, such as no immediate family in the area, what incentive is there for the defendant to remain in the jurisdiction of the court?

The prosecuting advocate might address the court in this way:

'Sir, you and your colleagues will be aware that this defendant has three previous convictions for absconding.'

'Madam, this defendant was granted bail on an earlier occasion and has failed to surrender. He appears before you this morning pursuant to a warrant for his arrest.'

'Sir, this defendant's community ties are poor. He is unable to offer a stable address in the area. He has no job and no reason to stay here.'

'The accused is a foreign national whose family resides abroad. She poses a flight risk.'

Risk of absconding from the defence perspective

It does no harm to remind the court of the presumption in favour of bail (s. 4 BA 1976) if it applies. If the defendant has a record for absconding, it is important for the defence solicitor to find out about the circumstances of the absconding offences. Were they deliberate? How long ago were they committed? Did the defendant ultimately surrender and plead guilty or was he arrested? If the defendant has a good bail record, this should be stressed! The defence solicitor should examine his client's community ties. Does he have a job, a mortgage, family or anything to keep him in the area?

It is pertinent to ask whether the defendant is going to be convicted of the offence he is charged with. This requires the defence solicitor to examine the strength of the evidence against his client. The defendant may indicate he is pleading not guilty and wishes to challenge the evidence against him. In these circumstances it is legitimate to point out that the defendant will not abscond because he wishes to clear his name of the charges faced. If the defendant is likely to plead guilty, the defence solicitor should consider whether a custodial sentence is a certainty. If not, he should make the appropriate representations.

Finally, the defence solicitor needs to consider what conditions to offer in order to allay the court's fear of the defendant absconding. Possibilities might include a condition of residence at a fixed address or at a bail hostel. In addition, the court may want the defendant to report to a police station on specified days and at certain times. A court may require the defendant to surrender his passport if he poses a flight risk. Less frequently, the court may only grant bail subject to the defendant providing a suitable surety or security.

The commission of further offences from the prosecution perspective

The prosecutor must ask himself why this particular defendant is likely to commit further offences if released on bail. This may be due to the defendant's extensive criminal record indicating that he is a prolific offender or because the defendant has a particular need to commit offences, for example to feed a drug addiction. Added to this the defendant may not have a stabilising influence in his life and even no fixed address. In some cases the risk of the commission of further offences may be due to the defendant's close proximity to the victim, for example in a domestic assault where the injured party fears reprisals if the defendant remains under the same roof.

The prosecuting advocate may address the court on these issues in this way:

'Madam, the defendant was already on bail for another similar offence when arrested in connection with these matters.'

'The defendant has a substantial criminal record for theft and burglary . . .'

'The defendant is a substance abuser who steals to fund his habit . . .'

'Sir, this defendant cannot keep out of trouble—you only have to examine his criminal record. You will also see he is the subject of an anti-social behaviour order made three months ago . . .'

'The defendant has committed offences whilst subject to a sentence of this court—in short, he cannot be trusted.'

Commission of further offences from the defence perspective

The defence solicitor should carefully consider the defendant's criminal record. Are the defendant's previous convictions recent? Have circumstances changed so that there is now a stabilising influence in the defendant's life? Does the defendant have responsibilities such as the care of a child who is likely to be taken into care if the defendant is remanded? Once again, what evidence connects the defendant to the offence with which he is charged? Does the defendant admit the charge for which he is already on bail? Looking at the defendant's past criminal record, is it possible to say whether no offences have been committed by the defendant whilst on bail?

Will imposing suitable conditions help to allay the magistrates' fears that this defendant will commit further offences? Possibilities might include imposing a curfew where a defendant has a history of committing offences at night. A condition that excludes the defendant from engaging in particular behaviour or going to a certain place may be effective, that is, a condition not to visit licensed premises or to go within a certain radius of a particular shop. The availability of an alternative address away from the area where the crime is alleged to have occurred may alleviate the risk.

Interference with witnesses or obstructing the course of justice from the prosecution perspective

This ground might be argued where, for example, there is more than one co-accused who is still at large. It could also cover the situation where the defendant is implicated in a burglary or robbery and there is stolen property that has yet to be recovered. It also extends to those situations where a defendant may know or be related to a victim or witness and may well wish to contact that person. Perhaps the defendant is predisposed to use violence or has a previous conviction for witness intimidation or harassment.

The prosecuting advocate may address the court on these issues in the following way:

'Sir, this defendant has previous convictions for violence.'

'Sir, this defendant has a previous conviction for perverting the course of justice.'

'Sir, there is as you can imagine a lot of ill-feeling in the area where the defendant resides. If released on bail the danger that the defendant might be embroiled in further confrontation cannot be ignored . . .'

'Madam, there is a large amount of stolen property that has still to be recovered and a co-accused still at large.'

Interference with witnesses or obstructing the course of justice from the defence perspective

Once again, if the defendant is not admitting the offence, assess the strength of the evidence against her. Point out that the defendant would not wish to make matters worse for herself by doing the things suggested. What was the date on which the offence is alleged to have occurred? Stolen property that is not immediately recovered is unlikely ever to be recovered. Consider whether there is any evidence that the defendant will threaten or interfere with a witness. Look at the defendant's record in this respect. Can conditions be suggested to allay the magistrates' or District Judge's fears? Possibilities include a condition that the defendant does not contact a witness or does not go within a certain radius of a particular area. The availability of alternative accommodation away from the witness or the area may greatly assist.

One of the factors a court should consider when deciding bail is the strength of the evidence against a defendant. From the defence perspective, if the defendant has not made damaging admissions and intends to plead not guilty, it is always worth challenging the evidence linking the defendant to the offence. It would be wholly unjust for a court to remand into custody on weak evidence, so consider whether to advance a defence at this stage.

10.12 PROCEDURE AT A CONTESTED BAIL HEARING

There is no prescribed procedure at a contested bail hearing. The usual practice after a court has decided to adjourn the case is for the prosecution to make representations against bail being granted. This will be based on the information contained in the police file. The defendant is then given an opportunity to put any relevant considerations before the court. This will usually be done through the defendant's solicitor or the duty solicitor in court.

Neither the prosecution nor the defence advocate is likely to have much time to prepare for the bail hearing. The provision of IDPC and the principles of TSJ as well as the common law duties of disclosure in *R v DPP, ex p. Lee* [1999] 2 Cr App R 304 (see Chapter 8 and Chapter 9, para. 9.16.1) should mean that the defence advocate or duty solicitor is in possession of sufficient disclosure of prosecution evidence at the first hearing before a magistrates' court to enable a bail application to be made.

A contested bail hearing takes the form of a mini-trial at which the rules of evidence are relaxed. The BA 1976 gives each side the framework for their representations. The prosecuting advocate will refer to the witness statements he has on file and the account the defendant gave at the police station in making the court aware of how the defendant came to be charged in connection with the matter(s) for which he appears. The prosecutor will outline his objections and hand in a copy of the defendant's previous convictions. The defence solicitor will then make his submissions, countering the arguments put by the prosecution. If the defendant has a job or an offer of work that is likely to be lost if remanded, the defence solicitor should try to obtain a letter from the employer to confirm this. If residence is likely to be a problem, the defence solicitor should have enquired about alternative accommodation.

Any available witnesses such as a surety or a person giving evidence of an alternative address will be put before the court. Having heard the representations from both sides, the magistrates will decide on the matter and announce their decision. You are able to view a contested bail hearing in the video clip section of our online resources in the *R v Lenny Wise* case study.

Before you do this you might attempt the exercise we have set in conjunction with the case study at the end of this chapter, together with two other scenarios designed to test your understanding of bail.

10.12.1 THE COURT'S DECISION—GIVING REASONS

Section 5 BA 1976 provides that where a court withholds bail or grants conditional bail, the reason(s) for doing so must be announced in open court. Where bail is refused, the defendant must be given a notice setting out the reason(s) for the magistrates' decision. It is the usual practice in magistrates' courts to give reasons for granting bail in all cases where bail has been opposed.

It should be stressed that bail is a decision for the court and it should be considered at every remand hearing, whether it is applied for or not. Magistrates can grant bail, notwithstanding prosecution objections, and may also remand a defendant in custody where there is no objection from the prosecutor.

A defendant who is 21 or over will be remanded to a prison if bail is denied. Between the ages of 17 and 20, remand is normally to a remand centre or an adult prison if no places are available at a remand centre.

It is important to remember that if convicted, the sentencing court can take into account the time served on remand when sentencing an offender to a period of imprisonment.

Instead of remanding the accused in custody, s. 128 Magistrates' Courts Act 1980 (MCA 1980) enables a magistrates' court to remand the defendant to a police station for a period not exceeding three clear days. This may be done only if it is necessary for enquiries to be made into any offence other than the one(s) for which he is appearing before the court. The defendant must be brought back to the magistrates' court as soon as the need to remand him at the police station ceases. Whilst on remand at the police station, the defendant is entitled to the same range of protections afforded by PACE 1984 and the Codes of Practice as any detainee who has been arrested on suspicion of having committed an offence (see Chapter 4).

10.13 REMAND PERIODS

When a magistrates' court remands a defendant in custody at his first appearance, the remand period must not exceed eight days.

It may be several weeks or even months before a case is ready for trial or for sending to the Crown Court. Provision is made in s. 128A MCA 1980 for an accused to be remanded for up to 28 days without his consent. The power only applies once a magistrates' court has set a date for the next stage of the proceedings to take place and decides the accused should be remanded in custody until that date. The power does not apply on a first remand. An accused is therefore allowed two bail applications before this power can be exercised. If the defendant is to be further remanded after 28 days, he must be produced at the next court hearing. The increasing use of TV video-links from prisons to some magistrates' courts and Crown Courts means prisoners do not have to be physically produced (see Chapter 9, para. 19.16.1 and 'virtual' courts).

After conviction a court may remand a defendant pending sentence where a pre-sentence report or some other report is required before sentence can be properly imposed. Where a court grants a defendant bail after conviction, the maximum period is four weeks. Where a defendant is remanded in custody pending completion of reports, the maximum period is three weeks.

10.13.1 CUSTODY TIME LIMITS

When an accused has been refused bail, s. 22 Prosecution of Offenders Act 1985 (POA 1985) imposes the following maximum time limits during which an accused may be remanded in custody between various stages in the proceedings before trial:

(a) 70 days between an accused's first appearance in the magistrates' court and sending to the Crown Court (see Chapter 11);

(b) 70 days between first appearance and summary trial for an offence triable either way (reduced to 56 days if the decision for summary trial is taken within 56 days);

(c) 56 days between first appearance and trial for a summary-only offence; and

(d) 112 days between sending for trial and arraignment in the Crown Court.

Where an indictable offence is sent straight to the Crown Court under s. 51 Crime and Disorder Act 1998 (see Chapter 13), the maximum custody time length is 182 days with time running from the date the case is sent up by the magistrates, less any time already spent in custody.

If the prosecution fails to comply with the custody time limits, the defendant has an absolute right to bail. A court can impose some conditions on the defendant's bail, such as reporting or a condition of residence, but cannot require the defendant to provide a surety or security as a condition of release.

The prosecution can apply for an extension of the custody time limit before it expires. The criteria for granting an extension are laid down in s. 22 POA 1985. For a detailed explanation of the extension of custody time limits, see the most recent edition of *Blackstone's Criminal Practice*.

10.14 HOW MANY BAIL APPLICATIONS CAN BE MADE?

While a court is under a duty to consider the grant of bail at each hearing after it has been refused, the defendant is prevented from making repeated applications by Sch. 1 Part IIA BA 1976 (as amended by s. 154(2) CJA 1988). This provides:

> 'At the first hearing after that at which the court decided not to grant the defendant bail he may support an application for bail with any further argument as to law or fact that he desires . . . At subsequent hearings the court need not hear arguments as to fact or law which it has heard previously . . .'

Where an accused has been refused bail at a previous hearing, the accused may make one further application only based on the same facts/arguments. Thereafter, unless there has been a 'change of circumstances' (i.e. new arguments as to the law or to facts are advanced), the court need not hear further argument at a subsequent hearing.

Consider the following examples of the operation of Part IIA:

X makes an unsuccessful application for bail on his first appearance. He makes a further unsuccessful application for bail on his second appearance. Thereafter Part IIA applies and the court need not hear a further application on his appearance unless there has been a change in circumstances.

X chooses not to make an application for bail on his first appearance. He makes an unsuccessful application for bail on his second appearance. Under Part IIA the court need not hear a further application on X's next appearance unless there has been a change in circumstances.

X makes an unsuccessful application for bail on his first appearance. He chooses not to make a further application on his second appearance. Part IIA applies and the court need not hear a further application on X's next appearance unless there has been a change in circumstances.

A change of circumstances need not be a major change either in the defendant's personal circumstances or in the proceedings connected with the case. So, for example, where an accused has been charged with an indictable offence and has been refused bail at two previous hearings, the fact that the case against the accused appears less strong when full pre-trial disclosure is made during the course of the proceedings, may amount to a change of circumstances. For judicial guidance on what may amount to a 'change in circumstances', please see *Nottingham Justices, ex p. Davies* [1981] 1 QB 38 and *R (B) v Brent Youth Court* [2010] EWHC 1893 (Admin).

10.15 WHERE BAIL IS REFUSED

Where magistrates have heard a full application for bail, the court must issue a full argument certificate. A copy must be given to the accused. Armed with this, an accused can apply for bail to a Crown Court judge under s. 81 Senior Courts Act 1981. The application must be made in writing to the Crown Court as soon as practicable after refusal and served on the prosecution. What needs to be included in the application notice is set out in

Crim PR, Part 14.8. Applications are usually listed for hearing within 48 hours of the initial refusal. The application will be conducted before a Crown Court judge in chambers and will take the form of a complete rehearing. Trainee solicitors and paralegal staff have full rights of audience before a Crown Court judge in chambers. The application to the Crown Court will be covered by an existing representation order.

10.16 APPEAL BY THE PROSECUTION

If bail is opposed by the prosecution but is granted to a person charged with or convicted of an offence carrying imprisonment or an offence of taking a vehicle without consent or aggravated vehicle-taking, s. 1 Bail (Amendment) Act 1993 gives the prosecution the right to appeal against the grant of bail to a Crown Court judge. There are strict procedural requirements governing the prosecution's right to appeal which are set out in Crim PR, Part 14.9. The prosecution must give oral notice of appeal at the conclusion of the proceedings in which bail was granted and before the defendant is released from custody. The oral notice must be confirmed in writing within two hours after the end of the proceedings. Pending the appeal, the magistrates must remand the defendant in custody. The Crown Court must hear the appeal within 48 hours and it will be a complete rehearing.

The prosecution now has a right to appeal to the High Court against the decision of a Crown Court judge to grant bail to a person charged with or convicted of an imprisonable offence (Sch. 11 LASPO 2012). This new route of appeal has no application to a decision of a judge of the Crown Court that was on appeal from the magistrates' court under the 1993 Act. The procedures are much the same as for appeals under the 1993 Act, requiring:

- prosecuting counsel to inform the Crown Court at the end of the hearing, before the defendant is released from custody, that the CPS intend to appeal, and to serve written notice of appeal on the Crown Court within two hours;

- the Crown Court to remand the defendant in custody until the appeal is determined or otherwise disposed of.

10.17 RECONSIDERING BAIL

Section 5B BA 1976 (inserted by the CJPOA 1994) allows a court to reconsider the grant of bail on application by the prosecution. The power only applies if the offence with which the defendant is charged is indictable only or triable either way. The application must be based on information that was not available to the court or the police at the last hearing. Therefore, new information must have come to light since the last bail hearing which puts the question of bail in a new light. Under s. 5B the court can vary the bail conditions imposed on the previous occasion or impose new ones or remand in custody.

10.18 VARYING BAIL CONDITIONS

Under s. 3(a) and (b) BA 1976 either side can apply to have bail conditions varied or, in the prosecution's case, to have conditions imposed on the grant of unconditional bail. It is not uncommon for a defendant to apply to have bail conditions varied. This requires an application to the court that imposed the conditions or to the Crown Court if a matter has already been sent there for trial or sentence.

Circumstances may have changed since the defendant was conditionally bailed that make the conditions impracticable or unworkable, that is, securing a job outside the immediate area or the need to change address. The CPS may or may not make a submission in relation

[handwritten margin note: → can be useful in saying that he had business documents by then argue that one of the conditions they gave was for him to collect his things with an officer.]

to the application. In a domestic violence prosecution where the alleged victim retracts her complaint and the defendant seeks to vary bail conditions (which may well exclude him from the family home), the CPS may call the complainant to testify on oath to her position in relation to bail.

Section 16 CJA 2003 amended BA 1976 to allow a defendant to appeal to the Crown Court against the imposition of any of the following conditions:

- residence away from a particular place;
- surety;
- curfew.

Such an appeal may not be brought if the defendant or the prosecution has already applied to a magistrates' court to have bail conditions varied and the matter has been dealt with or, in the case of the prosecution, it has applied for bail to be reconsidered in accordance with s. 5B BA 1976 and the matter has been determined.

10.19 WHERE AN ACCUSED FAILS TO SURRENDER TO BAIL

Section 6(1) BA 1976 creates the offence of absconding where the accused has been released on bail (whether by the police or by a court) and fails, without reasonable excuse, to surrender to custody at the time and date specified in the bail notice. Section 6(2) makes it an offence for a defendant who has a reasonable excuse for failing his bail, not to have then surrendered himself as soon as was thereafter reasonably practicable. Where the accused fails to surrender, the burden will be on the accused to prove that he had reasonable cause for failing to surrender.

Where the defendant is found guilty, absconding is punishable by up to three months' imprisonment and/or a maximum fine of £5,000 in the magistrates' court. Where bail was imposed by the Crown Court, the offence of absconding is treated as criminal contempt and is punishable by a maximum sentence of 12 months' imprisonment and/or an unlimited fine. A BA 1976 offence committed during the proceedings gives the court further grounds for refusing bail (see para. 10.6). Where an accused fails to surrender or having surrendered disappears before the case is heard, the court must decide what to do. Where there is no explanation for the accused's failure to appear, the court is likely to issue a warrant for the accused's immediate arrest. If the case has been listed for trial, the accused may be tried in his absence. Where some explanation is forthcoming to account for a defendant's absence, for example the defendant manages to contact his solicitor alerting him of a family emergency, the court is likely to grant bail in absence or issue a warrant backed with bail. The court will require proof for the absence, such as a medical certificate, to be produced on the next occasion.

10.20 BAIL GRANTED BY THE CROWN COURT

The Crown Court has an inherent jurisdiction (s. 81 Senior Courts Act 1981) to grant bail and can exercise its jurisdiction when:

- the defendant has been remanded in custody by a magistrates' court following an adjournment and the court has issued a certificate of full argument (see para. 10.15 above) under s. 5(6A) BA A1976;
- the defendant has been sent to the Crown Court for trial under s. 51/51A CDA 1998 (see Chapter 13, para. 13.3);
- the defendant has been summarily convicted, imprisoned and denied bail pending an appeal against conviction or sentence to the Crown Court;
- the defendant has been convicted and sentenced before a Crown Court and now wishes to appeal to the Court of Appeal.

10.21 BAIL AND THE HIGH COURT

[handwritten: → Idk what this is.]

The High Court may grant bail in the case of a convicted and imprisoned offender appealing against conviction or sentence by way of case stated or by judicial review.

10.22 HUMAN RIGHTS AND BAIL

The Law Commission in its Report No. 269, *Bail and the Human Rights Act 1998*, concluded that the existing law governing bail was broadly compliant with the ECHR 1950. Article 5 and not Article 6 governs decisions about bail. Article 5 guarantees an individual's right to liberty and security and therefore has clear relevance to bail decisions. Article 5(1) allows the right to be abrogated in defined circumstances and in accordance with a procedure prescribed by law. The prescribed circumstances include the lawful detention of a person after conviction by a competent court (Article 5(1)(a)) and the lawful arrest or detention of a person effected for the purpose of bringing him before a court on reasonable suspicion of having committed an offence or when it is reasonably necessary to prevent that person committing an offence or fleeing after having done so (Article 5(1)(c)).

[handwritten left margin: directed the conditions he get]

[handwritten right margin: → maybe useful to explain conditions he get so that they are in accordance with those articles.]

10.23 BAIL—THE PRACTICAL CONSIDERATIONS

The prosecutor is most likely to oppose bail in a case where the accused has been remanded in police custody upon being charged or is appearing before the magistrates' court in custody, either because it is alleged the accused has broken the conditions of his bail or has failed to surrender to the court's custody. The prosecutor must quickly assimilate the information on the police file and construct an argument opposing bail based on the grounds under BA 1976. Where bail is opposed but is granted by the magistrates, the prosecutor must be ready to give immediate notice of appeal if this is appropriate.

For the defence, it is important to realise that defendants tend to think of the short term. For them, gaining bail may be of considerable importance—more important than the final outcome.

The defence advocate must ensure he has sufficient disclosure of the prosecution's case (including a list of any previous convictions) to be able to deal with the prosecution's objections. The defence advocate should respond to each of the prosecutor's objections in turn and be prepared to advise his client on the further opportunities for applying for bail if it is refused. Bail conditions, such as an alternative address, should be canvassed with the client and if conditional bail is granted, the defence advocate should explain the importance of abiding by those conditions.

[handwritten right margin: → Can explain his breach.]

[handwritten right margin: → can be used to explain how he has his business partner as evidence to help him not oppose bail.]

[handwritten right margin: → can be used to explain to Paul what are the likely consequences since he breached bail.]

KEY POINT SUMMARY

- Be able to distinguish between the grounds for opposing bail and the factors used to substantiate the grounds.

- Know the circumstances where there is effectively a presumption against bail, making it more difficult for an accused to be granted bail.

- The defence advocate should anticipate the likely objections to bail and see what conditions the client can offer in an attempt to overcome the likely objections.

- Remember the rules of evidence are relaxed at a contested bail hearing.

- Be aware that the strength or weakness of the evidence against the accused is a relevant factor for the court to have regard to when reaching a decision on bail.

[handwritten: Note:- Idk if what I've written is notes but hopefully it does.]

- Remember that an accused has more than one opportunity to apply for bail, including the option of applying to a Crown Court judge in chambers where bail is refused by a magistrates' court.

- The prosecution has the right to appeal against the grant of bail in certain circumstances.

SELF-TEST QUESTIONS

To test your knowledge and understanding of the substantive law of bail, consider the following scenarios. Formulate what you consider would be your objections to bail being granted, having regard to the grounds for opposing bail and the factors the court is likely to have regard to. What submissions would you put forward to counter these objections to try and ensure bail is granted? An analysis of the scenarios is provided in the online resources.

Exercise 1: *R v Karl Green*

Karl Green is charged with wounding with intent, contrary to s. 18 Offences Against the Person Act 1861 (OAPA 1861). He appears before the magistrates' court. The prosecution seeks the usual eight-day adjournment to enable the case to be sent to the Crown Court. It is alleged that Karl assaulted David Murphy outside a public house on the housing estate where both the men live. The offence occurred two days ago. The injured party is presently in a coma. One witness, who is a friend of the injured party, has provided the police with a statement in which he identifies Karl Green as the person who punched his friend. In his statement he refers to the two men exchanging words. In one swift movement, he alleges, Green punched his friend with such force as to cause him to fall unconscious to the ground. An independent witness has provided a statement giving a similar account of the incident and a description of the man responsible being consistent with Green's appearance. The witness also states he observed the man who threw the punch flee the scene.

Karl Green is presently on conditional bail for a serious s. 18 OAPA 1861 assault on a police constable, alleged to have occurred six weeks earlier. He was seriously drunk at the time and one of the conditions of his bail, which includes him reporting to his local police station, prohibits him from visiting licensed premises. He appeared before the magistrates' court last week admitting a breach of his bail condition not to visit licensed premises. The magistrates were prepared to renew his bail, having regard to the explanation offered by Green which had been to fetch his sister who works at a public house as her baby was sick. According to his list of antecedents, Karl Green lives apart from his wife and is out of work. He has six previous convictions. The most recent relates to an assault occasioning actual bodily harm (s. 47 OAPA 1861) last year, for which Green received a six-month prison sentence suspended for 18 months. He has further convictions for assault dating some three and four years ago, two previous convictions for theft and a conviction for a public order offence. He was convicted of absconding three years ago.

In interview with his solicitor, Karl Green admits to throwing the punch. He maintains, however, that he acted in self-defence. Green claims the injured party was the aggressor and that, in self-defence, he threw one punch. When the injured party did not get up, Green panicked. His brother was with him when the incident occurred and will testify on his behalf. Green lives with his mother. He and his ex-wife are attempting a reconciliation. She had been dating the injured party but had terminated the relationship in recent weeks, believing she could salvage her marriage. She and Green have a son, Stephen, who is four years old. Karl says he is currently in work—he works for his cousin's skip-hire company. If remanded in custody he is likely to lose his job. His previous failure to surrender was due to sickness; however, no medical evidence was ever obtained. Green voluntarily surrendered himself and was fined for the offence of failing to answer his bail. So far as the assault on the policeman is concerned, he will be pleading guilty to a less serious charge of assault. He was seriously intoxicated at the time and does not recall much of what happened. He has expressed his deep remorse. Green tells his solicitor that he has a sister who may be prepared to offer him accommodation ten miles outside the area of the estate where he and his victim live.

Exercise 2: *R v Daniel Phillips*

Daniel Phillips has been charged with arson contrary to s. 1(3) Criminal Damage Act 1971 and with resisting a constable in the execution of his duty. The allegation is that he deliberately set fire to his former partner's house, causing extensive damage. He has been remanded into police custody pending his initial appearance before a magistrates' court. The case should be adjourned.

Daniel is 26. His former partner, Rachel Hughes, is 22. She has made a statement to the police. The couple have a child aged three who Rachel cares for. The relationship ended two years ago but Daniel has been reluctant to accept it. Rachel refused Daniel access to their son but this was resolved 18 months ago by court order. In recent weeks Rachel has formed a new relationship.

The police were called to Rachel Hughes's home at 6 am three days ago (a Saturday). Her property was on fire. Initial forensic tests have revealed the fire was started deliberately by someone pouring an accelerant through the front door letterbox and igniting it with a match. The finger of suspicion points to Daniel.

Daniel collected his son from Rachel for an access visit on the Saturday afternoon. She asked him to deliver their son back to her mother—the child was going to spend the night with his grandmother. She told Daniel Phillips that she would be staying with a friend of hers overnight. Her friend received a telephone call at 5.30 am. A male voice, which she thinks she recognised as Daniel, requested her to inform Rachel that her house was on fire.

Daniel was arrested three days later as the police were unable to locate him immediately—he was no longer living at his mother's address. There is no forensic evidence to link him to the crime scene as yet, but tests are continuing. Daniel made no comment in interview on the advice of his solicitor.

Rachel maintains she is absolutely terrified of Daniel, who has four previous convictions. He was convicted of criminal damage two years ago. Following an argument with Rachel he damaged her car. He was conditionally discharged for this offence for a period of one year. Six months later he was convicted of assault occasioning actual bodily harm and breach of a conditional discharge. The incident followed the breakdown of his relationship with Rachel. She started to date another man. When Daniel found out, he assaulted the man. He denied involvement but was found guilty by magistrates. He was given a community supervision order for two years. Last year Daniel was convicted of an offence under s. 2 Harassment Act 1997. He pleaded guilty before a Crown Court judge and was sentenced to six months' imprisonment, suspended for 18 months to run alongside his existing community supervision order. Daniel was also subject to a restraining order of five years forbidding him to contact or communicate with Rachel except when and for the sole purpose of collecting his son for an access visit. The harassment had taken the form of obscene text messages. Rachel was also bombarded with dozens of pictures taken of her, some of which were cut up. She started to receive menacing telephone calls in the early hours of the morning, which were eventually traced to a mobile telephone registered to Daniel.

In interview with his solicitor, Daniel steadfastly denies setting fire to the property. He maintains he has no axe to grind so far as Rachel is concerned. In fact he has formed a new relationship in recent months. His new girlfriend, Anita, aged 19, is pregnant with his baby. He was with her at the time of this alleged incident, at her mother's house. She and her mother will verify this. He left his mother's home several weeks ago, as he could not cope with her alcoholic mood swings. Daniel maintains the access visit with his son went off without problem and that he would not do anything to jeopardise his relationship with his son. Furthermore he is complying with the requirements of the community supervision order which is helping him to address the reason for his earlier offending. He is residing on a permanent basis with his new girlfriend and has a job as a mechanic. He denies resisting the police constable in the course of his arrest, maintaining the officer was much too heavy-handed.

Case study: *R v Lenny Wise*

Consider the initial disclosure of the prosecution case in relation to this case study, together with Lenny Wise's list of previous convictions (located in Appendix 2, Document 2). Assume you are the CPS lawyer and that this is Lenny's second appearance before a magistrates' court. He has been remanded in custody since being charged. Upon what grounds will you oppose bail and what factors will you have regard to in substantiating your objections? The prosecution's submission in this case can be viewed on the video section of our online resources. A transcript of the prosecuting solicitor's submission (Document 17) can be located on our Online Resource Centre in the case study section. For general consideration of the skills of advocacy, see Chapter 2.

Now look at this file from the perspective of the defence. Having regard to the prosecution's initial disclosure (Crim PR, Part 8) and to Lenny's statement (Document 6, located within Appendix 2), construct a defence submission in this case countering the prosecution's objections. How are you going to convince the court to grant bail in this case? The defence submission in this case can be viewed on the video section of our online resources. A transcript of the defence solicitor's submission can be located on our online resources in the case study section (Document 17).

An account of the magistrates' decision in relation to bail is contained in Document 15. You will see that Lenny applies to a judge in chambers in the Crown Court following the magistrates' court refusal to grant him bail and is subsequently granted conditional bail (Document 20). Documents 17–19 can be found in the case study section of our online resources, which contains a complete set of the documentation forming the *R v Lenny Wise* case study.

Case studies: *R v Roger Martin* and *R v William Hardy*

With regard to *R v William Hardy* and *R v Martin*, although there have been adjournments in each of these cases, there is no contentious issue as regards bail and each defendant is remanded on conditional bail during the proceedings.

FIGURE 10.1 COURT BAIL

EXCEPTIONS TO THE RIGHT TO BAIL

The Bail Act 1976 (s. 4) generally presumes the defendant should be granted bail. However:

- bail should only be granted exceptionally where a defendant is charged with murder, manslaughter, rape (or attempts) and he has previous convictions for one of these offences (s. 25 CJPOA 1994);

- bail may not be granted to a defendant charged with murder unless there is no significant risk that, if released, the defendant would commit an offence that would be likely to cause physical or mental injury;

- the defendant need not be granted bail if he is over 18 and is already on bail unless there is no significant risk of him committing an offence on bail (currently applies only to offences carrying life imprisonment (s.14 CJA 2003));

- the defendant need not be granted bail if he is over 18 and has previously been granted bail in the proceedings and has failed to surrender unless the court is satisfied there is no significant risk of the defendant failing to surrender if released on bail (currently applies only to offences carrying life imprisonment (s. 15 CJA 2003));

- the defendant need not be granted bail if he has tested positive to a Class A drug and is charged with an offence involving a specified Class A drug under the Misuse of Drugs Act 1971, or the court is satisfied that his offending is due to his drug dependency and the defendant refuses to undergo an assessment or follow-up treatment for his dependency (s. 19 CJA 2003).

REBUTTING THE PRESUMPTION TO BAIL

- The presumption to bail may be rebutted where the defendant is charged with an indictable imprisonable offence and where there is a real prospect of imprisonment; and

- the court is satisfied (Sch. 1 Part 1 Bail Act 1976) there are **substantial grounds** for believing the defendant will:
  - fail to surrender to custody; or
  - commit an offence while on bail; or
  - interfere with witnesses or obstruct the course of justice; or

- the defendant is already on bail for another offence and has been charged with an indictable offence; or

- the court is satisfied that the defendant should be kept in custody for his protection (or welfare where a juvenile); or

- the defendant is already serving a custodial sentence; or

- the defendant, having been released on bail, fails to surrender to bail or breaks a condition of that bail; or

- the court is satisfied it has not been practicable to obtain sufficient information to take a decision under the Bail Act 1976; or

- where the case has been adjourned for preparation of a report, it appears impracticable to complete the enquiries or report unless the defendant is in custody.

PARAGRAPH 9 FACTORS

- In deciding whether the ground(s) for refusing bail are made out, the court takes into account para. 9 Bail Act 1976 factors:
  - the nature and seriousness of the offence;
  - defendant's character, antecedents, community ties;
  - bail record;
  - strength of the evidence;
  - the risk that the defendant would engage in conduct that would be likely to cause physical or mental injury to another person; and
  - any other relevant matter.

BAIL CONDITIONS

- Bail can be unconditional or conditional;

- conditions ensure that the defendant:
  - will surrender to custody; or
  - will not commit further offences; or
  - will not interfere with witnesses or obstruct the course of justice; or
  - is available to assist with preparation of a pre-sentence report;

- conditions include:
  - reporting to a police station;
  - living at a specified address (possibly bail hostel);
  - curfew;
  - surety;
  - the defendant should not contact a specific individual;
  - exclusion from specified locality or place.

APPEALING BAIL DECISIONS

- Defence can 'appeal' against refusal of bail or bail conditions to Crown Court judge in chambers;

- prosecution can appeal to Crown Court against allowing bail where offence is punishable with imprisonment.

11 PROSECUTING AN EITHER-WAY OFFENCE

11.1	**Introduction**	**203**
11.2	**Plea before venue**	**204**
	11.2.1 Procedure at plea before venue (Crim PR, Part 9)	204
	11.2.2 Where the defendant indicates a guilty plea	205
	11.2.3 Where the defendant indicates a not guilty plea, gives no indication of plea or makes an equivocal plea	205
11.3	**The allocation hearing—ss.17–20 MCA 1980**	**205**
	11.3.1 The allocation guideline	205
	11.3.2 The statutory factors under s. 19 MCA 1980	206
	11.3.3 Relevant sentencing guidelines	206
	11.3.4 Prosecution and defence submissions	207
	11.3.5 Possible outcomes of the allocation hearing and subsequent steps	208
11.4	**The reasons for electing trial in the magistrates' court or in the Crown Court**	**210**
	11.4.1 Relative merits of trial on indictment	210
	11.4.2 Relative merits of summary trial	211
11.5	**The special procedure in criminal damage cases**	**212**
11.6	**Special rules relating to certain either-way offences**	**212**
11.7	**Sending an either-way offence to the Crown Court**	**212**
	11.7.1 Linked either-way or summary-only offences	213
	11.7.2 Position of co-accused jointly charged with an either-way offence	213
	11.7.3 Co-accused facing an either-way offence related to an indictable-only offence or a sent either-way offence	214
11.8	**Post-allocation matters where case is to be sent to the Crown Court**	**214**
	11.8.1 Bail	214
	11.8.2 Representation orders	214
	11.8.3 Disclosure of evidence and standard case progression directions	215
11.9	**Application for dismissal of the either-way offence sent to the Crown Court**	**215**
11.10	**Changing the allocation decision**	**216**

11.1 INTRODUCTION

Sections 17–21 Magistrates' Courts Act 1980 (MCA 1980) provide that where a defendant aged 18 or over is charged with an either-way offence, an allocation hearing must be held to determine whether the defendant should be tried summarily or on indictment.

It is therefore at the allocation hearing where the trial venue for either-way offences is decided. To understand the purpose of the allocation it is important to remember that there are a wide range of either-way offences including assault occasioning actual bodily harm, theft and burglary. Either-way offences can be committed with varying degrees of seriousness depending on the aggravating or mitigating features in the particular case. The more aggravating features, the more serious the offence will be regarded. Magistrates' court powers of sentence are limited compared to the Crown Court. If a magistrates' court considers its maximum sentencing powers (six months for a single either-way offence, increasing to 12 months where consecutive custodial sentences are imposed for two or more either-way offences) to be insufficient, the case will be sent to the Crown Court. Theft offences provide a good illustration. Theft can range from simple shoplifting to the appropriation of property worth millions of pounds (see the account of the Hatton Garden burglary in Chapter 8). Clearly, the offender charged with shoplifting would be most appropriately dealt with summarily while the more serious, very high-value theft should be dealt with in the Crown Court. These factors illustrate why allocation hearings are held in connection with either-way offences.

In this chapter we examine:

- the procedure for deciding where an either-way offence should be tried;
- the relative merits of summary trial and trial on indictment; and
- for those either-way offences that are to be tried in the Crown Court, the next stage of the proceedings.

The rules of court relevant to the allocation procedure are found in Crim PR, Part 9.

11.2 PLEA BEFORE VENUE

All defendants charged with an either-way offence are subject to the plea before venue procedure which precedes any allocation hearing (s. 17A MCA 1980/s. 50A (3) CDA 1998). The procedure provides the defendant with an opportunity to indicate how he intends to plead. The plea before venue is illustrated in the video section of our online resources in the *R v Lenny Wise* case study, which was filmed under the now redundant mode of trial procedure. Allocation hearings replaced mode of trial in 2013 (see Sch. 3 CJA 2003).

You are reminded that a defendant charged with an either-way offence is entitled to receive pre-trial disclosure of the prosecution's evidence in accordance with Crim PR, Part 8 (Initial Disclosure of the Prosecution's Case). Unless the matter is clear-cut, the defence lawyer should obtain IDPC before advising on plea. In accordance with TSJ (see Chapter 9, para. 9.15), the Crown Prosecution Service (CPS) is required to serve IDPC on the defendant prior to his first appearance before a magistrates' court to enable a plea to be indicated. Unless the defendant indicates a guilty plea, the magistrates' court will expect to conduct the allocation hearing at the first hearing. Where the defendant is making his first appearance in custody, the magistrates' court will still expect an indication of plea and progression to allocation, if required.

11.2.1 PROCEDURE AT PLEA BEFORE VENUE (CRIM PR, PART 9)

The court's legal adviser will outline the charge against the accused and explain in ordinary language that the charge is one that could be tried in the Crown Court or in the magistrates' court and that the defendant will be asked to indicate to the court whether he intends to plead guilty or not guilty. The legal adviser will also explain that if the defendant indicates a guilty plea, the magistrates' court will proceed to sentence and deal with him as if he had been found guilty and there will be no trial and no evidence will be called. The defendant will also be warned that notwithstanding an indication of a guilty plea, the magistrates' court may still commit him for sentence to the Crown Court under s. 3 Powers of Criminal Court (Sentencing) Act 2000 (PCC(S)A 2000) if the court considers its sentencing powers are insufficient or if the 'dangerousness' provisions explained in Chapter 22 apply (s. 3 PCC(S)A 2000). If the defendant indicates no plea or a not guilty plea the court will decide allocation. The legal adviser will then read the charge to the accused, who is asked to indicate his plea. A defendant has four possible responses. The defendant can:

- indicate a guilty plea;
- indicate a not guilty plea;

* give no indication of plea; or
* enter an equivocal plea.

11.2.2 WHERE THE DEFENDANT INDICATES A GUILTY PLEA

If the defendant indicates that he would plead guilty, he is taken to have pleaded guilty. Consequently, the magistrates' court will proceed to sentence him immediately or following an adjournment for the preparation of a pre-sentence report. The procedure upon sentence for a guilty plea and the possibility of committal for sentence to the Crown Court following the indication of a guilty plea to an either-way offence is explained in detail in Chapter 21.

11.2.3 WHERE THE DEFENDANT INDICATES A NOT GUILTY PLEA, GIVES NO INDICATION OF PLEA OR MAKES AN EQUIVOCAL PLEA

If at the plea before venue the defendant indicates that he will plead not guilty or makes no indication as to plea or makes an equivocal plea, the court will proceed to the allocation hearing. An equivocal plea is where the defendant's response to the charge is ambiguous. Where the court is uncertain about the defendant's plea, a not guilty plea will be entered on his behalf.

It is not unusual for an accused person to give no indication of plea on the advice of his solicitor. There may be reasons for this to do with the amount of disclosure that the police/CPS have provided at this early stage. There is also a financial incentive for the defence lawyer (based on current public funding fee scales) to have the magistrates' court decline summary jurisdiction subsequently followed by a prompt guilty plea by the defendant before the Crown Court. This is not however without risk for the defendant as s/he may well suffer a reduction in the overall amount of credit given for their guilty plea (see Chapter 21, para. 21.13). A defence lawyer might choose to adopt this tactical stance in a case where the allocation decision is on the cusp but knowing, at the end of the day, that his client may well plead guilty whether summary jurisdiction is accepted or declined. Once the magistrates' court has determined where the case is to be tried, the defendant may at this point be advised to indicate a guilty plea. Full sentencing discount credit may still be applied before the Crown Court where the defendant indicates an intention to plead guilty on the Better Case Management form (see para. 11.3.5 below) which will be sent to the Crown Court where jurisdiction has been declined.

11.3 THE ALLOCATION HEARING—SS.17–20 MCA 1980

At the allocation hearing the decision about whether an either-way offence should be tried summarily or on indictment is taken in the first instance by the magistrates or District Judge. This decision is based on:

* the requirements of the 2016 allocation guideline issued by the Sentencing Council;
* the statutory factors under s. 19 MCA 1980;
* any relevant sentencing guidelines issued by the Sentencing Council contained in the Magistrates' Court Sentencing Guidelines (MCSGs) (which are explained in Chapter 21); and
* prosecution and defence submissions.

11.3.1 THE ALLOCATION GUIDELINE

The practice at the allocation hearing is now largely influenced by the requirements of the allocation guideline issued by the Sentencing Council. The 2016 guideline is available at http://www.sentencingcouncil.org.uk/wp-content/uploads/Allocation_Guideline_2015.pdf. In view of its importance a copy of it is included in Appendix 3.

Whilst the requirements of s. 19 MCA 1980, the relevant sentencing guidelines and the parties' submissions are still significant factors in deciding place of trial, the revised guideline has changed the focus of the allocation hearing by establishing the overriding purpose of encouraging more cases to be tried and sentenced in the magistrates' court. In effect there is now presumption that either-way offences should be tried summarily unless there is a good reason against it. Cases should therefore only be sent to the Crown Court for trial when they are clearly unsuitable for trial in the magistrates' court.

Under the heading 'Venue for trial' the allocation guideline reminds the court that it is important to ensure that all cases are tried at the appropriate level. Generally, either-way offences should be tried summarily unless:

- the outcome would **clearly** be a sentence in excess of the magistrates' court's powers for the offence(s) charged after taking into account personal mitigation and any potential reduction for a guilty plea; or

- if the case has unusual legal, procedural, or factual complexities.

The exception covering unusual legal, procedural, or factual complexities may apply, for example, in cases where a very substantial fine is the likely sentence. Other circumstances where this exception will apply are likely to be rare and case specific and the court will rely on the submissions of the parties to identify relevant cases.

The guideline also reminds the court that in cases where there are no factual or legal complications consideration should always be given to the power to commit to the Crown Court for sentence under s. 3 Powers of Criminal Courts (Sentencing) Act 2000 (PCC(S)A 2000) after summary trial and thereby allowing the magistrates to retain jurisdiction notwithstanding that the likely sentence might exceed their sentencing powers.

11.3.2 THE STATUTORY FACTORS UNDER S. 19 MCA 1980

In addition to the allocation guideline in deciding the trial venue the court must also take into account the statutory factors under s. 19 MCA 1980 which provide:

(1) The court shall decide whether the offence appears to it more suitable for summary trial or for trial on indictment.

(2) Before making a decision under this section, the court—

   (a) shall give the prosecution an opportunity to inform the court of the accused's previous convictions (if any); and

   (b) shall give the prosecution and the accused an opportunity to make representations as to whether summary trial or trial on indictment would be more suitable.

(3) In making a decision under this section, the court shall consider—

   (a) whether the sentence which a magistrates' court would have power to impose for the offence would be adequate; and

   (b) any representations made by the prosecution or the accused under subsection (2)(b) above,

and shall have regard to any allocation guidelines (or revised allocation guidelines) issued as definitive guidelines.

11.3.3 RELEVANT SENTENCING GUIDELINES

In reaching a decision about trial venue the magistrates' court will also consider its sentencing powers on conviction. In assessing the likely sentence the court will apply any offence specific sentencing guidelines and/or any overarching sentencing guidelines to the particular case and any aggravating factors including the defendant's previous convictions.

The court will also take account of any defence submissions and any personal mitigation to which the defence may wish to refer.

If you recall the maximum sentence a magistrates' court can impose on conviction for an either-way offence is six months' imprisonment. This increases to a maximum of 12 months where the defendant is convicted of two or more either-way offences. The maximum fine that a magistrates' court could impose was £5,000 for a Level 5 offence. This is now unlimited for offences committed after 13 March 2015. This change has implications for the allocation of either-way cases likely to involve a very high fine. The Criminal Practice Direction requires the allocation of such cases to be determined by a District Judge authorised to deal with such cases. When making representations about the appropriate venue for trial for an either-way offence, the CPS advocate should provide the magistrates' court with current information on any applicable sentencing guideline.

In applying the s. 19 MCA 1980 statutory factors to the specific facts of the case before it, the magistrates' court will consider whether any aggravating features in the commission of the alleged offence, identified by the prosecuting advocate, may justify the case being tried in the Crown Court which has higher sentencing powers. Common aggravating features in the commission of an offence include where a defendant has acted in a premeditated way; where the victim of the crime was vulnerable; or where the property damaged or stolen was of high economic or sentimental value.

The MCSGs (see Appendix 3 for sample extracts) identify sentencing starting points and a sentence range (moving up and down from the starting point) for offences triable in the magistrates' court based on varying levels of seriousness in the ways in which an offence might be committed. When passing sentence, a court must follow any relevant sentencing guideline unless it would be contrary to the interests of justice. The starting point identified in the MCSGs for a particular offence might be committal for sentence to the Crown Court or committal might be within the range of sentences available. The guidelines also identify aggravating features in the commission of an offence which might lead the court to sentence at a higher starting point or even outside the sentencing range. Whilst the MCSGs are primarily applied when passing sentence, they are also highly relevant to the allocation hearing. They will be used by the prosecution and the defence in making their representations as to venue for trial and they will be used by the magistrates' court in reaching a decision about allocation for trial based on its maximum sentencing powers. The crucial importance of this will be more fully appreciated and understood after you have covered sentencing law and practice in Part V.

Remember that relevant sentencing guidelines can also be researched in a practitioner text such as *Blackstone's Criminal Practice*.

11.3.4 PROSECUTION AND DEFENCE SUBMISSIONS

At the allocation hearing all parties should be asked by the court to make representations as to whether the case is suitable for summary trial or trial on indictment. The prosecution will present a full outline of what the defendant is alleged to have done and disclose any of the defendant's previous convictions.

• The prosecution will then make representations as to whether the case should be tried summarily or whether jurisdiction should be declined and the case sent to the Crown Court. The prosecutor will need to explain the basis for her submissions.

• In some cases the CPS lawyer and the defence may agree about the appropriate trial venue. The only time there is likely to be disagreement between the parties is where the prosecution invites the court to decline to try the matter summarily because in its view the magistrates' sentencing powers would be insufficient, but the defendant seeks to persuade the court to retain summary jurisdiction. Given that the evidence remains untested at this point and that the accused may be indicating a not guilty plea, there may well be a limit on what the defence solicitor can say in representing that the case remain in the magistrates' court. Reference must be made to the applicable sentencing guidelines where the defence is seeking to have summary jurisdiction retained.

- It should not be forgotten that if jurisdiction to try a case summarily is accepted, the magistrates' court will still be able to commit for sentence on conviction if their powers are insufficient or if the offence is a specified offence and the 'dangerousness' provisions apply (see Chapter 22). This power has been emphasised in the revised allocation guideline, outlined above.

11.3.5 POSSIBLE OUTCOMES OF THE ALLOCATION HEARING AND SUBSEQUENT STEPS

(1) The magistrates' court declines jurisdiction

Where the magistrates' court decides that trial on indictment is more appropriate, the defendant has no right of election and the magistrates' court decision is communicated to him. The allocation hearing is adjourned and the defendant is sent forthwith to stand trial before the Crown Court (s. 51 CDA 1998) and a date will be set for the defendant's first appearance before the Crown Court at the **Plea and Trial Preparation Hearing (PTPH)—see Chapter 13, para. 13.5.** Upon sending, the parties will need to complete the Better Case Management form (BCM) which will be sent to the Crown Court. The form can be accessed at http://www.justice.gov.uk/courts/procedure-rules/criminal/forms-2015 and a copy of it is reproduced at Form 11.1 at the conclusion of this chapter. As explained above at para. 11.2.3, the defendant may indicate a guilty plea on the BCM form. Pending the adjournment (and in the absence of a guilty plea indication), the CPS will prepare and serve the case sent bundle on the defence (comprising used and unused prosecution evidence—see Chapters 8 and 13).

(2) The magistrates' court accepts jurisdiction

Where the magistrates' court decides that the case should be tried summarily, the legal adviser will explain to the defendant that he now has a choice. He can consent to be tried summarily (i.e. before the magistrates' court) or he can elect trial by jury in the Crown Court (i.e. trial on indictment). Under the allocation guideline it must be explained to the defendant that all possible sentencing options are available and if he chooses to be tried summarily and is convicted, he could still be committed to the Crown Court for sentence if the magistrates' court concludes, in the light of everything it has heard, that its sentencing powers are insufficient.

Before electing to be tried summarily or choosing trial on indictment the defendant can seek indication from the magistrates' court as to whether a non-custodial or custodial sentence would be imposed in the event of him pleading guilty. Any indication of sentence may influence the defendant as to which court to choose and whether to maintain a not guilty plea. A court is not obliged to give an indication of sentence and may refuse to do so. Very few indications are sought in practice.

Where an indication of sentence is given, the defendant will be asked whether they wish to reconsider any indication given at the earlier plea before venue. If the defendant then indicates a guilty plea, the court may not impose a custodial sentence unless such a sentence was indicated or the offence is a specified offence and the defendant is committed for sentence as a dangerous offender under s. 3A PCC(S)A 2000 (see Chapter 22).

If the defendant consents to summary trial, the magistrates' court will adjourn the allocation hearing and set a date for summary trial where the parties and the court will be governed by the principles of Transforming Summary Justice (TSJ—see Chapter 9, para. 9.15.2).

If the defendant elects trial on indictment, the allocation hearing will be adjourned and the case will be sent forthwith to the Crown Court accompanied by the parties' Better Case Management (BCM) form and a date set for the defendant's first appearance before the Crown Court at the Plea and Trial Preparation Hearing (PTPH). Pending the adjournment, the CPS will prepare and serve the case sent bundle on the defence as previously explained under **(1)**.

Of course the accused may still choose to enter a guilty plea where a decision to accept summary jurisdiction is made.

To assist further understanding of this important area and the roles undertaken by the prosecutor, defence lawyer and the court, consider this example.

 Example

Patryk, aged 35, is charged with assault occasioning actual bodily harm (s. 47 Offences Against the Person Act 1861) and criminal damage (s. 1(1) Criminal Damage Act 1971), and is due to make his initial appearance before the magistrates' court. His defence advocate has been served with advance information of the prosecution's evidence at court. From the evidence disclosed, it is alleged that Patryk assaulted a 45-year-old male with a baseball bat. The victim lives close to Patryk and there is bad feeling between them. The victim alleges that Patryk approached him in the street and started an argument.

When the victim threatened to call the police, it is alleged that Patryk went back into his house and emerged with a baseball bat. He proceeded to smash the windscreen of the victim's car, causing damage of £400. When the victim tried to prevent Patryk from causing any further damage, it is alleged that Patryk swung the bat at the victim's head causing a wound near to the victim's left eye, which required four stitches, and the loss of three teeth as well as severe bruising to the cheekbone and jaw. The wound will not leave any permanent scarring but dental treatment will be ongoing for some time.

Patryk, who exercised his right to remain silent at the police station, denies both offences. In relation to the assault, Patryk tells his solicitor that his neighbour started an argument and in the course of it he picked up a house brick and threatened Patryk with it. Patryk accepts he returned to his house to arm himself with a baseball bat because he feared further confrontation. When he re-emerged from his house, Patryk alleges that the victim started to verbally abuse him and in a fit of temper Patryk raised his baseball bat and aimed it at the victim's car resulting in the windscreen being smashed. Patryk maintains that he was then charged at by the victim and in self-defence he struck the victim with the bat not intending to cause serious injury. Patryk would prefer the matter to be dealt with summarily. Patryk has several previous convictions for drug-related offences and assault.

The prosecuting advocate will know that assault occasioning actual bodily harm (ABH) is an either-way offence and that criminal damage below £5,000 is a summary-only offence. Consequently, the maximum custodial sentence that the magistrates' court could pass in this case is six months' imprisonment. The CPS advocate will consider the sentencing guidelines for the offence of assault occasioning actual bodily harm. The guideline for assault contained in the MCSGs is reproduced in Appendix 3. [*Note the appearance of this offence-specific guideline is different from many of the others that appear in the MCSGs because it was formulated by the Sentencing Council for England and Wales, which adopts a different format from its predecessor, the Sentencing Guidelines Council.*] The prosecutor will say that based on what is alleged (premeditation, use of a weapon and serious injury), the magistrates' court sentencing guidelines suggest the assault should be sent to the Crown Court as it should be classed as a Category 1 s. 47 ABH. The prosecutor will disclose Patryk's previous convictions.

The defence advocate will use the sentencing guidelines to argue that the injury is not that serious and is non-permanent and therefore the magistrates' court would have sufficient sentencing powers on conviction as it could be classed as a Category 2 assault with a sentence starting point of 26 weeks in custody. The defence should remind the court of the revised allocation guideline (2016) and the firm presumption in favour of summary trial and the power of the Court to commit for sentence after trial. The magistrates conducting this allocation hearing will consider the representations made by the prosecution and the defence. On balance, they are likely to decline jurisdiction on the basis that their sentencing powers, in accordance with their sentencing guidelines, will be insufficient. In this event, Patryk will have no choice about where his case is tried.

11.4 THE REASONS FOR ELECTING TRIAL IN THE MAGISTRATES' COURT OR IN THE CROWN COURT

Where the magistrates believe the case is suitable for summary trial, the defendant has the right to elect trial by jury before the Crown Court or to consent to being tried summarily in the magistrates' court.

At a very early stage in the proceedings after receiving Initial Disclosure of the Prosecution Case (IDPC) from the CPS, the defendant's solicitor should assess the nature of the prosecution evidence against her client and be prepared to advise about the relative advantages of summary trial or trial on indictment if a plea of not guilty is to be maintained. Part of this advice will be based on a number of practical factors including how the defendant's case is funded and the defendant's personal circumstances. Clearly, if a defendant is privately funded or would be subject to a contribution order in the Crown Court, summary trial will be much cheaper than trial on indictment. If the defendant is vulnerable or has an anxious disposition, he may not be capable of dealing with the considerable pressures of a Crown Court trial.

In addition to any practical considerations, the defence lawyer should also consider the relative advantages and disadvantages of both types of proceedings having regard to the particular facts of her client's case. While it is part of the defence solicitor's professional duty to advise her client where his case should be tried, the decision ultimately lies with the client.

11.4.1 RELATIVE MERITS OF TRIAL ON INDICTMENT

Higher acquittal rate

In spite of inconclusive evidence, most defence lawyers believe that trial by jury provides a better chance of their client being acquitted. There is a commonly held perception that magistrates can be 'case-hardened' because they sit on a regular basis and often hear the same defence arguments. This is especially relevant in cases involving disputed police evidence, as magistrates may be more prepared to accept the evidence of the police in preference to that of the defendant. There is a widely held perception that jurors come to a case with a more open mind. For a defendant charged with theft who pleads not guilty because he lacked dishonest intent, 12 jurors hearing this defence for the first time may be more likely to give him the benefit of the doubt.

Disputed evidence

Where the case involves disputed evidence, the judge, as a legally qualified professional, is clearly much better placed to deal with points of law. A Crown Court judge will be more confident about excluding a disputed piece of evidence than a bench of lay magistrates. Also the separation of functions between judge and jury makes defence challenges about the admissibility of prosecution evidence during the trial much more effective as the jury is excluded from hearing arguments about the disputed point of law. Where the case involves disputing the admissibility of the prosecution's evidence (e.g. challenging the admissibility of a confession or evidence of identification), trial on indictment should be advised. Apart from the problems that some lay magistrates may experience in fully appreciating the advocate's legal submissions about the admissibility of prosecution evidence, if the defence submission is upheld, lay magistrates are required to put the excluded evidence to the back of their minds and continue trying the case. The increasing use of pre-trial hearings in the magistrates' court at which binding rulings on disputed evidence can be made means this problem arises less frequently than it used to. Of course some of these observations do not apply to summary trials conducted before a District Judge sitting in the magistrates' court.

Delay

It can take months before a case finally comes to trial in the Crown Court. Delay can be both an advantage and a disadvantage. The defence advocate might use the inevitable delay of trial in the Crown Court to prepare her client's case and to test the prosecution case.

Cost

Cost will be a significant factor for some defendants when deciding which trial venue to choose. Representation orders for summary proceedings are means tested. As explained in Chapter 9, the magistrates' court means test is an 'in or out' scheme. If the defendant qualifies for a representation order, he knows he will not have to contribute to any of his defence legal costs. If he does not qualify for a representation order, however, he will either have to represent himself or pay for legal representation out of his own funds. If acquitted, the defendant will be able to recover his privately paid costs out of central funds but this will be capped at legal aid rates if, and only if, he applied for legal aid but was determined to be ineligible (see Chapter 9, para. 9.13).

Means testing also applies to proceedings before the Crown Court. A Crown Court trial is considerably more expensive than a magistrates' court trial. Unless the defendant is 'passported' through the Crown Court means test or falls within the threshold for income and capital entitlement, he will be subject to a contribution order in the Crown Court unless his income is beyond the specified income threshold, in which case he will be ineligible (see Chapter 9, para. 9.10).

A further aspect of costs will arise if the defendant is convicted. In the event of conviction, prosecution costs (which most convicted defendants will be ordered to pay unless sentenced to custody) will be higher in the Crown Court than in the magistrates' court.

Powers of sentence

The Crown Court's powers of punishment greatly exceed those available to the magistrates' court. The Crown Court can impose a sentence up to the statutory maximum for the particular offence. Fines are also likely to be considerably higher in the Crown Court. This may be an important factor for a defendant.

11.4.2 RELATIVE MERITS OF SUMMARY TRIAL

Powers of sentence

If convicted in summary proceedings, the defendant is likely to receive a more lenient sentence, as the magistrates' court sentencing powers are limited compared to the Crown Court. As a matter of good practice, however, the defence advocate should remind her client about the magistrates' court power to commit to the Crown Court for sentence under s. 3 PCC(S)A 2000.

Delay

The delay in Crown Court proceedings may be a highly relevant consideration for some defendants, especially if the defendant is anxious or has been remanded in custody after being refused bail. The time between the date of the alleged offence and the date set for trial is often considerably shorter in summary cases enabling the case to be completed much sooner.

Publicity

Trial in the Crown Court will usually involve the defendant being exposed to greater publicity. Representatives of the local press and sometimes the national media will often take a greater interest in Crown Court proceedings. This is an important factor where the defendant is a public figure or the case is of particular public interest, for example where a teacher is charged with a sexual offence.

Stress

The relative informality of summary proceedings makes the magistrates' court more appropriate for a nervous client. By contrast, the atmosphere of the Crown Court is considerably more formal and intimidating.

Cost

As previously addressed, a trial in the magistrates' court can be conducted much more cheaply than a trial conducted before the Crown Court. For a defendant who does not pass the means test in the magistrates' court but who will be subject to a contribution order in the Crown Court, this will be an important consideration.

Defence pre-trial disclosure of evidence

Under the Criminal Procedure and Investigations Act 1996 (CPIA 1996), there is no obligation on the accused to serve a defence statement in summary proceedings (see Chapter 12, para. 12.7.5). In trials on indictment, after the prosecution has served 'initial' disclosure of 'unused' evidence, the accused is required to serve a defence statement (see Chapter 13, paras. 13.9.3–13.9.6). In summary proceedings, the service of a defence statement is voluntary.

Presenting advocate

If the defendant's trial is in the magistrates' court, the defendant is likely to have met his advocate before the trial. It is more likely that the advocate will be fully conversant with the facts, whereas at the Crown Court, instructions delivered to counsel are sometimes delivered at a very late stage and often there is no guarantee that the barrister instructed by the solicitor will be the person who represents her client at trial.

Appeal

An appeal from a Crown Court decision must be made to the Court of Appeal and requires leave. An appeal against summary conviction is made to a Crown Court. Leave is not required and the appeal is a complete rehearing of the case including, where appropriate, the admission of fresh evidence. The only disadvantage of an appeal to the Crown Court is that the sentence imposed by the magistrates' court can be increased if the appeal is unsuccessful but the appeal process is much more straightforward.

11.5 THE SPECIAL PROCEDURE IN CRIMINAL DAMAGE CASES

Where a defendant is charged with criminal damage contrary to s. 1 Criminal Damage Act 1971 unless the offence involves damage by fire, there are special rules regarding allocation. If the value of the damaged property is £5,000 or less, the case should be tried summarily. The defendant has no right of election to the Crown Court. The maximum sentence that a magistrates' court can impose for such an offence is three months' imprisonment and/or a £2,500 fine. If the damage to the property is over £5,000, the court is required to hold an allocation hearing in the normal way.

11.6 SPECIAL RULES RELATING TO CERTAIN EITHER-WAY OFFENCES

In the context of a third burglary offence, any previous convictions for burglary are important. If a defendant is charged with a third offence of domestic burglary the court will apply s. 111 PCC(S)A 2000, which requires a person convicted of a third domestic burglary offence (where all three of the offences were committed after 30 November 1999) to be given a custodial sentence of three years unless there are circumstances that do not justify imposing such a sentence. As this sentence is clearly in excess of the magistrates' court sentencing powers, it has no choice but to treat the offence as triable only on indictment, with the result that it must be sent to the Crown Court (s. 51 CDA 1998, see Chapter 13).

Whilst the offence of theft is triable either way, low-value shoplifting (defined as shoplifting where the value is of the stolen good does not exceed £200) is triable only summarily. However, in spite of this special classification an adult offender can still elect trial in the Crown Court if they wish.

11.7 SENDING AN EITHER-WAY OFFENCE TO THE CROWN COURT

Where the magistrates' court has decided at the allocation hearing that the case is more suitable for trial in the Crown Court or where the accused has elected trial on indictment after the magistrates' court has accepted jurisdiction to hold a summary trial, the case is sent forthwith to the Crown Court under s. 51 CDA 1998. The defendant's next appearance in connection with the either-way offence will be before the Crown Court at a Plea and Trial Preparation Hearing (PTPH). The conduct of the PTPH is covered in Chapter 13.

The s. 51 CDA 1998 'sending' procedure is the same procedure that is used to send an indictable-only offence and any related offence to the Crown Court following the accused's first appearance in connection with the matter before the magistrates' court. The s. 51 CDA 1998 procedure is outlined more fully in Chapter 13.

11.7.1 LINKED EITHER-WAY OR SUMMARY-ONLY OFFENCES

If the defendant is sent for trial in connection with an either-way offence, s. 51(3) CDA 1998 requires the magistrates' court also send a 'related' either-way (s. 51(3)(a)) or summary-only offence (s. 51(3)(b)) for trial on indictment. An either-way offence is 'related' where it can be joined in the same indictment because it is founded on the same facts or forms part of a series of offences of the same or similar character (s. 51E CDA 1998). The magistrates' court must also send any related summary offence for which the defendant appears at the same time (s. 51(3)(b) CDA 1998). A related summary offence must arise out of circumstances which are the same as or connected with the indictable-only offence and be punishable with imprisonment or disqualification (s. 51(11) CDA 1998). If the accused is convicted on indictment for the either-way offence, then if the judge considers that the summary-only offence is related to the indictable offence, the accused will be asked to enter a plea. If the accused pleads guilty, the Crown Court will pass sentence but its sentencing powers will be limited to those of the magistrates' court. If the defendant pleads not guilty and the prosecution wishes to proceed, the matter will have to be remitted back to the magistrates' court. Where a defendant appears before a magistrates' court on a separate occasion charged with a related either-way or summary offence, the magistrates have discretion to send the matter(s) up to the Crown Court so that they may be joined with the indictable-only matter(s) (s. 51(4) CDA 1998).

 Example

Brian is charged with burglary. At the allocation hearing, the magistrates' court determines that the offence should be heard on indictment. When the case sent papers are prepared, it appears that in order to escape from the crime scene Brian took a car without the owner's consent (a summary-only offence). The summary-only matter can be added to the indictment. Brian will be asked to plead to each count. If he pleads not guilty the jury will be sworn and the prosecution will present evidence to the court in respect of the burglary matter. If Brian is convicted of the burglary matter, he will be asked to enter a plea in relation to the vehicle-taking matter.

11.7.2 POSITION OF CO-ACCUSED JOINTLY CHARGED WITH AN EITHER-WAY OFFENCE

Suppose that A and B are jointly charged with an either-way offence and appear together. At the plea before venue, A indicates a guilty plea but B indicates a not guilty plea. In these circumstances, A will be sentenced by the magistrates' court (subject to possible committal for sentence to the Crown Court) and B will proceed to the allocation hearing.

What if both A and B indicate a not guilty plea? Both will be subject to the allocation hearing. If the magistrates' court declines summary jurisdiction, both will be sent forthwith to the Crown Court under s. 51 CDA 1998. If the magistrates' court accept summary jurisdiction, do A and B have an individual right of election? With the implementation of s. 51 CDA 1998 in relation to either-way offences, if either A or B elects trial on indictment, both will be sent forthwith to the Crown Court (s. 51(5) CDA 1998) irrespective of whether the other would have preferred summary trial. Crim PR, Part 9.2(6) requires this warning to be given to a co-accused as part of the plea before venue procedure outlined at para. 11.2.

11.7.3 CO-ACCUSED FACING AN EITHER-WAY OFFENCE RELATED TO AN INDICTABLE-ONLY OFFENCE OR A SENT EITHER-WAY OFFENCE

Where B is charged with an either-way offence which is related to an indictable-only offence with which A is charged, the either-way matter must be sent to the Crown Court in accordance with the requirements of s. 51 CDA 1998 (see Chapter 13). In these circumstances, the defendant (B) facing the either-way offence has no individual right of election. Any further related either-way offence or summary-only offence punishable with imprisonment or disqualification with which B is charged will also be sent.

 Example

A is charged with causing grievous bodily harm with intent contrary to s. 18 Offences Against the Person Act 1861 (indictable-only). B is charged with affray (triable either way). The affray allegation arises out of the s. 18 assault. A will be sent for trial in the Crown Court in connection with the indictable-only matter. If B appears before magistrates at the same time as A, B's case must also be sent to the Crown Court.

Where A, charged with an either-way offence, is sent for trial under s. 51 CDA 1998 and another adult (B), appears before the court, either on the same or subsequent occasion, charged jointly with A in connection with an either-way offence which appears to be related to the offence for which A was sent for trial, s. 51(5) CDA 1998 provides that where B appears on the same occasion as A, the court must also send B for trial to the Crown Court. Where B appears on a different occasion, the court has discretion to send the case. Any further related either-way offence or summary-only offence punishable with imprisonment or disqualification with which B is charged will also be sent.

11.8 POST-ALLOCATION MATTERS WHERE CASE IS TO BE SENT TO THE CROWN COURT

A number of important ancillary matters need to be considered once the either-way offence has been sent to the Crown Court.

11.8.1 BAIL

When the case is adjourned after the allocation hearing, the issue of a defendant's bail might well arise. Where the defendant has previously been refused bail, a fresh application for bail might be made depending on how many previous bail applications have been made (see Chapter 10, para. 10.15). Application may be made to the Crown Court. Generally the defendant's case being sent for trial at the Crown Court does not amount to a change in circumstances supporting a third application for bail, unless the evidence disclosed in the case sent bundle suggests the prosecution's case is not as strong as it originally appeared. This situation may satisfy the 'change of circumstances' test. The defence advocate should ensure bail is extended to cover the Crown Court proceedings where her client is currently subject to bail (conditional or otherwise).

11.8.2 REPRESENTATION ORDERS

If the defendant has qualified for a representation order before the magistrates' court, the representation order will cover the Crown Court proceedings upon the case being sent for trial. If the defendant applied for a representation order before the magistrates' court but failed the means test, he will (subject to the higher income threshold cut-off in the Crown Court) qualify for a representation order at this point but will be subject to a contribution order/notice based on his income and capital, declared on CRM15/CRM15C. If the defendant failed the interests of justice test initially but his case is subsequently sent to the Crown Court for trial, he will be passported through the interests of justice test.

11.8.3 DISCLOSURE OF EVIDENCE AND STANDARD CASE PROGRESSION DIRECTIONS

On sending a case for trial under s. 51 CDA 1998, a date will be set for a PTPH (see Chapter 13) in the Crown Court. In accordance with the Crim PR, Part 3, standard case progression directions apply which enable the parties to work towards the PTPH and ensure that the PTPH is an effective hearing. The standard directions make provision for the service of evidence (both used and unused material) by the CPS. The prosecution will be required to serve the case sent bundle on the defence (see Appendix 2, Documents 25–28) within 50 days if the defendant is in custody and 70 days in non-custody cases.

The case sent bundle will include:

- the draft indictment;
- all 'used' material including witness statements (primary prosecution disclosure);
- the schedule of unused material; and
- initial prosecution disclosure of unused material in accordance with s. 3 CPIA 1996.

Within 14 days of the service of the case sent bundle, the defence must notify the prosecution of their witness requirements (i.e. which prosecution witnesses the defence wish to attend court).

Within 28 days of the prosecutor completing or purporting to complete the disclosure obligations under s. 3 CPIA 1996, the defence must serve a defence statement (pursuant to s. 5 CPIA 1996), and details of any defence witnesses must be notified to the prosecution (s. 6C CPIA 1996). The rules on the disclosure of unused material and the requirement on the part of the defendant to serve a defence statement are considered in Chapter 13, which explores the conduct of trials on indictment.

Provision is also made in the standard case management progression form for the service of:

- any application for a special measures direction (see Chapter 16);
- notice to admit hearsay or evidence of bad character (see Chapters 18 and 19);
- defence notice objecting to the admission of hearsay or evidence of bad character.

11.9 APPLICATION FOR DISMISSAL OF THE EITHER-WAY OFFENCE SENT TO THE CROWN COURT

Committal hearings in either-way cases served as a mechanism for weeding out evidentially weak cases before they were committed to the Crown Court. Prior to the abolition of committal hearings, the prosecution was required to establish a prima facie case against the accused based on the evidence disclosed in the committal bundle. What is the position under the s. 51 CDA 1998 sending procedure? Once the accused has been served with the case sent bundle then, in accordance with Sch. 3 para. 2(1) CDA 1998, the defence can apply to the Crown Court to have the charge(s) dismissed. The application to dismiss is identical to the procedure that applies to indictable-only offences. The procedure is covered in greater detail in Chapter 13, para. 13.7. Reporting restrictions (limited to details of the defendant's name, age and bail arrangements) in relation to applications for dismissal of charges apply automatically but can be lifted.

What is the position where, because of some amendment to the charge(s) or a successful application to have charges dismissed before the Crown Court (outlined previously), an accused no longer faces the charge for which he was sent for trial? If he still faces an either-way offence, the Crown Court has to go through the plea before venue/allocation hearing as outlined at the start of this chapter.

11.10 **CHANGING THE ALLOCATION DECISION**

The abolition of committal proceedings for either-way offences means that it will no longer be possible to switch between committal proceedings and summary trial or vice versa. The power that previously permitted a switch from summary trial to committal is replaced by a new power under s. 25(2A) MCA 1980 for the prosecution to apply for an either-way offence which has been allocated for summary trial to be tried on indictment instead. The application must be made before the summary trial begins and before any application or issue in relation to the summary trial is dealt with. The court may grant the application if it is satisfied that the sentence which a magistrates' court would have power to impose would be inadequate.

KEY POINT SUMMARY IN RELATION TO EITHER-WAY OFFENCES

- In relation to all either-way offences, a defendant will be required to give an indication of his or her plea—this is known as the 'plea before venue'.

- The plea before venue will invariably be conducted at the defendant's initial appearance before the magistrates' court in accordance with TSJ.

- If the defendant indicates a guilty plea, the magistrates must accept jurisdiction to deal with the defendant summarily but can commit the defendant to the Crown Court for sentence if it concludes its maximum sentencing powers are insufficient.

- Where a not guilty plea or no plea is indicated, an allocation hearing must be held and the initial decision as to where the case shall be tried lies with the magistrates.

- If the magistrates' court declines summary jurisdiction, the defendant will have no choice—he will be tried on indictment in the Crown Court.

- If the magistrates' court accepts jurisdiction, the defendant will have the choice between a Crown Court trial or a trial before the magistrates' court.

- In reaching a decision as regards allocation, the magistrates will apply the statutory provisions under s. 19 MCA 1980 (as amended), the allocation guideline and specific sentencing guidelines and will consider, in particular, whether their maximum sentencing powers are likely to be sufficient in the event of conviction.

- When advising a client about allocation, the defence practitioner should not only consider the legal merits of advising in favour of summary trial or trial on indictment but also consider the client's personal circumstances and whether the client could cope with the considerable demands of a Crown Court trial.

- The defence advocate needs to find out in advance the prosecution's views on allocation and, if necessary, be prepared to argue against the CPS.

SELF-TEST QUESTIONS

Consider the following short scenarios.

- What representations do you consider the prosecution might make as regards allocation in each case?

- Applying s. 19 MCA 1980 factors, the allocation guideline and any applicable sentencing guidelines, do you consider the magistrates will accept or decline jurisdiction?

- Outline the procedure in relation to each possibility and consider, if the accused in each of the following exercises were given the choice as to election, what advice you would give in this regard?

 Analysis can be found in the online resources.

Exercise 1

Gunnar Erikson is 45 years old. He is charged with sexually assaulting a 12-year-old schoolgirl, contrary to s. 7 Sexual Offences Act 2003. It is alleged that he sat next to the girl when her friends left the bus they were all travelling on, leaving the girl and him alone on the upper deck. The girl alleges that Erikson tried to stroke her inner thigh and that he forcefully placed her hand on his clothed but erect penis. The girl promptly pushed him aside and quickly moved downstairs. The girl complained to her mother later that evening. Erikson was arrested several days later. He denies the offence and claims he is the victim of mistaken identification. Erikson has several previous convictions for theft and child sex offences. The girl turned 13 six days after the alleged offence.

 Exercise 2

Sinead Hogan is a 36-year-old pharmacist. She is charged with 16 offences of false accounting (s. 17 Theft Act 1968) and fraud worth £21,830 (s. 1 Fraud Act 2006) against the Prescription Pricing Authority. It is alleged that over a period of eight months she claimed expenditure for dispensing ordinary purpose syringes when her records show that she in fact dispensed a cheaper plastic disposable syringe. Sinead is a woman of impeccable character and denies the allegation.

Case study: *R v Lenny Wise*

Allocation

Take a look at *R v Lenny Wise* in the video section of our online resources. You will recall that Lenny is charged with domestic burglary. **(We would ask you to note that the Lenny Wise scenario was filmed under the pre-Sch. 3 CJA 2003 procedure and thus refers to the mode of trial enquiry. Consequently, Lenny's previous convictions were not disclosed for the purposes of what would have been mode of trial decision. They would have been disclosed under the new allocation hearing procedure.)** The plea before venue takes place at Lenny's second appearance before Lyme Magistrates. Lenny's solicitor gives him advice as regards allocation (previously mode of trial). The advice of Lenny's solicitor is contained in a file note (see Document 7 in Appendix 2).

On the video you can see Lenny indicates a not guilty plea at the plea before venue followed by his mode of trial enquiry/allocation hearing. You will also see the outline by the CPS lawyer inviting the court to decline jurisdiction to try the matter. At the conclusion of the mode of trial enquiry/allocation the magistrates decline jurisdiction and adjourn the matter and send the case to the Crown Court. Lenny is given the date for his Plea and Case Management Hearing (PCMH) before the Crown Court. The PCMH is now the Plea and Trial Preparation Hearing (PTPH). The reason for their decision is that they do not believe their sentencing powers would be sufficient in the event of conviction having regard to a number of aggravating factors in the commission of the alleged burglary. Lenny need not concern himself with means testing in the Crown Court. He will not be made the subject of a contribution order as he qualifies automatically in terms of his means (see Chapter 9).

FIGURE 11.1 EITHER-WAY OFFENCE—GENERAL SEQUENCE OF EVENTS

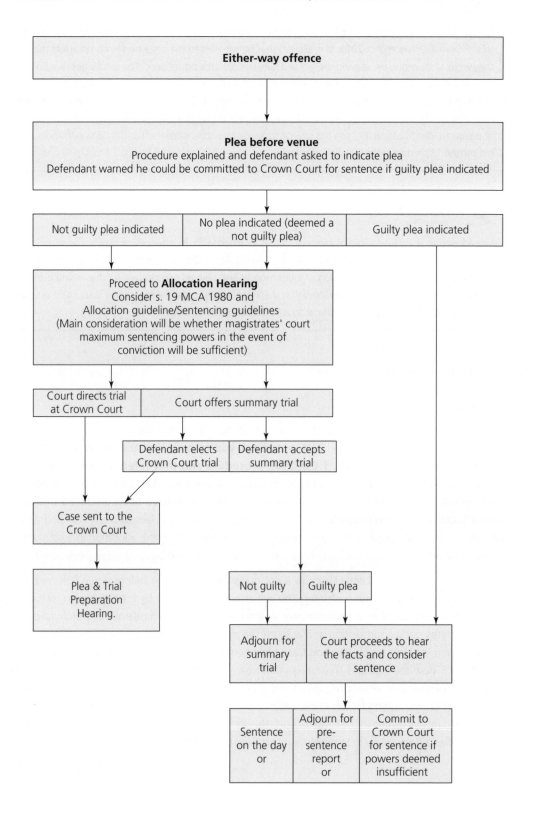

FORM 11.1 BETTER CASE MANAGEMENT FORM

Crown Court- Cases sent for trial

*In multi handed cases please complete **part one** for each defendant. However the court may complete **part two** on one form only to represent all defendants in the case.*

Part 1 - To be completed by the parties before the hearing

Name of defendant:	Date of Birth:	URN:

Solicitors firm representing (if any) :
Cjsm Email address:

Legal Aid Status:		Has the defendant been advised about credit for guilty pleas? ☐ Yes ☐ No
☐ Granted ☐ Applied for ☐ Will apply ☐ Private	☐ N/A	

Charges	Pleas (either way) or indicated pleas (ind only) or alternatives offered
1	1
2	2
3	3

Details of any other cases linked to this defendant:

In so far as known **Real issues in the case (concise details will be sufficient):**

What other areas of evidence do the prosecution anticipate serving before the PTPH?	
What other areas of evidence do the prosecution anticipate serving after the PTPH?	
Other evidence defence say they need prior to PTPH to make PTPH effective	

Any other information to assist the management of the case (e.g mental ill-health or other vulnerabilities or disabilities; reporting restrictions; likely press coverage):

Part 2 - To be completed by DJ(MC) / legal advisor after review of parties' information

Supplemental information about real issues gathered during the hearing:

☐ Child Witness Protocol- Witness under 10?   PTPH 14 days
☐ Case qualifies for s.28 pre-recorded cross-examination (where available) PTPH 28 days
  under s.16 ☐   under s.17 ☐

If a G Plea- was a PSR ordered? ☐ Yes ☐ No
NB: The type of report will be determined by the National Probation Service

Does the defendant require an interpreter? ☐ Yes ☐ No
Language/dialect:

Other information gathered during the hearing to assist the management of the case (e.g mental ill-health or other vulnerabilities or disabilities; reporting restrictions; likely press coverage):

Date of hearing in Crown Court:	☐ Bail or ☐ Custody – CTL expiry:

The court should remind the parties and the Defendant(s) that the Crown Court will expect before the PTPH that:
  ➢ The defendant(s) to have a conference with their legal advisors;
  ➢ The parties will engage to discuss pleas and outstanding issues (as necessary).

Name of DJ(MC)/ LA Completing Form: **Date:**

December 2017

12.1	**Introduction**	**220**
12.2	**Commencing a prosecution in the magistrates' court**	**221**
12.2.1	Time limits for the prosecution of summary-only offences	221
12.3	**Pleading guilty by post**	**222**
12.4	**Defendant unaware of court proceedings**	**222**
12.5	**Joinder of offences and defendants in the information**	**222**
12.5.1	Amending the written charge/information	223
12.6	**The early stages of a summary-only/either-way offence**	**224**
12.6.1	Taking a plea	224
12.6.2	Case management of a summary trial	224
12.7	**Preparing for trial (defence perspective)**	**226**
12.7.1	Visiting the crime scene	226
12.7.2	Tracing and interviewing potential defence witnesses	287
12.7.3	Instructing an expert witness	227
12.7.4	The pre-trial disclosure of evidence	227
12.7.5	'Unused' material and defence statements	227
12.7.6	Defence statements and summary trials	228
12.7.7	Evaluating the evidence	228
12.7.8	Securing the attendance of witnesses at trial	228
12.7.9	Disputed evidence	229
12.7.10	Preparing to mitigate on conviction	229
12.8	**Preparing for trial (prosecution perspective)**	**229**
12.9	**Rights of audience before magistrates' court and terms of address**	**230**
12.10	**Failure of the defendant to attend trial**	**230**
12.11	**The procedure at a summary trial on a not guilty plea**	**230**

12.1 INTRODUCTION

In this chapter we consider the steps in preparing for a summary trial. A summary trial will be held where a defendant pleads not guilty to a summary-only offence or pleads not guilty to an either-way offence where the magistrates' court has accepted jurisdiction to try the offence at the allocation hearing and the defendant has consented to summary trial.

This chapter should be read in conjunction with the latter part of Chapter 9 which provides an account of the early stages of a summary/either-way offence. In this chapter we specifically consider:

- pleading guilty by post;
- the circumstances in which a defendant can be summarily tried in her absence;
- the rules governing the drafting of a written charge/information;
- the pre-trial disclosure of evidence in a summary case;
- case management;

- the steps when preparing for summary trial;
- the procedure at a summary trial on a not guilty plea.

12.2 COMMENCING A PROSECUTION IN THE MAGISTRATES' COURT

Criminal proceedings are commenced either by the police charging an individual at the police station, or by the Crown Prosecution Service (CPS) issuing a 'written charge and postal requisition' under s. 29 Criminal Justice Act 2003 (CJA 2003). (Before s. 29 CJA 2003 came into force criminal proceedings were usually commenced either by the suspect being charged at the police station or by an information being laid in the magistrates' court and requesting the court issue a summons against the defendant. The summons required the defendant to attend court on a specified date to answer to the charge(s) in the information. The information and summons method is now used for private prosecutions only.)

The required content of the written charge/information is set out in Crim PR, Part 7.3(1). It is the formal accusation against the defendant. Crim PR, Part 7.3 provides that a 'written charge' or 'information' must contain:

(a) notice of when and where the defendant is required to attend the court; and

(b) a statement of the offence which describes in ordinary language and (if the offence is created by statute) identifies the legislation that creates it and sufficient particulars of the conduct constituting the commission of the offence to make clear what the prosecutor alleges against the defendant.

In the case of a 'requisition', the prosecutor must ensure service of both the 'written charge and the requisition' which may be contained within a single document on the defendant. Service is usually made by sending it by first-class post to an address where it is reasonably believed that the accused will receive it (Crim PR, Part 4). If the accused fails to appear and satisfactory service can be established, the court can adjourn the case or proceed in the defendant's absence or issue an arrest warrant for the accused either backed or not backed with bail.

Section 48 Criminal Justice and Courts Act 2015 permits certain cases to be tried by a single justice under the single justice procedure (SJP). The power currently relates to summary-only, non-imprisonable offences where the defendant is an adult and certain procedural requirements have been complied with. These procedural requirements are that the defendant has been served with a written charge (s. 29 CJA 2003) and a single justice procedure notice and any other documents that are prescribed by the Criminal Procedure Rules 2015 and that the defendant has not entered a plea of not guilty or specifically requested an oral hearing before a magistrates' court in response to receiving the single justice procedure notice.

As part of the Government's digital drive (https://www.gov.uk/government/consultations/transforming-our-courts-and-tribunals), an automatic online conviction procedure is likely to be introduced. Under this proposal, defendants who opt in to the online procedure and plead guilty will be offered the option to accept a pre-determined penalty (including the payment of any appropriate compensation and costs), be convicted, and pay the amount immediately. Secondary legislation will determine which offences will come within this proposed scheme and what the penalty will be.

12.2.1 TIME LIMITS FOR THE PROSECUTION OF SUMMARY-ONLY OFFENCES

A magistrates' court may not try a defendant for a summary offence unless the requisition/information was laid within six months of the commission of the alleged offence (s. 127(1)

Magistrates' Courts Act 1980 (MCA 1980)). This provision applies to most summary-only offences, although the time limit can be expressly overridden by statute.

12.3 PLEADING GUILTY BY POST

In some summary cases the defendant may plead guilty by sending a letter to the court without the need to attend the hearing. The practice of pleading guilty by post, which is governed by s.12 MCA 1980 and Crim PR, Part 24.8, can apply in the following circumstances:

(a) the offence is summary-only; and

(b) the proceedings have been started by requisition/summons.

The prosecution decides whether the accused should have the option of pleading guilty by post.

Where the defendant pleads guilty by post, the prosecution must serve on the defendant:

(i)   the requisition/summons;

(ii) a brief statement of the facts upon which the prosecution is to rely, or a copy of any statements written in compliance with s. 9 Criminal Justice Act 1967 (CJA 1967);

(iii) any information relating to the defendant that will be put before the court; and

(iv) a notice explaining the procedure.

If the defendant wishes to pleads guilty, she must notify the court and may submit a written statement in mitigation of sentence. The court proceeds on the basis of the written statements submitted by both sides which must be read to the court. The magistrates may refuse to accept a guilty plea if the statement in mitigation reveals a defence or the plea is unclear. If the guilty plea is accepted, the magistrates can sentence immediately, depending on the type of sentence or following an adjournment requiring the defendant's attendance.

12.4 DEFENDANT UNAWARE OF COURT PROCEEDINGS

If the defendant was unaware of the court proceedings then, within 21 days of finding out about the proceedings, s. 14 MCA 1980 permits the defendant to make a statutory declaration that she knew nothing of the proceedings. The declaration may be made before the court or a solicitor. The effect of the declaration is that the requisition/summons and all the proceedings are void. The written charge/information, however, is still valid.

12.5 JOINDER OF OFFENCES AND DEFENDANTS IN THE INFORMATION

At the commencement of a summary trial, the defendant is asked to plead guilty or not guilty to the information containing the charge(s).

The general rule is that a written charge/information may only charge one defendant with a single offence (Crim PR, Part 7.3) unless the prosecution alleges that the offence was committed jointly by more than one defendant.

 Example

Ben and Chris are charged with common assault arising out of a fight outside a nightclub on 23 January. The prosecution alleges both defendants assaulted the victim. As both defendants committed the offence jointly, each will be tried on the same written charge.

A written charge or information which charges more than one offence is bad for duplicity and the prosecutor must decide which charge he wishes to proceed with.

In some situations, where the defendant faces more than one charge or several accused are charged in separate written charges/informations, the court may try the charges together. Written charges/informations may be tried together where:

- the defence agree to the charges being tried together; or
- the court orders the offences to be tried together because it is in the interests of justice to do so and the offences form part of a series of offences of the same or similar character.

If the defence do not agree to the charges being tried together, for the alternative ground to apply the court must be satisfied that the offences are part of a series of offences of the same or similar character. This requires, first, that there should be some connection between them in time and place and the nature of the offences. Second, the court will take into account whether it is in 'the interests of justice' for the written charges to be tried together. Guidance on the application of the interest of justice test is provided by the House of Lords in *Chief Constable of Norfolk v Clayton* [1983] 2 AC 473. When applying the interests of justice test, the court must consider the convenience to the prosecution of having the charges/informations tried together against any injustice that might arise to the defendant. In most cases the defence will resist having the charges/informations tried together. A common submission is that it is not in the interests of justice as the evidence from one offence might unfairly prejudice the magistrates in deciding a defendant's guilt in respect to the other offence.

 Example

(a) Over the course of three days Leah commits four offences of theft and fraud by going from shop to shop and obtaining goods from each of them using a false credit card.

(b) In a domestic dispute over the course of two weeks, Neil commits common assault against his ex-girlfriend, her new boyfriend and his ex-girlfriend's mother.

(c) Julie steals two books from the library. The following day she commits an offence of careless driving.

In examples (a) and (b) the two conditions for the written charges to be tried together appear to be satisfied. First, the offences are part of a series of offences of the same or similar nature. There is also proximity between them in terms of time. Second, the court would rule that it is in the interests of justice for the charges to be tried together after considering the balance of convenience to the prosecution and the potential prejudice to Leah and Neil.

In example (c) the grounds for trying the charges together are not satisfied. As the defence will not agree and the offences are not the same or of a similar nature, Julie will be tried separately on each charge.

12.5.1 AMENDING THE WRITTEN CHARGE/INFORMATION

If the details contained in the written charge/information are incorrect or inconsistent with the evidence called by the prosecution, s. 123 MCA 1980 permits it to be amended at any stage of the proceedings provided the error has not caused injustice to the defendant. Examples of minor errors which would not cause injustice are where the defendant's name or the location of the offence is misspelt in the written charge. Where the error is regarded as 'substantial', the court may allow the amendment but will also grant an adjournment to allow the defence to deal with any issues arising out of the amendment (s. 123 MCA 1980).

 Example

Rashid is requisitioned with driving a motor vehicle with a defective tyre. The written charge details the defective tyre to be 'on the rear offside of the vehicle'. In fact, the defective tyre was on the rear nearside of the vehicle. In this situation, amending the written charge will be permitted and it is un-likely that the error would be regarded as substantial.

Majinder is requisitioned for common assault, which is wrongly specified in the written charge as having been committed on 23 March. In fact the alleged offence occurred on 26 March. As Majinder has an alibi for his whereabouts on 23 March, it is likely that the proposed amendment is 'substantial' and the court will adjourn the proceedings to enable the defence to deal with the amendment.

12.6 THE EARLY STAGES OF A SUMMARY-ONLY/EITHER-WAY OFFENCE

As we saw in Chapter 9, in the early stages of a summary-only or either-way offence the defence solicitor will advise the client about her plea. Before giving advice, the defence solicitor will need to:

- interview the client;
- obtain and evaluate initial disclosure of the prosecution's case (Crim PR, Part 8); and
- obtain a representation order on behalf of the client.

12.6.1 TAKING A PLEA

In accordance with various initiatives and now Transforming Summary Justice (TSJ)—(see Chapter 9, para. 9.15), the defendant is expected to enter a plea at the first hearing before the magistrates' court. To facilitate this, the CPS must serve initial disclosure of the prosecution's case on the accused before the first hearing (see Chapter 9, para. 9.15). A guilty plea will require the court to pass sentence either on the day or following an adjournment for a pre-sentence report. Sentencing practice is considered in Part V.

Where the defendant indicates a not guilty plea in a summary case, the requirements of TSJ, in conjunction with the Crim PR and the Criminal Practice Direction (2015) aim to en-sure that all contested trials in the magistrates' court are fully case managed from the first hearing and disposed with at the second hearing.

The court is required to actively manage the case by making standard directions, as ex-plained later. A summary case should normally be listed for trial within six to nine weeks of first appearance. This may be longer if, for example, the case is likely to involve defence expert evidence. The defendant will be remanded on bail or in custody to the trial date. Having set the trial date, some magistrates' courts additionally list the case for a pre-trial review/case management hearing usually one week before the date set for trial to avoid last minute difficulties which may lead to the trial being vacated on the day.

12.6.2 CASE MANAGEMENT OF A SUMMARY TRIAL

All parties are obliged to assist the court in its active management of cases under Crim PR, Part 3. Crim PR, Part 3.2 imposes specific duties on the court to further the overriding objective by actively managing cases.

'(2) Active case management includes—

    (a) the early identification of the real issues;

    (b) the early identification of the needs of witnesses;

    (c) achieving certainty as to what must be done, by whom, and when, in particular by the early setting of a timetable for the progress of the case;

    (d) monitoring the progress of the case and compliance with directions;

    (e) ensuring that evidence, whether disputed or not, is presented in the shortest and clearest way;

    (f) discouraging delay, dealing with as many aspects of the case as possible on the same occasion, and avoiding unnecessary hearings;

(g) encouraging the participants to co-operate in the progression of the case; and

(h) making use of technology.

(3) The court must actively manage the case by giving any direction appropriate to the needs of that case as early as possible.'

In setting a firm date for a summary trial at the first hearing, the magistrates' court will expect both the prosecution and the defence to assist in the completion of a trial preparation form (see Part 3 Case Management: Preparation for Effective Trial form (PET) available at https://www.justice.gov.uk/courts/procedure-rules/criminal/forms-2015) and its accompanying guidance. A copy of the PET form appears as Form 12.1 at the conclusion of this chapter.

The case management requirements of TSJ are entirely consistent with the overriding objective in Crim PR, Part 1 that cases will be dealt with justly, efficiently and expeditiously taking into account the gravity of the offence alleged, the complexity of what is in issue, the severity of the consequences for the defendant and others affected and the needs of other cases.

Take the time to look over the PET form reproduced at Form 12.1. The prosecutor must complete Parts 1, 2, and 4. Where a not guilty plea is anticipated, these parts should be completed and the form served on the defendant along with IDPC, before the first hearing. The defence must then complete Parts 1, 3, and 4 of the form, before or during the first hearing. Part 3 requires the defence advocate to confirm that he has advised his client about the potential sentencing credit for a guilty plea. The list on the final page of the form refers to the time limits that are prescribed by the Crim PR, or by other legislation, and any time limits and other directions that the court may wish to adopt.

In accordance with Crim PR, Part 3 and to effectively manage the case, the magistrates' court will require the parties to confirm:

• what the real issues in the case are;

• whether any point of law arises as part of their case;

• what witness evidence can be agreed and read out to the court under s. 9 CJA 1967 (see Chapter 18, para. 18.4.1);

• whether any evidence can be adduced by way of formal admissions in accordance with s. 10 CJA 1967;

• how many witnesses need to be called for each side and have dates for their availability (witnesses should only attend trial if they can testify on issues in dispute between the parties and the court must actively consider whether the witnesses' evidence can be agreed under s. 9 or 10 CJA 1967);

• whether the record of interview at the police station (ROTI) can be agreed;

• whether any applications for special measures or to admit evidence of bad character or hearsay are anticipated;

• what is a realistic time estimate for the trial.

Many of these matters are covered in Parts 8 and 9 of the PET form. Parts 11 and 12 of the form focus on potential witnesses in the case including the number of witnesses to be called; whether it is necessary for the witnesses to testify in person or whether their evidence could be agreed/edited and read in court in their absence and any special measures directions that may be required (see Chapter 17). Also in those cases where a not guilty plea is anticipated, the CPS should attend court with full witness availability. In relation to defence witnesses, the form asks only which defence witnesses are expected to give evidence in person.

Once the case has been listed for trial, the parties must comply with any directions that are given in relation to the service of unused evidence and any applications to admit or to oppose the admission of bad character and/or hearsay evidence at trial. Although the

Criminal Procedure Rules provide timescales for the service of a notice to admit bad character, the court can allow the application to be made orally at the case management stage (i.e. the first hearing), and will want to do so where it is obvious that an application could or should be made. Contested applications for special measures/bad character and hearsay may well be listed for a pre-trial hearing at which binding rulings under s. 45 Courts Act 2003 can be made.

Where any party anticipates there could be a problem with being ready by the trial date (this may be due to witness unavailability), Crim PR, Part 3 imposes a duty on the party to notify the court's case progression officer in good time so that an application can be made to vacate the date set for the trial.

Under TSJ an application by either side seeking an adjournment will be rigorously scrutinised in accordance with the principles outlined in *Crown Prosecution Service v Picton* [2006] EWHC 1108 (Admin). The near zero-tolerance approach to adjournments required by TSJ means that if the defence has complied with all its responsibilities and is fully ready for trial, but the prosecution has failed to comply with its responsibilities, then normally it would not be in the interest of justice for the prosecution to be allowed an adjournment and the prosecution may fail. If the failure lies with the defence and an adjournment is granted, the defence can expect to be subject to a wasted costs order.

Can the defence refuse to cooperate with the court's case management responsibilities?

What if the defendant simply indicates to the court when completing the case management form that he pleads not guilty and intends to put the prosecution to proof of his guilt? Can a defendant refuse to disclose the nature of his defence on the basis that it requires him to waive legal professional privilege or it violates his privilege against self-incrimination? If this is what the client instructs his solicitor to do, how does the solicitor reconcile his duties under the SRA Code of Conduct 2019 to uphold the rule of law and the proper administration of justice (*Principle 1*) and to act in the best interests of each client (*Principle 7*)?

The position is that the defence solicitor is under a duty to actively assist the court in its case management responsibilities under Crim PR, Part 3. This is reaffirmed by the Law Society in its Practice Note on the Criminal Procedure Rules 2015 (accessible at http://www.lawsociety.org.support-services/advice/practice-notes/the-criminal-procedure-rules-2015-solicitors-duties/). The guidance makes it clear that whilst a court cannot require a solicitor to act in a way which would override the presumption of innocence, the right to silence and the privilege against self-incrimination or legal professional privilege, a solicitor can be required by the Criminal Procedure Rules, or by a direction of the court (Crim PR, Part 3.5) made under its case management duties arising from Crim PR, Part 3, to provide information that will enable the court process to proceed efficiently. The Practice Note is essential reading and in particular s. 5 of the Note.

It is well established by case law that a defendant who advances a positive defence at trial having not previously disclosed it on the case management form can gain no advantage from ambushing the prosecution and failing to comply with his obligations under Crim PR, Part 3.3 to assist the court in its case management duties (see *Director of Public Prosecutions v Chorley Justices* [2006] EWHC 1795 (Admin)).

12.7 PREPARING FOR TRIAL (DEFENCE PERSPECTIVE)

Where the case is listed for trial (and having regard to the matters in Crim PR, Part 3 previously outlined), the defence solicitor should begin preparing for a summary trial as soon as possible. This may include some or all of the following.

12.7.1 VISITING THE CRIME SCENE

Visiting the crime scene can give the defence lawyer a better understanding of the location where the offence occurred. It is often useful to prepare a plan or take photographs, especially in road traffic collision cases where there is a dispute between the prosecution and the defendant about, for example, the position of the vehicle(s) on the road.

12.7.2 TRACING AND INTERVIEWING POTENTIAL DEFENCE WITNESSES

The practical effect of the stricter case management duties imposed by the courts places enormous pressure on a defence advocate to prepare for summary trial at the outset. Any potential defence witness should be contacted at the earliest opportunity for a statement to be taken. Sometimes, this may require the defence to make enquiries to identify the names and addresses of potential witnesses.

Whilst there is no property in a witness, it would be unusual for the defence to interview a prosecution witness before trial, and regard should always be had to the potential dangers that this could give rise to under the SRA Code of Conduct 2019, outlined in Chapter 1, para. 1.10.1 onwards. In this situation the guidance contained in the SRA Code of Conduct 2007 is still helpful:

> 'To avoid such allegations it would be wise, when seeking to interview a witness for the other side, to offer to interview them in the presence of the other side's representative.'

12.7.3 INSTRUCTING AN EXPERT WITNESS

Many summary offences do not require expert evidence but in those cases where expert evidence is required, the defence advocate should instruct an expert at the earliest opportunity. If the defendant has a representation order, the defence should obtain the written authority of the Legal Aid Agency (LAA) using Form CRM4 eForm, before formally instructing the expert. It is common practice to support the application with an explanation of why an expert is required and what the fee will be.

Where either the prosecution or the defence intends to call expert evidence at trial, Crim PR, Part 19 requires the pre-trial disclosure of the expert's report both to the court and to the other party (see Chapter 17, para. 17.9.3).

12.7.4 THE PRE-TRIAL DISCLOSURE OF EVIDENCE

Once an accused has pleaded not guilty to a matter that is to be tried summarily, the prosecution will come under further obligations to make pre-trial disclosure of evidence. This will include any 'used' material that the prosecution intends to rely on at trial which has not previously been disclosed as part of IDPC (Crim PR, Part 8) and any 'unused material' under the Criminal Procedure and Investigations Act 1996 (CPIA 1996).

12.7.5 'UNUSED' MATERIAL AND DEFENCE STATEMENTS

Section 3 CPIA 1996 requires the prosecution to serve the defendant with initial disclosure of any evidence not previously disclosed, which might reasonably be considered capable of undermining the case for the prosecution or of assisting the case for the accused. For a full explanation of the rules on disclosure of 'unused material' see Chapter 8, paras. 8.9 onwards.

The prosecution's obligation to serve 'unused' material arises in cases to be tried summarily where the defendant pleads not guilty. As explained in Chapter 8, para. 8.10.2 and Chapter 9, para. 9.15, and in accordance with TSJ, a streamlined disclosure certificate (SDC) detailing any 'unused' material will be served alongside IDPC prior to the first hearing.

On receiving initial prosecution disclosure of 'unused material', the defendant may choose to file a defence statement under s. 6 CPIA 1996, indicating on which matters the defendant takes issue with the prosecution case and for what reasons and giving particulars of any defence or alibi the defendant intends to rely on at trial. The detailed rules governing the service of defence statements are explained in Chapter 13, which outlines the steps for preparing for trial on indictment.

While the service of a defence statement is voluntary in summary cases, s. 6C CPIA 1996 requires the defendant to serve a defence witness notice giving details of all defence witnesses (other than an expert witness) he intends to call at trial. The provision is considered in more detail in Chapter 13, para. 13.6.13. The time limit for service of the defence witness notice in summary cases is 14 days after the prosecution's compliance or purported compliance with its initial disclosure duties under s. 3 CPIA 1996.

In those very exceptional situations when a defence statement is served in a summary case, the prosecution must fulfil its ongoing obligation to keep disclosure under review in accordance with s. 7A CPIA 1996. In particular the CPS must disclose any 'further' material which has not previously been disclosed and which might reasonably be expected to assist the accused's case as disclosed in the defence statement.

Apart from complying with the obligation under s. 6C CPIA 1996 (highlighted earlier) to disclose details of any witness to be called at trial, in view of the potential sanctions that apply to the service of a defence statement, why would a defence solicitor serve a defence statement in a summary trial?

12.7.6 DEFENCE STATEMENTS AND SUMMARY TRIALS

The answer to the question stated comes down to tactical considerations. The defence advocate knows that serving a defence statement will force the prosecutor to look again at the 'unused' material (s. 7A CPIA 1996) to see whether there is any previously undisclosed material that might assist the case for the defendant. The defence advocate therefore needs to carefully consider the disclosure schedule which is served with initial disclosure of unused material under s. 3 CPIA 1996, and decide whether serving a defence statement might unearth further useful disclosure. However, the service of a defence statement in summary proceedings remains rare as usually there is nothing to be gained by it. That said, para. 43 of the Attorney General's (2013) Guidelines on Disclosure states:

> 'In the magistrates' courts, where the provision of a defence statement is not mandatory, early identification of the material issues by the defence, whether through a defence statement, case management form or otherwise, will help the prosecution to focus its preparation of the case and allow any defence disclosure queries to be dealt with promptly and accurately.'

12.7.7 EVALUATING THE EVIDENCE

Having obtained full disclosure of the prosecution's case and an updated proof of evidence from the defendant and any defence witnesses, the defence solicitor should begin to evaluate the strength of the prosecution's case and to formulate a strategy for defending the case in court. In preparing for trial the elements of the offence(s) charged must be researched so the advocate knows the facts in issue which the prosecution must prove to secure the defendant's conviction. Research may also be necessary where the defence intends to challenge prosecution evidence at trial. The defence advocate should come to court prepared to cite relevant statutory provisions and case law in support of his submission to have prosecution evidence excluded.

Where the prosecution has served an application to allow one or more of its witnesses to give evidence under a special measures direction (see Chapter 16), or it has served an application to admit hearsay evidence (see Chapter 18), or to admit the defendant's bad character (see Chapter 19), the defence advocate must decide whether to oppose the application. If the application is opposed, the defence advocate should serve a notice in accordance with the standard directions or make an application to serve notice out of time, if necessary.

12.7.8 SECURING THE ATTENDANCE OF WITNESSES AT TRIAL

An important part of trial preparation is to decide which of the witnesses from whom he has taken a proof of evidence will be called to give evidence for the defence. Initially, the defence advocate will write to a prospective witness giving full details of the time and location of the court hearing asking the witness to attend voluntarily or to produce a document. If the witness does not reply or indicates that she is not willing to appear voluntarily it will be necessary to apply to the court for a witness summons to be issued.

The rules on the issue and service of a witness summons, which apply both to the prosecution and the defence, are contained in Crim PR, Part 17.

The application for a witness summons can be made orally or in writing. Special rules apply to a witness summons that seeks to have a witness produce a document.

Some witnesses will be reluctant to attend even where they have been served with a witness summons. In this situation, s. 97(2) MCA 1980 authorises an arrest warrant to be issued against the witness to ensure attendance.

12.7.9 DISPUTED EVIDENCE

Disputes about the admissibility of evidence do not arise as frequently in the magistrates' courts as at trials in the Crown Court. However, where evidence is disputed, the matter will be decided by the magistrates/District Judge at the beginning of the trial or during the trial. In some circumstances a *voir dire*, or trial within a trial, will be held (*R v Liverpool Juvenile Court, ex p. R* [1987] 2 All ER 668). At a *voir dire*, evidence may be called and legal submissions made as to why the disputed evidence should be excluded. If the magistrates decide the evidence is inadmissible, no further mention will be made of it and no reliance can be placed on it. A *voir dire* will commonly be held where the defendant disputes the admissibility of a confession or seeks to have identification evidence excluded for breaching Code D. The *voir dire* is much more effective in the Crown Court where there is a strict division of functions between the judge and the jury and issues of law and evidence are decided in the absence of the jury. This is not possible in the magistrates' court as the magistrates are arbiters of both fact and law. The use of pre-trial binding rulings under the Courts Act 2003 (highlighted at para. 12.6.2) goes some way to reducing the potential prejudice arising from the *voir dire* procedure in summary proceedings as the trial bench will be differently composed.

12.7.10 PREPARING TO MITIGATE ON CONVICTION

Unless the defendant is acquitted on all charges the defence advocate should be ready to make a plea in mitigation of sentence. Sentencing practice and procedure is explained in detail in Part V.

12.8 PREPARING FOR TRIAL (PROSECUTION PERSPECTIVE)

In preparing for trial, the prosecutor is likely to follow the same steps as the defence advocate.

In the short time available to prepare for summary trial, the prosecution advocate will have determined whether:

* an application for a special measures direction for one or more of its witnesses is required (see Chapter 16);
* an application to admit hearsay (see Chapter 18) or bad character evidence is required (see Chapter 19).

The prosecuting lawyer will, amongst other things, also:

* serve any unused material that is required to be disclosed in accordance with s. 3 CPIA 1996 (see para. 12.7.5);
* try to agree evidence with the defence in accordance with ss. 9 and 10 CJA 1967 (see para. 12.6.2 and Chapter 15, para. 15.8);

- research the elements of the offence so that she is clear what needs to be proved (see Chapter 15);

- determine which witnesses to call and in what order;

- ensure attendance of her witnesses with the assistance of the police and witness liaison;

- ensure any exhibits are available for production in court;

- be prepared to resist a defence argument to have prosecution evidence excluded;

- be prepared to assist the court on passing sentence if the accused is convicted, by referring the court to any of the defendant's relevant previous convictions and ask for ancillary orders where appropriate.

12.9 RIGHTS OF AUDIENCE BEFORE MAGISTRATES' COURT AND TERMS OF ADDRESS

Only solicitors/barristers, licensed CILEX advocates and associate prosecutors (to a limited degree) have a right of audience to conduct trials in a magistrates' court. If you are training to be a lawyer, although you may not have rights of audience at this stage, the magistrates' court is an invaluable learning experience—take full advantage to watch and learn.

When addressing a District Judge, the address is 'Sir' or 'Madam'. A lay bench can be addressed collectively as 'Your Worships'. Alternatively an advocate may choose to address the chairperson of the bench and say 'Madam and your colleagues' or 'Sir and your colleagues'. When referring to the magistrates' adviser, it is customary to state 'Your learned legal adviser' and when referring to your opposing advocate, you might say 'My friend for the prosecution' or, in the case of a barrister, 'My learned friend'.

12.10 FAILURE OF THE DEFENDANT TO ATTEND TRIAL

Unless it would be contrary to the interests of justice, s. 11(1)(b) MCA 1980 requires the trial to go ahead in the absence of an adult defendant. Much will depend on what explanation, if any, is advanced for the defendant's absence.

If the explanation is that the defendant is too ill to attend trial or has been faced with a family emergency, the court may accept a defence request for the trial to be adjourned to a later date and for bail to be extended. If the court decides to try the defendant in her absence and the defendant is represented, her solicitor can still put the prosecution to prove its case and make submissions and a closing speech. A trial in the defendant's absence, particularly an unrepresented defendant, is most likely to result in a conviction as the evidence against the defendant is not contradicted.

Having convicted an absent defendant, a court may also sentence in her absence or adjourn sentence and issue a warrant for the defendant's arrest. Where an offender is sentenced to imprisonment in her absence, she must be brought before the court before being taken to prison.

12.11 THE PROCEDURE AT A SUMMARY TRIAL ON A NOT GUILTY PLEA

Where the defendant pleads not guilty, the whole prosecution case is put in issue. The relevant rules of court relating to the conduct of summary trials are contained in Crim PR, Part 24.3:

(1) The hearing begins with the defendant's full name, address and date of birth and the name of her solicitor being given to the court.

(2) The charge(s) will be put to the defendant by the justices' legal adviser and the defendant confirms that she pleads not guilty to the charge(s).

(3) The prosecutor may make an opening speech by addressing the court with regard to:

– the prosecution's version of the facts;

– the witnesses to be called in support of the prosecution case; and

– any legal issues that will arise;

– to help the members of the court to understand the case and to resolve any issue in it, the court may invite the defendant concisely to identify what is in issue.

(4) The first prosecution witness is questioned by the prosecutor in examination-in-chief, the purpose of which is to obtain answers from the witness that support the prosecution case. All factual witnesses must remain outside the courtroom until they have given their evidence. Each witness called will first take the oath or affirmation and state their name. It is customary to point out to the witness that they should speak clearly and at a slow pace, addressing their answers to the bench. Certain witnesses may give their evidence with the benefit of special measures. The rules relating to witness testimony are explained in Chapter 16.

(5) The witness may then be cross-examined by the defence with a view to undermining the accuracy or truthfulness of what the witness said during examination-in-chief and/or to undermine the witness's credibility.

(6) The prosecution may re-examine the witness to repair any damage that may have been inflicted on the witness during cross-examination.

(7) The magistrates may ask the witness questions at any time but in most courts the convention applies that the witness will be questioned after the parties have finished asking questions.

(8) The process of witness testimony of examination-in-chief, cross-examination and re-examination continues until all the prosecution witnesses have testified.

(9) As well as calling witnesses to give oral evidence, the prosecution may also put its case to the court by presenting evidence in other forms including statements of witnesses who are not in court under s. 9 CJA 1967 (see earlier), or under the hearsay provisions, video recordings, tape recordings or real evidence such as an exhibit presented in court.

(10) At the conclusion of the prosecution's case, the defence may submit that there is no case to answer. Under Crim PR, Part 24(3)(c), the court may acquit on the ground that the prosecution evidence is insufficient for any reasonable court properly to convict. The test was more specifically defined under the now defunct *Practice Direction (Submission of No Case)* [1962] 1 WLR 227 as being a failure by the prosecution to establish an essential element of the alleged offence, or the prosecution evidence has been so discredited in cross-examination or is so manifestly unreliable that no reasonable tribunal could safely convict on it.

(11) Where a submission of no case to answer is not made or is unsuccessful, the defence may put its case to the court. The defence advocate may make an opening speech, but, as he is normally allowed only one speech, it is usual practice to reserve this to the end of the defence case so that he may have the advantage of the 'last word'.

(12) The defence calls its first witness, subjecting the witness to an examination-in-chief. Where the accused exercises her right to testify under s. 79 Police and Criminal Evidence Act 1984, the accused must be the first defence witness and has the right to leave the dock and give evidence from the witness box (*R v Farnham Justices, ex p. Andrew Gibson* [1991] Crim LR 642).

(13) The defence witness may then be cross-examined by the prosecution and any co-accused.

(14) The defence advocate may re-examine the witness to repair any damage that may have been inflicted on the witness during cross-examination.

(15) After any evidence called by the defence, the court may permit the prosecution or other party to adduce further evidence.

(16) The prosecution and the defence will usually close the proceedings by making a closing speech. The defence will have the last word.

(17) The court will then announce its decision of guilty or not guilty after retiring to consider the evidence. On finding the defendant guilty, the court will consider whether it is necessary to obtain a pre-sentence report. Where a pre-sentence report is ordered, the case will be adjourned to enable the report to be prepared. Before proceeding to sentence, the prosecution will disclose to the court the defendant's previous convictions (if any). The defence advocate will make a plea in mitigation. The court then passes sentence. In relation to an either-way offence, the court can commit the defendant for sentence to the Crown Court under s. 3 Power of Criminal Courts (Sentencing) Act 2000 (PCC(S)A 2000) where it is of the view that its powers of sentence are insufficient. Section 6 of the same Act enables the court to also commit any summary offence for which the defendant has been convicted alongside the either-way offence. The practice and procedure of sentencing, including the power to commit for sentence, are considered in Part V.

(18) Where the defendant is found not guilty, the defendant is free to leave. If the defendant is not legally aided she may apply to have her costs met out of central funds under s. 16 Prosecution of Offenders Act 1985. Such orders are at the discretion of the court but should normally be awarded unless it is felt that the accused brought suspicion on herself by her conduct and/or misled the prosecution into thinking the evidence against her was stronger than it in fact was. Guidance can be found in *Practice Direction (Crime: Costs)* [1991] WLR 498. The sum recoverable will be capped to legal aid rates (see Chapter 9, para. 9.13). A legally aided acquitted defendant's costs will be met under the representation order.

We further consider trial advocacy in the context of trials before the Crown Court in Chapter 14.

In conducting a summary trial you are reminded of the Principles and rules of professional conduct that could arise under the Solicitors' Code of Conduct 2019, which are considered in Chapter 1.

KEY POINT SUMMARY

- Be aware of the circumstances in which a defendant can be tried in his or her absence.
- Know the law which permits two or more written charges to be tried together and how you might challenge the 'interests of justice' test.
- Be familiar with the Preparation for Effective Trial Form (Form 12.1).
- Understand that summary cases where a not guilty plea is entered will be managed robustly at the first hearing so that a firm date can be set for a summary trial.
- Understand what the parties need to do and what information they need access to in order to assist the magistrates' court to set a firm date for summary trial, in accordance with Crim PR, Part 3.
- Know the responsibilities of each side in the pre-trial disclosure of evidence.
- Know the procedure for securing the attendance of witnesses at trial.
- Know the practice for admitting a witness's written statement in hearsay form under s. 9 CJA 1967.
- Be aware of the purpose of and the issues that will be covered by standard directions for trial and the duty of the parties to assist the court in the active management of cases under Crim PR, Part 3.

- Know the sequence of events where the defendant pleads not guilty.

- Know the test to support a submission of no case to answer.

SELF-TEST QUESTIONS

1. What is the test to determine whether a defendant can be tried for two or more written charges at the same time where the defendant does not consent?

2. Explain how the defence solicitor will find out what the prosecution's evidence comprises in advance of trial.

3. How can the solicitor ensure the attendance of witnesses?

4. What is the role of the legal adviser in a summary case (see Chapter 1)?

5. At what point might a submission of no case to answer be made and what is the test to support such a submission?

Analysis of these questions can be found on our online resources.

FIGURE 12.1 THE PROSECUTION OF A SUMMARY OFFENCE AND SUMMARY TRIAL

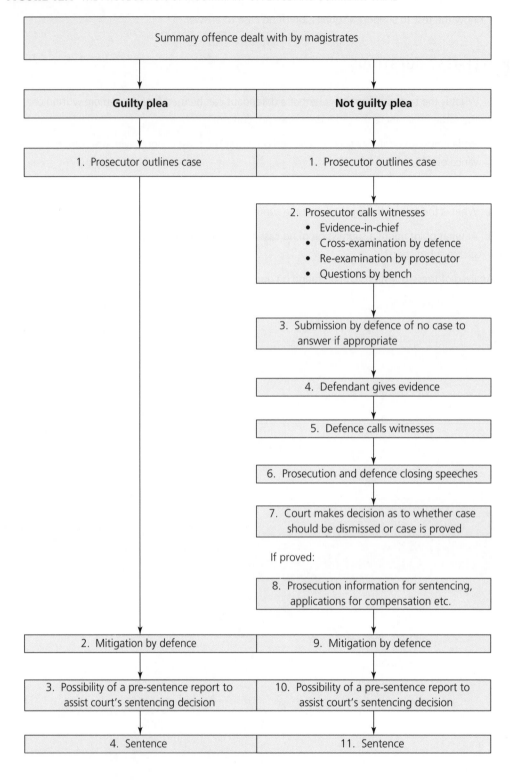

FORM 12.1 PREPARATION FOR EFFECTIVE TRIAL FORM

.... Magistrates' Court

Edition for use in courts in England

Preparation for effective trial
Criminal Procedure Rules Parts 1 & 3

■ This form:
  - collects information about the case that the court will need to arrange for an effective trial: CrimPR rules 3.2 and 3.3
  - records the court's directions: CrimPR rule 3.5.

■ After the court gives directions for trial, if:
  - information about the case changes, or
  - you think another direction is needed
  you must tell the court at once: CrimPR 1.2(1) & 3.10.

■ If the defendant pleads not guilty, and the court requires:
  - the prosecutor must complete Parts 1, 2 and 4
  - the defendant must complete Parts 1, 3 and 4
  - the court will record directions in Parts 4 and 5.

See the separate notes for guidance on the use of this form.

There is extra space on page 4, or attach extra sheets if required. The electronic version of this form will expand.*

A list of standard trial preparation time limits is at page 7.

Court contact details

Address		Phone
		Fax
Email		

Part 1: to be completed by the prosecutor and the defendant (or defendant's representative)

Defendant

	Date of birth:
	Age: years

☐ Summons ☐ Charge ☐ Bail
☐ Requisition ☐ Custody   Time limit expires:

Offence(s)

Police / CPS URN [   ]   **Date of first hearing** [   ]

1   Prosecution contact details

Prosecuting authority		Phone
		Fax
Email		

2   Defendant's contact details

Defendant	Address	Phone
		Mobile
	Email	

3   Defendant's representative *(if applicable)*

Solicitor		Phone
		Fax
		Ref
	Address	
	Email	

Representation is:
Defendant's representative to complete

legal aid granted ☐
legal aid applied for ☐
privately funded ☐

*Forms for use with the Rules are at: http://www.justice.gov.uk/courts/procedure-rules/criminal/formspage.

Part 2: to be completed by the prosecutor

---

4   **Case management information**

4.1   Are there any pending enquiries or lines of investigation?   ☐ Yes ☐ No
        If yes, give brief details:

4.2   Does the prosecutor intend to serve more evidence?   ☐ Yes ☐ No
        If yes, give brief details:

4.3   Does the prosecutor intend to serve a diagram, sketch map or photos?   ☐ Yes ☐ No
        If yes, give brief details:

4.4   The prosecution will rely on: defendant's admissions in interview   ☐
        Tick / delete as appropriate   defendant's failure to mention facts in interview   ☐
                                                [a summary] [a record] of the defendant's interview   ☐
                                                [expert] [hearsay] [bad character] evidence   ☐
                                                [CCTV] [electronically recorded] evidence   ☐

4.5   What equipment (live link, DVD or other media player, etc.) will the prosecutor need in the trial courtroom?
        The prosecutor must make sure that any DVD or other electronic media can be played in the courtroom.

4.6   Does the prosecutor presently expect the case to involve a complex, novel or unusual point of   ☐ Yes ☐ No
        law and / or fact? *This information will help the court officer to list the case effectively.*
        If so what?

4.7   Has the initial duty of disclosure of unused prosecution material been complied with?   ☐ Yes ☐ No
        If yes, when?

5   **Applications for directions**

5.1   Does the prosecutor want the court to vary a standard trial preparation time limit?   ☐ Yes ☐ No
        If yes, give details:

5.2   Does the prosecutor want the court to arrange a discussion of ground rules for questioning?   ☐ Yes ☐ No
        *If an intermediary is appointed, the court must discuss ground rules with the intermediary and
        advocates. A discussion may be helpful in other cases.*

5.3   Does the prosecutor want the court to make any other direction?   ☐ Yes ☐ No
        If yes, give details:

Part 3: to be completed by the defendant (or defendant's representative)

---

6   **Advice on plea and absence**

        Does the defendant understand that:

                        (a) he or she will receive credit for a guilty plea?   ☐ Yes ☐ No
                            *A guilty plea may affect the sentence and any order for costs
                            and other financial penalties / charges*

                        (b) the trial can go ahead even if he or she does not attend?   ☐ Yes ☐ No
                            CrimPR rule 24.12

7   **Partial or different guilty plea**

7.1   If more than one offence is alleged, does the defendant want to plead guilty to any of them?   ☐ Yes ☐ No ☐ N/A
If yes, which offence(s)?

7.2   Does the defendant want to plead guilty, but not on the facts alleged?   ☐ Yes ☐ No
If yes, the court must be given a written note of the facts on which the defendant wants to plead guilty.

7.3   Does the defendant want to plead guilty, but to a different offence?   ☐ Yes ☐ No
If yes, what offence?

8   **Case management information**

8.1   *Initial details of the prosecution case should have been served: CrimPR rule 8.2. The following statements are to help the court find out what is in dispute and give appropriate directions for trial. Tick as appropriate.*

The defendant [carried out] [took part in] the conduct alleged   ☐ Yes ☐ No ☐ N/A

The defendant was present at the scene of the offence alleged   ☐ Yes ☐ No ☐ N/A

The defendant was correctly identified   ☐ Yes ☐ No ☐ N/A

The defendant was arrested lawfully   ☐ Yes ☐ No ☐ N/A

[Nature of injury] [extent of loss or damage]   ☐ Yes ☐ No ☐ N/A
If not agreed, explain what is in dispute:

[Fingerprint] [DNA] evidence   ☐ Yes ☐ No ☐ N/A
If not agreed, explain what is in dispute:

[Medical] [identification of drug] [other scientific] evidence   ☐ Yes ☐ No ☐ N/A
If not agreed, explain what is in dispute:

The [alcohol] [drug] testing procedure was carried out correctly   ☐ Yes ☐ No ☐ N/A
If not agreed, explain what is in dispute:

Exhibits and samples were collected and delivered as stated (i.e. continuity)   ☐ Yes ☐ No ☐ N/A
If not agreed, explain what is in dispute:

Defendant's interview [summary] [record] is accurate   ☐ Yes ☐ No ☐ N/A
If not agreed, explain what is in dispute:

The defendant was [disqualified from driving] [subject to the alleged court order] at the time of the offence alleged   ☐ Yes ☐ No ☐ N/A

The list of the defendant's previous convictions is accurate   ☐ Yes ☐ No ☐ N/A
If not agreed, explain what is in dispute:

8.2   What are the **DISPUTED** issues of fact or law for trial, in addition to any identified in paragraph 8.1? *Give details. This question is to help the court find out what is in dispute and give appropriate directions for trial.*   *CrimPR rules 3.2(2)(a), 3.3(1)(a)*

8.3   Will the defendant give a defence statement? *Giving a defence statement is voluntary, but if one is given it must include the information collected in paragraphs 8.1 and 8.2 and must include particulars of facts relied on by the defence.*   ☐ Yes ☐ No

8.4   Will the defendant need any live link, or DVD or other media player, etc. equipment in the trial courtroom? *The defendant must make sure that any DVD or other electronic media can be played in the courtroom.*

8.5   Does the defendant presently expect the case to involve a complex, novel or unusual point of law and / or fact? *This information will help the court officer to list the case effectively.*   ☐ Yes ☐ No
If so what?

9   Admissions

Can any facts which are not in dispute be recorded in a written admission?   ☐ Yes ☐ No
Undisputed facts might include any statement accepted in paragraph 8.1.

If yes, a written admission [is set out here] [is attached] [will be served later].
Facts which are admitted are evidence: CrimPR rule 24.6 & Criminal Justice Act 1967, s.10.

If no, explain why:

10   Applications for directions

10.1   Does the defendant want the court to vary a standard trial preparation time limit?   ☐ Yes ☐ No
If yes, give details:

10.2   Does the defendant want the court to arrange a ground rules discussion?   ☐ Yes ☐ No
If an intermediary is appointed, the court must discuss ground rules with the intermediary and advocates. A discussion may be helpful in other cases.

10.3   Does the defendant want the court to make any other direction?   ☐ Yes ☐ No
If yes, give details:

Parts 2 & 3 continued: additional information

Use this space to record any additional information, or to continue an answer started above:

Defendant's name:

Part 4: to be completed by the prosecutor, the defendant (or the defendant's representative) and the court

11 Prosecution witnesses. *If this information changes, **you must tell the court at once**: CrimPR rule 1.2(1) & 3.10.*

	Prosecutor to complete				*Both parties to complete*		*For the court*	
Name of witness	Tick if under 18	Interpreter needed? If so, specify language and dialect.	Special or other measures e.g. live link needed? If so, specify.**	What disputed issue in the case makes it necessary for the witness to give evidence in person?	Tick if attendance proposed P / D		Tick if live link ordered	Evidence to be read ('R') or time required per witness *EinC X-exam*
1)	☐				☐	☐	☐	
2)	☐				☐	☐	☐	
3)	☐				☐	☐	☐	
4)	☐				☐	☐	☐	
5)	☐				☐	☐	☐	
6)	☐				☐	☐	☐	

12 Expected defence witnesses. *If this information changes, **you must tell the court at once**: CrimPR rule 1.2(1) & 3.10.*

	Defendant to complete				*Both parties to complete*		*For the court*	
Name of witness	Tick if under 18	Interpreter needed? If so, specify language and dialect.	Special or other measures e.g. live link needed? If so, specify.**	Why is it necessary for the witness to give evidence in person?	Tick if attendance proposed D / P		Tick if live link ordered	Evidence to be read ('R') or time required per witness *EinC X-exam*
1)*	☐				☐	☐	☐	
2)	☐				☐	☐	☐	
3)	☐				☐	☐	☐	

*If the defendant is likely to give evidence, list him or her as the first expected defence witness.   **Special or other measures may include screens, evidence by live link or in private, video recorded interview as evidence, intermediary, breaks in examination or other measures to accommodate disability.   They may increase the time needed for the witness.   In some cases, the defendant may not be allowed to cross-examine a prosecution witness.

Defendant's name:

Part 5: record of court's decisions and directions for effective trial

13   **Directions for trial** *The court must actively manage the case by giving any direction appropriate to the needs of that case as early as possible: CrimPR rule 3.2(3). Complete or delete the following as appropriate*

13.1   The prosecutor must serve any further evidence by: *(date)*

13.2   If the initial duty of disclosure has not been complied with, the prosecutor must comply by: *(date)*

13.3   A party who wants to use a DVD or other media, etc. must check <u>before</u> the trial that it can be played in the courtroom.

13.4   The court expects only the witnesses listed as attending in Part 4 to give evidence in person and the evidence of other witnesses to be read.

13.5   [Witness summons / warrant] [other steps to secure attendance] for witness(es): *insert name(s)*   *CrimPR Part 17; rule 3.9(3)*

13.6   Interpretation in the language(s) specified in Part 4 is required for: To be arranged by:

     (defendant)   Court staff   *CrimPR rule 3.9(5)*

     (witness)   Prosecutor ☐   Defendant ☐

13.7   Special or other measure, e.g. live link, are directed for: As specified in:

     (defendant)   Part 4 ☐   paragraph 13.11 ☐

     (witness)   Part 4 ☐   paragraph 13.11 ☐

     (witness)   Part 4 ☐   paragraph 13.11 ☐

13.8   The court will discuss ground rules for questioning on: *(date)*
If an intermediary is appointed for a witness or for the defendant, the court must discuss the ground rules for questioning with the intermediary and the advocates before the witness or defendant gives evidence. Sufficient time must be allowed for this.

13.9   The defendant in person may not cross-examine witness(es): *insert name(s)*   *CrimPR Part 23*
     and the court directs cross-examination for that purpose by: *name representative*

13.10   Standard trial preparation time limits apply [except] [with these variations]:

13.11   Other directions:

14   **Arrangements for trial**

		Court category:
Date:		
Time:		
Court:		
Estimated trial length:	.... hours	
including:	Evidence and submissions: .... Deliberations and decision:	
	A detailed trial timetable must be considered and attached if necessary: CrimPR rules 3.9 & 3.11	

After the court gives directions for trial, if information about the case changes, or you think another direction is needed, **you must tell the court at once**: CrimPR rules 1.2(1) & 3.10.

Signatures

     .... [on the direction of] [court]

Signed: .... for prosecution

Signed: .... [defendant] [defendant's solicitor]

Date: ....

Standard trial preparation time limits

*The court can vary any of these time limits. Time limits marked * are not prescribed by rules or other legislation.*
The total time needed to comply with all these time limits is 6 weeks (9 weeks if paragraph m applies).

Written admissions (Criminal Procedure Rules, r.24.6; Criminal Justice Act 1967, s.10)
a.   The parties must serve any written admissions of agreed facts within **14 days.***

Defence statement (Criminal Procedure Rules, r.15.4; Criminal Procedure and Investigations Act 1996, s.6)
b.   Any defence statement must be served within **14 days** of the prosecutor complying with the initial duty of disclosure.

Defence witnesses (Criminal Procedure and Investigations Act 1996, s.6C)
c.   Defence witness names, etc. must be notified within **14 days** of the prosecutor complying with the initial duty of disclosure.

Application for disclosure (Criminal Procedure Rules, rr.15.2 & 15.5; Criminal Procedure and Investigations Act 1996, s.8)
d.   The defendant must serve any application for an order for prosecution disclosure as soon as reasonably practicable after the prosecutor complies with the initial duty of disclosure.*   *Under s.8 of the Criminal Procedure and Investigations Act 1996, no such application may be made unless a defence statement has been served.*
e.   The prosecutor must serve any representations in response within **14 days after that**.

Witness statements (Criminal Procedure Rules, r.16.4; Criminal Justice Act 1967, s.9)
f.   The defendant must serve any defence witness statement to be read at trial at least **14 days before the trial.***
g.   Any objection to a witness statement being read at trial must be made within **7 days of service of the statement**. *This does not apply to the statements listed in Part 4.*

Measures to assist a witness or defendant to give evidence (Criminal Procedure Rules, rr.18.3, 18.13, 18.17, 18.22, 18.26)
h.   Any [further] application for special or other measures must be served within **28 days.**
i.   Any representations in response must be served within **14 days after that**.

Cross-examination where defendant not represented (Criminal Procedure Rules, rr.23.2, 23.4)
j.   The defendant must serve notice of any representative appointed to cross-examine within **7 days**.
k.   The prosecutor must serve any application to prohibit cross-examination by the defendant in person as soon as reasonably practicable.
l.   Any representations in response must be served within **14 days after that**.

Expert evidence (Criminal Procedure Rules, rr.19.3, 19.4)
m.   If either party relies on expert evidence, the directions below apply.
    (i)   The expert's report must be served within **28 days**.*
    (ii)   A party who wants that expert to attend the trial must give notice within **7 days after (i)**.*
    (iii)   A party who relies on expert evidence in response must serve it within **14 days after (ii)**.*
    (iv)   There must be a meeting of experts under rule 19.6 within **14 days after (iii)**.*
    (v)   The parties must notify the court **immediately after (iv)** if the length of the trial is affected by the outcome of the meeting.*

Hearsay evidence (Criminal Procedure Rules, rr.20.2, 20.3)
n.   The prosecutor must serve any notice to introduce hearsay evidence within **28 days**.
o.   The defendant must serve any notice to introduce hearsay evidence as soon as reasonably practicable.
p.   Any application to determine an objection to hearsay evidence must be served within **14 days of service** of the notice or evidence.

Bad character evidence (Criminal Procedure Rules, rr.21.2, 21.3, 21.4)
q.   The prosecutor must serve any notice to introduce evidence of the defendant's bad character within **28 days**.
r.   Any application to determine an objection to that notice must be served within **14 days after that**.
s.   Any application to introduce evidence of a non-defendant's bad character must be served within **14 days** of prosecution disclosure.
t.   Any notice of objection to that evidence must be served within **14 days after that**.

Previous sexual behaviour evidence (Criminal Procedure Rules, rr.22.2, 22.3, 22.4, 22.5)
u.   The defendant must serve any application for permission to introduce evidence of a complainant's previous sexual behaviour within **28 days** of prosecution disclosure.
v.   The prosecutor must serve any representations in response within **14 days after that**.

Point of law, including abuse of process etc. (Criminal Procedure Rules, rr.3.3, 3.10)
w.   Any skeleton argument must be served at least **14 days before the trial.***
x.   Any skeleton argument in reply must be served within **7 days after that.***

Trial readiness (Criminal Procedure Rules, rr.3.3, 3.10)
y.   The parties must certify readiness for trial at least **14 days before the trial**,* confirming which witnesses will give evidence in person and the trial time estimate.

November 2015

13 CROWN COURT PROCEEDINGS PRE-TRIAL

13.1	**Introduction**	**243**
13.2	**The Digital Case System (DCS)**	**243**
13.3	**The defendant's first court appearance for an indictable-only offence—s. 51 Crime and Disorder Act 1998**	**244**
	13.3.1 Sending 'related' offences to the Crown Court for trial	244
	13.3.2 Sending a linked co-defendant to the Crown Court	245
	13.3.3 Sending young offenders to the Crown Court	245
13.4	**Better Case Management (BCM)**	**245**
	13.4.1 Management of the indictable-only offence at the first hearing	245
13.5	**The Plea and Trial Preparation Hearing (PTPH)**	**246**
	13.5.1 The PTPH form	246
	13.5.2 Steps before the PTPH	247
	13.5.3 Conduct of the PTPH	247
	13.5.4 Case management directions	247
	13.5.5 Witness notification	248
	13.5.6 When will a Further Case Management Hearing (FCMH) be required?	248
13.6	**Crown Court bail**	**249**
13.7	**Preparatory steps in the early stages of an indictable-only offence**	**249**
13.8	**Disclosing 'used' material in indictable-only cases**	**249**
13.9	**Disclosing 'unused' material—CPIA 1996**	**250**
	13.9.1 Initial prosecution disclosure of unused material in Crown Court trials	250
	13.9.2 Defence disclosure obligations under the CPIA 1996	250
	13.9.3 The time limit to serve the defence statement	251
	13.9.4 What must a defence statement contain?	252
	13.9.5 Drafting a defence statement to avoid an adverse inference being drawn	252
	13.9.6 Drafting a defence statement—tactical considerations	253
	13.9.7 Prosecutor's continuing duty to keep disclosure under review	254
	13.9.8 Applying for further disclosure	254
	13.9.9 Disclosure and practical considerations	254
13.10	**What if the pre-trial disclosure of evidence reveals a weak prosecution case?**	**255**
	13.10.1 Making an application to dismiss the charge	255
	13.10.2 What happens to any related charges if the indictable-only offence is dismissed leaving only an either-way or summary offence?	255
13.11	**Preparatory hearings**	**255**
	13.11.1 Pre-trial rulings	255
13.12	**Preparing for trial**	**256**
	13.12.1 Witnesses	256
	13.12.2 Confirming the record of the tape-recorded interview (ROTI)	256
	13.12.3 Briefing the trial advocate	257

13.1 INTRODUCTION

Although indictable offences usually involve more complex issues of law, evidence and fact than summary cases, much of the preparatory work is the same. With much greater powers of punishment available to the Crown Court however, the potential consequences for a defendant are much more serious if the case is not properly prepared.

In January 2016 and in accordance with the Better Case Management (BCM) initiative, revised pre-trial procedures for cases to be tried on indictment were introduced based on changes introduced under the Transforming Summary Justice (TSJ) initiative that have been applied in the magistrates' courts. The significant developments explained in this chapter include the adoption of paperless trials in the Crown Court through the introduction of the Digital Case System (DCS), the requirement of engagement between the prosecution and the defence under Crim PR, Part 3.3, more robust case management responsibilities by the magistrates' court that sends the case for trial and the abolition of preliminary hearings and the Plea and Case Management Hearing which have been replaced by the Plea and Trial Preparation Hearing. Each of these changes is explained below.

You may wish to read this chapter in conjunction with the latter part of Chapter 9 which explains the provision of public funding for indictable-only cases and the initial preparatory steps that will occupy the defence practitioner when dealing with a client charged with an indictable-only offence.

This chapter deals with pre-trial practices and procedures of indictable-only offences. It covers:

- the Digital Case System (DCS);
- sending indictable-only cases to the Crown Court under s. 51 Crime and Disorder Act 1998 (CDA 1998);
- preparing for trial on indictment;
- pre-trial disclosure issues and defence statements;
- instructing counsel;
- the Plea and Trial Preparation Hearing (PTPH).

13.2 THE DIGITAL CASE SYSTEM (DCS)

The Digital Case System (DCS) runs in parallel with other changes (such as the Better Case Management initiative (BCM) explained below) that have streamlined the pre-trial procedures in the Crown Court. The effect of the DCS is to do away with all paper files in the Crown Court. This means that all key documents such as the indictment, witness statements, the defence statement, applications, and written orders are uploaded onto the DCS and accessed on computers, tablets, and smart phones. Paper copies continue to be supplied to unrepresented parties and to jurors.

Documents are served when they are uploaded onto the system and a notification is sent by e-mail to the other parties in the case. It is important to be aware that any paperwork handed over during the hearing will only be deemed to have been filed when it is uploaded onto the DCS. The elements of the new approach are reflected in the revised Crim PR, Part 4.6 which provides for the electronic service of court documents.

13.3 THE DEFENDANT'S FIRST COURT APPEARANCE FOR AN INDICTABLE-ONLY OFFENCE—S. 51 CRIME AND DISORDER ACT 1998

Even when charged with an indictable-only offence, the defendant will make his first appearance before a magistrates' court at which his entitlement to bail will be decided. Bail is more likely to be opposed by the prosecution where the offence is triable only on indictment because of the heightened risks of the defendant absconding given the serious nature of the offence charged. It should be recalled that whilst the rules relating to the pre-trial disclosure of evidence in accordance with Crim PR, Part 8 (IDPC) do not strictly apply to indictable-only offences, the Crown Prosecution Service (CPS) will normally provide this information before the defendant's first court appearance (see Chapter 8, para. 8.12).

You will be aware that either-way offences can also be tried on indictment in the Crown Court. As explained in Chapter 11, either-way offences that are to be sent to the Crown Court will go through the s. 51 CDA 1998 procedure. Once the indictable-only or either-way offence is sent to the Crown Court, a date is set for a PTPH. The PTPH was introduced as part of the BCM initiative. This has resulted in more robust management of Crown Court cases and the early identification of a likely guilty plea.

Before considering the PTPH and other preparatory steps we explain some specific provisions governing offences linked to an indictable offence sent to the Crown Court.

13.3.1 SENDING 'RELATED' OFFENCES TO THE CROWN COURT FOR TRIAL

Section 51(3) CDA 1998 provides that where an adult defendant is sent for trial under s. 51 in connection with an indictable-only offence, the magistrates' court must also send any related either-way offence for which the defendant appears at the same time. An either-way offence is 'related' where it can be joined in the same indictment because it is founded on the same facts or forms part of a series of offences of the same or similar character (s. 51E CDA 1998). The magistrates' court must also send any related summary offence for which the defendant appears at the same time (s. 51(3)(b) CDA 1998). A related summary offence must arise out of circumstances which are the same as or connected with the indictable-only offence and be punishable with imprisonment or disqualification (s. 51(11) CDA 1998).

Consider the following examples of how linked summary or either-way offences may also be sent to the Crown Court for trial.

 Example 1

Louis is charged with grievous bodily harm with intent, contrary to s. 18 Offences Against the Person Act 1861 (an indictable-only offence). He also faces an allegation of affray, contrary to s. 3 Public Order Act 1986 (either-way offence). Both incidents arise out of a brawl in the centre of town involving football supporters from rival clubs. The either-way offence is founded on the same facts as the indictable-only offence (s. 51E) and must therefore be sent to the Crown Court along with the indictable-only offence under s. 51(3)(a) CDA 1998.

 Example 2

Dennis is charged with driving while disqualified (a summary-only offence). In the course of the investigation into the offence he gives false particulars to the police leading to the arrest of someone other than himself. He is therefore charged with perverting the course of justice (an indictable-only offence). As the summary-only offence arises out of circumstances connected with the indictable-only offence and is punishable with imprisonment, both offences must be sent for trial to the Crown Court under s. 51(3)(b) CDA 1998.

Where a defendant appears before a magistrates' court on a separate occasion charged with a related either-way or summary offence, the magistrates have discretion to send the matter(s) up to the Crown Court so that they may be joined with the indictable-only matter(s) (s. 51(4) CDA 1998).

13.3.2 SENDING A LINKED CO-DEFENDANT TO THE CROWN COURT

 Example 3

What is the position where a co-accused is charged with an either-way offence which is related to the indictable-only offence? To take the example of Louis, assume that Tom is also charged with affray arising out of the brawl. In these circumstances, s. 51(5) CDA 1998 requires the magistrates' court to send Tom's case to the Crown Court along with Louis's indictable-only offence if Tom appears at the same time as Louis. Co-defendants facing an either-way offence which is related to an indictable-only offence therefore have no right of election in these circumstances. If Tom, who is charged with affray, appears in court after Louis's initial appearance, the magistrates would have discretion to send Tom's either-way offence to the Crown Court.

13.3.3 SENDING YOUNG OFFENDERS TO THE CROWN COURT

Where a young offender, aged under 18, is jointly charged with an indictable-only offence, s. 51(7) CDA 1998 provides that the magistrates' court shall send the young person for trial in the Crown Court along with the adult if it is in the interests of justice. If this power is exercised, the magistrates can also send any 'related' either-way or summary matter which the young person faces. (For an explanation of the interests of justice test and for full consideration of the young person in the criminal justice system, see Chapters 24, 25, and 26.)

13.4 BETTER CASE MANAGEMENT (BCM)

The principles of BCM are embodied in the Crim PR 2015 and supported by the Criminal Practice Direction (Part 3 Case Management). BCM is aligned to the DCS, outlined at para. 13.2, above.

13.4.1 MANAGEMENT OF THE INDICTABLE-ONLY OFFENCE AT THE FIRST HEARING

As outlined at para. 13.1, the defendant's first appearance in connection with an indictable-only offence is before the magistrates' court. Although the case must be sent forthwith to the Crown Court under s. 51 CDA 1998 and a date set for a PTPH, the court will also enquire whether the defendant is likely to plead guilty at the PTPH. The case will be sent along with the completed BCM form (see Chapter 11, para. 11.3.5 and Form 11.1).

Where the defendant has indicated an intention to plead guilty, the magistrates' court should request the preparation of a pre-sentence for use in the Crown Court. The PTPH represents the first formal opportunity for an accused to plead guilty to an indictable-only offence and to attract a full sentencing discount (see Chapter 21).

Where a not guilty plea is indicated the magistrates' court should, in accordance with BCM, explore with the parties:

- whether the defendant is prepared to plead to other offences;
- briefly identify with the parties the issues in the case; and
- any other information that is required by the parties to ensure an effective PTPH.

Under Crim PR, Part 3.5(3) the magistrates' court may also give other directions that are appropriate to the requirement of the case, although in most cases it is unlikely that any further directions will be necessary as the duties of the parties are clearly set out in the Criminal Procedure Rules 2015. The 'sending' magistrates' court will complete the 'Case sent to the Crown Court for trial—case management questionnaire' which is available at http://www.justice.gov.uk/courts/procedure-rules/criminal/forms-2015.

Having sent the indictable-only offence to the Crown Court, the PTPH must be held within 28 days of the case being sent to the Crown Court (Crim PR, Part 9.7(5)(a)(ii)).

There is a presumption under Crim PR, Part 3 that the parties will have communicated with each other prior to the PTPH. The parties must also have completed the PTPH form before the PTPH. A copy of the PTPH form can be found in Form 13.1 at the end of this chapter. An electronic version can be seen at http://www.justice.gov.uk/courts/procedure-rules/criminal). Part 1—Pre-Trial Information includes useful information which you should read. Any orders made by the judge at the PTPH are recorded on this form.

It will become clear that the PTPH requires a significant degree of preparation by both the prosecution and by the defence. Where the defendant continues to plead not guilty the judge will be required to robustly manage the case by making orders for the dates for the service of such matters as bad character or hearsay applications and response thereto. The judge will also want to set a firm date for the trial either by fixing a date or placing the case in the warned list for a given week.

13.5 THE PLEA AND TRIAL PREPARATION HEARING (PTPH)

13.5.1 THE PTPH FORM

The PTPH form is the primary record of the orders made in the case and is completed by the parties within the Digital Case System. single composite record of all the orders made in the case is therefore produced. This is particularly useful in multi-defendant cases.

The PTPH form is intended to:

- gather necessary information from the parties;

- monitor the extent to which the prosecution provide information prior to the PTPH;

- obtain an early indication of the prosecution witnesses who are likely to be required to attend the trial;

- allow the court to make, record and distribute clear orders timetabling the preparation of the case for trial (this is particularly important as it will address the need for those who have to act upon the orders to know exactly what the judge requires as part of their case management responsibilities);

- allow the court to provide for further hearings if they are necessary and useful.

Crown Court judges are encouraged to make standard orders within a single national process although where a case requires it bespoke orders may be made to deal with specific issues in the case—provided any order is made within the PTPH structure. The focus on establishing a clear set of case management orders at the PTPH should allow the case to proceed without the need for additional hearings.

After the PTPH the court will make electronic or paper copies of the form available to the parties.

As previously indicated in most cases the prosecution should prepare and circulate a draft copy of the form no less than seven days prior to the PTPH. The form can be edited online within the DCS.

13.5.2 **STEPS BEFORE THE PTPH**

In order to ensure the efficient progression of the case the prosecution is required to under-take the following actions before the PTPH:

- lodge a draft indictment no less than seven days prior to the PTPH; and
- serve the principal parts of the prosecution case, which in cases involving the police will usually consist of the MG5 form. The prosecution material is to be served:
  - if the defendant is on bail—by the sending hearing in the magistrates' court;
  - if the defendant is in custody—no less than seven days before the PTPH.

In addition the CPS must also prepare and circulate no less than seven days prior to the PTPH the draft PTPH form and have taken steps to confirm the availability of the prosecution witnesses to be called at trial.

Full details of what is expected to be served at the PTPH are set out in the Criminal Practice Direction (CPD) 3A.12–3A.20 and appear on the form. If there is a good reason why the CPS has not served all the materials listed before the PTPH, the court will usually proceed with the hearing rather than adjourn it.

What if the defendant wants to plead guilty before the PTPH?

The PTPH form is only intended for those cases where the defendant pleads not guilty. If, after the case has been sent to the Crown Court, the defendant decides to plead guilty, the defendant should not wait for the PTPH but instead inform the court and where appropriate apply for the preparation of a Fast Delivery Pre-Sentence Report or a Standard Delivery Pre-Sentence Report.

An application for a pre-sentence report will be considered by the court on an administrative basis and full reasons for requesting the report must be given. The court may adjourn the case for a Plea and Sentence Hearing (PSH) on a date when the report will be available. In most cases a court will order the preparation of a Pre-Sentence Report in an expedited format unless a good reason is advanced for a full report to be prepared.

13.5.3 **CONDUCT OF THE PTPH**

The PTPH presumes that the parties will have communicated with each other prior to the hearing and will continue to do so until the conclusion of the case.

At the PTPH the defendant will be arraigned (asked to enter pleas) unless there is a good reason not to.

Where a guilty plea is entered the defendant should, if possible, be sentenced on the day. Where the defendant pleads not guilty the court will:

- set the trial date;
- identify, so far as can be determined at that stage, the issues for trial;
- provide a timetable for the necessary pre-trial preparation and give appropriate directions to achieve an effective trial;
- make provision for any Further Case Management Hearing (FCMH) that must be listed on a firm date for it to achieve maximum effectiveness. As explained below a FCMH will only be held in complex cases.

All of the parties are under a duty to ensure that all the matters required to prepare for trial are satisfactorily dealt with and there must be a positive engagement between the parties and with the court.

13.5.4 **CASE MANAGEMENT DIRECTIONS**

The PTPH form includes standard directions. In individual cases the court may revise the standard directions or make other bespoke orders as necessary. However the form is designed so that the numbering of standard orders will not alter.

In most cases the court will be able to set four dates for the parties to complete their pre-trial preparation and therefore the judge or the court officer will need only to insert the dates for the four stages and delete any orders that are not required. The draft orders are grouped in a way intended to facilitate this approach.

The four stages are:

- **Stage 1** – for the service of most of the prosecution material. This date will ordinarily be 50 days (where the defendant is in custody) or 70 days (where the defendant is on bail) after the case was sent for trial. This requirement is consistent with the timetable for the service of the prosecution case provided for in the Crime and Disorder Act 1998 (Service of Prosecution Evidence) Regulations 2005. The court does not have power to abridge this time (without consent) but does have power to extend it.

- **Stage 2** – for the service of the defence response. This date will ordinarily be 28 days after Stage 1 reflecting the time provided for the service of a Defence Statement (DS).

- **Stage 3** – for the prosecution response to the Defence Statement and other issues raised by the defence. This date will ordinarily be 14 or 28 days after Stage 2 depending on the anticipated date of trial.

- **Stage 4** – for the defence to provide final materials or make applications that will commonly arise out of prosecution disclosure.

13.5.5 WITNESS NOTIFICATION

In many cases it will be possible for the defence to provide details of witness requirements at the PTPH and there is a presumption that they should do so.

In cases where this has not been possible a defendant's full witness requirements (with considered estimates of the time required) will have to be given at a later stage. The new Standard Witness List on the PTPH form must be used to notify witness requirements. Unless otherwise ordered it must be served by the defence on the prosecution at Stage 2 – at the same time as the Defence Statement is due (whether or not a Defence Statement is also actually served). Where a full Standard Witness List cannot be completed at the PTPH the defence should complete the section 'Witness Requirements Known at PTPH'.

13.5.6 WHEN WILL A FURTHER CASE MANAGEMENT HEARING (FCMH) BE REQUIRED?

After the PTPH it is anticipated that in most cases there will be no need to hold a Further Case Management Hearing (FCMH) before the trial unless:

- the court is informed that a guilty plea is to be entered; or

- it is necessary to give directions for an effective trial; or

- a Ground Rules Hearing (GRH) is required under Crim PR, Part 3.9(7) and the court directs that a FCMH is necessary to further the 'overriding objective' of the Crim PR.

The defendant will not usually be required to attend the FCMH unless there is good reason. A FCMH is most likely to be ordered in a range of cases including—

- Class 1 cases including murder, manslaughter, and robbery;

- Class 2 cases which carry a maximum penalty of ten years or more;

- Cases involving a vulnerable witness or a child or the witnesses are otherwise under disability or require special assistance;

- Cases involving an unrepresented defendant;

- Cases in which expert evidence is to be introduced.

The Court may also order a FCMH where—

- The defendant requests a hearing to enter a guilty plea; or

- Cases in which an application to dismiss or stay has been made; or
- Cases in which arraignment has not taken place for some reason.

For full details see Criminal Practice Direction 2015 (D I 3A. 21).

If the defendant has been released on bail and the case is in the Crown Court's warned list it is common for the defence solicitors to be informed of the trial date at short notice. It is the defence team's responsibility to ensure that their client is informed of the date of the forthcoming trial. A contact number for the accused is therefore essential. Some firms require their clients to telephone the office on a daily basis during the warned period to find out if the trial has been listed to start the following day. The defendant should be reminded that a failure to appear at court when required to do so will result in them committing the offence of absconding under the Bail Act 1976. If they fail to attend court a warrant without bail is likely to be issued for their arrest.

Twenty-eight days before the trial, the defence must service a Certificate of Readiness.

13.6 CROWN COURT BAIL

Where the defendant pleads not guilty at the PTPH, the case will be adjourned for trial or to a FCMH. Where a case is adjourned, the question of the defendant's bail may arise again. The defendant can make two contested bail applications, after which Sch. 1 Part IIA Bail Act 1976 applies (see Chapter 10, para. 10.14) requiring a change in circumstances. The defendant may already have made an unsuccessful bail application at a previous appearance before the magistrates' court. A second application is permitted before the Crown Court.

13.7 PREPARATORY STEPS IN THE EARLY STAGES OF AN INDICTABLE-ONLY OFFENCE

The preparatory work undertaken in the early stages of all criminal cases, including indictable cases, are considered in Chapter 9. The early stages of an indictable-only matter will require the defence lawyer to:

- interview her client;
- prepare a proof of evidence based on the initial interview;
- contact the CPS to:
  - obtain pre-trial disclosure of the prosecution's case;
  - request a copy of her client's criminal record;
  - obtain a record of any police interviews with her client;
  - obtain a copy of her client's custody record;
- identify, locate and interview potential defence witnesses;
- visit the crime scene if thought to be helpful;
- instruct an expert witnesses if necessary.

The actual date for service of 'used' and 'unused' material will be set by the PTPH judge. For an illustration of these steps please refer to the *R v Lenny Wise* case study in our online resources.

13.8 DISCLOSING 'USED' MATERIAL IN INDICTABLE-ONLY CASES

In indictable-only cases, the defence lawyer will not usually be in a position to advise her client on plea until the prosecution has made a full disclosure of the case against him. The standard directions which apply to a case sent for trial by a magistrates' court under s. 51

CDA 1998, require the service of prosecution case papers ('case sent bundle') to be made within 50 days where the defendant is in custody and within 70 days in other cases.

The 'case sent bundle' will include:

- the draft indictment;
- all 'used' material including witness statements (primary prosecution disclosure);
- list of exhibits;
- the schedule of unused material; and
- initial prosecution disclosure in accordance with s. 3 Criminal Procedure and Investigations Act 1996 (CPIA 1996).

See the *R v Lenny Wise* case study in our online resources, which includes a sent bundle, and see also Chapter 11.

Once the prosecution has served the 'case sent bundle', an important part of the defence solicitor's case preparation will be to carefully scrutinise the prosecution witness statements and other evidence to assess the strength of the case against her client. This assessment will be very important when advising a client whether to plead guilty or not guilty.

13.9 DISCLOSING 'UNUSED' MATERIAL—CPIA 1996

In addition to the prosecution's obligation to disclose evidence it intends to rely on at trial, the CPIA 1996 requires the prosecution to disclose the evidence which it will not use at trial. This is known as 'unused' material. The prosecution's obligation to serve 'used' and 'unused' material is explained in detail in Chapter 8. For the purpose of this chapter we briefly remind you of the key provisions. You may find it helpful to review the flowchart on disclosure which can be found at the end of Chapter 8 (Figure 8.3).

13.9.1 INITIAL PROSECUTION DISCLOSURE OF UNUSED MATERIAL IN CROWN COURT TRIALS

Section 3 CPIA 1996 requires the prosecution to provide the defendant with initial disclosure defined as any evidence not previously disclosed, which might reasonably be considered capable of undermining the case for the prosecution or of assisting the case for the accused. Practice differs between CPS areas. In some areas the CPS will comply with its obligations under s. 3 CPIA 1996 when it serves the 'case sent bundle' in an indictable-only offence or in an either-way offence to be tried on indictment. In other areas, s. 3 CPIA 1996 disclosure is made in accordance with standard directions upon the sending of the case or as directed by the PTPH judge before the Crown Court.

13.9.2 DEFENCE DISCLOSURE OBLIGATIONS UNDER THE CPIA 1996

After initial disclosure of unused material, the defence is required first to notify the CPS and the court whether it intends to call any witnesses at trial: s. 6C CPIA 1996 as amended by s. 34 Criminal Justice Act 2003 (CJA 2003). (Section 6C applies to both Crown Court and magistrates' court proceedings.)

What are the specific requirements under s. 6C CPIA 1996?

The defence witness notification must:

(a) give the name, address and date of birth of each proposed witness, or as many of those details as are known to the accused when the notice is given;

(b) provide any information in the accused's possession which might be of material assistance in identifying or finding any such proposed witness in whose case any of the details mentioned in paragraph (a) are not known to the accused when the notice is given.

What is the time limit for compliance?

It is the same time limit as for the service of a defence statement (i.e. 28 days for a Crown Court case and 14 days for a case that is to be tried summarily). Time starts to run from when the prosecutor complies or purports to comply with her duty to serve initial disclosure (see Chapter 13, para. 13.6.1).

What are the consequences of failing to comply with s. 6C CPIA 1996?

If the accused serves his s. 6C CPIA 1996 notice late, or at his trial calls a witness (other than himself) not included, or not adequately identified, in the witness notice, an adverse inference under s. 11 CPIA 1996 may be drawn by the magistrates or jury.

If things change, must an amended notice be served?

Yes. Section 6C(4) CPIA 1996 imposes a duty to serve an amended notice when:

- the defence decides not to call a witness;

- the defence decides to call other witnesses;

- further information is discovered that may enable the identification or finding of any proposed witness.

In response to this new obligation, the Law Society has issued a Practice Note on Defence Witness Notices which all defence lawyers should read at https://www.lawsociety.org.uk/support-services/advice/practice-notes/defence-witness-notices/.

The rationale behind s. 6C CPIA 1996 is that it enables the police to run checks on the character of a proposed defence witness in advance of trial and, if considered appropriate, enables the police to interview the witness. (The Code of Practice governing this type of interview can be accessed at http://www.opsi.gov.uk/acts/acts1996/related/ukpga-cop_19960025_en.pdf). The Code requires the police to:

- ask the witness whether he or she is prepared to consent to be interviewed;

- inform the witness that he or she is not obliged to attend the interview and that he or she is entitled to be accompanied by a solicitor (though this will not be publicly funded);

- ask whether the witness consents to a solicitor attending the interview on behalf of an accused as an observer.

The Code requires the police to inform the accused or his legal representative that an interview has been requested and to indicate whether the witness has consented to be interviewed in the presence of a solicitor attending on behalf of the accused as an observer. The police must notify the accused of the date, time and place of the interview. The interview must be recorded and a copy must be served on the accused.

Second, the defence must comply with the statutory requirement to file a defence statement which is mandatory for cases to be tried on indictment. Section 5 CPIA 1996 requires that a defence statement should be served on the court and the CPS. The defence statement must be served within 28 days of initial disclosure. A defence statement is mandatory in cases to be tried on indictment. Failure to serve the defence statement can lead to adverse comment and inferences being drawn by the court under s. 11 CPIA 1996. The importance of correctly drafting a defence statement cannot be overstated and is considered here.

Section 5 CPIA 1996 allows defence statements to be served on a co-accused on the application of any party or by the court of its own motion.

13.9.3 THE TIME LIMIT TO SERVE THE DEFENCE STATEMENT

The accused has 28 days to file a defence statement under s. 5 CPIA 1996 for trials on indictment. Time runs from the date on which the prosecution complies or purports to comply with its initial disclosure obligations under s. 3 CPIA 1996. The inclusion of the words 'purporting to comply' is worth highlighting. It implies partial disclosure is enough to trigger the defence disclosure obligation under s. 5. The defence can apply to the court for an extension of the time limit before it expires.

13.9.4 WHAT MUST A DEFENCE STATEMENT CONTAIN?

Section 6A CPIA 1996 requires that a defence statement must be in writing and must:

• set out the nature of the accused's defence including any particular defences on which he intends to rely;

• indicate the matters of fact on which the accused takes issue with the prosecution;

• set out, in the case of each matter, why the accused takes issue with the prosecution case;

• set out the particular facts on which the accused intends to rely for his defence; and

• indicate any point of law (including any point as to the admissibility of evidence) which the accused wishes to take, and any authority on which he intends to rely for that purpose.

A defence statement that discloses an alibi must give particulars including the witness's name, address and date of birth or as many of these details that are known to the accused when the statement is given, including any information in the accused's possession which might be of material assistance in identifying or finding the alibi witness. There is a continuing duty on the accused to provide this information if it comes to light after service of the defence statement.

Progressive reforms mean that defence statements are much more detailed than were originally required. This level of detail can cause practical difficulties for defence solicitors who may struggle to obtain clear instructions from a client within a very tight time frame. In addition to the obligations under s. 6A CPIA 1996, s. 6C requires the defence to serve a notice on the CPS and the court giving details of any witnesses it intends to call at the trial.

13.9.5 DRAFTING A DEFENCE STATEMENT TO AVOID AN ADVERSE INFERENCE BEING DRAWN

Section 11 CPIA 1996 states that where the accused:

• fails to serve a defence statement (where this is compulsory);

• fails to serve a defence statement within the time limit;

• sets out inconsistent defences in the defence statement;

• puts forward at his trial a different defence than that set out in the defence statement; or

• adduces evidence in support of alibi without having given the necessary particulars of the alibi,

the court or any other party (with the court's leave) may make such comment as appears appropriate and the court or jury may draw such inferences as appear proper in determining the defendant's guilt in connection with the offence for which he is being tried.

In practical terms, s. 11 CPIA 1996 is very important. Whether a defence statement is compulsory (indictable cases) or voluntary (summary cases), careful drafting is needed to avoid comment and an adverse inference being drawn.

Section 11(5) gives a court discretion to decide whether comment is permitted and as a consequence whether an inference might be drawn. Importantly, under s. 11(10), a person cannot be convicted solely on an adverse inference drawn under s. 11 CPIA 1996.

In exercising discretion under s. 11(5) what must the court take into account? The defendant is entitled to put forward an explanation as to why an adverse inference should not be drawn. Section 11(8) specifically requires a court to have regard to the defendant's reasons where the defendant has set out inconsistent defences before making or permitting comment. The nature of the inference drawn will therefore depend on the type of omission under s. 11 CPIA 1996 and the reasons for it. It may be that an alternative defence is put forward at trial because of a change in the prosecution's case from that indicated in the service of the case sent papers. It must be assumed that in this situation no adverse comment would be made. In other circumstances, the probable effect of an adverse inference drawn under s. 11 CPIA 1996 will be to cast doubt on the accused's defence. The evidential effect is similar to an adverse inference drawn from a suspect's silence under the Criminal Justice and Public Order Act 1994, which was considered in Chapter 5, and for this reason it is compatible with Article 6 European Convention on Human Rights 1950 (*R v Essa* [2009] EWCA Crim 43).

13.9.6 **DRAFTING A DEFENCE STATEMENT—TACTICAL CONSIDERATIONS**

In the light of s. 11 CPIA 1996, great care should be taken when drafting a defence statement if an adverse inference is not to be drawn. The defence practitioner must avoid putting forward inconsistent defences so she always needs to ensure that her client's instructions will not change or the trial advocate will not adopt an alternative approach. Disclosing a client's defence has implications for legal professional privilege which should be discussed with the client. The client needs to be given comprehensive and accurate advice regarding his defence statement and its implications before he checks, signs and dates it.

A tactical judgement has to be made about how much information the defence statement should contain. The more detail, the easier it is to facilitate further disclosure and the less the risk of an adverse inference being drawn from non-disclosure. Conversely, a more detailed defence statement will assist the prosecution in identifying the potential lines of cross-examination that may be raised against prosecution witnesses at trial. It is doubtful, in the light of the changes brought about by the CJA 2003 requiring a greater degree of specificity, that simply stating 'self-defence', or 'no dishonest intent' or 'mistaken identity' would be sufficient to avoid an adverse inference under s. 11 (*R v Tibbs* [2001] 2 Cr App R 309). Also consider the guidance given to defence practitioners in the Attorney General's Guidelines on Disclosure 2013 at paras. 39–43 (accessible at https://www.gov.uk/government/uploads/system/uploads/attachment_data/file/262994/AG_Disclosure_Guidelines_-_December_2013.pdf).

An important decision on whether a defence statement is compulsory in cases to be tried on indictment is *GR* [2010] EWCA Crim 1928 in which the Court of Appeal stated that defence advocates should never advise a client not to serve a defence statement and should always explain to a client what the statutory obligation is and what the consequences will be if a defence statement is not served or if something is omitted from the statement. Where the defence case is simply to put the prosecution to proof, a defence statement must still be served, stating the defendant does not admit the offence, putting the prosecution to strict proof and that the defendant will not be advancing a positive case at trial.

Reference must be made to the Practice Note on the Criminal Procedure Rules 2015 (accessible at https://www.lawsociety.org.uk/support-services/advice/practice-notes/the-criminal-procedure-rules-2015-solicitors-duties/#cpr12). The Practice Note reaffirms the defence solicitor's duties in relation to the defence statement and the solicitor's duty to assist in the active management of cases under Crim PR, Part 3.

A final observation in relation to defence statements is made with reference to the Attorney General's Guidelines on Disclosure 2013 paras. 32–33:

'32. It is vital that prosecutors consider defence statements thoroughly. Prosecutors cannot comment upon, or invite inferences to be drawn from, failures in defence disclosure otherwise than in accordance with section 11 of the CPIA. Prosecutors may cross-examine the accused on differences between the defence case put at trial and that set out in his or her defence statement. In doing so, it may be appropriate to apply to the judge under section 6E of the CPIA for copies of the statement to be given to a jury, edited if necessary to remove inadmissible material. Prosecutors should examine the defence statement to see whether it points to other lines of enquiry.

33. Prosecutors should challenge the lack of, or inadequate, defence statements in writing, copying the document to the court and the defence and seeking directions from the court to require the provision of an adequate statement from the defence.'

Paragraph 9 of the Guidelines should also be noted:

'9.

Disclosure must not be an open-ended trawl of unused material. A critical element to fair and proper disclosure is that the defence play their role to ensure that the prosecution are directed to material which might reasonably be considered capable of undermining the prosecution case or assisting the case for the accused. This process is key to ensuring prosecutors make informed determinations about disclosure of unused material. The defence statement is important in identifying the issues in the case and why it is suggested that the material meets the test for disclosure.'

A comprehensive defence statement assists the participants in the trial to ensure that it is fair. The trial process is not well served if the defence make general and unspecified allegations and then seek far-reaching disclosure in the hope that material may turn up to make them good. The more detail a defence statement contains the more likely it is that the prosecutor will make an informed decision about whether any remaining undisclosed material might reasonably be considered capable of undermining the prosecution case or assisting the case for the accused, or whether to advise the investigator to undertake further enquiries. It also helps in the management of the trial by narrowing down and focusing on the issues in dispute. It may result in the prosecution discontinuing the case. Defence practitioners should be aware of these considerations when advising their clients.

13.9.7 PROSECUTOR'S CONTINUING DUTY TO KEEP DISCLOSURE UNDER REVIEW

Section 7A CPIA 1996 (as amended by the CJA 2003) provides that after the prosecutor has complied with initial disclosure under s. 3 CPIA 1996 and before the accused is acquitted or convicted or the prosecutor decides not to proceed with the case (particularly following service of the defence statement), the prosecutor must keep under review whether there is any further prosecution material that might reasonably be considered capable of undermining the prosecution case against the accused or of assisting the defence case. Following the service of a defence statement, if the prosecution concludes there is no further evidence to disclose, this should be communicated to the defendant.

13.9.8 APPLYING FOR FURTHER DISCLOSURE

Under s. 8 CPIA 1996 the accused can apply to the court for further disclosure if he has grounds to believe there may be material which satisfies the objective test for disclosure provided he has filed a defence statement in accordance with the requirements of s. 5 or s. 6 of the Act. The defendant must prove to the court that he reasonably believes there is prosecution material which may assist his defence. The defendant must have settled grounds for the application and may not use s. 8 CPIA 1996 as a 'fishing expedition'.

13.9.9 DISCLOSURE AND PRACTICAL CONSIDERATIONS

Both the prosecution and the defence should be aware of disclosure issues at all stages in the prosecution of an indictable offence. The defence must always pursue legitimate requests for disclosure. A failure by the prosecution to disclose material within the definition of initial disclosure will give grounds for an appeal against conviction based on a material irregularity at trial—although there is no guarantee the conviction will be quashed (*R v Craven* [2001] 2 Cr App R 181). The prosecutor will be keen to scrutinise the defence statement for any deficiencies.

The practical aspects of disclosure under the CPIA 1996 are considered further in the context of our case study, *R v Lenny Wise*. The scenario includes illustrations of used and unused material and an example of a defence statement. The full documentation supporting this case study can be found in the online resources.

13.10 **WHAT IF THE PRE-TRIAL DISCLOSURE OF EVIDENCE REVEALS A WEAK PROSECUTION CASE?**

Where the 'case sent bundle' indicates a weak prosecution case, the defence may apply to the Crown Court to dismiss the charge(s).

13.10.1 MAKING AN APPLICATION TO DISMISS THE CHARGE

Under Sch. 3 CDA 1998, the defence may make an oral or a written application to the Crown Court to dismiss the charge(s) against the defendant. In most cases, the application will be decided on the basis of written submissions unless the defendant requests that oral evidence should be heard and the judge considers that it is in the interests of justice that oral evidence should be heard. In this situation, prosecution witnesses may be required to attend the hearing and be cross-examined. (The option to call oral evidence is prospectively repealed by Sch. 3 CJA 2003.) The defence may also seek to have disputed evidence excluded under s. 76 or s. 78 Police and Criminal Evidence Act 1984 (see Chapter 6). The rules governing the procedure to dismiss a charge(s) to be tried in the Crown Court are contained in Crim PR, Part 9. On hearing the representations from each side, the judge will dismiss the charge(s) where there is insufficient evidence for a jury to properly convict the accused. Where the application to dismiss is unsuccessful, the date will be confirmed for the PTPH. Reporting restrictions will apply at a hearing to dismiss although a defendant can apply to have reporting restrictions lifted (Sch. 3 para. 3 CDA 1998).

13.10.2 WHAT HAPPENS TO ANY RELATED CHARGES IF THE INDICTABLE-ONLY OFFENCE IS DISMISSED LEAVING ONLY AN EITHER-WAY OR SUMMARY OFFENCE?

The procedure under Sch. 3 paras. 7–15 CDA 1998 requires the Crown Court to conduct the plea before venue procedure in relation to an either-way offence. If the defendant indicates a not guilty plea or makes no indication at all, the allocation hearing must be conducted. If it is decided to deal with the either-way offence summarily, the case will be remitted to the magistrates' court. A summary-only offence would also be remitted to the magistrates where the linked indictable offence has been dismissed.

13.11 PREPARATORY HEARINGS

A preparatory hearing (see ss. 28–38 CPIA 1996 and Crim PR, Part 3.14) is appropriate for long and complex cases to be heard in the Crown Court. The judge decides whether there should be a preparatory hearing following an application by either party or by the court's own motion. In practice, the decision whether to hold a preparatory hearing is likely to be made at the PTPH.

Where a preparatory hearing is held, it takes place before the jury is sworn, and may clarify any difficult or contentious issue which will assist the jury's understanding of any matter in the case, identify issues which are likely to be material to the jury's verdict and expedite the proceedings or assist the judge's management of the trial. The preparatory hearing is part of the trial process.

13.11.1 PRE-TRIAL RULINGS

Sections 31–39 CPIA 1996 provide that a judge may make a binding ruling at the PTPH on matters relating to the admissibility of evidence and/or a question of law. Where a disputed point of law arises between the parties, the judge may well direct each party to serve skeleton arguments on the matter in dispute within prescribed time limits prior to giving a ruling on the matter.

Where a pre-trial ruling has been made, it may only be varied or discharged where it is in the 'interests of justice'. An application to vary a binding ruling will not be heard unless there has been a 'material change of circumstances' since the making of the original ruling. The CPIA 1996 provides a right of appeal to the Court of Appeal against a pre-trial ruling.

Matters of law and evidence likely to be determined at a pre-trial hearing could include:

* determining the competency of a witness;

* ruling on a special measures direction for a vulnerable or intimidated witness (see Chapter 16);

* deciding whether to hold a joint trial for two or more accused or whether to sever an indictment in a case where an accused faces more than one charge;

* resolving disputes as to the admissibility of hearsay evidence (see Chapter 18) or bad character evidence (see Chapter 19);

* determining a public interest immunity (PII) application to withhold evidence (see Chapter 8);

* making a ruling as to the admissibility of disputed confession evidence or evidence of identification (see Chapter 6).

The benefit of these rulings is that they should enable the trial to proceed on the day. An unfavourable pre-trial ruling may also influence an accused to change his plea to guilty. A judge is not obliged to give a pre-trial ruling on a disputed point of law in advance of trial and in some instances will wait until the prosecution has opened its case.

13.12 PREPARING FOR TRIAL

Much of the prosecution and defence lawyer's time when preparing for trial will be in connection with the PTPH. Typical preparatory matters are considered here.

13.12.1 WITNESSES

Both the defence and the prosecution must ensure the attendance of its witnesses at trial. Where it appears that a witness will not attend voluntarily, an application to summons the witness's attendance can be made under ss. 2–4 Criminal Procedure (Attendance of Witnesses) Act 1965. The rules relating to the issue of a witness summons are contained in Crim PR, Part 28.

13.12.2 CONFIRMING THE RECORD OF THE TAPE-RECORDED INTERVIEW (ROTI)

As we explained in Chapter 6, para. 6.4.1, Code E para. 3.1 requires that any interview between the police and a suspect in connection with an indictable or an either-way offence must be tape-recorded. A written statement of the tape-recorded interview and a copy of the tape recording will be sent to the defence as part of the prosecution's obligations to provide initial disclosure of the prosecution case under Crim PR, Part 8 (see Chapter 8).

Therefore, an important task undertaken by the defence team when preparing for trial is to listen to the ROTI and to compare it with a written transcript of the interview with your client provided by the police. This is likely to happen before instructing counsel or the solicitor-advocate as it is necessary to ensure that any potentially prejudicial or irrelevant material to your client's case should be excluded from the evidence to be heard by the court. Potentially prejudicial or irrelevant material will commonly include inaccurate statements of law and the investigating officers' opinions or statements made in interview disclosing your client's previous convictions.

Where necessary the defence solicitor can ask for advice on these points in their brief to counsel as explained in para. 13.12.3 below. After any suggested amendments have been identified by the defence team, the defence solicitor will write to the CPS to try to agree an edited version of the interview with the police.

If the final version of the interview transcript has not been agreed by the date of the PTPH, the judge will give directions that the edited version of the interview should be agreed if possible. If agreement cannot be reached with the CPS the defence will apply to the Crown Court for a pre-trial hearing to decide the issue. This hearing is known as a 'mention'.

13.12.3 BRIEFING THE TRIAL ADVOCATE

The defendant will need to be represented at the PTPH by a barrister or a solicitor-advocate. The CPS will also need to instruct a prosecuting advocate unless an in-house higher rights advocate is to appear. Counsel or a solicitor-advocate must be formally instructed or 'briefed'. The task of briefing counsel or a solicitor-advocate is commonly given to a trainee solicitor/paralegal or CPS caseworker. A properly drafted brief is a disciplined exercise requiring you to organise the materials in a file and to think very carefully about the issues in the case.

When to brief

The date set for the PTPH will dictate the time by which the brief should be delivered.

If the defence solicitor requires assistance in completing the defence statement, counsel should be instructed at an even earlier stage. It will obviously be easier to organise a conference with counsel in advance of the PTPH if the brief is sent in plenty of time.

It is preferable that the advocate who represents the defendant at the PTPH will also represent the defendant at trial. The CPS will instruct in-house barristers or solicitor-advocates or will use independent counsel based on their seniority. For the defence, unless a firm employs a solicitor-advocate with higher rights of audience, the instructing lawyer will have a preferred choice of barrister. All barristers' services are engaged through the clerk at the barrister's chambers. All the papers in the case and the instructions will be sent to the barrister in a brief to counsel.

What should a brief contain?

Whilst there is an etiquette to briefing the advocate, the precise practice may vary from firm to firm and your firm may have a preferred style. The brief we have drafted in conjunction with the *R v Lenny Wise* case study (see Appendix 2, Document 39) is written in the third person.

The brief should contain a back sheet with details of the case, the date and type of hearing, with the instructing solicitor's details on the right-hand side of the page. The left-hand side of the back page is left blank to enable counsel to handwrite endorsements onto it. If the case is legally aided, the back page of the brief should make this clear.

Where appropriate the brief may cover the advocate's representation at both the PTPH and at trial. In other cases separate briefs will be sent.

The front page of the brief should contain the case heading and a numbered list of enclosures. The list of enclosures depends entirely on the particular case you are dealing with, but would typically include:

- defendant's proof of evidence;
- draft indictment;
- case sent bundle;
- relevant correspondence with CPS;
- expert report(s).

The brief should begin with an introduction which deals with the defendant's personal details, the charge(s), the history of the case and any bail arrangements.

The brief should provide an analysis of the prosecution case by cross-referencing to the prosecution witness statements and other evidence that has been disclosed under the pre-trial disclosure rules and which will be included with the brief as enclosures. Any strengths or weaknesses in the prosecution case should be identified, as should the admissibility of items of prosecution evidence which may be challenged at trial.

The brief should also contain a summary of the defence case and identify any strengths or weaknesses.

The advocate should also be clearly directed on what advice is sought. This might relate to witness requirements, points of evidence, advice on plea or assistance with drafting a defence statement. The advocate's attention should also be directed to the factors that might be raised in mitigation in the event of your client being convicted.

Commonly, the brief will ask whether the advocate believes a conference with instructing solicitors will assist in the case preparation.

The brief will be sent to the advocate who should respond within the return date. At this stage, the solicitor needs to be mindful of key dates, particularly in relation to serving a defence statement, notifying the CPS which prosecution witnesses are required to attend trial to be cross-examined and responding to notices to admit bad character or hearsay. The advocate may send written advice in advance of the PTPH. It is important that the advocate's advice is followed up. This may involve further interviews with the defendant or witnesses or further correspondence with the CPS. If the barrister suggests a conference is needed, this must be organised by the instructing solicitor. This involves contacting counsel's clerk for available dates as well as contacting the defendant. The conference usually takes place at counsel's chambers.

KEY POINT SUMMARY

- Understand that all indictable-only offences must be sent to the Crown Court along with related (either-way/summary) offences in accordance with s. 51 CDA 1998 following an initial appearance before a magistrates' court.

- Trials on indictment cover not just indictable-only offences but either-way offences which have been sent for trial by a magistrates' court.

- Be aware of the rules dealing with the pre-trial disclosure of evidence by both the prosecution and the service of a defence statement under the CPIA 1996.

- The submission of a defence statement is mandatory in a case tried on indictment.

- Great care needs to be taken when drafting a defence statement in order to avoid an adverse inference from being drawn under s.11 CPIA 1996.

- The disclosure obligations on the defence are not as onerous compared to those on the prosecution but are still significant.

- Know the conventions about instructing/briefing counsel.

- Understand the purpose of the PTPH and the procedures where the defendant pleads guilty or not guilty at the arraignment.

SELF-TEST QUESTIONS

1. What is the purpose of the initial hearing in the magistrates' court where the defendant is charged with an indictable-only offence?

2. What obligation does the prosecution have in relation to the pre-trial disclosure of evidence in an indictable-only offence?

3. Explain the procedure at the application to dismiss the charge in the Crown Court.

4. Explain the purpose of the PTPH.

5. Consider once more Question 2 at the end of Chapter 8.

Case study: *R v Lenny Wise*

You will recall that Lenny Wise has been sent to stand trial on the burglary allegation and a date has been set for his Plea and Trial Preparation Hearing before Lyme Crown Court. Initial prosecution disclosure of unused material, in compliance with s. 3 CPIA 1996, is made (see Document 27). Before you look at the defence statement in relation to Lenny Wise you may wish to attempt a draft of your own. The defence statement submitted in this case is at Document 32. Further disclosure, in compliance with the CPS's duties under s. 7A CPIA 1996, are made in Documents 34, 35, and 36 (available in the online resources). Subject to the prosecution's duty to keep disclosure under review, the pre-trial disclosure of evidence in relation to *R v Lenny Wise* is complete. You will see that Lenny's solicitor has obtained a psychiatric report from Lenny's consultant, see Document 37. The requirement under Crim PR, Part 19 for the disclosure of expert reports to be adduced in court has been complied with.

You now have all the necessary information to undertake a brief to counsel. Our suggested brief to counsel in this case is included at Document 39.

You will see on Lenny Wise's file an account of his PTPH before Lyme Crown Court (Document 25a). Both sides must now work towards the Further Case Management Hearing (FCMH), which will consider the admissibility of Lenny Wise's confession. Shortly before the FCMH, counsel for the CPS concede that Lenny Wise's confession has been obtained in breach of PACE and Code C and that the CPS will not be relying on it. The FCMH is vacated. The matter is then listed for trial. A further, very short brief to counsel to represent Lenny Wise at trial is subsequently sent (see Document 41).

FIGURE 13.1 THE PROSECUTION OF INDICTABLE-ONLY OFFENCES AND TRIAL ON INDICTMENT

Defendant will make initial appearance before magistrates' court; matters relating to bail will be determined; advance information ought to be available.

Defendant's case is sent to the Crown Court under s. 51 CDA 1998 together with any related either-way offence or related summary offence if punishable with imprisonment or disqualification.

Defendant will make his initial appearance before Crown Court judge where he can plead guilty if he chooses otherwise the judge will devise a timetable for the pre-trial disclosure of evidence and will set a date for a Plea and Trial Preparation Hearing **(PTPH)**.

↓

- Prosecution will serve case sent bundle comprising used and unused material, the latter in compliance with s. 3 CPIA 1996;

- defence will be required to serve a defence statement in compliance with ss. 5 and 6 CPIA 1996 plus a defence witness notification (s. 6C CPIA 1996);

- prosecution will serve any further unused material in accordance with s. 7A CPIA 1996;

- defence can apply to have charges dismissed for insufficient evidence;

- case may need to be listed for a pre-trial hearing.

- Defendant will be asked to plead at his **PTPH**;

- defence should brief trial advocate in sufficient time to ensure attendance at **PTPH** and to advise on plea;

- if plea is to be not guilty, defence must notify CPS as to which witnesses it wants to cross-examine so that availability can be checked before **PTPH**.

↓

PTPH	**PTPH**
defendant pleads guilty; sentence will follow immediately unless pre-sentence is required.	defendant pleads not guilty; date will be set for Crown Court trial; defence and prosecution will prepare for trial.

FORM 13.1 PLEA AND TRIAL PREPARATION HEARING FORM

\#

PLEA AND TRIAL PREPARATION HEARING
PARTIES PRE-HEARING INFORMATION FORM
The pre-hearing information form must be completed for all cases sent to the Crown Court
where a trial is anticipated unless the case is expressly exempted by the CrimPR or CrimPD.

\#

\#

| Crown Court at: | | T: | | PTI URN: | |

	Defendant	DOB	Principal Charge(s)	Remand Status	Custody Time Limit	
D1				☐Unconditional Bail ☐Conditional Bail ☐ Custody ☐Youth Det. Remand		

	Real Issues and Time Estimate: Defence to set out below, so far as known, the real issues in the case - CrimPR 3.2;3.3;3.11- and provide provisional time estimate for overall trial length	*Streamlined Forensic Reports: Are the conclusions of any served Streamlined Forensics Report (SFR1) admitted as fact. If not identify the disputed issues concerning that conclusion? CrimPR 19.3. Make clear what is admitted and what is not admitted.*
D1		Choose Disputed Issues:

Other Proceedings:	
Particulars of any associated CRIMINAL proceedings?	
Particulars of any linked FAMILY proceedings?	

\#

Contact Information:

The parties must provide the information required below at the PTPH or if not then available it must promptly be provided to the court and other parties in writing. The court and other parties must be informed of any change and effective cover must be provided for sickness or absence. Legal professionals and investigators must provide CJSM emails. The names of individuals must be given but it is acceptable to provide group email addresses provided that they are effectively monitored and acted upon.

If the prosecution or defence have not allocated a trial advocate then the advocate at a hearing or, the prosecution Reviewing Lawyer or the defence solicitor is required to respond to issues in place of the trial advocate.

Court Case Progression	Name:	Phone:	Email:
Case Progression Officer:			

Prosecution Information	Name:	Phone:	Email:
Advocate at PTPH			
Advocate for trial			
Reviewing Lawyer			
Case Progression Officer (usually Paralegal)			
Officer in the Case (or equivalent)			

Defence Information		Name and Address for Service:	Phone:	CJSM Email for service:
D1	Defence Solicitors (or unrepresented defendant)			
	Case Progression Officer			
	Funding – Tick ☑	Private Funding ☐; Legal Rep applied for ☐; Legal Rep Order granted ☐ or Unrepresented ☐		
		Name:	Phone:	CJSM Email:
	Advocate at PTPH			
	Advocate for trial			

STATE OF PREPARATION AT PTPH

PROSECUTION			Yes/No/N/A	If not yet served they can be served by/Notes:
IND	Draft Indictment		Choose	
SUM	Summary of circumstances of the offence(s) and of any account given by defendant(s) in interview (this may be in Form MG5).		Choose	
EVI	Statements identified by prosecution as being of importance for the purpose of plea and initial case management.		Choose	

EVI	Exhibits identified by prosecution as being of importance for the purpose of plea and initial case management.	*Choose*	
TV	Relevant CCTV that would be relied upon by prosecution at trial.	*Choose*	
EXP	Streamlined Forensic Report(s) or indication of scientific evidence that the prosecution is likely to introduce.	*Choose*	
EXP	Indication of medical evidence that the prosecution is likely to introduce.	*Choose*	
EXP	Indication of other expert evidence that the prosecution is likely to introduce.	*Choose*	
BC	Indication of bad character evidence to be relied on.	*Choose*	
HS	Indication of any hearsay evidence to be relied on.	*Choose*	
SM	Indication of special measures to be sought.	*Choose*	
CRO	Defendant's criminal record if any.	*Choose*	
VPS	Victim Personal Statement if any.	*Choose*	

DEFENCE		*Yes/No/N/A*	*Particulars*
ABU FTP	Are there preliminary issues such as Abuse of Process or Fitness to Plead?	*Choose*	
DMS	Is an application for Dismissal anticipated after time for service elapses?	*Choose*	
SEV	Is an application for Severance anticipated? CrimPR 3.21	*Choose*	
ARR	Can the defendant be arraigned at PTPH? If not set out the reason.	*Choose*	
ALT	Is the defendant willing to offer a plea to another offence and/or a plea on a limited basis?	*Choose*	
DS	Is a Defence Statement available at this stage?	*Choose*	
PNC	Where there are joint defendants does this defendant agree to cross-disclosure of lists of previous convictions (the PNC print out)	*Choose*	
DS	Where there are joint defendants does this defendant agree to cross-disclosure of Defence Statements (If agreed Defence Statements may be uploaded on the Joint DCS file, If not agreed they will have to be served separately)	*Choose*	

THIRD PARTY DISCLOSURE		*Yes/No/N/A*	*Particulars*
TPD	Is it believed that any third party holds potentially disclosible material?	*Choose*	
TPD	Will the prosecution be making enquiries to review that material?	*Choose*	

WITNESS REQUIREMENTS KNOWN AT PTPH: To be populated with names of prosecution witnesses known at PTPH.
Prosecution to indicate any witness who the Prosecution intend to call live regardless of Defence requirements (write "**P**" in the "Required by" column.
Each Defendant is required to identify which prosecution witnesses it can be predicted will be required to give evidence and those whose evidence is not disputed by that defendant (write "**D1**" etc as appropriate in the relevant column AND where a witness is required identify the relevant disputed issue for **that** defendant.
Parties are expected to provide a considered list and must not simply indicate "all witnesses". Where a witness is named but no statement has been provided parties are not expected to indicate requirements.

FORM - PTPH NG 1

Witness Orders: The judge will review the witness requirements and the witness orders will be given in the Judge's Orders therefore the names listed here must be repeated there. A witness will not be warned unless he or she is shown as required in the Judge's orders section.
Unless otherwise ordered the Defence must also complete the Standard Witness Table at Stage 2.

Name of witness	Required by:	Not disputed by:	Relevant disputed issue etc.	Mark if availability known
				☐
				☐
				☐
				☐
				☐
				☐
				☐
				☐
				☐
				☐
				☐
				☐

\#

FORM - PTPH NG 1

PLEA AND TRIAL PREPARATION HEARING
JUDICIAL ORDERS

This form is the primary record of all orders made at PTPH and all orders of the court at PTPH must be incorporated. Any subsequent variation must be by further order.

Crown Court at:		T:		PTI URN:	

PLEAS

1	Judicial warning and notes of judicial comment (if any)	☐ Credit for Plea
2	Pleas entered at PTPH:	
3	Reason if not arraigned at PTPH:	

PRE-ARRAIGNMENT FCMH IF REQUIRED	Date:		⏱ Time Estimate
4	**Pre-Arraignment Further Case Management Hearing to resolve ☑:** ☐ Abuse of Process; ☐ Dismissal application; ☐ Joinder/Severance. ☐ Other:	☐ Defendant not required ☐ Defendant must attend ☐ Suitable for PVL ☐ Application/skeleton and supporting materials by: ☐ Response and supporting materials by:	minutes hours

PRE-ARRAIGNMENT FCMH ON FITNESS TO PLEAD	Date:	☑	⏱ Time Estimate
	☐ Fitness to Plead;	☐ Defendant not required ☐ Defendant must attend ☐ Suitable for PVL or Hospital Link ☐ Defence first medical report by: ☐ Prosecution to notify defence if the prosecution do OR do not intend to obtain medical report within 7 days or by:	minutes hours

PLEA AND TRIAL PREPARATION HEARING FORM for DCS – Page 5 of 12

FORM - PTPH NG 1

| | | ☐ If Prosecution are to serve medical report then to be served by; | |
| | | ☐ If Prosecution are not to serve medical report then defence to serve any second medical report by: | |

WITNESS REQUIREMENTS KNOWN AT PTPH and JUDGE'S WITNESS ORDERS THAT CAN BE MADE AT PTPH WITHOUT FURTHER FORMALITY

To be populated with witness names as in Part 1.

The Court has agreed that prosecution witnesses marked confirmed are likely to be required to give evidence.

Where it can be done justly without further formality the judge may make orders such as:

SMEAS – Special measures in which case the Court should specify which special measures are provided for;

SUMM – ordering the issue of a witness summons for the witness where grounds are made out;

UKLINK – ordering a UK live link <u>if available</u> – for example for police officers, other investigators, or experts to give evidence remotely;

SAT – ordering a satellite link from abroad.

Unless otherwise ordered the Defence must also complete the Standard Witness Table at Stage 2.

Name of witness	Confirmed by Court	SMEAS etc.	Details/Relevant disputed issue/ Judge's additional directions or observations

\#

STANDARD ORDERS FOR WITNESSES

5	SM	Where Special measures are provided above:	In respect of any witness who has provided an ABE interview, the ABE interview as edited by agreement or by order of the court shall stand as that witness' evidence in chief unless otherwise ordered.
			Any witness who has provided an ABE interview shall view that interview in the week preceding the trial in the presence of the officer in the case (or equivalent) or other suitable police officer (or investigator equivalent) who shall record any comment the witness shall make and pass that record to the prosecutor.
			Any application for screens or live link shall be made after a court visit and shall include the witness' reasons for the preference.
			The attendance of any such witness at trial must be timetabled for the time when the witness is expected to commence examination.
6	WIT	Young or vulnerable witnesses CrimPR 18 & 3.9(7)	Young or vulnerable witnesses to which an Advocates' Gateway toolkit applies are to be examined and cross-examined in accordance with that toolkit unless that is superseded by specific ground rules.

7	SAT	Where provision is made for a witness by UKLINK or SAT:	Particulars of the link must be provided not less than three weeks before trial - CrimPD 18.23-4):
8	EXP	Expert witnesses – CrimPR 19	Expert witnesses of comparable disciplines must liaise and serve on the parties and the Court a statement of the points on which they agree and disagree with reasons no less than 14 days prior to the trial OR by such date as may be inserted here:
9		Other orders about witnesses:	

YJCEA 1999 s.28 CASES (where implemented)

10	A s.28 direction is made for the following witnesses and their ABE interviews shall stand as their evidence in chief and they shall be cross examined in advance of the trial: Witnesses:

The intermediary's report shall be filed by:

		Date:	Time:		⏱ Time Estimate
11	Ground Rules Hearing			Ground Rules Form filed by: ☐ Defendant not required ☐ Defendant must attend ☐ Suitable for PVL ☐ The intermediary shall attend the Ground Rules Hearing	minutes hours
12	s.28 Cross-examination Hearing			☐ Defendant not required ☐ Defendant must attend	minutes hours

13	**Supplemental Orders for s.28 cases**
	Any intermediary shall attend the hearing.
	Date for witness to refresh their memory [date]:
	The officer in the case or another suitable police officer (or investigator equivalent) shall attend during the memory refreshing and make a note of anything said by the witness
	The judge (and advocates) shall meet the witness on [date}:...
	The advocates are not to meet the witness without the judge.
	s.4 Contempt of Court Act 1981 order has been made for ☐ the Ground Rules Hearing ☐ s.28 hearing
	The case is allocated to [Judge]:
	The future management of the case will be under the supervision of the trial judge.
	Other:

TRIAL	Date:		☑ Facilities required:	⏱ Time Estimate
14		☐ Fixture ☐ Backer ☐ Fixed Floater ☐ Warned List commencing.	☐ CCTV ☐ Live Link ☐ Satellite Link from: ☐ Interpreter for defendant(s) (language): ☐ Other	days weeks

FORM - PTPH NG 1

| 15 | | | Certificates of Readiness to be filed by all parties
(If no date is inserted then to be 28 days before trial date) | ☒ |

STAGE 1 - UNLESS INDIVIDUAL DATES ARE PROVIDED THE PROSECUTION SHALL SERVE THE FOLLOWING BY:				*Date:*
Ordinarily 50 days (custody cases) or 70 days (bail cases) after sending.				

		ITEM	*Date :*	*Additional requirements/particulars/directions if any:*
16	EVI	Service of prosecution case.		To include making available ABE transcripts and recordings.
17	DCL	Initial disclosure (if not yet served).		
18	TV	CCTV relied upon.		To be served in format compatible with systems available at court. Otherwise party to provide system.
19	IV	Written record of defendant's taped Interview(s) (ROTI).		Unless otherwise ordered where there is a substantially "no comment" interview a short summary rather than a full transcript is sufficient. In any event the parties are expected to engage pre-trial to agree a summary or editing.
20	IV	Audio recording of defendant's tape interviews(s).		
21	999	999 call transcript(s) and recording(s) relied upon.		
22	TEL	Telephone records to be relied upon.		
23	FOR	Service of forensic statements (SFR 2 or MG11) that can be served by Stage 1 CrimPR 19.3.		This order only applies where, in relation to SFR1 (or other served summary of expert's conclusions), the defendant has identified on the PTPH form a conclusion that is not admitted and what the disputed issues are. The SFR2 or MG11 will be limited to those identified issues.
24	BC	Bad character notice(s) CrimPR 21		To include, if to be relied upon, evidence of facts of bad character.
25	HSY	Hearsay application(s) CrimPR 20		
26	SM	Special measures application(s) CrimPR 18		
27		Other:		
28		Other:		

THIRD PARTY DISCLOSURE: It is ordered:			*Date:*
	TPD	The following areas of third party material have been identified:	
29	TPD	Prosecution shall either make requests to third party, OR notify defence in writing that it does not intend to make any application for third party disclosure by:	
30	TPD	Prosecution to apply for any necessary third party disclosure summons by:	
	TPD	Prosecution to make any application required to the Family Court by:	

31	TPD	If the prosecution is to pursue third party disclosure then the prosecution must serve a report in writing on the outcome of efforts to identify potentially disclosible materials held by third parties and any ongoing enquiries not yet completed by:	
32	TPD	Any disclosible third party disclosure shall be served on the defence by:	
		Other:	

STAGE 2 - UNLESS INDIVIDUAL DATES ARE PROVIDED IT IS ORDERED THAT THE DEFENCE SHALL SERVE THE FOLLOWING BY: Ordinarily 28 days after Stage 1.				DATE:
		ITEM	*Date:*	*Additional requirements/particulars/directions:*
33	DS	Defence Statement. (In single defendant cases to be uploaded. In multi-defendant cases to be uploaded if cross-service was agreed and if not to be served separately)		To include particulars of alibi; and requests for disclosure, describing the material and explaining, by reference to the issues in the case, why it is disclosible.
34	WIT	Final list of prosecution witnesses required to give live evidence; defence witnesses and interpreter requirements.		To be submitted in the Standard Witness Table with time estimates.
35	FOR	Response to Summary of Expert Conclusions (SFR1)		Stating which, if any, of the expert's conclusions are admitted as fact and where a conclusion is not admitted stating what are the disputed issues concerning that conclusion. A defendant who did not identify such issues on the PTPH form and does not serve such a response is taken to admit as fact the conclusions of the summary (SFR1).
36	SM	Special measures application for defendant or defence witnesses.		Any reply from prosecution or other party to be served within 14 days.
37	ABE	List of editing requests or objections to ABE interview recording.		
38	IV	List of editing requests for the Defendant's ROTI (if any).		
39	BC	Response to prosecution bad character notice(s) - CrimPR 21.		
40	HSY	Response to prosecution hearsay application(s) – CrimPR 20.		
41	SM	Response to prosecution special measures application(s) - CrimPR 18.		
42	EXP	Defence expert evidence to be relied upon - CrimPR 19.		
43		Other:		
44		Other:		

STAGE 3 – UNLESS INDIVIDUAL DATES ARE PROVIDED IT IS ORDERED THAT THE PROSECUTION SHALL SERVE THE FOLLOWING BY: Ordinarily 14 or 28 days after Stage 2	DATE:

PLEA AND TRIAL PREPARATION HEARING FORM for DCS – Page 9 of 12

		ITEM	Date for Service	Additional requirements/particulars/directions:
45	DCL	Further disclosure.		Items required to be disclosed under CPIA resulting from or requested by the Defence Statement.
46	EVI	Further evidence to be relied upon that could not be served by Stage 1.		
47	FOR	Forensic science statements (SFR2 or MG11) required as a result of the Defence response to a summary of conclusions (SFR1) - CrimPR 19.3		
48	EXP	Expert medical evidence.		
49	EXP	Psychiatric evidence.		
50	EXP	Other (specify) expert evidence.		
51	SAT	Satellite/Live link application(s) CrimPD 18.23-24		
52	TEL	Cell site analysis.		
53	INT	Intermediary report(s) with draft specific Ground Rules if required. CrimPR 18 & 3.9(7)		For Witness:
54		Other:		
55		Other:		

STAGE 4 – UNLESS INDIVIDUAL DATES ARE GIVEN IT IS ORDERED THAT THE DEFENCE SHALL SERVE THE FOLLOWING BY: Ordinarily 14 or 28 days after Stage 3.				DATE:
		ITEM	Date:	Additional requirements/particulars/directions:
56	DCL	Complaint about prosecution non-disclosure		To comply with s.8 CPIA and CrimPR 15.5.
57	DCL	Application(s) for witness summons for Third Party Disclosure if the prosecution indicates at PTPH that it will not be pursuing any TPD issues OR any Defendant is dissatisfied with the outcome of prosecution enquiries.		To comply with CrimPR 17.5
58	EXP	Defence expert evidence to be relied upon that could not be served by Stage 2 - CrimPR 19		
59	BC	s.100 or 101 bad character of non-defendant application - CrimPR 21		Any reply from prosecution or other party to be served within 14 days
60	SXB	s.41 Evidence of sexual behaviour application - CrimPR 22		Any reply from prosecution or other party to be served within 14 days
61	SM	Response to prosecution intermediary Report(s) - CrimPR 18		

62	**INT**	Intermediary report for defendant or defence witnesses with draft Ground Rules		Any reply from prosecution or other party to be served within 14 days
63	**SAT**	Satellite/Live link application(s) CrimPD 18.23-24		
64		Other:		
65		Other:		

Trial Preparation (these orders will only be required in more substantial cases)			
Prosecution	*Date*	*Defence*	*Date:*
Prosecution Opening Note		Notice of objections or comments	
Prosecution draft agreed facts (admissions)		Defence response	
Prosecution draft jury bundle index		Defence response including any requests for the inclusion of additional material	
Prosecution draft edited defendant's interview		Defence response	
Other:			

FURTHER MANAGEMENT IF REQUIRED	*Date:*	☑	⏱ *Time Estimate*
66	**Further Case Management Hearing** (including Preparatory Hearing or Pre-Trial Hearing). Particular issues:		☐ Defendant not required ☐ Defendant must attend ☐ Suitable for PVL	minutes hours
67	**Pre-Trial Review**. The PTR may be vacated on <u>all</u> parties informing the Court CPO in writing that they are fully trial ready and no orders are required.		☐ Defendant not required ☐ Defendant must attend ☐ Suitable for PVL	minutes hours
68	**Welfare and Ground Rules Hearing**		☐ Defendant not required ☐ Defendant must attend ☐ Suitable for PVL ☐ Not an intermediary case ☐ Other:	minutes hours

ADDITIONAL ORDERS:	*Date:*
69	
70	
71	

PLEA AND TRIAL PREPARATION HEARING FORM for DCS – Page 11 of 12

FORM - PTPH NG 1

FINAL JUDICIAL WARNINGS		
72	Judicial warnings given	☐ Warning that failure to provide a sufficiently detailed Defence Statement may count against the Defendant
		☐ Failure to attend is a separate offence
		☐ Trial in absence in which case advocates may withdraw
		☐ Other:

Parties are reminded that:

All participants have a duty to prepare and conduct the case in accordance with the overriding objective; to comply with the CrimPR, practice directions and directions of the court; and at once to inform the court and all parties of any significant failure - CrimPR1.2.

Prosecution and Defence Case Progression Officers are reminded of their duties to monitor compliance with directions; make sure the court is kept informed of events that may affect the progress of the case; make sure that he or she can be contacted promptly about the case during ordinary business hours; act promptly and reasonably in response to communications about the case and, if he or she will be unavailable appoint a substitute to fulfil his or her duties and inform the other Case Progression Officers - CrimPR3.4.

Parties must actively assist the court to fulfil the overriding objective and engage with other parties to further the overriding objective without or if necessary with a direction - CrimPR3.3. Provided they promptly inform the court Case Progression Officer parties may agree to vary a time limit fixed by a direction if the variation will not affect the date of any hearing that has been fixed or significantly affect the progress of the case in any other way -CrimPR 3.7

After the hearing Case Progression Officers and OICs must ensure that they receive and act upon the orders made.

JUDICIAL SIGNATURE Where the Judge him or herself has made the entries on the DCS it is not necessary to enter a name		
73	HHJ/Recorder:	Date:

14 TRIAL BEFORE THE CROWN COURT

14.1	**Introduction**	**274**
14.2	**The indictment**	**274**
	14.2.1 What counts may be included on the indictment?	275
	14.2.2 Duplicity	275
	14.2.3 Joinder of counts in an indictment	275
	14.2.4 Joinder of defendants	276
	14.2.5 Amending the indictment	276
14.3	**Supporting the advocate at trial**	**277**
14.4	**Last-minute checklist**	**277**
	14.4.1 Which witnesses must the prosecution call?	278
14.5	**First day of the trial**	**278**
	14.5.1 Conference with the advocate	278
14.6	**Plea bargaining**	**278**
14.7	**Arraignment and pleas**	**279**
	14.7.1 Pleading guilty	279
	14.7.2 procedure following a guilty plea	280
	14.7.3 Changing a plea	280
14.8	**During the trial**	**280**
	14.8.1 Empanelling the jury—Crim PR, Part 25.6–8	280
	14.8.2 Asking a juror to 'stand by'	280
	14.8.3 Challenge for cause	281
	14.8.4 Judicial challenges	281
	14.8.5 The composition of the jury	281
	14.8.6 Can the defendant be tried on indictment in his absence?	281
14.9	**The course of trial on indictment—Crim PR, Part 25.9**	**281**
	14.9.1 The prosecution's opening speech	281
14.10	**The course of trial—Presenting evidence—Crim PR, Part 25.11**	**282**
	14.10.1 Examination-in-chief	283
	14.10.2 Cross-examination	283
	14.10.3 Re-examination	284
14.11	**Defence submission of no case to answer**	**284**
14.12	**The defence case**	**284**
14.13	**The closing speeches**	**285**
14.14	**The summing-up and directing the jury—Crim PR, Part 25.14**	**285**
14.15	**The verdict**	**287**
	14.15.1 A unanimous or a majority verdict?	287
	14.15.2 What if the jury cannot reach a verdict?	287
14.16	**The procedure after the jury's decision—Crim PR, Part 25.16**	**288**
14.17	**Acquitted defendants**	**288**
	14.17.1 The double jeopardy rule	288
14.18	**The prosecution's right of appeal**	**288**
14.19	**Judge-only trials on indictment**	**289**

14.1 **INTRODUCTION**

Where the defendant pleads not guilty when arraigned at the Plea and Trial Preparation Hearing (PTPH), the judge will set the date for the trial in the Crown Court in accordance with the PTPH procedure outlined in Chapter 13. This chapter considers the procedural and practical steps at a trial on indictment by examining the following:

- the rules dealing with the indictment;
- supporting the advocate at trial;
- empanelling the jury;
- the presentation of the prosecution and defence cases;
- the judge's summing-up; and
- the jury's verdict.

The rules governing the conduct of the trial and sentence in the Crown Court can be found in Crim PR, Part 25.

14.2 **THE INDICTMENT**

Where the accused has been sent for trial in the Crown Court, the prosecution is required to draw up the indictment. The indictment is the formal document that contains the charge(s) the accused will plead to at trial, and is often included in the case sent bundle. Each charge on the indictment is known as a count, and the defendant will plead guilty or not guilty to each count at the PTPH or at trial.

The provisions that govern the drafting and use of indictments are principally found in Crim PR, Part 10, Criminal Practice Directions Part 2 Preliminary proceedings and the Indictments Act 1915 (IA 1915):

'(1) The heading should consist of the word "indictment", followed by the name of the place where the Crown Court is sitting and the name of the case.

(2) After the name of the case ("The Queen v John Smith and Adrian Green") should be written the presentment ("John Smith and Adrian Green are charged as follows:").

(3) It must include a paragraph headed "count".

(4) There must be a statement of the offence charged which:
- describes the offence in ordinary language, and
- identifies any legislation that creates it; and
- identifies particulars of the conduct constituting the commission of the offence as to make clear what the prosecutor alleges against the defendant.

(5) More than one incident relating to the commission of the offence may be included in a count if, by having regard to the time, place or purpose of those incidents taken together they amount to a single course of criminal conduct.

(6) An indictment may contain more than one count if all the offences charged are founded on the same facts; or form or are part of a series of offences of the same or similar character.

(7) If there is more than one count the counts are required to be numbered consecutively.

(8) An indictment may contain any count charging substantially the same offence as one specified in the notice of the offence or offences for which the defendant was sent for trial.

(9) Two or more accused persons may be charged in one count where the allegation is that they acted together to commit the offence.

(10) Two or more accused persons, not alleged to have acted together, may be charged in a single indictment (but in separate counts).

(11) The indictment must be signed by an appropriate officer of the Crown.'

The prosecution must draw up the indictment within prescribed time limits. The draft indictment should be lodged with the Crown Court no less than seven days prior to the PTPH. After being signed by a court officer, the draft indictment becomes the indictment on which the defendant is tried. An example of a draft indictment is featured in our online resources in our case study *R v Lenny Wise* (see Appendix 2, case sent bundle).

While the detailed rules about drafting indictments are outside the scope of this manual, some important general principles are here explained.

14.2.1 WHAT COUNTS MAY BE INCLUDED ON THE INDICTMENT?

Subject to the rules on 'joinder' of offences, a draft indictment may include charges for any indictable offence disclosed by the evidence after it has been sent for trial under s. 51 Crime and Disorder Act 1998 (CDA 1998).

In addition to indicting the accused for those offences for which he has been sent for trial, the indictment may also include counts for certain summary offences (see Chapter 13, para. 13.2.1).

An indictment may contain several counts but each count must allege only one offence. If the wording of the count shows that it is alleging two or more offences, the count is said to be 'bad for duplicity' and will be quashed. Should the judge wrongly reject a defence motion to have a duplicitous count quashed, the accused will have a good ground for appeal against conviction if found guilty.

The rules on 'joinder' determine what counts may be properly joined in the same indictment. Before the rules on 'joinder' of counts are briefly considered, when would a single count be bad for duplicity?

14.2.2 DUPLICITY

Each count in an indictment must allege only one offence. A single count alleging that Ian Brown stole razor blades belonging to Tesco on 13 July, and stole a DVD player from Asda on the 14 July would be bad for duplicity. It discloses two different offences allegedly committed on different days involving different victims. A count charging Ian with theft of razor blades and a DVD player from Tesco on 14 July would be perfectly valid. Although it might be said that two separate thefts have been committed, a degree of pragmatism is applied. Several criminal acts may be alleged in one count if they are so closely linked together as to form one activity or transaction (*DPP v Merriman* [1973] AC 584) or they 'amount to a course of conduct' within the meaning of Crim PR, Part 10.2(2). For example, where a defendant is accused of stealing cash or property from the same victim on several unspecified occasions, it is permissible to state in a single count that D stole £2,500 from V on a day or days unknown during a period between May 2018 and July 2018.

14.2.3 JOINDER OF COUNTS IN AN INDICTMENT

The long established rule which required an indictment containing more than one count to include only offences founded on the same facts, or offences which constitute all or part of a series of the same or similar character has been abolished.

However, if an indictment charges more than one offence and if at least one of those offences does not meet the criteria outlined in Crim PR, Part 3.21(4)(a) the court will order separate trials. Crim PR, Part 3.21(4)(a) requires that the court will order separate trials unless the offences included on the indictment are: (i) founded on the same facts; or (ii) form or are part of a series of offences of the same or a similar character.

Subject to the requirement Crim PR, Part 3.21(4)(a) it is for the court to decide which allegations against whom should be tried at the same time having regard to the prosecutor's submissions, the party's representatives, s. 5(3) Indictments Act 1915 and the Crim PR's 'overriding objective'.

Where the court is invited to exercise those powers as it is generally undesirable for a large number of counts to be tried at the same time and it may be appropriate for the prosecutor to identify selection of counts on which the trial should proceed leaving the decision to be taken later whether to try any of the remainder.

14.2.4 JOINDER OF DEFENDANTS

An indictment can charge two or more defendants jointly either as principal offenders or as secondary parties and an indictment can charge defendants in separate counts but in the same indictment, providing there is a linking factor between the counts. The defendants might have been acting in concert, for example, but committing separate offences. In *R v Assim* [1966] 2 QB 249, two defendants were charged in a single indictment, one with unlawfully wounding X and the other with assaulting Y occasioning him actual bodily harm. They could not be charged in a single count because their respective acts of violence had separate victims. However, both assaults were perpetrated on the same night at the same nightclub where the two defendants were both employed.

All parties to a single offence may be jointly charged in a single count, but it remains open to the jury to acquit some defendants but convict others. Similarly, the trial judge has a discretionary power to order the separate trial of defendants jointly charged in a single count, although this should be exercised exceptionally as a single trial saves times and spares witnesses.

Consider the following example of the joinder of counts and defendants on a single indictment.

 Example

Arif is charged with Count 1, affray. William is charged with wounding, Count 2. Both charges arise out of a disturbance when both defendants were refused entry to a nightclub.

All counts may be joined in the same indictment under Crim PR, Part 10.2(2) if taken together amount to a course of conduct having regard to the time, place, or purpose of commission of the offence(s).

14.2.5 AMENDING THE INDICTMENT

The power to amend an indictment, once it has been served, is provided by s. 5 IA 1915, and may be exercised unless the judge considers that such amendment would cause 'injustice'. The power to amend may be exercised at any stage during the trial. Any defect can be remedied by amendment whether the defect is trivial or more fundamental. Amendment may also take the form of inserting new counts in the indictment either in substitution for or in addition to those originally drafted.

For detailed analysis of the rules on drafting indictments, see *Blackstone's Criminal Practice*.

14.3 **SUPPORTING THE ADVOCATE AT TRIAL**

Supporting the prosecution or defence counsel or a solicitor-advocate is a task that is commonly allocated to a trainee solicitor, paralegal or Crown Prosecution Service (CPS) caseworker. In defence firms and in the CPS, the staff member is often handed a file at short notice and told to act as a 'watching brief' in the Crown Court. This role requires the staff member to quickly assimilate the information contained in the file.

As a result of changes to the funding of criminal cases, a defence representative is only paid for attending the advocate at trial where the proceedings come within one of the following categories:

- very serious indictable offences;
- serious fraud cases;
- where the defendant is a child or a young person;
- where the defendant will not be able to follow the proceedings because of illness, disability or inadequate command of English; or
- on the day that the client is likely to be given a custodial sentence.

If the accused's case falls outside one of the above categories, a paralegal or trainee solicitor's attendance for the defence at the Crown Court may still be paid for where the judge issues a litigator certificate. A litigator certificate is likely to be issued where:

- there are a significant number of defence witnesses to be marshalled on any given day; or
- there are a significant number of defence documents; or
- the defence advocate is representing more than one accused; or
- the accused is likely to be disruptive if the advocate appeared alone; or
- the advocate will need notes taken for the proper conduct of the defence; or
- there are any other exceptional circumstances.

14.4 **LAST-MINUTE CHECKLIST**

In the period leading up to the trial date a member of the prosecution or the defence team should ensure, where appropriate, that:

- any matters arising out of counsel's written advice or raised in conference have been complied with;
- there are sufficient copies of the defence and prosecution documentation (trial bundles) for the judge and jury;
- from the prosecution perspective, there is an obligation to keep disclosure of evidence under review (see Chapters 8 and 13) and if further evidence is to be relied on at trial that has not previously been disclosed the prosecution must serve a notice of additional evidence on the defence complying with the requirements of s. 9 Criminal Justice Act 1967 (CJA 1967). If the defence do not object within seven days, the statement will be read to the court as evidence at the trial without calling the witness;
- the prosecution will also need to ensure that any exhibits have been properly packaged and are available;
- each witness has been warned to attend trial or summonsed if necessary; and
- any domestic arrangements for the witnesses have been made, for example that hotel accommodation has been booked.

14.4.1 WHICH WITNESSES MUST THE PROSECUTION CALL?

As a matter of practice and as a general rule, the prosecution must ensure the attendance of all witnesses 'whose names are on the back of the indictment' (i.e. those witnesses whose statements have been served as part of the case sent bundle). The service of a witness statement is an indication that the prosecution will call that witness and will secure the attendance of the witness at trial even if the prosecutor now believes the evidence the witness will give may be unhelpful to the prosecution case.

It is unnecessary, however, for the prosecution to call a witness whose evidence is to be given as hearsay either under s. 9 CJA 1967 or s. 114 CJA 2003: see Chapter 18.

14.5 FIRST DAY OF THE TRIAL

On the first day of the trial you should arrive at court as early as possible. Ensure that you have all the relevant documentation and contact numbers for your barrister and witnesses in case of emergencies. Confirm with the court staff in which court the case is being heard. If you have any immediate concerns, the court usher is usually an invaluable source of information. When representing the accused, you will look out for the defendant and the defence witnesses and ensure that your witnesses are ready to give evidence when called. This is a time when you will need good interpersonal skills to allay any of your side's apprehension. The prosecution witnesses will normally be met by Witness Support staff.

Contact your advocate and confirm that he has everything he needs. It is common immediately before the start of the trial to be given last-minute tasks such as:

- photocopying;
- providing witnesses with copies of their statements to enable them to refresh their memory before testifying;
- liaising with witnesses, as the advocate cannot talk directly to the witnesses who are to be called;
- if assisting the defence advocate, you may be asked to take a proof of evidence from a defence witness whose identity has just come to light or to take a further proof of evidence with a view to clarifying some aspect of a witness's evidence;
- familiarising the witnesses with the layout of the courtroom; and
- undertaking last minute legal research.

14.5.1 CONFERENCE WITH THE ADVOCATE

The defence advocate will wish to speak with the defendant. This may be the first time the defendant has met her advocate. You will be required to make the introductions and to keep a careful note of the matters covered in the conference.

The advocate may give advice that a client does not wish to hear—most commonly that she should consider pleading guilty to some or all of the charges. Negotiations between opposing trial advocates on plea bargaining is not uncommon on the first day of a trial.

14.6 PLEA BARGAINING

There is no formal system of plea bargaining in England and Wales, and it remains of central importance that a defendant has a genuine choice whether to plead guilty or not guilty. It is common for the prosecution and the defence to negotiate about the gravity of the charge and the defendant's plea. Where a guilty plea to a lesser alternative charge is acceptable to all sides, the prosecution will offer no evidence on the more serious charge or ask for the charge to lie on the court file. Where a defendant faces multiple counts and indicates guilty pleas to some of those counts which are acceptable to the prosecution, the remaining counts can either be withdrawn or allowed to lie on file.

A Crown Court judge cannot be party to any plea bargaining as a defendant's decision to plead guilty must be unfettered. In *R v Goodyear* [2005] 3 All ER 117, the Court of Appeal stated that a trial judge can, at the invitation of the defence, give a binding indication of the maximum sentence in the event of a guilty plea. Any indication of the maximum sentence must be on an agreed basis of plea and not on hypothetical facts or charges. The court went on to give guidance on the procedure to be adopted when giving an indication of sentence.

'(1) An indication should not be given unless requested by the defendant.

(2) The indication request should not be made unless the legal representative obtains signed authority from his client.

(3) The judge should refuse to consider the indication if he has not been provided with a written basis of plea.

(4) The hearing should be conducted in open court.

(5) The judge should not do anything that would constitute a plea bargain.

(6) The judge has discretion without stating his reasons not to give an indication of sentence or can decide that he will give an indication at a later stage in the proceedings.

(7) Advance indication should be limited to the maximum sentence if a guilty plea was given at the time of the request.'

For full guidance on plea bargaining see the *Goodyear* judgment.

14.7 ARRAIGNMENT AND PLEAS

The trial formally begins with the defendant's arraignment. If the defendant has already been arraigned at the PTPH (which is the normal practice) and has pleaded not guilty, the count(s) in the indictment will simply be read out to the defendant again. Where a not guilty plea is maintained and a trial is to be held, the jury is empanelled. Only in exceptional circumstances will a defendant be arraigned at the start of the trial where, for example, he was not arraigned at the PTPH. A defendant would only be re-arraigned at the start of a trial if the indictment has been amended in a significant way or the defendant has decided to change his plea.

14.7.1 PLEADING GUILTY

A guilty plea entered by the accused must be unambiguous and voluntary. If a plea remains ambiguous, a not guilty plea must be entered instead. A voluntary plea must be of the accused's own free will and not the result of any external pressure. Such pressure, which will result in the quashing of a conviction, may come from either the judge or from counsel (*R v Turner* [1970] 2 QB 321 and *R v Barnes* (1970) 55 Cr App R 100). As outlined at para. 14.6, the defendant may choose to plead guilty having been given an indication as to the likely maximum sentence following a *Goodyear* direction. It is not uncommon for defendants to plead guilty to matters after being advised by counsel whom the defendant may be meeting for the first time either at the PTPH or on the day of trial.

Where the accused pleads guilty to a lesser alternative charge or only to some counts on a multiple count indictment, the decision to accept the plea, therefore avoiding the need for a trial, rests with the prosecution. If the plea is not acceptable to the prosecution, a jury is empanelled and evidence is then called in the normal way. If the defendant pleads guilty to a lesser offence (i.e. guilty to manslaughter but not guilty to murder) and the plea is accepted by the prosecution, the defendant stands acquitted of the offence charged and the court proceeds to sentence him for the lesser matter.

14.7.2 **PROCEDURE FOLLOWING A GUILTY PLEA**

If a defendant pleads guilty, a jury will not be empanelled and the court may sentence immediately or adjourn for the preparation of a pre-sentence report (see Chapters 20 and 21 for a full account of sentencing practice and procedure). If the accused pleads guilty to one count but will be tried on other counts, the judge will postpone sentence on the guilty plea until the outcome of his trial on the outstanding counts.

14.7.3 **CHANGING A PLEA**

An accused may change his plea from not guilty to guilty at any stage of the trial prior to the jury returning their verdict.

The judge has discretion to permit an accused to change a guilty plea to a plea of not guilty at any time until the court passes sentence. In practice, however, this discretion is used very sparingly (see *Revitt v DPP* [2006] 1 WLR 3172).

14.8 **DURING THE TRIAL**

In your supporting role in the Crown Court, you will sit behind the advocate taking a careful note of the proceedings and will be available to give any assistance. If the defendant wishes to communicate with her advocate, this often has to be done through the support staff. It is especially important to keep an accurate note of the answers given by the prosecution witnesses during cross-examination and by the defence witnesses during examination-in-chief, as the advocate is unlikely to make a written record of the witness's answers whilst asking questions. The same practices apply to the prosecution support staff who are the point of contact between the advocate and the lead investigating police officer.

There may be times during the trial when the advocate has missed an important point or you have an idea that might be useful to your party's case. Write a legible note summarising the point and slide it forward to bring it to the advocate's attention. If a more serious issue arises, it may be necessary to hold a conference with the advocate at the end of the day or even at an adjournment during the main proceedings.

14.8.1 **EMPANELLING THE JURY—CRIM PR, PART 25.6–8**

The jury will be empanelled or selected from a jury in waiting of 20 or more people who have been summonsed for jury service at the Crown Court. The clerk of the court calls out the potential jurors' names from a recently shuffled pack of cards, each card bearing a juror's name. This fulfils the requirement under s. 11 Juries Act 1974 that jurors should be selected randomly.

Once 12 names have been selected, the individuals are called forward to take the jury oath. Before being sworn, each juror may be asked to 'stand by' by the prosecution or challenged 'for cause' by either the prosecution or the defence. In the event of a successful challenge to a juror to 'stand by' or a challenge by the prosecution for 'cause', a replacement juror is drawn from the jury in waiting.

14.8.2 **ASKING A JUROR TO 'STAND BY'**

The prosecutor can ask a juror to 'stand by' as the juror is about to take the oath. Although the prosecutor does not have to give a reason to ask a juror to 'stand by', most commonly it is as the result of the jury panel being vetted by the police. The practice of asking a juror to 'stand by' has been severely curtailed by the Attorney General's Guidelines on Exercise by the Crown Court of its Right of Stand-by (2012 update).

14.8.3 **CHALLENGE FOR CAUSE**

Both the prosecution and the defence may challenge a juror for cause (s. 12(3) Juries Act 1974). This is done orally immediately before the juror is sworn. The party making the challenge has the burden of proving that:

- the juror is not qualified to serve;
- the juror is biased; or
- the juror may reasonably be suspected of being biased.

14.8.4 **JUDICIAL CHALLENGES**

The judge has a residual power to remove a juror where, for example, the juror is illiterate or otherwise is deemed unsuitable or incapable of sitting as a juror. A juror may be discharged by the judge during the trial where, for example, the juror is ill or for 'any other good reason'.

14.8.5 **THE COMPOSITION OF THE JURY**

An empanelled jury should consist of 12 jurors, although cases are regularly heard with 11 or even 10 jurors.

14.8.6 **CAN THE DEFENDANT BE TRIED ON INDICTMENT IN HIS ABSENCE?**

As a general principle, an accused should be present throughout his trial. Attendance is secured by a remand into custody or release on bail (see Chapter 10). In exceptional circumstances the accused's presence in court may be dispensed with because of the accused's misbehaviour or through his voluntary absence or ill health. Where the accused fails to surrender to bail or escapes from custody, the judge has discretion to hold the trial in the accused's absence. See the guidance on this point from the Court of Appeal in *R v Hayward* [2001] 3 WLR 125 and by the House of Lords in *R v Jones (Anthony William)* [2003] 1 AC 1.

14.9 **THE COURSE OF TRIAL ON INDICTMENT—CRIM PR, PART 25.9**

After the jury has been empanelled, the formal part of the trial begins with the prosecution advocate making an opening speech. The presentation of evidence in a criminal trial is governed and shaped by rules of evidence which are explained in Chapters 4 to 7 and 15 to 20. The opening speech by the prosecution is best understood in the context of the rules which determine the burden of proof, explained in Chapter 15.

It is no part of the prosecutor's role to win the case at all costs and the prosecutor must act as minister of justice by, for example, complying with the pre-trial disclosure of unused evidence to the defence. In *R v Gonez* [1999] All ER (D) 674, the Court of Appeal endorsed the prosecutor's role as a minister of justice and section 2.4 of the Code for Crown Prosecutors reflects this position by stating: *'Prosecutors must always act in the interests of justice and not solely for the purpose of obtaining a conviction.'* See Chapter 8 for a detailed explanation of the principles and operation of the Code and the prosecution's obligations to disclose used and unused evidence and other material to the defence before the trial.

14.9.1 **THE PROSECUTION'S OPENING SPEECH**

The purpose of the opening speech is to outline the case in a simple, narrative form by explaining the alleged facts and the evidence the prosecution intends to rely on to prove its case against the accused.

Whilst the opening speech gives the advocate the opportunity to advance the prosecution's theory of the case the prosecutor should not use emotive language however unpleasant or sensational the facts of the offence(s) may be, nor should the prosecutor play on the jurors' feelings or emotions.

The advocate will often begin her opening speech in this way: '*It is the prosecution who brings this case and it is the prosecution who has the burden of satisfying you so that you are sure that the defendant is guilty of this offence. If you are unsure, the defendant is entitled to the benefit of the doubt.*'

After this introduction the prosecutor will proceed with the opening speech by:

- outlining the facts;
- instructing the jury that it is the prosecution which brings the case and that the prosecution must prove the defendant's guilt;
- briefly explaining the relevant points of law, whilst acknowledging that the judge is the sole arbiter on points of law;
- identifying the witnesses to be called and provide an outline of what each witness is expected to testify to the court.

Most disputes about the admissibility of evidence will have been dealt with at a pre-trial hearing and be the subject of a binding ruling by the trial judge. Where items of disputed evidence remain to be decided, the prosecutor must not refer to the disputed evidence during the opening speech. Any outstanding evidential issues will be decided in a *voir dire*, that is, at a trial within the main trial conducted in the absence of the jury.

Under Crim PR, Part 25.9 the trial judge may invite the defence, after the prosecution's opening speech, to concisely identify the issues in dispute to the jury. If the defence declines to do so, the judge can direct that the jurors are given a copy of any defence statement served under r. 15.4, edited if necessary to exclude any reference to inappropriate matters or to any inadmissible evidence.

14.10 THE COURSE OF TRIAL—PRESENTING EVIDENCE—CRIM PR, PART 25.11

Having been sworn or affirmed, each prosecution witness gives evidence in the following order:

- examination-in-chief by the prosecution advocate;
- cross-examination by the defence advocate;
- re-examination (where appropriate) by the prosecution advocate.

As a matter of practice the prosecutor should call or read the statement of all witnesses whose statements have been served on the defence or, to use the traditional phrase, those 'witnesses whose names appear on the back of the indictment'. The service of the witness statement is an indication the prosecution will call that witness and will secure the attendance of the witness at trial and therefore there is no requirement for the defence to ensure the witness attends trial. Therefore, to avoid the defence being prejudiced by the court not having the opportunity to cross-examine a witness on her evidence, the prosecution is generally obliged to call the witness at the trial.

Even where the prosecution does not call a witness whose name appears on the back of the indictment (see para. 14.4.1), the prosecution has a duty to ensure that the witness is present at court for the trial so that the defence may call him if they wish. As an alternative to calling a witness and subjecting him to examination-in-chief, it is open to the prosecuting advocate to tender the witness for cross-examination. The advocate would, in these circumstances, call the witness, establish his name and address and then invite the defence to ask questions in cross-examination.

Evidence may also be presented by the prosecution (and by the defence) in written form, through formal admissions under s. 10 CJA 1967 or by agreement under s. 9 CJA 1967 or where the reason for the witness's absence from trial is governed by s. 116(2) CJA 2003. Do not forget the prosecution evidence will also commonly include exhibits such as items of real evidence, for example a murder weapon.

Questioning of witnesses through examination-in-chief or cross-examination must be conducted in accordance with the rules of evidence and in compliance with the advocate's professional conduct responsibilities (see Chapter 1 with specific reference to the Principles and rules under the Solicitors Code of Conduct 2019).

An effective examination of all witnesses requires the trial advocate to:

- always be in control of the witness;
- have clear objectives when examining the witness and an awareness of how those objectives can be achieved;
- know what the witness is going to say and how the witness is going to say it—the examination of a witness at trial is not about ascertaining the truth; it is about getting the witness to say something that supports the advocate's case. Whether in a summary trial or a trial on indictment, pre-trial preparation based on the disclosure of evidence will have alerted the advocate to the questions that should be put to witnesses in examination-in-chief or in cross-examination.

It should not be forgotten that a witness may be giving evidence with the benefit of a special measures direction (see Chapter 16).

14.10.1 EXAMINATION-IN-CHIEF

The purpose of examination-in-chief is to obtain evidence in support of the party calling the witness. It must be conducted in accordance with the rules of evidence. The mechanics of conducting an examination-in-chief and the applicable rules of evidence are considered in Chapter 16, para. 16.8. We briefly illustrate the process of examination-in-chief in our case study of *R v Lenny Wise* with the inclusion of an extract from the examination of the eye-witness Shirley Lewis (see Document 45 in our online resources).

14.10.2 CROSS-EXAMINATION

Cross-examination has a number of purposes, and provides the opportunity to:

- obtain helpful replies or concessions from a witness;
- expose errors, weaknesses or inconsistencies in the witness's account;
- undermine the witness's personal credibility—subject to the permissible limits allowed by the rules of evidence (see s. 100 CJA 2003 discussed in Chapter 16, para. 16.9.4).

The rules relating to cross-examination are explained in Chapter 16, paras. 16.9–16.12. Great importance is attached to cross-examination in the adversarial system of criminal justice. It may seem an obvious point, but witnesses are far from infallible. Witnesses may be biased. They may not come to court to tell the truth, the whole truth and nothing but the truth. Memory fades over time. The witness's actual perception of the event may not have been made in ideal circumstances. All of these fallibilities can be exposed and explored in cross-examination. Cross-examination also gives the advocate a chance to put his case to the opponent's witness. We briefly illustrate the process of cross-examination in our case study of *R v Lenny Wise*. At Document 45, located in our online resources in the case study section, we have included an extract from the examination of the eye-witness Shirley Lewis.

Where two or more defendants are separately represented, each may cross-examine prosecution witnesses in the order in which they appear on the indictment.

14.10.3 **RE-EXAMINATION**

In asking questions of his witness in re-examination, the advocate is restricted to matters that have arisen in cross-examination. The advocate cannot introduce new matters which he omitted to ask the witness in examination-in-chief. Re-examination is generally regarded as a damage limitation exercise. It can be used to rehabilitate the witness in the eyes of the court where this is necessary.

14.11 DEFENCE SUBMISSION OF NO CASE TO ANSWER

At the close of the prosecution case, the defence may make a submission of 'no case to answer'. The decision is made by the judge in the absence of the jury. The basis of a submission of no case to answer in the Crown Court was explained by Lord Lane in *R v Galbraith* [1981] 2 All ER 1060, in the following terms:

> 'How then should the judge approach a submission of "no case"? (1) If there is no evidence that the crime alleged has been committed by the defendant, there is no difficulty. The judge of course will stop the case. (2) The difficulty arises where there is some evidence but it is of a tenuous character, for example because of the inherent weakness or vagueness or because it is inconsistent with other evidence. (a) Where the judge comes to the conclusion that the Crown's evidence, taken at its highest, is such that a jury properly directed could not properly convict on it, it is his duty, on a submission being made, to stop the case. (b) Where however the Crown's evidence is such that its strength or weakness depends on the view to be taken of a witness's reliability, or other matters which are generally speaking within the province of the jury and where on one possible view of the facts there is evidence on which a jury could properly come to the conclusion that the defendant is guilty, then the judge should allow the matter to be tried by the jury.'

Where the submission of no case to answer is rejected by the court, or a submission is not made, it is likely that the defence will call evidence to support the accused's plea of not guilty.

Whilst the defence would normally make a submission of no case to answer at the close of the prosecution case there is also nothing to prevent a submission being made at the conclusion of the defence case (*R v Anderson* (1998), *The Independent*, 13 July 1998).

14.12 THE DEFENCE CASE

If the defence intend to call evidence other than, or in addition to, the testimony of the accused, the defence advocate has a right to make an opening speech at the beginning of the defence case. Where the defence case begins with an opening speech it will outline the evidence the defence intends to call and perhaps comment on the prosecution case indicating how the defence evidence will seek to rebut the evidence against the defendant.

On a not guilty plea the defence is not obliged to call evidence, nor is the accused compelled to testify in support of her own case. If the defence calls no evidence and the accused does not give evidence, the defence advocate will make a closing speech at the prosecution's closing speech.

In most cases, however, if the accused is pleading not guilty the defence will put some evidence before the court to support its case. If the accused chooses to give evidence on oath, the defendant will be the first defence witness to testify (s. 79 Police and Criminal Evidence Act 1984 (PACE 1984)). Whether the defendant should give evidence at his trial or not requires careful consideration. The evidential consequences of the defendant choosing not to give evidence on oath and the factors that influence the decision are considered in Chapter 19, para. 19.4.1.

Following examination-in-chief it is the prosecutor's opportunity to cross-examine the accused.

If necessary the defence advocate may then re-examine the accused to repair any damage that may have been inflicted on the defence case in cross-examination.

Once the court has heard the accused's evidence the defence may call other evidence in support of its case including any admissible hearsay evidence, exhibits, documentary evidence and the oral testimony of other defence witnesses who will each give evidence in the following order:

- examination-in-chief by the defence advocate;
- cross-examination by the prosecution advocate and co-accused (if applicable);
- re-examination (where appropriate) by the defence advocate.

If the defendant chooses to give evidence on oath, the defendant will be the first defence witness to testify (s. 79 PACE 1984). Whether the defendant should give evidence at his trial or not requires careful consideration. The evidential consequences of the defendant choosing not to give evidence on oath and the factors that influence the decision are considered in Chapter 19, para. 19.4.1.

Where there are two or more defendants separately represented, each may be cross-examined by the other and then by the prosecution.

14.13 THE CLOSING SPEECHES

At the close of the defence case, the prosecution advocate and then the defence advocate make a closing speech to the judge and jury. The closing speech is the advocate's final opportunity to persuade the jury of the merits of his party's case and to summarise the nature of the evidence that the jury has heard.

The closing speeches should therefore be delivered with full persuasive effect using a combination of logic and emotion. Each advocate will attempt to present his case in the most favourable light by identifying any evidence that supports his case and discrediting evidence that undermines it. In the course of making their speeches, the prosecution will obviously emphasise points in its favour (including, if applicable, the accused's failure to give evidence or to have mentioned his defence at the police station). The quality of any identification evidence often figures prominently in both the prosecution and defence advocate's closing speeches and the directions to be found in the case of *R v Turnbull* [1977] QB 224 will be advanced to the jury. (The *Turnbull* guidelines are considered in Chapter 17.)

The defence advocate may suggest to the jury inconsistencies, improbabilities and other weaknesses in the prosecution case. If, for example, prosecution witnesses have had their previous convictions admitted in evidence during the trial, the defence advocate may suggest that their credibility is such that they cannot be believed on oath. The defence advocate may also remind the jury of the prosecution's opening speech and highlight any disparities between what was said by the prosecutor at the start of the trial and how the prosecution evidence was presented at trial. Finally, the defence advocate should remind the jurors that if they are left in any doubt about the defendant's guilt, they must acquit.

14.14 THE SUMMING-UP AND DIRECTING THE JURY—CRIM PR, PART 25.14

Following the defence advocate's closing speech the judge will sum up the case to the jury. The judge directs the jurors on points of law and evidence, and helps them to consider the facts. The approach that judges use when summing-up differs considerably, but, in judicial training sessions, considerable attention is paid to the summing-up, which is a critical part of the Crown Court trial. Some judges go to considerable lengths to withhold their own feelings about the evidence in the case from the jury whilst others appear to make little secret of the way in which they view the evidence. It is, however, essential that the judge stresses consistently that it is for the jury only to decide the accused's guilt or innocence on the facts of the case.

The following issues are commonly referred to in the summing-up:

- an explanation that the jury are the sole arbiters of the facts in the case, but they must accept the judge's direction on points of law and evidence;

- an explanation of the offence(s) charged including an examination of each of the elements;

- a clear direction on the burden and standard of proof;

- an assessment of the evidence put before the court. The judge may comment on the evidence presented by each party as counsel might have done in their closing speeches. The judge may direct the jurors' attention to any answers from a witness which might appear to be implausible or to examine why a particular witness might have a motive to lie;

- depending on the issues in the case, the trial judge may be required to direct the jury on the following evidential issues:

  – the dangers of relying on identification evidence;

  – the dangers of relying on certain types of uncorroborated evidence;

  – the use that can be made of evidence of a defendant's bad character;

  – the use that can be made of the defendant's good character;

  – the precise circumstances in which an adverse inference from the defendant's silence might be drawn under ss. 34, 35, 36 and 37 Criminal Justice and Public Order Act 1994;

  – the special considerations that apply to expert evidence;

  – the need to consider the evidence in relation to each count separately unless the rules of evidence dictate otherwise;

  – the rules relating to confession evidence;

  – the dangers of relying on hearsay evidence;

  – the significance of lies told by the defendant.

Many of the directions the judge is required to give are explained in the *Crown Court Compendium 2017* available at http://www.judiciary.gov.uk/publications/crown-court-bench-book-directing-the-jury-2/. It is good practice for the trial judge to discuss her directions with the advocates before directing the jury.

In lengthy cases or where the case is factually and/or legally complex the judge may consider if it would assist the jury to provide a Written Route to Verdict and/or Written Directions of Law. In practice a Written Route to Verdict is no more than a logical sequence of questions which addresses the essential legal issues to be answered by the jury to enable them to arrive at their verdict. The Written Directions of Law is an aide-memoire that provides legal definitions for the jury's use. If the judge intends to provide either document for the jury, the documents should, if circumstances allow, be shown to the advocates before the closing speeches and certainly before the judge delivers her summing-up.

When attending with counsel or a solicitor-advocate in the Crown Court, it is very important that you take a verbatim record of the trial judge's directions. An error in the summing-up or appearance of bias in favour of the prosecution can provide a defendant with grounds for appeal in the event of a conviction.

At the end of the summing-up the judge advises the jury to appoint a foreman and instructs the jury to retire to seek a unanimous verdict.

On occasion, after the jury retires to make its decision, the jury may ask the judge for further explanation of matters of law or to remind them of any part of the evidence. If the jury ask for information about a point on which no evidence has been given, the judge must tell them there is no evidence on the matter and they must reach their verdict on the basis of the evidence they have heard. Where the jury have a question, it will be delivered by the jury bailiff (see later), who passes it on to the judge. The judge then asks for the trial advocates and the accused to return to court. The note is then read out and the advocates will be invited to make representations as to how the judge should deal with the question. The jury are brought back in to court whereupon the judge will confirm the question asked and the answer that is given along with any further direction deemed necessary.

For further information on jury related issues, see *Blackstone's Criminal Practice*.

14.15 **THE VERDICT**

When the judge has concluded her summing-up, a court usher (jury bailiff) takes the oath to keep the jury in some 'private and convenient place'. The jury deliberates in private, free from outside interference. If the jury reaches a unanimous verdict the jurors return to the courtroom and the judge asks whether they have reached such a verdict. If the answer is 'Yes', the jury foreman reads out the verdict to each count on the indictment. The jury must return a verdict on each count and in respect of each accused joined in the count, unless they are discharged from giving a verdict on a certain count. Where the indictment contains alternative counts, for example counts of handling stolen goods or theft, the jury will only return a verdict on one count. An indictment may expressly, or impliedly, include a lesser alternative offence such as manslaughter in place of murder. The jury may find the defendant not guilty of the count charged but guilty of the lesser offence. The decision to leave alternative counts to the jury is a matter for discussion between the advocates and the trial judge.

14.15.1 **A UNANIMOUS OR A MAJORITY VERDICT?**

In her summing-up the judge will direct the jury to try to reach a unanimous verdict. However, where it is not possible for all the jurors to agree, s. 17 Juries Act 1974 allows for majority verdicts of 11:1 or 10:2 or, if the jury is reduced below 12, a majority of 10:1 or 9:1. The defendant may either be convicted or acquitted by a majority verdict.

Before a majority verdict can be considered, the jury must have retired for at least two hours or such longer period as is reasonable, having regard to the nature and complexity of the case. If at the end of that time the jury indicates there is no possibility of reaching a unanimous verdict, the judge may send them out for a further period. If the judge decides that she is willing to accept a majority verdict, the jurors are directed they should continue to reach a unanimous verdict but if they cannot, a majority verdict will be accepted.

There is a great deal of authority which stresses that no pressure should be placed on a jury to arrive at a verdict. If there is such pressure, any conviction is liable to be quashed.

14.15.2 **WHAT IF THE JURY CANNOT REACH A VERDICT?**

If a jury cannot agree on a verdict, the judge discharges them from giving a verdict. The accused is not acquitted and may be retried before a different jury. It is for the prosecution to determine whether there should be a retrial. In the absence of reasons to the contrary, it is the practice to have a retrial following a failure by one jury to agree.

14.16 **THE PROCEDURE AFTER THE JURY'S DECISION—CRIM PR, PART 25.16**

Where the accused is found guilty, the court will sentence either on the day or, following an adjournment, for a pre-sentence report to enable the court to enquire into the accused's background. Part V of this work covers sentencing. Where the defendant is remanded in custody pending sentence, it will be necessary for defence counsel and whoever may be assisting him to see the defendant in the cells to discuss the verdict and any possible grounds for appeal. The defence representative may also be required to provide emotional support to the defendant and his family about the outcome.

If the convicted defendant was granted a representation order subject to a capital-based contribution (see Chapter 9), the specified capital sum will now be payable. If you are representing an acquitted defendant, this is the time to express your relief and to celebrate the result!

Depending on the verdict it may be necessary for the CPS staff member to meet with the prosecution advocate and the police investigating team to discuss any further action in the case.

At the conclusion of the case both CPS and defence support staff should write a full note of the court's decision and ensure that the brief is properly endorsed and that all the accompanying papers are received back from counsel.

14.17 **ACQUITTED DEFENDANTS**

A legally aided acquitted defendant's costs will be met under the representation order. Any income-based contributions made by the defendant will be reimbursed by the LAA with interest.

Privately funded defendants who are acquitted are generally entitled to an award of costs from central funds under s. 16 Prosecution of Offenders Act 1985. Such orders are at the discretion of the court but should normally be awarded unless it is felt that the accused brought suspicion on herself by her own conduct or misled the prosecution into thinking the evidence against her was stronger than it in fact was. The Legal Aid, Sentencing and Punishment of Offenders Act 2012 (LASPO 2012), however, has both curtailed and, in some instances, prohibited the amount of costs that can be recovered in the Crown Court (see Chapter 9, para. 9.13).

14.17.1 **THE DOUBLE JEOPARDY RULE**

Section 75(1) CJA 2003 abolished the rule against double jeopardy for certain serious qualifying of-fences that resulted in acquittal following trial on indictment or quashed on appeal. The 'qualifying offences' are listed in Sch. 5 CJA 2003 and include murder, manslaughter, kidnapping, and rape.

The procedure, which includes obtaining the DPP's consent and the leave of the Court of Appeal, is set out in ss. 76–80 CJA 2003. The DPP must be satisfied that there is new and compelling evidence, and that it is in the public interest to proceed with an application to the Court of Appeal. 'New' means evidence that was not adduced at the previous trial; 'compelling' evidence must be highly probative of the case against the acquitted person (s. 78). The Court of Appeal must be satisfied that there is evidence of such quality and relevance as to create a very real chance of conviction and that it is in the interests of justice to order a second trial.

14.18 **THE PROSECUTION'S RIGHT OF APPEAL**

In relation to trials on indictment, the prosecution enjoys a right of interlocutory appeal against binding rulings made by a trial judge at a preparatory hearing in accordance with ss. 35 and 36 Criminal Procedure and Investigations Act 1996 (Crim PR, Part 37).

Under s. 58 CJA 2003 the prosecution may appeal to the Court of Appeal against a terminating ruling made by the judge in relation to an issue at a trial on indictment and which cannot otherwise be the subject of an appeal to the Court of Appeal. The appeal can be against any judicial ruling made during the trial until the beginning of the summing-up to the jury. The prosecution's right to appeal arising out of decisions in the Crown Court is considered in more detail in Chapter 23, para. 23.11.

14.19 JUDGE-ONLY TRIALS ON INDICTMENT

Sections 43–50 CJA 2003 and s. 17 Domestic Violence, Crime and Victims Act 2004 (DVCVA 2004) introduced trial on indictment without a jury. Where these sections apply the defendant can, on application by the prosecution, be tried by a judge. These are known as judge-only trials.

Judge-only trial arises in three different circumstances:

'(1) Section 43 CJA 2003—on application by the prosecution where the case is a serious and complex fraud. This is not yet in force.

(2) Section 44 CJA 2003—on application by the prosecution where there is a risk of "jury tampering". This provision came into force 24 July 2006. There are two different types of application.

(a) An application made before the start of the trial. The prosecution will need to demonstrate that there is evidence of a real and present danger of jury tampering and that the risk of jury tampering is so substantial that it is necessary in the interests of justice for the trial to be conducted without a jury, notwithstanding any steps (e.g. police protection) that might reasonably be taken to prevent the risk.

(b) An application, made after the discharge of the jury where the discharge is a result of jury tampering, to continue the trial as a judge-only trial. The judge must hear representations from both the defence and the prosecution. The judge will consider the same issues as set out above.'

Under ss. 45 and 47 CJA 2003 both the prosecution and the defence have the right of appeal to the Court of Appeal regarding any decision implementing a judge-only trial. If the defendant is convicted the judge must, under s. 48 CJA 2003, give reasons for the decision.

The first trial without jury before the Crown Court against four men charged with a £1.75 million robbery at a warehouse in Heathrow committed in 2005, commenced on 13 January 2010. The four were subsequently found guilty by the judge.

Guidance on the use of judge-only trials was provided by the Court of Appeal in *R v J, S and M* [2011] 1 Cr App R 5:

'(3) Section 17 DVCVA 2004—on application by the prosecution the jury try only sample counts and a judge sitting alone tries the remaining counts. This provision came into force on 8 January 2007. The prosecution must satisfy the following conditions, that:

(a) the number of counts in the indictment is such that a trial of them all by jury would not be practicable;

(b) each count tried by the jury is a sample of counts which could for their part be tried by judge-only trial; and

(c) that it is the interests of justice to make the s. 17 DVCVA 2004 order.'

█ KEY POINT SUMMARY

- Be aware of the circumstances in which a defendant can be tried for more than one offence and can be tried jointly with others.

- On the day of trial the trainee solicitor/paralegal's role is to support the trial advocate and (if the defence representative) support the accused and his family.

- Be aware that although there is no formal system of plea bargaining, the defence advocate may, with the defendant's express consent, negotiate or take up an offer to plead guilty to a less serious alternative offence or seek a binding indication of sentence from the judge in the event of a guilty plea being entered.

- Keep clear written notes of the conduct of the proceedings including what is said by counsel in conference; during the course of the evidence and in the trial judge's summing-up.

- Understand the various stages of the trial on indictment and the verdicts which a jury can return.

SELF-TEST QUESTIONS

1. What is a draft indictment?

2. What is the test for joining more than one count in an indictment?

3. What test does the defence have to meet in order to successfully make a submission of no case to answer at a trial in the Crown Court?

4. What procedure should be adopted in the Crown Court if a point of law arises?

5. Why is the trial judge's summing-up so important?

6. What is an attendance/litigation certificate?

 Analysis of these questions can be found in our online resources.

Part IV

PROVING THE CASE—THE RULES OF CRIMINAL EVIDENCE

In Part IV we consider further the rules of criminal evidence. In doing so, we build on those rules of criminal evidence already covered in Chapters 5–7.

We begin in Chapter 15 by considering the rules that determine which party has the legal and evidential burdens of proving the issues in a contested case either before a Crown Court or before a magistrates' court. In Chapters 16 and 17 we consider a number of rules associated with witnesses giving evidence at trial. Chapter 18 addresses the admissibility of hearsay evidence, whilst Chapter 19 explores the important area of the admission of a defendant's bad character. We conclude Part IV with a brief consideration of the rules on private privilege in Chapter 20.

<table>
<tr><td>15</td><td colspan="3">THE BURDEN OF PROOF</td></tr>
</table>

15.1	**Introduction**	**293**
15.2	**The legal burden of proof—the general rule**	**293**
15.3	**Exceptions to *Woolmington*—reverse burden clauses**	**294**
	15.3.1 The reverse burden clause at common law	294
	15.3.2 Express statutory reverse burden clauses	294
	15.3.3 Implied statutory reverse burden clauses	294
15.4	**The standard of proof required to discharge the legal burden**	**295**
15.5	**The evidential burden**	**295**
	15.5.1 The evidential burden and the prosecution	295
	15.5.2 The evidential burden and the defence	295
15.6	**Discharging the legal and evidential burdens of proof—an example**	**296**
15.7	**Challenges to reverse burden clauses under Article 6 European Convention on Human Rights 1950 (ECHR 1950)**	**296**
	15.7.1 Reverse burden clauses—the guiding principles	297
15.8	**Formal admissions—s. 10 CJA 1967**	**297**
15.9	**Burdens of proof—practical considerations**	**298**

15.1 INTRODUCTION

In this chapter we explain the rules governing the legal and evidential burdens of proof that decide which party has the responsibility of proving a fact in issue to the court. We then explain the degree of persuasiveness the evidence must attain to satisfy the appropriate standard of proof and briefly consider the human rights issues in those exceptional situations where the accused has the legal burden of proof. For both the prosecution and the defence, the rules that allocate the burden of proof and the degree of proof are fundamental to the outcome of a case at trial.

15.2 THE LEGAL BURDEN OF PROOF—THE GENERAL RULE

Generally the prosecution has the legal burden of proving a defendant's guilt. This fundamental rule was famously enshrined in *Woolmington v DPP* [1935] AC 463 and is known as the '*Woolmington*' principle.

As a practical illustration of the *Woolmington* principle, remind yourself of the example in Chapter 2 of the theft offence under s. 1 Theft Act 1968. The prosecution has the legal burden of proving the facts in issue in the case—the *actus reus* of the offence, that is, the defendant appropriated property belonging to another and the *mens rea,* i.e. that the defendant was dishonest and had the intention to permanently deprive. Where the defendant is pleading not guilty and is not putting forward a defence, the defence has neither a legal nor an evidential burden to prove anything.

15.3 EXCEPTIONS TO *WOOLMINGTON*—REVERSE BURDEN CLAUSES

Whilst the *Woolmington* principle applies in most criminal cases, including the most serious offences such as murder and robbery, a number of exceptions apply at common law or under statute where the defence has the legal burden of proving one or more of the facts in issue. These are known as reverse burden clauses because they effectively reverse the presumption of innocence. Where a reverse burden clause applies, human rights considerations will almost inevitably arise at trial. These are considered at para. 15.7.

15.3.1 THE REVERSE BURDEN CLAUSE AT COMMON LAW

At common law where the accused submits that at the time of the offence he was insane within the meaning of *McNaghten's Rules* (1843) 10 Cl & F 200, the defence has the legal burden of proving insanity at trial.

15.3.2 EXPRESS STATUTORY REVERSE BURDEN CLAUSES

In a number of statutes, Parliament has expressly passed the legal burden to the accused to prove one or more facts in issue. For example, s. 139 Criminal Justice Act 1988 (CJA 1988) prohibits a person from possessing a knife in a public place. Under s. 139(4) CJA 1988, the accused has a defence where he can show 'good reason or lawful authority' for possessing the knife in a public place. Once the prosecution has discharged the legal burden of proving that the accused was found in possession of a knife in a public place, the defence then has the legal burden of proving that he had good reason or lawful authority for possessing the knife.

Another example is s. 2 Homicide Act 1957 (HA 1957) as amended, where Parliament has expressly provided that the accused has the legal burden of proving the partial defence of diminished responsibility under s. 2 HA 1957 on a charge of murder.

15.3.3 IMPLIED STATUTORY REVERSE BURDEN CLAUSES

In other statutes, Parliament has impliedly placed the legal burden on the accused to prove a fact in issue. In summary cases s. 101 Magistrates' Courts Act 1980 (MCA 1980) provides:

> 'Where the defendant to an information or complaint relies for his defence on any exception, exemption, proviso, excuse or qualification, whether or not it accompanies the description of the offence or matter of complaint in the enactment creating the offence or on which the complaint is founded, the burden of proving the exception, exemption, proviso, excuse or qualification shall be on him; and this notwithstanding that the information or complaint contains an allegation negating the exception, exemption, proviso, excuse or qualification.'

An example of s. 101 MCA 1980 is provided by s. 143 Road Traffic Act 1988, which makes it an offence to drive a motor vehicle without insurance. Once the prosecution has discharged its legal burden by proving that on the date specified in the information or written charge the defendant drove a motor vehicle on the public highway, the legal burden passes to the accused to prove that at the time he was driving he was insured to do so. If the defendant successfully discharges the legal burden on this issue, he will be acquitted. Section 101 most commonly applies to regulatory offences which prohibit or restrict certain activities such as selling alcohol unless the defendant has a licence to do so or is permitted to engage in a specified activity that is otherwise illegal.

The rationale behind the common law and statutory exceptions to the *Woolmington* principle is that the facts in issue which are covered by a reverse burden clause are within the defendant's exclusive knowledge or control and it is therefore easier for the defendant to prove the fact(s) in issue rather than for the prosecution to disprove them.

15.4 **THE STANDARD OF PROOF REQUIRED TO DISCHARGE THE LEGAL BURDEN**

Where the legal burden falls on either the prosecution or the defence the evidence presented to support the fact must have the necessary degree of persuasiveness to convince the court. This is known as the standard of proof. If the prosecution has the legal burden of proving a fact in issue, the standard of proof is 'beyond a reasonable doubt'. This phrase is defined in the Judicial Studies Board specimen directions in the following terms:

> 'How does the prosecution succeed in proving the defendant's guilt? The answer is—by making you sure of it. Nothing less than that will do. If after considering all the evidence you are sure that the defendant is guilty, you must return a verdict of "Guilty". If you are not sure, your verdict must be "Not Guilty".'

Where the defence has the legal burden, the standard is on the balance of probabilities. In *Re H (Minors) (Sexual Abuse: Standard of Proof)* [1996] 1 All ER 1, Lord Justice Nicholls suggested the phrase meant the following:

> 'The balance of probability standard means that the court is satisfied an event occurred if the court considers that, on the evidence, the occurrence of the event was more likely than not.'

15.5 **THE EVIDENTIAL BURDEN**

A party will prove its case and discharge its legal burden, by putting evidence before the court to support its version of the facts and interpretation of the law. This is known as discharging the evidential burden. Generally, the party which has a legal burden of proof will have an evidential burden. To state the obvious: the legal burden of proof cannot be discharged without adducing evidence!

The evidential burden will be discharged in a number of ways by:

- calling witnesses to give oral evidence;
- tendering documentary evidence;
- showing photographs or video evidence;
- producing items of real evidence, for example the murder weapon at a trial for murder or CCTV/mobile telephone records;
- producing expert opinion evidence to prove, for example the presence of the defendant's DNA at the crime scene.

15.5.1 **THE EVIDENTIAL BURDEN AND THE PROSECUTION**

It is always open to the defence to make a submission of no case to answer at the close of the prosecution's case. Where the submission is successful the defendant will be acquitted. Such a submission will succeed in the Crown Court if the test outlined in Chapter 14, para. 14.11 is met. To paraphrase the '*Galbraith*' test: if, at the close of its case, the prosecution has failed to prove an essential element of its case or its evidence has been so thoroughly discredited such that no jury, properly directed on it could properly convict, a submission of no case to answer will be upheld. Quite simply, the prosecution will have failed to discharge its evidential burden. Even an unsuccessful submission does not mean that the prosecution has discharged its legal burden of proof, since this is determined by the jury/magistrates at the conclusion of the case on all the evidence presented by both sides in deciding the defendant's guilt.

15.5.2 **THE EVIDENTIAL BURDEN AND THE DEFENCE**

Where the accused merely pleads not guilty and does not put forward a defence, the defence advocate may cross-examine the prosecution witnesses to instigate reasonable doubt in the mind of the magistrates or jurors about the accused's guilt. In this sense the defendant does not bear an evidential burden.

However where the defence puts forward an affirmative defence such as self-defence or duress, it has an evidential burden to put some evidence in support of the defence before the court. The evidential burden will be discharged where, if believed and left uncontradicted, the evidence would induce a reasonable doubt in the mind of the magistrates or the jury as to whether the defence case might be true or not. Where the defendant has discharged the evidential burden, the prosecution then has the legal burden to disprove the accused's defence. If the accused has not adduced any evidence of his defence, the trial judge is not obliged to leave the defence to the jury.

The example in para. 15.6 provides a practical illustration of the rules governing the allocation of the legal and evidential burdens of proof.

15.6 DISCHARGING THE LEGAL AND EVIDENTIAL BURDENS OF PROOF—AN EXAMPLE

 Example

Ali is charged with robbery. He pleads not guilty by suggesting that he is the victim of mistaken identification. The Crown Prosecutor knows that to discharge the legal burden of proof, the prosecution will have to prove in accordance with s. 8(1) Theft Act 1968, that Ali dishonestly appropriated property belonging to another with the intention to permanently deprive and that before or at the time of doing so and in order to do so, Ali used force on any person or put any person in fear of force being used.

To discharge the legal burden of proof, the prosecution must adduce evidence (i.e. discharge its evidential burden) by calling, for example, the investigating officers to testify. The officers will give evidence in examination-in-chief about the investigation including whether incriminating items were found in Ali's possession linking him to the robbery. The officers will also be able to tell the court if Ali had made incriminating admissions to the police during the investigation or at the police station. Other prosecution witnesses might be called to testify in examination-in-chief that immediately before the robbery they saw Ali at the crime scene. The victim is likely to be an important prosecution witness. She may give evidence in examination-in-chief about the property that was stolen from her and the force that was used against her.

Other types of evidence may also be tendered by the prosecution including real evidence, footage of CCTV recordings and documentary evidence, and quite possibly forensic evidence in the form of expert opinion evidence.

The defence will try to undermine the prosecution case by cross-examining each defence witness by challenging the witness's factual evidence and/or attempt to undermine the witness's personal credibility as a witness. The defence may also put evidence before the court in support of Ali's defence. If, for example, Ali is pleading not guilty because he has an alibi, evidence should be put before the court to prove Ali's alleged whereabouts at the time of the offence. However, in this case there is no legal burden of proof on Ali and, as he is not advancing an affirmative defence, there is no evidential burden on him either. His only burden is a tactical one which is to adduce some evidence to raise a reasonable doubt in the mind of the jury.

Where the prosecution fails to adduce evidence in support of an element of the *actus reus* or the *mens rea* of robbery, at the close of the prosecution case, the defence may make a submission of no case to answer, as outlined in *R v Galbraith* [1981] 2 All ER 1060.

Assuming a submission of no case to answer is not made in this case or, if it is made, it is unsuccessful following a direction from the judge, the jury will decide whether Ali is guilty on the evidence presented.

15.7 CHALLENGES TO REVERSE BURDEN CLAUSES UNDER ARTICLE 6 EUROPEAN CONVENTION ON HUMAN RIGHTS 1950 (ECHR 1950)

Imposing a legal burden of proof on a defendant to prove one or more of the facts in issue effectively requires the defendant to prove his innocence. At first reading this requirement appears incompatible with Article 6(2) ECHR 1950 which explicitly provides that everybody charged with a criminal offence shall be presumed innocent until proven guilty.

In several prominent cases since the implementation of the Human Rights Act 1998, defence lawyers have argued that imposing a legal burden on the defendant to prove a fact in issue infringes the presumption of innocence under Article 6(2) ECHR 1950. The principles identified here suggest the courts are dealing with these arguments on a case-by-case basis. In a case where a court concludes that imposing a legal burden on a defendant violates the presumption of innocence under Article 6, it will use its interpretive power under s. 3 Human Rights Act 1998 (see Chapter 1, para. 1.9.1), to read the statutory provision down so as to impose only an evidential burden of proof on the accused (*R v Lambert* [2002] 2 AC 545).

15.7.1 REVERSE BURDEN CLAUSES—THE GUIDING PRINCIPLES

The following guiding principles can be distilled from the cases decided on this issue so far:

- A reverse burden clause is not automatically incompatible with the presumption of innocence under Article 6(2) provided the legal burden imposed on the defence is not unreasonable and is proportionate to the aim of the provision (*Salabiaku v France* (1988) 13 EHRR 370).

- A reverse burden clause is more easily justified where the overall burden to prove the essential ingredients of the offence remains on the prosecution.

- A reverse burden clause imposing an evidential burden only on the accused will not contravene the presumption of innocence under Article 6(2).

- A legal burden is more easily justified where the defendant is required to prove something within his own knowledge so that it is easier for the defendant to prove the fact than for the prosecution to disprove it.

- The stronger the public interest in preventing the type of harm covered by the legislation, the more likely that a legal burden will be placed on the accused provided it is proportionate to the aims of the legislation, for example:
  - imposing a legal burden of proof on the defendant under s. 139 CJA 1988 was a proportionate response to the social problem of people carrying knives in public (*R v Matthews* [2004] QB 690 and *L v DPP* [2002] 1 Cr App R 32);
  - s. 11(1) Terrorism Act 2000 was not proportionate, given the extraordinary breadth of the provision and the practical difficulty an accused would have in establishing a defence (*Attorney-General's Reference (No. 1 of 2004)* [2004] 1 WLR 2111).

- The more severe the penalty available to the court on conviction the more reasonable it would be to impose an evidential burden only on the accused.

- It is easier to justify the imposition of a legal burden of proof in a regulatory offence, for example *R (Grundy and Co. Excavations Ltd and the Forestry Commission) v Halton Division Magistrates Court* [2003] 167 JP 387.

For further judicial guidance on reverse burden clauses and the presumption of innocence, see the following cases: *R v Lambert* [2002] 2 AC 545; *R v Mathews* [2004] QB 690; *R v Drummond* [2002] 2 Cr App R 352; *R v Johnstone* [2003] 2 Cr App R 33; *Attorney-General's Reference (No. 1 of 2004)* [2004] 1 WLR 2111; and most authoritatively the House of Lords decision in *Attorney-General's Reference (No. 4 of 2002); Sheldrake v DPP* [2005] 1 AC 264.

In *R v Williams (Oretto)* [2012] EWCA Crim 2162, it was held that s. 1(5) Firearms Act 1983 placed a legal burden on an accused charged with an offence of possession of a readily convertible imitation firearm, to prove that he did not know, nor had reason to suspect, that the firearm was readily convertible. The Court of Appeal took the view that this was justified and proportionate having regard to the number of other firearms offences which are defined in strict liability terms, the protection of the public and the fact that the person best positioned to explain how he came into possession of the firearm was the accused.

15.8 FORMAL ADMISSIONS—S. 10 CJA 1967

Under s. 10 CJA 1967, an admission can be made by either the prosecution or the defence before or at the trial. If made before the trial, the admission must be in writing and, where the defendant is legally represented, must be made by his solicitor or barrister. Where a party formally admits a fact in issue, the fact does not have to be proved at trial by relevant and admissible evidence.

15.9 **BURDENS OF PROOF—PRACTICAL CONSIDERATIONS**

The incidence of the legal and evidential burdens of proof play a highly practical role at all stages of a criminal case for both the prosecution and the defence.

Prosecution perspective

* A vital early task for the Crown Prosecution Service (CPS) lawyer when advising the police about charge, is to research the elements of the offence(s) for which the suspect has been detained and then to assess the evidence obtained by the police during the police investigation. This is necessary to enable the CPS lawyer to form a view about whether there is sufficient evidence to charge and, if so, with which offence.

* This exercise will be repeated more formally by the Crown Prosecutor when applying the 'evidential' test under the Code for Crown Prosecutors to ensure there is a 'realistic' prospect of a conviction in the case (see Chapter 8).

* The principles covering the incidence of the legal and evidential burdens of proof are also fundamentally important at trial. On a not guilty plea, the prosecution will only be able to prove the defendant's guilt by fully discharging its legal and evidential burdens of proof.

* When opening the case for the prosecution at trial, the Crown Prosecutor should explain what the prosecution has to prove in the case and the meaning of 'beyond reasonable doubt'.

* The Crown Prosecutor must be prepared to defend a possible submission of no case to answer which could arise at the close of its case, having presented the evidence in support of the prosecution's case.

Defence perspective

* The defence lawyer at the police station must also carefully consider the essential elements of the offence(s) when assessing the strength of the evidence against her client before offering advice about whether, for example, her client should remain silent in the police interview or to negotiate her client's release from custody. These considerations also extend to where the offence(s) impose a legal burden and/or an evidential burden on the client.

* If the client is subsequently charged, the legal adviser's assessment of the evidence will form the basis of advising her client about whether to give an early indication of a guilty plea to attract a 'full' sentencing discount.

* At trial, the defence should be alert to the possibility of making a submission of no case to answer at the close of the prosecution's case where the prosecution has not established a prima facie case against the accused.

* The defence advocate needs to be aware if the trial judge in the Crown Court misdirects the jury on the burden and standard of proof and a conviction results as this will provide grounds to appeal against conviction.

KEY POINT SUMMARY

* The rules relating to the incidence of legal and evidential burdens of proof are of considerable practical importance.

* Know the general rule about the incidence of the legal burden of proof in a criminal case.

* Know the exceptions to the '*Woolmington*' principle.

* Be able to explain the relationship between the legal burden and the evidential burden.

* Be aware of the standard of proof that a party has to satisfy in order to discharge its legal burden.

* Understand that where a legal burden of proof is imposed on a defendant an issue of compatibility with Article 6(2) ECHR 1950 might arise.

- Know the evidential effect of a formal admission in a criminal case.

- Be able to apply these basic evidential rules to your client's case.

SELF-TEST QUESTIONS

1. What is the general rule about the incidence of the legal burden of proof in a criminal case?

2. Explain the meaning of the phrase 'reverse burden clause'.

3. What factors do the courts take into account in deciding the compatibility of a reverse burden clause with Article 6(2) ECHR 1950?

Analysis of these questions can be found in our online resources.

FIGURE 15.1 THE LEGAL AND EVIDENTIAL BURDENS OF PROOF

THE LEGAL BURDEN OF PROOF

- As a general rule and as a fundamental component of Article 6 the prosecution has the legal burden of proving the defendant's guilt (*Woolmington v DPP*);
- the prosecution will not know whether it has succeeded in discharging its legal burden of proof until the jury/magistrates return a verdict.

EXCEPTIONS TO THE *WOOLMINGTON* PRINCIPLE WHERE THE DEFENDANT HAS A LEGAL BURDEN OF PROOF (REVERSE BURDEN CLAUSES)

- At common law where the defendant pleads insanity under the *McNaghten Rules* 1843;
- express or implied statutory exceptions (e.g. s. 2 Homicide Act 1957, s. 101 Magistrates' Courts Act 1980 in summary proceedings);
- reverse burden clauses give rise to a potential Article 6 argument.

THE STANDARD OF PROOF

- The legal burden of proof must be discharged 'beyond reasonable doubt';
- 'on the balance of probabilities' wherever legal burden falls on the defence, i.e. the court considers that, on the evidence, the occurrence of the event was more likely than not (*Re H (Minors) (Sexual Abuse: Standard of Proof)*).

THE EVIDENTIAL BURDEN OF PROOF

- The general rule is that the party with the legal burden also has an evidential burden;
- it is a burden to adduce some evidence;
- a failure by the prosecution to discharge its evidential burden at the close of the prosecution's case will result in a successful submission of no case to answer by the defence (*R v Galbraith* for Crown Court trials; *Practice Direction (Submission of No Case)* in summary cases);
- there is always a tactical burden on the defendant to exploit the 'reasonable doubt';
- where the defendant raises an affirmative defence, there is an obligation to adduce some evidence of it.

16.1	**Introduction**	**300**
16.2	**Dealing with witnesses before testifying**	**301**
16.3	**Witness evidence—the preliminary issues**	**301**
	16.3.1 The presumption in favour of competency	302
	16.3.2 Challenging the competence of a witness—s. 54 YJCEA 1999	302
	16.3.3 Compellable witnesses	303
16.4	**Testifying under a special measures direction**	**304**
	16.4.1 Vulnerable witnesses	304
	16.4.2 Intimidated witnesses	304
16.5	**Types of special measures**	**305**
	16.5.1 Giving evidence from behind a screen—s. 23 YJCEA 1999	305
	16.5.2 Giving evidence through a live television link—s. 24 YJCEA 1999	305
	16.5.3 Giving evidence in private—s. 25 YJCEA 1999	305
	16.5.4 Removal of wigs and gowns—s. 26 YJCEA 1999	305
	16.5.5 Video-recorded evidence-in-chief—s. 27 YJCEA 1999	305
	16.5.6 Video-recorded cross-examination or re-examination—s. 28 YJCEA 1999	306
	16.5.7 Examination of a witness through an intermediary—s. 29 YJCEA 1999	306
	16.5.8 Aids to communication—s. 30 YJCEA 1999	306
	16.5.9 Anonymous witness evidence	306
	16.5.10 Procedure for seeking a special measures direction	308
	16.5.11 Use of live-link other than for vulnerable witnesses	308
16.6	**The practical issues of witness evidence**	**308**
16.7	**Taking the oath or affirming**	**309**
16.8	**Examination-in-chief**	**309**
	16.8.1 Leading questions	309
	16.8.2 The witness refreshing his memory	310
	16.8.3 Admitting a witness's previous consistent statement	311
	16.8.4 Unfavourable or hostile witness	312
16.9	**Cross-examination**	**313**
	16.9.1 Challenging the witness's factual evidence	313
	16.9.2 Attacking the witness's credibility	314
	16.9.3 Proving a previous inconsistent statement	314
	16.9.4 Admissibility of a non-defendant's bad character—s. 100 CJA 2003	314
16.10	**Cross-examining the witness on his physical or mental disability**	**317**
16.11	**Re-examination**	**318**
16.12	**Cross-examining the complainant in a sexual offence**	**318**

16.1 INTRODUCTION

This chapter deals with the important topic of witness evidence. Where a defendant pleads not guilty, the law governing witness evidence plays a vital part in assisting the court to decide the ultimate issue in the case—the defendant's guilt or innocence.

From their earliest involvement, both prosecution and defence lawyers will formulate their strategies and advice with the trial in mind. Is the prosecution evidence sufficiently strong and credible for the Crown Prosecution Service (CPS) to prove its case at trial beyond reasonable doubt? Can the defence successfully challenge the prosecution evidence to induce reasonable doubt in the minds of the jury or magistrates about the defendant's guilt? All the preparatory work in the case, research, interviews, the taking of witness statements, written correspondence, meetings with the defendant client or the investigating police officers and conferences with expert witnesses have one aim in mind—to prepare their party's case for the trial.

This chapter explains the law, procedure and the practical issues associated with witness evidence. (The special position of a defendant as a witness in his own defence is considered in Chapter 19.) In this chapter, the following issues are addressed:

* the circumstances in which a witness can refresh his memory from an earlier written statement;
* the test to decide a witness's competence to give evidence;
* the compellability of a witness;
* the assistance available to 'vulnerable' or 'intimidated' witnesses to give evidence under a special measures direction;
* a witness taking the oath or affirming;
* the rules associated with examination-in-chief;
* the rules associated with cross-examination and re-examination.

16.2 DEALING WITH WITNESSES BEFORE TESTIFYING

On the day of the trial both prosecution and defence teams have a number of duties in relation to their witnesses. These tasks are often given to a trainee defence solicitor or a paralegal, or for the CPS, a caseworker or a person from the witness support service.

First, each side must ensure that its witnesses are present at court and available to give evidence. A witness remains out of court until called to testify to ensure she is not influenced by hearing other evidence. This practice is subject to two exceptions: (a) an expert witness will usually be in court before testifying; and (b) the police officer in charge of the case may also be in court provided the defence consent as this recognises the officer's position as the prosecution client. The officer is available to advise the prosecutor on any issues arising during the trial.

Second, a witness should be encouraged to refresh his memory. As the witness is likely to have made his statement some months earlier to the police or a member of the defence team, while waiting to give evidence the witness should read over his statement to remind himself of the matters about which he is going to testify (see *R v Richardson* [1971] 2 QB 484). The witness should be reminded not to compare or discuss his evidence with other witnesses.

Third, a witness should be available to give evidence when called. Both sides have discretion in which order to call its witnesses, subject to s. 79 Police and Criminal Evidence Act 1984 (PACE 1984), which requires that the defendant should be called before any other defence witness.

16.3 WITNESS EVIDENCE—THE PRELIMINARY ISSUES

Once called to give evidence a number of preliminary issues will be dealt with by the court before the witness begins to testify.

16.3.1 THE PRESUMPTION IN FAVOUR OF COMPETENCY

Before a witness can testify, the court must be satisfied that the witness is competent to give evidence. A witness is competent where, as a matter of law, the court can receive his evidence. Section 53(1) Youth Justice and Criminal Evidence Act 1999 (YJCEA 1999) presumes that all witnesses are competent to testify by providing: *'At every stage in criminal proceedings all persons are (whatever their age) competent to give evidence.'* A witness may give sworn or unsworn evidence depending on age, emotional maturity and understanding. Under s. 55(2) YJCEA 1999, a witness aged 14 years and over is presumed competent to give sworn evidence where the witness has sufficient appreciation of the solemnity of the occasion and the particular responsibility of telling the truth which is involved in taking an oath. Where a witness aged 14 years and over fails the sworn evidence test, he may give unsworn evidence (s. 56(1) YJCEA 1999).

A 'child' is a witness under the age of 14 years and is presumed competent to give unsworn evidence where it appears to the court that he is able to understand questions put to him and give answers to them which can be understood. This satisfies the test of 'intelligible testimony' (s. 53(3) YJCEA 1999).

16.3.2 CHALLENGING THE COMPETENCE OF A WITNESS—S. 54 YJCEA 1999

It is rare for a party (or the court) to challenge a witness's competence and is only likely to be made against a very young or a mentally impaired witness. The application is usually made pre-trial in summary proceedings or at the Plea and Trial Preparation Hearing in the Crown Court. If made at trial, the challenge is likely to be either immediately before or after the witness has begun to testify. The challenge may relate to the witness's competence *itself* or competence to give sworn evidence. In the Crown Court the issue is determined in the jury's absence.

In deciding the issue of competence, the court may hear expert evidence and take into account whether the witness is eligible for a 'special measures direction' under s. 19 YJCEA 1999 (see paras. 16.4 and 16.5).

The issue of a child's competence to give evidence was graphically illustrated in April 2009 when a four-year-old girl, known as X, became the youngest witness ever to testify at the Old Bailey. X gave evidence under a special measures direction about being anally raped when she was under the age of three by the defendant. The charges were denied. X's examination-in-chief was received via pre-recorded video interview conducted by a specially trained police officer (see para. 16.5.5). X was cross-examined via a live-link (see para. 16.5.2). The trial judge had considered X's competence before the trial commenced. Having reviewed X's pre-recorded video and having heard evidence from experts on both sides, he concluded that X was a competent witness. In the course of the trial, X was subject to cross-examination. It is evident from the transcript of the proceedings that X struggled to answer some of the questions put in cross-examination. At the conclusion of cross-examination, defence counsel invited the judge to revisit X's competency because X's age had made it impossible to effectively cross-examine X and to put his client's case to her. The trial judge concluded that when X had been asked simple questions she had been able to answer them and was therefore competent. In summing-up, the trial judge directed the jury about the issue of the child's age, emphasising that X's reliability, credibility and truthfulness should be assessed in the same way as any other witness.

The defendant was convicted and appealed against his conviction and sentence. In dismissing the appeal, the Court of Appeal in *R v Barker* [2010] EWCA Crim 4 stated that issues about the competence of a witness to give evidence under s. 53 YJCEA 1999 was not limited to child witnesses. The provisions equally applied to the infirm or those of unsound mind. The Lord Chief Justice stated:

> 'The question is entirely witness or child specific. There are no presumptions or preconceptions. The witness need not understand the special importance that the truth should be told in court, and the witness need not understand every single question or give a readily understood answer to every

question. Many competent adult witnesses would fail such a competency test. Dealing with it broadly and fairly, provided the witness can understand the questions put to him and can also provide understandable answers, he or she is competent. If the witness cannot understand the questions or his answers to questions which he understands cannot themselves be understood he is not. The questions come, of course, from both sides. If the child is called as a witness by the prosecution he or she must have the ability to understand the questions put to him by the defence as well as the prosecution and to provide answers to them which are understandable . . . The trial process must, of course, and increasingly has, catered for the needs of child witnesses, as indeed it has increasingly catered for the use of adult witnesses whose evidence in former years would not have been heard, by, for example, the now well understood and valuable use of intermediaries. In short, the competency test is not failed because the forensic techniques of the advocate (in particular in relation to cross-examination) or the processes of the court (for example, in relation to the patient expenditure of time) have to be adapted to enable the child to give the best evidence of which he or she is capable. At the same time the right of the defendant to a fair trial must be undiminished. When the issue is whether the child is lying or mistaken in claiming that the defendant behaved indecently towards him or her, it should not be over-problematic for the advocate to formulate short, simple questions which put the essential elements of the defendant's case to the witness, and fully to ventilate before the jury the areas of evidence which bear on the child's credibility.'

In upholding Barker's conviction, the Court of Appeal concluded that the trial judge's ruling on competence had been correct.

16.3.3 COMPELLABLE WITNESSES

Where a person is competent to testify, he will also generally be compellable. A witness is compellable if, as a matter of law, he can be made to give evidence, and a failure to testify can result in the person being committed to prison for contempt of court.

There are two main exceptions to the general rule about a witness's compellability. The first exception relates to the defendant, whose position is explained in Chapter 19. The second exception relates to the defendant's spouse under s. 80 PACE 1984, which establishes that:

- The defendant's spouse or civil partner is competent and compellable to give evidence for the defence unless the spouse or civil partner is jointly charged in the proceedings (s. 80(4) PACE 1984).

- The defendant's spouse or civil partner is a competent but not a compellable prosecution witness except where the defendant is charged with:

  – an assault on, or injury or a threat of injury to, the wife, husband or civil partner or on a person who was at the material time under the age of 16; or

  – is charged with a sexual offence alleged to have been committed in respect of a person who was at the material time under the age of 16 *except* where the spouse or civil partner is jointly charged with such an offence unless he or she no longer stands to be convicted (s. 80(3) PACE 1984).

 Example

Gordon is pleading not guilty to separate offences of assaulting Rob, aged 37, and assaulting Lucy, his 15-year-old step-daughter.

Moira, who is Gordon's wife, is a competent and a compellable *defence* witness for both offences. If the *prosecution* wishes to call Moira to give evidence against Gordon, she will be a competent but not a compellable witness at Gordon's trial for assaulting Rob. If the prosecution wishes to call Moira to give evidence against Gordon at his trial for assaulting Lucy, Moira will be both competent and compellable. She will be compellable as the offence of assault on a person under the age of 16 falls within s. 80(3) PACE 1984.

16.4 TESTIFYING UNDER A SPECIAL MEASURES DIRECTION

To reduce the trauma of giving evidence, the prosecution or the defence or the court can apply under Crim PR, Part 18 for the witness to testify under a special measures direction. (The availability of special measures is also taken into account by the court when deciding a witness's competence: see para. 16.3.1.)

Special measures will be ordered where the witness is either 'vulnerable' (s. 16 YJCEA 1999) or 'intimidated' (s. 17 YJCEA 1999) and the court is satisfied that it will improve the quality of the witness's evidence (s. 19(2) YJCEA 1999).

16.4.1 VULNERABLE WITNESSES

Section 16 YJCEA 1999 defines a vulnerable witness as:

* a person under 18 at the time of the court hearing; or
* a person who has a significant impairment of intelligence and social functioning, mental disability, mental or physical disorder or a physical disability.

A vulnerable witness automatically attracts a special measures direction entitling him to a range of facilities to assist him to give oral evidence. Section 21 YJCEA 1999 provides additional safeguards for all child witnesses whilst s. 22A YJCEA 1999 makes special provision for complainants in a sexual offence where the case is to be tried in the Crown Court.

In the *Barker* case, noted at para. 16.3.2, the four-year-old rape victim testified at the Old Bailey under a special measures direction by a pre-recorded video interview (admitted as her evidence-in-chief) and cross-examination through a closed circuit television link. When conducting the witness examination the barristers removed their wigs and used their first names.

16.4.2 INTIMIDATED WITNESSES

To be eligible for a special measures direction as an intimidated witness under s. 17 YJCEA 1999, the court must be satisfied that the quality of the witness's evidence would be diminished by his fear or distress connected with testifying in the proceedings. In determining this, a court shall have regard to the following under s. 17(2):

* the nature and facts of the alleged offence;
* the witness's age;
* the witness's social and cultural background and ethnic origin;
* the witness's domestic and employment circumstances;
* the witness's religious and political beliefs;
* the behaviour of the accused and/or his family and/or his associates towards the witness; and
* any views expressed by the witness.

A complainant in a sexual offence and a witness in proceedings relating to a 'relevant' offence (this includes a wide range of violent crimes involving the use of a gun or knife) automatically fall within this section and therefore the court does not need to be satisfied that the quality of the witness's evidence will be diminished for the purposes of establishing eligibility to special measures as an intimidated witness. A witness to a 'relevant offence' can inform the court that he or she does not wish to be eligible for assistance.

Irrespective of whether the witness falls within s. 16 or s. 17, under s. 19 YJCEA 1999, the court must be sure that the special measures will improve the quality of the witness's evidence and if so decide which of the measures available will maximise the quality of the witness's testimony and whether any such measure(s) might inhibit the evidence being effectively tested.

16.5 TYPES OF SPECIAL MEASURES

The facilities available under a special measures direction depend on whether the witness is a child, a vulnerable adult or an intimidated witness and whether the appropriate facilities are available in either the Crown Court or in the magistrates' court.

→ 'Son (Jamie)

16.5.1 GIVING EVIDENCE FROM BEHIND A SCREEN—S. 23 YJCEA 1999

- Prevents the witness from being seen by the accused while testifying.

- The witness will be seen by the judge and jury or the justices and the advocates.

- The facility is available for a child, a vulnerable adult or an intimidated witness in both the Crown Court and in the magistrates' court.

→ can work for the mum & child.

16.5.2 GIVING EVIDENCE THROUGH A LIVE TELEVISION LINK—S. 24 YJCEA 1999

- This facility is available to all vulnerable and intimidated witnesses in the Crown Court and in the magistrates' court. *→ may the wife & child are so this could work,*

- A witness testifying through a live television link does not infringe the defendant's right to a fair trial under Article 6 European Convention on Human Rights 1950 (ECHR 1950) (see the House of Lords decision in *Camberwell Green Youth Court, ex p. D and Others* [2005] 2 Cr App R 1).

- The C&JA 2009 provides that when making a live-link direction, a court can also direct that a person specified by the court can accompany the witness when the witness is giving evidence by live-link. The court must take the witness's wishes into account when it determines who is to accompany the witness.

16.5.3 GIVING EVIDENCE IN PRIVATE—S. 25 YJCEA 1999

- This provision excludes from the court those persons specified in the direction where:
  - the proceedings relate to a sexual offence; or
  - it appears to the court that there are reasonable grounds for believing that any other person than the accused has sought or will seek to intimidate the witness in connection with testifying in the proceedings.

- The defendant or the defendant's legal representatives or an interpreter appointed to assist the witness or a court reporter cannot be excluded. *can help → if there are picture*

- Giving evidence in private is available for all vulnerable witnesses and intimidated witness in both the Crown Court and in the magistrates' court.

16.5.4 REMOVAL OF WIGS AND GOWNS—S. 26 YJCEA 1999

- Available for a child, a vulnerable adult or an intimidated witness in the Crown Court.

→ Son

16.5.5 VIDEO-RECORDED EVIDENCE-IN-CHIEF—S. 27 YJCEA 1999

- This special measure provides for the video recording of an interview with the witness which may be admitted as the evidence-in-chief of that witness, unless it would not be in 'the interests of justice' to allow the recording to be admitted.

→ can be used for the wife.

- A s. 27 special measure is potentially available to all vulnerable and intimidated witnesses—but special rules require that the measure should mandatorily apply to child witnesses and complainants in sexual offences that are tried in the Crown Court.

- Section 21 YJCEA 1999 (as amended by C&JA 2009) creates a primary rule requiring all child witnesses to give evidence-in-chief by a video-recorded statement and any further evidence by live-link, unless the court is satisfied that to do so will not improve the quality of that child's evidence. A child witness is allowed to 'opt out' of this 'primary rule' provided the court is satisfied, after taking into account certain factors, that not giving evidence in that way will not diminish the quality of the child's evidence.

- Also, in sexual offences to be tried in the Crown Court, s. 22A YJCEA 1999 requires that the complainant's video-recorded statement should be admitted under s. 27 where it would maximise the quality of the complainant's evidence.

 Looking Ahead

If s. 137 Criminal Justice Act 2003 (CJA 2003) comes into force, wider use could be made of video-recorded witness evidence in cases involving serious crimes to be admitted as the evidence-in-chief subject to compliance with certain conditions.

16.5.6 VIDEO-RECORDED CROSS-EXAMINATION OR RE-EXAMINATION—S. 28 YJCEA 1999

- Where the video recording is admitted as the witness's evidence-in-chief, the direction may also provide that any cross-examination or re-examination should be video-recorded.

- The recording must be made in the presence of the judge or justices and the legal representatives acting in the proceedings but not the accused.

Section 28 was piloted in three Crown Court areas from December 2013 for child witnesses of sexual offences under the age of 16 and those eligible for assistance by reason of disability. The government remains committed to a national roll-out of s. 28 and proposes that it will additionally cover adult victims of sexual offences.

16.5.7 EXAMINATION OF A WITNESS THROUGH AN INTERMEDIARY—S. 29 YJCEA 1999

- Permits the witness to be examined through an interpreter or through any other person as the court may direct.

- Available to all vulnerable witnesses in the Crown Court and in certain magistrates' courts.

16.5.8 AIDS TO COMMUNICATION—S. 30 YJCEA 1999

- This facility permits the witness while testifying to be provided with such a device as the court considers appropriate to enable questions to be put to the witness or receive answers from him to overcome any disorder or disability or other impairment.

- Available to all vulnerable witnesses in the Crown Court and a magistrates' court.

16.5.9 ANONYMOUS WITNESS EVIDENCE

Anonymous witness orders are available to deal with the problem of witness intimidation. Section 86 of Coroners and Justice Act 2009 provides that:

- The court may make an anonymous witness order where it considers appropriate to ensure the identity of a witness in the proceedings is not disclosed (s. 86(1)).

- The order will specify the type of special measures to be made under s. 86(1) to secure the witness's anonymity including:

  - withholding a witness's name (s. 86(2)(a));

  - permitting the witness to use a pseudonym (s. 86(2)(b));

  - screening the witness (s. 86(2)(d)); and

  - disguising the witness's voice by modulation (s. 86(2)(d)).

- Section 86(4) requires a witness who is subject to an anonymous witness order to be seen by the judge and other members of the court, the jury (if there is one) and any other person appointed to assist the court such as an interpreter.

- Section 87 permits an application for an anonymous witness order to be made by either the prosecution or by the defence although a defence application would require the identity of the witness to be disclosed to the prosecution.

- The conditions for making an order are set out in s. 88: an order may be made if three conditions are met:

  - Condition A (s. 88(3)): that the order is necessary to:

    (a) protect the safety of the witness or another person or to prevent any serious damage to property (a court must have regard to the witness's reasonable fear of these consequences if identified); or

    (b) prevent real harm to the public interest;

  - Condition B (s. 88(4)): that having regard to all the circumstances the measures would be consistent with a defendant receiving a fair trial; and

  - Condition C (s. 88(5)): the importance of the witness's testimony is such that the witness ought to testify; and:

    (a) the witness would not testify unless the order was made; or

    (b) there would be real harm to the public interest if the witness were to testify without the order being made.

- In deciding whether Conditions A–C are met, s. 88(2) requires a court to have regard to:

  (a) the defendant's general right to know a witness's identity;

  (b) the extent to which a witness's credibility is a relevant factor in the case;

  (c) whether evidence given by the witness may be the sole or decisive evidence;

  (d) whether the witness's evidence may be properly tested without his identity being disclosed;

  (e) whether there is any reason to believe that the witness:

    (i) has a tendency to be dishonest, or

    (ii) has any motive to be dishonest in the circumstances of the case, having regard (in particular) to any previous convictions of the witness and to any relationship between the witness and the defendant or any associates of the defendant;

  (f) whether it would be reasonably practicable to protect the witness by any means other than by making a witness anonymity order specifying the measures that are under consideration by the court.

- In jury trials a further safeguard is provided by s. 90 where the judge is required to give the jury an appropriate warning to ensure that the defendant is not prejudiced by a witness giving evidence anonymously.

For the first judicial guidance on witness anonymity orders see *R v Mayers and Others* [2008] EWCA Crim 1418.

16.5.10 PROCEDURE FOR SEEKING A SPECIAL MEASURES DIRECTION

Detailed rules on the procedure and time limits for applying for a special measures direction are contained in Crim PR, Part 18. In the Crown Court, the prosecution should serve the notice of application on the defendant and the court within 28 days of the case sent bundle. In summary cases, the notice should be served within 14 days of the defendant indicating a not guilty plea. A party opposing the application must serve the notice of opposition within 14 days of the date upon which the application was served on him. The magistrates' court or Crown Court will make directions as to the date for service as part of its case management duties (see Chapter 12, para. 12.6.2 and Chapter 13, para. 13.5.3). Applications for a special measures direction can be made out of time and can be made orally at the trial. The application for a special measures direction can be found in the forms section on the Criminal Procedure Rules web pages Part 18 (https://www.justice.gov.uk/courts/procedure-rules/criminal/forms-2015).

Limited special measures are available to some eligible defendants and are considered in Chapter 19, para. 19.3.1.

16.5.11 USE OF LIVE-LINK OTHER THAN FOR VULNERABLE WITNESSES

Section 51 CJA 2003 permits a court to allow any witnesses (other than the defendant) to give evidence by a live-link from any suitable facility (it is not limited to those in a court building) if the court is satisfied that it is in the interests of the efficient and effective administration of justice and where the necessary facilities are already available. In deciding whether to give a direction the court must consider all the circumstances of the case and a list of statutory factors under s. 51(7). The provision is appropriate for witnesses with limited availability, such as professional witnesses, or those with mobility issues who do not qualify for live-links under the 1999 Act. The written application requesting a witness to give evidence via live-link should be made at the earliest opportunity, stating the grounds upon which such application is made by reference to the factors listed in s. 51(7). Increasingly you will find police officers giving evidence to magistrates' courts via live video feeds in a bid to save their time.

16.6 THE PRACTICAL ISSUES OF WITNESS EVIDENCE

Good case preparation will have identified and anticipated any problems that might arise about the competence of a witness and the need for special measures.

The difficulties encountered with the competence and credibility of the main prosecution witness during the first well-publicised Damilola Taylor murder trial is a good illustration of what might happen when potentially important issues relating to witnesses are not properly addressed during case preparation. Damilola Taylor was a ten-year-old schoolboy who bled to death in November 2000 on the stairwell of a block of flats on the North Peckham Estate in south London. Two 16-year-old brothers were charged with murder. In pleading not guilty, the defence claimed the boy had injured himself accidentally.

A key prosecution witness was a 14-year-old girl, known only as witness Bromley, who claimed that she had witnessed the attack. However, the reliability of her testimony was tainted after it was suggested in cross-examination that she was only giving evidence to claim a £50,000 reward offered by the *Daily Mail* in connection with the conviction of Damilola's murderers. As a result of the attacks on the witness's credibility, the prosecution case collapsed and the brothers were acquitted. Since 2008, a CPS lawyer can carry out an audio-taped pre-trial witness interview, if felt to be necessary, and in accordance with the prescribed guidelines. It is easier for a defence solicitor to assess credibility issues in relation to a defence witness as the defence team will have direct contact with the witness.

16.7 TAKING THE OATH OR AFFIRMING

Once any preliminaries have been dealt with but before testifying, the witness will take the oath or affirm. Where the witness is a religious observer, s. 1 Oaths Act 1978 allows the oath to be taken on the New Testament or in the case of a Jewish witness, on the Old Testament. The witness will be required to state: 'I swear by Almighty God . . .' and then the appropriate form of words as prescribed by law.

Where the witness follows another faith, an appropriate form of oath will be taken. For example, a Muslim witness is sworn on the Koran 'I swear by Allah . . .'. A Sikh will swear on the Sunder Gutka 'I swear by Waheguru . . .'.

If the witness refuses to take an oath or the oath is contrary to his religion, s. 5 Oaths Act 1978 allows the witness to make a solemn affirmation in the following form: 'I [name] do solemnly, sincerely and truly declare and affirm . . .'.

Having been sworn or affirmed, the party calling the witness will begin the examination-in-chief.

16.8 EXAMINATION-IN-CHIEF

This is the stage where the advocate questions her own witness with the following purposes:

- to obtain answers from the witness about his factual evidence which supports the party's case;
- to put questions to the witness which enhance the witness's personal credibility;
- to raise any matters which the advocate anticipates might be raised in cross-examination.

Having previously taken the witness's statement when events were fresh in the witness's memory, the advocate expects the answers to be consistent with his written statement. A question should not be asked in examination-in-chief to which the witness or the advocate does not know the answer!

16.8.1 LEADING QUESTIONS

Leading questions are not generally permitted in examination-in-chief. A leading question either suggests to the witness the answer desired by the advocate or assumes the existence of disputed facts that have not yet been satisfactorily proven.

 Example

Consider these examples of leading questions.

'The car you saw the defendant drive away from the crime scene was a blue Ford Escort, wasn't it?'

'Is it correct to suggest that when you saw the defendant she was acting suspiciously?'

These questions clearly offend the rule against leading questions, as the witness is led into giving the answer the advocate desires.

Where a leading question is asked in error, the judge or the magistrates' adviser will suggest to the advocate that the question should be put differently. There are two situations where leading questions are permitted. First, at the start of a witness's testimony leading questions are permitted about introductory matters, such as the witness's name, address and occupation. Second, leading questions can be asked to establish a fact that is not in dispute between the parties.

Consider the following short illustration of an examination-in-chief.

Example

In a prosecution for a domestic assault the prosecutor could start his examination-in-chief of the complainant in the following way:

Q: Mrs Dougherty, can you recall what you were doing in the early evening of 6 April?

A: Yes. I was at home preparing supper.

Q: Who else was at home with you?

A: My children. They were upstairs playing with their computer games.

Q: Was your husband home at this time?

A: No. He was down the pub.

Q: What time did your husband come home?

A: He came home at around 7.30 in the evening.

Q: Can you describe your husband's demeanour when he came in?

A: I'm sorry, I don't understand the question.

Q: Can you tell the court what you observed about your husband when he walked in?

A: I could tell he was drunk.

Q: How could you tell he was drunk?

A: He was unsteady on his feet and he smelt of alcohol.

Q: In your own words can you tell the court what happened next . . .

16.8.2 THE WITNESS REFRESHING HIS MEMORY

Under s. 139 CJA 2003, a witness can refresh his memory from a document or transcript of a sound recording at any stage while testifying, provided:

- the document was made or verified by the witness on an earlier occasion; and
- the witness states in his oral evidence that the document records his recollection of the matter at the earlier time; and
- his recollection of the matters about which he is testifying is likely to have been significantly better at that time than it is at the time of his oral evidence.

Before the witness uses the document, it must be produced for inspection by the court and by the opposing advocate. Where the witness is cross-examined on those parts of the document which the witness used to refresh his memory, the document does not form part of the evidence in the case.

Where the cross-examiner strays outside those parts of the document that the witness used to refresh his memory, the whole document may be put in evidence to be considered by the jury/magistrates as evidence of the truth of what it states (s. 120(3) CJA 2003). If the document fails to refresh the witness's memory, it cannot be admitted as evidence of the truth of matters stated in the case (*R v Chinn* [2012] EWCA Crim 501).

 Example

The most commonly encountered memory-refreshing document is a police officer's notebook. Where the officer wishes to refresh his memory during examination-in-chief, it is customary for the following exchange to take place between the advocate and the officer.

Police officer: 'May I refer to my pocket book?'

Advocate: 'When did you make up your pocket book, officer?'

Police officer: 'When I returned to the police station.'

Advocate: 'Were the events still fresh in your mind when you made up your pocket book?'

Police officer: 'Yes they were.'

The court usher will then pass the notebook to be inspected by the court and the defence advocate. The defence advocate should carefully note the parts used by the officer to refresh his memory and should restrict cross-examination to those parts to avoid the whole document becoming part of the evidence in the case.

16.8.3 ADMITTING A WITNESS'S PREVIOUS CONSISTENT STATEMENT

In a criminal trial the 'best' evidence is a witness giving oral testimony in court of facts within the witness's personal knowledge. There is a general common law rule excluding previous consistent (or self-serving) statements. Such previous consistent statements are deemed to have little or no evidential value (*R v Roberts* [1942] 1 All ER 187)). However, there are several exceptions to the general rule where a witness's previous consistent statement may be admitted. The exceptions have largely been codified by s. 120 CJA 2003.

Under s. 120 CJA 2003 a witness's previous consistent statement can be admitted as evidence of any matter stated in it in order to rebut the allegation that the witness's evidence has been recently fabricated, s. 120(2) CJA 2003 (this is dealt with at para. 16.11 in the context of re-examination)

Providing the conditions under s. 120(4) are satisfied (namely that while giving evidence the witness indicates that to the best of his belief he made the statement, and that to the best of his belief it states the truth), a witness's previous consistent statement can also be admitted as evidence of facts stated in the following situations:

- the statement identifies or describes a person, object, or place, s. 120(4) and (5) (the obvious application of this would be a witness's previous identification of an accused at an identification procedure);

- the statement was made by the witness when the matters stated were fresh in his memory but he does not remember them, and cannot reasonably be expected to remember them, well enough to give oral evidence of them in the proceedings (s. 120(4) and (6));

- where the victim of the alleged crime has made a previous statement about the commission of the alleged offence against her to another person and the statement was not made as a result of a threat or promise (s. 120(4) and (7)). This is known as making a previous complaint. A previous complaint can only be admitted into evidence if the complainant gives oral evidence in connection with its subject matter.

A previous consistent statement admitted under s. 120 CJA 2003 can be admitted as evidence of the truth of its content as well as evidence of the witness's consistency. It will be a matter for the jury or magistrates to determine how much weight should be attached to the earlier statement.

 Example

Gill is the victim of a street robbery. Heavily traumatised by the incident, she goes home and tells her brother Chris about the robbery and describes the assailant.

Under s. 120(7) CJA 2003, evidence of the conversation may be admitted in evidence at the trial of the person accused of robbing Gill, providing Gill gives a first-hand account of what occurred. Where Gill's previous consistent statement is admitted under s. 120(7) CJA 2003, it is admissible as evidence of the truth of the statement's contents—that is, that Gill was the victim of a street robbery committed by the person Gill described to her brother.

Debbie claims to have been raped by a man she met over the internet. Two days after the alleged rape, Debbie confides to her best friend Rosie that she has been raped but begs her not to tell anyone because she (Debbie) cannot come to terms with what has happened. Debbie makes a formal complaint to the police several weeks later leading to Robert being arrested and charged. Robert's defence is consent. At trial, and assuming Debbie gives evidence, the prosecution will be able to call Rosie to give evidence of Debbie's earlier complaint under s. 120(7) CJA 2003.

16.8.4 **UNFAVOURABLE OR HOSTILE WITNESS**

At an early stage in the proceedings the prosecution and the defence will take a proof of evidence from each witness it intends to call to give evidence to support its case at trial. Most witnesses will give the answers expected of them and their oral evidence will be consistent with their earlier statement. In this situation, a witness is said to 'come up to proof'. Where a witness does not give the answers expected of him during examination-in-chief he may be either 'unfavourable' or 'hostile'.

An unfavourable witness is a witness who does not 'come up to proof'. This means the witness cannot, for whatever reason, recall a fact(s) about his testimony even after refreshing his memory. The advocate cannot assist the witness by asking leading questions or by prompting him—even though the witness's inability to answer his questions may damage his side's case. It is good practice to get an unfavourable witness out of the witness box as soon as possible—subject to the other party's right to cross-examine the witness.

While an unfavourable witness can be damaging, a more serious situation arises for the advocate when a witness turns hostile. A witness is hostile where he shows no desire to tell the truth in support of the party calling him. An example would be where, in his oral testimony, the witness deliberately and maliciously changes his evidence from what was contained in his written statement or conveniently can 'no longer recall the incident'.

In the Crown Court, if the advocate believes his witness is hostile, the advocate will apply to the judge in the jury's absence for leave to treat the witness as hostile. In summary proceedings a submission is made to the District Judge or magistrates.

The judge or magistrates will then be shown the witness's previous written statement to support the application to have the witness ruled as hostile. The court will then decide whether the witness is hostile or merely unfavourable by considering the witness's demeanour, attitude and any other relevant factor.

Where the witness is ruled hostile:

- the advocate may cross-examine his witness; and/or

- the advocate may ask his witness whether or not he has made an earlier statement which is inconsistent with his present oral testimony—s. 3 Criminal Procedure Act 1865.

Where the witness adopts his earlier written statement as his evidence or the written statement is proven against him, the statement becomes evidence of any matter stated in it of which oral evidence would have been admissible (s. 119(1) CJA 2003).

 Example

Josef is being prosecuted for assaulting his wife, Sandra. The police were called to the couple's home and witnessed Sandra in a state of distress with a split, bleeding lip. In her initial statement to the police Sandra states that Josef assaulted her whilst he was in a drunken rage. Shortly before summary trial, Sandra and Josef are reconciled. Having taken the oath in the witness box, Sandra testifies that she cannot recall the incident. What can the prosecutor do in this situation?

The prosecutor can apply to the magistrates to have Sandra declared hostile. The magistrates will be shown Sandra's earlier signed statement and will have observed her demeanour in the witness box. If Sandra is declared to be a hostile witness, the prosecutor will ask Sandra if she has made a statement on an earlier occasion which is inconsistent with what she is now saying on oath. Sandra may say that the content of her earlier statement is untrue. Having established that Sandra made the earlier inconsistent statement, it will be a matter for the magistrates trying the case to decide where the truth lies and whether, in the circumstances, they can convict Josef beyond reasonable doubt on the basis of the earlier statement alone.

16.9 **CROSS-EXAMINATION**

Cross-examination is where the advocate questions the other side's witness and has the following purposes:

- to obtain factual evidence from the witness which supports the case of the cross-examiner; and
- to test the truthfulness of the evidence the witness has given in examination-in-chief or to cast doubt on the witness's evidence; and
- to undermine the witness's credibility.

16.9.1 **CHALLENGING THE WITNESS'S FACTUAL EVIDENCE**

Where in cross-examination the advocate contradicts the witness's factual evidence, the cross-examiner should put his client's version of the facts to the witness to give the witness the opportunity to explain the contradiction. A failure to cross-examine a witness on his factual evidence is taken by the court as accepting the witness's evidence-in-chief on that issue.

Questions asked in cross-examination are not restricted to issues arising in examination-in-chief but may be directed to any fact in issue or to attacking the witness's credibility.

Leading questions are not only allowed but are essential for effective cross-examination. Consider the following example of cross-examination.

 Example

Continuing the example of the domestic violence assault highlighted earlier in the context of examination-in-chief, the defence advocate might cross-examine the complainant as follows:

Q: It's simply not true is it, Mrs Dougherty, that your husband launched an unprovoked attack on you?

A: He did.

Q: In fact it was you who had been drinking, hadn't you Mrs Dougherty?

A: No.

Q: Your husband says there was a half empty bottle of vodka on the kitchen table.

A: It's not true.

Q: Is it true that you have had counselling for drink problems in the recent past?

A: I have been depressed. I wasn't drunk.

Q: So you accept you sometimes drink to escape your problems?

A: I sometimes have a drink but I wasn't drunk.

Q: In fact you have been having a lot of problems in your marriage recently, haven't you?

A: Yes.

Q: Your husband has been seeing someone else, hasn't he, and that must have made you feel very angry and hurt.

A: He assaulted me.

Q: Your husband was intending to leave you that night, wasn't he?

A: I don't know.

Q: When he came in to the house it was with the intention of collecting some personal belongings, wasn't it?

A: No—he asked me why his supper wasn't ready. He started shouting at me like he always does.

Q: No—that's not how it happened, is it? You tried to stop him getting past you. He pushed you to one side and you lost your temper, didn't you?

A further example of the way in which witness testimony is obtained in court is provided in the *R v Lenny Wise* case study in relation to the eye-witness, Shirley Lewis. The complete version can be accessed in our online resources.

A: No.

Q: You lost your temper and attacked him. In defending himself he pushed you back and you fell against the kitchen sink—that's how you cut your head, isn't it?

16.9.2 ATTACKING THE WITNESS'S CREDIBILITY

The cross-examiner may also attack the witness's credibility to persuade the jury or the magistrates to give little or no weight to the witness's oral evidence by suggesting the witness is biased or has previous convictions. Matters affecting the credibility of a witness's evidence are said to be collateral issues in the case and subject to the finality rule which means that evidence cannot be called to rebut the witness's answer.

However, as exceptions to the finality rule, the cross-examining advocate is allowed to adduce evidence to contradict the answer given by the witness where he has suggested the witness:

• is biased; or

• has made a previous inconsistent statement; or

• has previous convictions (s. 100 CJA 2003); or

• suffers from a physical or mental disability.

16.9.3 PROVING A PREVIOUS INCONSISTENT STATEMENT

In cross-examination the defence advocate will have a copy of the prosecution witness's earlier statement disclosed under the pre-trial disclosure of evidence rules (see Chapter 8) and will expect answers that are consistent with the witness's written statement. However, where the witness gives answers that are inconsistent with his earlier written statement, s. 5 Criminal Procedure Act 1865 permits the witness to be cross-examined about those parts of his written statement that are inconsistent with his oral evidence.

If the witness denies that he made a written statement that is inconsistent with his present oral testimony and the advocate wishes to contradict the witness, the advocate must draw the witness's attention to those parts of his statement that are inconsistent with his oral testimony. The witness will then be asked whether he wishes the court to adopt the version of his evidence contained in the written statement or his oral evidence.

Section 4 Criminal Procedure Act 1865 provides a similar provision in relation to an inconsistency between a witness's previous oral statement and his oral testimony in court. The cross-examiner can point out the inconsistencies to the witness and ask him which version he wishes the court to adopt as his evidence.

Section 119(1) CJA 2003 provides that where a previous inconsistent statement is proved, the statement becomes evidence of any matter stated in it of which oral evidence would have been admissible. The jury or magistrates must decide where the truth lies. Whether the witness offers an explanation for the inconsistency or not, his credibility is undermined.

16.9.4 ADMISSIBILITY OF A NON-DEFENDANT'S BAD CHARACTER—S. 100 CJA 2003

Either party may adduce evidence of a witness's previous convictions or other bad character evidence to undermine the witness's credibility. The rules governing the admission of bad character of both the defendant and non-defendants were substantially reformed by the CJA 2003. The provisions that apply to a defendant can be found in s. 101 CJA 2003 and are considered at length in Chapter 19. The rules relating to the admissibility of non-defendant bad character are contained in s. 100 CJA 2003, which provides:

'(1) In criminal proceedings evidence of the bad character of a person other than the defendant is admissible if and only if—

(a) it is important explanatory evidence;

(b) it has substantial probative value in relation to a matter which—

    (i) is a matter in issue in the proceedings, and

    (ii) is of substantial importance in the context of the case as a whole;

    or

    (c) all parties to the proceedings agree to the evidence being admissible.'

Section 100 applies not only to the witnesses in the case but to any person other than the defendant. In most cases an application under s. 100 will relate to a witness and can be made by either the prosecution or the defence.

The following conditions apply before the evidence of a non-defendant's bad character can be admitted.

(1) The evidence must fall within the definition of bad character under s. 98 CJA 2003

Bad character is defined in s. 98 CJA 2003 as:

- evidence of or a disposition towards misconduct other than evidence which has to do with the alleged facts of the offence for which the defendant is charged; or

- evidence of misconduct in connection with the investigation or prosecution of that offence.

Section 98 clearly covers a witness's previous convictions or other disreputable conduct which, if heard by the court, would undermine the witness's credibility. As s. 98 specifically excludes conduct related to the facts of the offence being tried, it would not be necessary for the defence to seek leave to question the investigating police officer that she planted the evidence on the defendant or that she fabricated the defendant's confession. These suggestions clearly relate to evidence of misconduct during the investigation. Arguably, no leave is required where a defendant suggests the witness committed the crime as this would be questioning to do with the alleged facts of the offence.

(2) Leave must be granted by the court to admit the evidence

If the evidence falls within s. 98, the court's leave must be granted before evidence of a non-defendant's bad character may be adduced—unless the parties agree to the bad character evidence being disclosed (s. 100(1)(c) CJA 2003).

A party seeking leave will be required to give notice to the court in accordance with Crim PR, Part 21.3. The party who receives the notice may oppose the application by giving notice in writing. Such matters can be dealt with at trial or more likely at a pre-trial hearing.

(3) The reasons for admitting a non-defendant's bad character

Leave will only be granted if the court is satisfied that the bad character evidence should be admitted because:

- it is important as explanatory evidence (s. 100(1)(a) CJA 2003); or

- it has substantial probative value in relation to a matter raised in the proceedings and is of substantial importance in the context of the case as a whole (s. 100(1)(b) CJA 2003).

(a) Important as explanatory evidence (s. 100(1)(a) CJA 2003)

A non-defendant's bad character will only be admitted as explanatory evidence where, without it, the court would find it impossible or difficult to properly understand the other evidence in the case and its value for understanding the case as a whole is substantial. In some situations it will be necessary for a party to give explanatory background information to the offence, which may result in part or the whole of the witness's bad character being disclosed.

 Example

Nigel is charged with arson by starting a fire in the hostel for resettling young offenders in which he was living at the time of the alleged offence. Nigel has previous convictions for dishonesty and drug-related offences. He denies the offence.

Wasswa testifies for the prosecution that on the day of the fire, he saw Nigel storing five large containers of barbeque fuel and firelighters under his bed. In providing the court with the background facts of the arson offence, the prosecutor will refer to the fact that Wasswa was residing at the hostel. This will obviously imply that Wasswa has a criminal record. In this situation it will be unnecessary for the prosecution to disclose full details of that criminal record.

(b) The evidence has substantial probative value in relation to a matter in the proceedings (s. 100(1)(b) CJA 2003)

Section 100(1)(b) permits the admission of a non-defendant's bad character into evidence only where it satisfies the test of enhanced relevance. Evidence relating to the credibility of a witness falls within s. 100 (*R v Weir* [2006] 1 WLR 1885). Evidence that has only marginal value or no real significance or goes to a trivial or minor issue in the case may not be admissible.

In deciding the 'substantial probative value' test, s. 100(3)(a), (b) and (c) CJA 2003 set out a non-exhaustive list of factors for the court to consider, including:

- the nature and number of the events or other things to which the evidence relates;
- when those events or things are alleged to have happened or existed;
- that it is evidence of the person's misconduct and it is suggested that the evidence has probative value by reason of the similarity between that misconduct and other misconduct.

To highlight some of the potential difficulties in the operation of s. 100, we include some worked examples for you to consider.

 Example 1

Consider the earlier example of Nigel, accused of starting a fire in a hostel for the resettling of young offenders. Nigel denies the offence and states Wasswa is responsible. Wasswa has previous convictions for arson. Nigel wishes to adduce evidence of Wasswa's previous convictions. Arguably, Nigel does not require leave to accuse Wasswa of having committed the offence, since it has to do with the alleged facts (s. 98 CJA 2003). In substantiating that allegation, Nigel would want to adduce evidence of Wasswa's propensity to cause damage by fire as Wasswa's propensity is clearly relevant to Nigel's defence. If this falls within the definition of s. 98 CJA 2003, leave will not be required. If it does not and the parties do not agree, leave will be required.

Alternatively Nigel might deny the offence and simply accuse Wasswa of lying when he states he saw Nigel storing lighter fuel under his bed. If Wasswa's previous convictions relate to criminal damage and drug misuse, it is difficult to see how these can be said to have substantial relevance in relation to the issues in this case. If Wasswa's previous convictions, however, related to theft and burglary, they would arguably assume the necessary substantial probative value as they cast Wasswa's credibility as a witness in a different light.

 Example 2

Dominic is on trial for burglary. He calls Andrew to give evidence of alibi. Andrew has two recent convictions for dishonesty. Will the prosecution be able to put these convictions to Andrew? If the defence does not agree, the prosecution will seek leave under s. 100 CJA 2003. Arguably the previous convictions cast doubt on the credibility of Andrew who is obviously an important defence witness.

Guidance on the application of s. 100(1)(b) CJA 2003 is provided by *R v Brewster and Cromwell* [2010] EWCA Crim 1194. The Court of Appeal observed:

'. . . the purpose of section 100 was to remove from the criminal trial the right to introduce by cross-examination old or irrelevant or trivial behaviour in an attempt unfairly to diminish in the eyes of the tribunal of fact the standing of the witness or to permit unsubstantiated attacks on credit.'

In relation to the test that ought to be applied, the Court of Appeal further observed:

> 'The first question for the trial judge under section 100(1) (b) is whether creditworthiness is a matter in issue which is of substantial importance in the context of the case as a whole. This is a significant hurdle. Just because a witness has convictions does not mean that the opposing party is entitled to attack the witness' credibility. If it is shown that creditworthiness is an issue of substantial importance, the second question is whether the bad character relied upon is of substantial probative value in relation to that issue. Whether convictions have persuasive value on the issue of creditworthiness will, it seems to us, depend principally on the nature, number and age of the convictions. However, we do not consider that the conviction must, in order to qualify for admission in evidence, demonstrate any tendency towards dishonesty or untruthfulness. The question is whether a fair-minded tribunal would regard them as affecting the worth of the witness' evidence.'

(c) Practical issues associated with s. 100 CJA 2003

Unless the parties agree to the admission of a non-defendant's bad character, s. 100(1)(a) or (b) CJA 2003 is triggered. When considering a defence application to admit the bad character of a prosecution witness, the judge will be mindful of the risk of appeal in the event of conviction if the application is refused. It should be remembered that generally there is no burden of proof on the defendant. All the defendant has to do to be acquitted is to raise a reasonable doubt and for this reason it is likely to be easier for the defence to demonstrate that the line of questioning has substantial probative value in support of the defence case to undermine the credibility of a prosecution witness (*R v Weir* [2006] 1 WLR 1885).

More significantly, both prosecutors and defence advocates will be aware that if leave is granted and evidence of a prosecution witness's bad character is admitted, on the tit-for-tat principle, the defendant's previous convictions may be disclosed under s. 101(1)(g) CJA 2003 (see Chapter 19). A steady stream of case law on bad character is emerging. If it is relevant to your core Criminal Litigation course or to your elective in Advanced Criminal Litigation you can access the 'Bad Character Case Compendium' which is held on the student resource section of our online resources. The compendium contains a summary of the most important cases on bad character to date, including some recent cases on s. 100 CJA 2003.

Finally, you should be aware that questioning a witness with a view to exposing wrongdoing is subject to *Principles 1* and *2* of the Solicitors Code of Conduct 2019.

16.10 CROSS-EXAMINING THE WITNESS ON HIS PHYSICAL OR MENTAL DISABILITY

Medical evidence may be introduced during cross-examination to prove that the witness suffers from a physical or mental disability that may undermine the accuracy of his testimony (*Toohey v Metropolitan Police Commissioner* [1965] AC 595). The law requires the evidence of unreliability to come from a recognised medical specialist so that if you intend to challenge an aspect of a witness's physical or psychiatric fitness to give evidence, you will have to instruct an expert witness to testify.

Example

The witness states that she saw the defendant at a distance of 100 metres breaking into a car. There is evidence to suggest the witness was not wearing her glasses at the time. To rebut this identification, evidence could be introduced by the defence to prove that the witness is short-sighted and cannot see any further than 40 metres without corrective lenses.

16.11 **RE-EXAMINATION**

The third stage of witness testimony is re-examination, where the party calling the witness may ask further questions of the witness following cross-examination. Re-examination enables the advocate to repair the damage done to the witness's credibility during cross-examination and to explain any confusion or ambiguities in the witness's evidence. Leading questions are not permitted because, as with examination-in-chief, the advocate is dealing with his own witness. Re-examination is confined to matters arising out of cross-examination. The advocate cannot ask the witness about a matter he omitted to cover in examination-in-chief.

As noted in para. 16.8.3, an issue that may arise during re-examination is where, in cross-examination, it was suggested that the witness has recently made up or fabricated his evidence. This is a potentially serious attack on the witness's credibility and re-examination provides an opportunity to rebut this allegation of recent fabrication. Section 120(2) CJA 2003 permits the witness's previous statement to be admitted in evidence to show that his evidence has not been recently made up. Where the previous consistent statement is admitted, it becomes evidence of the truth of the matters stated in it. See *R v Oyesiku* (1971) 56 Cr App R 240 for an example of where an allegation of recent fabrication was rebutted.

16.12 **CROSS-EXAMINING THE COMPLAINANT IN A SEXUAL OFFENCE**

Special rules apply to the cross-examination of a complainant in a sexual offence. The rules contained in ss. 41–43 YJCEA 1999 prohibit a defendant from asking a complainant about any of his or her past sexual behaviour involving the defendant or any other person, except with the leave of the court in defined circumstances. The law was unsuccessfully challenged as being incompatible with a defendant's right to a fair trial in the leading authority of *A (No 2)* [2002] 1 AC 45. These complex rules are outside the scope of this work but may be researched in the current edition of *Blackstone's Criminal Practice*.

KEY POINT SUMMARY

- All witnesses are presumed to be competent to give evidence.

- Know the test that a witness has to satisfy to be competent and to be able to give sworn evidence or unsworn evidence.

- Anticipate and be prepared to argue against any challenges to the competence of your witnesses and to raise argument as to the competency of an opposing party's witness.

- Be aware that special measures and/or anonymous witness orders are available to assist vulnerable or intimidated witnesses to give evidence.

- Know the practice and procedure for applying for a special measures direction and/or an anonymous witness order and the facilities that are available.

- Be aware of the purposes of examination-in-chief and the need to prepare questions that will elicit answers from the witness that are favourable to your case.

- Know the general rule against asking leading questions in examination-in-chief and the limited circumstances in which leading questions are permitted.

- Be aware of the purpose of cross-examination and the purpose of the advocate being permitted to ask leading questions.

- Understand that s. 100 CJA 2003 now regulates the admissibility of evidence of a non-defendant's bad character and that, in the absence of agreement between the parties, leave of the court in accordance with s. 100 is required.

- Be aware of the purpose of re-examination and its limitations.

SELF-TEST QUESTIONS

1. David is charged with sexual assault on his step-daughter, Florence, aged 14. Florence has learning difficulties. David is pleading not guilty. The prosecution has witness statements from Susie, David's wife, and their son, Aaron, aged 7.

   (a) Is Susie a competent and compellable witness for the prosecution?

   (b) Which type of evidence will Florence be presumed competent to give?

   (c) Consider why there may be doubts about Florence's competence to give this type or any other type of evidence.

   (d) Which type of evidence will Aaron be presumed competent to give?

   (e) What provisions are there to assist Florence and Aaron to give evidence?

2. Are leading questions permitted during examination-in-chief?

3. What conditions are required by s. 139 CJA 2003 for a document to be used by a witness to refresh his memory during examination-in-chief?

4. Explain the purposes of cross-examination.

5. (a) Kyle is on trial for grievous bodily harm. The incident occurred in a nightclub. The victim is Ben. Chris, a key witness for the prosecution, is a good friend of Ben. Kyle states he acted in self-defence when he was attacked by Ben and Chris. Ben has a recent previous conviction for affray committed during a disturbance in a town centre. Chris has recent previous convictions for public order offences and assault. Should Kyle be allowed to adduce evidence of these previous convictions?

   (b) If the facts in the scenario in (a) are changed such that Chris has a previous conviction for perverting the course of justice (he gave false particulars to the police in order to avoid a driving-related prosecution), would leave be granted to put this conviction to the witness?

Case study: *R v Lenny Wise*

With reference to the *R v Lenny Wise* case study, consider whether any of the potential witnesses in this case might qualify in terms of a special measures direction.

Analysis of all the above questions can be found in our online resources.

FIGURE 16.1 WITNESS COMPETENCE AND COMPELLABILITY

COMPETENCY

- A witness is competent where as a matter of law his evidence can be received by the court;

- all witnesses are presumed competent to give evidence (s. 53(1) YJCEA 1999);

- a witnesses aged 14 years and above will be presumed competent to give sworn evidence;

- a witness aged under 14 years will be presumed competent to give unsworn evidence;

- where a witness's competence is challenged, s. 54 YJCEA 1999 lays down the procedure for the court to decide the issue;

- the court must be satisfied that the witness is able to understand questions put to him and give answers to them which can be understood (s. 53(3) YJCEA 1999);

- a witness may be granted the benefit of a special measures direction before a determination as to competency is made (s. 54(3) YJCEA 1999).

COMPELLABILITY

- A witness is compellable where he can be made to give evidence and a failure to testify may result in him suffering a penalty;

- generally, all witnesses are competent and compellable for the prosecution, except:

  - the defendant and co-defendant; and

  - the defendant's spouse BUT see s. 80(3) PACE 1984.

SPECIAL MEASURES DIRECTION, S. 19 YJCEA 1999

- A special measures direction seeks to reduce the trauma of a 'vulnerable' or an 'intimidated' witness to give evidence;

- s. 16 YJCEA 1999 defines a 'vulnerable' witness as:

  - a witness under 18 years; or

  - a witness who suffers from significant impairment of intelligence and social functioning;

- s. 17 YJCEA 1999 defines an intimidated witness as:

  - a witness whose quality of evidence is diminished by fear or distress associated with testifying;

- where a special measures direction is made under s. 19 YJCEA 1999, the court may order the following, subject to availability:

  - witness may give evidence from behind a screen, s. 23 YJCEA 1999;

  - witness may give evidence through a live TV link, s. 24 YJCEA 1999;

  - witness may give evidence in private, s. 25 YJCEA 1999;

  - removal of lawyers' wigs, s. 26 YJCEA 1999;

  - witness may video-record his evidence-in-chief, s. 27 YJCEA 1999;

  - witness may video-record his cross-examination and re-examination, s. 28 YJCEA 1999;

  - witness may give evidence through an intermediary, s. 29 YJCEA 1999;

  - witness may give evidence with the benefit of a communication aid, s. 30 YJCEA 1999;

- witness anonymity orders are subject to special rules.

FIGURE 16.2 WITNESS TESTIMONY

EXAMINATION-IN-CHIEF

- Purpose of questions in examination-in-chief is to:
  - elicit factual evidence which supports the party's case;
  - enhance the witness's personal credibility;
  - anticipate issues to be raised in cross-examination.
- Leading questions are generally not permitted.

Memory refreshing by a witness

- S. 139 CJA 2003 permits a witness to refresh his memory from a document made or verified by him if he states:
  - the document records his recollection at an earlier time; and
  - his recollection of the matter is likely to have been significantly better at that time.

Admissibility of previous consistent statements by a witness

- S. 120 CJA 2003 permits evidence of the witness's previous consistent statement to be admitted as evidence of its truth, including where the victim of the crime made a voluntary complaint to another person, s. 120(7) CJA 2003.

Unfavourable witness

- Is a witness who cannot recall some facts about his testimony and simply does not come up to proof.

Hostile witness

- Is a witness who shows no desire to tell the truth at the behest of the party calling him:
  - where the witness is ruled hostile, the advocate can cross-examine his own witness and under s. 3 Criminal Procedure Act 1865 put his previous statement to the witness;
  - where the previous statement is proven against the witness; or
  - where the witness adopts his previous statement, s. 119(1) CJA 2003 makes his statement evidence of the truth of any matter stated in it.

CROSS-EXAMINATION

- The purpose of cross-examination is to:
  - elicit factual evidence which supports the cross-examiner's case;
  - test the truthfulness of the witness's evidence in examination-in-chief; and
  - undermine the witness's credibility.

  Leading questions are permitted.

- Proving the witness has made a previous inconsistent statement, s. 4 Criminal Procedure Act 1865:
  - where the previous statement is proven against the witness; or
  - the witness adopts his previous statement:
  - s.119(1) CJA 2003 makes his statement evidence of the truth of any matter stated in it.

- Undermining the witness's general credibility:
  Such questioning is subject to the finality rule in that the cross-examiner must take the witness's answer as being final unless the cross-examiner submits the witness:
  - is biased;
  - has previous convictions;
  - has a physical or mental disability which undermines the reliability of his evidence.

- Adducing evidence of a witness's bad character:
  - usually raised in cross-examination;
  - under s.100(1)(a) CJA 2003, the court may only grant leave to admit evidence of the bad character of someone other than the accused if:
    - it is important explanatory evidence;
    - it has substantial probative value in relation to a matter which is a matter in issue in the proceedings *and* is of substantial importance in the context of the case as a whole; or
    - all parties agree;
  - s. 100 CJA 2003 has no application if the witness's misconduct is connected with the investigation or prosecution of the present offence, see s. 98 CJA 2003;
  - adducing evidence of another person's bad character can result in the accused's bad character being revealed to the court (s. 101(1)(g) CJA 2003).

RE-EXAMINATION

- The purpose of re-examination is to:
  - repair any damage inflicted during cross-examination.
- Leading questions are not permitted.
- A witness may rebut an allegation of recent fabrication by adducing evidence of an earlier previous inconsistent statement, which (if admitted) will be evidence of what it states (s. 120(2) CJA 2003).

17 CORROBORATION, THE *'TURNBULL* GUIDELINES' AND OPINION EVIDENCE

17.1	**Introduction**	**323**
17.2	**What is meant by corroboration?**	**324**
	17.2.1 When is corroborative evidence required?	324
17.3	**Corroboration required as a matter of law**	**324**
17.4	**Corroboration and the exercise of judicial discretion**	**324**
	17.4.1 When might a corroboration warning be given?	325
	17.4.2 Warnings in relation to a defendant's lies	325
17.5	**The requirements of corroborative evidence**	**326**
17.6	**The '*Turnbull* guidelines'**	**326**
	17.6.1 Eye-witness identification in 'good' conditions	328
	17.6.2 Eye-witness identification in 'poor' conditions	328
	17.6.3 The *Turnbull* guidelines in summary proceedings	328
	17.6.4 Failure to give a *Turnbull* warning	328
	17.6.5 When do the *Turnbull* guidelines not apply?	328
	17.6.6 *Turnbull*—the practical considerations	329
17.7	**Opinion evidence**	**330**
17.8	**Facts personally perceived by the witness**	**330**
17.9	**Expert witnesses**	**330**
	17.9.1 Who is an expert?	330
	17.9.2 The expert's duties	331
	17.9.3 The pre-trial disclosure of expert evidence	331
	17.9.4 The content of an expert's report served under Crim PR, Part 19.4	332
17.10	**Expert evidence—practical considerations**	**333**

17.1 INTRODUCTION

There is a link between the first two evidential rules explained in this chapter. The law governing corroborative or supporting evidence and the application of the '*Turnbull* guidelines' in cases involving disputed evidence of eye-witness identification seek to ensure the court reaches its verdict on 'reliable' evidence to prevent miscarriages of justice or convictions being overturned on appeal as 'unsafe'.

This chapter considers:

- the nature of corroborative evidence;
- the situations where corroborative evidence is required as a matter of law;
- the situations where a corroboration warning might be given as a matter of judicial discretion;
- the application of the '*Turnbull* guidelines' in cases where eye-witness identification is disputed.

Finally, the rules relating to opinion evidence and to expert opinion evidence in particular are explained.

17.2 **WHAT IS MEANT BY CORROBORATION?**

Corroborative evidence is independent evidence which supports or confirms other evidence in the case.

Evidence that requires corroboration is said to be unreliable or deficient or tainted in some way. A common example is where a witness may have a purpose of his own to serve by testifying for the prosecution against the accused.

When evaluating the evidence in a case, both prosecution and defence lawyers should always assess their witness's credibility. How will the witness appear to the jury/magistrates? Is the witness likely to be believed? Does the witness have a motive for giving false evidence? These all involve considerations of weight. Where a witness's evidence may be questionable, a corroboration warning might be appropriate. Such a warning alerts the jury/magistrates to the dangers of relying solely on the witness's testimony and the need for independent evidence which is capable of supporting what the witness has to say.

17.2.1 **WHEN IS CORROBORATIVE EVIDENCE REQUIRED?**

While corroboration has assumed less formal significance in criminal trials in recent years, corroborative evidence may still be encountered in two situations:

- where the offence charged requires corroborative or supporting evidence as a matter of law before the accused can be convicted; and

- where the court considers it appropriate as a matter of discretion to give a warning about the evidence of an 'unreliable' witness.

17.3 **CORROBORATION REQUIRED AS A MATTER OF LAW**

A limited number of statutes require prosecution evidence to be corroborated as a matter of law before the defendant can be convicted of the offence, including perjury (s. 13 Perjury Act 1911) and treason (s. 1 Treason Act 1795).

The only offence in this category which you might encounter is where a defendant is charged with speeding. Section 89(2) Road Traffic Regulation Act 1984 (RTRA 1984) requires that the defendant cannot be convicted of speeding on the opinion evidence of one witness. The vehicle's speed has to be corroborated by the opinion evidence of another witness. In practice, s. 89 RTRA 1984 has been superseded by modern technology, as in most prosecutions the vehicle's speed is proved by an electronic device such as a radar gun or the police vehicle's speedometer reading which do not need to be supported by independent evidence.

17.4 **CORROBORATION AND THE EXERCISE OF JUDICIAL DISCRETION**

Traditionally, the evidence of certain witnesses such as children, the complainant in a sexual offence and an accomplice (a person initially charged in the proceedings but who has pleaded guilty and testifies for the prosecution against the accused) was regarded as less reliable than the testimony of other witnesses. When directing the jury about the evidence of these witnesses, the judge was required, as a matter of law, to give a mandatory warning about the dangers of convicting the accused on the unsupported evidence of these witnesses.

The mandatory requirement to give a corroboration warning in relation to these three types of witnesses has been abolished. The present position is that a corroboration warning is discretionary and depends on the facts of each case. The key case on corroboration is *R v Makanjuola; R v Easton* [1995] 3 All ER 730, where the Court of Appeal laid down the following general guidelines:

- A corroboration warning is not a mandatory requirement because the witness is a child giving unsworn evidence or an accomplice or the complainant of a sexual offence.

- It is matter for the judge's discretion what, if any, warning is considered appropriate in relation to the evidence of a particular witness.

- In some cases, it may be appropriate for the judge to warn the jury to exercise caution before acting on the unsupported evidence of a witness. There will need to be an evidential basis for suggesting that the evidence of the witness may be unreliable.

- If any question arises whether a special warning should be given in respect of a witness, it is desirable that the question be resolved with counsel in the absence of the jury before final speeches.

- Where the judge decides to give a warning in respect of a witness, it will be appropriate to do so as part of the judge's review of the evidence and the manner in which the judge gives a direction is a matter for the judge's discretion.

- The Court of Appeal will not interfere with the trial judge's discretion except where the judge acted in an 'unreasonable' way as explained in *Associated Picture Houses Ltd v Wednesbury Corporation* [1948] 1 KB 223.

17.4.1 WHEN MIGHT A CORROBORATION WARNING BE GIVEN?

Both prosecution and defence advocates must be alert to the need for a corroboration warning in the case where a witness's evidence might be regarded as unreliable or tainted. The defence advocate might try to persuade the judge to give a corroboration warning to the jury, or raise it as a relevant consideration before a magistrates' court in her closing speech in any of the following situations:

- a prosecution witness has an 'axe to grind' against the defendant or stands to profit from the defendant's conviction, including an accomplice (see *R v Cheema* [1994] 1 WLR 147) and a co-defendant who runs a cut-throat defence against another co-accused (see *R v Jones* [2004] 1 Cr App R 5);

- a prosecution witness who has a propensity to be untruthful;

- there is evidence to suggest collusion between witnesses or some ulterior motive for the evidence that has been given;

- the witness is mentally unstable or is otherwise regarded as unreliable.

A trial judge cannot be compelled to give a corroboration warning as the decision is discretionary. However, an unreasonable failure to give a warning, in a case where a conviction results, may give the defendant grounds for an appeal against conviction. Where a warning is considered appropriate, the *Makanjuola* guidelines give the court discretion to tailor the warning to the specific facts of the case.

17.4.2 WARNINGS IN RELATION TO A DEFENDANT'S LIES

Whenever a lie told by an accused is relied on by the prosecution or may be used by the jury as evidence of guilt, a 'Lucas direction' (*R v Lucas* [1981] QB 720), should be given to the jury, instructing them that:

- the lie (which must be admitted or proved beyond reasonable doubt) must be deliberate and relate to a material issue in the case;

- they must be satisfied that there is no innocent motive for the lie as some people may lie for reasons other than perhaps hiding their guilt for the present offence, including where the accused may lie out of shame, or to bolster a defence, or out of a wish to conceal their disgraceful behaviour from their family;

- the lie must be proved to be a lie by other evidence.

The need for a *Lucas* direction only arises in cases where the prosecution, or the judge, anticipates that the jury may believe a proven lie is evidence against the accused. The purpose of the *Lucas* direction is to alert the jury to the fact that a lie told by a defendant does not, of itself, necessarily indicate guilt because he may have had some other reason for lying.

17.5 THE REQUIREMENTS OF CORROBORATIVE EVIDENCE

For evidence to be corroborative, it needs to be:

- admissible in its own right; and
- independent of the evidence to be corroborated.

Corroborative evidence may come from any other evidence in the case, including:

- the oral testimony of another witness;
- an incriminating admission made by a defendant;
- documentary evidence;
- real evidence;
- other circumstantial evidence in the case;
- lies told by the defendant can support the prosecution (see para. 17.4.2);
- forensic evidence such as DNA linking the defendant to the crime scene;
- the defendant's refusal, without good cause, to consent to give an intimate sample under s. 62 Police and Criminal Evidence Act 1984 (PACE 1984);
- inferences from a defendant's silence under ss. 34–37 Criminal Justice and Public Order Act 1994 (CJPOA 1994) (see Chapter 5);
- a defendant's previous convictions where they show a propensity for the defendant to behave in a way that is relevant to proving the facts of the present offence (see Chapter 19).

17.6 THE '*TURNBULL* GUIDELINES'

The *Turnbull* guidelines are of considerable practical importance in trials where the defendant claims to be the victim of mistaken eye-witness identification.

In Chapter 7 we explained the pre-trial safeguards in Code D of the Codes of Practice in dealing with identification procedures used by the police during the investigation to confirm or exclude the defendant's involvement in an offence. Identification evidence obtained in breach of these procedures is vulnerable to challenge under s. 78 PACE 1984.

Disputed evidence of eye-witness identification is treated with caution as extensive psychological research has highlighted the errors eye-witnesses make when they observe, interpret and recall information. An honest witness may be a very convincing witness but may still be mistaken in identifying the defendant at the crime scene. In order to minimise the risk of a miscarriage of justice based on mistaken identification, the Court of Appeal has developed guidelines about how the courts should deal with evidence of disputed eye-witness identification. The guidelines were formulated in *R v Turnbull* [1977] QB 224 and are known as the '*Turnbull* guidelines'.

The *Turnbull* guidelines apply in a case where the defendant disputes the accuracy of eye-witness identification and are fundamental to ensuring that the defendant enjoys a fair trial.

A slightly abridged version of the *Turnbull* guidelines appears here. The trial judge must adapt the guidelines, when directing the jury, to the particular facts of the case. The guidelines provide:

'First, whenever the case against an accused depends wholly or substantially on the correctness of one or more identifications of the accused which the defence alleges to be mistaken, the judge must warn the jury of the special need for caution before convicting the accused in reliance on the correctness of the identification . . . In addition he should instruct them as to the reason for the need for such a warning and should make some reference to the possibility that a mistaken witness can be a convincing one and that a number of such witnesses can all be mistaken.

Secondly, the judge should direct the jury to examine closely the circumstances in which the identification by each witness came to be made. How long did the witness have the accused under observation? At what distance? In what light? Was the observation impeded in any way, as for example by passing traffic or a press of people? Had the witness ever seen the accused before? How often? If only occasionally, had he any special reason for remembering the accused? How long elapsed between the original observation and the subsequent identification to the police. Was there any material discrepancy between the description of the accused given to the police by the witness when first seen by them and his actual appearance? . . . Finally, he should remind the jury of any specific weaknesses which had appeared in the identification evidence.

Recognition may be more reliable than identification of a stranger; but even when a witness is purporting to recognise someone he knows, the jury should be reminded that mistakes in recognition of close relatives or friends are sometimes made.

All these matters go to the quality of the identification. If the quality is good at the close of the accused's case, the danger of a mistaken identification is lessened; but the poorer the quality, the greater the danger.

. . . when the quality is good, as for example when the identification is made over a long period of observation, or in satisfactory conditions by a relative or neighbour, a close friend, a workmate and the like, the jury can safely be left to assess the value of the identifying evidence even where there is no other evidence to support it; provided always, however, that an adequate warning has been given about the special need for caution.

When, in the judgment of the trial judge, the quality of the identifying evidence is poor, as for example a fleeting glimpse of a witness or a longer observation made in difficult conditions, the situation is very different. The judge should then withdraw the case from the jury and direct an acquittal unless there is other evidence which goes to support the correctness of the identification. This may be corroboration in the sense lawyers use that word; but it need not be so if its effect is to make the jury sure that there has been no mistaken identification . . .

The judge should identify to the jury the evidence capable of supporting the identification. If there is any evidence or circumstances which the jury might think was supporting when it did not have this quality, the judge should say so . . .

Care should be taken by the judge when directing the jury about the support for an identification which may be derived from the fact that they have rejected an alibi. False alibis may be put forward for many reasons: an accused, for example, who has only his own truthful evidence to rely on may stupidly fabricate an alibi and get lying witnesses to support it out of fear that his own evidence may not be enough. Further, alibi witnesses can make genuine mistakes about dates and occasions like any other witnesses can. It is only when the jury is satisfied that the sole reason for the fabrication was to deceive them and there is no explanation for its being put forward can fabrication provide any sort of identification evidence. The jury should be reminded that providing the accused has told lies about where he was at the material time does not of itself prove that he was where the identifying witness says he was.'

The *Turnbull* guidelines require the judge to make an initial qualitative assessment of the eye-witness identification. If the trial judge concludes the identification evidence is poor and is unsupported by any other evidence in the case, the judge must withdraw the case from the jury and direct an acquittal. If the trial judge concludes the evidence is poor but is supported by other evidence in the case or the identification evidence is good, the judge can leave the case to the jury but must direct the jury in accordance with the *Turnbull* guidelines and stress the special need for caution. In a case where the evidence of identification is poor but supported, the judge must point out the evidence that is capable of providing the support. Supporting evidence will be similar to corroborative evidence as outlined in para. 17.5.

In accordance with the guidelines, the judge must explain why there is a special need for caution with such evidence and direct that, while an honest witness may be a very convincing witness, the witness may nevertheless be mistaken. The judge should invite the jury to consider the circumstances in which the witness purportedly identified the defendant and point out any specific weaknesses in the identification including:

- a witness's failure to make a positive identification;
- a breach of Code D, such as a failure to convene a formal identification procedure;
- inconsistencies between witnesses' original descriptions.

17.6.1 EYE-WITNESS IDENTIFICATION IN 'GOOD' CONDITIONS

The *Turnbull* guidelines give examples of identification in 'good' conditions including where:

- the identification is made over a long period of observation; or
- the identification is made by a relative or neighbour or a close friend or a workmate, etc.

17.6.2 EYE-WITNESS IDENTIFICATION IN 'POOR' CONDITIONS

The *Turnbull* guidelines give examples of identification in 'poor' conditions including where:

- the witness has a fleeting glimpse of the crime scene; or
- the observation is made in difficult lighting or weather conditions; or
- the witness has only a distant view of the crime scene.

17.6.3 THE *TURNBULL* GUIDELINES IN SUMMARY PROCEEDINGS

The *Turnbull* guidelines equally apply to trials in the magistrates' court. In a summary case involving disputed identification evidence of the accused, the legal adviser will remind the magistrates of the guidelines in open court and the special need for caution.

17.6.4 FAILURE TO GIVE A *TURNBULL* WARNING

The failure to give a *Turnbull* warning in cases of disputed eye-witness identification will invariably provide a convicted defendant with a ground for appeal against conviction on the basis that his conviction is 'unsafe'.

17.6.5 WHEN DO THE *TURNBULL* GUIDELINES NOT APPLY?

The *Turnbull* guidelines should be followed in all cases where the possible mistaken identification of the accused is in issue. The guidelines will not apply to:

- cases involving the identification of motor vehicles;
- the evidence of police officers who base their identification on long periods of observation or surveillance;
- cases in which there has been no formal identification of the defendant, only evidence of a description;

- cases where the accused maintains that the eye-witness is fabricating his evidence (*R v Cape* [1996] 1 Cr App R 191);

- in most cases where the accused admits his presence at the crime scene but note the guidance in *R v Thornton* [1995] 1 Cr App R 578.

17.6.6 *TURNBULL*—THE PRACTICAL CONSIDERATIONS

The application of the *Turnbull* guidelines to the facts of the case is a significant consideration for the prosecuting lawyer in a number of situations. These include giving pre-charge advice to the police or when applying the evidential test under the Code for Crown Prosecutors. A further consideration will be whether the prosecution can prove its case if the identification evidence is critically scrutinised under the *Turnbull* guidelines at trial.

The guidelines are also a relevant consideration for the defence advocate in a contested case based on mistaken identification where the examination-in-chief and cross-examination of eye-witnesses will be based around the guidelines. The defence advocate should also carefully scrutinise the trial judge's direction to the jury to ensure it complies with the requirements laid down in *R v Turnbull*.

You are reminded that our fictional case study *R v Lenny Wise* is a case based on alleged mistaken identification.

 Example

Francis is 21 and has been arrested on suspicion of burglary of commercial premises. He is white, of medium build, 6' tall with bleached white hair. The break-in occurred at 3.30 am. A description of the alleged assailant is provided by a security guard. He explains that when the alarm bell was activated, he chased the assailant across the yard of the factory for approximately 40–50 seconds before the assailant climbed over a wall. The yard was partially illuminated and he saw the person from a distance of approximately 30 yards. The security guard describes the youth as white, average height (about 5'10") and build, aged in his early twenties. The youth had fair hair and was wearing denims and a black short jacket. The assailant ripped his clothing on wire meshing covering the top of the wall.

At 3.45 am on the night in question, two officers in a police patrol vehicle arrested Francis. At the time of the arrest, Francis was wearing dark trousers and blue T-shirt. No jacket was found.

Francis chose not to be represented by a solicitor at the police station and proceeded to deny any involvement in the burglary. He agreed to participate in a video identification procedure. In interview he refused to answer questions and failed to account for a large tear in his jeans. Francis was released on police bail. Four days after witnessing the incident, the security guard attended the identification suite to view the video parade. After some hesitation he selected Francis's image. Francis was subsequently charged with burglary. Francis denies the offence and calls evidence of alibi at his trial.

At Francis's trial, a *Turnbull* direction would be given about the evidence of the security guard's eye-witness identification. The judge or magistrates would be required to assess the quality of the security guard's identification evidence. If the judge concludes the evidence is poor quality and is unsupported by other evidence, the case will be withdrawn from the court. If the identification evidence is supported by other independent evidence, it can be left to the jury or the magistrates to assess the reliability of the evidence by examining the circumstances in which the identification was made.

In this case the judge may conclude that the evidence is weak but is supported by the fact that Francis refused to answer questions at the police station and failed to give an account of the tear in his jeans. If the case is left to the jury, the judge will invite them to consider the fact that the initial observation of the assailant was in less than ideal circumstances. The security guard had the person under observation for only a short period of time, and at a distance. The lighting was good, however, although it does not appear that Francis is known to the security guard. Although an honest witness, the security guard may nevertheless be mistaken. The judge should remind the jury that the security guard was hesitant before making a formal identification of Francis.

17.7 OPINION EVIDENCE

In a criminal case a witness is called to court to give factual evidence based on what the witness perceived with his own senses. The general rule in criminal proceedings is that opinion evidence is inadmissible. A witness is not permitted to state orally or to write that the 'defendant is obviously guilty' or the 'defendant was up to no good'. In addition to being inadmissible, a witness's opinion is irrelevant and offends the 'ultimate issue' rule. The 'ultimate issue' relates to the defendant's guilt or innocence, which must be decided by the magistrates or the jury on the basis of all the evidence in the case.

There are two important exceptions to the general rule where opinion evidence is admissible: facts personally perceived by the witness, and opinion evidence given by expert witnesses.

17.8 FACTS PERSONALLY PERCEIVED BY THE WITNESS

A lay witness may give an opinion on a fact that she has personally perceived not requiring expertise. For example, it would be admissible for the witness to state that 'the defendant was drunk' or 'the defendant's car was speeding as it approached the road junction'.

In each example, the witness is giving her opinion on a matter within her personal knowledge and experience that does not require expertise or training. In effect these statements are statements of fact and are necessary to communicate to the court an accurate impression of the events the witness is testifying about.

17.9 EXPERT WITNESSES

An expert witness may give her opinion on an issue that goes beyond the ordinary competence of the court. The list of matters upon which expert evidence is required in criminal proceedings continues to grow and includes:

- accident investigation;
- ballistics;
- tool mark analysis;
- blood-alcohol levels;
- fingerprints;
- handwriting;
- computer technologies;
- facial mapping and facial identification;
- the defendant's state of mind when pleading insanity or diminished responsibility;
- medical;
- scientific/forensic investigations (DNA and statistical analysis).

Although these are highly technical matters of which the court has no knowledge or experience, expert evidence is like any other evidence in the case and is subject to an assessment of the weight to be accorded to it by the jury/magistrates.

17.9.1 WHO IS AN EXPERT?

Whether a witness is competent to give 'expert' evidence is a matter of law to be decided by the court. In deciding this issue, reference will be made to the witness's education, academic qualifications and professional experience. In the cases of *R v Clare and Peach* [1995] 2 Cr

App R 333 and *R v Hodges and Walker* [2003] 2 Cr App R 247, the witnesses qualified as an expert because of their practical experience as police officers.

At the trial of Hodges and Walker for supplying heroin, expert evidence was admitted from a detective constable in the drugs squad with 17 years' experience. The officer testified that the drugs paraphernalia, the large quantity of heroin and the amount of money discovered at W's property was inconsistent with W's claim that the drugs were for his personal use. On appeal, the Court of Appeal held that the officer's testimony had correctly been admitted as expert evidence. While the officer did not have medical or toxicological qualifications, he was entitled to refer to his expertise as a result of talking to drug users and to drug dealers.

Therefore, one of the first questions to be asked in examination-in-chief of an expert will be to establish the witness's credentials as an expert in his particular field. As a practical illustration of the principles to be applied in deciding whether a prospective witness is competent to testify as an expert consider the case of *R v Clarke (Earl St John)* [2013] EWCA Crim 162 in which the Court of Appeal made some important observations about the competence of a witness to give expert evidence about the causes of death in a homicide case.

17.9.2 THE EXPERT'S DUTIES

The duties of an expert witness are set out in Crim PR, Part 19.2:

(1) An expert must help the court to achieve the overriding objective by giving an unbiased opinion on matters within his expertise and must actively assist the court in fulfilling its case management duties under Crim PR, Part 3.2 by (i) complying with directions made by the court, and (ii) at once informing the court of any significant failure (by the expert or another) to take any step required by such a direction.

(2) This duty overrides any obligation to the person from whom he receives instructions or by whom he is paid.

(3) This duty includes an obligation to inform all parties and the court if the expert's opinion changes from that contained in a report served as evidence or given in a statement (Crim PR, Part 19.2 (3)(c)).

17.9.3 THE PRE-TRIAL DISCLOSURE OF EXPERT EVIDENCE

It may be unnecessary for either party to serve a full report on the other side and the court if the opposing party can accept a summary of the expert's conclusion. Crim PR, Part 19.3 provides:

(1) A party who wants another party to admit as fact a summary of an expert's conclusions must serve that summary

    (a) on the court and on each party from whom that admission is sought;

    (b) as soon as practicable after the defendant whom it affects pleads not guilty.

(2) A party on whom such a summary is served must

    (a) serve a response stating

        (i) which, if any, of the expert's conclusions are admitted as fact, and

        (ii) where a conclusion is not admitted, what are the disputed issues concerning that conclusion; and

    (b) serve the response

        (i) on the court and on the party who served the summary

        (ii) as soon as practicable, and in any event not more than 14 days after service of the summary.

(3) A party who wants to introduce expert evidence otherwise than as admitted fact must

(a) serve a report by the expert which complies with rule 19.4 (see below) on

(i) the court, and

(ii) each other party;

(b) serve the report as soon as practicable, and in any event with any application in support of which that party relies on that evidence;

(c) serve with the report notice of anything of which the party serving it is aware which might reasonably be thought capable of detracting substantially from the credibility of that expert;

(d) if another party so requires, give that party a copy of, or a reasonable opportunity to inspect

(i) a record of any examination, measurement, test or experiment on which the expert's findings and opinion are based, or that were carried out in the course of reaching those findings and opinion, and

(ii) anything on which any such examination, measurement, test or experiment was carried out.

(4) Unless the parties otherwise agree or the court directs, a party may not

(a) introduce expert evidence if that party has not complied with paragraph (3);

(b) introduce in evidence an expert report if the expert does not give evidence in person.

Therefore, under Crim PR, Part 19.3, where either party proposes to rely on expert evidence at a summary trial or at a trial on indictment it must be served in advance of the trial and as soon as is practicable on the court and any other party in the case. A failure to comply with the rules may result in the expert evidence not being admitted unless the court gives permission or the other parties agree that it should be admitted.

The rules do not detract from the prosecutor's general duty of disclosure in relation to used material and to unused material under the Criminal Procedure and Investigations Act 1996 (CPIA 1996) (see Chapter 8) and it is usual for the prosecution's expert evidence to be disclosed under the general disclosure rules.

Section 30 Criminal Justice Act 1988 permits an expert's report to be admitted in evidence whether or not the report's author attends to give oral evidence.

17.9.4 THE CONTENT OF AN EXPERT'S REPORT SERVED UNDER CRIM PR, PART 19.4

The required content of an expert's report is set out in Crim PR, Part 19.4. An expert's report must:

(a) give details of the expert's qualifications, relevant experience, and accreditation;

(b) give details of any literature or other information which the expert has relied on in making the report;

(c) contain a statement setting out the substance of all facts given to the expert which are material to the opinions expressed in the report, or upon which those opinions are based;

(d) make clear which of the facts stated in the report are within the expert's own knowledge;

(e) say who carried out any examination, measurement, test or experiment which the expert has used for the report and (i) give the qualifications, relevant experience, and accreditation of that person, (ii) say whether or not the examination, measurement, test or experiment was carried out under the expert's supervision, and (iii) summarise the findings on which the expert relies;

(f) where there is a range of opinion on the matters dealt with in the report—(i) summarise the range of opinion, and (ii) give reasons for the expert's own opinion;

(g) if the expert is not able to give an opinion without qualification, state the qualification;

(h) include such information as the court may need to decide whether the expert's opinion is sufficiently reliable to be admissible as evidence;

(i) contain a summary of the conclusions reached;

(j) contain a statement that the expert understands an expert's duty to the court, and has complied and will continue to comply with that duty; and

(k) contain the same declaration of truth as a witness statement.

Under Crim PR, Part 19.6 the court may direct that the experts instructed by both parties should discuss the issues within their area(s) of expertise and prepare a statement for the court of the matters on which they agree and disagree, giving their reasons.

The court also has the power under Crim PR, Part 19.7 to direct the use of a single joint expert in the case of co-defendants both seeking to instruct different experts.

Disclosing an unfavourable expert's report

As Crim PR, Part 19.4 does not override legal professional privilege, the defence is not obliged to disclose an unfavourable expert report which is not to be used at trial. The prosecution's position, however, is different, as an unhelpful report which is not to be used at trial will be disclosed under the 'unused' material rules on the pre-trial disclosure of evidence explained in Chapter 8.

Note that when s. 6(D) CPIA 1996 (as amended by the Criminal Justice Act 2003) comes into force, an accused who instructs an expert witness with a view to providing an opinion for use as evidence at trial, must give to the court and the prosecutor a notice specifying the person's name and address unless specified in the defence statement (see Chapter 13, para. 13.6.14).

17.10 **EXPERT EVIDENCE—PRACTICAL CONSIDERATIONS**

The decision to instruct an expert witness rests entirely with the parties. During the criminal investigation the police may instruct several expert witnesses including forensic scientists. The provision of expert evidence may be a significant factor for the prosecuting lawyer in determining whether to charge. Reliable and credible expert evidence as part of the prosecution case can be a significant factor in persuading a defendant to plead guilty.

Funding is obviously a highly relevant consideration for a privately paying defendant. If the defendant is publicly funded, the defence lawyer should obtain the Legal Aid Agency's authorisation before incurring the expense of instructing an expert witness (see Chapter 9, para. 9.11). As there is no definitive directory of defence expert witnesses, defence lawyers tend to instruct on the basis of a recommendation or/and having instructed the expert in an earlier case.

Both parties should always have in mind that if they intend to rely on expert evidence at trial, disclosure of the expert's report must be made in accordance with Crim PR, Part 19.

KEY POINT SUMMARY

- Understand and be able to recognise the circumstances in which a corroboration warning might be called for.

- Understand and be able to recognise the circumstances in which the *Turnbull* guidelines are applicable.

- The decision to give a corroboration warning lies with the judge/magistrates, with the relevant guidance provided by the decision in *R v Makanjuola*.

- A failure to give a *Turnbull* warning in a case where it must be given affords a convicted defendant strong grounds for appeal against conviction.

- Expert opinion evidence is admissible in relation to an issue which is outside the competency of the court.

- An expert witness's competency is determined by his qualification and/or relevant experience.

- Where a party seeks to rely on expert evidence notice must be given in accordance with Crim PR, Part 19 and case management directions.

- Expert evidence must comply with the requirements of Crim PR, Part 19 as it defines the duties of an expert; the content of any report and the rules of service, and the management of such evidence.

SELF-TEST QUESTIONS

Consider this factual scenario and answer the questions that follow.

You act for Stefan who has been charged with causing grievous bodily harm with intent, contrary to s. 18 Offences Against the Person Act 1861 (OAPA 1861). The assault is alleged to have been racially motivated. He pleads not guilty at his trial, giving evidence on oath that he was not involved in the crime. He calls his girlfriend to substantiate his defence of alibi.

The assault occurred outside a public house at 11.30 pm in a busy city centre street. Witnesses describe two white youths attacking an Asian youth. Eye-witnesses provided varying descriptions of the attackers. An anonymous witness has told the police that Stefan and Andrew (also charged in connection with the proceedings) were involved. Upon his arrest and having been confronted with positive identification evidence, Andrew admitted his limited involvement and implicated Stefan as being the principal instigator of the attack and of being completely out of control.

Stefan was subsequently arrested. His solicitor advised him not to answer police questions as he considered the evidence against Stefan to be very weak. Stefan followed his advice. In the interview, Stefan was cautioned and asked to account for visible bruising to his nose. He offered no explanation. Stefan consented to participating in a video identification procedure.

It was several days before the victim was able to assist the police. Shortly after being hospitalised, the victim was shown several sets of photographs of convicted offenders (which included a photograph of Stefan) to see if he could spot his attacker. He selected Stefan's photograph. Three weeks later the victim was well enough to view the video parade and selected Stefan's image.

At trial, the prosecution accepts Andrew's guilty plea to a much less serious offence of assault occasioning actual bodily harm (s. 47 OAPA 1861) and agrees to withdraw the s. 18 charge. Andrew gives evidence for the prosecution, putting the blame on Stefan as being the person responsible for kicking the youth while he was on the ground.

Stefan maintains Andrew is lying in order to cover up his own involvement in a serious offence. Stefan denies being at the scene. Andrew is to be married in a few weeks, time to a woman whose brother is a member of the investigative team.

In evidence, Stefan states that, while he and his girlfriend were in the city centre on the evening in question and had a drink with Andrew and some of his friends, they left before any trouble occurred.

CCTV footage is available of the incident. Sergeant Peter Taylor is called for the prosecution to give evidence of the fact that the blurred image on one of the stills is that of Stefan. The sergeant has studied the stills for a number of hours using video enhancing equipment.

Questions

- Do you have any concerns as regards the manner in which the evidence of identification has been obtained in this case? If so, is there anything you can do about this?

- On what basis will Sergeant Taylor's evidence be admitted?

- Is this a case which calls for a *Turnbull* direction? If so, explain why. What will the requirements of that warning be?

- Is this is a case which calls for a corroboration warning? If so, explain why.

Case study: *R v Lenny Wise*

Consider whether a *Turnbull* warning would need to be given in *R v Lenny Wise*, and whether any issues in relation to expert opinion evidence arise in this case.

Analysis can be found on our online resources.

FIGURE 17.1 CORROBORATION

CORROBORATIVE EVIDENCE

- **What is it?**
  Corroborative evidence is independent evidence which supports or confirms other evidence in the case (see *R v Baskerville*).

- **What type of witness might it apply to?**
  Where there is reason to doubt the reliability/truthfulness of a prosecution witness (perhaps because the witness has a purpose of his own to serve in giving false/unreliable evidence), a corroboration warning about the dangers of relying upon the unsupported evidence of the witness may be required.

- **Where might supporting evidence come from?**
  - Another witness's oral testimony; or
  - documentary or real evidence; or
  - forensic evidence; or
  - the defendant's lies or admissions (*R v Lucas*).

- **Corroboration as a matter of judicial discretion**
  A judge may choose to give a corroboration warning to a jury (or magistrates can warn themselves) about the dangers of relying on the uncorroborated evidence of a 'suspect' witness where 'there is an evidential basis for it' (see *R v Makanjuola and Easton*).

THE '*TURNBULL* GUIDELINES'

- Guidelines laid down by the decision in *R v Turnbull*.
- '*Turnbull*' applies to evidence of eye-witness identification where the defendant disputes his presence at the crime scene.
- *Turnbull* guidelines require:
  - the court to proceed with caution as an honest witness may be a mistaken witness;
  - the jury or magistrates' court should consider the circumstances of the eye-witness identification, including:
    - the length of time the witness allegedly observed the defendant;
    - the light and distance etc. in which the identification occurred;
    - did the witness have a special reason for remembering/recognising the defendant etc.
- Where the identification took place in 'good' conditions, the jury or magistrates may assess the value of the identifying evidence.
- Where the identification take place in poor conditions, the evidence should be withdrawn unless there is supporting evidence about the correctness of the identification.
- Jury/magistrates should be reminded of any specific weakness in the evidence of identification, including breaches of Code D (under PACE 1984).

OPINION EVIDENCE

- Generally inadmissible in a criminal case, except:
  - facts personally perceived by the witness which does not require expertise; or
  - expert evidence on an issue beyond the ordinary competence of the court, including:
    - forensic science;
    - facial mapping;
    - accident investigation.
- The expert's role is to provide impartial information to assist the court reach a decision in the case.
- If a party wishes to rely on expert evidence at trial, a copy of the expert's report must be served (Crim PR, Part 19).

18 HEARSAY EVIDENCE

18.1	**Introduction**	**337**
18.2	**Hearsay evidence—the general rule**	**338**
18.3	**Identifying hearsay evidence**	**338**
	18.3.1 Definitional difficulties with hearsay evidence	339
	18.3.2 Implied assertions	339
	18.3.3 Statements produced by mechanical devices—hearsay or real evidence?	340
	18.3.4 Statements produced by a computer—hearsay or real evidence?	340
18.4	**The statutory exceptions to the hearsay rule**	**341**
	18.4.1 Section 9 CJA 1967	341
18.5	**Hearsay evidence under the CJA 2003**	**341**
18.6	**The unavailable witness—s. 116 (first-hand hearsay)**	**342**
	18.6.1 The reasons for a witness's unavailability	342
18.7	**Business documents—s. 117**	**344**
	18.7.1 Documents prepared for a criminal investigation or criminal proceedings—special rules	344
18.8	**Hearsay admissible under the preserved common law rules—s. 118 CJA 2003**	**345**
	18.8.1 *Res gestae* statements—s. 118(4)(a)–(c) CJA 2003	345
	18.8.2 Statements in public documents—s. 118(1) CJA 2003	346
	18.8.3 Confession evidence—s. 118(5) CJA 2003	346
18.9	**Admitting hearsay by agreement—s. 114(1)(c) CJA 2003**	**347**
18.10	**The 'safety-valve'—s. 114(1)(d) and s. 121 CJA 2003**	**347**
18.11	**Miscellaneous hearsay provisions**	**349**
18.12	**Important safeguards when admitting hearsay evidence**	**349**
	18.12.1 Restricting multiple hearsay—s. 121 CJA 2003	349
	18.12.2 The witness's capability to make the statement—s. 123 CJA 2003	350
	18.12.3 Challenging the witness's credibility—s. 124 CJA 2003	350
	18.12.4 Stopping the case where evidence is unconvincing—s. 125 CJA 2003	350
	18.12.5 Excluding unnecessary hearsay—s. 126 CJA 2003	350
	18.12.6 Discretion to exclude hearsay—s. 126 CJA 2003	350
	18.12.7 Directing the jury	350
18.13	**Procedure for admitting hearsay evidence—Crim PR, Part 20**	**351**
18.14	**Hearsay evidence and the ECHR 1950**	**351**
18.15	**Hearsay evidence—trial considerations**	**353**

18.1 INTRODUCTION

Hearsay evidence is often described as 'second-hand' evidence and offends the preferred way in which evidence is presented at a criminal trial which requires witnesses to attend court to give oral evidence about facts of which they have personal knowledge. This is the most reliable evidence on which the court decides the defendant's guilt or innocence. Hearsay evidence is therefore inferior to the original witness's direct oral testimony, because it cannot be tested by cross-examination.

Hearsay evidence in criminal cases most often arises in two situations:

- if a witness testifies about facts of which he has no personal knowledge because the facts were communicated to the witness by another person who is not in court; and

- where a witness's written statement is put before the court because the witness is unable to attend court to give oral evidence.

Consider the following example of hearsay evidence.

> ### 💡 Example
>
> Jessie witnesses a robbery in which a pensioner's handbag is stolen. She tells her friend Ben that the person responsible was a white male of average height, wearing a black jogging top and baggy black trousers with a tattoo on the left-hand side of his face. If Jessie cannot attend court to give a first-hand account of what she witnessed, can Ben be called to repeat what Jessie told him about the circumstances of the robbery? The answer is no because Ben's evidence infringes the rule against admitting hearsay evidence as Ben has no personal knowledge of the facts about which he is testifying, as he did not see the man alleged to be responsible for the robbery. As Ben is relying on what Jessie has told him, he cannot be effectively cross-examined.
>
> Alternatively, if Jessie makes a written witness statement to the police but is unable to attend trial to give oral evidence, can the prosecution adduce Jessie's written statement in place of her oral testimony? The written statement constitutes hearsay evidence. As in the first example, it will not be possible to cross-examine Jessie to test the reliability and truthfulness of her evidence, and once again, the court would be relying on 'second-hand' evidence.

Hearsay evidence can be first-hand hearsay or multi-hand hearsay where a statement has gone through more than one intermediary. Suppose in this example that Ben is unable to attend trial but tells Toby what Jessie told him. If Toby is called to give evidence, this would constitute multi-hand hearsay. The same would be true if a written statement by Ben, recounting what Jessie said to him was to be admitted as evidence, as this would be two steps removed from the original source.

18.2 HEARSAY EVIDENCE—THE GENERAL RULE

The general rule in criminal cases is that hearsay evidence is inadmissible for the reasons explained in the introduction to this chapter. Unless the hearsay comes within a recognised common law or statutory exception it is inadmissible, although the Criminal Justice Act 2003 (CJA 2003) has *considerably* widened the basis for admitting hearsay evidence.

Section 114 CJA 2003 makes clear that hearsay is excluded unless the provisions set out in the Act make the hearsay admissible:

> (1) In criminal proceedings a statement not made in oral evidence in the proceedings is admissible as evidence of **any matter stated** if, but only if—
>
> (a) any provision of this chapter or any other statutory provision makes it admissible,
>
> (b) any rule of law preserved by section 118 makes it admissible,
>
> (c) all parties to the proceedings agree to it being admissible, or
>
> (d) the court is satisfied that it is in the interests of justice for it to be admissible.

18.3 IDENTIFYING HEARSAY EVIDENCE

Hearsay has been defined as follows:

> 'Any statement other than one made by a person while giving oral evidence in the proceedings is inadmissible to prove the truth of any fact stated in it.' (*R v Kearley* [1992] 2 AC 228)

To come within the definition of hearsay, the evidence will consist of the following elements:

(a) The evidence must be contained in a 'statement' and covers all forms of communication including:

– a written witness statement;

– a document compiled in the course of a business or by a public authority;

– a witness's oral evidence;

– a witness's evidence recorded on an audio or video tape;

– evidence on a computer disc;

– a gesture by a witness (*R v Gibson* [1887] LR 18 QBD).

(b) The statement must have been made by the witness other than while giving evidence in the present proceedings.

(c) The statement must be put in evidence to prove the truth of the statement's contents and not for any other reason, for example to prove the statement was made or to show the witness's state of mind at the time the statement was made.

A confession is a good illustration of evidence containing the constituent elements of a hearsay statement:

• the confession will be contained in a 'statement'—that is, a written transcript of the interview with the police or a tape recording of the interview;

• the confession will be made on an occasion other than while the defendant gives evidence in the present proceedings—that is, the defendant will confess at the police station during the investigation of the alleged crime; and

• the purpose of putting the statement before the court is to prove its truth—that is, that the accused admits his involvement in the offence as charged.

Confession evidence is admissible as an exception to the hearsay rule in accordance with the principles explained in Chapter 6.

A statutory definition of hearsay is provided under s. 115 CJA 2003: *[handwritten: & Statutory Defn.]*

> (2) A **statement** is any representation of fact or opinion made by a person by whatever means; and it includes a representation made in a sketch, photofit or other pictorial form.
>
> (3) **A matter stated** is one to which this chapter applies if (and only if) the purpose, or one of the purposes, of the person making the statement appears to the court to have been—
>
> (a) to cause another person to believe the matter, or
>
> (b) to cause another person to act or a machine to operate on the basis that the matter is as stated.

18.3.1 DEFINITIONAL DIFFICULTIES WITH HEARSAY EVIDENCE

Not every out-of-court statement is hearsay. If the earlier out-of-court statement is adduced for a reason other than proving the truth of facts asserted, the statement will not be hearsay. In *R v Davis* [1998] Crim LR 659, the defendant attempted to prevent adverse inferences being drawn against his silence under s. 34 Criminal Justice and Public Order Act 1994 (see Chapter 5) by trying to repeat on oath the advice his legal adviser had given him at the police station to remain silent. The defendant was prevented from doing so by the judge who ruled it as hearsay. The Court of Appeal held the trial judge was wrong as the evidence was not hearsay because the defendant was not seeking to prove the truth of anything his legal adviser had said, but was merely trying to show the effect the advice had on him in explaining his decision to remain silent.

18.3.2 IMPLIED ASSERTIONS

An implied assertion is a statement which is not intended by its maker to explicitly assert a fact but does so by implication. Implied assertions are excluded from the definition of hearsay by s. 115(3) CJA 2003. The hearsay provisions under the CJA 2003 only apply to a statement that appears to have been made:

> 'to cause another person to believe the matter, or to cause another person to act or a machine to operate on the basis that the matter is as stated . . .'

In practice, unless the statement's maker intended to assert a fact, the hearsay rule does not apply and the evidence may be admitted as direct evidence of a fact provided it is relevant to the particular case.

In *R v Twist* [2011] 2 Cr App R 17, the Court of Appeal devised a three-stage test to assist the trial court to decide whether a statement of fact or opinion to be admitted in evidence was a 'statement' within the meaning of s. 115(3) CJA 2003. The test requires the trial judge to:

(i)   identify what relevant fact (matter) it is sought to prove;

(ii) ask whether there is a statement of *that matter* in the communication. If no, then no question of hearsay arises (whatever other matters may be contained in the communication); and

(iii) if yes, ask whether it was one of the purposes (not necessarily the only or dominant purpose) of the maker of the communication that the recipient, or any other person, should believe *that matter* or act upon it as true? If yes, it is hearsay. If no, it is not.

For an illustration of the '*Twist*' test, see *R v Midmore* [2017] EWCA Crim 533. M (a drug dealer) was charged with aiding and abetting B, his half-brother, in causing grievous bodily harm to C by means of an acid attack.

The disputed hearsay evidence concerned a *WhatsApp* message sent from B's mobile phone to his girlfriend's phone shortly after he made a purchase of the 'One Shot' sulphuric acid, which included a picture of the 'One Shot' with the caption: 'This is the one face melter'. M, who was with B at the time of the purchase, contended he thought the acid was going to be used to clear a blocked drain. The prosecution relied on the message as an implied assertion of intent on B's part to use it to cause serious injury. The trial judge ruled the evidence was not hearsay within the definition of s. 115(3) CJA 2003 and should not be excluded under s.78 PACE. On appeal the Court of Appeal concluded the message had not been not sent to cause B's girlfriend to believe that the product would actually melt a face or to cause her to act on that basis. The evidence was rightly admitted against M on the basis of its relevance.

18.3.3   STATEMENTS PRODUCED BY MECHANICAL DEVICES—HEARSAY OR REAL EVIDENCE?

Section 115(2) CJA 2003 confines the hearsay provisions to statements made by a person. Would CCTV images, photographic stills and audio recordings fall within the hearsay rule? These forms of recording events, which are commonly admitted in evidence, are examples of real evidence and are excluded from the hearsay rule. The provenance of the evidence will still need to be proven and therefore it is necessary to adduce evidence of when the video was filmed and by whom.

18.3.4   STATEMENTS PRODUCED BY A COMPUTER—HEARSAY OR REAL EVIDENCE?

Does a document created by a computer constitute hearsay? Where the computer performs an entirely automated process which does not involve any human input of information, the printout or calculation that the computer performs is real evidence. This means that readings from a speedometer, police radar gun and Intoximeter are not hearsay. Similarly, the automated telephone exchange records which log the dates, times and numbers of telephone calls made and received are frequently admitted in evidence as items of real evidence. Section 129(2) CJA 2003 creates a rebuttable presumption as to the correct functioning of a mechanical device.

Where a computer is used to perform a task based on information inputted by a human being, the evidence is likely to come within the hearsay rule if the purpose of using the computer printout is to prove the truth of some fact asserted by the person who entered the information. Such computer-generated evidence is admissible under s. 129(1) CJA 2003 which provides that:

'where a representation of fact:

(a) is made otherwise than by a person, but

(b) depends for its accuracy on information supplied (directly or indirectly) by a person,

the representation is not admissible in criminal proceedings as evidence of the fact unless it is proved that the information was accurate.'

For other types of information stored on computers such as e-mail correspondence, business records, invoices, etc., which comprise statements made by a person, their admissibility is subject to s. 116 or s. 117 CJA 2003 (see paras. 18.6 and 18.7).

Having considered the constituent elements of a hearsay statement, we will examine the common law and statutory exceptions to the general exclusionary rule which allow hearsay evidence to be admitted at trial.

18.4 THE STATUTORY EXCEPTIONS TO THE HEARSAY RULE

Most statutory exceptions to the hearsay rule are contained in the CJA 2003, which has codified the most important exceptions to the rule—although some cases from the 'old' law under the CJA 1988 continue to be relevant. Before we consider the CJA 2003 provisions, two other important statutory exceptions to the hearsay rule should be noted.

18.4.1 SECTION 9 CJA 1967

In practice s. 9 CJA 1967 is the most important exception to the hearsay rule, and is in daily use in all Crown Courts and magistrates' courts. Section 9 CJA 1967 permits a witness's written statement to be read to the court without the witness attending the trial where:

- the statement is signed by the maker; and
- contains a declaration in specified words as to the statement's truth; and
- the statement has been served on the opposing party; and
- within seven days of its service the opposing party has not objected to the statement being admitted as hearsay.

The key point about a 'section 9 statement' is the other side's consent must be obtained before the statement may be admitted as hearsay unless the statement falls within another admissible hearsay provision. If the other side objects, for whatever reason, the court has no power to overrule the objection and admit the statement in evidence. An advocate is only likely to agree to a witness's evidence being read to the court under s. 9 CJA 1967 if she does not wish to cross-examine the witness because nothing the witness says in their statement is disputed.

When preparing a case for trial and, in accordance with Crim PR, Part 3, both prosecution and defence lawyers should consider whether there are any witnesses whose evidence could be read to the court under s. 9 CJA 1967. In our *R v Lenny Wise* case study, you will see that in preparing for trial, several prosecution witness statements have been agreed and will be admitted as 'section 9 statements'.

18.5 HEARSAY EVIDENCE UNDER THE CJA 2003

Section 114 CJA 2003 comprehensively codifies the exceptions that permit hearsay evidence to be admitted in a criminal case. The section provides:

'a statement not made in oral evidence in the proceedings is admissible as evidence of any matter stated if it comes within one of the four exceptions'.

Section 114(1)(a)–(d) identifies the following four situations where hearsay will be admissible under the Act:

- s. 114(1)(a)—hearsay will be admissible where it comes within one of the categories of admissible hearsay evidence under the Act (mainly where a witness is unavailable to give evidence—ss. 116 and 117 CJA 2003) and any other preserved statutory section (s. 9 CJA 1967 and Sch. 2 CPIA 1996, see earlier);

- s. 114(1)(b)—hearsay will be admissible where it comes within one of the preserved common law rules (s. 118);

- s. 114(1)(c)—hearsay will be admissible where the parties agree to the evidence being admitted;

- s. 114(1)(d)—hearsay will be admissible where the court is satisfied that it is in the 'interests of justice' for the hearsay statement to be admitted (the so-called 'safety-valve').

The main statutory gateways for admitting hearsay are provided by ss. 116 and 117 CJA 2003.

18.6 THE UNAVAILABLE WITNESS—S. 116 (FIRST-HAND HEARSAY)

A statement will only be admissible under s. 116(1) CJA 2003 where:

- the person could have given oral evidence if he had attended court; and

- the person who made the statement is identified to the court's satisfaction; and

- the person who made the statement had the requisite capability (s. 123 CJA 2003) at the time he made the statement.

The definition of capability is the same as the competence test to give oral evidence under s. 53 Youth Justice and Criminal Evidence Act 1999, that is, can the witness understand questions put to him and give answers that can be understood (see Chapter 16).

Section 116 CJA 2003 permits a statement to be admitted where the witness is unable to attend court for one of the following reasons:

- the witness is dead or is unfit because of his bodily or mental condition (s. 116(2)(a) and (b));

- the witness is outside the UK and it is not reasonably practicable for him to attend (s. 116(2)(c));

- the witness cannot be found although such steps as it is reasonably practical to take to find him have been taken (s. 116(2)(d));

- that through fear the witness does not give evidence (or does not continue to give evidence) (s. 116(2)(e)).

Under s. 116 CJA 2003 it is immaterial whether the hearsay statement is contained in a document or was made orally. Once the condition for admitting the statement is proved under s. 116, the evidence can be admitted.

The burden of proving the relevant condition rests on the party seeking to adduce the hearsay evidence. Disputes about the statement's admissibility are likely to be determined at a pre-trial hearing.

18.6.1 THE REASONS FOR A WITNESS'S UNAVAILABILITY

Reason 1—the witness is dead or unfit

R v Setz-Dempsey (1993) 98 Cr App R 23 confirms that an assessment of the witness's 'unfitness to attend' can include mental or physical capacity. A death certificate or medical report should discharge the burden of proving this ground.

Reason 2—the witness is (a) outside the UK and (b) it is not reasonably practicable to secure his attendance

If the witness's statement is to be given as hearsay, both conditions have to be satisfied by the party seeking to rely on s. 116(2)(d) CJA 2003. In *R v Castillo* [1996] 1 Cr App R 438, the Court of Appeal identified a number of factors that should be considered in determining whether it is practicable for the witness to attend, including:

- the importance of the evidence the witness could give;
- the expense and inconvenience of securing the attendance of the witness;
- the seriousness of the offence;
- whether the witness's evidence could be given via live television link; and
- the prejudice likely to be caused to the defendant given that the defendant would have no opportunity to cross-examine.

Reason 3—all reasonable steps have been taken to find the witness, but he cannot be found

The party seeking to use the hearsay at trial must prove that all reasonable steps have been taken to find the witness including indicating the steps taken to trace the witness (see *R v T(D)*, 4 June 2009, unreported).

Reason 4—the witness does not give evidence through fear

Fear is widely defined in s. 116(3) to include fear of death or injury of another person or financial loss. The witness's fear must be genuine and should be proved by admissible evidence. In *R v Rutherford* [1998] Crim LR 490, fear was proved by a signed written statement from the witness. A witness may still be in fear notwithstanding that the fear was not induced by or on behalf of the accused (*R v Horncastle and Others* [2009] EWCA Crim 964).

Where a party relies on the 'fear' ground under s. 116(2)(e), the court may grant leave under s. 116(4) where it would be in the interests of justice to admit the statement having regard to:

(a) the statement's contents;

(b) any risk that its admission or exclusion will result in unfairness to any party (with particular reference to how difficult it will be to challenge the statement if the relevant person does not give evidence);

(c) in appropriate cases, the fact that a special measures direction could be made in relation to the relevant person (see Chapter 16);

(d) any other relevant circumstance.

The requirement to seek leave under this ground is an important safeguard in protecting the defendant's right to a fair trial under Article 6. The relationship between hearsay evidence and Article 6 is considered at para. 18.13.

Consider the following examples of admitting hearsay under s. 116 CJA 2003.

 Example 1

Ethel, aged 84, is the victim of a burglary. She describes the burglar to her daughter Dianna. Ethel suffers a stroke soon after and is unable to provide a formal written statement to the police or indeed to attend trial. Can the prosecution call Dianna so that she may repeat in court what her mother told her about the burglar? This would clearly constitute hearsay evidence. Hearsay evidence is generally inadmissible unless it comes within the exceptions under the CJA 2003. Assume Ethel was capable at the time she spoke with her daughter. On the face of it, the conditions for admissibility under s. 116 CJA 2003 would appear to be satisfied. The identity of the maker of the statement is not in dispute and Ethel is unable to attend trial for a prescribed reason under s. 116(2)(b).

Example 2

Serge is the victim of a homophobic assault. He gives the police a detailed description of his attackers in a written witness statement. Serge refuses to give evidence in court as he fears for his personal safety. Can the prosecution adduce Serge's written statement as hearsay evidence? Serge's statement would appear to be admissible under s. 116(2)(e) CJA 2003. Serge is clearly identifiable as the maker of the statement and is unavailable to give oral evidence out of fear. In choosing to admit Serge's statement the court must have regard to the factors set out in s. 116(4) CJA 2003, including the availability of special measures to assist witnesses like Serge to give evidence.

18.7 BUSINESS DOCUMENTS—S. 117

Business documents are admissible under s. 117 CJA 2003 and take into account modern business practice where millions of documents are created on a daily basis. As it is impossible to require every person who had personal knowledge of the document's contents to testify in court, s. 117(2) makes business documents admissible as hearsay where the following conditions are satisfied:

- the document was created or received in the course of a trade, business, profession or other occupation, or as the holder of a paid or unpaid office (s. 117(2)(a)); and
- the person who supplied the information contained in the statement (the relevant person) had or might reasonably be expected to have had personal knowledge of the matters dealt with in the statement (s. 117(2)(b)); and
- each person (if any) through whom the information was supplied from the relevant person received the information in the course of a trade, business, profession or other occupation or as the holder of a paid or unpaid office (s. 117(2)(c)).

Section 117 permits the admission at trial of multiple hearsay which satisfies the requirements of the section. In each case:

- the person creating or receiving the document must be acting in the course of a trade, business or profession or as the holder of a paid or unpaid office; and
- the person who supplied the information contained in the statement must reasonably be supposed to have personal knowledge of the matters dealt with; and
- if the information came through an intermediary, the information must have been received by a person in the course of a trade, business or profession or as the holder of a paid or unpaid office.

Business records, ledgers, invoices, hospital records, etc. will all be admissible under s. 117(2).

18.7.1 DOCUMENTS PREPARED FOR A CRIMINAL INVESTIGATION OR CRIMINAL PROCEEDINGS—SPECIAL RULES

Section 117(4) provides documents prepared for pending or contemplated criminal proceedings and which are to be admitted as hearsay, must satisfy the conditions laid down in s. 117(5). Such statements are admissible providing any of the five conditions set out in s. 116(2) CJA 2003 relating to the absence of the relevant person is satisfied (see para. 18.6.1), or, as an additional reason, the relevant person (the person who supplied the information contained in the document) cannot reasonably be expected to have any recollection of the matters dealt with in the statement having regard to the length of time since he supplied the information and all other circumstances (s. 117(5)(b)).

Section 117(7) CJA 2003 incorporates an important safeguard to documents to be admitted under s. 117 in providing that a court may make a direction to exclude a statement if the statement's reliability as evidence for the purpose for which it is tendered is doubtful in view of:

- its contents;
- the source of the information contained in it;
- the way in which or the circumstances in which the information was supplied or received; or
- the way in which or the circumstances in which the document concerned was created or received.

Consider the following example of admitting hearsay under s. 117(4) CJA 2003.

 Example

> Take the example of Ethel which we considered earlier in the context of s. 116. Assume Ethel has been able to provide the police with a written statement, but is then unable to attend trial. Her written statement would be admissible under s. 117(4)–(5) CJA 2003. It comprises a document prepared for the purposes of criminal proceedings and a prescribed reason for not calling Ethel is made out, namely she is not well enough to attend trial (s. 116(2)(b)). There would appear to be no obvious reason for doubting the reliability of her statement (s. 117(7)).

18.8 HEARSAY ADMISSIBLE UNDER THE PRESERVED COMMON LAW RULES—S. 118 CJA 2003

The CJA 2003 specifically preserves some common law exceptions to the hearsay rule including the most important—*res gestae* and confessions.

18.8.1 *RES GESTAE* STATEMENTS—S. 118(4)(A)–(C) CJA 2003

Res gestae means transaction, or series of events. The label is given to statements that characterise or explain an event or transaction. There are various situations which cover the admission of evidence under the *res gestae* rule under s. 118(4) CJA 2003 including the 'spontaneous utterance rule'. The leading case on the '**spontaneous utterance rule**' is *R v Andrews* [1987] AC 281, where the House of Lords held that a statement made by a fatally stabbed man naming his two attackers soon after he was attacked was properly admitted under the *res gestae* rule.

Section 118(4)(a) CJA 2003 preserves the 'spontaneous utterance rule' and allows an earlier out-of-court statement to be adduced in evidence providing the statement was made by a person 'so emotionally overpowered by an event that the possibility of concoction or distortion can be disregarded'.

A *res gestae* statement can also be admitted where the witness is available to give evidence. The admissibility of hearsay evidence under the *res gestae* principle remains subject to the court's discretion to refuse to admit the statement under s. 78 Police and Criminal Evidence Act 1984 (PACE 1984) on the grounds of unfairness (s. 126(2) CJA 2003).

In *R v W* [2003] 2 Cr App R 29 the defendant was accused of a very serious assault on his mother. She had been pushed down the stairs and had her hair set on fire. There were several witnesses to the aftermath of the attack during which the victim told each of them that her son had gone berserk and attacked her. Later, however, the victim refused to give a statement to the police and gave a deposition before a magistrates' court in which she retracted her oral allegation, claiming she had accidentally fallen downstairs. She declined to comment on how her hair had been burned.

Realising that there would be little point in calling the victim to testify, the prosecution called the witnesses to whom the victim had spoken immediately after the assault to give evidence under the *res gestae* principle. The Court of Appeal held there was nothing in *R v Andrews* which prohibited a *res gestae* statement being admitted, even though the witness to the facts was available to give evidence. As with other prosecution evidence, the *res gestae* statement was subject to the court's exclusionary discretion under s. 78 PACE 1984. However, on the facts and given the importance of this witness to the prosecution's case and the inability of the defendant to cross-examine the hearsay witness, the defendant could not have enjoyed a fair trial as required by Article 6 European Convention on Human Rights 1950 (ECHR 1950).

Use of *res gestae* in domestic violence prosecutions

The use of *res gestae* statements can be significant evidence in domestic violence cases and especially in the prosecution of so-called 'victimless' crimes. A good illustration of these principles is provided by *Barnaby v DPP* [2015] EWHC 232. The complainant made three urgent 999 telephone calls. She was sobbing as she asked for police assistance because her partner, B, had tried to strangle her and she was frightened of him. She asked the police not to tell B that she had called. When officers arrived at her home, she repeated her allegation and had visible reddening and marks on her face. She refused to give a statement to the police, expressing concern that B would hurt her and her son. At trial, neither the prosecution nor the defence called the complainant. Instead the prosecution sought to adduce the 999 calls and her account to the police officers. The magistrates admitted the statements under the *res gestae* principle.

Upholding the decision, the High Court concluded that the complainant's utterances had been instinctive and spontaneous in the circumstances and any possibility of concoction or distortion could be dismissed.

The increasing use of body worn cameras by the police, which capture both a complainant's words and demeanour in the immediate aftermath of an alleged domestic violence incident, will undoubtedly mean more *res gestae* admissions in complainant unsupported prosecutions.

18.8.2 STATEMENTS IN PUBLIC DOCUMENTS—S. 118(1) CJA 2003

Statements contained in a public document or certified true copies are admissible at common law as evidence of the truth of their contents. This exception to the hearsay rule has long been recognised because such evidence was considered to be reliable and very often the public official who compiled the document would have no recollection of the facts, or be dead, or be unfit to testify. Many statutes provide for the admissibility of certain classes of documents, such as certified true copies of entries in a register of deaths compiled by the Registrar of Births, Deaths and Marriages, as evidence of the date of a person's death where this is a relevant fact in issue in any proceedings.

In addition to such specific provisions, most statements in public documents will be admissible in criminal cases by virtue of s. 117 CJA 2003.

18.8.3 CONFESSION EVIDENCE—S. 118(5) CJA 2003

A confession is a statement made on an earlier out-of-court occasion which is being relied on in court to prove the truth of facts asserted in it. For that reason it comprises hearsay evidence. Confession evidence has always been admissible as a common law exception to the hearsay rule. Having read Chapter 6, you will be aware that the defendant may oppose the admission of confession evidence under ss. 76 and 78 PACE 1984. It is normally the prosecution that seeks to have the defendant's confession adduced into evidence. Sometimes however, a co-accused will seek to adduce another co-accused's confession into evidence because it assists his defence.

Suppose co-accused A makes a confession, which in whole or in part exonerates B. The prosecution do not propose to rely on A's confession in evidence. Can B adduce A's confession as hearsay? The answer is 'yes'. This scenario arose in the case of *R v Myers* [1998] AC 124, where the House of Lords effectively created a further exception to the hearsay rule by allowing B to adduce evidence of A's confession provided it had not been obtained by means of 'oppression' and was not 'unreliable'. As a consequence of the decision in *Myers*, s. 76 PACE 1984 (the main statutory section which regulates the admissibility of disputed confession evidence—see Chapter 6) was amended to allow one co-defendant *charged in the same proceedings* to admit in evidence a confession made by a second co-defendant where the confession supports the defence of the first co-defendant (s. 76A PACE 1984).

18.9 ADMITTING HEARSAY BY AGREEMENT—S. 114(1)(C) CJA 2003

This ground is self-explanatory.

18.10 THE 'SAFETY-VALVE'—S. 114(1)(D) AND S. 121 CJA 2003

Section 114(1)(d) gives a court discretion to admit hearsay evidence which does not come within one of the other specified categories for admitting hearsay evidence under the CJA 2003. A court may only admit such evidence where it is in the interests of justice.

In applying the discretionary 'interests of justice' test the court will apply the following factors laid down in s. 114(2)(a)–(i):

(a) how much probative value the statement has (assuming it to be true) in relation to a matter in issue in the proceedings, or how valuable it is for the understanding of other evidence in the case;

(b) what other evidence has been, or can be, given on the matter or evidence mentioned in para. (a);

(c) how important the matter or evidence mentioned in para. (a) is in the context of the case as a whole;

(d) the circumstances in which the statement was made;

(e) how reliable the maker of the statement appears to be;

(f) how reliable the evidence of the making of the statement appears to be;

(g) whether oral evidence of the matter stated can be given and, if not, why it cannot;

(h) the amount of difficulty involved in challenging the statement;

(i) the extent to which that difficulty would be likely to prejudice the party facing it.

The 'safety-valve' gives the court a limited inclusionary discretion to admit hearsay where it is in the interests of justice. The Law Commission intended the provision to be used in only 'exceptional circumstances' where hearsay evidence cannot be admitted under any other provision.

As the cases detailed below and in our online case compendium show, the courts are using s. 114(1)(d) to extend the boundaries of admissible hearsay. For example, in *RL v R* [2008] 2 Cr App R 18, L was charged with four counts of rape and five counts of indecent assault against his daughter. L attempted to explain the presence of a towel with his semen on it at the crime scene by suggesting that it had been left in his daughter's flat after L and his wife had had sex during an earlier visit. The police obtained a statement from Mrs L in which she stated she could not remember having sex with L as he had alleged. As L's wife was not a compellable prosecution witness at trial (see Chapter 16), the prosecution sought to put Mrs L's statement in evidence under s. 114(1)(d) CJA 2003 as being in the interests of justice. The trial judge admitted the statement and L was convicted. On appeal, the Court of Appeal ruled that the evidence had been properly admitted under s. 114(1)(d) CJA 2003. For a further illustration in a spousal context, see *R v Horsnell* [2012] EWCA Crim 227.

In *R v Stewart John Burton* [2011] EWCA Crim 1990, B appealed against his conviction for sexual activity with a child. B had been arrested following the discovery of letters from him to a 14-year-old girl (X). Gifts from B and pregnancy test kits were also found in X's bedroom. The letters referred to them having kissed and cuddled. X refused to discuss the matter with her mother but told a police officer that she and B had been boyfriend and girlfriend. She said they had kissed and cuddled but denied having had sexual intercourse with him. She later refused to provide a statement or be interviewed. The Crown sought to adduce evidence of what X had said to the police officer, under s. 114(1)(d) CJA 2003. The conversation between X and the police officer could not be admitted under s. 116 CJA 2003 because X was available to give evidence, albeit refused to do so. The prosecution could have witness summonsed X but concluded that would have been counterproductive. The only basis upon which the conversation between X and the police officer could have been admitted was under s. 114(1)(d). B objected on the basis that the Crown was trying to circumvent the restrictions on admitting hearsay evidence under s. 116 CJA 2003. The judge concluded that given her age, the Crown was right not to force X to give oral evidence and that the admission of the evidence was in the interests of justice.

Upholding the conviction, the Court of Appeal concluded that this was an exceptional case and therefore it was in the interests of justice that the evidence be admitted. Particular emphasis was placed on the fact that the absent witness was a child of 14 who clearly had feelings for the accused. She was not best placed to assess what was in her best interests and there was a clear public interest in protecting young people from sexual exploitation by older men.

Whilst the boundaries for admitting hearsay evidence may have been extended by the 'safety-valve', the Court of Appeal is vigilant to ensure that it is not used to subvert the express provisions under ss. 116–118, see *R v Horncastle* at para. 18.6.1 above. Nor should the 'safety-valve' be used to rescue the prosecution from the consequences of its own failure when a key witness failed to attend trial (*McEwan v DPP* [2007] EWHC 740). In *R v Z* [2009] 1 Cr App R 34, the Court of Appeal quashed a conviction for sexual assault where hearsay evidence of unrelated earlier alleged sexual assaults on two women (denied by Z) was admitted as evidence of X's propensity/bad character (see Chapter 19). One of the witnesses, who had since died, made a complaint at the time but had never pursued it. The other witness had also made a complaint at the time. She was available to give evidence at Z's trial but was extremely reluctant to do so. The Court of Appeal concluded that it had been wrong for the judge to admit the evidence. On this point, the Court of Appeal observed: 'Cases must be rare indeed in which such significant potentially prejudicial evidence as that of D should be admitted as hearsay where the maker of the statement is alive and well and able, although reluctant, to testify, and her reluctance is not due to fear (within the meaning of s 116(2)(e) CJA 2003).' Note that *R v Stewart John Burton* [2011] EWCA Crim 1990 (considered earlier) is an example of a rare case involving a reluctant witness.

Finally, in *R v Ford* [2010] EWCA Crim 2250, the Court of Appeal held that anonymous hearsay evidence was not admissible under s. 114(1)(d).

 Example 1

Recall the earlier example of Ethel aged 84 who is the victim of the burglary. If Ethel gives a description of the perpetrator to her neighbour Arthur and Arthur relays the information to his son Thomas, will the prosecution be able to call Thomas to give evidence of what Ethel said to Arthur which in turn was said to him if both Ethel and Arthur are unable through illness to give oral evidence at trial?

This example raises the issue of multiple hearsay evidence. The original statement has gone through more than one stage of reporting. It cannot therefore be admitted under s. 116 CJA 2003 and it is not admissible under s. 117 CJA 2003 as that section is restricted to documentary hearsay. The only possibility in this instance is the safety-valve. Assume there is no reason to doubt the credibility of any of the witnesses. The statement is of importance to the prosecution. There is a good reason for Ethel's unavailability to give oral evidence and the defence can still challenge the evidence. On balance, the court might choose to admit the evidence given its reliability and probative value.

18.11 MISCELLANEOUS HEARSAY PROVISIONS

The CJA 2003 has formally brought into the hearsay rules a number of miscellaneous provisions dealing with a witness's written statement where the witness testifies at trial.

- Section 119 CJA 2003 provides that where a witness admits making a previous inconsistent statement or it has been proved that he has made such a statement, the statement can now be admitted as evidence of the truth of what it asserts. (For the rules on proving a previous inconsistent statement, see Chapter 16, para. 16.9.3.)

- Section 120 CJA 2003 enables a witness's previous consistent statement to be admitted as evidence of the truth of what it asserts. This includes previous consistent statements used to rebut a suggestion of recent fabrication, recent complaints, and statements used to refresh a witness's memory upon which the witness is cross-examined, resulting in the statement being put in evidence (see Chapter 16).

- Section 120(4) CJA 2003 provides that a witness's previous statement may be admissible as evidence of the facts stated, if while giving evidence the witness indicates that to the best of his belief he made the statement, that it states the truth and the statement falls within one of the prescribed categories under s. 120(5), (6), and (7) (see Chapter 16).

18.12 IMPORTANT SAFEGUARDS WHEN ADMITTING HEARSAY EVIDENCE

Although the CJA 2003 introduces a more liberal regime for admitting hearsay, even where the conditions for admissibility are satisfied, the Act provides safeguards to limit multiple hearsay and provisions for challenging the capability and credibility of a hearsay witness. The availability of these safeguards will be taken into account by the court when determining disputes between the prosecution and defence regarding the CJA 2003 hearsay provisions and their compatibility with the defendant's right to a fair trial under Article 6 (see para. 18.14).

18.12.1 RESTRICTING MULTIPLE HEARSAY—S. 121 CJA 2003

Multiple hearsay occurs when a statement passes through more than one intermediary.

Section 121 provides that a hearsay statement is not admissible to prove the fact that an earlier hearsay statement was made unless:

- either of the statements is admissible under s. 117 CJA 2003; or under s. 119 as a previous inconsistent statement; or under s. 120 as a previous consistent statement; or

- the parties agree to it being admitted (s. 121(1)(b)); or

- the court is satisfied that the value of the evidence, taking into account how reliable the statement appears to be, is so high, that the interests of justice require it to be admitted (s. 121(1)(c)).

Section 121(1)(c) is regarded as a second safety-valve. In assessing the interests of justice under s. 121(1)(c), a court should additionally consider the factors set out in s. 114(2) (a)–(i) (*see Maher v DPP* [2006] EWHC 1271 (Admin)). The factors in s. 114(a)–(i) are outlined at para. 18.9. For a case where s. 121(1)(c) was applied, see *R v Xhabri* [2005] EWCA Crim 3135.

18.12.2 **THE WITNESS'S CAPABILITY TO MAKE THE STATEMENT—S. 123 CJA 2003**

Nothing in s. 116, 119 or 120 makes a statement admissible as evidence if it was made by a person who did not have the requisite capability at the time when he made the statement. The same requirement applies to statements admitted under s. 117(2) in relation to the person who supplied or received the information or created or received the document.

18.12.3 **CHALLENGING THE WITNESS'S CREDIBILITY—S. 124 CJA 2003**

Section 124 CJA 2003 permits the opposing party to challenge the hearsay witness's credibility in the same way as if the witness had given oral evidence. In *Riat, Doran, Wilson, Claire, Bennett* [2012] EWCA Crim 1509, the Court of Appeal described s. 124 CJA 2003 as being a critical safeguard in ensuring compliance with Article 6 (see para. 18.14 below). If the hearsay is important prosecution evidence, the judge is entitled to expect that very full inquiries have been made as to the witness's credibility and all relevant material disclosed (including but not limited to any previous convictions of the absent witness). If the hearsay is part of the defence case the judge will expect the defendant to supply sufficient information about the witness to enable proper checks to be made about their credibility.

18.12.4 **STOPPING THE CASE WHERE EVIDENCE IS UNCONVINCING—S. 125 CJA 2003**

Section 125 requires the court to stop the case and to acquit the defendant where the case against him is based wholly or partly on an out-of-court statement which is so unconvincing that, considering its importance to the case, a conviction would be unsafe. This provision applies only to trials on indictment. In quashing the conviction on count 1 in *Ibrahim v R* [2012] EWCA Crim 1509, the Court of Appeal concluded that in the light of serious credibility issues associated with the victim, s. 125 CJA 2003 should have been applied. *Riat* [2012] stresses the importance of s. 125 in the management of hearsay evidence during the trial and that the provision should be kept under constant review by the trial judge.

18.12.5 **EXCLUDING UNNECESSARY HEARSAY—S. 126 CJA 2003**

Section 126(1) CJA 2003 gives the court discretion to exclude hearsay evidence where the court is satisfied that the value of the evidence is substantially outweighed by the undue waste of time which its admission would cause.

18.12.6 **DISCRETION TO EXCLUDE HEARSAY—S. 126 CJA 2003**

Section 126(2) CJA 2003 preserves the discretion under s. 78 PACE 1984 (unfairness) and at common law under s. 82(3) PACE 1984 (probative value outweighed by prejudicial effect) to exclude hearsay evidence. This important safeguard ensures that a defendant enjoys a fair trial under the CJA 2003 hearsay provisions. In *Riat* [2012], the Court of Appeal stated that s. 126 provided a free-standing jurisdiction to refuse to admit hearsay evidence and went further than s. 78 PACE 1984 because it applies also to evidence tendered by a defendant.

18.12.7 **DIRECTING THE JURY**

In accordance with the guidance provided to judges in the *Crown Court Compendium Part 1: Jury and Trial Management and Summing Up (December 2018)* and as an important safeguard the judge should point out to the jury the limitations of hearsay evidence, namely, the jury has not had the benefit of seeing or hearing the witness, nor has the witness been subject to cross-examination. In a summary trial, the advocate against whom the hearsay evidence has been adduced should remind the magistrates of the limitations of such evidence in his closing speech.

18.13 PROCEDURE FOR ADMITTING HEARSAY EVIDENCE—CRIM PR, PART 20

A party seeking to introduce hearsay evidence must give notice to the court and all other parties in advance of trial, on a prescribed form, in accordance with time limits laid down in Crim PR, Part 20. A copy of the relevant form can be found at https://www.justice.gov.uk/courts/procedure-rules/criminal/forms-2015.

Where the case is to be tried summarily, notice is usually served at the same time that the prosecution complies with its obligations to serve 'unused' material as directed by the court as part of its case management duties (see Chapter 12). Where a case has been sent for trial under s. 51 Criminal Disorder Act 1998, a hearsay notice must be served in accordance with the directions (usually standard directions) given by the judge at the PTPH (see Chapter 13). Having received notice of hearsay evidence, a party may oppose its admission by giving notice within 14 days (or as required by the PTPH judge) on a prescribed form. Provision is made in the rules to allow a court to vary the notice requirements or even dispense with them (Crim PR, Part 20). A dispute between the parties is likely to result in a pre-trial ruling on the matter.

18.14 HEARSAY EVIDENCE AND THE ECHR 1950

Article 6(3)(d) confers on a defendant the right to examine or have examined witnesses against him and to obtain the attendance and examination of witnesses on his behalf under the same conditions as the witnesses against him. Where evidence is admitted as hearsay, the defendant is unable to cross-examine the witness. Is the admission of hearsay evidence intrinsically unfair?

The case law of the ECHR 1950 suggests that hearsay does not automatically conflict with Article 6, provided there are counterbalancing measures in place which enable the defendant to effectively challenge the evidence (*Kostovski v Netherlands* (1990) 12 EHRR 434). In *Luca v Italy* (2003) 36 EHRR 46, the European Court of Human Rights (ECtHR) observed that Article 6 would invariably be breached in a case where hearsay evidence is the sole or decisive evidence against the defendant. This proposition was rejected by the Court of Appeal in *R v M* [2003] 2 Cr App R 21 and *R v Sellick and Sellick* [2005] 1 WLR 3257. In both cases there was evidence to suggest that the accused was directly or indirectly responsible for the hearsay witness being unavailable to give evidence.

In a number of domestic cases, including *R v Sellick and Sellick* and *R v Al-Khawaja* [2006] 1 Cr App R 184, the Court of Appeal has acknowledged the wide range of safeguards (see para. 18.12) in relation to the admission of hearsay evidence, including the specific preservation of s. 78 PACE 1984, by s. 126 CJA 2003, as important protections to ensure the defendant's right to a fair trial. Recent attention has however been paid to the important decision of the ECtHR in *Al-Khawaja and Tahery v UK* [2009] 1 EHRR 49. Al-Khawaja was a doctor who was convicted of sexually assaulting two female patients. One of his victims committed suicide before the trial. Her evidence, which was of particular importance to the prosecution's case, was admitted at trial as hearsay. Following Dr Al-Khawaja's unsuccessful appeal against his conviction, he took his case to the ECtHR which, following the principle in *Luca v Italy*, declared that the admission of hearsay evidence at his trial did violate Article 6(1), specifically Article 6(3)(d). The British government appealed the decision of the ECtHR in this case to the Grand Chamber of the Court.

In the meantime, in *Horncastle and Others v R* [2009] EWCA Crim 964, a powerfully composed Court of Appeal with five members considered the practical effects of *Al-Khawaja and Tahery v UK* and concluded that provided the hearsay safeguards in the CJA 2003 were observed, a conviction based solely or decisively on hearsay evidence would not in fact breach Article 6(3)(d). The key element in assessing the fairness of the trial was whether in admitting the hearsay a trial court was satisfied the hearsay evidence was reliable and its reliability had been properly tested and assessed. Following the Court of Appeal's decision in *Horncastle and Others v R*, leave to appeal to the then House of Lords was granted on a point of law of public importance as to whether a defendant could enjoy a fair trial under Article 6(1) and (3)(d) where the evidence against him was wholly or to a decisive extent based on the evidence of witnesses whom the defendants had no opportunity to cross-examine.

In *R v Horncastle and Others* [2009] UKSC 14, in its reconstituted form as the Supreme Court, the court strongly affirmed the approach taken by the Court of Appeal. In giving the judgment of the court, Lord Phillips, whilst acknowledging the important protections provided to a defendant by Article 6(3)(d), held the principle was not absolute. There were sufficient safeguards in the rules for admitting hearsay under the CJA 2003 to ensure that prosecution hearsay evidence would not be admitted in contravention of the defendants' right to a fair trial under Article 6. Accordingly the sole or decisive evidence test propounded by the ECtHR in *Al-Khawaja* was rejected.

Following the Supreme Court's judgment in *Horncastle*, the long-anticipated Grand Chamber judgment in the case of *Al-Khawaja and Tahery* was delivered ([2011] ECHR 2127). Reversing the decision of the ECtHR in Al-Khawaja's case (by concluding overall that Al-Khawaja had enjoyed a fair trial in accordance with Article 6), but affirming its decision in Tahery's case (where the absent witness did not attend trial out of fear not orchestrated by the defendant or his associates), the Grand Chamber concluded that the 'sole and decisive rule' articulated in previous judgments of the ECtHR was not to be applied in an inflexible manner, and that where hearsay evidence is the sole or decisive evidence against a defendant, its admission as evidence will not automatically result in a breach of Article 6. However, a good reason for the witness's non-availability and 'sufficient counterbalancing factors, including the existence of strong procedural safeguards' were required so as to permit a fair and proper assessment of the reliability of the evidence. In the view of the Grand Chamber, the safeguards under CJA 2003 outlined at para. 18.12 and the requirement for leave where fear is relied on as the reason for a witness's absence are, in principle, strong safeguards/counterbalancing factors designed to ensure fairness.

The Grand Chamber also held that when an absent witness's fear is attributable to the defendant or those acting on his behalf, the defendant is taken to have waived his Article 6 rights, no matter how important the absent witness is to the prosecution's case.

In the light of the Grand Chamber's decision in *Al-Khawaja and Tahery v UK* [2011] and the Supreme Court in *Horncastle* (2009), further clarification has been provided by the Court of Appeal in the conjoined appeals of *Riat, Doran, Wilson, Claire, Bennett* [2012] EWCA Crim 1509. In giving judgment, the Vice-President set out five crucial propositions about the relationship between the CJA 2003 hearsay provisions and the right to a fair trial:

- The law to be applied is that in the 2003 Act.

- If there is any difference, on close analysis, between the judgment of the Supreme Court in *Horncastle* and that of the ECtHR in *Al-Khawaja and Tahery v UK*, the obligation of a domestic court is to follow the guidance of the Supreme Court.

- There is no overarching rule, either under Convention law or in domestic law, that hearsay evidence which is 'sole or decisive' evidence against an accused automatically conflicts with the fair trial requirements under Article 6.

- In deciding whether to admit hearsay evidence, a trial judge need not ordinarily look further than the provisions of the CJA 2003 and the guidance in *Horncastle*.

- Neither under the statute, nor under *Horncastle*, can hearsay simply be treated as if it were first-hand evidence and be automatically admissible. It is a second-hand form of evidence and therefore more difficult to test and assess its credibility and probative value.

Further refinement of the ECtHR's position can be found in *Schatschaschwili v Germany* [2015] ECHR 1113 where it was held that the lack of a good reason for the witness's unavailability was not conclusive but was a factor to consider when assessing the overall fairness of the proceedings. Counterbalancing safeguards, it would seem, appear to be far more important in cases where the absent witness's evidence is the sole or decisive evidence.

18.15 **HEARSAY EVIDENCE—TRIAL CONSIDERATIONS**

Whilst the rules governing the admission of hearsay apply equally to both prosecution and the defence, in most cases hearsay evidence is usually admitted as part of the prosecution case. Having read Chapter 16 you will be aware that there are a number of special measures that are open to some vulnerable and intimidated witnesses. It is for the police and the Crown Prosecution Service lawyer to identify these witnesses and to make an application for special measures on their behalf. However, it is far from uncommon for a witness to fail to attend trial. Where either party becomes aware of a problem before trial, consideration should be given to the possible admission of the witness's evidence under the hearsay provisions. If time permits, an application should be made in accordance with Crim PR, Part 20.

Where the defence is served with notice to admit hearsay evidence, either in advance or at trial, the defence must serve notice to oppose the admission (time permitting) if the hearsay is opposed. Opposition may be based on the fact that the prosecution cannot establish a ground for its admission or, more likely, that the admission of hearsay evidence will lead to an unfair trial.

For all parties it may be appropriate for hearsay to be admitted by agreement either under s. 9 CJA 1967 or under s. 114(1)(c) CJA 2003.

KEY POINT SUMMARY

- Understand what hearsay evidence is. It is any out-of-court statement which is repeated in court for the purpose of proving the truth of a fact or facts asserted in the earlier out-of-court statement. In other words, the earlier statement is being relied on 'testimonially'.

- Understand that as a general rule, hearsay evidence is inadmissible in criminal cases unless it falls within a recognised common law or statutory exception. (Note: the categories for admission have been significantly broadened by the CJA 2003.)

- Recognised common law exceptions admitting hearsay evidence include statements admitted as part of the spontaneous utterance rule (*res gestae*) and confession evidence.

- Hearsay evidence can be admitted with the agreement of the parties under s. 9 CJA 1967 (agreement will be confined to those written statements that do not contain contentious facts requiring the witness to be cross-examined).

- The main statutory basis for admitting hearsay is contained in s. 114 CJA 2003.

- The statutory requirements of ss. 116 (unavailable witness) and 117 CJA 2003 (business documents) must be proved before hearsay evidence can be admitted.

- Understand the categories for admission of hearsay under the CJA 2003 include the safety-valve s. 114(1)(d), which covers hearsay that is not capable of being admitted under any other provision in the Act providing it is in the interests of justice.

- Be aware of the statutory safeguards that will apply in the context of the CJA 2003 and the need to ensure the admission of hearsay evidence does not prejudice a defendant's right to a fair trial in accordance with Article 6.

SELF-TEST QUESTIONS

The CPS is prosecuting an armed robbery involving several defendants. Duane (who has provided the police with a detailed statement during the investigation) is a key prosecution witness. He has received a number of menacing telephone calls warning him against testifying. He has a young family and tells the police he will not testify in court. What evidential problem does this development give rise to and how can the prosecution get around it?

For analysis, see our online resources.

FIGURE 18.1 HEARSAY EVIDENCE

THE GENERAL RULE

- Hearsay is any statement made on an earlier out-of-court occasion which is being adduced in court to prove the truth of facts asserted in that earlier out-of-court statement.

- Section 114 CJA 2003 provides that hearsay evidence being 'a statement not made in oral evidence in the proceedings, is admissible as evidence of any matter stated in it, if it comes within one of the four exceptions', s. 114 CJA 2003.

- The exceptions which permit the reception of hearsay evidence in criminal cases are set out in s. 114(1)(a)–(d) CJA 2003.

- The exceptions include:
  - s. 116 CJA 2003 (unavailable witness providing the witness is identified);
  - s. 117 CJA 2003 (business documents);
  - s. 114(1)(b) CJA 2003 (it comes within one of the preserved common law exceptions);
  - s. 114(1)(c) CJA 2003 (the parties agree to the hearsay being admitted); or
  - s. 114 (1)(d) CJA 2003 (court decides that it is 'in the interests of justice' for the hearsay to be admitted);
  - s. 9 CJA 1967 (agreed witness statements).

- The CJA 2003 contains a number of safeguards, including the application of s. 78 PACE to ensure use of hearsay evidence is compatible with Article 6 and special provisions as regards multiple hearsay.

REASONS FOR WITNESS UNAVAILABILITY (S. 116 CJA 2003)

- Witness is dead, s. 116(2)(a) CJA 2003; or

- witness is ill, s. 116(2)(b) CJA 2003; or

- cannot be found, s. 116(2)(c) CJA 2003; or

- is outside the UK and it is not reasonably practicable for him to attend, s. 116(2)(d) CJA 2003; or

- witness is in fear, s. 116(2)(e) CJA 2003 (leave required).

ADMITTING A BUSINESS DOCUMENT AS HEARSAY

- Under s. 117 CJA 2003, a business document may be admitted as hearsay where:
  - the document was created or received in the course of a business or trade or profession, etc.; and
  - the person who supplied the information contained in the statement had or might reasonably be expected to have had personal knowledge of the matters dealt with in the statement; and
  - if the document passed through an intermediary, each intermediary was acting in the course of a trade, profession, etc.

PRESERVED COMMON LAW EXCEPTIONS TO THE HEARSAY RULE

- Hearsay is admissible under s. 118 CJA 2003 where the statement falls within one of the preserved common law exceptions, including:
  - the *res gestae* rule;
  - public documents.

ADMITTING HEARSAY WHERE IT IS 'IN THE INTERESTS OF JUSTICE'

- Where a hearsay statement does not come within one of the recognised exceptions under s. 114(1)(a)–(c) CJA 2003, the court may admit the statement under s. 114(1)(d) CJA 2003 where 'it is in the interests of justice'.

- The following factors under s. 114(2) must be taken into account when exercising discretion, including:
  - the credibility of the statement's maker;
  - the statement's probative value;
  - the reason why oral evidence cannot be given;
  - the statement's importance to the party's case;
  - the difficulty to the other side in challenging the hearsay.

19.1	**Introduction**	**355**
19.2	**The accused as a competent defence witness**	**356**
	19.2.1 The defendant as a prosecution witness	356
19.3	**The course of the defendant's evidence**	**356**
	19.3.1 Can the defendant give evidence under a special measures direction?	356
19.4	**Adverse inferences from the defendant's silence at trial—s. 35 CJPOA 1994**	**357**
	19.4.1 Advising a defendant whether to testify at trial	358
19.5	**Disclosing evidence of the defendant's character**	**359**
	19.5.1 The defendant's good character	359
	19.5.2 Obtaining evidence of good character	360
19.6	**Admitting evidence of the defendant's bad character**	**361**
	19.6.1 Statutory definition of bad character	361
19.7	**Gateways to admission**	**362**
	19.7.1 The statutory discretion to exclude bad character evidence	362
	19.7.2 Admitting bad character by agreement—s. 101(1)(a) CJA 2003	363
	19.7.3 Voluntarily disclosing bad character—s. 101(1)(b) CJA 2003	363
	19.7.4 Bad character as important explanatory evidence—s. 101(1)(c) CJA 2003	363
	19.7.5 Bad character as an important issue between the defendant and the prosecution— s. 101(1)(d) CJA 2003	364
19.8	**Bad character admitted between co-defendants—s. 101(1)(e) CJA 2003**	**371**
19.9	**Bad character to correct a false impression given by the defendant—s. 101(1)(f) CJA 2003**	**374**
19.10	**Bad character admitted under s. 101(1)(g) CJA 2003**	**375**
	19.10.1 What amounts to an attack?	375
	19.10.2 The exercise of discretion in relation to gateway (g)	376
19.11	**The practice and procedure for admitting evidence of a defendant's bad character**	**377**
19.12	**Relevance and use that can be made of bad character adduced under s. 101 and the importance of the direction to the jury**	**378**
19.13	**Miscellaneous matters**	**379**

19.1 INTRODUCTION

In this chapter we examine the evidential rules that apply to the defendant at trial, including:

- the defendant's competence and compellability;

- the course of the defendant's evidence;

- drawing an adverse inference under s. 35 Criminal Justice and Public Order Act 1994 (CJPOA 1994) from the defendant's silence at his trial;

- disclosure of a defendant's past character;

- should the defendant give evidence—arguments for and against.

19.2 THE ACCUSED AS A COMPETENT DEFENCE WITNESS

Under s. 53(1) Youth Justice and Criminal Evidence Act 1999 (YJCEA 1999), the defendant is a competent witness in his defence at every stage of the proceedings and, as a matter of law, can testify at his own trial.

While the defendant is a competent defence witness, he is not a compellable witness—that is, he has the right not to give evidence and unlike any other witness who refuses to testify he will not be in contempt of court (s. 1(1) Criminal Evidence Act 1898 (CEA 1898)). However, if the defendant remains silent, adverse inferences may be drawn from his silence under s. 35 CJPOA 1994, which is considered at para. 19.4. An accused is a competent but a non-compellable witness for a co-accused under s. 53 YJCEA 1999.

19.2.1 THE DEFENDANT AS A PROSECUTION WITNESS

The defendant is not a competent prosecution witness, whether he is charged alone or jointly with another defendant (s. 53(4) YJCEA 1999). In practice, s. 53(4) YJCEA 1999 is only relevant where one accused (X), is jointly charged with another (Y). A co-accused cannot give evidence for the prosecution while he remains a party to the proceedings. Under s. 53(5) YJCEA 1999, however, where co-accused (X) ceases to be a party in the proceedings, he becomes a competent and compellable prosecution witness against any other person who has been charged in the same proceedings. This occurs where:

- X has been acquitted or has pleaded guilty at an earlier hearing and has been sentenced by the court; or

- X makes a successful submission of no case to answer at the close of the prosecution's case; or

- proceedings against X are discontinued; or

- X is tried separately from Y as a result of a successful application to sever a joint trial.

In any of these situations X may give evidence for the prosecution against Y and anyone else charged in the proceedings. X's status will then change from a co-accused to an accomplice. The defence advocate may submit to the judge or magistrates that the accomplice's evidence should be accompanied by a corroboration warning in accordance with the principles in *R v Makanjuola* [1995] 1 WLR 1348 (see Chapter 17).

19.3 THE COURSE OF THE DEFENDANT'S EVIDENCE

Section 79 Police and Criminal Evidence Act 1984 (PACE 1984) stipulates that if a defendant is to give evidence, he must normally testify before any other defence witness. The defendant's evidence follows the same course as any other witness, including swearing an oath or affirming; examination-in-chief; cross-examination and, where appropriate, re-examination.

19.3.1 CAN THE DEFENDANT GIVE EVIDENCE UNDER A SPECIAL MEASURES DIRECTION?

A 'vulnerable' defendant can apply to the court to give evidence on oath through a live TV link under s. 47 Police and Justice Act 2006 (PJA 2006). A court will only grant leave if it is in the interests of justice and the conditions under s. 47(4) or (5) are met. Where the defendant is under the age of 18, the conditions under s. 47(4) are:

(a) his ability to participate effectively in the proceedings as a witness giving oral evidence in court is compromised by his level of intellectual ability or social functioning; and

(b) use of a live-link would enable him to participate more effectively in the proceedings as a witness (whether by improving the quality of his evidence or otherwise).

Where the defendant is over the age of 18, the conditions under s. 47(5) are:

(a) he suffers from a mental disorder (within the meaning of the Mental Health Act 1983) or otherwise has a significant impairment of intelligence and social function;

(b) for that reason he is unable to participate effectively in the proceedings as a witness giving oral evidence in court; and

(c) the use of a live-link would enable him to participate more effectively in the proceedings as a witness (whether by improving the quality of his evidence or otherwise).

Section 33BA(3) YJCEA 1999 permits an accused to testify through an intermediary where under s. 33BA(2) the accused:

- suffers from a mental disorder within the meaning of the Mental Health Act 1983 or otherwise has a significant impairment of intelligence and social function; and

- for that reason is unable to participate effectively in the proceedings as a witness giving oral evidence in court, s. 33BA(6); and

- the order is necessary to ensure the accused enjoys a fair trial, s. 33BA(2)(b).

An order can be made on behalf of an accused under the age of 18, where his ability to effectively participate in the proceedings as a witness is compromised by his intellectual ability or social functioning.

19.4 ADVERSE INFERENCES FROM THE DEFENDANT'S SILENCE AT TRIAL—S. 35 CJPOA 1994

Where the defendant does not testify, s. 35 CJPOA 1994 permits the prosecution to comment on the defendant's silence and, where appropriate, call for inferences to be drawn by the court. Section 35 CJPOA provides:

'(1) At the trial of any person for an offence, subsections (2) and (3) below apply unless—

(a) the accused's guilt is not in issue; or

(b) it appears to the court that the physical or mental condition of the accused makes it undesirable for him to give evidence; . . .

(2) Where this subsection applies, the court shall, at the conclusion of the evidence for the prosecution, satisfy itself (in the case of proceedings on indictment, in the presence of the jury) that the accused is aware that the stage has been reached at which evidence can be given for the defence and that he can, if he wishes, give evidence and that, if he chooses not to give evidence, or having been sworn, without good cause refuses to answer any question, it will be permissible for the court or jury to draw such inference as appears proper from his failure to give evidence or his refusal, without good cause, to answer any question.

(3) Where this subsection applies, the court or jury, in determining whether the accused is guilty of the offence charged, may draw such inferences as appear proper from the failure of the accused to give evidence, or his refusal without good cause to answer any question.

(4) This section does not render the accused compellable to give evidence on his own behalf, and he shall accordingly not be guilty of contempt of court by reason of a failure to do so.'

Before adverse inferences can be drawn under s. 35 CJPOA 1994, the following conditions must be satisfied if the defendant is to enjoy a fair trial:

(a) At the close of the prosecution's case, the judge is required to put the following question to the defence advocate:

'Have you advised your client that the stage has now been reached at which he may give evidence and, if he chooses not to do so, or having been sworn without good cause refuses to answer any question, the jury may draw such inferences as appear proper from his failure to do so?' (*Practice Direction (Criminal: Consolidated)* [2002] 3 All ER 904)

(b) If the defendant remains silent, the jury (or the magistrates) should be directed in the following terms in accordance with the guidance laid down by the Court of Appeal in *R v Cowan, Gayle and Riccardi* [1995] 4 All ER 939:

– the legal burden of proof remains on the prosecution;

– the defendant is entitled to remain silent;

– before drawing an adverse inference from the defendant's silence, the jury/magistrates have to be satisfied that there is a case to answer on the prosecution evidence; and

– if the jury or magistrates conclude that the only sensible explanation for the accused's silence is that he has no answer to the prosecution's case, or none that would stand up to cross-examination, adverse inferences may be drawn.

An adverse inference drawn from the accused's failure to give evidence cannot be the sole finding of guilt (s. 38(3) CJPOA 1994).

It is common for a defendant to submit that a particular physical or mental condition prevented him from testifying. A 'physical condition' would include an epileptic attack. A mental condition would include latent schizophrenia. If after the defence has discharged an evidential burden to prove the condition, it appears to the judge in the *voir dire* that the defendant's physical or mental condition makes it undesirable for him to give evidence, the jury will be directed that adverse inferences should not be drawn (see *R v Friend* [1997] 2 Cr App R 231).

19.4.1 ADVISING A DEFENDANT WHETHER TO TESTIFY AT TRIAL

As the defendant is a competent but not a compellable witness at his trial an important part of the defence case preparation is to advise their client whether to give evidence. The advice will be based on both practical considerations and the potential legal implications of testifying or remaining silent.

The practical considerations include:

(1) The nature of the prosecution and defence case

Some offences, for example a sexual offence, may involve only two participants—the victim and the defendant. In this situation it is almost inevitable that the defendant must testify, as there is no other way in which the defence evidence can be put to the court. This may also apply where one co-accused blames the other. If there are credible and reliable witnesses who can give evidence in support of the defendant's case, it might not be necessary to call the defendant.

(2) Where a legal burden of proof is placed on the defendant

Where a legal burden of proof is placed on a defendant to establish his innocence (see Chapter 15), often the accused is the only person who can testify in support of that defence.

(3) Will the defendant be a credible witness?

Sometimes the best prosecution witness is the defendant! The defence advocate will assess how her client will come across in the witness box. Will she appear believable and credible? Will she cope with cross-examination? Is the defendant sufficiently articulate to create a good impression? Does she have the mental strength to cope with testifying, as appearing as a witness in a criminal trial is highly stressful?

(4) Strength of the prosecution's case

Where objectively assessed the prosecution's evidence is unlikely to persuade a jury of the defendant's guilt beyond reasonable doubt, the defence advocate may not wish to assist the prosecution by calling her client to testify if she has doubts about her client's ability to cope with cross-examination. The decision about whether to allow the defendant to testify may have to wait until after the cross-examination of the prosecution witnesses.

(5) The legal considerations

As well as the practical factors, the decision whether the defendant should testify also involves an important legal consideration because if the defendant does not give evidence, adverse inferences may be drawn under s. 35 CJPOA 1994 (see para. 19.4).

19.5 DISCLOSING EVIDENCE OF THE DEFENDANT'S CHARACTER

While most attention is directed towards the admission of a defendant's past bad character, a defendant's good character also has important evidential value.

19.5.1 THE DEFENDANT'S GOOD CHARACTER

Evidence of the defendant's good character is admissible to show that he is not the type of person who would commit the offence(s) charged and/or it may be relevant to assessing the defendant's credibility (i.e. whether the defendant is likely to be telling the truth).

'Good character' will usually mean the absence of a criminal record, but particularly praiseworthy activities such as a good military service record, public service or charitable acts may also be used to enhance a defendant client's character.

The approach taken by the courts when dealing with a defendant's good character was laid down by the Court of Appeal in *R v Vye and Others* (1993) 97 Cr App R 134:

- A defendant with no convictions is entitled to a good character direction as to his propensity (i.e. the defendant is less likely to have committed this offence because he is a person of past good character). This direction must be given irrespective of whether or not the defendant gives evidence in the case. **This is known as the propensity limb.**

- A defendant with no convictions is also entitled to a good character direction as to his credibility where, before trial, he has asserted his innocence either at the police station and/or has given evidence on oath at his trial. **This is known as the credibility limb.**

In the Crown Court, the trial judge is required to direct the jury in accordance with the principles in *R v Vye*. A failure to give a good character direction will provide a defendant with a good ground to appeal against his conviction. In a summary trial, the defence advocate should remind the magistrates of the relevance of good character evidence.

The court retains discretion to give a modified good character direction where an accused has one or more previous convictions but they are of a minor nature, unrelated to the current charge or dated or has no previous convictions but admits to past serious reprehensible conduct (*R v Aziz* [1995] 3 WLR 53). *Aziz* affirmed that a judge is not obliged to give absurd or meaningless directions. In *R v Hamer* [2010] EWCA Crim 2053, the Court of Appeal held that an accused who had no previous convictions or cautions but who had been issued with a fixed penalty notice for disorder (PND) was entitled to an unfettered '*Vye*' direction. In *R v Styles* [2015] EWCA Crim 1619, the Court of Appeal held that the accused was entitled to a modified good character direction in a case where his earlier misconduct was of a minor and unrelated nature to the serious charge he was facing at trial.

Reference must also be made to the recent and important Court of Appeal decision in *R v Hunter and others* [2015] EWCA Crim 631. This decision was a response to the growing number of appeals against conviction following a refusal by the trial judge to give a modified good character direction. All the appeals in *Hunter* concerned cases where the defence had voluntarily adduced evidence of their bad character under s. 101(1)(b) (see para. 19.7.3 later) on a tactical basis to persuade the jury that the defendant was less likely to have committed the offences charged which were of a sexual nature. The *Vye* propensity direction had been given in each case but not a full credibility direction. *Hunter* acknowledges that the relaxation of the rules permitting evidence of defendant bad character in a wider number of instances under CJA 2003 have had an impact on the relevance and admissibility of good character evidence. In *Hunter*, the Court of Appeal observed that whilst the principles enunciated in *Vye* and *Aziz* started as good practice, they had been extended to the point where defendants with bad criminal records, or those who had no right to claim good character, were claiming entitlement to a good character direction and many judges felt required to give absurd or meaningless directions, or ones which were far too generous to a defendant.

In *Hunter* the Court of Appeal took the opportunity to clarify and promote consistency in an increasingly complex area of the law of evidence by identifying different categories of good character as follows:

(1) A defendant with **'absolute good character'** is taken to mean **no previous convictions or cautions recorded against them and no other reprehensible conduct alleged, admitted, or proven** and is **entitled to both limbs** of the *Vye* direction.

(2) Where the defendant can be labelled as having **'effective good character'** because they have previous convictions or cautions recorded which are old or minor and have no relevance to the charge, the judge must make a judgment as to whether or not to treat the defendant as a person of effective good character. **If the judge** decides to treat a defendant as a person of effective good character, **the judge must give both limbs of the *Vye* direction, modified as necessary** to reflect the other matters and thereby ensuring that the jury is not misled.

(3) Where the **defendant has adduced his previous convictions or cautions under s. 101(1)(b) CJA 2003**, he has no entitlement to either limb of the good character direction. **It is a matter for the judge's discretion.** The discretion is a broad one of the 'open textured variety' described in *R v Aziz* whether to give any part of the direction and if so on what terms. It is not narrowly circumscribed. **The judge will decide what is fair on the facts** of the case and the **Court of Appeal will have proper regard for the exercise of discretion by the trial judge**.

(4) Where the defendant has **no previous convictions or cautions, but evidence is admitted and relied on by the prosecution of other misconduct**, the judge is obliged to give a bad character direction. **There may be instances where, in the interests of ensuring fairness, the judge might choose to give a modified good character direction.** However, where the defendant has previous convictions and bad character is relied on, **it is difficult to envisage a good character direction that would not offend the absurdity principle.**

(5) Where the defendant has **no previous convictions but admits other reprehensible behaviour that is not relied on by the prosecution as being probative of guilt**, then in accordance with *Aziz*, the judge **retains a residual discretion to give the good character direction, unless it would defy common sense.** The discretion in this instance is no longer narrowly circumscribed and is to be left to the good sense of the trial judge.

(6) Where the trial judge gets it wrong, the failure will not necessarily or usually be fatal. Due regard will be given to the exercise of discretion because the trial judge is the person best placed to exercise it, and the Court of Appeal will thus be slow to interfere in the future.

(7) As a matter of good practice, defendants should put the court on notice as early as possible that character and character directions are an issue that may need to be resolved. The judge can then decide whether a good character direction should be given and if so, in what terms. Provision as to giving notice has been made in the Criminal Procedure Rules 2015.

19.5.2 OBTAINING EVIDENCE OF GOOD CHARACTER

When preparing the defence case for trial, it is necessary to obtain character evidence in support of a client with good character. Character evidence can be presented orally by calling a witness to give evidence on oath, or in a witness statement admitted with the prosecution's agreement, under s. 9 Criminal Justice Act 1967 (CJA 1967) (see Chapter 12, para. 12.6.2). The defendant's previous convictions (if any) will have been disclosed under the prosecution's pre-trial disclosure of evidence obligations, enabling the defence advocate to assess whether the accused is entitled to a good character direction.

19.6 ADMITTING EVIDENCE OF THE DEFENDANT'S BAD CHARACTER

Part 11 CJA 2003 provides a comprehensive statutory framework for admitting the bad character evidence of both the defendant and non-defendant. The provisions covering non-defendants are explained in Chapter 16.

The 2003 Act undermines many of the traditional immunities which generally gave the defendant a shield, or protection against having evidence of his bad character disclosed to the court.

The 'old law' (abolished by s. 99 CJA 2003) was based on an exclusionary approach. Evidence of a defendant's bad character was generally inadmissible to show that because of past offending, the defendant was guilty of the current offence and was limited to a number of exceptions which included the admission of a defendant's bad character under the 'similar fact' evidence rule.

The justification for the former exclusionary approach was to protect the defendant from the prejudice that such knowledge would engender in the minds of the jury or magistrates. The knowledge that X has previous convictions for theft and burglary, on a current charge of burglary, would make it much more likely that X would be convicted as it was thought that juries and magistrates would attach too much significance to the defendant's criminal record and insufficient attention to the evidence linking the defendant to the present offence.

The CJA 2003 considerably extends the boundaries for admitting evidence of a defendant's bad character with fewer safeguards.

19.6.1 STATUTORY DEFINITION OF BAD CHARACTER

Section 98 CJA 2003 defines evidence of a person's bad character as 'evidence of, or of a disposition towards, misconduct on his part . . .'.

The term 'misconduct' is further defined by s. 112 CJA 2003, as the commission of an offence or other 'reprehensible' behaviour.

The definition of bad character under the Act is wide and includes:

- evidence of the defendant's previous convictions;
- evidence relating to an offence(s) with which the defendant was charged but not convicted;
- evidence relating to an offence(s) with which the defendant has been charged but acquitted;
- evidence not amounting to criminal conduct but which constitutes 'reprehensible' behaviour.

While the definition of bad character under the CJA 2003 is generally clear, there is uncertainty about the precise limits of what amounts to 'reprehensible behaviour'.

Section 98 further provides that the Act *does not* apply to evidence of, or of a disposition towards, misconduct on his part which:

'(a) has to do with the alleged facts of the offence with which the defendant is charged, or

(b) is evidence of misconduct in connection with the investigation or prosecution of that offence.'

Evidence of misconduct going directly to the facts of the offence for which the defendant is being tried is excluded from the CJA 2003 bad character provisions. The admissibility of this evidence is governed by its relevance to the issues in the current case. Consider the following examples:

Example 1

Nigel is charged with arson by starting a fire in a hostel for resettling young offenders in which he was living at the time of the alleged offence. The fire occurred shortly after a dispute between Nigel and a member of the hostel staff who accused Nigel of breaking the hostel's curfew rules. In proving the facts, the prosecutor will have to refer to the fact that Nigel was residing at a hostel for the resettling of young offenders. It has to do with the facts of the offence and therefore does not trigger the character provisions under the Act (s. 98(a)).

Example 2

Gina is accused of a serious offence of assault. The prosecution wishes to adduce evidence that Gina has tried to bribe a prosecution witness not to give evidence. The evidence of the bribe is admissible as it is evidence connected with the prosecution of the offence (s. 98(b)).

19.7 GATEWAYS TO ADMISSION

Section 101(1) CJA 2003 is very significant and is reproduced below in full. It provides seven gateways through which evidence of a defendant's bad character can be admitted.

'**101   Defendant's bad character**

(1) In criminal proceedings evidence of the defendant's bad character is admissible if, but only if—

    (a) all parties to the proceedings agree to the evidence being admissible,

    (b) the evidence is adduced by the defendant or is given in answer to a question asked by him in cross-examination,

    (c) it is important explanatory evidence,

    (d) it is relevant to an important matter in issue between the defendant and the prosecution,

    (e) it has substantial probative value in relation to an important matter in issue between the defendant and a co-defendant,

    (f) it is evidence to correct a false impression given by the defendant, or

    (g) the defendant has made an attack on another person's character.

(2) Sections 102 to 106 contain provisions supplementing subsection (1).

(3) The court must not admit evidence under subsection (1)(d) or (g) if, on an application by the defendant to exclude it, it appears to the court that the admission of the evidence would have such an adverse effect on the fairness of the proceedings that the court ought not to admit it.

(4) On an application to exclude evidence under subsection (3) the court must have regard, in particular, to the length of time between the matters to which that evidence relates and the matters which form the subject of the offence charged.'

Each of the gateways is explained in detail later but before we do so, we will consider the following important question—does the court retain discretion to exclude evidence of a defendant's bad character?

19.7.1 THE STATUTORY DISCRETION TO EXCLUDE BAD CHARACTER EVIDENCE

Under s. 101(3) CJA 2003 the defence may apply to the court to exclude evidence of bad character under either gateway (d) or (g) *only* if the admission of the evidence would have an adverse effect on the fairness of the proceedings. Section 101(3) specifically provides:

'The court must not admit evidence under subsection 1(d) or (g), if on application by the defendant to exclude it, it appears to the court the admission of the evidence would have such an adverse effect on the fairness of the proceedings that the court ought not admit it.'

In *R v Hanson; R v Gilmore; R v Pickstone* [2005] 2 Cr App R 21, the Court of Appeal stated that the discretion under s. 101(1)(3) was stronger than under s. 78 PACE 1984 as under the former the court 'must not admit' the evidence where its admission would have such an adverse effect on the fairness of the proceedings whereas under s. 78 PACE 1984, the court 'may refuse to allow' the evidence.

In exercising discretion under s. 101(3) CJA 2003 the court is specifically required to have regard to the length of time that has passed since the bad character sought to be admitted was committed (s. 101(4) CJA 2003).

While the discretion to exclude bad character evidence under s. 101(3) is specific to gateways (d) and (g), what is the position under the other gateways? In the absence of an express provision excluding the operation of s. 78 PACE 1984, it must be assumed that it applies to the admission of the defendant's bad character under the 2003 Act. This proposition is supported by statements in the Court of Appeal's decision in *R v Highton; R v Van Nguyen; R v Carp* [2005] 1 WLR 3472.

19.7.2 ADMITTING BAD CHARACTER BY AGREEMENT—S. 101(1)(A) CJA 2003

All parties to the proceedings agree to the defendant's bad character being admitted in evidence.

19.7.3 VOLUNTARILY DISCLOSING BAD CHARACTER—S. 101(1)(B) CJA 2003

Evidence of the defendant's bad character is given by the defendant himself or is given in answer to a question asked by him in cross-examination with the intention of disclosing his bad character.

Section 101(1)(a) and (b) is largely self-explanatory. In relation to s. 101(1)(b), there may be tactical advantages to a defendant choosing to adduce evidence of his bad character where the prosecution has chosen not to put the bad character in evidence as part of its case.

Prosecution might use.

19.7.4 BAD CHARACTER AS IMPORTANT EXPLANATORY EVIDENCE—S. 101(1)(C) CJA 2003

This gateway is further defined in s. 102, and is available only to the prosecution. It is not relied on in practice to any significant extent.

⇓ Conditions.

> '102 Important explanatory evidence
>
> For the purposes of s. 101(1)(c) evidence is important explanatory evidence if—
>
> (a) without it, the court or jury would find it impossible or difficult properly to understand other evidence in the case, and
>
> (b) its value for understanding the case as a whole is substantial.'

In some cases it will be necessary for the prosecution to give background information about the offence, which may result in part or the whole of the defendant's bad character being disclosed. Section 101(1)(c) CJA 2003 gives statutory effect to the previous position at common law.

The Court of Appeal in *R v Edwards; Fysh; Duggan and Chohan* [2006] 1 Cr App R 3 (specifically the appeal of Chohan) provides a useful illustration of gateway (c). Chohan was charged with burglary. He denied the offence. The main prosecution evidence came from an eye-witness who identified him at an identification parade. The identification of Chohan was based on recognition as the eye-witness claimed Chohan had been her drug dealer. Chohan denied involvement in the burglary and accused the eye-witness of fabricating her evidence because he had terminated a sexual relationship with her. Chohan denied supplying drugs to her. The trial judge permitted the evidence to be adduced under gateway (c) as the supply of drugs clearly constituted reprehensible behaviour and it comprised important explanatory evidence. It explained the basis of the eye-witness's identification and why she was so confident that her identification of Chohan was accurate.

Gateway (c) overlaps with s. 98 (above) and with gateway (d), the propensity gateway (see below). The test for admission under gateway (c) is strict. The evidence admitted under this gateway is often very prejudicial, so careful consideration must be given to its admission. To further illustrate the operation of gateway (c) review *R v Awoyemi and others* [2016] 2 Cr App R 302 in the Bad Character Case Compendium.

19.7.5 BAD CHARACTER AS AN IMPORTANT ISSUE BETWEEN THE DEFENDANT AND THE PROSECUTION—S. 101(1)(D) CJA 2003

Evidence of the defendant's bad character is relevant to an important matter in issue between the defendant and the prosecution. This is an important gateway for the prosecution.

Gateway (d) is further defined in s. 103 and is available only to the prosecution.

'103   Matter in issue between the defendant and the prosecution

(1) For the purposes of section 101(1)(d) the matters in issue between the defendant and the prosecution include—

(a) the question whether the defendant has a propensity to commit offences of the kind with which he is charged, except where his having such a propensity makes it no more likely that he is guilty of the offence;

(b) the question whether the defendant has a propensity to be untruthful, except where it is not suggested that the defendant's case is untruthful in any respect.

(2) Where subsection (1)(a) applies, a defendant's propensity to commit offences of the kind with which he is charged may (without prejudice to any other way of doing so) be established by evidence that he has been convicted of—

(a) an offence of the same description as the one with which he is charged, or

(b) an offence of the same category as the one with which he is charged.

(3) Subsection (2) does not apply in the case of a particular defendant if the court is satisfied, by reason of the length of time since the conviction or for any other reason, that it would be unjust for it to apply in his case.

(4) For the purposes of subsection (2)—

(a) two offences are of the same description as each other if the statement of the offence in a written charge or indictment would, in each case, be in the same terms;

(b) two offences are of the same category as each other if they belong to the same category of offences prescribed for the purposes of this section by an order made by the Secretary of State.

(5) A category prescribed by an order under subsection (4)(b) must consist of offences of the same type.

(6) Only prosecution evidence is admissible under section 101(1)(d).'

An important matter in issue between the prosecution and the defence includes:

- the question whether the defendant has a propensity to commit offences of the kind with which he is currently charged (unless the propensity makes him no more likely to be guilty of the offence with which he is charged); and/or

- the question whether the defendant has a propensity to be untruthful (unless it is not suggested that the defendant's case is untruthful).

Section 144 Coroners and Justice Act 2009 extended the application of s. 103 CJA 2003 to include a defendant's conviction(s) from a foreign jurisdiction where the conviction(s) would have been admissible in England and Wales.

Gateway (d) is very significant because it makes it considerably easier for a defendant's bad character to be admitted than previously at common law under the similar fact evidence rule. Previous convictions and other 'reprehensible behaviour' will be admitted against the defendant under gateway (d) provided they are relevant to an important matter in issue between the prosecution and the defence, subject to the discretion to exclude under s. 101(3).

In the light of the more relaxed rules governing the admission of the defendant's bad character in *R v Hanson; R v Gilmore; R v Pickstone* [2005] 2 Cr App R 21, the Court of Appeal warned prosecutors that bad character applications should not be routinely made simply because a defendant has previous convictions.

(1) Propensity to commit offences of the kind with which the defendant is charged

Under s. 103(2) CJA 2003, propensity to commit offences of the kind with which the defendant is charged *may* be established by evidence that the defendant has been convicted of an offence of the same description or an offence of the same category as the offence(s) with which he is charged. Section 103(2) does not apply if a court concludes that by reason of length of time since conviction or for any other reason, it would be unjust to infer propensity from the defendant's criminal record (s. 103(3)).

(2) An offence of the same description/category

An offence will be of the same description if the statement of offence would in each case be the same (s. 103(4)(a)). For example, if X is charged with assault occasioning actual bodily harm contrary to s. 47 Offences Against the Person Act 1861 and has a previous conviction for a s. 47 assault, this would constitute an offence of the same description and would therefore be admissible to show X's propensity to commit violent assault.

Offences of the same category have to be prescribed in an Order made by the Secretary of State (s. 103(4)(b)). Currently the two categories of offences that fall within the same category are theft and child sex offences.

Theft offences of the same category include theft, robbery, burglary, aggravated burglary, taking a motor car without consent, aggravated vehicle-taking, handling stolen goods, going equipped to steal, making off without payment and inchoate offences of the same description. In relation to sexual offences against persons under the age of 16, the Order includes a full list of all such offences in Part 2 including rape, indecent assault, unlawful sexual intercourse and incest, together with the new offences involving children under the Sexual Offences Act 2003.

Where the defendant is on trial for either a theft or child sex offence and has a conviction(s) for an offence(s) which fall within the same category, there is a strong presumption that the conviction(s) should be revealed to the jury.

(3) Proving propensity to commit an offence of the kind in other ways

Proof of propensity to commit an offence of the kind with which the defendant is charged is not confined to previous convictions for offences of the same description or category. For example, Letitia is charged with a serious assault arising out of an incident in a nightclub. She claims to have acted in self-defence maintaining she was the victim of an unprovoked attack. She has previous convictions for affray and for a public order offence under s. 5 Public Order Act 1986. Although Letitia's previous convictions are not of the same description or category as the current charge, the prosecution could legitimately argue that they indicate a propensity on Letitia's part to engage in acts of violence and public disturbance, making her defence less credible. Her previous convictions are therefore relevant to an important matter in issue between the prosecution and the defence.

Evidence of a defendant's propensity is not restricted solely to proof of previous convictions and can be proved in other ways (s. 103(2) CJA 2003). In *R v Weir* [2005] EWCA Crim 2866, the Court of Appeal held that propensity could be established by proof that the defendant had been given a police caution. Weir was charged with sexual assault of a 10-year-old girl. His denied any wrongdoing. Five years previously, he had received a caution for taking an indecent photograph of a child. Also see *Olu* [2010] EWCA Crim 2975 in the Bad Character Case Compendium, for the particular considerations that apply when admitting a caution as evidence of propensity where the defendant denies he is guilty of the offence for which he was given the caution. (A diversionary caution cannot be given unless there is an admission of guilt (see Chapter 8).)

Propensity can be established by proof of conduct that is not criminal (provided it is reprehensible). In the pre-2003 Act case of *R v Butler* (1987) 84 Cr App R 12, B denied committing a very degrading sexual assault on a woman in the back of the woman's car after he had flagged her car down, maintaining the woman's identification of him was mistaken. The prosecution was allowed to adduce evidence from the defendant's former girlfriend of the degrading and very similar sexual acts she had allowed him to perform on her. Although the evidence disclosed no criminal acts on the defendant's part, as his former girlfriend had consented, it provided significant probative value on the issue of the accuracy of the victim's identification of her attacker.

Propensity can also be established by unproven past allegations of misconduct, even where this resulted in an acquittal, provided the evidence is relevant. In the pre-2003 Act case of *R v Z* [2000] 3 WLR 117, the defendant denied a charge of rape, maintaining his victim had consented. At his trial evidence was heard that he had previously been tried and acquitted of rape in three separate trials, having used the same defence in each case. The victims in each of the previous cases were permitted to give evidence against Z as their evidence was relevant to the issue of consent in the case being tried. In *R v Smith* [2005] EWCA Crim 3244, a case heard under the 2003 Act, the Court of Appeal endorsed the approach taken in *R v Z* about the admissibility under gateway (d) of earlier allegations against the accused for which he was not prosecuted but which showed propensity to commit the offences charged in the later proceedings. To ensure the defendant is not unfairly prejudiced by this approach the Court of Appeal specifically emphasised that the defendant's protection comes through the judge's discretion to exclude the evidence of bad character under s. 101(3) or, where appropriate, through s. 78 PACE 1984.

For a more detailed consideration of the difficulties of establishing propensity from unproven past accusations, see *R v McKenzie* [2008] EWCA Crim 758; *R v O'Dowd* [2009] EWCA Crim 905 and the Supreme Court's decision in *R v Mitchell* [2017] Crim LR 310. In our Bad Character Case Compendium, which is found in the student resource section of our online resources.

(4) *R v Hanson* and its importance in relation to propensity and the exercise of discretion under s. 101(3)

In one of the first key decisions on the bad character provisions under the CJA 2003, the Court of Appeal provided the following guidance in *R v Hanson; R v Gilmore; R v Pickstone* [2005] 2 Cr App R 21:

(a) Where the prosecution relies on the defendant's propensity to commit offences, there are three questions to be answered:

   (i) Does the history of conviction(s) establish a propensity to commit offences of the kind charged?

   (ii) Does that propensity make it more likely that the defendant committed the offence charged?

   (iii) Is it unjust to rely on the conviction(s) of the same description or category; and, in any event, will the proceedings be unfair if they are admitted?

(b) Propensity is not confined to offences of the same description or category. As such s. 103(2) is not exhaustive of the types of convictions which might be relied on to show evidence of propensity to commit offences of the same kind. Equally, simply because an offence falls within the same description or category is not necessarily sufficient to show a propensity.

(c) There is no minimum number of events that are required to show propensity. The fewer the number of convictions, the weaker the evidence of propensity is likely to be. A single previous conviction may show evidence of propensity where the offence discloses unusual tendencies or the *modus operandi* discloses significant features such as to give the previous misconduct probative force.

> 'Child sexual abuse or fire setting, are comparatively clear examples of such unusual behaviour but we attempt no exhaustive list. Circumstances demonstrating probative force are not confined to those sharing striking similarity. So, a single conviction for shoplifting will not, without more, be admissible to show propensity to steal. But if the modus operandi has significant features shared by the offence charged, it may show propensity.'

(d) Having regard to the exercise of judicial discretion under s. 101(3), and under s. 103(3), the court should take into consideration:

(i) the degree of similarity between the previous conviction and the offence charged, albeit they are both within the same description or prescribed category. For example, theft and assault occasioning actual bodily harm may each embrace a wide spectrum of conduct. This does not, however, mean that what used to be referred as striking similarity must be shown before convictions become admissible;

(ii) the respective gravity of the past and present offences;

(iii) a key factor will be an assessment of the strength of the prosecution's case. If there is little or no evidence, it is unlikely to be just to admit a defendant's previous convictions.

(e) The date of the commission of an offence will often be more significant than the date of conviction. Old convictions, with no special features shared with the offence charged, are likely to have an adverse effect on the fairness of the proceedings.

(f) It will often be necessary, before determining admissibility and even when considering offences of the same description or category, to examine each individual conviction rather than merely to look at the name of the offence or at the defendant's record as a whole.

(g) The sentence passed will not normally be probative or admissible at the behest of the Crown, though it may be at the behest of the defence.

(h) Where past events are disputed, the judge should be careful not to permit the trial to drift into satellite litigation by a prolonged investigation into the circumstances of the past misconduct:

> '. . . the Crown needs to decide, at the time of giving notice of the application, whether it proposes to rely simply upon the fact of conviction or also upon the circumstances of it. The former may be enough when the circumstances of the conviction are sufficiently apparent from its description, to justify a finding that it can establish propensity, either to commit an offence of the kind charged or to be untruthful and that the requirements of ss. 103(3) and 101(3) can, subject to any particular matter raised on behalf of the defendant, be satisfied. For example, a succession of convictions for dwelling-house burglary, where the same is now charged, may well call for no further evidence than proof of the fact of the convictions. But where, as will often be the case, the Crown needs and proposes to rely on the circumstances of the previous convictions, those circumstances and the manner in which they are to be proved must be set out in the application. There is a similar obligation of frankness upon the defendant, which will be reinforced by the general obligation contained in the new Criminal Procedure Rules to give active assistance to the court in its case management (see r. 3.3). Routine applications by defendants for disclosure of the circumstances of previous convictions are likely to be met by a requirement that the request be justified by identification of the reason why it is said that those circumstances may show the convictions to be inadmissible. We would expect the relevant circumstances of previous convictions generally to be capable of agreement, and that, subject to the trial judge's ruling as to admissibility, they will be put before the jury by way of admission. Even where the circumstances are genuinely in dispute, we would expect the minimum indisputable facts to be thus admitted. It will be very rare indeed for it to be necessary for the judge to hear evidence before ruling on admissibility under this Act.'

(i) The importance of correctly directing the jury is also stressed. In any case where bad character is admitted, the jury should be instructed not to place undue reliance on bad character evidence:

> 'Evidence of bad character cannot be used simply to bolster a weak case, or to prejudice the minds of a jury against a defendant. In particular, the jury should be directed; that they should not conclude that the defendant is guilty or untruthful merely because he has these convictions; that, although the convictions may show a propensity, this does not mean that he has committed this offence or been untruthful in this case; that whether they in fact show a propensity is for them to decide; that they must take into account what the defendant has said about his

previous convictions; and that, although they are entitled, if they find propensity as shown, to take this into account when determining guilt, propensity is only one relevant factor and they must assess its significance in the light of all the other evidence in the case.'

(j) If a judge has directed himself or herself correctly, the Court of Appeal will be slow to interfere with a ruling as to admissibility.

What of the specific appeals in Hanson?

In *Hanson*, the charge was theft of money from the living accommodation above a public house. The circumstantial evidence linking Hanson to the crime clearly indicated he had a case to answer, although it was not overwhelming. He denied the offence but had previous convictions for dishonesty, including dwelling-house burglary, theft from premises, a previous conviction for robbery and aggravated vehicle-taking. On the facts in this case, the Court of Appeal observed:

'Convictions for handling and aggravated vehicle taking, although within the theft category, do not, in our judgment, show, without more pertinent information, propensity to burgle as indicted or to steal, to which the applicant pleaded guilty. The applicant's robbery conviction, albeit also within the theft category, might, had it been analysed, have been regarded as being so prejudicial as to adversely affect the fairness of the proceedings in relation to the offence charged. But the applicant had a considerable number of convictions for burglary and theft from private property that were plainly properly admissible to show propensity to commit an offence of the kind here charged.'

In *Gilmore,* an offence of theft was denied. Gilmore was arrested in the early hours of the morning. He had in his possession a bag containing very recently stolen items. Gilmore claimed to have come across the items innocently, believing them to be rubbish. The evidence linking him to the theft was strong. Three recent previous convictions for theft were properly admitted. They were indicative of a recent propensity to steal.

In *Pickstone,* the charges included the rape and indecent assault of P's step-daughter. P denied the offences. There was medical evidence to support the fact of sexual interference. P stated the girl was making up the allegation against him. The respective credibility of the complainant and the defendant was very much in issue. Nine years previous to the current allegation, P had been convicted of the indecent assault of an 11-year-old girl. The trial judge admitted the previous conviction under gateways (d) and (g). He expressly took into account the length of time since the previous conviction, concluding the 'defendant's sexual mores and motivations are not necessarily affected by the passage of time'. In this context, the admission of the evidence under gateways (d) and (g) would not adversely affect the fairness of the proceedings.

(5) Can an old or single previous conviction prove propensity?

In *R v Sully* (2007) 151 SJLB 1564, two convictions for sexual assault on children which were over 30 years old were correctly admitted on a charge of sexual assault of a female under 13. Similarly in *R v Cox* [2007] EWCA Crim 3365, on a charge of sexually assaulting a 13-year-old babysitter, the defendant's previous convictions for sexual assault and attempted unlawful sexual intercourse with a 12-year-old girl, committed 20 years previously, were admitted. By contrast, in *R v Michael M* [2007] Crim LR 637, a 20-year-old conviction for possessing a sawn-off shotgun was wrongly admitted as evidence of propensity on a charge of possession of a firearm with intent to cause fear of violence. These cases show that what constitutes propensity is a question of fact in each case but that the dicta in *R v Hanson* are being applied in the context of offences showing 'unusual features', for example sexual offences involving children.

(6) Propensity to be untruthful—s. 103(1)(b)

Section 101(1)(d) CJA 2003 further permits the prosecution to adduce evidence of a defendant's bad character where the defendant's propensity to be untruthful is an important matter in issue between the prosecution and the defence. In *R v Hanson* [2005] 2 Cr App R 21, the Court of Appeal observed that a propensity to be untruthful is not the same as a propensity to dishonesty (s. 103(1)(b)) and therefore the prosecution should not simply adduce evidence of previous convictions for dishonesty with the explicit purpose of showing the accused has a propensity for untruthfulness.

This statement must now be read in the light of the comments made by Lord Phillips CJ in *R v Campbell* [2007] 1 WLR 2798 which appear to render s. 103(1)(b) virtually obsolete. Lord Phillips observed that a defendant's truthfulness is likely to be in issue in any case where he pleads not guilty and so propensity to be untruthful cannot normally be described as being an important matter in issue.

> 'A propensity for untruthfulness will not of itself, go very far to establishing the committal of a criminal offence. To suggest that a propensity for untruthfulness makes it more likely that a defendant has lied to the jury is not likely to help them. If they apply common sense they will conclude that a defendant who has committed a criminal offence may well be prepared to lie about it, even if he has not shown a propensity for lying whereas a defendant who has not committed the offence charged will be likely to tell the truth, even if he has shown a propensity for telling lies. In short, whether or not a defendant is telling the truth to the jury is likely to depend simply on whether or not he committed the offence charged. The jury should focus on the latter question rather than on whether or not he has a propensity for telling lies. For these reasons, the only circumstance in which there is likely to be an important issue as to whether a defendant has a propensity to tell lies is where telling lies is an element of the offence charged. Even then, the propensity to tell lies is only likely to be significant if the lying is in the context of committing criminal offences, in which case the evidence is likely to be admissible under section 103(1)(a).'

Lord Phillips' reasoning appears to ignore the clear wording in s. 103(1)(b) CJA 2003 which deems a propensity to be untruthful to be a matter in issue between the prosecution and the defence and is contrary to the dicta in *R v Hanson* [2005] which give guidance as to what types of previous convictions are relevant to a determination of a defendant's propensity to be untruthful. In a case where the jury is required to assess the credibility of two conflicting accounts (the defendant's version and the version of a prosecution witness), the fact that the defendant has convictions for fraud or deception is surely relevant to an important matter in issue?

(7) Evidence of propensity—the practical issues

For the Crown Prosecution Service (CPS), gateway (d) is the most common route for the defendant's bad character to be disclosed under the CJA 2003. The reason for this is the wide test under gateway (d), which admits evidence of the defendant's propensity to commit offences or to be untruthful where it is 'relevant to an important issue between the prosecution and the defence'. Most CPS applications involve disclosing previous convictions to prove propensity. In practice the reprehensible ground is not frequently invoked by the CPS due, in part, to uncertainty about what constitutes reprehensible behaviour. Included in this ground might be where the defendant had previously harassed his rape victim or reported incidents of earlier domestic violence in a later offence of serious domestic assault. Note has also been taken of the Court of Appeal's warning in *R v Hanson; R v Gilmore; R v Pickstone* [2005] Cr App R 21, urging restraint by prosecutors not to routinely make bad character applications to bolster an otherwise weak evidential case.

Even though the test for admitting evidence under gateway (d) is interpreted widely, a prosecution application to show propensity should not go unchallenged by the defence. The defence should require the court to ask itself: 'Is the defendant's propensity (as identified by the prosecution) truly relevant to the facts in issue?' or 'Does the defendant's propensity make it more likely that he committed the offence?' Even if the answer to either question is yes, the defence should still apply to have the evidence excluded under s. 101(3) CJA 2003 (see para. 19.7.1) on the basis that it would have an adverse effect on the fairness of the proceedings. The nature of the defence relied on will be significant in determining the relevance and therefore the admissibility of bad character evidence.

Issues of propensity to commit offences of the kind with which the defendant is charged will involve difficult questions of fact for the judge/magistrates. It may be insufficient for the prosecution to rely on the defendant's criminal record as the court may need to hear the facts behind the conviction to determine its true relevance and whether it is indicative of the defendant's propensity. Suppose a defendant is facing a disputed allegation of common assault but has a previous conviction for assault contrary to s. 47 Offences Against the Person Act 1861 (OAPA 1861). This is an offence of the same description, but an assault can be committed in different ways and for many different reasons.

The following examples illustrate the possible application of gateway 101(1)(d).

 Example 1

Barry is charged with assault occasioning actual bodily harm on his neighbour. He pleads not guilty, maintaining he acted in self-defence. Barry has a previous conviction for a violent assault, contrary to s. 20 OAPA 1861, six years earlier. He was involved in a fracas in a public house following a football match and pleaded guilty. The prosecution would say that he has a previous conviction for an offence of the same description/ type which shows Barry has a propensity to use violence. The defence should oppose the application to have this previous conviction admitted. Applying the dicta in *Hanson* (this being one previous conviction only with no special feature), can this single previous conviction amount to propensity? It should also be noted that the manner in which the earlier assault came to be committed is somewhat different from the present alleged assault. In addition, regard should be had to s. 103(3)—this previous conviction is six years old. Aside from challenging propensity, the defence should make an application under s. 101(3) to have it excluded on the basis that its admission would have an adverse effect on the fairness of the proceedings.

In exercising discretion regard should be had to the guidance in *Hanson*. In particular, the previous offence was more serious than that current offence and the circumstances were different. A pertinent factor will be an assessment of how strong the prosecution's case is, as bad character evidence should not be adduced to bolster an evidentially weak case. If the evidence was admitted, the judge would need to carefully direct the jury not to place too much reliance on the fact of previous convictions. If the evidence is not admitted under gateway (d) it might be admitted under gateway (g) if Barry's defence involves an attack on a prosecution witness. It would be up to the judge to decide how to direct the jury in terms of the relevance of the evidence (see para. 19.12).

In this example, assume instead that Barry has three previous convictions for theft. Could these convictions be admitted as evidence of Barry's propensity to be untruthful?

In the light of the statements in *Hanson*, the answer is arguably no. A propensity towards dishonesty is not the same thing as a propensity to be untruthful. It would be important to ascertain whether Barry pleaded guilty to any or all of his previous offences or was found guilty after having given evidence on oath. In the light of Lord Phillips' statement in *R v Campbell* [2007], the evidence would appear to assume no relevance at all. The evidence could, however, be admitted under gateway (g) if Barry's defence involves an attack on a prosecution witness (see later).

 Example 2

Deepak is charged with burglary. He denies the offence, maintaining a defence of mistaken identity. He intends to call his girlfriend as an alibi. Deepak has an extensive criminal record which includes a conviction for violent robbery four years ago, and several previous convictions for theft, burglary and possession of drugs over the past 12 years. Will the fact of these previous convictions be admissible?

The prosecution will want to adduce Deepak's previous convictions for dishonesty related offences under s. 101(1)(d), both as evidence of Deepak's propensity to commit offences of the kind with which he is charged and as evidence of his propensity to be untruthful. The previous convictions for robbery, theft and burglary are all offences of the same description/category as the current offence. The assumption will therefore be that they show Deepak's propensity to commit offences of dishonesty.

What can the defence argue in this situation? How relevant is Deepak's propensity to the issue of whether the witness's identification is correct or not, especially as Deepak denies being at the scene? Would it not adversely affect the fairness of the proceedings if they were to be admitted? Wouldn't the jury inevitably disregard the evidence of identification and conclude Deepak is guilty because of his track record? If Deepak's defence is mistaken identity, in what sense is he putting forward an untruthful defence? While the previous convictions for theft and burglary may be admitted on the issue of his propensity, the admission of the robbery conviction might be regarded as being particularly prejudicial. *Hanson* suggests the court should have regard to the respective gravity of past and present offences and the strength of the prosecution's case. Applying the dicta in *Hanson* (and subject to the caveat raised by Lord Phillips in *R v Campbell*), previous convictions for offences of dishonesty do not necessarily indicate a propensity to be untruthful.

Once again, if the evidence was admitted, the judge should carefully direct the jury not to place too much reliance on the fact of previous convictions.

 Example 3

Frank is charged with sexually assaulting his nine-year-old nephew. He denies the offence, maintaining that the child is lying. Frank received a caution 18 months earlier for possession of indecent photographs of young boys which were found on his computer. He only accepted the caution because he felt under pressure and wanted to avoid unwanted publicity as he was working as a teacher. He does not know how the images appeared on his computer. Can the prosecution use this fact in evidence against him at his trial for sexual assault?

The prosecution would argue that the caution suggests Frank has a paedophilic disposition, making it less likely that the nephew is making up the allegation. Although he has only a caution recorded against his name, *Hanson* suggests that sex offences involving children are indicative of unusual behaviour.

The defence advocate might argue that the earlier offence is very different to that currently alleged, and for this reason its relevance in the context of the current case must be doubted. Furthermore, there is doubt as to the safety and reliability of the previous caution. Consequently, the admission of such evidence would prejudice Frank's right to a fair trial on the basis that its prejudicial value exceeds its probative effect. Does it make it more likely that the boy is telling the truth?

---

(8) Relevance aside from propensity

It should not be forgotten that gateway (d) is not confined exclusively to propensity evidence. Any evidence 'relevant to an important matter in issue between the defendant and the prosecution' is potentially admissible under this gateway. Relevance may lie in the fact that the evidence casts doubt on the defence advanced such as innocent association or mistaken identification (see the accounts of *Elliott* [2010] EWCA Crim 2378, *R v Zafran Akhtar Saleem* [2007] EWCA Crim 1923, and *R v Awoyemi and others* [2016] 2 Cr App R 302 in the Bad Character Case Compendium).

19.8 BAD CHARACTER ADMITTED BETWEEN CO-DEFENDANTS—S. 101(1)(E) CJA 2003

Evidence of a defendant's bad character has substantial probative value to an important issue between the defendant and a co-defendant.

Section 101(1)(e) CJA 2003 is defined further in s. 104, and applies only to a co-defendant.

> **'104 Matter in issue between the defendant and a co-defendant**
>
> (1) Evidence which is relevant to the question whether the defendant has a propensity to be untruthful is admissible on that basis under section 101(1)(e) only if the nature or conduct of his defence is such as to undermine the co-defendant's defence.
>
> (2) Only evidence—
>
> (a) which is to be (or has been) adduced by the co-defendant, or
>
> (b) which a witness is to be invited to give (or has given) in cross-examination by the co-defendant is admissible under section 101(1)(e).'

This subsection may apply where co-accused (A) wishes to lead evidence of a fellow co-accused's (B's) propensity to commit offences of a certain kind to show that it was more likely that B committed the offence in question. A good example of this gateway is provided by *R v Randall* [2004] 1 Cr App R 26 where it was not entirely clear which of the co-accused had inflicted the final, fatal injury in an allegation of murder. Each blamed the other. Co-accused A sought to introduce B's previous convictions for serious violence to suggest that B was more likely to have inflicted the fatal injury. By contrast, A's previous convictions were for minor offences. The House of Lords quashed A's conviction for murder, maintaining the trial judge should have directed the jury that B's criminal past was relevant to A's defence, and that they could consider B's past when determining the involvement of each in the offence.

R v Randall must now be re-considered in the light of the recent case of *R v Platt* [2016] EWCA Crim 4. P, the appellant, and his co-accused, M, were jointly tried for a murder committed in a hostel that housed ex-offenders, many of whom had drug or alcohol related problems. The murder victim was a sex offender who had often been bullied in the hostel and whose body was found with multiple injuries to his face, including facial fractures. The victim had also had accelerant poured on him and had been set on fire. The prosecution case was that the murder had been jointly committed. There was strong circumstantial evidence against P and evidence linking M to the crime. At the trial, P and M ran 'cut throat' defences. P denied involvement in the killing and whilst not positively asserting that the blame lay with M, P contended that M was amongst those who might have killed the deceased. M persuaded the trial judge to admit P's previous conviction for arson committed when P was 15, and two convictions for s. 20 causing grievous bodily harm. The first s. 20 offence arose out of an assault at a football match and was also committed when P was 15. The later s. 20 offence was when P had punched and broke the jaw of a man who it was accepted had jumped on him. The trial judge admitted the convictions under s. 101(1)(e) as having substantial probative value in relation to the appellant's credibility, which was an important matter in issue between him and his co-accused. In reaching her decision, the trial judge relied on *R v Randall*. It will be recalled that in *Randall*, the evidence of the co-accused's bad character had been admitted as evidence of his propensity to commit an offence of the kind charged, making it less likely that R had inflicted the fatal blows.

Concluding that the trial judge had erred when she admitted P's previous convictions under s. 101 (1)(e), the Court of Appeal stated:

(1) The test of 'substantial probative value' to an important matter in issue between a defendant and a co-defendant under s. 101(1)(e) is higher than that applicable under s. 101(1)(d), which is the test of 'relevance' to an important matter in issue between the defendant and the prosecution because there is no discretion under s. 101(1)(e) to exclude the bad character evidence if it is admitted.

(2) The word 'substantial' should be given its ordinary, unelaborated meaning and needed no gloss.

(3) When applying the test in s. 101(1)(e), the judge, as is explained in the Court of Appeal's decision in *R v Phillips* [2012] 1 Cr App R 332 (25) at 347, has to answer two questions in relation to propensity: (1) whether the evidence has substantial probative value and (2) whether the matter in respect of which the evidence is substantially probative, is a matter of substantial importance in the context of the case as a whole.

(4) Where statute has abolished the common law applicable to a subject and provided a clear statutory code, it is neither necessary nor desirable to refer to the old law, and this is particularly so in relation to the Criminal Justice Act 2003, which has been in force for some ten years and those editing textbooks might well consider that the time had come for a substantial revision to remove the old law!

On the facts, the evidence lacked the requisite 'substantial probative value'. They were certainly not relevant to P's credibility and indeed, no application had been made under s. 104(1). In relation to propensity, the conviction for arson was dated and a completely different type of offence to the murder and the s. 20 matters were again of some age and in a completely different context. Although concluding that the trial judge had erred, the Court of Appeal upheld the conviction as being safe in the light of the other evidence in the case and the fact that the trial judge has stressed the limited value of the bad character evidence.

The key factor is whether the evidence has substantial probative value on an important matter in issue between co-defendants.

Where one co-accused wishes to adduce evidence of the other's propensity to be untruthful, s. 104(1) specifically stipulates that this will only be allowed where the nature and conduct of the co-accused's defence **undermines the defence of his fellow co-accused**. In *R v Lawson* [2007] 1 WLR 1191, it was suggested that convictions for shoplifting and stealing are relevant to untruthfulness and that the statements in *R v Hanson*, which suggest there is a difference between dishonesty and untruthfulness (see para. 19.7.5(6)), should not be applied to gateway (e).

The following guidelines are taken from the pre-2003 Act case of *R v Varley* [1982] 2 All ER 519 which, it is submitted notwithstanding statements made about the relevance of pre-2003 Act authorities by the Court of Appeal in *Platt*, continue to apply to gateway (e).

- It has to be decided objectively whether the evidence either supports the prosecution case in a material respect or undermines the defence of the co-accused.

- In relation to undermining a co-accused's defence, care must be taken to see that the evidence clearly undermines the defence. Inconvenience to or inconsistency with the other's defence is not of itself sufficient.

- Mere denial of participation in a joint venture is not of itself sufficient to rank as evidence against the co-defendant. Such denial must lead to the conclusion that if the witness did not participate then it must have been the other who did.

The following should be noted about s. 101(1)(e) CJA 2003:

- Where the grounds for admitting evidence of a co-accused's bad character are satisfied, there is no discretion to disallow cross-examination (provided the safeguard that the evidence must have substantial probative value in relation to an important matter in issue between the co-accused is satisfied).

- Evidence of a bad character disclosed under this gateway is not limited to undermining a co-accused's credibility as a witness, and may (subject to how the judge chooses to direct the jury) be used as evidence going towards the co-accused's guilt.

Consider this example of the operation of s. 101(1)(e) CJA 2003.

 Example

Wayne and Jordan are jointly charged with murder. The prosecution alleges that the victim was fatally wounded as a result of being knifed by one or both of the defendants. Wayne and Jordan are pleading not guilty and are running cut-throat defences by blaming each other. Wayne has several previous convictions. Last year he was convicted of possession of an offensive weapon, namely a knuckle-duster. Five years previously, following a trial at which he gave evidence on oath, he was convicted of robbery, during which an iron bar was used to inflict a serious injury on a security guard. Wayne has several previous convictions for theft, deception and burglary over a 10-year period. In his examination-in-chief, Wayne states that it was Jordan who knifed the victim. Jordan has one recent previous conviction for theft and a conviction for affray four years previously in respect of which she pleaded guilty.

Jordan's counsel may seek to cross-examine Wayne about his previous convictions on the basis that:

- Wayne's previous convictions have substantial probative value in relation to an important issue between the co-accused—that is, the identity of the person who inflicted the fatal knife injury on the deceased; and
- in giving evidence, Wayne has undermined Jordan's defence.

Provided these conditions are satisfied, the court has no discretion to prevent Jordan from adducing evidence of Wayne's previous convictions. The bad character evidence is arguably relevant both to undermining Wayne's credibility as a witness (as his previous convictions show that he has a propensity to be dishonest) and to the likelihood that it was more likely to have been Wayne who inflicted the fatal stab wound as his previous recent conviction for possession of an offensive weapon and his conviction for a violent robbery indicate a propensity to commit violent assaults.

For a case that illustrates the application of gateway (e), see *R v Edwards; Rowlands; McClean; Gray and Smith* [2005] EWCA Crim 3244.

19.9 BAD CHARACTER TO CORRECT A FALSE IMPRESSION GIVEN BY THE DEFENDANT—S. 101(1)(F) CJA 2003

Evidence of the defendant's bad character is admissible to correct a false impression given by the defendant.

Section 101(1)(f) CJA 2003 is further defined by s. 105 and is available only to the prosecution:

'105   Evidence to correct a false impression

(1) For the purposes of section 101(1)(f)—

(a) the defendant gives a false impression if he is responsible for the making of an express or implied assertion which is apt to give the court or jury a false or misleading impression about the defendant;

(b) evidence to correct such an impression is evidence which has probative value in correcting it.

(2) A defendant is treated as being responsible for the making of an assertion if—

(a) the assertion is made by the defendant in the proceedings (whether or not in evidence given by him);

(b) the assertion was made by the defendant—

(i) on being questioned under caution, before charge, about the offence with which he is charged, or

(ii) on being charged with the offence or officially informed that he might be prosecuted for it, and evidence of the assertion is given in the proceedings,

(c) the assertion is made by a witness called by the defendant;

(d) the assertion is made by any witness in cross-examination in response to a question asked by the defendant that is intended to elicit it, or is likely to do so; or

(e) the assertion was made by any person out of court, and the defendant adduces evidence of it in the proceedings.

(3) A defendant who would otherwise be treated as responsible for the making of an assertion shall not be so treated if, or to the extent that, he withdraws it or disassociates himself from it.

(4) Where it appears to the court that a defendant, by means of his conduct (other than the giving of evidence) in the proceedings, is seeking to give the court or jury an impression about himself that is false or misleading, the court may if it appears just to do so treat the defendant as being responsible for the making of an assertion which is apt to give that impression.

(5) In subsection (4) 'conduct' includes appearance or dress.

(6) Evidence is admissible under section 101(1)(f) only if it goes no further than is necessary to correct the false impression.

(7) Only prosecution evidence is admissible under section 101(1)(f).'

A defendant gives a false impression if he makes an express or implied assertion which gives the court a false or misleading impression about him. A defendant can create a false impression through an assertion made at the police station or by what he says on oath at trial or through his conduct in the proceedings (s. 105(4)). As with all the gateways, it applies irrespective of whether the defendant gives evidence in his defence. Gateway (f) may be avoided if the defendant withdraws or disassociates himself from the assertion (s. 105(3)). In *Renda* [2005] EWCA Crim 2826, gateway (f) was triggered at the police station when R made false statements regarding his work history. The Court of Appeal held that a concession extracted from a defendant in cross-examination will not amount to a withdrawal or disassociation from a previously made misleading statement.

The prosecution may only introduce evidence of the defendant's bad character sufficient to rebut the false impression that was made about the defendant's character (s. 105(6)). It may not be necessary, therefore, for the whole of the defendant's bad character to be disclosed.

There is nothing in the Act which suggests that, having adduced evidence of the defendant's bad character under this gateway, the court cannot use the information to infer guilt. Equally, there is nothing to prevent the judge from directing the jury to make limited evidential use of such evidence. As the discretion under s. 101(3) does not apply to this gateway, the admissibility of the defendant's bad character can be challenged under s. 78 PACE 1984 and the common law discretion under s. 82(3) PACE 1984 (see *R v Stokes* [2015] EWCA Crim 1911).

 Example

Saeeda is charged with handling a consignment of stolen designer clothes. Both during the police investigation and at trial, Saeeda asserts that she would never do anything dishonest where her business interests are concerned. To rebut this false assertion about her unimpeachable business ethics, the prosecution wish to put in evidence Saeeda's conviction for a VAT fraud committed while she was a director of an unrelated business venture six years ago. The prosecution would be able to put Saeeda's conviction into evidence to rebut the misleading impression she has created about her business affairs. Had Saeeda made her assertion solely in the course of the interview, the gateway could still be triggered by the investigating officer giving evidence of the assertion in interview. In either instance, Saeeda should be advised to withdraw the statement she made in interview before trial. In these circumstances the gateway under s. 101(1)(f) would not be triggered.

19.10 BAD CHARACTER ADMITTED UNDER S. 101(1)(G) CJA 2003

Evidence of the defendant's bad character is admissible after the defendant has made an attack on another person's character.

This is another significant gateway for the prosecution and is further defined in s. 106:

'106 Attack on another person's character

(1) For the purposes of section 101(1)(g) a defendant makes an attack on another person's character if—

(a) he adduces evidence attacking the other person's character, or

(b) he (or any legal representative appointed under section 38(4) of the Youth Justice and Criminal Evidence Act 1999 to cross-examine a witness in his interests) asks questions in cross-examination that are intended to elicit such evidence, or are likely to do so, or

(c) evidence is given of an imputation about the other person made by the defendant—

(i) on being questioned under caution, before charge, about the offence with which he is charged, or

(ii) on being charged with the offence or officially informed that he might be prosecuted for it.

(2) In subsection (1) "evidence attacking the other person's character" means evidence to the effect that the other person—

(a) has committed an offence (whether a different offence from the one with which the defendant is charged or the same one), or

(b) has behaved, or is disposed to behave, in a reprehensible way; and "imputation about the other person" means an assertion to that effect.

(3) Only prosecution evidence is admissible under section 101(1)(g).'

19.10.1 WHAT AMOUNTS TO AN ATTACK?

Gateway (g) replaces the old law under s. 1(3)(ii) CEA 1898, which gave a defendant a shield against the revelation of past bad character whilst giving evidence on oath. The defendant would lose his shield if his defence led to the character of a prosecution witness being impugned. In *R v Hanson* [2005] 2 Cr App R 21, the Court of Appeal observed:

'As to s. 101(1)(g), the pre-2003 Act authorities will continue to apply when assessing whether an attack has been made on another person's character, to the extent that they are compatible with s. 106.'

This means that authorities such as *Selvey v DPP* [1970] AC 304 and *R v Britzman* [1983] 1 WLR 350 on what constitutes an 'attack' continue to apply. In *Selvey* it was held that a defendant still loses his shield notwithstanding that attacking the character of another is a necessary part of his defence. Some latitude was given to defendants under the 1898 Act in that a denial of guilt, however emphatic, would not amount to an attack. The cases at common law went so far as to suggest that even calling a witness a liar would not amount to an attack, but a suggestion that the witness had a motive for lying would do so. This may no longer be the case under CJA 2003.

Based on the pre-2003 Act authorities, the following situations would constitute an 'attack' on another:

- an allegation that a prosecution witness is biased;
- an allegation that the police have fabricated evidence;
- cross-examining a prosecution witness on any previous convictions they might have;
- accusing a prosecution witness of perjury;
- accusing the investigating officers of deliberately flouting PACE and the Codes of Practice.

It will probably not amount to an 'attack' to suggest that:

- a prosecution witness is mistaken, confused or simply wrong;
- the police have 'misinterpreted' a provision under the PACE Codes of Practice;
- a prosecution witness is lying (based on statements in the pre-2003 Act case of *R v Britzman*).

Gateway (g) is wider than its CEA 1898 predecessor. It refers to attacking another person's character and is therefore not limited to witnesses giving evidence in the case. It is now irrelevant whether the defendant testifies and it can be engaged at the police station when answering questions in interview. In *R v Lamaletie* [2008] EWCA Crim 314, L denied in his police interview an allegation of violent assault claiming he had acted in self-defence. The trial judge permitted the admission of L's previous convictions under gateway (g) as L had *'made an attack on another person's character'*: On appeal against his conviction, L argued that his statements in interview amounted to no more than an 'emphatic denial'. The Court of Appeal disagreed saying L had gone further by alleging not simply that victim had struck the first blow but that he 'was attacking me everywhere'. Even the allegation that he had started the fight would probably be an assertion of reprehensible behaviour within the meaning of s. 106 (2)(b).

The ease with which this gateway can be engaged by answering questions in interview at the police station is further illustrated in *R v Ball* [2005] EWCA Crim 2826 B's use the word 'slag' during a police interview when seeking to defend an allegation of rape. This comment was sufficient to trigger gateway (g). Suppose the investigating officer says to the suspect '. . . so are you saying that witness X is lying . . . ?' If the suspect answers this affirmatively, he might be regarded as attacking another person's character, triggering the admission of his previous convictions at any subsequent trial. This provision makes the difficult role of the legal adviser at the police station (considered in the additional chapter 'Advising at the Police Station' available in the online resources) even more challenging.

You will recall that the defendant will only be able to 'attack' the character of a witness if he is granted leave under s. 100 CJA 2003, see Chapter 16, para. 16.9.4. Even where a defendant is granted leave to adduce evidence disclosing the character of another under s. 100 CJA 2003, gateway (g) will still be triggered, as this is regarded as making an attack on the character of another person.

19.10.2 THE EXERCISE OF DISCRETION IN RELATION TO GATEWAY (G)

As with s. 101(1)(d), the defence can apply to have the evidence excluded under s. 101(3) CJA 2003 on the basis of 'unfairness'. Under the pre-2003 Act, the discretion to exclude evidence of a defendant's previous convictions following the loss of his shield, even where his previous convictions were similar to the offence for which he was being tried, was exercised restrictively. In *R v Burke* (1986) 82 Cr App R 156, while acknowledging that 'cases must occur in which it would be unjust to admit evidence of a character gravely prejudicial to the accused, even though there may be some tenuous grounds for holding it technically admissible', the Court of Appeal nevertheless went on to say that:

> 'In the ordinary and normal case the trial judge may feel that if the credit of the prosecutor or his witnesses has been attacked, it is only fair that the jury should have before them material on which they can form their judgment whether the accused person is any more worthy to be believed than those he has attacked. It is obviously unfair that the jury should be left in the dark about an accused person's character if the conduct of his defence has attacked the character of the prosecutor or the witnesses for the prosecution.'

For a helpful illustration of the operation and rationale of gateway (g), consider the case of *R v Royston Lewis* [2007] EWCA Crim 3030 in the Bad Character Case Compendium. Also, see the account of the recent case of *R v Omotoso* [2018] EWCA Crim 1394 in the compendium.

 Example

Consider the following example of s. 101(1)(g) CJA 2003. Lim is charged with assaulting his cohabitee on two separate occasions. The couple have a volatile relationship. Lim denies the allegation and claims he acted in self-defence, maintaining the injured party flew at him in a drunken rage. Lim has previously obtained a civil injunction against his partner. Lim seeks leave under s. 100 CJA 2003 to adduce evidence of his partner's violent acts against him. This is clearly an attack on her character. As a consequence, the prosecution serves notice under s. 101(1)(g) to admit Lim's previous convictions for wounding with intent, assault occasioning actual bodily harm and assault on a police officer (the most recent committed eight years ago), offences of theft, handling and deception committed 12 years ago and two drink-related driving offences (failing to provide a specimen and driving with excess alcohol) committed in the last five years. None of his assaults were perpetrated on females. If leave is granted under s. 100 CJA 2003, it is inevitable that gateway (g) will be opened. The defence could apply to have the evidence excluded (s. 101(3) CJA 2003) on the basis that to admit them would be unduly prejudicial. Lim will say that his previous convictions for violence are considerably dated and that none of them involved him using violence against women. If admitted, Lim might persuade the court to confine their relevance to an assessment of his credibility only. However, given the statements in *Highton* and *Campbell,* there is nothing to prevent the court from using the previous convictions on the issue of Lim's propensity if they are relevant. Previous convictions for deception may well be used as evidence indicating a propensity to be untruthful subject to the statements in *Campbell* on this point.

19.11 THE PRACTICE AND PROCEDURE FOR ADMITTING EVIDENCE OF A DEFENDANT'S BAD CHARACTER

With the exception of gateways (a), (b), and (e), it is the Crown Prosecutor's decision whether to make a bad character application.

Where a bad character application is made, the police will provide evidence of the defendant's bad character from the Police National Computer (PNC), which details a person's previous offending.

The procedure for applying is set out in Crim PR, Part 21. On receiving the defendant's antecedents from the PNC the prosecution must serve the notice in the prescribed form when seeking to admit evidence of the defendant's bad character under gateways (c)–(g), excluding (e). Most applications are in writing and in accordance with strict time limits. Where the defence seeks to adduce bad character under gateway (b), notice on the correct form must also be given. The forms can be found under Part 21. Where the application is opposed by the defence, the notice to oppose must be served on the prescribed form and returned within set time limits.

In the Crown Court, a contested bad character application may be made the subject of a pre-trial ruling with prosecution and defence advocates sometimes required to submit a skeleton argument in support of their applications. More frequently, a contested application will usually be left to be heard on the day of the trial before the jury is empanelled.

Both prosecutors and defence advocates will be aware that a binding ruling in favour of admitting evidence of a defendant's bad character made before the trial may persuade a defendant to plead guilty.

In cases that are to be tried before the magistrates' court, a contested application is normally listed for consideration at the pre-trial hearing where a District Judge or magistrates will hear legal arguments and make a binding ruling.

When making a binding ruling on the admissibility of bad character evidence, the court must give written reasons for reaching its decision (s. 110 CJA 2003).

In assessing the evidence and preparing the case for trial the CPS lawyer requires an excellent understanding of the statutory framework and the leading case law because where bad character is admissible, in most cases it will significantly enhance the prosecution's case and increase the chance of a successful prosecution.

The defence lawyer should also be similarly vigilant and be prepared to rigorously persuade the court that either the test for admitting the bad character under the gateway specified by the CPS in the application is not made out or argue persuasively that the court should exercise its exclusionary discretion under s. 78 PACE 1984 and/or s. 101(1)(3) CJA 2003.

Our case study *R v Lenny Wise* includes an application by the prosecution to admit evidence of Lenny Wise's criminal convictions under s. 101(1) CJA 2003 in Document 28 of the case study. The defence notice to oppose the admission of Lenny's bad character is illustrated in Document 33. For a further illustration of a bad character application please refer to the *R v Nicholas Jones* case study. All of the relevant documentation and video-links can be accessed from our online resources.

19.12 RELEVANCE AND USE THAT CAN BE MADE OF BAD CHARACTER ADDUCED UNDER S. 101 AND THE IMPORTANCE OF THE DIRECTION TO THE JURY

The CJA 2003 makes no stipulation as to the use that can be made of bad character under the Act. In *R v Highton; R v Van Nguyen; R v Carp* [2005] 1 WLR 3472 the Court of Appeal stated:

> 'In the case of gateway (g), for example, admissibility depends on the defendant having made an attack on another person's character, but once the evidence is admitted, it may, depending on the particular facts, be relevant not only to credibility but also to propensity to commit offences of the kind with which the defendant is charged.'

This view is supported by statements made in *R v Campbell* [2007] 1 WLR 2798. Lord Phillips observed that once bad character is admitted it can be used for any purpose for which it assumes relevance. This means that bad character admitted through gateway (g) may be used by a jury as evidence of the defendant's propensity even though the bad character has not been admitted under gateway (d) and vice versa. It is for the judge to decide what relevance the evidence can assume. The jury should be directed accordingly.

The importance of correctly directing the jury about the relevance of bad character evidence and the need not to place undue reliance upon it is stressed in *Highton*. (See also the Crown Court Compendium (part 1) available at https://www.judiciary.gov.uk/wp-content/uploads/2016/05/crown-court-compendium-part-i-jury-and-trial-management-and-summing-up.pdf). The Part 1 of the *Crown Court Compendium* requires judges to explain to the jury why they have heard bad character evidence and what use they can and cannot make of it.

In relation to misuse and in the case of propensity evidence, the jury must be warned that if they accept the evidence does indicate a tendency on the part of the defendant to commit offences of the kind charged that does not mean that the defendant committed the offence on this occasion but that it may provide some support for the prosecution's case. The jury must be instructed not to convict the defendant wholly or mainly on the basis of previous convictions or past bad behaviour. In relation to gateway (g), the jury will be instructed that simply because the defendant has previous convictions this does not necessarily mean that he or she is telling lies.

A failure to properly direct a jury on the use it may make of bad character evidence will afford grounds for an appeal against conviction.

19.13 MISCELLANEOUS MATTERS

Under s. 107 CJA 2003 power is given to a trial judge to stop a trial on indictment at any time before the close of the prosecution's case where evidence has been admitted under s. 101(1)(c)–(g) CJA 2003 and the court is satisfied that the evidence is contaminated, with the result that any conviction would be regarded as being unsafe. There are also special rules relating to childhood convictions under s. 108 CJA 2003, which provide that where a person (aged 21 or over) is being tried, evidence of any previous convictions committed by him under the age of 14 shall not be admissible unless both of the offences are triable on indictment and the court is satisfied that the interests of justice require the evidence to be admitted.

Postscript

A steady stream of case law on bad character is emerging. If it is relevant to your core Criminal Litigation course or to your elective in Advanced Criminal Litigation you can access the 'Bad Character Case Compendium', which is held on the student resource section of our online resources. The compendium contains further analysis of bad character evidence and a summary of the most important cases on bad character to date. A number of recent decisions are illustrative of the arguments typically advanced at first instance.

Some decisions show how far the pendulum has swung in favour of the prosecution in admitting evidence of the defendant's bad character. This has serious implications for defendants because if bad character is admitted, it can significantly strengthen the prosecution's case. However, only a handful of cases go to appeal and most decisions on admitting bad character are made at first instance by judges, District Judges and magistrates on the facts in each case. A defence advocate can therefore influence the way in which law is applied and developed on a day-to-day basis.

Further postscript

In the Lecturer Resource section of the online resources, you will find a free-standing video case study entitled *R v Nicholas Jones*. The case involves applications to admit both defendant and non-defendant bad character. The applications were not scripted and were argued before a judge of the Crown Court, who gives a detailed ruling on each application. Full instructions on how you might use this learning resource are given.

KEY POINT SUMMARY

- Be aware of the evidential value of a defendant's good character. Evidence of a defendant's past good character should always be advanced.

- The admissibility of evidence of a defendant's past bad character is regulated by the provisions of the CJA 2003.

- Bad character is very widely defined to include any reprehensible behaviour and is not confined to previous convictions.

- Understand that there are seven gateways in s. 101 through which evidence of a defendant's bad character may be adduced, and that each gateway is further defined in ss. 102–106.

- The application of judicial discretion under s. 101(3) CJA 2003 may prove to be a crucial safeguard in ensuring the defendant can enjoy a fair trial as it gives the court discretion (at least in the context of the most frequently engaged gateways (d) and (g)) to exclude bad character evidence if it would have an adverse effect on the fairness of the proceedings.

- Guidance on what constitutes propensity to commit offences of the kind charged and how judicial discretion to exclude evidence of propensity might be exercised has been provided by the Court of Appeal in *Hanson* and *Highton*.

- The defence must oppose the application of bad character if it is to be excluded—the decision to admit or exclude such evidence may well depend on the quality of the arguments put forward by opposing advocates!

- The defendant is not a compellable witness in a criminal case, but a failure to give evidence without good cause is subject to the risk of having an adverse inference drawn under s. 35 CJPOA 1994.

- Understand the factors that may be taken into consideration when advising clients about whether or not to testify at their trial.

SELF-TEST QUESTIONS

1. Aaron is charged with possession of drugs with intent to supply. The drugs were found under the bonnet of a car he was driving. Aaron pleads not guilty, maintaining he had no knowledge of the presence of the drugs having borrowed the car. Twelve months ago, Aaron was convicted of possession of crack cocaine with intent to supply. He pleaded guilty on the basis that he was a mere custodian of the drugs for a friend. He was given a community sentence which is considered lenient for such an offence. Upon what basis do you feel the prosecution would seek admission of Aaron's previous conviction? If you were the defence advocate, what arguments would you advance in opposition?

2. (a) Brian is charged with the rape of a 15-year-old girl. His defence is that the girl consented. He was convicted five years ago of an offence of unlawful sexual activity with a 14-year-old girl following a guilty plea. Will the prosecution be able to rely on this earlier conviction? What representations would the defence make opposing the prosecution application to adduce his previous conviction?

   (b) Vary the facts slightly. Brian is still charged with the rape of a 15-year-old. His defence is that his victim consented. Brian has a previous conviction for raping his former 26-year-old partner, eight years ago. On that occasion, he ran the same defence. Would this previous conviction be admissible? If so, on what basis?

3. Barry and Tina are accused of the murder of Sean, aged three. Barry was Sean's step-father and Tina was his natural mother. The child died as a result of head injuries. Barry denies murder and states that the child died while in his mother's care and that she has a vicious temper and punched the child while in a drunken stupor. Tina denies murder and claims Barry struck Sean about the head while high on drugs. She maintains she is terrified of Barry and was powerless to do anything. The pathologist's report discloses that the child was malnourished and that his body was covered in bruises and cigarette burns. Barry has several previous convictions for drug-related offences and theft, a previous conviction for criminal damage and one previous conviction for assault occasioning actual bodily harm. Tina has a previous conviction for theft. She will give evidence in support of her defence. Should Barry give evidence? Does the conduct of his defence give you cause for concern? If so, why?

4. Danielle is charged with causing grievous bodily harm with intent. It is alleged she 'glassed' a man in the face causing facial injuries. She denies the offence. She has no previous convictions. What evidential use can be derived from the last-mentioned fact?

Analysis of these questions can be found on our online resources.

Case study: *R v Lenny Wise*

You are reminded that the complete documentation in relation to this case study can be accessed from our online resources.

You will be aware of the issues in this case. The prosecution have served notice to admit Lenny Wise's previous convictions under s. 101(1)(d) CJA 2003. The defence have served notice opposing their admission.

Do you consider that Lenny's previous convictions would be admissible?

Consider whether it would be advisable for Lenny to give evidence in his defence. What factors would have a bearing on your advice?

FIGURE 19.1 EVIDENTIAL RULES RELEVANT TO THE ACCUSED

COMPETENCE AND COMPELLABILITY OF THE ACCUSED

- The accused is:
  - a competent but non-compellable witness for the defence, s. 53 YJCEA 1999;
  - neither a competent nor compellable witness for the prosecution, s. 53(4) YJCEA 1999.
- A co-accused is also not a competent or compellable witness for the prosecution unless he ceases to be a party to the proceedings (s. 53(5) YJCEA 1999).

THE COURSE OF THE ACCUSED'S EVIDENCE

- Section 79 PACE 1984 requires the accused to testify as the first defence witness.
- Where the accused does not give evidence at his trial, adverse inferences may be drawn against his silence under s. 35 CJPOA 1994, providing:
  - the accused is made aware of his right to testify and the possible consequences of remaining silent, Practice Direction (Criminal Consolidated) [2002]; and the jury or magistrates are reminded that:
- the legal burden of proving the accused's guilt lies with the prosecution; and
- the defendant is entitled to remain silent; and
- the prosecution must have established a prima facie case against the accused; and
- adverse inferences cannot be the sole reason for finding the accused guilty, s.38(3) CJPOA 994; and
- adverse inferences may only be drawn where the only explanation for the accused's silence is that he has no answer to the prosecution case; or none that would stand up to cross-examination (see *R v Cowan, Gayle and Riccardi* [1995]).

GOOD CHARACTER

- A defendant with good character is entitled to a good character direction, see *R v Vye and Others* [1993] as to:
  - propensity (a defendant of good character is less likely to have committed the offence); and
  - credibility as a witness (where the defendant before trial asserts his innocence and/or gives evidence at trial).

ADDUCING THE DEFENDANT'S BAD CHARACTER

- Bad character is defined by s. 98 CJA 2003 as evidence of or a disposition towards misconduct or other reprehensible behaviour.
- Section101(a)–(g) CJA 2003 provides seven gateways through which evidence of a defendant's bad character can be admitted:

  (a) all parties agree to the evidence being admitted;

  (b) the evidence is adduced by the defendant or is given in answer during the defendant's cross-examination;

  (c) it is important explanatory evidence;

  (d) it is relevant to an important matter in issue between D and P;

  (e) it has substantial probative value in relation to an important matter in issue between a defendant and co-defendant;

  (f) it is evidence to correct a false impression given by a defendant; or

  (g) the defendant has made an attack on another person's character.

- Evidence of bad character sought to be admitted under s. 101(1)(d) and (g) is subject to exclusionary discretion in s. 101(3) CJA 2003 based on the fairness of admitting the evidence which is triggered by the defence.
- *R v Hanson* [2005] provides important guidance on what constitutes propensity to commit offences of the kind and propensity to be untruthful.
- In exercising discretion in terms of what is just under s. 103(3) and the fairness of the proceedings under s. 101(3), *Hanson* says the following factors are important:

  - the similarity between past and present offences;

  - the respective gravity of past and present offending;

  - the age of any previous convictions;

  - the strength of the prosecution's case.

20 PRIVATE PRIVILEGE

20.1	**Introduction**	**382**
20.2	**Legal professional privilege in criminal cases**	**383**
	20.2.1 Communications between the lawyer and client—s. 10(1)(a) PACE 1984	383
	20.2.2 Communications with third parties—s. 10(1)(b) PACE 1984	384
20.3	**The rationale for legal professional privilege**	**384**
20.4	**Legal professional privilege and the courts**	**384**
20.5	**Waiving/losing legal professional privilege**	**385**
20.6	**Powers of search and legal professional privilege**	**386**
20.7	**The privilege against self-incrimination**	**386**
	20.7.1 Asserting and waiving the privilege	386
	20.7.2 Statutory exceptions to the privilege against self-incrimination	386
	20.7.3 The privilege against self-incrimination and the ECHR 1950	387

20.1 INTRODUCTION

The term 'private privilege' relates to separate privileges that prevent evidence from being disclosed in litigation, or witnesses from being compelled to answer questions at trial. In a criminal case, privilege may be claimed in two situations:

- legal professional privilege;
- the privilege against self-incrimination.

While it is generally in the public interest for cases to be decided on all available admissible and relevant evidence, private privilege recognises that in certain situations it is in the wider public interest to maintain the confidentiality of communications between a lawyer and his client even where the court is denied the benefit of otherwise admissible and relevant evidence.

In this chapter we consider:

- legal professional privilege in criminal cases;
- legal professional privilege and the courts;
- waiving legal professional privilege;
- the privilege against self-incrimination;
- the privilege against self-incrimination and the European Convention on Human Rights 1950.

Whilst the evidential effect of claiming private privilege is the same as claiming public interest immunity (see Chapter 8, para. 8.15), an important difference between them is that private privilege is a personal right belonging to the client or to a witness and cannot be claimed by any other person. Conversely public interest immunity seeks to protect the 'confidentiality' of the work of organisations operating in the 'public' domain, such as the police, security services and HM Revenue and Customs.

20.2 **LEGAL PROFESSIONAL PRIVILEGE IN CRIMINAL CASES**

Legal professional privilege in criminal cases is defined by s. 10(1) Police and Criminal Evidence Act 1984 (PACE 1984), to include:

> '(a) communications between a professional legal adviser and his client or any person representing his client made in connection with the giving of legal advice to the client;
>
> (b) communications between a professional legal adviser and his client or any person representing his client or between such an adviser or his client or any such representative and any other person made in connection with or in contemplation of legal proceedings and for the purpose of such proceedings; and
>
> (c) items enclosed with or referred to in such communications and made—
>
> (i) in connection with the giving of legal advice; or
>
> (ii) in connection with or in the contemplation of legal proceedings and for the purposes of such proceedings;
>
> when they are in the possession of a person who is entitled to possession of them.'

Under s. 10(2) PACE 1984, legal professional privilege does not apply to communications between legal adviser and client where it is used to commit or to conceal the commission of a crime.

It is immaterial whether the lawyer was aware of the illicit purpose of the communication and the 'crime' may relate to an offence either under UK law or in a foreign jurisdiction, see *R v Cox and Railton* [1884] 14 QBD 153.

Legal professional privilege applies in the following two situations.

20.2.1 **COMMUNICATIONS BETWEEN THE LAWYER AND CLIENT—S. 10(1)(A) PACE 1984**

All communications between the lawyer and client for the purpose of giving or obtaining legal advice, will be privileged from disclosure. The privilege belongs always with the client and even survives the death of a lawyer's client. The only person who can waive privilege and permit disclosure is the client or his or her personal representatives. In the important case of *Three Rivers District Council v Bank of England (No 6)* [2004] UKHL 48, the House of Lords observed that if a communication or document qualifies for legal professional privilege, the privilege is absolute. It cannot be overridden by some supposedly greater public interest.

In *Balabel v Air India* [1988] 2 All ER 246, the Court of Appeal held that 'giving legal advice' is not restricted to communications that specifically request or give legal advice, but also includes communications and correspondence that are part of the ongoing relationship between the lawyer and the client.

Therefore, legal professional privilege will attach to:

- all communications between a lawyer and his client;
- communications with counsel;
- communications to salaried legal advisers whether or not they hold a formal legal qualification; and
- communications with foreign lawyers.

The most obvious example of the privilege is that a client cannot be compelled to disclose any oral or written advice given to her by her lawyer or counsel in connection with the case.

While the phrase 'giving legal advice' is broadly interpreted, the courts will not apply the principle to all client–lawyer communications.

Legal professional privilege does not apply to:

- a record of a conveyancing transaction (*R v Crown Court at Inner London Sessions, ex p. Baines and Baines* [1987] 3 All ER 1025);
- a solicitor's documentary records of time spent with a client;

- time sheets;
- fee records;
- the record of a client's appointment in a solicitor's appointment diary (see *R v Manchester Crown Court, ex p. R (Legal Professional Privilege)* [1999] 1 WLR 832).

These documents are not covered by legal professional privilege as they are not concerned with the giving of legal advice. Similarly, a pre-existing document not brought into existence for the purpose of giving or obtaining legal advice or in preparation for litigation (see below) is not privileged from disclosure.

20.2.2 COMMUNICATIONS WITH THIRD PARTIES—S. 10(1)(B) PACE 1984

Legal professional privilege will attach to communications between the client, the legal adviser and a third party where the sole or dominant purpose of the communication was in connection with actual or pending litigation.

In deciding the 'dominant purpose test', the court will adopt an objective view of all the evidence, taking into account the intention of the document's author and the purpose of preparing the document. The key requirement in maintaining the privileged status of communications with third parties is that the communication must relate to pending or contemplated litigation.

20.3 THE RATIONALE FOR LEGAL PROFESSIONAL PRIVILEGE

There are sound policy reasons behind legal professional/ litigation privilege. It is in the public interest that when seeking the advice of her lawyer, a client should be able to openly discuss her case, and to make a full disclosure of all relevant information to her lawyer in the knowledge that she cannot be compelled to disclose the content of those discussions, nor will she be compelled to give evidence about them in court. The rationale is succinctly explained by Lord Rogers in *Three Rivers District Council v Bank of England (No 6)* [2004] UKHL 48:

'If the advice given by lawyers is to be sound, their clients must make them aware of all the relevant circumstances of the problem. Clients will be reluctant to do so, however, unless they can be sure that what they say about any potentially damaging or embarrassing circumstances will not be revealed later. So it is settled that, in the absence of a waiver by the client, communications between clients and their lawyers for the purpose of obtaining legal advice must be kept confidential and cannot be made the subject of evidence. Of course, this means that, from time to time, a tribunal will be deprived of potentially useful evidence but the public interest in people being properly advised on matters of law is held to outweigh the competing public interest in making that evidence available.'

20.4 LEGAL PROFESSIONAL PRIVILEGE AND THE COURTS

As legal professional privilege underpins the administration of criminal justice, the courts adopt a strict approach to enforcing its application. The position is illustrated by the House of Lords in *R v Derby Magistrates' Court, ex p. B* [1996] AC 487.

R v Derby Magistrates' Court, ex p. B [1996] AC 487

A 16-year-old girl was murdered. The appellant was arrested and made a statement to the police that he alone was responsible for the murder. He later retracted the statement and alleged that although he had been present at the scene of the crime, it was his step-father who had killed the girl. Relying on this second statement, the appellant was acquitted in the Crown Court.

Later, the appellant's step-father was charged with the murder. At the step-father's committal, the appellant was called as a witness for the prosecution and repeated the statement that his step-father had killed the girl. He was cross-examined by the defence about the instructions he had given to his solicitor concerning the murder. The appellant claimed legal professional privilege but the magistrates issued a summons (s. 97 Magistrates' Courts Act 1980) directing the appellant and his solicitor to produce the relevant proofs of evidence as they would be 'likely to be material evidence'.

On appeal, the House of Lords held that a summons could not be issued under s. 97 Magistrates' Courts Act 1980 to compel the production of documents protected by legal professional privilege unless the privilege had been waived, which in the present case, it had not. In reaffirming its status, the House of Lords stated that legal professional privilege is much more than an ordinary rule of evidence; it is a fundamental condition on which the administration of justice rests.

The importance that the European Court of Human Rights attaches to the right of a client to consult a lawyer in private has been stressed on a number of occasions.

20.5 **WAIVING/LOSING LEGAL PROFESSIONAL PRIVILEGE**

Privileged material may be relied on by an opposing party if the privilege is waived or lost. As legal professional privilege vests in the client, only she can waive it, either at the pre-trial stage or during the trial. If the client expressly or impliedly waives the privilege a lawyer can be compelled to reveal the contents of the communications between himself and the client, or between himself and a third party. As explained in Chapter 5, the question of waiver commonly arises where the accused is required to explain her silence in response to questions at the police station, by disclosing the reasons that she was given by her lawyer for refusing to answer. In this situation both the accused and the legal adviser may be cross-examined about the content of the advice given at the police station.

Also, in *R v Brown (formerly Latham)* [2015] EWCA Crim 1328 the Court of Appeal recognised a further, narrow common law qualification to the inviolable nature of legal professional privilege by permitting particular individuals to be present at discussions between a legal adviser and her client. This qualification would apply if there was a real possibility that the meeting would be misused for a purpose or conducted in a manner that amounted to 'impropriety'. In Latham, at least two nurses had been ordered to be present at a meeting between the defendant and his legal adviser to protect both the defendant from self-harming and to protect the solicitor as the defendant had previously made threats to kill his solicitor.

The rules on legal professional privilege attaching to communications to an expert witness should be read in conjunction with the obligation on both the prosecution and the defence to disclose any expert report either side intends to rely on at trial (see Chapter 17). Disclosing a report automatically waives any privilege attached to the report. An expert's report which the defence does not use in evidence at trial is covered by legal professional privilege and therefore does not have to be disclosed.

Legal professional privilege may be lost accidentally (see *R v Tompkins* (1977) 67 Cr App R 181). It needs to be closely guarded at all times. In *Cottrill* [1997] Crim LR 56, solicitors acting for the defendant accidentally, but voluntarily, sent a copy of the defendant's proof of evidence to the prosecution. The defendant knew nothing of what had happened. He gave evidence at trial which was inconsistent with the contents of his earlier proof. It was held that the prosecution could properly use the earlier proof when the defendant was cross-examined. Its admissibility and use were subject to the exercise of discretion under s. 78 PACE 1984 (see Chapter 5).

20.6 POWERS OF SEARCH AND LEGAL PROFESSIONAL PRIVILEGE

While the police have extensive powers of search during an investigation (see Chapter 3), Parliament has been careful to exclude items that are subject to legal professional privilege from the ambit of a search warrant issued under s. 8 PACE 1984. This general principle is qualified in part by the exception recognised under the Regulation of Investigatory Powers Act 2000 (RIPA 2000) and confirmed by the House of Lords in the combined appeals of *Re McE and Others* [2009] UKHL 15 in which a majority held that on a proper construction s. 27 RIPA 2000 was intended to override a suspect's right to have a private consultation with a solicitor.

Although the House of Lords was not called upon to decide whether evidence lawfully obtained in breach of legal professional privilege would be admissible at trial, Lord Carswell observed that the principle expounded in *R v Derby Magistrates' Court, ex p. B*, which prohibits the use of evidence obtained in breach of legal professional privilege, remained absolute.

20.7 THE PRIVILEGE AGAINST SELF-INCRIMINATION

The privilege against self-incrimination is an important right enjoyed by all UK citizens. The right to silence (see Chapter 5) is an important component of this privilege. The privilege against self-incrimination applies throughout the investigation process and continues through to trial. Once a defendant has chosen to give evidence on oath in support of his defence, he cannot refuse to answer questions in cross-examination on the ground that it would incriminate him as to the offence charged! However, no witness (including the defendant) need answer any question or produce documents or items at trial which would expose the witness to the possibility of future prosecution under UK law.

20.7.1 ASSERTING AND WAIVING THE PRIVILEGE

The privilege belongs to the witness and must therefore be claimed by the witness during the proceedings. Only the witness may waive the privilege. If answering a question or producing a document could potentially violate a witness's privilege not to self-incriminate, the modern practice is for the judge or the magistrates' legal adviser to warn the witness that she does not have to answer the question. Once the court is satisfied that the privilege applies, the witness will not be compelled to answer even if her motive for remaining silent is based in bad faith or she has a motive of her own to serve.

Where the witness waives the privilege or does not assert the privilege, her answers can be used in evidence against her in subsequent criminal proceedings.

20.7.2 STATUTORY EXCEPTIONS TO THE PRIVILEGE AGAINST SELF-INCRIMINATION

Various statutes compel an individual to answer questions and provide information in a criminal investigation. A failure to comply with the statutory requirement will lead to the designated person being liable to a penalty. A commonly invoked provision is s. 172 Road Traffic Act 1988. Section 172(2)(a) Road Traffic Act 1988 requires the keeper of a motor vehicle to answer questions as to the identity of the driver of the vehicle where the driver is suspected of being involved in a road traffic offence. Failure to provide such information is an offence under s. 172(3) Road Traffic Act 1988, punishable with a fine and the endorsement of penalty points on the driver's licence. A similar example is provided by s. 31 Theft Act 1968, which states that a witness may not refuse to answer any questions in proceedings for the recovery or administration of property or the execution of a trust on the ground that to do so might incriminate him or his spouse (or civil partner) of an offence under the Act. The point raised by defence lawyers in this area is that where an individual is compelled to answer questions or provide evidence which could later be used in evidence against him, is the use of such evidence compatible with Article 6 and the right to a fair trial? The point is considered here.

20.7.3 THE PRIVILEGE AGAINST SELF-INCRIMINATION AND THE ECHR 1950

In *Saunders v UK* (1997) 23 EHRR 313, the defendant had been compelled to answer questions about his business dealings during an investigation by the Department of Trade and Industry. The statute containing the compulsory powers did not prevent the answers obtained from being used in evidence in subsequent criminal proceedings. In fact, they were used against Saunders in a later prosecution under the Companies Act 1985. In finding that there had been a violation of Article 6, the European Court of Human Rights observed:

'The Court recalls that, although not specifically mentioned in Article 6 of the Convention, the right to silence and the right not to incriminate oneself are generally recognised international standards which lie at the heart of the notion of a fair procedure under Article 6. Their rationale lies, *inter alia*, in the protection of the accused against improper compulsion by the authorities thereby contributing to the avoidance of miscarriages of justice and to the fulfilment of the aims of Article 6. The right not to incriminate oneself, in particular, presupposes that the prosecution in a criminal case seek to prove their case against the accused without resort to evidence obtained through methods of coercion or oppression in defiance of the will of the accused. In this sense the right is closely linked to the presumption of innocence contained in article 6(2) of the Convention.'

The *Saunders* decision was relied on in the case of *Brown v Stott* [2001] 2 WLR 817, which concerned s. 172 Road Traffic Act 1988 and which requires the keeper of a motor vehicle to answer questions as to the identity of the driver of the vehicle where the driver is suspected of being involved in a road traffic offence. Failure to provide such information is an offence under s. 172(3) Road Traffic Act 1988, punishable with a fine and endorsement.

Brown v Stott [2001] 2 WLR 817

The police were called to an all-night superstore, where B was suspected of having stolen a bottle of gin. The officers thought that B had been drinking and asked her how she had got to the store. She replied that she had driven there and pointed to a car that she said was hers. At the police station, car keys were found in her handbag, and pursuant to s. 172(2) Road Traffic Act 1988, the police required her to say who had driven the car to the store. B replied that she had driven the car. A breath test was administered that proved positive. B was charged with driving after consuming excess alcohol under s. 5(1)(a) Road Traffic Act 1988.

On appeal, the Privy Council held that evidence of B's admission that she had driven the vehicle to the all-night store did not infringe her privilege against self-incrimination or her right to a fair hearing under Article 6 for the following reasons:

- the rights under Article 6 are not absolute and may be qualified in respect to a proper clear public objective such as road safety;
- there was a clear public interest in enforcement of road traffic legislation and that properly applied, s. 172 Road Traffic Act 1988 did not represent a disproportionate response to this serious social problem:
  - s. 172 Road Traffic Act 1988 permitted the police to ask a suspect a simple question, the answer to which does not incriminate the accused per se;
  - the penalty for refusing to answer the question is moderate and non-custodial;
  - if there was evidence of coercion by the police, the court had discretion to exclude the suspect's answer.

The same conclusion was reached by the European Court of Human Rights in *O'Halloran v UK* (2007) 47 EHRR 397. Whilst the privilege against self-incrimination is an important human right, it is not an absolute right.

KEY POINT SUMMARY

- Know the situations where legal professional privilege can be claimed.

- Be aware of the circumstances in which legal professional privilege may be lost.

- Understand the privilege against self-incrimination and its limitations.

SELF-TEST QUESTIONS

1. Are all communications passing between a solicitor and his or her client privileged from disclosure?

2. What is the dominant purpose test for legal privilege to attach to communications between the client, solicitor and a third party?

3. In whom does legal privilege vest?

4. Explain the privilege against self-incrimination.

Analysis of these questions can be found on our online resources.

FIGURE 20.1 PRIVATE PRIVILEGE

LEGAL PROFESSIONAL PRIVILEGE

- Prevents the disclosure of all communications between the lawyer/client in connection with the giving or obtaining of legal advice, including (s. 10(1)(a) PACE);

  – letters, memoranda containing legal advice; and

  – communications with counsel.

- Prevents the disclosure of all communications between the client, lawyer and a third party where the sole or dominant purpose is in connection with actual or pending litigation including communications in connection with advice sought from an expert witness (s. 10(1)(b) PACE).

- The courts take a strict approach to enforcing the privilege, see *R v Derby Magistrates' Court, ex p. B.*

- The privilege will be lifted where:

  – it is waived by the client; or

  – it used to further a crime; or

  – it is lost accidentally.

PRIVILEGE AGAINST SELF-INCRIMINATION

- Permits a witness to refuse to answer a question on oath where the answer would expose the witness to the possibility of a criminal charge being laid against him.

- The privilege applies to individuals who are compelled to answer questions by investigating bodies, the answers to which are then used in evidence against that individual in criminal proceedings.

- The privilege belongs to the witness.

- The witness may waive the privilege.

- The privilege is not an absolute right under Article 6 ECHR 1950 and may be qualified where:

  – there is a clear public interest in the privilege not applying; and

  – it is proportionate to the aim of the legislation, see *Brown v Stott.*

Part V

POST-CONVICTION: SENTENCING AND APPEALS

Part V covers all aspects of sentencing in the Crown Court and magistrates' court.

In Chapter 21 we consider the procedure on passing sentence and the general principles that inform the process of sentencing.

In Chapter 22 we explain specific types of sentence and provide guidance on how a defence solicitor might prepare and deliver a plea in mitigation.

The final chapter in this section, Chapter 23, considers the process of appeal against sentence and conviction.

The special considerations that apply to the sentencing of road traffic offences are covered in a separate chapter which can be found in the online resources. Only consider this specialist chapter after you have digested Chapters 21 and 22.

21 SENTENCING PROCEDURE AND THE GENERAL PRINCIPLES OF SENTENCING

21.1	**Introduction**	**391**
21.2	**New developments—warning**	**392**
21.3	**The role of the CPS on sentence**	**392**
21.4	**The procedure on sentencing**	**393**
	21.4.1 Procedure following a finding of guilt	393
	21.4.2 Procedure following a guilty plea	393
	21.4.3 Agreed basis of plea and *Newton* hearings	394
21.5	**Hierarchy of sentences**	**394**
21.6	**Sentencing aims**	**395**
21.7	**The basis of sentencing under the CJA 2003**	**395**
	21.7.1 Defining the seriousness of an offence	395
	21.7.2 The totality principle	396
21.8	**Sentencing Council for England and Wales**	**396**
	21.8.1 How are offence-specific guidelines issued by the Sentencing Council applied?	397
21.9	**Sentencing guidelines in the Crown Court**	**399**
21.10	**How does the defence solicitor assess the seriousness of an offence?**	**399**
21.11	**Magistrates' Court Sentencing Guidelines (MCSGs 2017)**	**399**
21.12	**Personal offender mitigation**	**400**
21.13	**Discount for timely guilty pleas**	**400**
21.14	**What constrains sentencing?**	**401**
	21.14.1 The limits of the magistrates' court's sentencing powers	401
	21.14.2 Power to commit for sentence under s. 3 PCC(S)A 2000	401
	21.14.3 Committal for sentence under s. 4 PCC(S)A 2000	402
21.15	**The Crown Court's sentencing powers**	**402**
	21.15 .1 The fifty-six day slip rule	402
	21.15.2 Mandatory sentences in the Crown Court	403
21.16	**What informs the process of sentencing?**	**403**
	21.16.1 Pre-sentence reports—s. 156 CJA 2003	403
21.17	**Victim impact statements**	**404**
21.18	**Taking other offences into consideration**	**404**

21.1 INTRODUCTION

A defendant will be sentenced before the Crown Court or magistrates' court upon conviction, either after pleading guilty or having been found guilty after a trial. As the vast majority of defendants plead guilty to some or all of the charges against them, a considerable amount of a prosecutor's time and even more of a defence lawyer's time is taken up with the question of sentence.

A criminal defence practitioner will:

(a) advise his client on the likely sentence after a guilty plea or on conviction;

(b) represent his client at a sentencing hearing by making a plea in mitigation;

(c) advise his client on the prospects of a successful appeal against sentence.

In dealing with any of these tasks, the well-prepared defence advocate will require a thorough knowledge of sentencing principles and practice. It is worth highlighting that sentencing considerations are also relevant to the grant of a representation order (Chapter 9), the grant of bail (Chapter 10) and, of course, allocation (Chapter 11).

Sentencing law and practice is complex and for this reason the subject is covered in two chapters to assist understanding. In this chapter we explain the procedure on passing sentence and consider the general principles that govern a court's decision when passing sentence. In Chapter 22 specific types of sentence are explained and strategies suggested for preparing and delivering an effective plea in mitigation are explored.

21.2 NEW DEVELOPMENTS—WARNING

Sentencing is a fast-changing area of criminal practice. The Sentencing Council for England and Wales regularly issues new and revised sentencing guidelines. For example, a definitive guideline for sentencing breach offences came into effect from 1 October 2018. The guideline covers sentencing for a range of breaches including breaching a community order, breaching a suspended sentence, and a failure to surrender to bail. Other recent guidelines include the Definitive Guideline on Intimidatory Offences (in force on 1 October 2018), the Definitive Guideline on Manslaughter (in force on 1 November 2018), and the Definitive Guideline on Child Cruelty (in force 1 January 2019).

Also the Court of Appeal hands down sentencing guidance when deciding appeals against sentence. Keeping up to date with developments in sentencing is therefore important for the well-informed law student and the busy criminal practitioner.

Sentencing is a very politicised aspect of criminal justice. You may wish to consider the speech delivered by current Justice Secretary David Gauke on 18 February 2019, entitled: *Beyond prison, redefining punishment* in which he expressed strong support for the abolition of short custodial sentences of six months or less in favour of robust community-based alternatives.

21.3 THE ROLE OF THE CPS ON SENTENCE

Whilst the prosecutor does not take an active role in sentencing, she represents the public interest. In deciding whether to accept a guilty plea, the prosecutor must apply the guidance summarised at para. 21.4.3 and in the Attorney General's guidance on the acceptance of guilty pleas (see web-links section of the online resources) and at s.9 of its Code of Conduct (2018). Prosecutors must assist the court in reaching an appropriate sentence by drawing the court's attention to:

• any victim impact statement;

• any evidence of the impact the offending has had on the community;

• any relevant sentencing guidelines or guideline cases;

• the aggravating and mitigating factors of the offence;

• any other relevant sentencing provisions and ancillary orders sought.

The prosecutor should also challenge any assertion by the defence in mitigation that is derogatory to a person's character and may also assist the court by making submissions as to the sentencing range within which the current offence falls (see para. 21.8.1 later).

21.4 **THE PROCEDURE ON SENTENCING**

The procedure is generally the same whether the offender is sentenced in the Crown Court or magistrates' court.

The court will pass sentence where the defendant has pleaded guilty or after being found guilty. Sentence may be adjourned to obtain a pre-sentence report (see para. 21.16.1), or to await the conclusion of other outstanding criminal proceedings against the defendant where it would make good sense to sentence on the totality of the defendant's criminal behaviour.

21.4.1 **PROCEDURE FOLLOWING A FINDING OF GUILT**

Where a defendant has been found guilty, the court will know the circumstances of the offence and the defendant's involvement. The prosecutor's role in this situation is largely restricted to reading out any victim impact statement in the case; referring the court to the defendant's antecedent history; detailing any requests for compensation and asking for ancillary orders (see Chapter 22.20), including prosecution costs.

The defence advocate will be invited to make a plea in mitigation of sentence. If the advocate or the court believes that further information about the defendant is required before sentence can be passed, the hearing will be adjourned for a pre-sentence report (PSR) (see para. 21.16.1) prepared by the Probation Service. The vast majority of PSRs in magistrates' courts are prepared on the day of conviction following trial or a guilty plea. Where a full PSR needs to be prepared, an adjournment will be necessary. Where a court adjourns sentence for a full PSR, it can remand the defendant in custody or on bail. If remanded in custody, a court can adjourn sentence for no more than three weeks. Bail may be conditional or unconditional and can include a condition that the defendant co-operates with the Probation Service in the preparation of the report. An adjournment on bail can be for no more than four weeks or to avoid an adjournment, a magistrates' court will ask for a fast delivery pre-sentence report wherever possible (see para. 21.16.1).

Whenever a PRS is required, the defence advocate will often reserve what he or she wishes to say by way of mitigation until the full sentencing hearing can proceed.

21.4.2 **PROCEDURE FOLLOWING A GUILTY PLEA**

Although the procedure is broadly similar in both the Crown Court (see Crim PR, Part 25) and the magistrates' court, the relevant rules governing the procedure that a magistrates' court should follow upon conviction are laid down in Crim PR, Part 24. Where a defendant pleads guilty, avoiding the need for a trial, the sentencing hearing will begin with the prosecution outlining the circumstances of the offence. This will be based on the evidence contained in witness statements and the defendant's interview and/or any agreed basis of plea between the parties. Sometimes, the prosecution may include CCTV footage as part of its outline and may also refer the court to any victim impact statement.

The prosecutor will then provide the court with a copy of the defendant's criminal record, drawing attention to any relevant previous convictions. If the current conviction places the defendant in breach of an existing court order, the prosecutor should provide details of the earlier offence. The same applies following conviction after trial. If the offence involves injury to an individual or damage to property, the prosecutor should provide full details and hand in any applications for compensation. In the case of an injury or damage, the prosecutor may refer the court to any photographs of the injured party or the damaged caused.

The prosecutor should present the facts fully and fairly. If there are any offences to be taken into consideration (see para. 21.18), these will be referred to by the prosecutor and an agreed schedule submitted to the court. Finally, the prosecutor will ask for any ancillary order and prosecution costs in a specified sum.

Having heard the prosecution, the defence will then submit a plea in mitigation. Once again, if the defence solicitor feels a PSR might be required, she will invite the court to adjourn for the report to be prepared before addressing the court in any great detail on the matter of sentence.

21.4.3 AGREED BASIS OF PLEA AND *NEWTON* HEARINGS

Before an accused enters a guilty plea it is good practice for the defence advocate to discuss the basis of his client's plea with the prosecution, as a guilty plea does not necessarily mean that the accused accepts everything outlined by the prosecution. A defendant may wish to plead guilty to some charges but not others. A defendant may be prepared to plead guilty to assault but deny the use of a weapon in the commission of the assault. In deciding whether to accept a guilty plea, the prosecutor must apply section 9 of the Code for Crown Prosecutors, which provides:

> 'Crown Prosecutors should only accept the defendant's plea if they think the court is able to pass a sentence that matches the seriousness of the offending, particularly where there are aggravating features (9.2).
>
> Crown Prosecutors must never accept a guilty plea just because it is convenient (9.4).
>
> In considering whether the pleas offered are acceptable, Crown Prosecutors should ensure that the interests of the victim and, where possible, any views expressed by the victim or victim's family, are taken into account when deciding whether it is in the public interest to accept the plea. However, the decision rests with the Crown Prosecutor.
>
> It must be made clear to the court on what basis any plea is advanced and accepted. In cases where a defendant pleads guilty to the charges but on the basis of facts that are different from the prosecution case, and where this may significantly affect sentence, the court should be invited to hear evidence to determine what happened, and then sentence on that basis.'

If a basis of plea is accepted, the defence advocate must make sure that the court sentences her client on the agreed basis of plea which should be in writing and signed by all the parties. Where, despite a guilty plea, there is a significant dispute between the prosecution and the defence about the facts of the offence which cannot be resolved, and the dispute would materially affect the sentence, a *Newton* hearing (*R v Newton* (1982) 77 Cr App R 13) may be required to determine the disputed fact. A *Newton* hearing takes the form of a trial of the disputed issue. Witnesses will be called to give evidence (if required) and the formal rules of evidence apply. The burden of proof on the disputed issue rests with the prosecution and the standard of proof is beyond reasonable doubt. Where the prosecution case is believed, the defendant may lose some or all credit for pleading guilty (see para. 21.13). If the contested issue is resolved in the defendant's favour, the credit due to him should not be reduced. The principles in *Newton* should also be considered alongside *R v Underwood* [2005] 1 Cr App R 178, where the Court of Appeal provided important guidance on the approach to an agreed basis of plea in the Crown Court (see Criminal Practice Direction (CPD 2013) Sentencing B).

The case law on *Newton* hearings is covered in *Blackstone's Criminal Practice*. Once the court has heard the outline of the facts from the prosecution and has considered the defendant's plea in mitigation, it is in a position to determine the appropriate sentence in accordance with the principles about to be outlined.

21.5 HIERARCHY OF SENTENCES

The magistrates' court and the Crown Court can pass a range of sentences under the Criminal Justice Act 2003 (CJA 2003) which we list here in decreasing order of severity:

* custody—immediate/suspended;
* community sentence (combining requirements such as unpaid work/programme activity/curfew);

- fine/compensation order;
- conditional or an absolute discharge.

We consider the specifics of each sentence in Chapter 22.

In addition, upon conviction for certain offences, a court may and in some cases must also endorse the offender's driving licence or disqualify him from driving or order the destruction or confiscation of property acquired by criminal activities or order the seizure of criminal assets. In sexual offences the court will require the offender to register on the Sex Offenders' Register.

21.6 SENTENCING AIMS

When a sentence is passed on an offender over the age of 18, s. 142 CJA 2003 requires the court to have regard to one or more of the following purposes of sentencing. They include:

(a) the punishment of offenders;

(b) reduction in crime (including its reduction by deterrence);

(c) the reform and rehabilitation of the offender;

(d) the protection of the public;

(e) the making of reparation by the offender to people affected by their offences.

The CJA 2003 does not indicate that any one purpose is more important than any other. **In formulating a realistic sentencing objective for the plea in mitigation, the defence solicitor should consider what the court's sentencing aims are likely to be.**

Punitive sentences include custody and certain types of community sentence where the offender must undertake unpaid work or abide by a curfew. These sentences deprive the offender of his liberty. In some cases a large fine can be punishment. In particularly serious cases where an offender has used violence, perhaps not for the first time, or has committed a serious sexual offence, there will be a need to protect the public, and the offender can expect a lengthy custodial sentence.

Where the offence is less serious and there are underlying reasons for an offender's behaviour, a rehabilitative sentence might be appropriate which aims to prevent further offending. The most obvious example is a community sentence with a supervision requirement, or a drug rehabilitation requirement. For a first-time offender whose offence is not serious, a conditional discharge might be appropriate.

In terms of reparation as a sentencing objective, a court ordering an offender to pay compensation to his victim for injury, loss or damage is a good example.

21.7 THE BASIS OF SENTENCING UNDER THE CJA 2003

The CJA 2003 adopts the fundamental principle that a sentence should not be more severe than the seriousness of the offence warrants. **The sentence a court chooses to impose should therefore reflect the seriousness of the offence.** The concept of 'seriousness' is the engine which drives sentencing practice in England and Wales. So how is 'seriousness' assessed?

21.7.1 DEFINING THE SERIOUSNESS OF AN OFFENCE

Section 143(1) CJA 2003 states that in assessing the seriousness of any offence, the court must consider:

- **the offender's culpability in committing the offence; and**
- **any harm which the offence has caused or was intended to cause or might foreseeably have caused.**

Culpability includes such matters as the defendant's intention when committing an offence, whether he acted recklessly or had knowledge of the risk he was taking. Harm and risk of harm can include harm to the victim but also to the wider community.

Statutory aggravating factors affecting the seriousness of an offence are identified in ss. 143–146 CJA 2003.

- Section 143(2) requires a court to treat an offender's previous convictions as an aggravating factor if the court considers it reasonable to do so, having regard to the nature of the offence and the time that has elapsed since conviction. **Recent and relevant previous convictions will therefore be regarded as aggravating the seriousness of the current offence before the court**.

- Section 143(3) requires the court to treat any offence committed while on bail as being an aggravating factor in determining the seriousness of the offence.

- Sections 145 and 146 provide that where an offence is either racially or religiously motivated or is motivated out of hostility towards a person's sexual or presumed sexual orientation or transgender identity or presumed transgender identity, disability or presumed disability, this shall be regarded as an aggravating feature in determining the seriousness of the offence.

In addition to any statutory aggravating factors, the court will also consider any aggravating and mitigating features of the offence itself with reference to any applicable sentencing guidelines for the offence.

In its publication *Overarching Principles: Seriousness*, the Sentencing Guidelines Council (see para. 21.8) provides general guidance on assessing an offender's culpability for the purposes of s. 143 CJA 2003. Culpability is determined by such matters as the offender's motivation in committing the offence; whether it was planned or spontaneous and whether the offender was in a position of trust. A further relevant factor includes the deliberate targeting of a vulnerable victim by reference to their age, disability or by virtue of their job. The guidance offers an extensive list of typical aggravating and mitigating features to an offence.

To remind you—the starting point when sentencing an offender is an assessment by the court of the seriousness of the offence.

21.7.2 THE TOTALITY PRINCIPLE

Whilst an offender who stands to be sentenced for several matters will be given a sentence for each offence, in determining the composition of the total sentence, a court must have regard to the totality principle which requires that the sentence passed must not be disproportionate to the seriousness of the overall offending behaviour (s. 66(3) CJA 2003). This may be reflected in concurrent or consecutive custodial sentences or the overall composition of a community sentence or overall amount of a financial penalty. The Sentencing Council for England and Wales (see para. 21.8) has issued guidance on the application of the totality principle which came into force in June 2012. The guidelines include specific examples of the application of the totality principle in practice. The totality principle is not without its complexity.

21.8 SENTENCING COUNCIL FOR ENGLAND AND WALES

Sentencing practice in England and Wales is underpinned by sentencing guidelines formulated by the Sentencing Council for England and Wales (SC) and its predecessor, the Sentencing Guidelines Council (SGC). The SGC was created under the CJA 2003 with a statutory duty to provide authoritative guidance on sentencing to be applied by the courts, a role which had traditionally been undertaken by the Court of Appeal in relation to sentencing in the Crown Court.

To assist in the development of a consistent approach to sentencing across England and Wales, the SC and SGC have issued a number of definitive general sentencing guidelines, including guidance on reduction for guilty plea (recently revised), overarching principles relating to seriousness, and to youth offenders; the totality principle and revised guidance on the imposition of custodial and community sentences. In addition, the SC has produced an extensive list of offence-specific guidelines and the all-important, Magistrates' Court Sentencing Guidelines (MCSGs) (revised 2017). All previous SGC guidelines now come under the ownership of the SC. Until such time as a SGC guideline is revised by the SC, it will continue to apply.

The importance of the SC in terms of sentencing practice cannot be overstated. The courts must follow the sentencing guidelines unless it is 'in the interests of justice' not to do so, s.125 Coroners and Justice Act (C&JA) 2009. Final guidelines produced by the SC can be accessed at http://sentencingcouncil.judiciary.gov.uk/sentencing-guidelines.htm. Our online resources include a link to the SC in the web-links section. Underpinning sentencing practice in the magistrates' court are the Magistrates' Court Sentencing Guidelines 2017 (MCSGs)—see para. 21.11.

21.8.1 HOW ARE OFFENCE-SPECIFIC GUIDELINES ISSUED BY THE SENTENCING COUNCIL APPLIED?

The format of SC guidelines is best illustrated by reference to a specific example.

In Appendix 3, you will find a copy of the guideline applicable to s. 47 Offences Against the Person Act 1861 (ABH). As assault occasioning actual bodily harm contrary to s. 47 OAPA 1861 is triable either way. The guideline applies to cases sentenced before the Crown Court (where the maximum sentence is five years' imprisonment) and in the magistrates' court (where the maximum sentence is six months' imprisonment) for a single either-way offence. In order to fully understand what follows, please take a look at the guideline.

Each SC guideline identifies the **range of sentences** (*'the offence range'*) which it may be appropriate for a court to impose on an offender convicted of that offence. The *offence range* identified by the SC for a s. 47 ABH ranges from a fine at the lowest end up to three years' imprisonment if tried on indictment.

The guideline requires a step-by-step approach as you will see from the 'Assault' guideline in Appendix 3. **Step 1** requires the sentencing court to **categorise** the assault. This is a crucial first step as the category determines the **sentencing starting point**. The category into which a particular offence falls is decided by reference to the **offender's culpability and/or the harm caused by the offence(s) and any other specifically relevant factor(s) identified in the guideline**. Each SC guideline specifies both a *starting point* for each *category range* and a *range of sentence either side of the starting point*. The starting point is the sentence the SC considers to be appropriate for all offenders in all cases. This contrasts with SGC guidelines where the sentencing starting point is based on a first-time offender who has pleaded not guilty.

The 'Assault' guideline defines three offence **categories** for all assault offences including ss. 18, 20, 47 OAPA 1861 and common assault. The most serious is **category 1**.

- A category 1 assault (whether it be a s. 18 GBH or a common assault) will involve *greater harm* (serious injury must normally be present) and *higher culpability*.

- A category 2 assault will involve *greater harm* (serious injury must normally be present) and *lower culpability* or *lesser harm* but *higher culpability*.

- A category 3 assault involves *lesser harm* and *lower culpability*.

The guideline identifies factors specific to greater and lesser harm and factors specific to higher culpability and lower culpability. A court should have regard to these aggravating and mitigating factors in deciding which *category* the present case falls within. Identifying the correct category range enables the court to identify the sentencing **starting point** and **range** of sentence available. **The categorisation of the offence before the court is not an exact** science and the defence advocate may well need to make representations as to why (in the particular case) it ought to be pitched in a lower category.

Having completed step 1 the court will proceed to **step 2**, which identifies the starting point for sentence based on the **category** choice. A sentencing starting point is exactly that: a starting point. Step 2 requires the court to then consider whether there are any additional statutory or other aggravating factors (discussed at para. 21.7.1) or indeed whether there are any mitigating factors in the commission of the offence or personal offender mitigation which should result in an **upward or downward adjustment from the starting point**.

The court will then follow steps 3–9 of the guideline.

Step 4 requires the court to take into account any reduction applicable for a guilty plea (see para. 21.13), as well as the totality principle (see para. 21.7.2) and any time spent on remand in custody in reaching its final sentencing outcome. A summary of the step-by-step approach, extracted from the MCSGs, can be found in Appendix 3: 'Using Sentencing Council Guidelines'. Having considered the s. 47 guideline, take a look at the domestic burglary guideline, also reproduced in Appendix 3.

The importance of accessing, understanding, and applying sentencing guidelines cannot be overstated. The effect of them has been to make the sentencing exercise before both a magistrates' court or a Crown Court a much more prescriptive and predictable exercise.

 Example

Do you recall the example of Patryk in Chapter 11, para. 11.3.5 in the context of the allocation hearing? As explained in Chapter 11, sentencing guidelines are inextricably linked with the allocation decision. Patryk is sent for trial before the Crown Court and decides to plead guilty. It is accepted by the prosecution that there has been long-standing ill feeling between Patryk and his neighbour and Patryk, who had been subjected to a substantial degree of provocation, had armed himself with the bat with the intention to only damage his neighbour's car. His victim is not 'vulnerable' and, whilst dental treatment will continue for the next three months, the wound will heal with no permanent scarring and there is no lasting psychological injury. A pre-sentence report has been prepared which suggests Patryk is remorseful for the injuries he has caused. He has written a letter of apology to his victim. The report describes Patryk as a reformed drug addict who was recently bereaved and is receiving treatment from his doctor for chronic depression. Since the offence he has left his flat and lives elsewhere.

In determining allocation, we concluded that this could be a **category 1** offence due to greater harm and higher culpability caused by several aggravating factors (use of a weapon; premeditation; serious injury). This is why the magistrates' court declined jurisdiction. **In determining the actual sentence, the Crown Court will apply the s. 47 ABH guideline**. The category range for this offence is outlined in Table 21.1.

TABLE 21.1 S. 47 ASSAULT—SENTENCING GUIDELINES

Offence category	Starting point	Category range
Category 1	1 year 6 months' custody	1–3 years' custody
Category 2	26 weeks' custody	Low level community order–51 weeks' custody
Category 3	Medium level community order	Band A—High level community order

The sentencing starting point based on a **category 1** assault occasioning actual bodily harm sentenced before a Crown Court is 1 year and 6 months' custody. Given that the injuries are non-permanent and given that it is accepted that there was a substantial degree of provocation by the victim, a judge may be persuaded that this is a **category 2** offence with a sentencing starting point of 26 weeks in custody but with a range that takes it down to a community order. Aggravating factors include Patryk's previous convictions. Mitigating factors include Patryk's remorse and clinical depression. If the judge concludes that the custody threshold is passed (see Chapter 22, para. 22.2.1) which is whether it is classed as a **category 1 or 2 ABH**, she might choose to impose a suspended sentence of imprisonment based on the mitigating factors in this case, which would be within the range of sentence suggested under the guideline for this offence. Credit will then be applied for Patryk's guilty plea.

21.9 SENTENCING GUIDELINES IN THE CROWN COURT

Sentencing in the Crown Court has historically been informed by decisions of the Court of Appeal. Whilst the role of formulating sentencing guidelines now belongs to the SC, in cases where there is no definitive SGC or SC guideline, Court of Appeal decisions continue to apply. The Court of Appeal will hear an appeal arising out of a sentencing decision in the Crown Court where it is contended by the defence that the sentence imposed was 'manifestly excessive'. In hearing the appeal the Court of Appeal will often make observations about the application of the sentencing guidelines, which must be applied by Crown Court judges when passing sentence in subsequent cases. For an excellent illustration of the Court of Appeal's reviewing process, consider the case of *R v Grant Christopher Smith* [2015] EWCA Crim 1482, where the court had to decide whether the sentencing judge was correct to treat the s. 18 wounding with intent to cause grievous bodily harm as a category 1 or a category 2 offence. In allowing the appeal against sentence and reducing a 12-year custodial term to a nine-year term, the Court of Appeal stated that *'the sorts of harm and violence which will justify placing a case within category 1 must be significantly above the serious level of harm which is normal for the purposes of section 18.'*

The case is a good illustration of both an appeal against sentence and the application of an offence specific guideline in practice. Whilst sentencing has become a much more scientific and prescriptive process with the advent of sentencing guidelines, it is an imperfect science and the guidelines are open to interpretation by both the defence advocate in mitigation of sentence and by the judge or magistrates when sentencing the defendant.

Most Court of Appeal sentencing decisions are reported in the Criminal Appeal Sentencing Reports and summarised in *Blackstone's Criminal Practice*, making it an excellent starting point for your research into the relevant sentencing guidelines applicable to cases to be sentenced before the Crown Court.

21.10 HOW DOES THE DEFENCE SOLICITOR ASSESS THE SERIOUSNESS OF AN OFFENCE?

Defence solicitors must consider their client's role in the particular offence and consider which factors aggravate and which factors mitigate the seriousness of the offence. These include the statutory aggravating factors identified at para. 21.7.2 and in the SGC's 2004 guideline: *Overarching Principles–Seriousness* and (see Appendix 2) the factors identified in an offence-specific guideline.

21.11 MAGISTRATES' COURT SENTENCING GUIDELINES (MCSGs 2017)

The MCSGs cover virtually all offences that are commonly dealt with in the adult magistrates' court. You can access an online version of the MCSGs (2017) via the Sentencing Council's website. The online version is always the up-to-date version. Some of the more recently revised offence-specific guidelines in the MCSGs (2017) are formatted in the **SC style** explained at para. 21.8.1 whilst others are still based on the previous **SGC** format (**'old style'**). The 'old style' MCSGs are based on a first-time offender convicted after trial and stipulate a *starting point* based on the nature of the activity that best describes what the offender is said to have done. The guidelines also specify a sentence range that can fall either side of the *starting point*. The court may depart from the starting point to reflect any aggravating (statutory or otherwise) or mitigating features in the commission of the offence as specified in the guideline. For an illustration of an 'old style' MCSG guideline, see the affray guideline which is reproduced at the end of Appendix 3. In time, the entire MCSGs will be re-formatted in the SC style.

21.12 PERSONAL OFFENDER MITIGATION

The seriousness of an offence (informed by offence-specific guidelines) will indicate a particular type of sentence. However, **every offender must be sentenced on an individual basis**. The court must therefore have regard to any personal offender mitigation that might apply in the case. It is the combination of the seriousness of the offence, and any personal offender mitigation that will determine the appropriate sentence. The seriousness of the offence may indicate a custodial sentence but there may be strong personal mitigating factors which suggest a community-based disposal as the most appropriate sentence. Personal offender mitigation will clearly be highlighted by the defence in the plea in mitigation (which we consider in Chapter 22) and in any pre-sentence report.

21.13 DISCOUNT FOR TIMELY GUILTY PLEAS

Section 144 CJA 2003 provides as follows:

'(1) In determining what sentence to pass on an offender who has pleaded guilty to an offence in proceedings before that or another court, a court shall take into account—

(a) the stage in the proceedings for the offence at which the offender indicated his intention to plead guilty, and

(b) the circumstances in which this indication was given.'

Section 174(2)(b) CJA 2003 provides that in passing sentence on an offender, the court must state in open court in ordinary language that it has given the offender the benefit of a discount under s. 144 CJA 2003.

Timely guilty pleas save cost, court time and, most importantly, spare victims and witnesses from having to give evidence. Whilst s. 144 CJA 2003 does not specify the amount of discount a court might award the new SC guideline on the 'Reduction in Sentence for a Guilty Plea' which came into effect on 1 June 2017 provides some guidance.

Where a guilty plea is indicated at the first stage of proceedings a reduction of one-third should be made (this is subject to exceptions in section 4 of the guideline). The first stage will normally be the first hearing at which a plea or indication of plea is sought and recorded by the court. After this a sliding scale is applied with a maximum of one-quarter after the first stage and down to a maximum of one-tenth if a guilty plea is entered on the first day of a trial.

The discount is a significant factor for many defendants and defence solicitors must ensure that their client understands the advantages of pleading guilty at the earliest opportunity. Of course, no client should feel pressurised into pleading guilty for this reason alone and no client should be advised to plead guilty if they have a credible defence or there is a reasonable doubt as to their guilt.

Sentencing discounts do not apply to ancillary orders which include compensation orders or to the minimum periods of disqualification and the mandatory imposition of penalty points for driving offences.

21.14 **WHAT CONSTRAINS SENTENCING?**

There are a number of factors that constrain sentencing, including:

* the statute creating the offence (statutes creating an offence will specify a maximum penalty for the particular offence);

* whether the sentence is being imposed in the Crown Court or in the magistrates' court (magistrates' courts' powers of sentence are limited);

* statutory sentencing requirements laid down by Parliament (in some instances Parliament has removed judicial discretion and requires the imposition of a mandatory sentence of imprisonment or other ancillary penalty);

* the defendant's age (the sentencing of offenders under the age of 18 is considered in Chapter 26);

* whether the defendant pleaded guilty or was found guilty (timely guilty pleas attract a reduction in the length of sentence).

21.14.1 **THE LIMITS OF THE MAGISTRATES' COURT'S SENTENCING POWERS**

The maximum custodial sentence that a magistrates' court can currently pass for an imprisonable offence is six months upon conviction of a summary matter (s. 78 Powers of Criminal Courts (Sentencing) Act 2000 (PCC(S)A 2000) and s. 133 Magistrates' Courts Act 1980 (MCA 1980)) unless the statute creating the offence specifies a lesser maximum sentence. It does not matter that a defendant is convicted of two or more summary matters on the same occasion: the maximum prescribed by statute is six months. The six-month maximum can rise to 12 months where consecutive prison sentences of six months are imposed on a defendant convicted of two or more either-way offences (proviso to s. 133(1) and (2) MCA 1980), although a court would need to have regard to the totality principle, highlighted at para. 21.7.1. The magistrates' court is no longer constrained in terms of the size of the fine it can impose at Level 5. The maximum fine at Level 5 was £5,000 but a Level 5 fine is now unlimited for offences committed after 13 March 2015.

The magistrates' sentencing jurisdiction is closely related to the allocation hearing for either-way offences as one of the principal reasons for a magistrates' court declining jurisdiction to try an either-way matter is that the magistrates consider their maximum sentencing powers, in the event of conviction, are insufficient. See Chapter 11 for further details.

21.14.2 **POWER TO COMMIT FOR SENTENCE UNDER S. 3 PCC(S)A 2000**

Upon summary conviction for an either-way offence, a magistrate's court has the power to commit a defendant to the Crown Court for sentence under s. 3 PCC(S)A 2000 where it considers its maximum powers of punishment (see para. 21.14.1 above) to be insufficient, having regard to the seriousness of the offence. Where this power is exercised, a magistrate's court can also commit the offender for sentence on any other offences for which the defendant has been convicted (s. 6 PCC(S)A 2000). This enables the Crown Court to deal with all outstanding matters including any other less serious either-way or summary matters the defendant has been convicted of and any suspended sentence or breach of a community penalty or conditional discharge imposed by a magistrates' court for which the accused now stands to be dealt with. However, the Crown Court's sentencing powers are limited to those of the magistrates and the summary offence(s) must be punishable with imprisonment or disqualification.

The power to commit for sentence can be used where a defendant pleads guilty to an either-way offence at the plea before venue (see Chapter 11) or is found guilty after summary trial in a case in which the magistrates' court has accepted summary jurisdiction to try the case following an allocation hearing and subsequent trial. In the not too distant past, when allocation was referred to as the mode of trial procedure, it was frequently argued that the decision to accept summary jurisdiction following mode of trial created a legitimate expectation in the accused that he would not be sent to the Crown Court for sentence in the event of conviction. This proposition was in fact firmly doubted by the Divisional Court in *North Sefton Magistrates' Court, ex p. Marsh* (1994) 16 Cr App R (S) 401, which held that the magistrate's court discretion under s. 3 (in a case where summary jurisdiction had been accepted), was unfettered. Any doubt as to the position in a case where the magistrates' court has accepted summary jurisdiction following an allocation hearing is laid to rest by the clear requirement under the 'Allocation Guideline' for the court to: '*warn the defendant that all sentencing options remain open and, if the defendant consents to summary trial and is convicted by the court or pleads guilty, the defendant may be committed to the Crown Court for sentence.*'

If the defendant is committed for sentence under s. 3 PCC(S)A 2000, the Crown Court will proceed to deal with the defendant as if he had been convicted on indictment.

The funding provisions to cover representation before the Crown Court upon committal for sentence are outlined in Chapter 9, para. 9.10.2.

21.14.3 COMMITTAL FOR SENTENCE UNDER S. 4 PCC(S)A 2000

Where an accused has indicated a guilty plea to an either-way offence but has been committed for trial in the Crown Court on a related either-way offence, the magistrates' court can commit the defendant to the Crown Court for sentence on the matter to which he has indicated a guilty plea under s. 4 PCC(S)A 2000. If the Crown Court convicts the defendant on the related either-way matter, or if the magistrates' court, on committal for sentence under s. 4, states that it also had the power to do so under s. 3, the Crown Court can sentence on the offence as if the defendant had been convicted on indictment; otherwise its powers are limited to those upon summary conviction.

21.15 THE CROWN COURT'S SENTENCING POWERS

The Crown Court's sentencing powers are considerably greater than those of the magistrates' court. Theft is a good illustration of this point. Conviction for a single offence of theft under the Theft Act 1968 in a magistrates' court currently carries a maximum six months' custodial sentence. Conviction on indictment in the Crown Court carries a maximum custodial sentence of seven years and an unlimited fine.

The more extensive sentencing powers available to the Crown Court are an important factor in an accused's decision whether to elect trial in the Crown Court if he is given the choice at the allocation hearing (see Chapter 11).

Where a Crown Court passes sentence on a defendant who has been convicted of or has pleaded guilty to a summary offence which has been committed to the Crown Court alongside an either-way offence under s. 51(3)(b) Crime and Disorder Act 1998, the powers of the Crown Court are limited to those of a magistrates' court.

21.15.1 THE FIFTY-SIX DAY SLIP RULE

Under s. 155 Powers of Criminal Courts (Sentencing) Act 2000, the Crown Court has the power to alter a sentence made by the Crown Court within 56 days of sentence. The usual reason for altering the sentence is that further information relevant to the sentence, has become known since sentencing or the court has overlooked some statutory provision limiting its powers. The power has been exercised in cases where the original sentence was based on mitigation subsequently found to be false. In a Crown Court case in March 2017, Mustafa Bashir (who was originally sentenced to what can only be described as a somewhat lenient 18-month suspended prison sentence for beating his wife with a cricket bat and forcing her to drink bleach, largely on the basis that he was about to sign a contract with Leicester Cricket Club which would have been lost if sentenced to an immediate custody), had his sentence altered under the slip rule to an immediate 18-month term when this fact was proved to be untrue.

21.15.2 MANDATORY SENTENCES IN THE CROWN COURT

Recent reforms have removed the discretionary element in sentencing in favour of mandatory sentences which have primarily affected sentencing in the Crown Court. Sections 110 and 111 PCC(S)A 2000 require a minimum sentence of seven years for a third conviction of Class A drug trafficking and a minimum three years for a third conviction of domestic burglary. In relation to domestic burglary, the defendant must have committed his second burglary after being convicted of his first and, in addition, both burglary convictions must post-date 1 December 1999. The court need not impose the minimum term if it is of the opinion that it would be unjust to do so. A court may go below the minimum sentence in order to grant a discount for a timely guilty plea.

Life imprisonment is mandatory for murder. It is up to the court to fix the minimum term in accordance with s. 269 CJA 2003 and *R v Jones* [2005] EWCA Crim 3115.

Sections 224–229 CJA 2003 make special provision for 'dangerous' offenders. These are considered in more detail in Chapter 22, para. 22.8.

21.16 WHAT INFORMS THE PROCESS OF SENTENCING?

The sentencing process is informed by the sentencing guidelines, pre-sentence reports and personal offender mitigation.

It is essential to realise that before a client can be advised about the possible sentence and before any plea in mitigation is prepared, the relevant sentencing guidelines for the offence charged must be researched. In serious cases, a defence solicitor may wish to take the advice of counsel or a solicitor-advocate on the question of sentence.

21.16.1 PRE-SENTENCE REPORTS—S. 156 CJA 2003

The importance of a pre-sentence report cannot be underestimated. When the court requires more information about an offender before it decides the appropriate sentence, the information may be provided by a pre-sentence report (PSR), prepared by a probation officer. The report's purpose is to assist the court to find the most appropriate sentence for the offender and commonly includes an assessment of the offender's attitude to the offence and his awareness of the consequences of his actions, the offender's personal history, previous convictions, education, employment position and health. Importantly the report will assess the offender's risk of reoffending based on the current offence and his attitude to it and address such matters as the defendant's suitability for certain types of sentence. The report will propose what the Probation Service considers to be the most appropriate sentence for the offender, consistent with any sentencing aims expressed by the court. A court is not bound to follow the proposal. If the proposal is helpful to the defendant, however, his solicitor or barrister will no doubt place much emphasis on it.

Pre-sentence reports are usually ordered when the court is considering a custodial or community sentence, although s. 156 CJA 2003 empowers the courts to sentence persons over 18 without the benefit of a PSR if a report is considered 'unnecessary'.

When requesting a PSR, the court may give a broad indication of the sentencing direction it is leaning towards or, more usually, it will say that it is keeping all of its sentencing options open. This is a euphemism to mean the court is not ruling out custody. If the court is not ruling out committal for sentence to the Crown Court (in the case of an either-way offence), it should make this explicitly clear so as not to create any legitimate expectation on the offender's part that he will be sentenced in a particular way. When a court requests a PSR, the probation officer in court will consider whether a standard delivery report (SDR) or a fast delivery report (FDR) should be provided. An SDR will take the Probation Service three to four weeks to prepare and will require an adjournment. It is a very comprehensive report. An FDR (which is the norm in magistrates' courts) can be prepared within an hour or two of the defendant being convicted or pleading guilty and therefore requires a much shorter adjournment. Most FDRs are either presented to the court in a short, written form or are delivered orally by the probation officer who has prepared it. The implementation of TSJ in summary proceedings (see Chapter 9) has resulted in the much greater use of FDRs, meaning many more offenders are being sentenced on their first appearance before the magistrates' court following a guilty plea. It really is simple, speedy, summary justice.

21.17 **VICTIM IMPACT STATEMENTS**

There has been a significant move to acknowledge victims' rights within the criminal justice system in recent years. Since October 2001, it has been possible for victims to make a 'victim impact statement' detailing the effect that the offence has had on them. Guidance on the use of such statements is contained in the MCSGs and the Consolidated Criminal Practice Direction Part III, 28.

21.18 **TAKING OTHER OFFENCES INTO CONSIDERATION**

'The defendant pleads guilty to the offence of theft charged against him and asks that you take a further 26 offences of a like nature into consideration . . .'

A defendant is normally sentenced on those offences for which he has been convicted except for offences which the defendant asks to be 'TIC'd'—that is, taken into consideration. The defendant is not convicted of these offences but admits the offences in court and asks for them to be taken into consideration upon passing sentence.

There are mutual benefits to this arrangement. For the prosecution, it assists in the clear-up rate for crimes. For the defendant, although he receives a higher sentence because of the increased number of offences, he knows he cannot be later prosecuted for the offences 'TIC'd'.

Any offences to be taken into consideration should be listed on a schedule which is signed by the defendant. In court, the defendant will be asked to confirm he is admitting the offences listed on the schedule and that he wishes for them to be taken into consideration when the court passes sentence. The procedure can be initiated by the police during the defendant's detention and by the prosecutor in court after a finding of guilt.

The procedure does not apply to driving offences which carry endorsement and/or disqualification. Courts should not allow offences of a different nature to be taken into consideration, and a magistrates' court should not take into consideration indictable-only offences.

Important guidance on sentencing in relation to offences taken into consideration is provided in the Divisional Court's decision in *R v Miles* [2006] EWCA 256.

The SC has issued guidance on taking offences into consideration which came into force in June 2012. The guideline states: '*The presence of TICs should generally be treated as an aggravating feature that justifies an upward adjustment from the starting point. Where there is a large number of TICs, it may be appropriate to move outside the category range, although this must be considered in the context of the case and subject to the principle of totality.*'

KEY POINT SUMMARY

- An understanding of the way in which a court will reach sentence in a particular case is a necessary prerequisite of being able to advise a defendant client about sentence and in constructing a plea in mitigation of sentence.

- Sentencing practice requires courts to sentence on the basis of the seriousness of the offence.

- Seriousness is based on the offender's culpability and the harm caused as well as on any aggravating or mitigating features within the offence itself and any statutory aggravating factors.

- The court's assessment of offence seriousness will:
  - determine which of the sentencing thresholds has been crossed;
  - indicate whether a custodial, community or fine is the most appropriate;
  - be a key factor in deciding the length of a custodial sentence, the number and nature of requirements to be incorporated in a community sentence and the amount of any fine imposed.

- Research and utilise available sentencing guidelines—including any specific offence sentencing guidelines issued by the SC and/or Court of Appeal decisions for sentencing in the Crown Court and the Magistrates' Court Sentencing Guidelines for cases that are to be sentenced summarily— as these will provide you with a broad indication of likely sentence.

- Understand that although an offence might be regarded as serious and warrant a particular sentence, a court will have regard to personal offender mitigation in arriving at the most appropriate sentence.

- Anticipate the need for a pre-sentence report (PSR) and understand why such a report is often influential in informing the sentencing process.

- If a defendant client accepts he is guilty but disputes a material aspect of the prosecution's version of events, anticipate the need for a *Newton* hearing.

- Guilty pleas always attract a sentencing discount: the more timely the guilty plea, the greater the discount.

SELF-TEST QUESTIONS

Consider the following scenario and then try to answer the questions that follow by taking the structured approach to sentencing as explained in this chapter.

Scott is charged with assault occasioning actual bodily harm contrary to s. 47 Offences Against the Person Act 1861. It is alleged that Scott, aged 23, was drunk, and while at a kebab takeaway he and a group of other youths started shouting racial abuse at a group of Asian youths. A fight broke out and it is alleged Scott punched and head-butted one of the Asian youths causing a cut just above the young man's eye and a fracture to his nose. The cut did not require stitches and the fracture will heal in a few weeks.

Scott initially denies the offence in interview but pleads guilty at his first appearance in connection with the matter.

At the time of this offence Scott was on bail for an alleged offence of theft but was later acquitted. Scott's previous convictions include:

- 15 months ago: assault occasioning actual bodily harm—s. 47 Offences Against the Person Act 1861 (Community Order, 12 months);

- 24 months ago: public order—threatening behaviour—s. 5 Public Order Act 1968 (fine);

- 36 months ago: theft—s. 1 Theft Act 1968 (conditional discharge).

Questions

- What is the starting point in terms of sentencing for an assault contrary to s. 47 according to the Magistrates' Court Sentencing Guidelines? The relevant guideline is included in Appendix 3.

- Try to gauge the seriousness of this offence—what factors aggravate the seriousness of this assault?

- Is this a case where a pre-sentence report is likely to be requested?

- Is Scott entitled to a sentencing discount?

Case studies: *R v Roger Martin; R v Lenny Wise; R v William Hardy*

In relation to *R v Hardy* and *R v Martin*, you will be able to see the plea in mitigation and the sentencing process on the video clips contained within our online resources. Before you view these, however, it is important that you engage in the process which culminates in the plea in mitigation. This can only be done by considering this chapter and Chapter 22 and attempting to engage in the tasks we have set in relation to the case studies throughout this chapter and Chapter 22.

R v Roger Martin

If you have considered the documentation in relation to this web-based only case study, you will be aware that Roger Martin has been advised to plead guilty to the offences of common assault, careless driving and failing to stop and report after an accident. All these matters are summary-only and Roger Martin must therefore be sentenced before a magistrates' court. You will note that the solicitor's ability to negotiate a reduced charge of dangerous driving down to careless driving has been of enormous benefit to Roger Martin. He no longer faces the risk of a committal to the Crown Court and of course, dangerous driving carries with it a mandatory disqualification period of 12 months.

- Ignoring the driving penalties for the time being, assess the level of seriousness of the common assault. Research any relevant sentencing guidelines.

- Try to ascertain what you consider will be the worst outcome for Roger Martin in terms of sentence.

- Do you consider a pre-sentence report should be obtained in these circumstances?

The questions posed in relation to *R v Roger Martin* are considered further in our online resources.

R v William Hardy

It will be recalled that William Hardy has been advised to plead guilty to an offence of engaging in sexual activity with a child contrary to s. 9(2) Sexual Offences Act 2003. The offence is indictable-only.

- What is the maximum sentence for this offence?

- Research any relevant sentencing guidelines for this offence in an attempt to gauge the level of seriousness and the likely sentence.

- Do you consider a pre-sentence report should be obtained in this case?

All of these matters are considered in the online resources.

R v Lenny Wise

You will be aware that Lenny Wise was acquitted of the offence of domestic dwelling burglary. Had Lenny Wise been convicted before the Crown Court, what would have been the maximum sentence the judge could have passed? Research the relevant sentencing guidelines for burglary offences tried on indictment. You will find the guideline specific to the offence of domestic dwelling burglary in Appendix 3.

- What sentence do you consider Lenny would have received?

- Would it have been necessary for a pre-sentence report to have been ordered?

FIGURE 21.1 SENTENCING PROCEDURE

SENTENCING PROCEDURE WHERE DEFENDANT IS FOUND GUILTY

- Procedure generally same in Crown Court and magistrates' court.

- Court will be aware of facts of case and the defendant's role; defendant's criminal record will be disclosed to the court by the prosecutor who will seek any ancillary orders.

- The case may be adjourned for a pre-sentence report (SDR or FDR).

- Defendant may be bailed or remanded in custody pending preparation of reports.

- Defence make a plea in mitigation.

- Defendant sentenced with court giving reasons.

SENTENCING PROCEDURE WHERE DEFENDANT PLEADS GUILTY

- Procedure generally same in Crown Court and magistrates' court.

- Where dispute between prosecution and defence about facts of the offence, which would materially affect sentencing outcome, a *Newton* hearing (*R v Newton*) may be held.

- Prosecution outline facts of the offence and the defendant's role, seeking any ancillary orders.

- Defendant's criminal record will be disclosed to the court.

- The case may be adjourned for pre-sentence report (SDR or FDR).

- Defence make plea in mitigation.

- Defendant sentenced with court giving reasons.

FIGURE 21.2 STRUCTURED APPROACH TO SENTENCING UNDER MCSGs

Structured approach to sentencing under MCSGs

- Sentence is based on the seriousness of the offence defined by the offender's culpability in committing the offence and the risk of harm caused (s. 143 CJA 2003).
- A court will have a sentencing purpose in mind (s. 142 CJA 2003) when imposing a particular sentence.
- The seriousness of the offence/s is determined by:

Statutory aggravating factors which include

- offence committed while on bail (s. 143);
- previous offending (s. 143);
- religiously aggravated (s. 145);
- racially aggravated (s. 145);
- motivated by a person's sexual orientation, transgender identity or disability (s. 146).

Aggravating and mitigating features of the offence itself as identified by sentencing guidelines

(whether they be Magistrates' Court Sentencing Guidelines/Court of Appeal judgments/Sentencing Council general and specific guidelines) will give an indication of the starting point in terms of the type of sentence and length, i.e. custody/community sentence/fine/discharge.

Court will consider personal offender mitigation based on the plea in mitigation and addressed in any pre-sentence report.

Court arrives at a sentence.

Court applies any sentencing discount to take account of a guilty plea (s. 144 CJA 2003).

Court passes sentence and explains its reasons (s. 174 CJA 2003).

22 SPECIFIC TYPES OF SENTENCE AND THE PLEA IN MITIGATION

22.1	**Introduction**	**410**
22.2	**When can a discretionary custodial sentence be imposed?**	**410**
	22.2.1 The custody threshold test—s. 152(2) CJA 2003	410
	22.2.2 What if the custody threshold test is finely balanced?	411
22.3	**Custody between the ages of 18 and 21**	**411**
22.4	**Length of custodial sentence**	**411**
	22.4.1 The totality principle and custodial sentences	412
	22.4.2 Release from custody on licence	412
	22.4.3 Credit for guilty plea	413
	22.4.4 Time spent remanded in custody	414
22.5	**Suspended sentence of imprisonment**	**414**
22.6	**Concluding remarks on discretionary custodial sentences with reference to SC guidelines**	**414**
22.7	**Fixed-length sentences**	**415**
22.8	**Sentencing dangerous offenders**	**415**
22.9	**Community sentences**	**419**
	22.9.1 The threshold for imposing a community sentence	419
	22.9.2 Is the offence serious enough?	420
22.10	**Community sentences under the CJA 2003**	**420**
	22.10.1 How will the type of order be determined?	420
22.11	**The requirements**	421
	22.11.1 Unpaid work—s. 199 CJA 2003	421
	22.11.2 Rehabilitation activity requirement—s. 200A CJA 2003	421
	22.11.3 Programme requirement—s. 202 CJA 2003	422
	22.11.4 Prohibited activity requirement—s. 203 CJA 2003	422
	22.11.5 Curfew requirement—s. 204 CJA 2003	422
	22.11.6 Exclusion requirement—s. 205 CJA 2003	422
	22.11.7 Residence requirement—s. 206 CJA 2003	423
	22.11.8 Mental health treatment requirement—s. 207 CJA 2003	423
	22.11.9 Drug rehabilitation requirement—s. 208 CJA 2003	423
	22.11.10 Alcohol treatment requirement—s. 212 CJA 2003	423
	22.11.11 Attendance centre requirement (where offender is aged under 25)—s. 214 CJA 2003	423
22.12	**Guilty plea credit/time spent on remand and community orders**	**423**
22.13	**Enforcement of community orders under the CJA 2003—Sch. 8**	**424**
22.14	**Deferring sentence—ss. 1 and 2 PCC(S)A 2000**	**424**
22.15	**Fines**	**424**
	22.15.1 Victim surcharge	426

22.16	**Compensation orders**	**426**
22.17	**Conditional discharge**	**427**
22.18	**Absolute discharge**	**428**
22.19	**Bind over**	**428**
22.20	**Ancillary orders**	**429**
	22.20.1 Prosecution costs	429
	22.20.2 Confiscation and forfeiture	429
	22.20.3 Criminal Behaviour Order (CBO)	430
	22.20.4 Restraining order	430
22.21	**The plea in mitigation**	**431**
	22.21.1 Delivering an effective plea in mitigation	431
	22.21.2 Preparing a plea in mitigation	431
	22.21.3 Using the pre-sentence report in preparation	432
	22.21.4 Presenting character evidence or other evidence in a plea in mitigation	432
22.22	**Structuring a plea in mitigation**	**432**
22.23	**Advocacy and the plea in mitigation**	**435**
22.24	**Professional conduct**	**436**

22.1 INTRODUCTION

The general principles of sentencing practice are considered in Chapter 21; this chapter explains the range of disposals available to a court when passing sentence on an adult offender and provides guidance about making a plea in mitigation.

22.2 WHEN CAN A DISCRETIONARY CUSTODIAL SENTENCE BE IMPOSED?

Even where an offence carries a custodial sentence this does not mean that custody will be automatically imposed. Section 152(2) Criminal Justice Act 2003 (CJA 2003) defines the custody threshold test by providing that:

'(2) The court must not pass a custodial sentence on the offender unless it is of the opinion that the offence, or combination of the offence and one or more offences associated with it, was so serious that neither a fine alone or a community sentence can be justified for the offence.

(3) Nothing in subsection (2) prevents the court from passing a custodial sentence on the offender if—

(a) he fails to express his willingness to comply with a requirement which is proposed by the court to be included in a community order and which requires an expression of willingness; or

(b) he fails to comply with an order under section 161(2) (pre-sentence drug testing).'

Section 152(2) CJA 2003 acknowledges that custody should be a sentence of last resort.

In passing a custodial sentence, s. 174(2)(b) CJA 2003 requires a court to state in open court why it is of the opinion that the offence is so serious that no other sentence apart from custody is justified.

22.2.1 THE CUSTODY THRESHOLD TEST—S. 152(2) CJA 2003

Section 152(2) CJA 2003 establishes the 'custody threshold test': 'Is the offence so serious that neither a community sentence nor fine can be imposed?' Only if this question is answered affirmatively can a custodial sentence be imposed. As explained in Chapter 21, the seriousness of an offence is assessed according to the defendant's culpability and the harm caused and the presence of aggravating and/or mitigating factors, as defined in the relevant sentencing guidelines. Where the court considers the offence is so serious that it merits a custodial sentence, there may be personal offender mitigation which persuades a court to impose a less draconian disposal than custody.

It is obvious that in many cases where an offender is convicted of a serious indictable offence, a custodial sentence is almost inevitable. Sentencing guidelines will help the defence advocate to determine whether the custody threshold is likely to be met in a particular case.

22.2.2 WHAT IF THE CUSTODY THRESHOLD TEST IS FINELY BALANCED?

Where the custody threshold test is finely balanced, the defence advocate has everything to play for in his plea in mitigation. In support of the defence advocate's argument that his client should not receive a custodial sentence, assistance may be provided by case law. For example, in *R v Kefford* [2002] 2 Cr App R (S) 106, the Court of Appeal reduced the original sentence of 12 months imposed on a building society employee for several dishonesty-related offences totalling £11,120 to four months because of prison overcrowding. In *R v Mills* [2002] EWCA Crim 26, the Court of Appeal substituted a six-month community order for an eight-month custodial term on a mother convicted of two offences of obtaining property by deception. The defendant who had committed the offences because she was in debt had no previous convictions and was the sole carer for her young children. The Court of Appeal considered that it was relevant that the offences involved no violence and were perpetrated against a commercial organisation and that whilst the 'clang of the prison gates' was an important deterrent, there were limitations on the beneficial impact that such a short custodial term would have on the defendant. In addition, where the defendant was the sole carer of young children, the court had to consider how the imposition of a custodial term would affect the children. More recently the problem of prison overcrowding and the inability of short prison sentences to deliver opportunities for rehabilitation has been further highlighted by the Court of Appeal in *R v Seed* [2007] 2 Cr App R (S) 69.

The decision to impose a custodial sentence is both complex and considered. See further at para. 22.6.

22.3 CUSTODY BETWEEN THE AGES OF 18 AND 21

An offender under the age of 21 cannot be sentenced to a term of imprisonment in an adult prison (s. 89(1) Powers of Criminal Courts (Sentencing) Act 2000 (PCC(S)A 2000)). Offenders under the age of 21 but over 18, who are subject to a custodial sentence, will serve their time at a young offenders' institution. A minimum custodial sentence of 21 days must be imposed for offenders aged 18–20.

22.4 LENGTH OF CUSTODIAL SENTENCE

Section 153(2) CJA 2003 requires a custodial sentence to be for the shortest term that is commensurate with the seriousness of the offence, or the combination of the offence and one or more offences associated with it—although this does not apply to a sentence fixed by law and indeterminate and extended sentences for certain violent and sexual offences passed under ss. 224–229 CJA 2003 (see para. 22.8).

Guidance from the Court of Appeal in several cases including *R v Ollerenshaw* [1999] 1 Cr App R (S) 65, *R v Kefford* [2002] 2 Cr App R (S) 495 and *R v Seed* [2007] 2 Cr App R (S) 69 require courts to keep custodial sentences as short as possible, consistent with the court's duty to protect the public interest and to punish and deter the offender. The well-publicised concern about prison overcrowding reinforces the point.

22.4.1 THE TOTALITY PRINCIPLE AND CUSTODIAL SENTENCES

Section 153(2) CJA 2003 states that when imposing custody for more than one offence, a court must have regard to the totality principle, which requires that the sentence passed must not be disproportionate to the seriousness of the overall offending behaviour. The totality principle most often arises in deciding whether two or more custodial sentences should be served concurrently or consecutively.

Assume a sentence of three months' imprisonment is imposed for possessing an offensive weapon and a further custodial sentence of three months for driving whilst disqualified. The sentences are ordered to run consecutively which means the offender is required to serve a total of six months' imprisonment. Had the two sentences been passed to run concurrently, the offender would be required to serve a total of three months in custody. In deciding whether to impose consecutive custodial sentences, the court must have regard to the totality of the defendant's actions and the need to sentence proportionately (see Chapter 21, para. 21.7.2). The SC has produced a guideline on the totality principle which can be accessed via the SC's website.

22.4.2 RELEASE FROM CUSTODY ON LICENCE

The CJA 2003 draws a distinction between custodial terms of less than 12 months and custodial terms of more than 12 months. In relation to custodial terms of 12 months or more, relevant provisions are contained in ss. 237–268 CJA 2003. A prison sentence of 12 months or more is served in full, although half the sentence is served on licence in the community with the offender being subject to requirements. In passing sentence, the court will be able to recommend certain licence requirements, although they will not be binding on the Probation Service. The Probation Service will be able to attach specific requirements to the second half of the custodial sentence to prevent reoffending and to protect the public. A failure to abide by the requirements will result in the offender being recalled to custody. The provisions do not apply to 'dangerous' offenders nor to those offenders subject to extended sentences (see para. 22.8).

Where a court passes a custodial sentence of less than 12 months (which obviously covers the magistrates' court), half the sentence is served in custody. For the remainder of the term, the offender is on unconditional licence in the community. If the offender commits a further offence whilst on licence she can be ordered to return to custody to serve the balance of the original sentence.

The Offender Rehabilitation Act 2014 has introduced some significant changes by extending the supervision of offenders released from short custodial sentences.

A new s. 256AA CJA 2003 creates a new period of post-sentence supervision supervision for offenders serving custodial sentences of more than one day but less than two years. The supervision period begins at the end of the sentence and ends on the expiry of 12 months from the date of release. This means that an offender serves half their custodial sentence in custody and the second half under licence in the community. The post-sentence supervision period applies until the offender has spent 12 months in the community since their automatic release date.

The following examples illustrate how these provisions apply for different sentence lengths compared with the sentences before the law was amended. The Explanatory Notes

TABLE 22.1 SUMMARY OF THE CONDITIONS FOR IMPOSING A CUSTODIAL SENTENCE

Sentence imposed by court	Custodial period before the provisions were in force	Custodial period now the provisions of the Act are in force	Arrangements on release before the provisions of the Act were in force	Arrangements on release now the provisions of the Act are in force
6 month sentence	3 months	3 months	3 months in community, but with no licence conditions or supervision	3 months' licence
				9 months' post-sentence supervision Total supervision 12 months
10 month sentence	5 months	5 months	5 months in community, but with no licence conditions or supervision	5 months' licence
				7 months' post-sentence supervision Total supervision 12 months
18 month sentence	9 months	9 months	9 months' licence	9 months' licence
				3 months' post-sentence supervision Total supervision 12 months

accompanying the Offender Rehabilitation Act 2014 provide a helpful table to illustrate the changes.

Provision is made for a breach of post-sentence the supervision requirements. A court may issue a summons or warrant for the offender's arrest where it is proved to the court's satisfaction that the offender has without reasonable excuse failed to comply with a requirement during the supervision period. The sanctions available to the court are:

- Committal to prison for a period not exceeding 14 days.

- A fine not exceeding level 3 on the standard scale.

- A 'supervision default order' imposing either an unpaid work requirement or a curfew requirement.

22.4.3 **CREDIT FOR GUILTY PLEA**

As noted in Chapter 21, para. 21.13, where a custodial sentence is to be imposed, s. 144 CJA 2003 requires that the defendant should be given credit for a timely guilty plea and the court should reduce the term to take account of the guilty plea. The application of the reduction principle can reduce a custodial sentence to a community sentence or a community sentence to a fine. Section 174(2)(d) CJA 2003 imposes a duty on the court to state in open court that as a result of the guilty plea, the court has imposed a less severe sentence than it otherwise would have done.

22.4.4 **TIME SPENT REMANDED IN CUSTODY**

Time spent on remand in prison automatically counts as timed served (s. 240ZA CJA 2003). The time spent on bail subject to an electronically monitored curfew of not less than nine hours in any given day must also normally count as time served by the offender as part of the sentence but the court must make a direction to this effect (s. 240A CJA 2003) and the credit period needs to be calculated by the sentencing court in accordance with s. 240 A(3) CJA 2003.

22.5 **SUSPENDED SENTENCE OF IMPRISONMENT**

A suspended sentence of imprisonment can be imposed on an offender aged 18 or over where the custody threshold is met.

A suspended sentence is available in the Crown Court for a custodial sentence of 24 months or less and in the magistrates' court for a custodial sentence of six months or less. Custodial sentences of less than 14 days cannot be suspended. The period of suspension can be between six months and two years. As part of the suspended sentence, the court can order the offender to undertake requirements in the community during the supervision period. The list of requirements is the same as that for a community order (see para. 22.10). Any requirements must be commensurate with the seriousness of the offence. If the offender fails to comply with the requirements, or commits a further offence (whether or not punishable with imprisonment), the court has a number of options under Sch. 12 para. 8 CJA 2003. It can order that the suspended sentence be activated for the original custodial term or a lesser term unless it would be unjust to do so having regard to the extent to which the offender has complied with the community requirements of the suspended order, or amend the order extending the operational period or impose more onerous requirements. It can impose a fine for breach if it decides not to imprison.

22.6 **CONCLUDING REMARKS ON DISCRETIONARY CUSTODIAL SENTENCES WITH REFERENCE TO SC GUIDELINES**

We end this section on discretionary custodial sentences with reference to the SC's recently published revised guideline: 'Imposition of Community and Custodial Sentences' which came into force on 1 February 2017.

'General Principles

The approach to the imposition of a custodial sentence should be as follows:

1) A custodial sentence must not be imposed unless the offence or the combination of the offence and one or more offences associated with it was so serious that neither a fine alone nor a community sentence can be justified for the offence.

- There is no general definition of where the custody threshold lies. The circumstances of the individual offence and the factors assessed by offence-specific guidelines will determine whether an offence is so serious that neither a fine alone nor a community sentence can be justified. Where no offence specific guideline is available to determine seriousness, the harm caused by the offence, the culpability of the offender and any previous convictions will be relevant to the assessment.

- The clear intention of the threshold test is to reserve prison as a punishment for the most serious offences.

2) Is it unavoidable that a sentence of imprisonment be imposed?

- Passing the custody threshold does not mean that a custodial sentence should be deemed inevitable. Custody should not be imposed where a community order could provide sufficient restriction on an offender's liberty (by way of punishment) while addressing the rehabilitation of the offender to prevent future crime.

- For offenders on the cusp of custody, imprisonment should not be imposed where there would be an impact on dependants which would make a custodial sentence disproportionate to achieving the aims of sentencing.

3) What is the shortest term commensurate with the seriousness of the offence?

- In considering this the court MUST NOT consider any licence or post sentence supervision requirements which may subsequently be imposed upon the offender's release.

4) Can the sentence be suspended?

- A suspended sentence MUST NOT be imposed as a more severe form of community order. A suspended sentence is a custodial sentence. Sentencers should be clear that they would impose an immediate custodial sentence if the power to suspend were not available. If not, a non-custodial sentence should be imposed.'

22.7 FIXED-LENGTH SENTENCES

In some cases the length of a custodial sentence is fixed by law. This applies to a conviction for murder and mandatory minimum sentences (under ss. 110 and 111 PCC(S)A 2000) for a third conviction in connection with Class A drug trafficking and burglary. Mandatory minimum periods also apply to certain firearms offences. For each of these offences, a court is required to impose the minimum statutory term unless it would be 'unjust' to do so. Where the offender has been assessed as a 'dangerous' offender within s. 226 CJA 2003 (see later), a mandatory sentence of life or an indeterminate sentence for public protection must be passed.

22.8 SENTENCING DANGEROUS OFFENDERS

Sections 224–229 CJA 2003 introduced changes to sentencing 'dangerous' offenders. These provisions have been significantly amended by the Legal Aid, Sentencing and Punishment of Offenders Act (LASPO) 2012. A significant part of LASPO's sentencing reforms includes the repeal of ss. 225 and 226 CJA 2003 (s. 123 LASPO 2012), which made provision for sentences of imprisonment for public protection (indeterminate sentences) and detention for public protection (the equivalent sentence for persons under 18). The indeterminate sentence for public protection is replaced with a life sentence upon conviction for a second 'serious' offence in the case of an offender aged 18 and over and a revised approach to extended sentences for offenders assessed as 'dangerous' has been brought into force.

The provisions apply to adults as well as young offenders under the age of 18. The application of the dangerousness provisions in relation to young offenders is considered in Chapter 26, para. 26.18. An essential part of the dangerousness provisions is the distinction between 'specified' and 'serious' offences.

A 'specified offence' is a violent or a sexual offence specified in Sch. 15 CJA 2003 and which carries a sentence of between two and ten years' imprisonment. A 'serious offence' is a violent or sexual offence specified in Sch. 15 which carries a sentence of ten or more years' imprisonment in the case of an adult.

A sentence under the 'dangerousness' provisions can only be passed in the Crown Court, which is a relevant consideration for a magistrates' court in determining allocation and possible committal for sentence (see Chapter 11 and Chapter 21, para. 21.14.2).

An extended sentence comprises two parts: a custodial sentence for the offence for such length as the seriousness of the offence demands which must be at least four years, and an extended period on licence for such length as the court considers necessary to protect the public from serious harm.

Who qualifies for a life sentence under the dangerousness provisions?

Section 225(1) and (2) CJA 2003 provide the following conditions:

- where an offender is aged 18 or over and is convicted of a 'serious offence'; AND
- the court considers that the offender is dangerous (that is there is a significant risk to members of the public of serious harm (which includes death or serious personal/psychological injury) occasioned by the commission of further 'specified offences'); AND
- the offence carries a life sentence; AND
- the court considers that the seriousness of the offence is such as to justify imposing a sentence of life imprisonment,
- the court MUST impose a sentence of life imprisonment.

In *R v Turton* [2018] EWCA Crim 2091, the Court of Appeal confirmed that assessing the risk posed by the offender was to be taken at the time of sentencing and not some uncertain point in the future. Guidance on imposing a discretionary life sentence is provided by the Court of Appeal in *R v Kehoe* [2008] EWCA Crim 819. Unless the offence is so serious that imprisonment for a whole life term is justified, a minimum term which the offender will serve in custody must be set. The minimum term is normally one-half of the notional determinate sentence, which is set by taking into account the seriousness of the offence and any reduction for a guilty plea. Once the offender has served the minimum term, he will not be released on licence unless the Parole Board is satisfied that it is no longer necessary for the protection of the public that the offender be confined. The offender remains on licence for the rest of his life.

Life sentences to be imposed on conviction for a second serious offence

A new s. 224A CJA 2003 provides that a court *must* impose a life sentence on a person aged 18 or over who is convicted of an offence listed in Sch. 15B Part 1 CJA 2003 committed after 3 December 2012 which is *serious enough to justify a sentence of imprisonment of ten years or more, if* that person has *previously* been convicted of an offence listed in any Part of Sch. 15B and was sentenced to imprisonment for life or for a period of ten years or more in respect of that previous offence. However, the court *is not obliged to impose a life sentence* where it is of the opinion that there are particular circumstances which relate to the offence, the previous offence or the offender which would make it *unjust to do so* in all the circumstances.

Step 1: Was the offence committed on or after 3 December 2012?
If the answer is NO then the provisions do not apply.

Step 2: Is the offence listed in Sch. 15B Part 1 CJA 2003?
If the answer is NO then the provisions do not apply.

Step 3: At date of conviction was the offender aged at least 18 years?
If the answer is NO then the provisions do not apply.
   Section 224A (3) CJA 2003 sets out the *sentence condition*. The present offence must be serious enough to justify a sentence of imprisonment of ten years or more. The court must consider what sentence it would have imposed but for s. 224A (taking into account any guilty plea made by the offender, as well as any aggravating or mitigating factors, and ignoring the extended sentence available under s. 226A CJA 2003).
   Section 224A(4) sets out the previous *offence condition*. The offender must have been previously convicted of an offence listed in any part of Sch. 15B, and, on conviction, must have received a *relevant life sentence* or a *relevant determinate sentence*.

Step 4: But for consideration of these provisions, would the offence otherwise merit a determinate sentence (ignoring s. 226A CJA 2003) of at least ten years or more?
If the answer is NO then the provisions do not apply.

Step 5: At the time this offence was committed had the offender previously been convicted of an offence listed in Sch. 15B CJA 2003?

If the answer is NO then the provisions do not apply.

Step 6: Was that previous offence punished with either a relevant life sentence (see s. 224A(5) CJA 2003) or a relevant sentence of imprisonment/detention for a determinate period (see s. 224A(6)–(11)) CJA 2003?

If the answer is NO then the provisions do not apply.

Section 224A(5) CJA 2003 sets out what is meant by a *relevant* life sentence. A relevant life sentence is one where the offender was not eligible for release during the first five years of the sentence (not taking into account any period spent on remand or bail). The term 'life sentence' includes a sentence of imprisonment or detention for public protection.

Section 224A(6) and (7) CJA 2003 set out when an extended sentence is relevant. An extended sentence is relevant if the custodial term was ten years or more.

Section 224A(8) CJA 2003 provides that any other determinate sentence of imprisonment or detention of 10 years or more is a *relevant* sentence.

Step 7: The court must impose a life sentence unless factors relating to this offence, the previous offence, or the offender would make it unjust to do so.

Extended sentences

Section 226A(1) CJA 2003 provides that an extended sentence may be passed where:

(a) an offender aged 18 and over is convicted of a specified offence (whenever that offence was committed);

(b) the court considers that the offender presents a significant risk to members of the public of serious harm through the commission by the offender of further specified offences;

(c) the court is not obliged to impose a life sentence because of the seriousness of the offence by virtue of s. 224A (life sentence for second listed offence) or s. 225(2) CJA 2003 (life sentence for dangerous offenders); *and*

(d) either condition A **or** condition B is met.

Section 226A(2) CJA 2003 sets out condition A, which is that when the current offence was committed, the offender had a previous conviction for an offence listed in Sch. 15B.

Section 226A(3) CJA 2003 sets out condition B, which is that the current offence is serious enough that, if the court imposed an extended sentence under this section, it would specify an appropriate custodial term of at least four years.

Section 226A(5) CJA 2003 sets out the structure of the new extended sentence. It consists of the appropriate custodial term followed by an extension period, which is a further period during which the offender is to be subject to a licence. The offender will normally be released on a licence when he has served two-thirds of the custodial term.

Section 226A(6) CJA 2003 provides that the court must determine the custodial term.

Section 226A(7) CJA 2003 stipulates that the extension period must be a period of such length as the court considers necessary to protect the public from serious harm caused by the offender's commission of further offences listed in Sch. 15.

Section 226A(8) CJA 2003 sets out the maximum extension periods of five years for a violent offence and eight years for a sexual offence.

Section 226A(9) CJA 2003 stipulates that the appropriate custodial term and the extension period must not together exceed the maximum term of imprisonment that may be imposed for the offence.

How is an offender assessed as being dangerous?

In determining whether the offender is 'dangerous' the court must ask itself, does the offender pose a *significant* risk to members of the public of *serious harm* including death or serious personal/psychological injury occasioned by the commission of further '*specified offences*'?

Section 229 CJA 2003 provides that the court:

- *must* take into account all such information as is available as to the nature and circumstances of the offence;
- may take into account all available information about the nature and circumstances of any other offence(s) of which the offender has been convicted by a court anywhere in the world;
- may take into account any information it has about any pattern of behaviour of which any of the offences form part;
- may take into account any information it has before it about the offender.

It is the prosecutor's responsibility to direct the court to the possible application of the 'dangerousness' provisions. The pre-sentence report and any psychiatric report, as well as an offender's previous convictions and mental condition, will be essential in helping the court to determine whether someone is 'dangerous' within the meaning of s. 229 CJA 2003.

Important guidance was provided by the Court of Appeal in *R v Lang and Others* [2005] EWCA Crim 2864. Thirteen appeals were heard based on the 'dangerousness provisions' *as originally drafted under the CJA 2003*, prior to amendment by the Criminal Justice and Immigration Act 2008 (CJIA 2008) and LASPO 2012. In all but three cases, the Court of Appeal varied the sentence either because it felt 'dangerousness' was not established on the facts, or a sentence of public protection (now abolished by LASPO 2012) was more appropriate than a life sentence. The judgment contains the following guidance on the assessment of dangerous and its consequences:

'(i) The risk identified must be significant. This is a higher threshold than mere possibility of occurrence and in our view can be taken to mean (as in the Oxford Dictionary) "noteworthy, of considerable amount or importance."

(ii) In assessing the risk of further offences being committed, the sentencer should take into account the nature and circumstances of the current offence; the offender's history of offending including not just the kind of offence but its circumstances and the sentence passed, details of which the prosecution must have available, and, whether the offending demonstrates any pattern; social and economic factors in relation to the offender including accommodation, employability, education, associates, relationships and drug or alcohol abuse; and the offender's thinking, attitude towards offending and supervision and emotional state. Information in relation to these matters will most readily, though not exclusively, come from antecedents and pre-sentence probation and medical reports . . . The sentencer will be guided, but not bound by, the assessment of risk in such reports . . .

(iii) If the foreseen specified offence is serious, there will clearly be some cases, though not by any means all, in which there may be a significant risk of serious harm. For example, robbery is a serious offence. But it can be committed in a wide variety of ways many of which do not give rise to a significant risk of serious harm. Sentencers must therefore guard against assuming there is a significant risk of serious harm merely because the foreseen specified offence is serious. A pre-sentence report should usually be obtained before any sentence is passed which is based on significant risk of serious harm. In a small number of cases, where the circumstances of the current offence or the history of the offender suggest mental abnormality on his part, a medical report may be necessary before risk can properly be assessed.

(iv) If the foreseen specified offence is not serious, there will be comparatively few cases in which a risk of serious harm will properly be regarded as significant. The huge variety of offences in Schedule 15 includes many which, in themselves, are not suggestive of serious harm. Repetitive violent or sexual offending at a relatively low level without serious harm does not of itself give rise to a significant risk of serious harm in the future. There may, in such cases, be some risk of future victims being more adversely affected than past victims but this, of itself, does not give rise to significant risk of serious harm.

(v) In relation to the rebuttable assumption to which section 229(3) gives rise, the court is accorded a discretion if, in the light of information about the current offence, the offender and his previous offences, it would be unreasonable to conclude that there is a significant risk. The exercise of such discretion is, historically, at the very heart of judicial sentencing and the language of the statute indicates that judges are expected, albeit starting from the assumption, to exercise their ability to reach a reasonable conclusion in the light of the information before them. It is to be noted that the assumption will be rebutted, if at all, as an exercise of judgment: the statute includes no reference to the burden or standard of proof. As we indicated earlier, it will usually be unreasonable to conclude that the assumption applies unless information about the offences, pattern of behaviour and offender show a significant risk of serious harm from further offences. [*Note: the presumption of dangerousness referred was repealed by the amendments made to the dangerousness provisions under CJIA 2008.*]

(vi) In relation to offenders under 18 and adults with no relevant previous convictions at the time the specified offence was committed, the court's discretion under section 229(2) is not constrained by any initial assumption such as, under section 229(3), applies to adults with previous convictions. It is still necessary, when sentencing young offenders, to bear in mind that, within a shorter time than adults, they may change and develop. This and their level of maturity may be highly pertinent when assessing what their future conduct may be and whether it may give rise to significant risk of serious harm.

(vii) In relation to a particularly young offender, an indeterminate sentence (since abolished by LASPO 2012) may be inappropriate even where a serious offence has been committed and there is a significant risk of serious harm from further offences (see for example, *R v D* [2005] EWCA Crim 2282).

(viii) It cannot have been Parliament's intention, in a statute dealing with the liberty of the subject, to require the imposition of indeterminate sentences (since abolished by LASPO 2012) for the commission of relatively minor offences.

(ix) Sentencers should usually, and in accordance with section 174(1)(a) of the Criminal Justice Act 2003, give reasons for all their conclusions: in particular, that there is or is not a significant risk of further offences or serious harm; where the assumption under section 229(3) arises for making or not making the assumption which the statute requires unless this would be unreasonable; and for not imposing an extended sentence under sections 227 and 228. Sentencers should, in giving reasons, briefly identify the information which they have taken into account.'

22.9 COMMUNITY SENTENCES

As the name suggests, a community sentence is served in the community. Courts are encouraged to use community-based sentences as alternatives to custody. They are commonly proposed by the Probation Service in pre-sentence reports.

The CJA 2003 introduced significant changes to the structure and enforcement of community-based sentences. Courts now pass a generic community order with one or more specified requirements.

Contrary to popular perception, community-based sentences are demanding and rigorously enforced.

22.9.1 THE THRESHOLD FOR IMPOSING A COMMUNITY SENTENCE

As with custodial sentences, there is a threshold test for imposing a community order which must be met before a court can impose a community sentence. Section 148 CJA 2003 provides:

'A court must not pass a community sentence on an offender unless it is of the opinion that the offence, or the combination of the offence and one or more offences associated with it, is serious enough to warrant such a sentence.'

A community-based sentence can only be imposed for an offence which is considered to be 'serious enough' to warrant it. It cannot be imposed for an offence which is not punishable with imprisonment (s. 150A CJA 2003).

22.9.2 **IS THE OFFENCE SERIOUS ENOUGH?**

In assessing whether an offence is serious enough to warrant a community sentence, the Magistrates' Court Sentencing Guidelines (MCSGs) provide assistance. If you consult the guidelines, you will see there are several offences, including theft from a person and handling stolen goods, which suggest a sentencing range to include a community order. As previously indicated the balance of aggravating and mitigating features in the particular case may tilt the sentence down towards a fine or upwards beyond the community sentence threshold. The sentencing guidelines indicate the basic starting point.

22.10 **COMMUNITY SENTENCES UNDER THE CJA 2003**

Section 177 CJA 2003 creates a single, generic community order which will impose one or more requirements on the offender. The community order is available for all offenders aged 18 or over and can last for up to three years. The order must specify an end date, which can be no longer than the longest requirement.

The requirements that can be imposed under a community order include:

- unpaid work—s. 199;
- rehabilitation activity requirement—s. 200A;
- a programme requirement—s. 202;
- a prohibited activity requirement—s. 203;
- a curfew requirement—s. 204;
- an exclusion requirement—s. 205;
- a residence requirement—s. 206;
- a foreign travel prohibition requirement—s. 206A;
- a mental health requirement—s. 207;
- a drug rehabilitation requirement—s. 209;
- an alcohol treatment requirement—s. 212;
- an alcohol abstinence and monitoring requirement—s. 212A (currently being piloted);
- in the case of an offender under 25, an attendance centre requirement—s. 214.

Where a court makes a community order imposing a curfew requirement or an exclusion requirement, the court must also impose an electronic monitoring requirement (s. 177(3)). Section 177(2A) CJA 2003 has recently been amended by Sch. 16 Crimes and Courts Act 2013. All community orders must now include at least one requirement imposed for the purpose of punishment and/or impose a fine unless there are 'exceptional circumstances', which relate to the offence or the offender, which would make it 'unjust' in all the circumstances to do so.

22.10.1 **HOW WILL THE TYPE OF ORDER BE DETERMINED?**

Section 148(3) CJA 2003 provides that where the court passes a community sentence:

'(a) the particular requirement or requirements forming part of the order must be such as, in the opinion of the court is, or taken together are, the most suitable for the offenders; and

(b) the restrictions on liberty imposed by the order . . . are commensurate with the seriousness of the offence, or the combination of the offence and one or more offences associated with it.'

In determining the requirements for a community order, the court will have regard to one or more of the sentencing objectives contained in s. 142(1) CJA 2003 (see Chapter 21).

The seriousness of the offence and the risk of harm posed by the offender will determine the nature and combination of requirements and the intensity of those requirements.

Important guidance on community orders is provided in the SC's recently published revised guideline *Imposition of Community and Custodial Sentences*, which came into force on 1 February 2017. The guideline can be accessed via the SC's website. The 'seriousness' of the offence (informed by specific sentencing guidelines) is an important factor in deciding whether the court chooses a low, medium or high range of requirements. Proportionality and suitability will be the guiding principles.

Generally the guidelines suggest the lowest range of community sentence should be reserved for low level types of offence. Such an order might contain just one requirement for a short duration. The most requirements would be reserved for those offenders whose offences fall just short of the custodial threshold. The nature and severity of the requirements to be imposed should be guided by:

(a) the assessment of the offence's seriousness (low/medium/high);

(b) the purpose(s) of sentencing the court wishes to achieve;

(c) the risk of reoffending;

(d) the ability of the offender to comply; and

(e) the availability of requirements in the local area.

The SC guideline includes examples of the type of requirements that might be imposed based on an offence of low/medium/high seriousness.

The guidelines stress the importance of obtaining a pre-sentence report (whether that be a written or oral report prepared by the Probation Service in court) to help determine the particular requirements or combination of requirements in a specific case.

22.11 **THE REQUIREMENTS**

22.11.1 **UNPAID WORK—S. 199 CJA 2003**

The offender is required to perform unpaid work in the community under the supervision of a responsible officer. A court cannot impose an unpaid work requirement unless the court is satisfied that the offender is a suitable person to perform such work. For this reason, a court will invariably require a pre-sentence report to assess the offender's suitability.

When imposing a community order with an unpaid work requirement, the court gives the offender the chance to make amends to the community in which the offence has been committed. It is punitive in nature. A supervising officer oversees the community work placement which might involve painting, decorating or gardening for organisations or individuals.

The number of hours of unpaid work must not be less than 40 and not more than 300 and should be proportional to the seriousness of the offence(s) committed. An unpaid work requirement may be combined with any further requirement(s) as the court deems fit.

22.11.2 **REHABILITATION ACTIVITY REQUIREMENT—S. 200A CJA 2003**

Section 200A(2) requires the court when imposing this requirement to specify the maximum number of days for which the offender may be instructed to participate in the specified activities. Section 200A(3) makes clear that the instructions under this requirement must be given with a view to promoting the rehabilitation of the offender, although they may also serve other purposes. Section 200A(4) permits the offender to be instructed to attend appointments with the responsible officer or another person. Instructions may require the offender to participate in specified activities or to go to a specified place and comply with instructions given by the person in charge of the activities at that place. Activities can include restorative justice with the co-operation of those affected by the offending behaviour.

22.11.3   **PROGRAMME REQUIREMENT—S. 202 CJA 2003**

An offender would be required to participate in an activity programme which has been accredited by a body established by the Secretary of State. A pre-sentence report would be required in order to check the offender's suitability and the availability of such an accredited programme.

The aims of these programmes are to:

- make offenders accept responsibility for their offences;
- avoid further offending;
- attempt to resolve any difficulties linked to offending behaviour, for example homelessness, marital or relationship breakdown, unemployment, illiteracy, addiction.

Such programmes have traditionally included:

- Enhanced Thinking Skills Programme. This requires the offender to participate in group work with a view to enabling poorly educated offenders to attain basic literacy and numeracy skills.
- Sex Offender Programme. This is aimed at offenders convicted of sexual offences who have been assessed as suitable for the programme.
- Drink Impaired Drivers Programme. This is aimed primarily at offenders convicted of drink-driving offences.

A programme requirement will invariably be combined with a supervision requirement (undertaken by a probation officer) under the community order.

22.11.4   **PROHIBITED ACTIVITY REQUIREMENT—S. 203 CJA 2003**

This requires the offender to refrain from participating in specified activities named in the order on any day or days specified during the requirement period. The requirements that may be included in a prohibited activity requirement are not limited and may include the prohibition of activities that would otherwise be lawful. Possibilities include prohibiting the defendant from visiting a particular place, for example nightclubs, or undertaking a particular activity such as driving, drinking alcohol or attending football matches.

22.11.5   **CURFEW REQUIREMENT—S. 204 CJA 2003**

A curfew requires a convicted offender to stay at an agreed address for a specified time of between two and 16 hours, for example between 7 pm and 7 am for a period of between one and seven days. A curfew can be imposed for a total of 12 months.

Curfew orders are enforced by electronic 'tagging' and are intended make it harder for an offender to commit further crimes by helping to break patterns of offending behaviour by forcing the offender to stay at the specified address.

A tag is attached to the offender's wrist or ankle and is linked to a monitoring machine installed in the place where the offender is living. The machine is linked via a telephone line to a monitoring centre. Monitoring centre staff are made immediately aware if the curfew is broken.

In imposing a curfew requirement, the court will take account of the offender's religious beliefs, employment or attendance at an educational establishment and its compatibility with any other requirements imposed as part of the community order. A pre-sentence report may well be required in order for the court to be satisfied that suitable accommodation is available to the offender.

22.11.6   **EXCLUSION REQUIREMENT—S. 205 CJA 2003**

This directs the offender not to enter a place or an area specified in the order. An exclusion requirement must not exceed two years and will be monitored electronically. The order can provide for the prohibition to operate only during specified periods and may specify different periods or days during the order.

22.11.7 RESIDENCE REQUIREMENT—S. 206 CJA 2003

This requires the offender to reside at a place specified in the order. It could include a hostel or institution recommended by a probation officer.

22.11.8 MENTAL HEALTH TREATMENT REQUIREMENT—S. 207 CJA 2003

Rehabilitative in nature, a mental health requirement requires the offender to be treated by a medical practitioner or psychologist. Before a court can impose such a requirement it must be satisfied that the offender is in need of such treatment and the offender is willing to comply.

22.11.9 DRUG REHABILITATION REQUIREMENT—S. 208 CJA 2003

A drug rehabilitation requirement (DRR) involves assessment and treatment for drug dependency. The treatment and testing period must be a minimum of six months and a maximum of three years. Before a court can impose a drug treatment requirement, it must be satisfied the defendant is dependent on drugs and can be treated. The defendant must consent to the order. The pre-sentence report must include an assessment from a treatment provider and a place must be available to the defendant. A DRR is a high-intensity community order designed to get offenders to change their drug use, thereby reducing their offending. The order will involve frequent drug testing and a high level of contact and supervision coupled with a regular monthly review by the courts.

22.11.10 ALCOHOL TREATMENT REQUIREMENT—S. 212 CJA 2003

This requirement is specifically aimed at offenders who are dependent on alcohol and whose dependency may respond to treatment. The offender must be willing to comply with the requirement. The period of treatment cannot be for less than six months.

22.11.11 ATTENDANCE CENTRE REQUIREMENT (WHERE OFFENDER IS AGED UNDER 25)— S. 214 CJA 2003

An attendance centre requirement obliges the offender to attend at a centre for between 12 and 36 hours. Attendance is limited to one occasion a day and for not more than three hours at any time. The attendance centre must be reasonably accessible to the offender.

22.12 GUILTY PLEA CREDIT/TIME SPENT ON REMAND AND COMMUNITY ORDERS

Where a community sentence is to be imposed, the court should take account of s. 144 CJA 2003. This may be reflected in the number of requirements or duration of requirements under a community order. In its definitive guideline on *Reduction in Sentence for a Guilty Plea* (July 2017), the SC says that, where an offence crosses the threshold for imposing a community sentence, the application of the reduction principle under s. 144 CA 2003 may properly form the basis for imposing a fine.

Time spent on remand or subject to an electronically monitored curfew of not less than nine hours a day may be taken into account by the court in determining the nature and number of restrictions to their liberty that are imposed as part of a community order.

22.13 ENFORCEMENT OF COMMUNITY ORDERS UNDER THE CJA 2003—SCH. 8

The court will explain the consequence of the offender's failure to comply with a community order. An offender can breach a community order by failing to comply with its requirements or by committing further offences while subject to a community order.

Where a breach occurs the Probation Service will issue a single warning about a failure to comply and any further failure will result in breach proceedings being commenced against the offender. The Probation Service can apply to have the order revoked by requiring the offender to be returned to court. In dealing with an offender for breaching the requirements, the court must take into account the extent to which the offender has complied with the order.

The court has a range of powers including to fine; take no action; impose more onerous requirements on the existing order; revoke the order if it is in the interest of justice to do so and resentence the offender for the original offence; and in the case of an offender aged over 18 (who was convicted of an imprisonable offence in the first instance and has wilfully and persistently failed to comply with the requirements of the order), the court may impose a prison sentence not exceeding six months.

The Sentencing Council is developing a definitive guideline on breach of orders.

22.14 DEFERRING SENTENCE—SS. 1 AND 2 PCC(S)A 2000

Section 1:

> 'The Crown Court or magistrates' court may defer passing sentence on an offender for the purposes of enabling the court, or any court to which it falls to deal with him, to have regard in dealing with him to . . .
>
> (a) his conduct after conviction (including, where appropriate, the making by him of reparation for his offence) or;
>
> (b) any change in his circumstances . . .'

Deferment can only be imposed with the offender's consent and if it is in the interests of justice to do so, having regard to the nature of the offence and the character and circumstances of the defendant.

Deferment may be for up to six months and results in an adjournment of the proceedings. The power to defer sentence is most appropriately exercised where there has been an offer by the offender to make reparation to her victim or a change is expected in the offender's life which may produce a stabilising influence, for example a new job or marriage.

The power to defer should be exercised sparingly. In accordance with Sch. 23 CJA 2003 a court can impose requirements on the offender (similar to those imposed on a community order) during the period of deferment, including, if appropriate, supervision by a probation officer plus a new restorative justice requirement. If the court is satisfied that the offender has failed to comply with one or more requirements, the offender can be brought back to court to be sentenced. The expectation is that if the offender stays out of trouble and does what is required of her, she will not receive a custodial sentence for the offence for which she has been convicted.

22.15 FINES

Fines are frequently imposed in the magistrates' courts. The power to impose a financial penalty is contained in ss. 126–129 PCC(S)A 2000. Fines are suitable punishment for offences which are not serious enough to merit a community sentence, nor so serious that a custodial sentence must be considered. A high fine can be regarded as punitive and aimed at deterring an offender from repeat offending.

A fine must not exceed the statutory limit for the offence which is defined in terms of levels. The maximums are as follows:

Level 1 (£250)

Level 2 (£500)

Level 3 (£1,000)

Level 4 (£2,500)

The maximum amount for a Level 5 fine was £5,000. For offences committed after 15 March 2015 however, a Level 5 fine is now unlimited in the magistrates' court. The Crown Court's power to impose a fine is unlimited.

Section 164 CJA 2003 importantly provides:

'(1) Before fixing the amount of any fine to be imposed on an offender who is an individual, a court shall inquire into his financial circumstances.

(2) The amount of any fine fixed by the court shall be such as, in the opinion of the court, reflects the seriousness of the offence.

(3) In fixing the amount of any fine to be imposed on an offender (whether an individual or other person), a court shall take into account the circumstances of the case including, among other things, the financial circumstances of the offender so far as they are known, or appear, to the court . . .'

Section 162 CJA 2003 enables the court to order an offender to disclose his financial means when considering imposing a fine.

It is good practice for the defence lawyer to obtain a written statement of his client's means which can be handed to the court including a full breakdown of his client's income and outgoings.

The MCSGs provide detailed guidance on the imposition of fines in the magistrates' court. Some offences in the guidelines have a fine as the initial starting point when passing sentence. For the purposes of the MCSGs a fine is based on one of six bands (A, B, C, D, E, and F) as detailed in Table 22.2.

TABLE 22.2 MAGISTRATES' COURT SENTENCING GUIDELINES FINE BANDS

	Starting point	Range
Fine Band A	50% of weekly income	25–75% of relevant weekly income
Fine Band B	100% of weekly income	75–125% of relevant weekly income
Fine Band C	150% cent of weekly income	125–175% of relevant weekly income
Fine Band D	250% of relevant weekly income	200–300% of relevant weekly income
Fine Band E	400% of relevant weekly income	300–500% of relevant weekly income
Fine Band F	600% of relevant weekly income	500–700% of relevant weekly income

In practice and in accordance with offence specific guidelines, Bands A–C are more likely to be used than Bands D–F. The choice of the fine band and the position of the offence within the range for that band is decided by the court's assessment of the overall seriousness of the offence. The size of the fine is then determined by the application of the defendant's relevant weekly income (RWI) to the choice of fine band and the position within it. The MCSGs include guidance on the definition of relevant weekly income based on the offender's income from employment or self-employment after deduction of tax and National Insurance. Payments received from tax credits, housing and child benefits are excluded from determining the relevant weekly income. The minimum relevant weekly income for an offender in receipt of welfare benefits or generally in receipt of a very low income is £120. Where there is no reliable information on relevant weekly income, the guidelines require the court to assume the offender has a relevant weekly income of £440. In deciding the proportions of relevant weekly income that are starting points and ranges for each fine band, account has been taken of reasonable living expenses.

Credit must be given to take account of a guilty plea in accordance with principles previously discussed (see Chapter 21, para. 21.13).

Example

Bupinda pleads guilty to an offence of careless driving. She was driving too quickly in wet conditions and failed to notice a pedestrian stepping into the road. Bupinda applied her brakes but collided with the pedestrian causing minor injury. Bupinda has a previous conviction for speeding. Applying the MCSGs for this offence (you can access this offence specific guideline in MCSGs 2017, available via the SC website), the starting point for a fine based on what occurred would appear to be Band B. Aggravating features of the offence include injury to a pedestrian and the fact that Bupinda has a previous conviction for speeding. The magistrates' court decides that Band B is the appropriate band but that the fine should be calculated at 110% of relevant weekly income to take account of the aggravating features. Bupinda has a weekly income of £200. She can expect a fine in the region of £220 and she will be entitled to a one-third reduction for her timely guilty plea. She will therefore have to pay a fine of £150 plus a victim surcharge (see later).

Financial penalties (including fines/compensation orders/victim surcharges/prosecution costs) may be paid by instalments. Where a financial penalty cannot be discharged immediately, a fines collection order will be made with the court setting the rate of payment. Court-appointed fines collection officers may take enforcement proceedings in the event of default.

Whilst a fine is usually imposed as a sentence in its own right it can be combined with a community order, a compensation order and with disqualification from driving. It cannot be combined with a discharge as a sentence for a single offence. In theory, a fine can be combined with custody but in practice this is rare as imprisonment will deprive the offender of the ability to pay.

22.15.1 VICTIM SURCHARGE

Whenever a court imposes a fine it must order the offender to pay a victim surcharge, as detailed in Table 22.3.

TABLE 22.3 VICTIM SURCHARGE LEVELS

Sentence imposed	Victim surcharge
conditional discharge	£20
fine	10% of total fine, but minimum of £30, maximum £170
community order	£85
custodial sentence	6 months or less: £115
	over 6 months and up to 2 years: £140. Over 2 years £170 (only in the Crown Court)
suspended custodial sentence	6 months and below: £115. Over 6 months: £140

22.16 COMPENSATION ORDERS

It is a legitimate expectation for a victim of a criminal offence to receive compensation for any injury, loss or damage suffered as a result of a convicted individual's actions. Section 130 PCC(S)A 2000 imposes a duty on the court to consider making a compensation order in such amount as it considers appropriate and to give reasons for not making an order when it is empowered to do so.

Until recently, magistrates could award compensation of up to £5,000 per offence. This limit has now been removed in the case of adult offenders. In the Crown Court, the amounts are unlimited. The MCSGs contain a table of guideline compensation awards for personal injury. In fixing the level of compensation, the offender's means must be taken into account. Priority is given to compensation orders over victim surcharges; fines and prosecution costs.

Example 1

Harry is convicted of assault. The victim sustains a broken nose requiring some manipulation. Based on the guidelines, Harry can expect to be ordered to pay compensation in the region of £2,000. Clearly, if Harry is in receipt of welfare benefits this sum is likely to be substantially reduced.

 Example 2

Tilly is convicted of resisting a police constable in the execution of his duty. The officer falls to the floor during the arrest, sustaining bruising to both knees. The court is considering a fine for the offence. Based on the MCSGs, compensation in the region of £50–£100 may well be ordered. If Tilly is in receipt of welfare benefits and cannot afford to pay a fine as well as compensation, the court will give priority to the compensation element.

 Example 3

Alice is convicted of criminal damage. She pleads guilty to breaking a door. The cost of replacing the door is estimated at £150. Alice can expect to be asked to pay some or all of this sum by way of compensation, depending on her means.

Compensation can be awarded for psychological injury. For the purposes of a compensation order, the injured party can be an individual or a company/organisation.

Where injury or damage has occurred through a road traffic offence, compensation is not awarded by the courts. Such compensation is left to compulsory driving insurance schemes. If the offender is uninsured and the Motor Insurers' Bureau will not cover the loss, an award can be made in these circumstances.

The prosecution should normally have compensation details to hand at the point of sentencing. Where personal injury has resulted, the CPS should have the necessary details, including photographic evidence, if available. Where damage has occurred the court will expect to see an invoice for repairs or an estimate for replacement.

Where a defendant disputes the amount of compensation requested, the court will hear representations. If the matter is incapable of being resolved, the question of compensation may be adjourned for further enquiries to be made or a possible *Newton* hearing (see Chapter 21, para. 21.4.3).

Where more than one offender caused the victim's injury, loss or damage, the court may apportion the compensation to be paid according to each offender's culpability and his or her ability to pay.

Can the court order compensation when it sends the offender to prison? Whilst it is not usual to do so, it is possible and the Court of Appeal has stated that such an order is not wrong in principle providing the court is satisfied the offender has the means to pay or will have sufficient earning capacity when released from prison (*R v Jonge* [1999] 2 Cr App R (S) 1).

22.17 CONDITIONAL DISCHARGE

A conditional discharge may be ordered under s. 12 PCC(S)A 2000 and is a common disposal in the magistrates' courts but may also be imposed by a Crown Court. The offender can be conditionally discharged for a period of up to three years. There is no minimum period specified.

It must be explained to the defendant that, if she does not reoffend during the period of the conditional discharge, she will not be punished for the offence for which she has been convicted. However, if she is convicted of a further offence, especially if it is of a similar type, the conditional discharge can be revoked and the defendant will be sentenced not only in connection with the new matter, but could also be resentenced for the offence for which she received the conditional discharge.

A conditional discharge therefore has a deterrent element. It would not be imposed for a serious offence, but it is particularly suitable for first-time offenders, and those who may not have offended in the recent past whose offence is not serious enough to warrant a community sentence. A conditional discharge is usually passed as a sentence in its own right but can be combined with an award of compensation and/or costs.

22.18 ABSOLUTE DISCHARGE

An absolute discharge may be imposed under s. 12 PCC(S)A 2000—although the sentence is rarely passed. In effect, the defendant is not being punished, although the conviction is recorded against her. It might be imposed on a defendant who, although technically guilty, is morally blameless, or in connection with a very trivial offence. Where the offence is very trivial the prosecutor may be required to explain why the prosecution was brought at all.

22.19 BIND OVER

The bind over is an ancient power available to the criminal courts. A bind over does not rank as a conviction. The power to bind over can arise either on complaint or of the court's own motion under common law powers and is also contained in s. 1(7) Justices of the Peace Act 1968. It enables a magistrates' court to bind over an individual to keep the Queen's Peace for a specified period of time and in a sum of money. It can be imposed where the court is satisfied that there has been a breach of the peace or there is a real risk of a breach in the future. The offender must consent to be bound over. No money is taken from the offender but it must be explained to the offender that, if she fails to keep the peace, she will be required to forfeit all or part of the sum specified. In court, it would be expressed in the following way:

> Chair: 'Stand up—You will be bound over in the sum of £100 for a period of 12 months to keep the peace towards X. This means that you do not have to pay any money now. But if you break the order, you can be ordered to pay all or part of that sum. Do you agree to be bound over?'
>
> Defendant: 'Yes . . .'

In practice, a bind over is a matter of negotiation between the defence and the prosecution. They are most commonly imposed in connection with less serious matters such as minor domestic disputes or disputes between neighbours which have resulted in court proceedings. In these cases, the defendant may feel aggrieved that she is the one being prosecuted when others might be regarded as being equally culpable. The offer of a bind over may therefore be the most pragmatic way of resolving the proceedings. The substantive offence which led the defendant to appear before the magistrates is then withdrawn when a bind over is imposed. The precise terms of the bind over must be explained. This could include refraining from specified types of conduct or activities.

If the defendant does not consent to the bind over and pleads not guilty to the substantive offence a trial date will be fixed and the matter tried. The benefits of a bind over ought to be explained to the defendant, as a guilty verdict will result in a criminal record and most probably an order that the defendant pays the prosecution's costs.

22.20 **ANCILLARY ORDER**

There are a number of ancillary orders that a court can impose upon sentence. They include:

* criminal behaviour orders;
* compensation orders;
* confiscation orders (Crown Court only);
* deprivation orders;
* disqualification from driving;
* drink banning orders;
* disqualification from being a company director;
* financial reporting order;
* football banning orders;
* forfeiture orders;
* parenting orders;
* restitution orders;
* restraining orders;
* serious crime prevention order (Crown Court only); and
* sexual harm prevention orders.

22.20.1 **PROSECUTION COSTS**

It is common for courts to award some or all of the prosecution's costs in the event of a conviction (s. 17 Prosecution of Offences Act 1985) although priority is given to the payment of compensation orders and fines.

R v Northallerton Magistrates' Court, ex p. Dove [2000] 1 Cr App R (S) 136 provides the guidance on awarding prosecution costs:

* The purpose of an award is to compensate the prosecution and not to punish the defendant.
* An award should not exceed the sum which the prosecutor has actually and reasonably incurred.
* Account must be taken of the offender's ability to pay, particularly having regard to any other financial penalties to be imposed, that is, compensation/fine.

The amount sought by the prosecution depends on the nature of the offence and the degree of preparation that the prosecutor has had to undertake. The court may order all or part of the costs sought, or make no order as to costs.

22.20.2 **CONFISCATION AND FORFEITURE**

We briefly refer to confiscation and forfeiture orders as the detail falls outside the scope of this text. The provisions are contained in the Proceeds of Crime Act 2002 and are notoriously complex and draconian. The Act gives the Crown Court powers to confiscate assets which are the result of the particular criminal conduct of which the defendant has been convicted. The most obvious example would be the proceeds of drug trafficking. However, the Act also permits a court to confiscate assets which it believes have been acquired as a result of general criminal conduct in circumstances where the offender is enjoying a 'criminal lifestyle'. There is a protracted procedure requiring the prosecution to provide a statement of information to which the defendant must respond. The provisions are not restricted to particular offences and can apply whenever a defendant is convicted before a Crown Court or if the defendant has been committed to the Crown Court for sentence.

Although the court of its own motion can initiate the process, the application is likely to be made by the prosecution.

Section 143 PCC(S)A 2000 gives a court the power to order forfeiture of any property lawfully seized from the defendant (or which is in the defendant's possession or under her control at the time she was apprehended) which has been used for the purpose of committing or facilitating the commission of an offence or which was intended by the defendant to be used for such purpose. In utilising this power, a court should have regard to the totality of sentence for the particular offence. Provision is included in s. 145 PCC(S)A 2000 to allow the sale of property connected with an offence in order to pay compensation to the victim, but only where the offender's means are such that she would otherwise not be in a position to discharge the compensation figure.

22.20.3 CRIMINAL BEHAVIOUR ORDER (CBO)

The CBO replaces the ASBO (Anti-Social Behaviour Order) and was introduced by the Anti-Social Behaviour, Crime and Policing Act 2014. The CBO is available on conviction for any criminal offence in any criminal court. However, the order is aimed at tackling the most serious and persistent offenders where their behaviour has brought them before the court. CBOs include prohibitions to stop anti-social behaviour, and may also include requirements to address the underlying causes of the offender's behaviour. The order could include prohibitive and/or positive requirements including not being in possession of a can of spray paint in a public place or not entering a particular area, or not being drunk in a particular place. The court may make a CBO against an offender only on the application of the prosecution and which will usually be instigated by the police or local authority. The CBO can also be imposed alongside another sentence including a conditional discharge but not an absolute discharge. In the case of an adult, the CBO must either be for a fixed two-year period or more or for an indefinite duration. A court can vary or discharge an order upon the application of the offender or the prosecution. A breach of a CBO is punishable with up to five years' imprisonment.

For a CBO to be made the court must be satisfied, beyond reasonable doubt that the offender has engaged in behaviour that caused, or was likely to cause, harassment, alarm, or distress to any person and that making the order will help in preventing the offender from engaging in such behaviour. More extensive guidance on CBOs can be found on the CPS website at http://www.cps.gov.uk/legal/a_to_c/criminal_behaviour_orders/.

For more details on these and other ancillary orders, see *Blackstone's Criminal Practice*.

22.20.4 RESTRAINING ORDER

Reforms introduced under s. 12 Domestic Violence, Crime and Victims Act 2004 enable a court to impose a restraining order upon an individual. In the past the power to impose such an order was restricted to cases where the offender had been convicted of an offence under the Harassment Act 1977. As a consequence of the 2004 Act, restraining orders can be imposed in relation to any offence and even in the case of an acquittal. A restraining order can be imposed upon conviction for any offence for the purpose of protecting a person from conduct which amounts to harassment or will cause a fear of violence. Such an order can be imposed in the event of an acquittal where the court concludes that it is necessary to protect the person from harassment by the defendant. Recent guidance on imposing a restraining order following an acquittal can be found in the Court of Appeal decision in *R v Tara Major* [2010] EWCA Crim 3016.

The terms of a restraining order must be clear, precise and easily understood. The order must also be proportionate to the nature of the harassment and can be imposed for a specified period or until a further order is issued.

It is an offence to do anything prohibited by a restraining order without reasonable excuse (s. 5(5)). The maximum penalty for breach of an order is five years' imprisonment following conviction on indictment and six months summarily (s. 5(6) Harassment Act 1997).

An application for a further order to vary or discharge the existing order can be made by the prosecution, defendant or any person mentioned in the order (s. 5(4)).

Having covered all the necessary background information relevant to the sentencing process, we finally consider how the defence solicitor might construct and deliver a plea in mitigation.

22.21 THE PLEA IN MITIGATION

As previously explained, the sentence a defendant receives will largely be determined by the seriousness of the offence. However, in arriving at the most appropriate sentence, the court will consider the defendant's personal circumstances and any personal offender mitigation.

The plea in mitigation is important because it should assist the court to determine the seriousness of the offence and direct the court's attention to any relevant personal offender mitigation.

22.21.1 DELIVERING AN EFFECTIVE PLEA IN MITIGATION

An effective plea in mitigation requires the defence advocate to combine a thorough knowledge of sentencing law and practice with good advocacy skills. There are, in our view, three fundamental requirements for a competent plea in mitigation.

First, the advocate must understand the theory of sentencing and the importance of researching the relevant sentencing guidelines.

Second, the advocate must have in mind a realistic sentencing objective, having regard to the theory behind sentencing and after considering the relevant sentencing guidelines. Formulating a realistic sentencing objective requires a combination of common sense and experience of sentencing.

Third, the advocate needs good advocacy skills.

An effective plea in mitigation should be well thought through, carefully constructed and persuasively delivered. Preparation is the key.

22.21.2 PREPARING A PLEA IN MITIGATION

The starting point for a plea in mitigation is an awareness of the sentence a court can impose for the particular offence(s) and any applicable sentencing guidelines.

The defence advocate will know the prosecution's version of the facts having considered the pre-trial disclosure of evidence (advance information) and from hearing the prosecutor's submission to the court outlining the circumstances of the offence. Assuming you are acting for the defendant, you will have taken your client's detailed instructions about the offence and considered and discussed with him the contents of any pre-sentence. You should be able to assess the balance of any aggravating and mitigating features and be able to assess the seriousness of the offence with reference to any applicable offence-specific guideline.

As sentencing is based on the seriousness of the offence, you need to make an assessment of seriousness by asking 'What would I like to achieve for my client?' Then put yourself in the court's position and consider what sentencing objective the court is likely to follow. Will it want to punish your client/rehabilitate him/prevent the commission of further offences/protect the public/put your client on trust as to his future behaviour? By engaging in this exercise you should arrive at a realistic sentencing objective which gives you the basis upon which to build your plea in mitigation.

If you conclude that a custodial sentence is a possibility for your client, consider whether the custody threshold test is met on the case facts. Consider *R v Kefford* [2002] 2 Cr App R (S) 495 and other cases that are relevant to passing a custodial sentence. Can you use them in your plea in mitigation?

If your preparation leads you to conclude that the court might impose a community sentence, consider whether the criteria for such sentence are met.

If a financial penalty or a compensation order is likely, make sure you have an up-to-date statement of your client's financial means.

22.21.3 USING THE PRE-SENTENCE REPORT IN PREPARATION

In preparing a plea the defence advocate must discuss the content of any pre-sentence report (PSR) with his client. This applies to either a written report or a report that is orally delivered. Advocates should be selective and refer the sentencing court to relevant portions of the pre-sentence report which assist the plea being put forward.

22.21.4 PRESENTING CHARACTER EVIDENCE OR OTHER EVIDENCE IN A PLEA IN MITIGATION

The defence advocate should consider whether personal testimonial evidence will assist the plea in mitigation by presenting the court with background information about your client. If your client is of good character and is charged with an offence which is likely to damage her reputation, it is useful to hand in to the court a short character reference. If your client has a medical condition that is relevant to sentencing, consider obtaining a written note from her GP, or if your client has a job offer or a helpful letter from an employer, it is good mitigation to obtain written confirmation to present to the court.

22.22 STRUCTURING A PLEA IN MITIGATION

There is no approved structure for a plea in mitigation as every plea in mitigation must be tailored to the individual case. Having regard to all that has been said in this and the preceding chapters, we include a checklist of the possible factors an advocate might have regard to in preparing a plea in mitigation.

Introduction

If your client has pleaded guilty, you may wish to introduce yourself to the bench before beginning your plea in mitigation. You may also want to say a few words to introduce your client:

'Madam . . . my client is a young woman. She is 24. She has a job and resides with her partner . . .'

Acknowledge the prosecution's presentation of the facts

Consider thanking the prosecution for its fair outline of the facts of the case, if this is appropriate:

'Madam, I am grateful to my friend for fairly outlining the facts in this case . . .'

If there are aspects of the prosecution's presentation with which you disagree, highlight them at this stage. You might continue:

'There is, however, one matter which I feel I ought to clarify/bring to your attention at the outset and before going any further . . .'

Using a pre-sentence report

If a written pre-sentence report has been prepared, ascertain from the bench at an early stage in your plea whether they have had the opportunity to consider its content. If not, politely suggest that the bench may wish to do so before you continue with your plea. Think about court etiquette. Be polite:

'Madam, I wonder if you have had the opportunity to consider the pre-sentence report that has been prepared in connection with this matter? You have; I am grateful for that indication . . .'

Use the pre-sentence report selectively, if it is to your benefit:

'I wonder if I might direct Madam's attention to paragraph 12 of the pre-sentence report where Miss James speaks favourably of a community-based disposal in this matter . . .'

If the PRS is delivered orally, this will normally be before the defence makes its plea in mitigation.

Acknowledge your client's predicament

'Madam, let me say at the outset that my client is a deeply anxious individual . . . my client fully appreciates that she stands to be sentenced today for a serious offence/that she could be sent to prison for these offences today . . . she expresses her complete remorse for her wrongdoing . . . understands the need for punishment but also seeks the help of the court in dealing with her offending behaviour . . .'

Can you play down the seriousness of the offence?

Can you use the MCSGs, or other applicable guidelines, to play down the seriousness of the offence? Consider the aggravating and mitigating factors. Are you absolutely clear as to the basis of your client's guilty plea if your client is pleading guilty?

If your client has pleaded guilty to an offence of assault, relevant mitigating factors may include provocation, a minor injury, etc. If your client has been found guilty of a theft offence, relevant mitigating features would include the fact that it was committed spontaneously, the amount involved is small or that the theft or deception was not committed for personal gain. If the offence to be sentenced was burglary, relevant factors would include the fact that the property was empty or disused and that no damage was caused in the course of the burglary. Have the stolen items been recovered? Was the crime committed in a sophisticated way?

Be tactful when exploring the victim's role in the commission of the offence. You do not want to score an own goal. It is your client who stands to be punished for the offence, not the victim.

If custody is a distinct possibility

Consider the applicable criteria. Is the offence 'so serious' that only custody can be justified? Be prepared to make representations based on the aggravating and mitigating features. Once again, refer to the sentencing guidelines and the case law considered in Chapter 21 and make the point that if a custodial sentence is to be imposed, its length should be commensurate with the seriousness of the offence (s. 153 CJA 2003). You might refer to the current problems of prison overcrowding highlighted in *Kefford* [2002] 2 Cr App R (S) 106 and *Seed* [2007] 2 Cr App R (S) 69, with a view to trying to persuade the court to keep any custodial sentence to as short a length as possible. You might ask the court to suspend a period of imprisonment.

Can you play down your client's role in the offence?

Was your client led into temptation? Perhaps your client was not the instigator or 'ring leader'. Was your client provoked? Was your client intoxicated or under the influence of an unlawful substance? You have to be careful with regard to the aforementioned. Drink and drugs do not excuse an offender's behaviour, but they may go some way to explain why your client acted in the way she did.

Can you offer an explanation as to why your client has offended?

Do not seek to excuse the offence, but see if you can offer an explanation for your client's offending. Common factors include low self-esteem, mental health issues, complete lack of self-control, dire financial straits, homelessness and addictive behaviour such as alcoholism, drug abuse, gambling.

Are there any personal factors at work that might put the offending behaviour into context?

Is your client getting divorced? Maybe your client is in the grips of an acrimonious breakdown of a relationship. Perhaps your client is frustrated because she cannot gain access to her children resulting in a sense of frustration and anger. Is your client presently facing an uncertain future? Maybe she is ill, bereaved, redundant or about to be made redundant, being sued or going through some personal crisis. Consider whether any of the above can be substantiated by evidence, perhaps in the form of a short medical report or letter from an employer.

What is your client's attitude to the offence?

Some clients will give you more scope in this respect than others. Attitude may be reflected in a timely guilty plea and cooperation with the police. A guilty plea spares witnesses. You will want to remind the bench that it should give credit for a timely guilty plea.

Your client's attitude might be expressed in a pre-sentence report if one is ordered and you should highlight this and bring it to the attention of the court. How candid has your client been in engaging with the Probation Service?

Most advocates will express their clients' regret and remorse and perhaps offer an apology. Of course, actions speak louder than words. If your client has sought to make reparation to the victim (by paying compensation or repairing any damage) or has personally expressed an apology this is very useful mitigation.

What effect will the conviction have on your client?

Will this conviction result in a damaged reputation? This will be of particular relevance in the case of a first-time offender, especially if convicted of an offence relating to dishonesty. A first-time conviction for a sexual offence will result in damage to your client's reputation.

What has been the effect of court proceedings on your client's family? Is the court sentencing a mother who has the sole care of her children? What effect have the proceedings had on your client? Has your client been put under stress by the court appearances? What were the circumstances of your client's arrest? Was it public? Did your client have to spend a night or two in a police cell? Is it an experience your client wishes to repeat? Does your client face the loss of her job as a result of this conviction?

No previous convictions?

The fact that your client has no previous convictions is excellent mitigation. It means that this offence is completely out of character and is a one-off. The court may want to place your client on trust as to her future behaviour, depending on the seriousness of the offence.

What if your client has a criminal record?

Can you use your client's criminal record to your advantage? Perhaps the last conviction was some time ago. Consider whether your client has been subject to a community order and has found it to be beneficial. Has your client made brave attempts to rehabilitate herself in the meantime? Maybe steps have been taken to overcome drug addiction. Should your client be given the benefit of the doubt on this occasion? Can you detect a trend in the nature of the offences that have been committed that now needs to be addressed?

Do you have any character witnesses you might call to give evidence or to submit in written form to the court?

Your preparation for the plea in mitigation should have alerted you to this possibility. Ensure you have enough copies of any character references to distribute to the court.

What has your client done since to assist matters?

Has your client made good any damage or offered to pay voluntary sums of compensation? Has your client been able to obtain employment? Has your client begun to address the reason for her offending? If alcoholism or drug abuse is the problem, has your client sought help from professionals? If the offending behaviour is set against the backdrop of a marital or relationship breakdown, consider whether your client has come to terms with matters and is seeking help, perhaps from a solicitor or a counselling agency.

In short, is there evidence you can point to which suggests your client has some insight into her offending behaviour and wants to do something about it?

Finances

Given that the fine is a popular sentencing option in magistrates' courts (see para. 22.15), you must be in a position to provide the court with details of your client's finances, including weekly income and outgoings, savings and debts. A fine should always reflect an individual's ability to pay, and you may need to make representations on this basis. Imposing a fine could, of course, have a detrimental effect on your client's family. Where your client has an outstanding account with the court, you can expect the legal adviser to check whether your client's existing payments are up to date.

Miscellaneous considerations

Do not overlook the fact that if the current conviction puts your client in breach of an existing penalty, you will need to address this and the circumstances pertaining to that previous offence, as your client is likely to be resentenced or punished in some way for it. If your client has admitted an offence of absconding during the currency of the proceedings you will need to address the court on this as it constitutes a separate offence. Remember that if you are mitigating on a driving matter, different considerations might apply. You might need to argue special reasons or mitigating circumstances such as exceptional hardship (see the Additional Chapter 'Sentencing in Road Traffic Cases' in the online resources).

Finally, your conclusion . . .

What are you seeking to persuade the sentencing court to do? Are you looking for leniency, or a sentence to address your client's needs and the need to punish? Close your submission:

'Unless I can assist you further Madam . . . those are my submissions . . .'

The foregoing checklist assumes your client has pleaded guilty to the offence, obviating the need for a trial. If your client has been found guilty following a trial, whilst you can still address the court on the mitigating features of the offence, it is pointless to disagree with the verdict and to seek to minimise your client's role. By finding your client guilty, the court has already made up its mind about your client's involvement. You must, however, explain your client's personal circumstances so that the court is appraised of the sort of individual it is sentencing.

22.23 ADVOCACY AND THE PLEA IN MITIGATION

Please refer to our comments in respect of advocacy skills in Chapter 2. We highlight a handful of key features in relation to pleas in mitigation.

Use powerful words

Use words that are inclusive:

'Let us examine the circumstances surrounding the commission of this offence . . . you will see . . . you will no doubt appreciate the position my client found herself in . . .'

Use a structure

There is no predetermined structure to a plea in mitigation. Consequently, you will need to devise a structure that gives coherence to your submission. Use the checklist at para. 22.22 as your starting point. Consider ways in which you can link the various portions of your submissions:

'Madam, having looked at the circumstances of the offence, let us now turn to my client's personal situation . . .'

Remember, if you find yourself making a plea in mitigation before a District Judge, you will need to be succinct. An experienced District Judge may well indicate at the outset what sentence they are thinking of imposing on your client. Be prepared to hold your ground.

22.24 **PROFESSIONAL CONDUCT**

In submitting a plea in mitigation, the defence advocate should bear in mind the professional conduct rules outlined in the Code of Conduct for Solicitors (2019) as explained in Chapter 1. Specific considerations will include compliance with *Principle 1*, the duty to uphold the rule of law and the proper administration of justice, *Principle 4* to act with honesty and *Principle 5* to act with integrity. Therefore, when delivering a plea in mitigation the advocate must not attempt to deceive or knowingly or recklessly mislead the court and must not be complicit in another person deceiving or misleading the court.

KEY POINT SUMMARY

- A custodial sentence is the most draconian sentence a court can pass.

- For a custodial sentence to be imposed, the custody threshold test defined in s. 152 CJA 2003 must be met.

- The threshold test under the CJA 2003 requires the offence to be so serious that neither a fine alone, nor a community order, can be justified.

- The duration of a custodial sentence must be commensurate with the seriousness of the offence.

- A custodial sentence can be immediate or suspended.

- A suspended sentence may only be imposed where the custody threshold test is met. The offender may have one or more requirements imposed upon him to complete during the period of suspension.

- The threshold test for a community sentence is whether the offence is 'serious enough'. Community sentences involve one or more requirements based on the seriousness of the overall offending behaviour.

- Understand the range of sentencing options available to a court and the requisite criteria for each of them.

- When acting for the defendant, try to formulate a realistic sentencing objective for your client having regard to the offence your client has committed and the range of sentencing disposals available to the court.

- Try to think in terms of the worst case scenario for your client, and what you feel you can and would realistically like to achieve.

- If a custodial sentence is a distinct possibility, consider whether the custody threshold test is met: be prepared to cite supporting case law on this. Consider whether a community penalty might be a constructive alternative to custody.

- Given that a financial penalty is common, be sure to have a statement of means from your client and be prepared to make appropriate representations based on those means.

- Anticipate an ancillary order such as prosecution costs.

- All of the above underscore the importance of researching the penalties for the offence you are considering and any specific sentencing guidelines.

SELF-TEST QUESTIONS

1. Explain the basis upon which a court can impose a term of imprisonment upon a convicted offender.

2. What principles determine the length of a custodial sentence?

3. What types of custodial terms may be imposed?

4. Consider the short scenarios below and try to answer the following questions:

   - What sentence do you feel the court is likely to pass, and why? Research the applicable sentencing guidelines (see Appendix 3 for assistance, although note that you may have to look up some of the offence-specific guidelines using the Magistrates' Court Sentencing Guideline which can be accessed via the Sentencing Council's website: https://www.sentencingcouncil.judiciary.gov.uk/).

Exercise 1

Celia appears before the magistrates' court represented by the duty solicitor. She pleads guilty to stealing a gold bracelet worth £150 from a counter display. Without trying to conceal anything she picked up the bracelet, tried it on her wrist and left the shop without paying, prompting the sale's assistant to call shop security. She was stopped a few yards from the shop and admitted the theft. When interviewed by the police, she was cooperative but very tearful and frightened as to what her husband would say. She has no idea why she took the item. She had her credit cards on her at the time and could have paid.

Celia is married. She is 52. She has two grown-up children who live away from the family home. Her husband is a well-respected professional person. Celia has no employment. She has rheumatoid arthritis and has felt depressed of late. Celia is well thought of in her community and is an active member of a number of charitable concerns. Six months ago, Celia was conditionally discharged for 12 months for stealing items of underwear from a department store. She is in breach of this order by virtue of the current offence.

 Exercise 2

Louise pleads guilty to theft before the magistrates' court. She worked as a trainee in a hairdresser's shop. She had access to the till and took small amounts (£150 in total) over a period of several weeks. The thefts caused a bad atmosphere as everyone in the salon was under suspicion. Louise says she took the money because an acquaintance was putting pressure on her to repay a debt. She says she fully intended to repay the money from her tips. Louise is 18, has no previous convictions and pleads guilty at the first opportunity. She is now unemployed and receiving income support and housing benefit. She lives in a bedsit.

 Exercise 3

Andrew was found cultivating five cannabis plants in his bedroom. He says he was growing them for personal use and for the use of his disabled partner who suffers from a chronic illness and finds the effects alleviate some of his discomfort. Andrew pleaded guilty before the magistrates' court at the first opportunity. He has several previous convictions for theft and possession of drugs. Andrew and his partner receive invalidity benefit of £130 per week.

 Exercise 4

Darren is charged with assaulting a police constable in the execution of his duty contrary to s. 89 Police Act 1996. Darren and some of his friends had been celebrating their football team's win. They had been drinking and were rowdy. They were stopped by police on the High Street who asked them to calm down. While most of the youths dispersed, Darren (who accepts he was drunk) entered into an argument with one of the police officers. A scuffle ensued in which the police officer fell over. While the officer lay on the ground, he was kicked several times by Darren. The officer suffered a bloody nose and extensive bruising to his face and left arm and was off sick for three weeks. A pre-sentence report assesses Darren's risk of reoffending as being medium. It highlights Darren's alcohol consumption as being the motivation for the offence. Darren is deemed suitable for a community sentence including an unpaid work requirement. Darren is 21 and has previous convictions for possession of an offensive weapon and common assault. He completed a community order with a 120-hour unpaid work requirement for the offensive weapon offence last year. He pleads guilty before the magistrates' court to the assault on the officer and expresses his remorse. Darren is employed as a shop assistant and brings home £150 per week. He will lose his job if sent to prison. He lives with his mother and gives her £25 per week towards his keep. He owns a car and therefore has related car expenditure.

- If you were the defence solicitor, what would you hope to persuade the court to do in terms of sentence?

Analysis can be found in our Online resources.

Case study: *R v William Hardy*

You will recall that William Hardy has pleaded guilty to the offence of unlawful sexual activity with a child, which is an indictable-only offence.

Your file to date contains:

- William Hardy's proof of evidence;

- initial disclosure of prosecution case;

- pre-sentence report;

- character references;

- an agreed basis of plea;

- your research of the relevant sentencing guidelines for an offence of this type (see analysis of self-test question in relation to Chapter 21).

In the light of all that we have considered in relation to sentencing, we invite you to draft a plea in mitigation on behalf of William Hardy.

You can see the full sentencing hearing in relation to *R v William Hardy* in the video section of our online resources. In the video clips you will see the outline of the case presented by the solicitor-advocate for the CPS, followed by the plea in mitigation delivered by William Hardy's solicitor-advocate. A transcript (based for the most part on the plea) is included and analysis of the proceedings is provided on the video. You will also see the Crown Court judge pass sentence on William Hardy.

Case study: *R v Roger Martin*

Taking into consideration our study of sentencing theory and practice, it is your turn to draft a plea in mitigation on behalf of Roger Martin.

You are able to see the final determination of the *R v Roger Martin* case study by viewing his sentencing hearing in the video section of our online resources. In the video clips you will see the outline of the case presented by an associate prosecutor for the CPS, followed by the plea in mitigation delivered by Roger Martin's solicitor. Analysis of the proceedings is provided in the video. You will see the sentence passed by the magistrates. We would ask you to note that this scenario was filmed before the CJA 2003 came into force and before the Sentencing Council's 'Assault' guideline came into effect. Were the same facts to be sentenced under the CJA 2003, Roger Martin would have been subject to a generic community order with specified requirements, which would include an element of supervision and unpaid work in the community.

FIGURE 22.1 THE CONDITIONS FOR IMPOSING A CUSTODIAL SENTENCE ON AN ADULT

- A custodial sentence may only be imposed if the threshold test is satisfied where:
  - the offence, or combination of offences; or associated offences;
  - is so 'serious' that neither a fine alone nor a community sentence can be justified, s. 152(2) CJA 2003; or
  - where the offender fails to consent to a requirement to be included in a community order.
- Discount for pleading guilty will be applied, s. 144 CJA 2003.
- The length of custody should be commensurate with the seriousness of the offence, s. 153(2) CJA 2003.
- The length of custodial sentences passed by a magistrates' court is restricted compared to the Crown Court.
- The court should give reasons in open court for imposing the sentence passed, s. 174(2) CJA 2003.
- Before deciding to suspend a prison sentence, the custody threshold test must be met.
- Time spent on remand shall count as time served when imposing a custodial sentence, s. 240 CJA 2003.
- A magistrates' court can pass a maximum custodial sentence of six months (12 months for two or more either-way offences).
- Custodial sentences can be suspended for a period of between six months and two years and requirements may be imposed on the offender during the period of suspension.

FIGURE 22.2 NON-CUSTODIAL SENTENCES

COMMUNITY SENTENCES UNDER THE CJA 2003

- Imposed where the court is satisfied the:

  - offence; or
  - combination of offences; or
  - associated offences

  is/are 'serious enough' to warrant it, s. 148(1) CJA 2003.

- Section 177 CJA 2003 creates a single community sentence which will impose one or more requirements on the offender, e.g.:
  - unpaid work, s. 199 CJA 2003;
  - curfew requirement, s. 204 CJA 2003;
  - exclusion requirement, s. 205 CJA 2003;
  - residence requirement, s. 206 CJA 2003;
  - drug and/or alcohol rehabilitation requirement, ss. 209 and 221 CJA 2003.

- The requirement(s) imposed on the offender should be:

  - suitable for the offender; and
  - where the offender's liberty is restricted, commensurate with the 'seriousness' of the offence, s. 148(3) CJA 2003.

- Sentencing discount for guilty plea will apply.

- Pre-sentence report will invariably be required.

FINES

- Court must consider offender's financial circumstances before imposing a fine, s. 162(1) CJA 2003.

- Fine must reflect the 'seriousness' of the offence, s. 164(2) CJA 2003.

- Sentencing discount will apply for a guilty plea.

- Fines are higher in the Crown Court.

OTHER TYPES OF SENTENCE

- Conditional discharge;

- Absolute discharge.

ANCILLARY ORDERS

- Compensation orders:
  - on conviction s. 130 PCC(S)A 2000 requires court to order compensation for any injury, loss, damage etc.;
  - court must give reason for not making compensation order;
  - magistrates can order compensation up to £5,000;
  - see Magistrates' Court Sentencing Guidelines for compensation for personal injury;
  - compensation in Crown Court is unlimited;
  - priority given to compensation orders over fines, prosecution costs etc.

- Defendant pays prosecution costs:
  - purpose to compensate prosecution;
  - sum should not exceed costs reasonably incurred;
  - court must account for offender's ability to pay;
  - confiscation and forfeiture orders, see Proceeds of Crime Act 2002.
- Anti-Social Behaviour Orders.
- Notification under Sex Offenders' Register.
- Football banning order.
- Restraining order.
- Deportation.

23 APPEALS

23.1	**Introduction**	**442**
23.2	**Reopening a case—s. 142 MCA 1980**	**443**
23.3	**Appeal to the Crown Court—s. 108 MCA 1980 (Crim PR, Part 34)**	**443**
	23.3.1 The procedure for appealing to the Crown Court (Crim PR, Part 34.2)	443
	23.3.2 Hearing the appeal	444
23.4	**Appeal by way of case stated—s. 111 MCA 1980 and s. 28 Senior Courts Act 1981 (Crim PR, Part 35)**	**444**
	23.4.1 The procedure for stating a case	445
	23.4.2 Is further appeal possible?	445
	23.4.3 May the same issue be appealed to the Crown Court and by way of case stated?	445
23.5	**Judicial review**	**445**
	23.5.1 Applying for judicial review	446
23.6	**Appeal from the Crown Court (Crim PR, Parts 36 and 39)**	**446**
	23.6.1 Obtaining leave to appeal	446
	23.6.2 Funding an appeal to the Court of Appeal	446
	23.6.3 What is a direction for loss of time?	447
	23.6.4 Granting bail on appeal	447
	23.6.5 Appeals against conviction (Crim PR, Part 39)	447
	23.6.6 Disposals available to the Court of Appeal	448
23.7	**Appeal against sentence from the Crown Court (Crim PR, Part 39)**	**448**
23.8	**Appeal to the Supreme Court (Crim PR, Part 43)**	**449**
23.9	**Attorney General's references (Crim PR, Part 41)**	**449**
23.10	**Criminal cases review commission**	**449**
	23.10.1 What test must be satisfied before the commission can refer a case?	449
23.11	**Does the prosecution enjoy a right to appeal?**	**450**

23.1 INTRODUCTION

This chapter examines the practice and procedure involved in appealing against a decision of the magistrates' court or the Crown Court. In most cases, the defendant will appeal against the 'safety' of the conviction and/or the severity of the sentence. Some procedures for challenging the trial court's decision, such as appeal by way of case stated or judicial review are available to both the prosecution and the defence. An increasing number of appeal procedures are available only to the prosecution. The procedures explained in this chapter include:

- reopening a case—s. 142 Magistrates' Courts Act 1980 (MCA 1980);
- appeal from the magistrates' court to the Crown Court;
- appeal by way of case stated;
- judicial review;
- appeal to the Court of Appeal;
- Attorney General's Reference;
- Criminal Cases Review Commission;
- appeals under the Criminal Justice Act 2003 (CJA 2003).

The rules of court relating to appeals are now contained in Crim PR, Parts 34–44.

23.2 **REOPENING A CASE—S. 142 MCA 1980**

Following conviction by a magistrates' court, s. 142(2) MCA 1980 enables a defendant to ask the magistrates to set the conviction aside or to vary or rescind a sentence. The application may be made whether the defendant pleaded guilty or not guilty at the original trial.

In deciding whether to grant the application, the court will exercise its discretion under s. 142 MCA 1980 where it is 'in the interests of justice' to do so. Factors considered include the interests of the court and the inconvenience to other parties of reopening the case.

There is no time limit for making an application under s. 142 MCA 1980 but an unreasonable delay will be taken into account in determining the interests of justice test.

If the conviction is set aside, the case is reheard by a different set of magistrates.

A common use of s. 142(2) MCA 1980 is to rectify an obvious mistake made during the defendant's trial. It is also used to reopen cases where a defendant has been convicted in her absence. The defence lawyer may advise his client to make an application under s. 142 MCA 1980 if it will provide a speedier remedy than an appeal to the Crown Court.

Section 142(1) allows a magistrates' court to vary or rescind its decision as to sentence if it is in the interests of justice to do so. This power is frequently used to reopen sentencing decisions (most notably the imposition of a fine or penalty points) following a conviction in the defendant's absence.

 Example

Kemal is summonsed for careless driving. He fails to respond to the summons and is convicted by the magistrates' court in his absence. He applies under s. 142 MCA 1980 to have his conviction set aside. In deciding the interests of justice test, the magistrates will consider the inconvenience to the prosecution, the prosecution witnesses and to the court of the case being reheard. These interests will be balanced against the defendant's general right to have the opportunity to defend himself.

If Kemal has strong mitigating reasons for failing to attend trial because, for example, he was out of the country or was genuinely preoccupied with family or business problems the court may decide that it is in the interests of justice to rehear the case. If Kemal simply forgot to attend court, it is likely that his application under s. 142 MCA 1980 will fail.

23.3 **APPEAL TO THE CROWN COURT—S. 108 MCA 1980 (CRIM PR, PART 34)**

A defendant convicted before a magistrates' court may appeal against conviction and/or sentence to the Crown Court. Where the defendant pleaded guilty, the defendant may only appeal against the sentence. Appeal to the Crown Court is not available to the prosecution.

23.3.1 **THE PROCEDURE FOR APPEALING TO THE CROWN COURT (CRIM PR, PART 34.2)**

A written notice of appeal must be made within 21 days of the conviction and/or the sentence and sent to the magistrates' court that heard the case. The time for giving notice of appeal may be extended by the Crown Court.

The notice of appeal does not have to specify any detail other than indicating whether the appeal is against conviction and/or sentence. It is common to use a form of appeal which merely states that the 'defendant proposes to appeal on the ground that the magistrates erred in fact and in law in convicting him' or 'the defendant proposes to appeal against sentence on the ground that it was excessive in all the circumstances'.

There is no filter procedure and the court has no discretion not to accept the notice of appeal.

Where a custodial sentence was passed in the magistrates' court, the appellant may apply to be released on bail until the appeal hearing although the presumption to bail does not apply in this situation. If bail is refused, a further application may be made to the Crown Court (see Chapter 10).

23.3.2 HEARING THE APPEAL

The appeal in the Crown Court is a complete rehearing of the case (see s. 79(3) Senior Courts Act 1981) before a Crown Court judge sitting with not less than two and no more than four lay magistrates. None of the magistrates should have been previously involved in the case under appeal. New evidence may be heard if it has become available since the original trial. The decision of the Crown Court may be a majority decision; as the lay justices can out-vote the judge. The Crown Court can confirm, vary or reverse any part of the magistrates' court's original decision (i.e. quash a conviction or vary sentence) or remit the matter back to the convicting magistrates' court with its opinion (s. 48 Senior Courts Act 1981).

A convicted defendant should be warned that if his appeal fails, the Crown Court can impose any sentence that was available to the magistrates' court. This may result in a convicted defendant receiving a more severe penalty (although not one that would have been beyond the maximum sentence which the magistrates' court could have passed). An unsuccessful appeal may additionally result in the defendant paying some or all of the prosecution's costs.

23.4 APPEAL BY WAY OF CASE STATED—S. 111 MCA 1980 AND S. 28 SENIOR COURTS ACT 1981 (CRIM PR, PART 35)

Section 111 MCA 1980 provides:

'(1) Any person who was a party to any proceeding before a magistrates' court or is aggrieved by the conviction, order, determination or other proceeding of the court may question the proceeding on the ground that it is wrong in law or is in excess of jurisdiction by applying to the justices composing the court to state a case for the opinion of the Divisional Court (High Court) on the question of law or jurisdiction involved;

(2) An application under subsection (1) above shall be made within 21 days after the day on which the decision of the magistrates' court was given.'

Appeal by way of case stated to the Divisional Court may be made by any party to the proceedings before the magistrates' court who seeks to challenge the conviction or any order or determination made by the court during the proceedings.

The grounds for making an appeal by way of case stated are that the magistrates' court was:

• wrong in law; or

• in excess of its jurisdiction.

The issues that are commonly raised in a case stated application include whether:

• the justices had jurisdiction to try the case; or

• the justices were correct to find that there was a case to answer; or

• admissible evidence was excluded; or

• inadmissible evidence was admitted in evidence; or

• the justices' interpretation of the law was wrong.

Although much less common under s. 28 Senior Courts Act 1981, an appeal by case stated to the Divisional Court may also be made by any party against a decision of the Crown Court. The appeal can be against any order, judgment, or other decision on the basis that it was wrong in law, or in excess of its jurisdiction.

23.4.1 THE PROCEDURE FOR STATING A CASE

- Within 21 days of the acquittal, conviction or sentence, the party must apply in writing (usually by letter), requiring the magistrates who heard the case to state a case for the Divisional Court's consideration. The party should identify the question of law on which the Divisional Court's opinion is sought.

- Within 21 days of receiving the application, a statement of case is prepared by the magistrates' legal adviser in consultation with the magistrates, which will:
  - outline the facts called into question;
  - state the facts as found by the magistrates;
  - state the magistrates' finding on the point of law being challenged, listing any authority cited; and
  - state the question for the Divisional Court to answer.

- Drafts of the case are then sent to the parties who may suggest amendments.

- The final form of the case stated is then sent to the appellant who must lodge it at the Crown Office of the Royal Courts of Justice in London. Notice and a copy of the case stated must be given to the respondent.

- The appeal is heard by the Divisional Court usually before three judges. Evidence is not called and the hearing takes the form of legal argument on the facts of the case as stated.

- The Divisional Court may reverse, amend or affirm the magistrates' decision or may remit the matter back to the magistrates with its opinion and a direction that the magistrates' court should, for example, convict the defendant or acquit him or the case should be tried again before a different Bench.

- Costs may be awarded to either party out of central funds.

Magistrates may bail a defendant who has received a custodial sentence pending the hearing of his appeal (s. 113 MCA 1980). If bail is refused, an application can be made to a High Court judge in chambers.

23.4.2 IS FURTHER APPEAL POSSIBLE?

No—unless the matter is appealed to the Supreme Court on a point of law of public importance and either the Divisional Court or the Supreme Court grants leave.

23.4.3 MAY THE SAME ISSUE BE APPEALED TO THE CROWN COURT AND BY WAY OF CASE STATED?

No—the right of appeal to the Crown Court is lost once an application is made to state the case. It is possible to appeal by way of case stated to challenge the conviction and to appeal to the Crown Court against the sentence in the same case. For this reason, the first avenue of appeal is usually the Crown Court (para. 23.3).

23.5 JUDICIAL REVIEW

Judicial review is available to a party in a criminal case where a magistrates' court as a 'public law' body has exercised its legal powers illegally or has failed to follow the correct procedure or has acted irrationally. Judicial review proceedings are governed by the Civil Procedure Rules, Part 54. State funding for judicial review is through a civil funding certificate.

Judicial review will be appropriate to challenge a decision where the magistrates' court acted in excess of its jurisdiction by failing to follow the statute which confers jurisdiction, or by acting in breach of the rules of natural justice, by, for example failing to allow an adjournment requested by a defendant on proper grounds or failing to give proper time to prepare a defence, see *R v Thames Magistrates' Court, ex p. Polemis* [1974] 1 WLR 1371. Judicial review will also be appropriate where there are grounds for suspecting bias on the part of the legal adviser or one or more of the magistrates.

23.5.1 APPLYING FOR JUDICIAL REVIEW

The Civil Procedure Rules, Part 54 prescribes a two-stage procedure for applying for judicial review. The first stage is an application for leave to a High Court judge to obtain permission to proceed. A notice of application on the appropriate claim form setting out the grounds for review must be filed by the defendant. The claim form must:

- identify the applicant;
- identify the relief sought;
- identify the grounds on which the application is made; and
- include an affidavit (i.e. a sworn statement) that verifies those grounds and adds further argument.

A single judge usually determines the application for leave without a hearing and in the absence of the other side (the respondent).

If leave is granted, the judicial review hearing will be before the Administrative Court, which hears arguments from the applicant, the respondent and any other body affected by the magistrates' decision. In a criminal case this will usually be the Crown Prosecution Service (CPS), the Ministry of Justice or the Home Office.

Bail pending the hearing of an application for judicial review may be granted by a judge in chambers.

At the end of the hearing, the court makes its decision, and if the applicant's case is proven, will grant relief by making a mandatory order; and/or a prohibiting order or a quashing order.

23.6 APPEAL FROM THE CROWN COURT (CRIM PR, PARTS 36 AND 39)

A person convicted of an offence on indictment may appeal to the Court of Appeal against his conviction and/or sentence where he pleaded not guilty, or against sentence only where he pleaded guilty, s. 1 Criminal Appeal Act 1968 (CAA 1968). The advice of counsel or a solicitor-advocate should always be sought before commencing an appeal against conviction and/or sentence to the Court of Appeal.

23.6.1 OBTAINING LEAVE TO APPEAL

Leave to appeal against conviction and/or sentence to the Court of Appeal is always required. Leave may be given by the trial judge granting a certificate that the case is fit for appeal or the Court of Appeal can grant leave.

Where leave is required from the Court of Appeal, within 28 days of conviction or sentence, the appellant must serve on the Registrar of Criminal Appeals, a notice of application for leave to appeal, accompanied by draft grounds of appeal. The draft grounds will be settled by counsel or a solicitor-advocate.

23.6.2 FUNDING AN APPEAL TO THE COURT OF APPEAL

Where a defendant has been granted a representation order for trial on indictment, the order will cover advice in connection with a possible appeal, drafting the grounds of appeal and seeking leave. Once the notice and grounds of appeal have been lodged, the registrar will determine whether a representation order should be granted.

If the appeal is against conviction, a transcript should be provided of either of the judge's summing-up or of some part of the evidence or where appropriate, the full transcript of the trial. The court's shorthand writer will then be asked by the registrar to transcribe the appropriate part of his notes. The papers are then put before a single judge.

This is a filtering stage at which a single judge considers whether leave ought to be given. If leave to appeal is given, public funding will be available for the hearing itself.

If the single judge refuses leave to appeal, the appellant has 14 further days in which to serve notice on the registrar that he wishes to renew the application before the full court. The papers are then put before the 'full' court, which considers the issue. If leave is refused, the application is lost and the appellant may be subject to a loss of time direction.

23.6.3 WHAT IS A DIRECTION FOR LOSS OF TIME?

Usually, any time spent in custody by an appellant between sentence being passed and his appeal hearing counts as part of any custodial sentence. A direction to the contrary called 'direction for loss of time' may be given by the court when refusing leave to appeal or dismissing an appeal purely on the grounds of law (s. 29 CAA 1968). This is a means of penalising an appellant for pursuing a frivolous appeal, although directions for loss of time are very rarely made if counsel has advised on an appeal. A direction for loss of time would normally be made against an appellant who proceeds with an appeal against counsel's advice.

23.6.4 GRANTING BAIL ON APPEAL

The Court of Appeal may grant bail to an appellant pending the determination of his appeal (s. 19 CAA 1968). This may be exercised by the single judge when he considers the papers. Where the trial judge certifies that a case is fit for appeal, he may also grant bail pending determination of the appeal (s. 81 Senior Courts Act 1981).

23.6.5 APPEALS AGAINST CONVICTION (CRIM PR, PART 39)

The Court of Appeal may only allow an appeal against conviction if it thinks that the conviction is 'unsafe' (s. 2(1)(a) CAA 1968, as amended by the Criminal Appeal Act 1995).

In deciding whether the conviction is 'unsafe', the Court of Appeal will hear legal argument from each side and may, exceptionally, hear fresh evidence under s. 23 CAA 1968. Fresh evidence will only be received under s. 23 CAA 1968 if it is:

- capable of belief;
- capable of founding a ground of appeal;
- it would have been admissible at the original trial; and
- there is a reasonable explanation for the failure to adduce the evidence.

The common practice is for an appellant to refer to specific legal or procedural errors that arose at trial, and then supplement these specific claims with the general ground that the conviction is unsafe.

The test to decide whether a conviction is 'unsafe' is subjective. Each member of the Court of Appeal must ask: 'Have I a reasonable doubt, or even a lurking doubt, that this conviction may be unsafe?' If the answer is affirmative, the appeal should be allowed (*Stafford v DPP* [1974] AC 878). In *Pendleton* [2002] 1 WLR 72, the House of Lords held that the correct test in a case where the Court of Appeal receives fresh evidence on appeal under s. 23 CAA 1968, is whether the conviction was safe, not whether the defendant was guilty. In such cases the Court of Appeal must consider what effect the fresh evidence would have had on the jurors if it had been received at the original trial. If it might reasonably have affected the jurors' decision to convict, the conviction should be regarded as 'unsafe'.

There was concern that the amendment to the single ground of appeal by the CAA 1995, that the conviction is 'unsafe', had restricted the Court of Appeal's powers to quash a conviction. In *R v Chalkley; Jeffries* [1998] 2 Cr App R 79, the Court of Appeal confirmed that, following the amendment of s. 2(1) CAA 1968, the court had no power to allow an appeal if it did not consider the conviction to be unsafe but was in some other way dissatisfied with what had occurred at the trial, since the former tests of 'unsatisfactoriness' and 'material irregularity' were no longer available, except to determine the safety of a conviction.

In practice, however, the potentially restrictive interpretation of s. 2(1) CAA 1968 put forward in *Chalkley* has not been adopted and, in considering if a conviction is unsafe, the Court of Appeal is entitled to take into account:

- whether the conviction is unsatisfactory; or
- that the court made a wrong decision on a point of law; or
- there was a material irregularity in the course of the trial.

As a consequence, grounds for appeal against conviction can include:

- wrongful admission or exclusion of evidence;
- failure to properly exercise judicial discretion;
- errors on the part of counsel;
- defects in the indictment;
- conduct of the trial judge;
- errors in the trial judge's summing-up;
- problems associated with jurors.

23.6.6 DISPOSALS AVAILABLE TO THE COURT OF APPEAL

In deciding whether the appellant's conviction is unsafe, the Court of Appeal may:

- quash the conviction and order an acquittal;
- quash the conviction and order a retrial;
- find the appellant guilty of an alternative offence;
- allow part of the appeal; or
- dismiss the appeal.

23.7 APPEAL AGAINST SENTENCE FROM THE CROWN COURT (CRIM PR, PART 39)

An appeal against sentence follows the same procedure as an appeal against conviction except that an appeal against sentence only will not attract a loss of time direction. An appeal can be made on the basis that the sentence imposed was:

- wrong in law (i.e. the sentence imposed could not legally be passed);
- wrong in principle or was manifestly excessive (the fact that the sentence was merely severe will not be sufficient, but if the sentence passed was outside the appropriate range for the offence and the offender in question, it might be considered excessive. Further examples include where there has been a serious disparity in sentence between two or more co-accused which cannot in principle be justified, or if the defendant was given a legitimate expectation that he would receive a certain type of sentence giving him a

justifiable sense of grievance, or there was a failure to obtain a pre-sentence report or to hold a *Newton* hearing when one was clearly required).

In considering an appeal against sentence, the Court of Appeal can:

- quash any sentence or order; or
- impose any sentence or order that could have been available to the Crown Court except the appellant should not be dealt with more severely than at the Crown Court (s. 11(3) CAA 1968).

23.8 APPEAL TO THE SUPREME COURT (CRIM PR, PART 43)

Appeal from the Court of Appeal to the Supreme Court may only be made where the Court of Appeal or the Supreme Court certifies the case involves a point of law of general public importance.

23.9 ATTORNEY GENERAL'S REFERENCES (CRIM PR, PART 41)

Under s. 36 CJA 1988 (Crim PR, Part 41) the Attorney General may, with leave of the Court of Appeal, refer to that court any sentence imposed by the Crown Court where he considers the sentence was unduly lenient. The Court of Appeal may then quash the original sentence and substitute such sentence (usually heavier) as it thinks appropriate for the case and which the court below had power to pass when dealing with the offender.

Reference should also be made to the possibility of using the 56 day slip rule to 'correct' a sentence (see Chapter 21, para. 21.15.1).

The Attorney General also has the power to refer a case to the Court of Appeal for its opinion on a point of law which arose in the case. The power relates to a case where the defendant was acquitted following trial on indictment. Whatever the outcome of the appeal, the defendant remains acquitted.

23.10 CRIMINAL CASES REVIEW COMMISSION

The Criminal Cases Review Commission, which was established by the Criminal Appeal Act 1995, is located in Birmingham and investigates allegations of miscarriages of justice.

Under s. 9 CAA 1995, the Commission may refer to the Court of Appeal:

- a conviction for an offence on indictment;
- a sentence imposed for an offence on indictment;
- a finding of not guilty by insanity.

Under s. 11 CAA 1995, the Commission may refer to the Crown Court a conviction and/or sentence imposed by the magistrates' court.

23.10.1 WHAT TEST MUST BE SATISFIED BEFORE THE COMMISSION CAN REFER A CASE?

The Commission may only refer a case to the Court of Appeal or to the Crown Court where, under s. 13 CAA 1995, the Commission considers that there is a real possibility that the verdict or sentence would not be upheld if the reference was made.

Section 15 CAA 1995 enables the Court of Appeal to direct the Commission to investigate a particular matter 'in such manner as the Commission thinks fit'. Sections 17–21 CAA 1995 provide the Commission with the power to obtain documents and direct officers to investigate and report on a relevant matter.

23.11 **DOES THE PROSECUTION ENJOY A RIGHT TO APPEAL?**

Traditionally the prosecution enjoyed only limited rights to appeal and had no right to appeal against the acquittal of a defendant following a summary trial or trial on indictment. The only exception to this was the prosecutor's right to appeal a decision by a magistrates' court by way of case stated.

In relation to trials on indictment, the prosecution now enjoys a right of interlocutory appeal against binding rulings made by a trial judge at a preparatory hearing in accordance with ss. 35 and 36 Criminal Procedure and Investigations Act 1996 (Crim PR, Part 37).

The right of the prosecution to appeal against sentence is set out in Chapter 24, para. 24.9. It requires a reference to be made by the Attorney General.

The CJA 2003 extended the prosecution's right of appeal in a number of important situations.

First, under s. 58 CJA 2003 the prosecution may appeal to the Court of Appeal against a terminating ruling (Crim PR, Part 38) made by the judge in relation to an issue at a trial on indictment and which cannot otherwise be the subject of an appeal to the Court of Appeal. The appeal can be against any judicial ruling made during the trial until the beginning of the summing-up to the jury. The procedure of appealing against a terminating ruling is detailed in Crim PR, Part 38. It includes a prosecution appeal against:

- a successful submission of no case to answer by the defence; or
- a ruling on a public interest immunity (PII) application in favour of the defence; or
- a decision to stay the proceedings for an abuse of process; or
- a successful defence application to sever the counts on the indictment.

In making the application the prosecution must agree that in the event of failing to obtain leave to appeal or if the appeal is abandoned, the defendant will be automatically acquitted.

Under the procedure, which is laid down in ss. 57–61 CJA 2003, the appeal can follow an expedited or non-expedited route. It is for the trial judge to decide which route is appropriate. In an expedited appeal, the trial may be adjourned to await the Court of Appeal's ruling. In a non-expedited appeal, the trial may be adjourned or the jury discharged.

Under s. 61 CJA 2003 the Court of Appeal may confirm or reverse or vary any ruling which the prosecution has appealed against. A ruling may only be reversed where the Court of Appeal is satisfied that:

- the ruling was wrong in law;
- the ruling involved an error in law or principle; or
- the ruling was not reasonable for the judge to make.

Where the court reverses or varies the terminating ruling, it must order either:

- the resumption of the Crown Court trial; or
- a fresh trial;
- or the defendant's acquittal (but only if he could not have a fair trial by resumption of the trial or ordering a new trial).

Second, the CJA 2003 has radically revised the traditional operation of autrefois acquit. Historically where a defendant has been found not guilty at trial and acquitted, the doctrine of autrefois acquit has prevented him from being retried for the same offence. With the DPP's consent, s. 76 CJA 2003 allows the prosecutor to apply to the Court of Appeal for an order to quash the defendant's acquittal for a qualifying offence and to order a new trial. Generally a qualifying offence is any offence which carries a sentence of life imprisonment.

The Court of Appeal must order a retrial if there is new and compelling evidence in the case and it is in the interests of justice for the order to be made (see *Blackstone's Criminal Practice* for further information).

 Looking Ahead

When in force, ss. 62 and 63 CJA 2003 give the prosecution the right of appeal on an evidential ruling made by the judge in relation to the admissibility of the prosecution evidence at trial. The appeal may be expedited or non-expedited and the Court of Appeal may confirm, reverse or vary the evidentiary ruling in question.

KEY POINT SUMMARY

- Understand the avenues of appeal from the magistrates' court and which might be the most appropriate appeal mechanism from a defendant's viewpoint.

- Know the time limits and procedures that apply to a defendant who wishes to appeal against conviction/sentence.

- Be aware of the procedural steps in appealing from the Crown Court to the Court of Appeal.

- Understand what is meant by an 'unsafe' conviction under s. 2(1)(a) CAA 1968.

SELF-TEST QUESTIONS

1. When might it be appropriate to apply for the case to be reheard under s. 142 MCA 1980?

2. What is the potential danger to a defendant who appeals against sentence to the Crown Court?

3. Who may appeal by way of case stated?

4. Must leave be obtained to appeal from the Crown Court to the Court of Appeal?

5. On what ground may the Court of Appeal allow an appeal against conviction?

Analysis of all the above can be found in the online resources.

FIGURE 23.1 APPEALS

APPEALS FROM THE MAGISTRATES' COURT

- **Rehearing the case,** s. 142 MCA 1980

  - on the defendant's application, the magistrates' court may set the conviction/sentence aside;

  - the application will be granted where 'it is in the interests of justice';

  - any retrial will be reheard by a different bench of magistrates.

- **Appeal to the Crown Court,** s. 108 MCA 1980

  - against conviction and/or sentence;

  - within 21 days of conviction and/or sentence, defendant applies to magistrates' court which heard his case;

  - the appeal in the Crown Court takes the form of a rehearing;

  - the Crown Court can confirm, vary or reverse the magistrates' decision;

  - where the appeal fails, the Crown Court can impose any sentence which the magistrates might have imposed (which might include a harsher penalty).

- **Appeal by way of case stated,** s. 111 MCA 1980

  - to the Administrative Court;

  - where the magistrates' court was wrong in law; or

  - acted in excess of jurisdiction;

  - application from any interested party within 21 days;

  - appeal is heard by three judges in the Administrative Court;

  - the Administrative Court may reverse, amend or affirm the magistrates' court decision or may remit the case back to the magistrates.

- **Judicial review,** Civil Procedure Rules, Part 54

  - application to the Administrative Court;

  - where a public law body acted irrationally or illegally or did not follow the correct procedure;

  - where applicant proves the case, the court may make a mandatory order or a prohibiting order or a quashing order.

APPEAL FROM THE CROWN COURT

- Defendant may appeal to the Court of Appeal against conviction (where pleaded not guilty) and/or sentence.

- Leave must be obtained from the trial judge or the Court of Appeal.

- Appeal against conviction will be allowed where the conviction is 'unsafe', s. 2(1)(a) CAA 1968.

- Where conviction is 'unsafe', the court may:

  - quash the conviction and order an acquittal; or

  - quash the conviction and order a retrial;

  - find the appellant guilty on an alternative offence; or

  - allow part of the appeal; or

  - dismiss the appeal.

- In deciding an appeal against sentence, the Court of Appeal can:

  - quash any sentence or order; or

  - impose any sentence or order that was available to the Crown Court provided the appellant is not dealt with more severely than at his trial.

- Prosecution's right to appeal against:

  - rulings made by the trial judge at a preparatory hearing, ss. 35, 36 Criminal Procedure and Investigations Act 1996;

  - appeal against a terminating ruling during a trial on indictment, ss. 57–61 CJA 2003;

  - application to the Court of Appeal for an order to quash the defendant's acquittal for a qualifying offence and to order a new trial, s. 76 CJA 2003.

Part VI

YOUTH JUSTICE

Part VI comprises three chapters which examine the special considerations that apply to young offenders under the age of 18.

24 YOUTH JUSTICE—INTRODUCTION

24.1	**Introduction**		**455**
24.2	**The terminology of youth justice**		**457**
	24.2.1	Persistent offenders (PO)	457
24.3	**The youth justice organisations**		**458**
24.4	**The statutory aims of the youth justice system**		**459**
24.5	**Parental responsibility**		**459**
24.6	**Police station detention and the young person**		**459**
	24.6.1	Determining the young person's age	459
	24.6.2	The custody officer's duties	460
	24.6.3	The appropriate adult	460
	24.6.4	The juvenile's other rights	461
24.7	**Dealing with a young client—a defence perspective**		**461**
24.8	**Preventing juvenile offending**		**462**
	24.8.1	Community resolution	462
	24.8.2	Youth cautions	463
	24.8.3	Youth conditional cautions	463
24.9	**The decision to prosecute**		**464**
24.10	**The procedure upon charge**		**465**
24.11	**Funding the young person's right to legal representation**		**465**

24.1 INTRODUCTION

The Audit Commission has estimated that approximately seven million crimes are committed each year by offenders under 18 years of age and that over £1 billion is spent annually dealing with offending by young people.

The youth justice statistics for 2017/18 published by the Youth Justice Board provide an interesting insight into the work of the youth justice system. Overall the number of young people in the youth justice system continues to decline. For the year ending March 2018 there were 14,400 first-time entrants into the youth justice system. This represents a fall of 14% compared to the previous year and a fall of 86% since the year ending March 2008. However, there has been another year-on-year increase in offences involving young people using knives and other offensive weapons.

In 2017/18 65,833 young offenders were arrested resulting in 10,999 youth cautions being issued by the police.

Over the same period just under 70,300 proven offences were committed by young people resulting in either a caution or a court conviction. The main offence types committed by children and young people involved violence against the person (29% of all proven offences). Other 'common' offences were theft and handling (11% of all proven offences), criminal damage (11% of all proven offences), vehicle theft and unauthorised taking (11% of all proven offences).

In 2017/18, 23,000 children and young people were sentenced in England and Wales, after being found guilty, including 1,600 who received immediate custody. Community sentences such as referral orders (approximately 11,200), Youth Rehabilitation Orders (approximately 6,200), and Reparation Orders (approximately 120) were the most common sentences, comprising 68% of total disposals. Just over 6,600 children and young people were sentenced to other types of disposals such as discharges and fines. The average population of young people in custody was 960. For an indictable offence, the average custodial term served by a young offender was 16.0 months. The average custodial term for those sentenced for summary offences was 4.5 months. These are the full custodial terms including any periods served in the community.

Although the principal aim of the youth justice system as required by s. 37(1) Crime and Disorder Act 1998 (CDA 1998) is to prevent offending and reoffending by children and young people, the statistics indicate there continues to be a relatively high reoffending rate amongst young offenders. During 2016/17, 42.2% of children or young people reoffended within 12 months from their release from custody or at the end of their previous sentence.

In spite of the overall reduction in youth offending it is clear that criminal and anti-social behaviour by children and young people continue to have important political, economic and social implications as well as making considerable demands on the criminal justice system and those who work in it. The final three chapters of *Criminal Litigation* explain the practice and procedures that apply in this specialist area of criminal practice.

While many of the practices and procedures of youth justice will be familiar to you and are based on the adult model, there are also important differences in recognition of the special position and vulnerabilities of young people in the criminal justice system. These special considerations are reflected, for example, in the relative informality of proceedings in the youth court and the requirement that all participants in the youth justice system are under a statutory duty to prevent offending and reoffending by children and young people. Therefore, the youth justice system is structured to address the needs of those juveniles who are involved in criminal and anti-social behaviour.

Youth justice also has a number of specialist organisations that formulate policy and deal with young offenders and their families on a daily basis. There are schemes which seek to divert young people from crime when they are in danger of offending for the first time and provision is also made for alternatives to prosecution where a young person admits an offence. Therefore, prevention from offending and the opportunities for the early rehabilitation of those who have offended are pervasive to the aims and procedures of youth justice. Whether you are acting for a young person or prosecuting, you will need a good working knowledge of these issues.

Chapter 25 deals with the rules governing where the young person is to be tried and Chapter 26 covers the disposals available to the youth court, Crown Court and the adult magistrates' court when sentencing young offenders. This chapter deals with the following issues:

- the terminology of youth justice;
- the youth justice organisations;
- the meaning of parental responsibility;
- the principal aims of the youth justice system;
- the early diversion procedures to prevent further offending;
- the juvenile at the police station;
- the alternatives to prosecution;
- the decision to charge.

We begin by considering the terminology of youth justice.

24.2 **THE TERMINOLOGY OF YOUTH JUSTICE**

The terminology of youth justice uses a number of key words and phrases to categorise an offender who is not classed as an adult. Be aware of the meaning of each term and understand the context in which the term is used. A commonly used word is 'juvenile', which, while not defined in legislation, is generally applied to a person who is under 18 years of age. The Code for Crown Prosecutors para. 4.14(d) acknowledges that a child or young person is someone under the age of 18. Similarly, in relation to his detention at the police station an arrested juvenile is anyone who appears to be under the age of 18, para. 1.5 Code C.

You will also come across the word 'child'. Some legislation, for example s. 107 Children and Young Persons Act 1933 (CYPA 1933), defines a child as a person under 14 years. However, in relation to a person in the care of the local authority, 'child' has an extended meaning to include a person aged under 18 years. The term 'young person' or 'young offender' or 'youth offender' is generally attributed to a person aged 14 to 17 years. This classification is relevant, for example, to sentencing where a distinction is drawn between the powers available over a child aged between 10 and 13 and a young person who is aged between 14 and 17.

In this chapter, as a matter of style, we adopt the generic terms of juvenile, youth, young person and young offender to mean a person under 18 years unless a different meaning is indicated.

24.2.1 **PERSISTENT OFFENDERS (PO)**

As a youth justice practitioner you will encounter a special category of young offender who has been assessed as a persistent offender. This classification is important for sentencing, because certain sentences are only available where the offender is classified as a persistent offender. These disposals include a Youth Rehabilitation Order with intensive supervision and surveillance or fostering (see Chapter 26, para. 26.9.17) and a DTO in relation to an offender aged between 12 and 14 (see Chapter 26, para. 26.10). Whilst there is no statutory definition of the term 'persistent offender' the Sentencing Council's *Sentencing Children and Young People—Definitive Guideline (2017)* at paras. 6.4–6.10 provides some guidance. Paragraph 6.5 of the Guideline states that a persistent offender will include where the child or young person has had previous contact with authority as result of their criminal behaviour (this will include findings of guilt as well as admissions of guilt and conditional cautions). Generally a young person who has committed one previous offence cannot reasonably be classed as a persistent offender and even a young offender who has committed two or more previous offences should not automatically be categorised as 'persistent'. In this situation the court should consider the lapse of time between the commission of the offences. Paragraph 6.7 suggests that where there have been three findings of guilt in the past 12 months for imprisonable offences of a comparable nature the court could justify classing the child or young person as a persistent offender. The guidance can be accessed through the Sentencing Council's website and via the weblinks section of the online resources.

It is for the court to decide whether a young person is a persistent offender by applying the Sentencing Council's guidance. In *R v L* [2012] EWCA Crim 1336, L, 14, appealed against a ten-month DTO imposed after his guilty plea to three offences of robbery and one attempted robbery. L had two reprimands for the theft of a bicycle and possession of an imitation firearm. L's appeal against sentence was allowed. A sentence of detention and training could only be passed on an offender aged 14 if he could be described as a 'persistent offender'. The two reprimands and three robberies committed on a single occasion did not justify the designation of 'persistent offender'.

24.3 **THE YOUTH JUSTICE ORGANISATIONS**

A number of specialist organisations operate in the youth justice system to develop and manage policies and resources or are involved in day-to-day contact with juveniles and their families. The Youth Justice Board for England and Wales (YJB) is an executive non-departmental public body which exercises a supervisory function over the youth justice system by working to prevent juvenile offending, to address the reasons for their offending and to ensure that when a juvenile is committed to custody, the accommodation is safe and secure.

The YJB's informative website can be accessed at http://www.gov.uk/government/organisations/youth-justice-board-for-england-and-wales.

At a local level in England and Wales the Criminal Justice Boards (CJBs) coordinate the work of the criminal justice agencies. There are 42 CJBs—one for each police force and Crown Prosecution Service area. Each CJB consists of the chief constable of the local constabulary, the area's chief crown prosecutor and chief probation officer and senior representatives from the local prison service and youth services. While CJBs play a strategic role in all aspects of local criminal justice matters, they play an especially important role in coordinating youth justice policies and practice.

The day-to-day administration of youth justice is undertaken by youth offending teams (YOTs), which are part of every local authority in England and Wales. The YOT, which is separate from the police and from the courts, works with the police; probation service; social services and education; the health authority; housing and drug, alcohol and substance misuse agencies, charities and the local community. Each YOT works with children and young people who get into trouble with the law by identifying the needs of young offenders and to manage specific programmes to prevent them from offending or reoffending. The YOT will also help to run local crime prevention programmes, assist young people at the police station when they are arrested and supervise young offenders who are serving a community sentence.

For defence lawyers establishing a good working relationship with the YOT to whom a client has been assigned is important, as often they are an invaluable source of information.

A good example of the collaborative project management undertaken by the youth justice agencies is provided by the Deter Young Offenders scheme (DYO). Since 2009, the CJBs have been implementing a multi-agency approach to dealing with young offenders who are classified as DYOs. DYOs are a small number of juveniles who have been assessed as posing the highest risk of causing harm and/or of reoffending. The scheme requires the early identification by the YOT of high risk offenders at their first conviction where a pre-sentence report or a youth panel report has been requested. In assessing whether an offender comes within the DYO scheme, the YOT is required to produce a profile (known as the Asset Core Profile) of the offender's attitude to a range of factors including their attitude to offending, level of educational attainment and job prospects as well as the level and nature of their previous offending. Based on the offender's Asset Core Profile, the YOT is then required to recommend a 'standard', 'enhanced' or 'intensive' level of intervention under a Youth Rehabilitation Order or under a Referral Order to deal with the offender's specific needs. The greater the perceived risk of the young person causing harm to others or of him reoffending, the greater the intensity of the intervention. It is for this reason that the project has been named by the Youth Justice Board as 'Youth Justice: The Scaled Approach'. The document, which provides guidance on the framework for assessment and interventions in the case of DYOs, can be downloaded from the Justice website at http://www.justice.gov.uk/downloads/youth-justice/scaled-approach/dyo-scheme-management-framework.pdf. Information on the 'Scaled Approach' is also available from the Justice website at http://www.justice.gov.uk/youth-justice/the-scaled-approach.

(Another youth organisation whose website contains helpful resources and guidance is the Youth Justice Legal Centre available at www.yjlc.uk.)

24.4 **THE STATUTORY AIMS OF THE YOUTH JUSTICE SYSTEM**

Section 37(1) Crime and Disorder Act 1998 (CDA 1998) states the principal aim of the youth justice system is to prevent offending by children and young people. In support of the principal aim, s. 37(2) CDA 1998 requires that:

> 'In addition to any other duty to which they are subject, it shall be the duty of all persons and bodies carrying out functions in relation to the youth justice system to have regard to that aim.'

All participants in the youth justice system including the police, the Crown Prosecution Service (CPS), defence lawyers, the local authority and the courts, must work towards and have regard to achieving this overriding principle.

A further duty is the 'welfare principle' imposed by s. 44(1) CYPA 1933, which requires:

> 'Every court in dealing with a child or young person who is brought before it, either as an offender or otherwise, shall have regard to the welfare of the child or young person and shall in a proper case take steps for removing from undesirable surroundings, and securing that proper provision is made for his education and training.'

When making submissions to the court about the appropriate action to be taken against a young offender, the welfare principle should also be considered.

24.5 **PARENTAL RESPONSIBILITY**

Integral to youth justice is the concept of parental responsibility which was introduced by the Children Act 1989. Parental responsibility is defined by s. 3(1) Children Act 1989 as 'all the rights, duties, powers, responsibilities and authority which by law a parent of a child has in relation to the child and his property'. The principle applies to the person(s) who has (have) responsibility for looking after the young person on a daily basis and make(s) decisions about his life.

Married parents and civil partners share parental responsibility for their child. If the parents are not married, parental responsibility is vested in the child's mother, although an unmarried father can acquire parental responsibility. Parental responsibility can be shared with or acquired by other legal bodies such as a local authority where, for example, the child is the subject of a care or supervision order.

Whilst liaising with the person with parental responsibility in the case is important to the police, it is especially important for the YOT and for the defence lawyer who will need to work closely with the person(s) having parental responsibility over the young person to ensure that the case has the best possible outcome. The person having parental responsibility may also be involved in other aspects of the case, such as acting as the young person's appropriate adult at the police station, or at the conclusion of the case, being made the subject of a parenting order or a parental bind over, or paying the fine imposed on the young person.

24.6 **POLICE STATION DETENTION AND THE YOUNG PERSON**

An explanation of the procedure for dealing with a suspect in police detention is covered in Part II of this book. Here we highlight the special rules that apply to juveniles who have been arrested and detained at the police station.

24.6.1 **DETERMINING THE YOUNG PERSON'S AGE**

Under s. 37(15) Police and Criminal Evidence Act 1984 (PACE 1984) (for the purpose of arrest) and Code C para. 1.5 (for the purpose of detention without charge at the police station), a juvenile is anyone who appears to be under the age of 18 and therefore all 17 year-olds are treated as children for the purposes of PACE 1984.

Therefore, if a suspect who may be a juvenile refuses to give his age to the custody officer or the officer believes the age the person has given is incorrect, the suspect must be treated as a juvenile. Remember that if the detained person is under 10 years of age he has no criminal liability and therefore cannot be detained.

In these circumstances, the custody officer will arrange for the child to be taken home or if there is concern for the child's physical or moral welfare, the local authority social services department will be contacted. A child safety order may be applied for.

Where the person is identified as a juvenile, he will be entitled to a range of special protections which are dealt with here.

24.6.2 THE CUSTODY OFFICER'S DUTIES

Code C requires the custody officer to identify the juvenile's needs and vulnerabilities (Code C paras. 3.5(c)–3.10). Under Code C para. 3.13 the custody officer must as soon as practicable identify the parent, guardian or local authority or other person who has parental responsibility for the juvenile's welfare and inform that person of the juvenile's arrest, the reasons for the arrest and the place where the juvenile is being held.

Code C para. 8.8 states that a juvenile shall not be placed in a police cell unless no other secure accommodation is available and the custody officer considers it is not practicable to supervise the juvenile if he is not placed in a cell or that a cell provides more comfortable accommodation than other secure accommodation in the station. A juvenile may not be placed in a cell with an adult detainee.

24.6.3 THE APPROPRIATE ADULT

A key protection under PACE 1984 that is available to children and young people (and to other vulnerable detainees) (see Chapter 4, specifically paras. 4.9 and 4.12.5) is the attendance of the appropriate adult. The appropriate adult's role is to assist and advise the juvenile while he is in police detention. It is essential for the appropriate adult to be independent of the police. Under Code C para.1.7, an appropriate adult for a juvenile means:

- the juvenile's parent or guardian;
- if the juvenile is in local authority care or in the care of a voluntary organisation, a person representing that organisation;
- a social worker from a local authority; or
- failing these, some other responsible adult aged 18 or over who is not a police officer, employed by the police, under the direction or control of the chief officer of a police force or a person who provides contractual arrangements (but without being employed by the chief officer of a police force), to assist that force in relation to the discharge of its chief officer's functions, whether or not they are on duty at the time.

The suitability of a person to be an appropriate adult is important because where the appropriate adult is considered incapable of effectively protecting the juvenile's interests, evidence obtained against the juvenile may be excluded at his trial. While it may appear that the juvenile's parent or carer will be the obvious choice, a parent may be incapable of acting through lack of experience or knowledge or through mental illness, or because the juvenile and parent are not on good terms. In these situations an alternative must be found. Depending on his age, the wishes of the juvenile as to who he wants to act as the appropriate adult should be taken into account. For example, in *R v Blake* (1989) 89 Cr App R 179, the police ignored the juvenile's request that her social worker act as the appropriate adult, asking the girl's father to attend the police station directly against the girl's wishes. In *R v Morse* [1991] Crim LR 195, the juvenile's father had an IQ of below 70 and was incapable of appreciating the importance of his role. In both cases the confession made by the juvenile in the presence of the appropriate adult was excluded at their trial.

A solicitor should not act as an appropriate adult as this leads to a conflict of interest between his role as a legal adviser and his role as an appropriate adult.

Code C para 1.7A, now makes clear the role of the AA:

The role of the appropriate adult is to safeguard the rights, entitlements, and welfare of juveniles and vulnerable persons . . . . For this reason, the appropriate adult is expected, amongst other things, to:

- support, advise, and assist them when, in accordance with this Code or any other Code of Practice, they are given or asked to provide information or participate in any procedure;

- observe whether the police are acting properly and fairly to respect their rights and entitlements, and inform an officer of the rank of inspector or above if they consider that they are not;

- assist them to communicate with the police whilst respecting their right to say nothing unless they want to as set out in the terms of the caution. . .);

- help them to understand their rights and ensure that those rights are protected and respected.

It is also important to make a juvenile client aware that, unlike his legal adviser, the appropriate adult is not bound by any duty of confidentiality or legal professional privilege. Best practice suggests that legal advisers at the police station should initially consult with their juvenile clients in the absence of the appropriate adult to warn them about the dangers of disclosing information that should remain confidential between lawyer and client.

It should be recalled that the juvenile may be attending at the police station as a volunteer (see Chapter 4. 2.1 for important safeguards).

24.6.4 THE JUVENILE'S OTHER RIGHTS

In addition to having an appropriate adult to support him, a juvenile is entitled to the full range of legal rights at the police station as other detainees (see Chapter 4). These include the right to inform someone of his arrest under s. 56 PACE 1984 and the right to legal advice under s. 58 PACE 1984.

While the grounds for suspending the right to legal advice under s. 58(8) PACE 1984 apply to a juvenile in the same way as for an adult detainee, once the appropriate adult has been requested to attend the police station, it is very difficult for the police to justify that one or more of the reasons for delaying legal advice under s. 58(8) PACE 1984 applies. While the time limits for detention without charge are the same for both a juvenile and an adult, in view of the juvenile's vulnerabilities every effort should be made to keep detention to a minimum, especially for a very young person. Generally a juvenile should not be held in a police cell unless there is no other way of guaranteeing his safety. Wherever the juvenile is detained, the custody officer must monitor his detention more closely than for an adult and undertake regular risk assessments.

With regard to the taking of an intimate sample from a juvenile, the consent of a parent or guardian must be given if the juvenile is under 14. If the juvenile is aged between 14 and 16, both his consent and that of his parent or guardian are required. A juvenile aged 17 can give consent to the taking of the intimate sample (s. 65 PACE 1984).

24.7 DEALING WITH A YOUNG CLIENT—A DEFENCE PERSPECTIVE

During an initial interview with a young person it is important for the defence practitioner to gain his trust and to encourage him to give a full and coherent response to the allegations that have been made against him. The defence practitioner should fully advise her client about the possible outcomes in the case, the consequences of admitting guilt and the possibility of being given a youth caution or youth conditional caution. Young offenders (and sometimes their parents or carers) can be the most challenging clients that a defence practitioner will encounter. Some young people have little respect for authority and are likely to test even the most patient defence lawyers. When acting for a young person, skilled interviewing techniques are required to encourage the young person to recognise that you are there to help and are not part of the law enforcement machinery.

For example, Leanne Black, aged 14 achieved national notoriety as a young offender. Black attacked the CPS lawyer and threw a jug of water at the magistrates as she was sentenced to four months' custody for her second offence of drink-driving. These dramatic events occurred shortly after her lawyer had submitted in mitigation that Leanne was a reformed character. The family's disruptive behaviour was not, however, limited to inside the courtroom. As she arrived at court Leanne hurled eggs at the media, and Nora Black, Leanne's mother, flashed her bare bottom, inviting them to 'film this'.

Other notorious young offenders have included twins Ben and Nathan Weeks, who became subject to ASBOs when they were just 10 after the court heard they had made life intolerable for their neighbours in Norfolk by shouting, swearing and shooting at residents' cars and windows with a ball-bearing gun.

24.8 PREVENTING JUVENILE OFFENDING

To support the statutory aims of youth justice there is the hierarchy of diversion procedures to prevent a young person from becoming a convicted offender in the mainstream court system or to achieve their early rehabilitation where the young person has committed low-level crime or anti-social behaviour. Research commissioned by the YJB shows the peak age for juvenile offending is 14 years, so that if a juvenile can be diverted from offending before he reaches this age, the chances of him offending in the future will be much diminished. With this aim in mind, a number of intervention programmes and out-of-court disposals are available to divert a young person from offending or reoffending.

Under the Legal Aid, Sentencing and Punishment of Offenders Act 2012, a framework of out-of-court disposals consisting of Community Resolution, Youth Cautions and Youth Conditional Cautions are available. These disposals provide the youth justice agencies with greater flexibility to deal with cases based on a number of factors including the seriousness of the offence, the offender's offending history, the likelihood of the offender's compliance with the requirements of any out-of-court scheme and the views of the victim. The disposals also focus on the public interest, public protection and welfare and the orders may be used in any sequence and are not limited to a strict incremental level of intervention to deal with the young person's offending.

24.8.1 COMMUNITY RESOLUTION

This is a non-statutory disposal which is based on local YOT practice in cooperation with the local police force. Community Resolution is aimed at low-level offending or anti-social behaviour and is an example of restorative justice. The young person may be required to make a written or verbal apology to the shop owner against whom the young person committed theft or the householder whose property has been damaged or undertake unpaid work in the community or to clear up any damage they have caused. For Community Resolution to apply it must be clear that an offence or an incident has occurred and there should be reasonable suspicion that the juvenile is responsible. The victim's views must be sought and in most cases the victim will agree that they do not want more formal action to be taken against the juvenile.

The young person must admit the offence and agree to participate and accept the conditions of the Community Resolution/Restorative Justice programme.

24.8.2 **YOUTH CAUTIONS**

Youth Cautions (YC) and Youth Conditional Cautions (YCC) replace the previous system of reprimands and final warnings. Under s. 66ZA Crime and Disorder Act a child or young person aged 10 to 17 years may be given a YC as an alternative to prosecution where:

- there is sufficient evidence for a realistic prospect of a conviction and it is in the public interest to give a YC rather than to prosecute (in accordance with the requirements of the Code for Crown Prosecutors);
- the child or young person admits the offence;
- the YC is given in the presence of an appropriate adult (s. 41 Criminal Justice and Courts Act 2015 extends the requirement for the attendance of an appropriate adult to offenders aged 17 years); and
- the police officer/prosecutor does not consider that the young person should be prosecuted or given a youth conditional caution.

A YC can be given to a child or young person as many times as it is considered appropriate, even where the child or young person has previously been convicted of an offence.

The offender will be automatically referred to the YOT, which will assess the offender and determine the level of intervention—usually in partnership with the police. A failure by the young person to comply with the intervention requirements is citable in court and may inform any future disposal decisions.

If a second YC is given, the offender must be assessed by the YOT and be offered a voluntary rehabilitation programme unless it is considered inappropriate. A YC is not a conviction but is a formal criminal justice disposal. Under the Rehabilitation of Offenders Act 1974 youth cautions are 'spent' at the point of issue so there is therefore generally no requirement on the young person to disclose caution unless the circumstances for their disclosure comes within one of the exempted categories under the 1974 Act such as where the young person applies to work with children or other vulnerable people. (This comment should be considered in the light of the Supreme Court's decision in *R (on the application of P,G, and W (Respondents) v Secretary of State for the Home Department and another (Appellants)* [2019] UKSC 3, in which these disclosure requirements were challenged under Article 8 ECHR 1950 under the legality test and the proportionality test).

You will find a link to the Youth Cautions guidance on the Justice website through the online resources (web-links—Youth Justice section) and also at http://www.justice.gov.uk/downloads/oocd/youth-cautions-guidance-police-yots-oocd.pdf.

24.8.3 **YOUTH CONDITIONAL CAUTIONS**

Under s. 66B Crime and Disorder Act 1998 a child or young person aged 10 to 17 years inclusive may be given a YCC as an alternative to prosecution where:

- the authorised person (police officer/prosecutor) believes there is sufficient evidence against the juvenile for a realistic prospect of a conviction and that it is in the public interest to administer a YCC rather than to prosecute (in accordance with the requirements of the Code for Crown Prosecutors);
- the young person must admit to the authorised person that he has committed the offence and accept the YCC and its conditions;
- the YCC is given in the presence of an appropriate adult (s. 41 Criminal Justice and Courts Act 2015 extends the requirement for the attendance of an appropriate adult to offenders aged 17 years);
- the authorised person must explain the effect of the YCC and warn the young person that, although it is not a criminal conviction, it will be recorded and form part of the

young person's criminal record and may be disclosed in certain circumstances and that a failure to comply with any conditions may result in prosecution for the original offence and;

- the young person must sign a document containing details of the offence, the admission to the authorised person, consent to be given a YCC and details of the conditions attached.

The conditions attached to a YCC must have one or more of the following objectives:

- rehabilitation—to modify the young person's behaviour to reduce the possibility of reoffending and to be supervised by the YOT;

- reparation—to repair the damage done by the young person's offending to the community at large or directly to the victim of the offence or through a payment to a local charitable community fund; and

- punishment—to punish the young person for their offending by requiring unpaid work or attendance at a specified place to undertake an agreed activity, provided in either case the period does not exceed 20 hours. A financial penalty should only be made where rehabilitative and reparative conditions are not suitable.

The YOT advises the police on the appropriate conditions to prevent reoffending and the YOT is also responsible for monitoring the offender's compliance. Non-compliance may result in prosecution for the original offence.

Whilst a young person can be given a YCC where he has previously been convicted of an offence, a YCC will not generally be appropriate where if prosecuted the likely penalty would be a substantial community order or imprisonment unless the wider public interest is met by giving the YCC. The YCC will form part of the young person's criminal record and may need to be disclosed to future employers if the offender is applying to be employed in certain occupations including working with children or other vulnerable people. (See the comments in para. 24.8.2 above about the requirement to disclose similar penalties following the Supreme Court's decision in *R (on the application of P,G, and W (Respondents) v Secretary of State for the Home Department and another (Appellants)* [2019] UKSC 3.

You will find a link to the *Code of Practice for Youth Conditional Cautions* in the online resources (web-links—Youth Justice section) and at http://www.gov.uk/government/publications/code-of-practice-for-youth-conditional-cautions.

24.9 **THE DECISION TO PROSECUTE**

This section should be read in conjunction with the first part of Chapter 8 which examines the charging process in greater depth. Except in the most serious offences, the decision about how the case will proceed will not be taken immediately by the police or the CPS. A young person will usually be bailed until the decision is made. The case file will often be referred to a CPS youth offender specialist to decide whether to prosecute or take alternative action.

When making the decision, the prosecutor will apply the evidential and public interest stages under the Code for Crown Prosecutors in the same way as for an adult (see Chapter 8). If the prosecutor is satisfied there is sufficient evidence to provide a realistic prospect of conviction, the public interest stage is then considered. Particular guidance is found in paragraph s.4.14(d) of the Code, which identifies the specific public interest considerations when the offender is aged under 18 at the time the offence. The Code acknowledges that the criminal justice system treats children and young people differently from adults and that significant weight must be attached to the suspect's age and their maturity. The best interests and welfare of the young person must be considered, including whether a prosecution could have an adverse impact on the young person's future prospects that is disproportionate to the seriousness of the offending. The prosecutor must also have regard to the principal aim of the youth justice system, which is to prevent offending by young people, and to the obligations under the United Nations 1989 Convention on the Rights of the Child.

The younger the suspect, the less likely a prosecution is required unless it is in the public interest to prosecute. The factors generally in favour of a prosecution include where:

- the offence is serious;

- the suspect's record suggests there is no alternative to prosecution;

- the absence of an admission means that out-of-court disposals that might have addressed the offending behaviour are not available.

24.10 THE PROCEDURE UPON CHARGE

The young person should be charged in the presence of the appropriate adult and his legal adviser. Having been charged, the custody officer must decide whether to release the young person on bail. As with an adult, the relevant criteria to be applied by the custody officer are set out under s. 38 PACE 1984 (see Chapter 4, para. 4.14.3) subject to an additional ground where it would not be in the young person's interests to be granted bail.

Where bail is refused, s. 38(6) PACE 1984 requires the custody officer to ensure that the young person is moved to local authority accommodation unless:

- it is impracticable to do so (in which case the officer must give reasons why this is so); or

- in the case of a child or young person aged between 12 and 17, no secure accommodation is available and it appears that local authority accommodation would not be adequate to protect the public from serious harm from that child or young person.

The principles of TSJ apply to the youth court in the same way as they apply in the adult court (see Chapter 9, para. 9.16).

24.11 FUNDING THE YOUNG PERSON'S RIGHT TO LEGAL REPRESENTATION

The cost of the young person attending the police station will be met under the Police Station Advice and Assistance scheme. The advice is free of charge. Post-charge, the defence practitioner will need to apply for a representation order as soon as possible using CRM14 eForm (see Chapter 9). The young person will need to satisfy the interests of justice test unless he is charged with an indictable-only offence. However, the means test has no application to applicants under the age of 18. The young person should sign CRM14 eForm.

KEY POINT SUMMARY

- All those involved in the provision of youth justice services must work in accordance with the statutory duties of the youth justice system under s. 37 CDA 1998 and the welfare principle under s. 44 CYPA 1933.

- Be aware of who has parental responsibility over a young person.

- Be aware of the role of the YOT representative.

- Know the procedures the police have to follow under Code C when the juvenile is detained at the police station.

- Have a good working knowledge of the diversion procedures as alternatives to prosecution. The defence practitioner may well want to argue with the police and/or the CPS about the suitability of these alternatives for their juvenile client.

SELF-TEST QUESTIONS

1. Explain the role of the appropriate adult.

2. Is a young person entitled to a representation order?

3. Explain the role of the Youth Offending Team (YOT).

4. Remi, aged 14, is a first-time offender charged with a minor offence of criminal damage contrary to s. 1 CDA 1971. Explain the factors the police and/or the CPS will take into account in dealing with Remi.

5. Charlie, aged 12, is accused of assaulting a teacher. It is alleged that Charlie lost his temper and forcefully pushed the teacher against a door resulting in the teacher fracturing her nose. Charlie has since apologised. He admits he should not have lost his temper; however, he was incensed about being accused of something he did not do. Charlie has been in and out of care. He received a reprimand six months ago for an offence of common assault involving a pupil at his previous school. His mother is a drug addict and finds it difficult to cope with Charlie. Charlie's behaviour at school has been poor. He has poor concentration levels and is frequently in trouble for fighting. He has been excluded from school as a result of this incident. Explain the factors the police will take into account in dealing with Charlie.

 An analysis of the above can be found in our online resources.

25.1	**Introduction**	**467**
25.2	**The young person's first court appearance**	**468**
	25.2.1 Court bail	469
	25.2.2 Remanding a young person	469
	25.2.3 Conditional bail	470
25.3	**Where will the young person be tried?**	**471**
	25.3.1 Trial of a young person in the Crown Court	471
	25.3.2 Plea before venue in relation to young persons (Crim PR, Part 9.13)	472
	25.3.3 'Grave' crimes	473
	25.3.4 Declining jurisdiction to try a young person under the dangerous offender provisions (ss. 226 and 228 CJA 2003)	475
	25.3.5 Deciding jurisdiction and the issue of dangerousness	476
	25.3.6 Sending the young person for trial under s. 51(7) CDA 1998 when jointly charged with an adult	477
25.4	**Safeguarding the young person's right to a fair trial in the Crown Court**	**478**
25.5	**Trial of a young person in the adult magistrates' court**	**479**
25.6	**Proceedings in the youth court**	**480**

25.1 INTRODUCTION

Where a prosecution is commenced against a child aged 10 to 13 years or against a young person aged 14 to 17 years, the general rule is that he will be tried and sentenced in the youth court. The youth court adopts more informal and less adversarial procedures to deal with the needs and vulnerabilities of young defendants. There is also a requirement that the parent(s) or guardian(s) of a defendant aged under 16 years must be present in court unless the court considers it to be 'unreasonable'. The procedures must also comply with the young person's right to a fair trial under Article 6 European Convention on Human Rights 1950 (ECHR 1950).

While young persons are normally tried in the youth court, there are exceptional situations where they will be tried in the Crown Court or in the adult magistrates' court. This chapter explains:

- the rules for deciding where a young person is to be tried;

- the rules for trying a young person in the Crown Court;

- the rules for trying a young person in the adult magistrates' court;

- the young defendant's right to court bail;

- the procedure in the youth court.

For further information and to access some useful flowcharts summarising key areas of this chapter, see the *Youth Court Bench Book* (2017), published by the Judicial College, available online at https://www.sentencingcouncil.org.uk/wp-content/uploads/youth-court-bench-book-august-2017.pdf. A link via the web-links section of our online resources (Youth Justice section) will take you there.

25.2 **THE YOUNG PERSON'S FIRST COURT APPEARANCE**

In virtually all cases and irrespective of the classification of the offence charged the young person's first court appearance will be in the youth court. The Criminal Procedure Rules and the principles of Transforming Summary Justice (TSJ) outlined in Chapter 9, para. 9.15.1 apply to the youth court.

The court's essential case management responsibilities, therefore, require it to ensure that each case proceeds as expeditiously as possible and in a way that is consistent with the interests of justice and the fair trial provisions in Article 6 ECHR 1950. Under Crim PR, Part 3 all the parties are under a duty to help the case to proceed efficiently under the supervision of the court including compliance with the overriding objectives of Crim PR, Part 1 that cases should be dealt with 'justly'.

Of significant importance is the court's duty to actively manage the case by giving any directions that are appropriate to the needs of the case as early as possible in the proceedings. Each party must actively assist the court to fulfil this duty. Consideration should also be given to the principal aim of the youth justice system to prevent children and young people from offending and reoffending under s. 37(1) CDA 1998.

There is an expectation that many cases will be dealt with at the first hearing and that in any event progress will be made at every hearing. In support of this expectation the prosecution must ensure that it has prepared sufficient information and evidence about its case to enable the first hearing to be effective and for a plea to be taken or to ensure that the case progresses.

Therefore before the first hearing the prosecution should disclose initial details of its case to the defence including the charge sheet, a summary of the evidence or a statement that sets out the facts of the case and the defendant's previous convictions (if any). Also under TSJ where a not guilty plea is anticipated the prosecution should have further information available such as the schedule of unused material.

Based on this disclosure the defence solicitor will advise their client about whether to plead guilty or not guilty at the first hearing.

The procedure at the first hearing depends on whether the young person indicates a guilty or not guilty plea.

Procedure on a guilty plea

If a guilty plea is entered at the first hearing the court should pass sentence on the same day if at all possible. If information is required about the defendant it may use a previous pre-sentence report or receive an oral or fast delivery report from the youth offending team (YOT).

Procedure on a not guilty plea

If a not guilty plea is entered the parties must fully complete the Preparation for Effective Trial form prior to the case being dealt with.

The court must identify the relevant disputed issues and the prosecution and the defence should indicate which witnesses are required to attend court and the dates of their availability. The need for special measures should be identified to enable the court to estimate the length of the trial and to put the appropriate arrangements in hand. Bad character and hearsay applications should be dealt with by binding pre-trial rulings, preferably at the first hearing.

The court should give directions to ensure the progress of the case and a trial date and trial time-table must be fixed as soon as possible.

At any adjournment the court will either remand the defendant in custody or release them on bail as explained at para. 25.2.1 below.

Note as exceptions to the general rule, the young person's first court appearance will be in the adult magistrates' court where the young person is:

• jointly charged with an adult (s. 46(1)(a) Children and Young Persons Act 1933 (CYPA 1933)); or

- charged with aiding and abetting an adult to commit an offence (s. 18(a) CYPA 1933, s. 46(1)(b) CYPA 1963); or
- charged with an offence which arises out of the same circumstances or is connected with the offence with which the adult is charged (s. 18(a) CYPA 1963).

25.2.1 COURT BAIL

As with adults, the young person's entitlement to bail will be dealt with at the first court appearance. All youths appearing before the youth court are entitled to unconditional bail unless the court considers that grounds exist for imposing bail conditions or refusing bail.

The law and procedure governing court bail under the Bail Act 1976 (as it applies to either-way/indictable-only offence/summary imprisonable offence and non-summary imprisonable offence) apply to a young person in much the same way as to an adult, except there is an additional ground on which bail can be refused where the young person should be kept in custody for their own protection or welfare (Sch. 1 Part 1 para. 2 Bail Act 1976). (For a more detailed consideration of the law and procedure governing court bail, see Chapter 10.)

In deciding to grant or refuse bail under Sch. 1 Part 1 para. 2 Bail Act 1976, the court will take into account the statutory factors identified in Sch. 1 para. 9 Bail Act 1976, including the nature and seriousness of the offence and the young person's bail record and community ties. The court must also have regard to the statutory aims of youth justice including the welfare principle under s. 44 CYPA 1933. In *R (B) v Brent Youth Court* [2010] EWHC 1893 (Admin) the Divisional Court ruled on the application of the welfare principle to repeated applications for bail by a young offender.

For offences carrying life imprisonment, paras. 9AA and 9AB have been inserted into the Bail Act 1976 requiring a court to give particular weight to the fact that the defendant was on bail on the date of the offence or that the defendant has failed to surrender during the conduct of the case. Where the young person is charged with murder, only a Crown Court judge can grant bail. The youth court must remand the accused in custody (see below) to appear before the Crown Court.

25.2.2 REMANDING A YOUNG PERSON

If bail is refused the court must give reasons for its decision. Section 91 Legal Aid, Sentencing and Punishment of Offenders Act 2012 (LASPO 2012) permits the court to remand a child in youth detention accommodation or in local authority accommodation (under s. 91(6) LASPO 2012 a child is classified as a person under the age of 18). In most cases the child will be remanded to designated local authority accommodation which will provide the child with appropriate community-led supervision, support, education and training. A child aged 10 to 11 years must be remanded in local authority accommodation.

A remand into local authority accommodation is a refusal of bail even where the local authority permits the child or a young person to reside at home with his or her parent or guardian. The court may impose conditions on the youth when it remands to local authority accommodation similar to those conditions imposed on bail. Electronic monitoring can only be imposed if the following requirements are met:

- the youth is 12 years or over; and
- is charged or convicted of an imprisonable offence; and
  - the offence (or one or more of the offences) is a violent or sexual offence; or is one for which an adult may receive a custodial sentence of 14 years or more; or
  - the offence (together with any other imprisonable offences of which the child has been convicted in any proceedings) amount or would, if the child were convicted of that offence, amount to a recent history of committing imprisonable offences while on bail or subject to a custodial remand.

- the court is satisfied that electronic monitoring is available in the area and the YOT is of the opinion that its imposition is suitable.

The court may also impose a condition that the youth must not be placed with a named person.

Remand to youth detention accommodation

Exceptionally, under ss. 98–101 LASPO 2012, a youth aged 12 to 17 years may be remanded in youth detention accommodation where the youth is either charged with a 'serious' offence or where the child has a history of offending whilst on bail.

The following conditions must apply before a youth charged with a 'serious' offence can be remanded to youth detention accommodation:

(a) **The age condition**: the youth is 12 years or over;

(b) **The offence condition**: the youth is charged with a violent or sexual offence or an offence for which an adult may receive a custodial sentence of 14 years or more;

(c) **The necessity condition**: the court must be of the opinion that after considering all of the options for remand that only remanding the youth to youth detention accommodation would be adequate to protect the public from death or serious personal injury; or prevent the commission by the youth of further imprisonable offences;

(d) **The legal representation condition**: the youth must be legally represented or was represented but the representation was withdrawn (due to the youth's conduct or their financial resources); or if the youth applied for legal representation but was refused (on the grounds of financial resources); or if the youth (having been informed of the right to apply for representation) refused or failed to apply.

The following conditions must apply before a youth who has a history of offending whilst on bail or on remand can be remanded to youth detention accommodation:

(a) **The age condition**: the youth is 12 years or over;

(b) **The sentencing condition**: the youth is 12 years or over;

(c) **The offence condition**: the offence must be an imprisonable offence;

(d) **The first or second history conditions**:

  (i) the youth has a recent history of absconding while subject to a custodial remand and the offence is alleged to have been or has been found to be committed while the youth was remanded to local authority accommodation or youth detention accommodation; or

  (ii) that the offence when taken with previous imprisonable offences for which they have been convicted amounts to or would amount to a recent history of committing imprisonable offences whilst on bail or subject to a custodial remand;

(e) **The necessity condition**: the court must be of the opinion that after considering all of the options for remand that only remanding the youth to youth detention accommodation would be adequate to protect the public from death or serious personal injury; or prevent the commission by the youth of further imprisonable offences;

(f) **The legal representation condition**: the youth must be legally represented or was represented but the representation was withdrawn (due to the youth's conduct or their financial resources); or the youth applied for legal representation but was refused (on the grounds of financial resources); or the youth (having been informed of the right to apply for representation) refused or failed to apply.

25.2.3 CONDITIONAL BAIL

Where bail is granted, it may be unconditional or conditional. Conditions can be imposed where the court considers it necessary to ensure the young person's attendance at the next court appearance or to prevent the young person from offending while on bail or interfering with witnesses or for the young person's welfare.

There are a wide range of conditions that can be attached to youth bail including bail supervision and support packages, electronic tagging and Intensive Supervision and Surveillance (ISSP). Where required, the YOT will be available to assist the court to reach a decision.

Electronic tagging may be imposed as a bail condition in relation to a 12- to 17-year-old where:

- the young person is charged with or convicted of a violent or sexual offence or an offence which in the case of an adult carries a sentence of 14 years' imprisonment; or

- the young person has a recent history of repeatedly committing imprisonable offences while remanded on bail or to a local authority; and

- the YOT certifies to the court that that the condition would be suitable.

    Electronic tagging can be imposed as a condition on its own or as part of a package and as a condition of remand to local authority accommodation. Given the availability of such a wide range of conditions, a remand to local authority accommodation should be viewed as a last resort.

For children aged 10 and 11, there is no power to impose a tagging condition or to remand to secure accommodation.

25.3 WHERE WILL THE YOUNG PERSON BE TRIED?

There is a clear and well-established principle that a young person will be tried in the youth court where:

- the young person is charged alone; or
- is charged with another young person.

Most young people are tried summarily in the youth court irrespective of the seriousness or the classification of the offence(s) with which they are charged. Section 24(1) Magistrates' Courts Act 1980 (MCA 1980) provides that this presumption applies even in the case of an indictable-only offence other than homicide.

Unlike an adult offender charged with an either-way offence, the young person has no right of election to the Crown Court. Therefore, if the youth court is considering declining jurisdiction by sending the case to the Crown Court, the only course of action available to the young person's advocate is to make representations against having the case tried before a judge and jury. In contrast to the adult magistrates' court, the youth court has a maximum sentencing power of 24 months in custody subject to the maximum term of imprisonment that the Crown Court could impose on an offender aged 21 or over for the same offence.

As exceptions to the general rule, the young person may be tried in the Crown Court in the situations explained here.

25.3.1 TRIAL OF A YOUNG PERSON IN THE CROWN COURT

There are a number of situations in which a defendant under 18 *may* and sometimes *must* be tried in the Crown Court.

- Where the young person is charged with homicide, s. 51A(2) and (3) Crime and Disorder Act 1998 (CDA 1998) states the case *must* be sent forthwith for trial in the Crown Court—the term 'homicide' is widely defined to include murder, manslaughter, and attempted murder.

- Where the young person is charged with a firearms offence subject to a mandatory minimum sentence of three years (and is over 16 years of age at the time of the offence) the case *must* be sent forthwith for trial in the Crown Court.

- Where the young person is charged with a specified offence under s. 224 CJA 2003 and it appears to the court that if found guilty he will be sentenced as a 'dangerous' offender under ss. 226 CJA 2003, s. 51A(3)(d) CDA 1998 requires the case *must* be sent forthwith for trial in the Crown Court.

In other cases, the court must follow the plea before venue procedure where:

- The young person is charged with a 'grave' crime *and* the youth court considers that the Crown Court should invoke its power under s. 91 Powers of Criminal Courts (Sentencing) Act 2000 (PCC(S)A 2000) to pass a lengthy custodial sentence, s. 51A(3)(b) CDA 1998.

- Where the young person is jointly charged with an adult and it is in the interests of justice for the defendants to be tried together, the case should be sent to the Crown Court for trial (s. 51(7) CDA 1998).

If the power to send the young person to the Crown Court is exercised, the court will also send for trial any 'related' either-way or qualifying summary-only offence with which the young person is charged (ss. 51A (4)) and 51(8) CDA 1998). A jointly charged adult appearing at the same time as the young person or charged with a related either-way offence or qualifying summary-only offence will also be sent for trial in the Crown Court (s. 51A(6) CDA 1998).

25.3.2 PLEA BEFORE VENUE IN RELATION TO YOUNG PERSONS (CRIM PR, PART 9.13)

The plea before venue procedure (PBV), as it applies to defendants under the age of 18, is set out in s. 24A MCA 1980 and Crim PR, Part 9.13. The PBV applies where there is a possibility of the young person being tried in the Crown Court either because he is charged with an indictable offence to which s. 91 PCC(S)A 2000 applies (see para. 25.3.3) or he is jointly charged with an adult and the magistrates' court needs to consider whether it is in the interests of justice to send the young person to the Crown Court alongside the adult (see para. 25.3.6).

In deciding where the young person's case will be heard in each of these situations, the court will conduct the PBV under s. 24(A)(6) MCA 1980. The young person will be asked to provide an informal indication of the likely plea. If a guilty plea is indicated, the youth court will consider the appropriate sentence taking into account the effect of the guilty plea, any offence-specific sentencing guidelines and the overarching principles contained in the Sentencing Council's *Sentencing Children and Young People—Definitive Guideline (2017)*. If the court considers that the offence is one to which s. 91 PCC(S)A 2000 applies (i.e. a custodial sentence in excess of 24 months is likely which can only be imposed by the Crown Court), the young person can be committed (in custody or on bail) to the Crown Court for sentence (s. 3B PCC(S)A 2000).

Where a court commits a youth for sentence, the court may also commit for sentence any other indictable offence or summary offence (provided it is punishable with imprisonment or disqualification) to which the youth pleads guilty.

Alternatively, if at the PBV the young person indicates a not guilty plea (or gives no indication as to plea), the youth court will hold an allocation hearing. (The allocation hearing as it applies to adult defendants is explained in Chapter 11.)

The allocation hearing and youths

At the allocation hearing, the court will hear representations from the prosecution and the defence about the appropriate trial venue. The court will also take into account the circumstances of the alleged offence, any previous convictions, and both the Allocation Guideline (2016) and section 2 of the *Sentencing Children and Young People–Overarching Principles—Definitive Guideline (2017)* (Unlike for an adult defendant at the allocation hearing, the young person cannot request an indication of sentence from the court.)

The youth court will also be aware of the very strong presumption that a person under 18 years of age should be tried summarily (see para. 2.1 *Sentencing Children and Young People— Definitive Guideline (2017)*) and its new power to commit for sentence where summary jurisdiction to try a 'grave' crime (see para. 25.3.3 below) is retained but on conviction, the youth court concludes that the youth should be committed for sentence to the Crown Court.

25.3.3 'GRAVE' CRIMES

Where the young person is charged with a 'grave' crime, the case may be sent to the Crown Court for trial. A 'grave' crime is an offence which is punishable with at least 14 years' imprisonment in the case of an adult offender. Numerous offences carry a maximum custodial term in excess of 14 years including rape, robbery and causing death by dangerous driving. Also classified as a 'grave' crime are specified offences under the Sexual Offences Act 2003 including sexual assault under s. 3.

It is important to realise that the youth court's maximum custodial sentencing powers are restricted. The maximum custodial term that can be passed by the youth court on a young offender is a 24-month Detention and Training Order (DTO). The youth court's power to impose a DTO is also restricted in the case of a young person under the age of 15 unless the young person is a persistent offender, s. 100 PCC(S)A 2000 (see Chapter 26, para. 26.10). These restrictions must be read in conjunction with s. 91(1) and (2) PCC(S)A 2000. Section 91 permits the Crown Court to sentence a young person who has been convicted of a 'serious' or 'grave' offence where the youth court is of the opinion that a longer sentence than it can impose is deserved. Only the Crown Court may impose a custodial term of more than 24 months on a young offender (s. 91 PCC(S)A 2000).

A highly relevant consideration for the youth court at the allocation hearing in connection with a grave crime will be whether its maximum sentencing powers on conviction will be sufficient if jurisdiction to deal with the matter is retained. More 'grave' crimes are likely to remain in the youth court as a result of an important change that was brought about for cases tried after 13 April 2015. A new s.3B(1) Powers of the Criminal Courts (Sentencing) Act 2003 enables a youth court to retain jurisdiction to try a 'grave' crime but to commit the young person for sentence to the Crown Court upon conviction, if the court considers its sentencing powers to be insufficient. Reference must now be made to para. 2.10 of the *Sentencing Children and Young People—Definitive Guideline (2017)* which provides: '*In most cases it is likely to be impossible to decide whether there is a real prospect that a sentence in excess of two years' detention will be imposed without knowing more about the facts of the case and the circumstances of the child or young person. In those circumstances the youth court should retain jurisdiction and commit for sentence if it is of the view, having heard more about the facts and the circumstances of the child or young person, that its powers of sentence are insufficient.*'

Where jurisdiction to try the child or young person for a 'grave' crime is retained, the young person will be warned that all available sentencing options remain open and, if found guilty, the child or young person may be committed to the Crown Court for sentence.

How then do the sentencing powers under s. 91 PCC(S)A 2000 inform the court's decision about trial venue? The short answer is if the youth court concludes that there is a real prospect, taking everything into account, that the young person will receive a custodial sentence of **substantially more than two years**, the case should be tried in the Crown Court. (This test is confirmed at para. 2.8 of the Sentencing Council's *Sentencing Children and Young People—Definitive Guideline (2017)*.)

The basis upon which the youth court should decide to decline jurisdiction to try the young person and send to the Crown Court for trial has been judicially considered in several cases. In *R (D) v Manchester City Youth Court* [2002] 1 Cr App R (S) 573, it was stated that the youth court should not decline jurisdiction unless the offence and the circumstances surrounding it and the offender are such as to make it more than a theoretical possibility that a sentence of detention for a long period may be passed.

An overriding consideration for the youth court is that trial in the Crown Court for a defendant under the age of 18 is inherently less suitable than in the youth court. This is especially significant where the young person is under 15 years of age. The most authoritative guidance on the issue of venue is provided by *R (H, A and O) v Southampton Youth Court* [2005] 2 Cr App R (S) 30, in which Leveson J in the Divisional Court stated as follows:

> 'In an effort to assist hard-pressed magistrates to determine this issue and thereby prevent the constant diet of cases of this nature before the court and, at the same time, seeking to avoid the need to trawl through the ever-growing list of authorities which touch on this point, with the approval of the Vice President of the Court of Appeal Criminal Division, I will attempt to summarise the matter in a way that can properly be put before the youth court whenever the situation arises.
>
> 1. The general policy of the legislature is that those who are under 18 years of age and in particular children of under 15 years of age should, wherever possible, be tried in the Youth Court. It is that court which is best designed to meet their specific needs. A trial in the Crown Court with the inevitably greater formality and greatly increased number of people involved (including a jury and the public) should be reserved for the most serious cases.
>
> 2. It is a further policy of the legislature that, generally speaking, first-time offenders aged 12 to 14 and all offenders under 12 should not be detained in custody and decisions as to jurisdiction should have regard to the fact that the exceptional power to detain for grave offences should not be used to water down the general principle. Those under 15 will rarely attract a period of detention and, even more rarely, those who are under 12.
>
> 3. In each case the court should ask itself whether there is a real prospect, having regard to his or her age, that this defendant whose case they are considering might require a sentence of, or in excess of, two years or, alternatively, whether although the sentence might be less than two years, there is some unusual feature of the case which justifies declining jurisdiction, bearing in mind that the absence of a power to impose a detention and training order because the defendant is under 15 is not an unusual feature.'

In the *Southampton Youth Court* case, the youth court declined jurisdiction to try a 14-year-old youth who was charged with indecent assault. The youth was not a persistent offender and for this reason and because he was under 15, he could not be sentenced to a DTO. The defendant successfully applied to the Divisional Court to judicially review the youth court's decision. The Divisional Court criticised the defence solicitor for not challenging the submissions made by the Crown Prosecution Service (CPS) and stressed the importance of ascertaining the seriousness of the offence and any relevant sentencing guidelines. The case was remitted to the youth court to continue hearing the matter.

The Sentencing Council's *Sentencing Children and Young People—Definitive Guideline (2017)* exhorts at para. 2.10 that: *'Children and young people should only be sent for trial or committed for sentence to the Crown Court when charged with or found guilty of an offence of such gravity that a custodial sentence **substantially exceeding two years** is a realistic possibility. For children aged 10 or 11, and children/young people aged 12–14 who are not persistent offenders, the court should take into account the normal prohibition on imposing custodial sentences.'*

In its legal guidance section, the CPS instructs its prosecutors as follows:

> 'Prosecutors should assist the court to determine venue in grave crimes by:
> * Drawing to the court's attention any relevant sentencing authorities;
> * Informing the court of the aggravating and mitigating features of the offence;
> * Providing the court with an accurate and agreed list of the youth's previous convictions, warnings and reprimands. This will assist the court to determine both the nature and length of sentence.'

If the defence opposes the application to decline jurisdiction, appropriate representations based on case law, applicable sentencing guidelines and possibly giving an informal indication of plea will need to be made.

Where jurisdiction to try the young person is declined by the youth court the case will be sent to the Crown Court and a date will be set for a Plea and Trial Preparation Hearing (PTPH)—see Chapter 13. The youth court may also send the young person for trial for any other indictable offence with which he is charged and which can properly be joined in the same indictment (s. 51A(4) CDA 1998).

A challenge by either the prosecution or the defence to the youth court's decision to either accept or decline jurisdiction to try a youth under the 'grave' crime provisions is by judicial review in the Administrative Court. A good illustration of this procedure and the approaches taken by the parties and the court is provided by *BH (a child) v Llandudno Youth Court* [2014] EWHC 1833 (Admin). The claimant was charged with a single offence of causing or inciting a boy under the age of 13 to engage in sexual activity of a non-penetrative nature, contrary to s. 8(1) and (3) Sexual Offences Act 2003. The claimant and his co-defendant, who were 11 years old at the time of the offence, had taken the complainant who was aged 10 into their school toilet where the claimant attempted to force the complainant's mouth towards the claimant's penis. There were no further relevant incidents involving the claimant or his co-defendant apart from general allegations of bullying by both of them.

On hearing the facts of the offence and representations from the prosecution and the defence, the district judge sitting in the youth court decided to commit the claimant for trial to the Crown Court under s. 24(1)(a) MCA 1980 (now s. 51A(3)(b) CDA 1998).

The defence challenged the youth court's decision to commit to the Crown Court by judicial review. In granting the claimant's application the Administrative Court was of the opinion that the judge had taken his starting point as the range of sentences that an adult offender might have received on similar facts as the offence charged and then applied a reduction for the claimant's age. On this basis the District Judge concluded that a custodial sentence was inevitable.

The Administrative Court held that the tariff an adult offender might receive for such an offence afforded no guidance to the sentence that an 11-year-old child would receive. The question that the judge should have asked was whether, bearing in mind the claimant's previous good character and by taking into account any other mitigating and aggravating factors, there was a real prospect the Crown Court would exercise its powers under s. 91 PCC(S)A 2000 to impose a custodial sentence substantially greater than the 24 months that the youth court could impose. On the facts it was clear that there was no real prospect the Crown Court would impose a custodial sentence under s. 91 and on this ground the decision to commit was quashed.

If a youth is sent to the Crown Court for one or more offences, the court may at the same time or on a subsequent occasion send them to the Crown Court for trial on any related indictable offence or summary offence punishable with imprisonment or disqualification. If the youth indicates an intention to plead guilty to the related offences, the court may commit them to the Crown Court for sentence along with the other matters.

25.3.4 DECLINING JURISDICTION TO TRY A YOUNG PERSON UNDER THE DANGEROUS OFFENDER PROVISIONS (SS. 226 AND 228 CJA 2003)

Section 51A(3)(d) CDA 1998 and paras. 2.3–2.7 of the Sentencing Council's *Sentencing Children and Young People—Definitive Guideline (2017)* requires the youth court to send the young person for trial in the Crown Court where the offence charged is a specified offence and it seems to the court that if found guilty the child or young person would meet the criteria for a sentence under the dangerous offender provisions. A sentence under the dangerous offender provisions can only be imposed if:

- the child or young person is found guilty of a specified violent or sexual offence; and

- the court is of the opinion that there is a significant risk to the public of serious harm caused by the child or young person committing further specified offences; and

- a custodial term of at least four years would be imposed for the offence.

A full list of the specified offences is found in Sch. 15 CJA 2003, and includes 'violent' offences such as manslaughter; kidnapping; offences under ss. 18 and 20 Offences Against the Person Act 1861 and 'sexual' offences, including rape, under s. 1 Sexual Offences Act 2003.

25.3.5 DECIDING JURISDICTION AND THE ISSUE OF DANGEROUSNESS

The dangerousness provisions as they apply to adult offenders are considered in Chapter 22, para. 22.8. A number of offences are 'specified' for this purpose. It follows that where a young person is charged with a 'specified' offence, the youth court has to consider whether the Crown Court would conclude that 'there is a significant risk to the public of serious harm occasioned by the commission by the offender of further specified offences'. Be aware that if a youth court tries a 'specified' offence, it retains the power to commit the young offender to the Crown Court for sentence if it concludes at that stage that the criteria for imposing a discretionary life sentence or an extended custodial sentence appear to be satisfied (s. 3C PCC(S)A 2000).

The main issue about whether to send the young person to the Crown Court for trial under s. 51A(3)(d) CDA 1998 is the assessment of whether the young person falls within the strict definition of a 'dangerous' offender (see Chapter 26, para. 26.18 and the guidance formulated in *R v Lang and Others* [2006] 1 WLR 2509 covered in Chapter 22, para. 22.8). A 'significant risk' is more than a mere possibility of occurrence. In deciding the issue of dangerousness, the court is required to take into account all the available information about the nature and circumstances of the offence and the offender. In many cases the court will not have sufficient details to make an informed decision at this early stage. A proper assessment of the dangerousness of the defendant is unlikely to be possible until a pre-sentence report has been prepared by the YOT, which can only occur once the young person is convicted.

It will be apparent that a 'specified' offence may also be classified as a 'grave' crime which may cause some practical difficulties. In considering whether to exercise its power under s. 51A(3)(d) CDA 1998 or under the 'grave' crime provisions, the Divisional Court observed in *CPS v South East Surrey Youth Court and MG* [2006] 1 WLR 2543 that the youth court should bear in mind:

(a) the policy of the legislature identified in *R (H, O and A) v Southampton Youth Court* [2005] 2 Cr App R (S) 30 (which was discussed earlier) that those under 18 years of age should be tried in the youth court, which is best designed to meet their specific needs;

(b) the guidance of the Court of Appeal in *R v Lang and Others* [2006] 1 WLR 2509, particularly in relation to non-serious specified offences (see Chapter 22, para. 22.8);

(c) the need, in relation to those under 18, to be particularly rigorous before concluding that there is a significant risk of serious harm by the commission of further offences (such a conclusion is unlikely to be appropriate in the absence of a pre-sentence report following assessment by the YOT); and

(d) in most cases where a non-serious specified offence is charged, an assessment of dangerousness will not be appropriate until after conviction, when, if the dangerousness criteria are met, the defendant can be committed to the Crown Court for sentence.

The Divisional Court tacitly approved the practice adopted by the Justice's Clerk for South East Surrey. In deciding whether the offence should be tried summarily or on indictment, the court should first consider whether the offence comes within the meaning of a 'grave' crime (see para. 25.3.3). If the offence is a 'grave' crime, the court is required to consider whether the defendant is 'dangerous'. If he is 'dangerous', the court can send him to the

Crown Court for trial under s. 51A(3)(d) CDA 1998. If he is not 'dangerous' but is charged with a 'grave' crime, the court can consider sending him to the Crown Court for trial under s. 51A(3)(b) CDA 1998 where the criteria outlined in the *Southampton Youth Court* case are satisfied. If the defendant is not charged with a 'grave' offence, the issue of 'dangerousness' should only be considered following the defendant's conviction at a summary trial. It should always be borne in mind that wherever possible those under 18 should be tried in the youth court.

The CPS guidance on youth offenders suggests that there will be few cases in which it will be appropriate to exercise the power conferred by s. 51(3)(d) CDA 1998 and that the power should only be used where there is sufficient information for the court to determine whether the offender is dangerous and it is in the interests of justice for the youth to be tried on indictment.

25.3.6 SENDING THE YOUNG PERSON FOR TRIAL UNDER S. 51(7) CDA 1998 WHEN JOINTLY CHARGED WITH AN ADULT

Under s. 51(7) CDA 1998, a defendant under the age of 18 may be sent to the Crown Court for trial where:

* the young person is jointly charged with an adult; and
* the adult is going to be tried in the Crown Court (either because the offence is indictable-only or an allocation hearing has decided to send an either-way offence for trial on indictment); and
* the court considers that it is necessary in the 'interests of justice' for the young person to be jointly tried with the adult in the Crown Court.

The decision about where the case will be tried will follow the same allocation hearing procedure as explained at para. 25.3.2) and will be based on whether the magistrates' court considers that it is in the interests of justice for the young person to be jointly tried at the Crown Court with an adult or to be tried in the youth court.

In applying the interests of justice test, the court will consider the representations made by each side, the strong general presumption that all young offenders should be tried and sentenced in the youth court and to the factors referred to in the allocation guidelines (March 2016) issued by the Sentencing Council which state as follows:

1. *if the adult is sent for trial to the Crown Court, the court should conclude that the youth must be tried separately in the youth court unless it is in the interests of justice for the youth and the adult to be tried jointly;*
2. *examples of factors that should be considered when deciding whether it is in the interests of justice to send the youth to the Crown Court (rather than having a trial in the youth court) include:*
   * *whether separate trials will cause injustice to witnesses or to the case as a whole (consideration should be given to the provisions of ss. 27 and 28 Youth Justice and Criminal Evidence Act 1999);*
   * *the age of the youth—the younger the youth, the greater the desirability that the youth be tried in the youth court;*
   * *the age gap between the youth and the adult—a substantial gap between the youth and the adult goes in favour of the youth being tried in the youth court;*
   * *the lack of maturity of the youth;*
   * *the relative culpability of the youth compared with the adult and whether the alleged role played by the youth was minor;*
   * *lack of previous convictions on the part of the youth.*

The allocation guidelines further provide that in deciding where the young offender is to be tried the youth court should also consider that it now has a general power to commit the youth for sentence to the Crown Court under s. 3B Powers of Criminal Courts (Sentencing) Act 2000 following summary conviction for a 'grave' offence. In appropriate cases this will allow the Crown Court to pass sentence on both the adult offender and on the youth even where they have been tried separately and convicted. This power can be exercised in relation to the young offender where the youth court considers its sentencing powers are inadequate.

These factors are reaffirmed in paras. 2.11–2.14 of the Sentencing Council's *Sentencing Children and Young People—Definitive Guideline (2017)*. Both the definitive sentencing guideline and the allocation guideline can be accessed via the SC's website.

If the court considers that it is in the interests of justice for the young person to be jointly tried with an adult in the Crown Court, the case will be sent forthwith to the Crown Court and a date will be set for the PTPH—see Chapter 13. If the court considers that it is in the interests of justice to hold separate trials, the matter will be adjourned to a trial date in the youth court.

It is generally accepted that to comply with the young person's right to a fair trial under Article 6 ECHR 1950, only rarely will it be in the interests of justice for the young person to be tried jointly with an adult and that the young person should not be exposed to the intimidating atmosphere in the Crown Court unless there are very strong and compelling reasons for overturning this presumption.

25.4 SAFEGUARDING THE YOUNG PERSON'S RIGHT TO A FAIR TRIAL IN THE CROWN COURT

If the court decides that trial in the Crown Court is appropriate for the young person, the Consolidated Criminal Practice Direction Part III requires that:

- the young defendant should visit the courtroom out of court hours to familiarise herself with the layout;

- where practicable, the trial should be held in a courtroom where all the participants are on the same level;

- a young defendant should normally be permitted to sit with her family and to engage in informal communication with her legal representative;

- the court should explain the course of proceedings to the young defendant in terms she understands and remind her legal representatives of their continuing responsibility to explain each stage of the proceedings to the young defendant;

- the trial should be conducted to a timetable which takes account of the young defendant's inability to concentrate for long periods;

- robes and gowns should not be worn unless the young defendant requests or the court considers there are good reasons for wearing robes and gowns;

- the court should be prepared to restrict attendance at court to those who have a direct interest in the outcome of the proceedings and to restrict the reporting of the proceedings by the media. As a trainee solicitor, it is likely that your principal will obtain the court's permission for you to attend the trial.

This practice has developed as a response to criticism from the European Court of Human Rights (ECtHR) in *T and V v UK* (2000) 30 EHRR 121, which held that the boys accused of killing James Bulger had not had a fair trial in the highly formal proceedings of Preston Crown Court. The trial, which lasted for three weeks in November 1993, was accompanied by widespread media frenzy and great public hostility.

In appealing to the ECtHR, T and V submitted that their trial in the Crown Court constituted inhuman and degrading treatment within the meaning of Article 3 ECHR 1950 and that they had been denied a fair trial under Article 6.

Whilst the ECtHR rejected the submission that T and V's trial breached Article 3, it did accept that their right to a fair trial under Article 6 had been violated. The Court concluded that the formality and ritual of the Crown Court must have seemed incomprehensible to the young defendants, making it impossible for them to effectively participate in the proceedings.

Even with these requirements in mind, the procedure for trying a young person in the Crown Court is generally the same as for adult defendants. One important difference is the reporting restrictions that are imposed on the media. Section 39(1) CYPA 1933 permits the court to direct that no newspaper report shall reveal the name, address or school of the young defendant or publish a photograph. A further difference is that s. 34A(1) CYPA 1933 requires that where the young defendant is aged under 16 years, her parent or guardian must attend court. Where the young person is aged 16 or 17, her parent or guardian may attend court.

25.5 TRIAL OF A YOUNG PERSON IN THE ADULT MAGISTRATES' COURT

The circumstances in which a young person will be tried before an adult magistrates' court will be relatively rare. A youth must be tried before an adult magistrates' court where the youth is jointly charged with an adult in connection with a matter that is to be tried summarily (this would include an either-way offence which is to remain in the magistrates' court) and both the adult and the youth plead not guilty.

If the young person is later convicted at trial or chooses to plead guilty, the powers of the adult magistrates' court to sentence the youth are restricted (see Chapter 26). In these circumstances the adult court will normally remit the youth to the youth court for sentence if it considers its sentencing powers to be restrictive.

If the adult defendant pleads guilty but the youth pleads not guilty, the adult court may try the youth. However, it is much more likely to remit the youth to the youth court for trial (s. 29 MCA 1980).

Consider the following examples of the factors to be taken into account in deciding the place of trial of a defendant under the age of 18.

 Example

Josh, aged 14, is charged with theft. As he is charged alone and is a juvenile, he will be tried in the youth court.

Josh, aged 14, is charged jointly with Sharon, who is 16, with theft. As both defendants are under 18, both will be tried in the youth court.

Josh, aged 14, is jointly charged with Giancarlo, aged 33, with robbery. Assuming Josh appears at the same time as Giancarlo, the magistrates' court will be required to send Giancarlo to the Crown Court under s. 51 CDA 1998. Josh will also be sent for trial if the magistrates consider it is in the interests of justice that Josh be tried with Giancarlo (regard being had to s. 51(7) CDA 1998).

Josh, aged 14, is charged with rape and will indicate a not guilty plea. As rape is a 'grave' offence, the youth court may decline jurisdiction to try the case in favour of the Crown Court's more extensive powers of sentence under s. 91 PCC(S)A 2000. Summary jurisdiction may be retained with the possibility of committal for sentence upon conviction under the new power in s. 3B(1) Powers of the Criminal Courts (Sentencing) Act 2000. Consideration will also be given to the 'dangerousness' provisions as rape is a specified offence (s. 226 CJA 2003).

Josh, aged 14, is jointly charged with Graham, aged 33, with common assault. If both Josh and Graham plead not guilty, the trial will be held in the adult magistrates' court. If Graham pleads guilty but Josh pleads not guilty, Josh will be tried in the youth court.

PROCEEDINGS IN THE YOUTH COURT

Most young defendants will be tried in the youth court where proceedings are more informal than in the adult court. The informality extends to the layout of the court, which enables the young person to fully participate in the proceedings (unless the defendant is remanded in custody). Magistrates are encouraged to sit on the same level as the other people present if the physical layout of the courtroom permits it. The witnesses usually remain seated during the proceedings, as do the advocates and other court officers. The defendant will be addressed by his first name and the language used should be appropriate to his age and maturity. The words 'conviction' and 'sentence' will be avoided as the phrases 'case proven' or 'not proven' are preferred. Sentences are described as 'disposals' and before disposing of the case, the court is required to inform the young person and her parent or guardian of the way it proposes to deal with the case. Magistrates who conduct cases before the youth court are specially trained. All youth court chairmen will have attended training about engaging with children and young people. You are reminded of the fact that the accused may be eligible for limited special measures (see Chapter 19, para. 19.3.1) and a wide range of special measures are available to vulnerable witnesses (defined to include a witness under the age of 18) to maximise the quality of the evidence provided (see Chapter 16, para. 16.4). The following may be present in court:

- court officers, including members of the YOT;
- the parties in the case including the young person, prosecution and defence lawyers and witnesses;
- the defendant's parents or guardians;
- the victim, unless it is not in the interests of justice for the victim to attend (this would be a rare occurrence);
- news reporters—although reports of the proceedings are generally restricted so as not to reveal the young person's identity, address, school, etc.

Even allowing for the greater informality, where the defendant denies the offence, the trial in the youth court will follow the same procedure as in the adult court:

- the prosecutor makes an opening speech;
- the first prosecution witness is examined in chief;
- the witness is cross-examined by the defence;
- the prosecutor may re-examine his witness;

(each prosecution witness gives evidence through this procedure);

- the prosecutor may also put before the court:
  - documentary evidence;
  - exhibits (known as real evidence); and
  - statements admissible under s. 9 CJA 1967, which permits the written statement of a witness who is not in court to be read to the bench;
- at the close of the prosecution case, the defence may make a submission of no case to answer where the prosecution has failed to prove an essential element of the offence or the prosecution evidence has been so discredited that the court could not find the case proven against the defendant;
- the first defence witness, usually the accused, is examined in chief;
- the witness is cross-examined by the prosecution;
- the defence advocate may re-examine his witness;

(each defence witness gives evidence through this procedure);

- the defence advocate may also put before the court:
  - documentary evidence;
  - exhibits (known as real evidence); and
  - statements admissible under s. 9 CJA 1967, which permits the written statement of a witness who is not in court to be read to the bench;
- the prosecutor and the defence advocate make a closing speech;
- the court decides whether the case is proven;
- if proven, the court will proceed to disposing of the case; or
- if the case is not proven the defendant is free to leave the court.

For further information on the conduct of cases before the youth court, see the Magistrates Association Youth Court Protocol contained in Appendix A of the *Youth Court Bench Book 2017* available at https://www.sentencingcouncil.org.uk/wp-content/uploads/youth-court-bench-book-august-2017.pdf.

KEY POINT SUMMARY

- The rules governing the grant or refusal of bail in relation to a young defendant are governed by the Bail Act 1976 and, subject to one or two exceptions, are applied in much the same way as they are to an adult accused.

- A remand in custody in relation to a young person under the age of 17 is a remand into the care of a local authority with or without a security requirement.

- A young person under the age of 12 cannot be remanded into the care of the local authority.

- There is a strong presumption that a defendant under 18 should be tried in the youth court which is specifically designed for the special needs of younger offenders, even in a case where the young person is charged with a serious offence.

- A youth has no right of election to the Crown Court when charged with an either-way offence.

- Understand the circumstances in which a youth must be tried in the Crown Court and the circumstances where he might be tried in the Crown Court.

- Understand the concept of a 'grave' crime and why this is important in relation to mode of trial considerations for a youth.

- Understand when the 'dangerousness' provisions under s. 224 CJA 2003 bite and why they are important in relation to mode of trial considerations for youths.

- Be able to explain the differences in procedure between the adult court and the youth court.

SELF-TEST QUESTIONS

1. What is the general rule about where a young defendant should be tried?

2. Tracey is 15. She has been charged with an offence of arson contrary to s. 1(1) and (3) CDA 1971. It is alleged that she and a group of other girls set fire to a mobile classroom in the grounds of a high school, resulting in £20,000 worth of damage. The fire began at around 10.30 at night. The classroom was unoccupied. Tracey has no criminal record but comes from a family beset by social problems. She has recently been suspended from school. No one else has been charged in connection with the incident. Consider the following questions:

- In which court will Tracey appear?

- In which court is Tracey likely to be tried and dealt with?

3. Barry, aged 15, is charged with causing death by dangerous driving. He denies the offence. He has several previous convictions, including convictions for robbery, violence and aggravated vehicle-taking. What considerations will the youth court have regard to in deciding whether to accept jurisdiction to try Barry?

 An analysis of the above can be found on our online resources.

FIGURE 25.1 YOUTH PROCEEDINGS

WHERE WILL A YOUNG PERSON BE TRIED?

Youth court (the vast majority of young defendants are tried before the youth court)

This will be the case where:

- youth is charged alone; or

- youth is charged with another youth.

Crown Court where the youth is:

- charged with homicide, which includes both murder and manslaughter, s. 51A CDA 1998 or Firearms Act 1968 offence carrying mandatory minimum term; or

- charged with a 'grave' offence, s. 51A(3(b)) CDA 1998—'grave' offence includes an offence for which an adult could be punished with imprisonment for 14 years or more (there must be a realistic possibility that the young person will receive a custodial sentence substantially beyond 24 months); or

- charged with a specified offence and the young person would, if found guilty, be sentenced as a 'dangerous' offender under s. 226 CJA 2003 (s. 51A(3)(d) CDA 1988); or

- jointly charged with an adult and the adult is to be tried on indictment and the court considers that 'it is in the interests of justice' for them to be tried together, s. 51(7) CDA 1998.

Adult magistrates' court where:

- young person is charged jointly with an adult with a summary offence BUT

- the summary offence may be remitted to the youth court where:

  - the adult pleads guilty; and

  - the young person pleads not guilty; or

  - the adult is sent for trial or is discharged and the young person pleads not guilty.

When charged with an either-way offence, the young person has no right of election.

Youth court proceedings:

- are more informal in terms of procedure and terminology;

- have limited right of public access;

- have reporting restrictions; and

- are tried before specially trained 'mixed' bench.

---

26 SENTENCING YOUNG OFFENDERS

26.1	**Introduction**		**484**
	26.1.1	What are the general principles that guide youth sentencing?	484
	26.1.2	The scaled approach	485
26.2	**Sentencing procedure in the youth court**		**486**
26.3	**Deferring sentence—s. 1 PCC(S)A 2000**		**486**
26.4	**Referral order—ss. 16 and 17 PCC(S)A 2000 and paras. 6.19–6.22 Sentencing Children and Young People—Definitive Guideline (2017)**		**487**
26.5	**Fine—Part VI PCC(S)A 2000 and paras. 6.17–6.18 Sentencing Children and Young People—Definitive Guideline (2017)**		**488**
26.6	**Conditional discharge—s. 12 PCC(S)A 2000 and para. 6.14 Sentencing Children and Young People—Definitive Guideline (2017)**		**489**
26.7	**Absolute discharge—s. 12 PCC(S)A 2000 and para. 6.13 Sentencing Children and Young People—Definitive Guideline (2017)**		**489**
26.8	**Reparation order—ss. 73–75 PCC(S)A 2000 and paras. 6.15–6.16 Sentencing Children and Young People—Definitive Guideline (2017)**		**489**
26.9	**Youth rehabilitation order (YRO)—s. 1 CJIA 2008 and paras. 6.23–6.41 Sentencing Children and Young People—Definitive Guideline (2017)**		**490**
	26.9.1	Activity requirement	490
	26.9.2	Supervision requirement	491
	26.9.3	Unpaid work requirement	491
	26.9.4	Programme requirement	491
	26.9.5	Attendance centre requirement	491
	26.9.6	Prohibited activity requirement	491
	26.9.7	Curfew requirement	491
	26.9.8	Exclusion requirement	491
	26.9.9	Residence requirement	491
	26.9.10	Local authority residence requirement	491
	26.9.11	Electronic monitoring requirement	491
	26.9.12	Mental health treatment requirement	492
	26.9.13	Drug treatment requirement	492
	26.9.14	Drug testing requirement	492
	26.9.15	Intoxicating substance treatment requirement	492
	26.9.16	Education requirement	492
	26.9.17	Intensive supervision and surveillance requirement	492
	26.9.18	Intensive fostering requirement	492
	26.9.19	Dealing with a breach of a YRO	492
26.10	**Detention and training order—ss. 100–107 PCC(S)A 2000 and paras. 6.50–6.53 Sentencing Children and Young People—Definitive Guideline (2017)**		**493**
26.11	**Endorsement or disqualification of the young offender's driving licence/record**		**494**
26.12	**Compensation order—ss. 130–135 PCC(S)A 2000**		**494**
26.13	**Parenting orders—ss. 8–10 CDA 1998 and para. 3.3 Sentencing Children and Young People—Definitive Guideline (2017)**		**495**
26.14	**Parental bind over—s. 150(1) PCC(S)A 2000 and para. 3.3 Sentencing Children and Young People—Definitive Guideline (2017)**		**495**
	26.14.1	Youth court bench book	495

26.15	**Criminal Behaviour Order (CBO) and an Anti-Social Behaviour Injunction (ASBI)**	**495**
26.16	**Victim surcharge**	**496**
26.17	**Sentencing the young offender in the adult magistrates' court**	**496**
26.18	**Sentencing the young offender in the Crown Court**	**496**
26.19	**Sentencing a 'dangerous' young offender**	**497**
	26.19.1 Detention for life	497
	26.19.2 Imposing an extended custodial sentence	498
	26.19.3 Assessing 'dangerousness'	498
26.20	**Crossing a significant age threshold between commission of an offence and sentence**	**498**

26.1   INTRODUCTION

This chapter deals with the range of disposals available where a young offender admits the offence(s) or a finding of guilt is recorded against him. While most young offenders will be sentenced by the youth court, as you saw in Chapter 25, in specified situations an adult magistrates' court or the Crown Court may try a young person and/or sentence him.

The issues explained in this chapter include:

* the principles which guide the sentencing of youths;

* the youth court's sentencing powers;

* the adult magistrates' court sentencing powers;

* the Crown Court's sentencing powers;

* sentencing a 'dangerous' young offender.

To fully understand the principles of sentencing in relation to youths, you should be aware of sentencing practice and procedure in relation to adults explained in Chapters 21 and 22. As you will soon appreciate, in comparison the sentencing of young offenders is more complex and much more directed at dealing with the young offender's specific needs.

26.1.1   WHAT ARE THE GENERAL PRINCIPLES THAT GUIDE YOUTH SENTENCING?

The Sentencing Council's *Sentencing Children and Young People—Overarching Principles—Definitive Guideline* (June 2017) set out the overarching principles to be applied by all courts when sentencing a young offender. The guideline can be accessed at https://www.sentencingcouncil.org.uk/wp-content/uploads/Sentencing-Children-and-young-people-Definitive-Guide_FINAL_WEB.pdf and via our online resources.

Paragraphs 1.1–1.21 of the Guideline summarise the overarching principles that should be taken into account by the court when sentencing a child or a young person. The first overarching principle is the requirement that when sentencing a young offender the court must have regard to the principal aim of the youth justice system (to prevent offending by children and young people) and the welfare of the child young person (para. 1.1). The factors to be taken into account in applying the welfare factor to sentencing are further specified at para. 1.12 to include any mental health problems or learning difficulties experienced by the young offender, any traumatic life experience including exposure to drug and alcohol abuse and any speech and language difficulties.

Paragraphs 4.1–4.10 of the guideline set out the general factors that should be taken into account by the court when determining the sentence. Although the seriousness of the offence (paras. 4.2–4.7) will be the starting point in deciding the appropriate disposal the guideline advises that the approach to sentencing a child or young person should be individualistic and focused on the offender as opposed to primarily being offence focused including the age and maturity of the child or young person (paras. 4.8–4.10). The young person will also receive a sentencing credit for admitting their guilt (paras. 5.1–5.8).

Particular regard should be taken of the young offender's background where, for example, they come from a deprived home or have low educational attainment or suffered abuse or neglect (para. 1.13).

Wherever possible the court should focus on the offender's rehabilitation and must always consider the positive and negative effects that the sentence is likely to have on the offender (para. 1.2). The court is also reminded that domestic and international law require that custody should always be a disposal of last resort for young offenders (para. 1.3). This principle is reflected by the custody threshold test being higher for youths than for adults (see para. 26.10).

The sentence passed by the court should avoid criminalising the young offender as the primary purpose of the youth justice system is to encourage children and young people to take responsibility for their own actions and promote their reintegration into society rather than to punish. There should therefore be an emphasis on a restorative justice disposal to encourage the offender to take responsibility for their actions and to understand the impact their offence may have had on others (para. 1.4).

Account must also be taken of the young offender's lack of emotional development and immaturity that has influenced their offending (para. 1.5), the much greater effect of punishment on a young offender compared to an adult (para. 1.8) and any restriction on their liberty must be commensurate with the seriousness of the offence including the young offender's culpability in committing the offence and any harm which the offence caused or was intended to cause or might foreseeably have caused (para. 1.9).

Whilst the same structured approach to sentencing applied to adults is adopted for young offenders, the guideline highlights key differences in the approach to be taken when sentencing a young offender. The structured approach to be taken in relation to sentence is articulated at s. 4 of the Definitive Guideline. Although extracts from the guideline are referred to below in relation to specific disposals, you are strongly advised to read the guideline in full.

In addition to the *Sentencing Children and Young People—Overarching Principles—Definitive Guideline (2017)*, s. 142A Criminal Justice Act 2003 (CJA 2003) also identifies the relevant considerations that apply when sentencing an offender under 18. A court must have regard to:

- the principal aim of the youth justice system which is to prevent offending and reoffending;
- the welfare of the offender; and
- the purposes of sentencing.

The statutory purposes of sentencing applicable to offenders under the age of 18 are listed under s. 142A CJA 2003 as being:

- punishment;
- reform and rehabilitation;
- protection of the public; and
- reparation to persons affected by the offence.

Section 142A CJA 2003 has curiously yet to be brought into effect. For all of these reasons, it is important for the court to have access to the fullest possible information about the young person to enable it to determine the most appropriate sentence commensurate with the seriousness of the offence. Such information will invariably be supplied by a youth offending team (YOT) in a pre-sentence report.

26.1.2 THE SCALED APPROACH

As explained in Chapter 24, para. 24.3, a significant factor in determining the appropriate disposal that should be passed on a juvenile are the factors set out in the 'Scaled Approach', which ensures that sentencing interventions recommended by the YOT are tailored to the individual defendant and based on an assessment of their risks and needs.

When a YOT prepares a pre-sentence report at the request of a court or a youth panel overseeing a referral order, it will assess the individual via the ASSET tool (which evaluates the likelihood of reoffending and the risk of serious harm) and will use the 'Scaled Approach'. Under the ASSET tool, the young offender's attitude to offending, level of educational attainment, employment prospects, lifestyle, living arrangements, and habits relating to alcohol and substance abuse are assessed along with such factors as the level and nature of his or her previous offending. These factors are scored to produce a numerical assessment of the offender's risk of reoffending as well as providing guidance on the appropriate level of intervention required to deal with the offender's individual needs. The higher the score, the greater the level of intervention required by the YOT. The required intervention will be classified as either being at standard, enhanced or intensive. This classification will help determine the overall length of a referral order, the duration and nature of any requirements imposed as part of any Youth Rehabilitation Order and the nature of supervision following release on licence from custody under a Detention and Training Order (DTO).

It should be noted that the Magistrates' Court Sentencing Guidelines, which provide offence-specific sentencing starting points when sentencing adult offenders, cannot easily be applied to young offenders, although they have some relevance where custody is the appropriate starting point for sentence in the case of an adult. Some definitive sentencing guidelines exist for youths aged 17 in relation to sexual offences and robbery (see the *Sentencing Children and Young People—Overarching Principles—Definitive Guideline (2017)*).

26.2 SENTENCING PROCEDURE IN THE YOUTH COURT

Where the case is proven against the young person or the offence is admitted, the youth court will proceed to sentence. As in the adult court, the Crown Prosecution Service (CPS) advocate will outline the full circumstances of the offence where a guilty plea is entered and will refer the court to any relevant previous convictions and any existing sentence of the court. The CPS lawyer may also ask for ancillary orders, such as prosecution costs. The defence advocate will submit a plea in mitigation on the young person's behalf. The young person and/or his or her parent or guardian will be given the opportunity to make a statement to the court. Before determining the appropriate sentence, it is common practice for the chair of the Bench to engage with the young person to determine whether they understand the reasons for their offending and the effect of their behaviour on the victim, on the community, and on their parents or guardian. Also, when deciding sentence, the court will consider any relevant information about the young person's general behaviour, home environment and school record. If the information is not immediately available, the court must consider adjournment for enquiries. In most cases a written pre-sentence report will be provided by the YOT (see para. 26.1.2).

When the youth court has all the necessary information, a range of disposals are available. Some disposals relate to the young offender only, while others can be imposed on his or her parent or guardian. Credit will be given for a guilty plea on the basis of current sentencing guidelines (see Chapter 21, para. 21.13).

26.3 DEFERRING SENTENCE—S. 1 PCC(S)A 2000

The youth court can defer sentence for up to six months. Sentence may be deferred:

- because of an imminent and significant change in lifestyle; or
- to allow the young person to save up to pay compensation to the victim.

The court must give reasons for the deferment and explain what is required of the young person during the deferred period. If another offence is committed during the deferred period, the offender may be sentenced for the new offence in addition to the previous offence. A deferred sentence is very rare.

26.4 REFERRAL ORDER—SS. 16 AND 17 PCC(S)A 2000 AND PARAS. 6.19–6.22 SENTENCING CHILDREN AND YOUNG PEOPLE— DEFINITIVE GUIDELINE (2017)

A referral order can be imposed by the youth court or by an adult magistrates' court. Under a referral order, the young person is referred to a Youth Offender Panel (YOP). The YOP is composed of two trained community volunteers and a member of the YOT. It will meet with the young person and his or her parent/guardian and agree a 'contract' with the offender. The contract should include a programme of interventions designed to address the causes of the young person's offending behaviour and to get the young person to take responsibility for the consequences of his or her actions. Where the offence crosses the custody threshold, but, as a first time guilty plea, a referral order is the only non-custodial alternative or has the discretion to do so instead of imposing a DTO, the referral order will include an *'intensive contract'*.

The victim of the offence may attend the YOP. The referral order is therefore capable of fulfilling two of the statutory aims of sentence: the prevention of offending and reparation through restorative justice.

Regular panel meetings are held to review the progress of a referral order. Importantly for the young person, the conviction is spent once the 'contract' is completed.

In some instances, a referral order is a mandatory sentence; in other situations a referral order is discretionary. Common to both the mandatory and discretionary referral order are the following requirements:

- the sentence for the offence must not be fixed by law; and
- neither a custodial sentence nor an absolute discharge is appropriate for the offence or any connected offence.

Any referral order must be for between three and 12 months.

Circumstances in which a referral order is mandatory

The 2017 Definitive Guideline and ss. 16 and 17 PCC(S)A 2000 provide that a referral order is the mandatory sentence in the youth court or adult magistrates' court where the young offender:

- is sentenced for an imprisonable offence; and
- has no previous convictions (a bind over and an absolute or conditional discharge are disregarded); and
- pleads guilty to an imprisonable offence and any connected offence; and
- an absolute or conditional discharge, hospital order or custody is not appropriate.

A referral order must therefore be imposed on a 'first-time' offender, who pleads guilty to an offence which is not suitable for a custodial sentence or any of the other prescribed disposals even though the offence might be regarded as a serious offence.

 Example 1

Adam, aged 16, pleads guilty to possession of a small amount of a Class A drug with intent to supply. Adam has received a youth caution and a conditional discharge for previous offences. In these circumstances and assuming the offence is not so serious that a custodial sentence should be imposed, the youth court must sentence Adam to a referral order.

Circumstances in which a discretionary referral order can be imposed

A court can impose a discretionary referral order for any offence where there has been a guilty plea regardless of the young person's previous offending, see para. 6.20 of the 2017 Definitive Guideline and ss. 16 and 17 PCC(S)A 2000. A discretionary referral order may be passed by the court taking into account the young person's age, plea, seriousness of the offence, and previous convictions. In theory there is no limit to the number of referral orders that a repeat offender can receive.

 Example 2

Lewis, aged 17, pleads guilty to possession of a small amount of a Class C drug with intent to supply. Lewis has several previous convictions. Lewis successfully completed a three-month referral order 24 months ago for an offence of criminal damage. He was made subject to a reparation order 18 months ago for an offence of theft, which he also completed successfully. The pre-sentence report recommends a second referral order. The youth court can subject Lewis to a referral order in these circumstances.

 Example 3

Jack, aged 16, pleads guilty to allowing himself to be carried in a stolen vehicle and is found guilty of being in possession of a small amount of a Class A drug after a trial. Jack has previously received a conditional discharge for other offences committed in the past. As Jack has been subject to a trial, he does not meet the criteria for a compulsory referral order. In these circumstances the youth court may sentence Jack to a discretionary referral order.

The length of a referral order, which is decided by the court, is based on the seriousness of the offence. The order can be between 3–12 months. Paragraph 6.22 of the 2017 Definitive Guideline specifies an order of between 3–5 months for an offence of low seriousness up to an order of between 10–12 months for an offence of very high seriousness. In accordance with the 'Scaled Approach' previously outlined, the YOT is more likely to recommend an intensive contract in a case where the court indicated that custody is being considered but, because it is a first time guilty plea, a referral order is the only non-custodial alternative. In such cases, the YOT should convene a Youth Offender Panel (YOP) at which the young offender is asked to attend and to agree an intensive contract. Whilst the court determines the length of the referral order a Referral Order Panel decides the requirements of the order.

A referral order is a sentence in its own right although it can be combined with a compensation order. The YOP must refer the young person back to court if they fail to sign the contract or fail to agree or comply with its terms or commits another offence. The youth court may then revoke the referral order and resentence for the original offence and any later offence(s) or under ss. 43 and 44 Criminal Justice and Courts Act 2015 may impose a fine up to a maximum of £2,500 or extend the youth offender contract for up to a maximum of 12 months, where it is 'appropriate to do so' to ensure that the restorative justice process is completed.

The youth court may also revoke a referral order if it is in the interests of justice where a young person is making good progress.

The statutory guidance on referral orders came into force in October 2018 and can be accessed at https://www.gov.uk/government/publications/young-offenders-referral-orders.

26.5 FINE—PART VI PCC(S)A 2000 AND PARAS. 6.17–6.18 SENTENCING CHILDREN AND YOUNG PEOPLE—DEFINITIVE GUIDELINE (2017)

While imposing a fine on an offender is a common sentence passed by the adult magistrates' court (see Chapter 22, para. 22.15), fining a young person is relatively rare, for obvious reasons. When the court considers imposing a fine, the following considerations apply:

- The fine may be imposed as a disposal in its own right.
- The court must take into account the offender's financial circumstances including any expenses incurred by the young person to attend school, college, or to an apprenticeship.

- The parent/guardian must attend the court hearing if the court is considering making him or her pay and the court must consider the parent's financial resources.
- Where the offender is under 16, the parent/guardian will be ordered to pay, unless:
  - the parent/guardian cannot be found; or
  - it would be unreasonable to expect him or her to pay.
- The maximum fine that can be imposed where the young offender is aged between 10 and 13 is £250.
- The maximum fine that can be imposed where the young offender is aged between 14 and 17 is £1,000.

Priority is given to a compensation order over a fine.

26.6 CONDITIONAL DISCHARGE—S. 12 PCC(S)A 2000 AND PARA. 6.14 SENTENCING CHILDREN AND YOUNG PEOPLE—DEFINITIVE GUIDELINE (2017)

A conditional discharge may be imposed on a young offender for an offence which has been proven or which the young person has admitted but the court considers that the offence is not serious enough to justify immediate punishment. In practice, they are reserved for the less serious offences and are relatively rare in the youth court given the availability of the referral order. The offender must not commit any further offences during the operational period of the conditional discharge, which can be up to a maximum of three years. If the young offender reoffends during the operational period, he or she may be punished for the later offence and for the original offence. Unless exceptional circumstances apply a conditional discharge may be imposed where:

- the young offender has received in the previous 24 months two or more cautions or a conditional caution followed by a caution.

26.7 ABSOLUTE DISCHARGE—S. 12 PCC(S)A 2000 AND PARA. 6.13 SENTENCING CHILDREN AND YOUNG PEOPLE—DEFINITIVE GUIDELINE (2017)

As with a conditional discharge, an absolute discharge is appropriate for very trivial offences where the court considers that punishment is not required. An absolute discharge may be imposed where:

- the case is proven against the young offender; and
- the court considers that no punishment is required; and
- the court considers there is no risk of further offending by the young person.

26.8 REPARATION ORDER—SS. 73–75 PCC(S)A 2000 AND PARAS. 6.15–6.16 SENTENCING CHILDREN AND YOUNG PEOPLE—DEFINITIVE GUIDELINE (2017)

A reparation order can require the young offender to make reparation to the victim of the offence or where the victim wishes to the community as a whole. In deciding whether to make a reparation order, the court will obtain a report from the young person's YOT who will suggest a suitable form of reparation. The order is designed to confront the offender with the consequences of his or her offending behaviour and can only be imposed for an imprisonable offence. The reparation element shall be commensurate with the seriousness of the offence. A reparation order cannot be combined with any other order. The following considerations apply to a reparation order:

- the young person is required to give reparation to a specified person or to the community;
- the work to be carried out is under the supervision of a probation officer or social worker;
- no more than 24 hours' work to be completed within three months of the order;
- the order is overseen by the YOT;
- in a case where a reparation order can be made, the court must give reasons for refusing to make one.

Failure to comply with a reparation order can lead the youth court to impose a fine not exceeding £1,000 or to resentence in some other way.

26.9 YOUTH REHABILITATION ORDER (YRO)—S. 1 CJIA 2008 AND PARAS. 6.23–6.41 SENTENCING CHILDREN AND YOUNG PEOPLE— DEFINITIVE GUIDELINE (2017)

A Youth Rehabilitation Order (YRO) is a single generic community sentence for all offenders under the age of 18. When passing a YRO on a young offender, the court must include one or more requirements designed to provide for punishment, protection of the public, reducing reoffending and reparation. A YRO can be imposed for any offence which is 'serious enough' (s. 148 CJA 2003) but the offence does not have to be imprisonable. The nature and number of requirements under the YRO must be proportionate and suitable and any restrictions on the young person's liberty must be commensurate with the seriousness of the offence. A pre-sentence report will invariably be required. The pre-sentence report will be prepared in accordance with the 'Scaled Approach' outlined earlier with the requirements under the YRO being based on the young person's profile assessed as either 'Standard', or 'Enhanced', or 'Intensive'. Reference should be made to the Sentencing Council's recently published *Sentencing Children and Young People—Overarching Principles—Definitive Guideline (2017)*, paras. 6. 23–6.41.

A young offender with a 'Standard' profile is assessed as posing a low likelihood of reoffending and a low risk of serious harm. Therefore the recommended requirements will be based on activities such as reparation or unpaid work or an attendance centre requirement. A young offender with an 'Enhanced' profile is assessed as posing a medium likelihood of reoffending or a medium risk of serious harm and the requirements will seek to repair the harm caused by their offending and enable the offender to facilitate change in their lives through a supervision requirement, reparation, or a requirement to deal with the reasons for their offending such as attendance for drug treatment or an offending behaviour programme. A young offender with an 'Intensive' profile is assessed as having a high likelihood of reoffending or very high risk of causing serious harm. Requirements will therefore seek to control the young person and enable them to change their offending habits through a supervision requirement or reparation or a curfew or prohibited activity requirement or combination.

Whilst there is no minimum period for a YRO the maximum length is three years. A YRO can, however, come to an end on the completion of all the requirements or can be extended for up to six months for the completion of all the requirements (s. 84 LASPO 2012).

A YRO is not available where the offender is before the court and the compulsory criteria for a referral order are present (see para. 26.4), or there is an existing reparation order or YRO in force. The requirements that may be attached to a YRO (which are similar to those for adults—see Chapter 22) are considered here.

26.9.1 ACTIVITY REQUIREMENT

This requires participation in activities for a specified number of days which must not exceed 90 days.

26.9.2 **SUPERVISION REQUIREMENT**

This is a requirement to attend appointments with a specified YOT officer. The period of supervision must be equal to the length of the order and will be used to address the young person's attitudes, behaviour and thinking that have contributed to their offending.

26.9.3 **UNPAID WORK REQUIREMENT**

This can only be passed on an offender aged 16 or 17 years and must be between 40 and 240 hours to be completed over a 12-month period.

26.9.4 **PROGRAMME REQUIREMENT**

A requirement to participate in a systematic set of activities recommended by the YOT to address the issues associated with their offending such as curbing their violent tendencies or increasing victim awareness.

26.9.5 **ATTENDANCE CENTRE REQUIREMENT**

This requires a young person to attend a centre to engage in and to receive instruction. For those aged 16+ the minimum length is 12 hours and the maximum 36. For those aged 14 and 15, the minimum is 12 hours and the maximum is 24 and for those under 13, the maximum is 12 hours.

26.9.6 **PROHIBITED ACTIVITY REQUIREMENT**

A requirement to refrain from participating in specified activities such as not entering licensed premises.

26.9.7 **CURFEW REQUIREMENT**

The offender must stay at a specified location such as a hostel for a specified period of time of between two and 16 hours in any one day. The maximum length of a curfew is 12 months. The curfew will be supported by electronic monitoring unless the court considers this to be inappropriate or it is not available.

26.9.8 **EXCLUSION REQUIREMENT**

This requirement cannot exceed three months and prohibits a young person from entering a specified place during a specified time period up to a maximum of three months. The court must also make an electronic monitoring requirement to ensure compliance.

26.9.9 **RESIDENCE REQUIREMENT**

This disposal applies only to those aged 16 and over and requires that the young person live with a specified person (who must consent) or at a specified place.

26.9.10 **LOCAL AUTHORITY RESIDENCE REQUIREMENT**

This is a requirement to reside in accommodation provided by a local authority for a specified period which must not exceed six months and which ceases to apply when the offender reaches 18. There are a number of prerequisites that apply before this requirement can be imposed.

26.9.11 **ELECTRONIC MONITORING REQUIREMENT**

This disposal will be imposed as part of a curfew requirement and the offender is tagged to ensure their compliance.

26.9.12 MENTAL HEALTH TREATMENT REQUIREMENT

This requires the offender's willingness to comply and is a requirement for residential or non-residential treatment for a diagnosed mental condition that is susceptible to treatment.

26.9.13 DRUG TREATMENT REQUIREMENT

The court must be satisfied that the young person requires treatment, that suitable arrangements have been made or can be made to deal with the young person's needs and that the young person consents to comply with the conditions of the treatment.

26.9.14 DRUG TESTING REQUIREMENT

This disposal operates alongside the drug treatment requirement and requires the offender to voluntarily provide urine samples for drug testing.

26.9.15 INTOXICATING SUBSTANCE TREATMENT REQUIREMENT

The court must be satisfied that the young person is dependent on or has a tendency to misuse intoxicating substances and that the dependency is susceptible to treatment. It requires the offender's willingness to comply.

26.9.16 EDUCATION REQUIREMENT

A requirement to comply with approved educational arrangements made by the parent or guardian and approved by the local education authority. The requirement must be necessary to secure the good conduct of the young person or to prevent further offending.

26.9.17 INTENSIVE SUPERVISION AND SURVEILLANCE REQUIREMENT

This requirement may only be included in an order where:

- the offence is imprisonable; and
- the custody threshold test is met (and in the case of an offender under the age of 15 at the time of conviction, the young person is a persistent offender).

A YRO combined with an intensive supervision and surveillance (ISS) requirement is a direct alternative to custody.

The order must include an 'extended activity requirement' of between 90 and 180 days, plus supervision, curfew, and electronic monitoring. This is a highly intensive community order.

26.9.18 INTENSIVE FOSTERING REQUIREMENT

This requirement (which is also an alternative to a DTO) can only be imposed where the same circumstances exist as are required for the intensive supervision and surveillance requirement. In addition, the court must be satisfied that a significant factor in the commission of the offence was the circumstances in which the young person was living at the time and that this requirement would assist in rehabilitation. Extensive consultation with the young person's parent/guardian and the local authority are needed before this requirement can be imposed. The order must specify the period during which the young person must reside with the foster parent, which must not exceed 12 months. The order cannot operate after the young person has attained 18.

26.9.19 DEALING WITH A BREACH OF A YRO

In the event of the young person failing to comply with a YRO, a court can choose to do any of the following:

- take no action (there is no obligation on the court to make a more onerous order, in contrast to the adult offender);

- impose a fine subject to the young offender's means to a maximum of £2,500 for 14- to 17-year-olds and £250 for offenders under 14. The order may still continue in its original form in spite of the fine;

- amend the terms of the order by increasing or substituting requirements (in doing so the court can impose any requirement it could have imposed when making the original order save for an 'extended activity' or fostering requirement); or

- revoke the order and resentence the offender (this could involve the offender being made subject to an 'extended activity' or fostering requirement or custody if the court is satisfied that the YOT has taken all necessary steps necessary to ensure the young person has been given appropriate opportunity and support necessary for compliance). Revocation and resentence is unlikely for a first breach as the primary aim is to ensure compliance with the order.

Where an offender has 'wilfully and persistently' failed to comply with the order and the court proposes to sentence again for the original offence, additional powers are available. These additional powers include the power to sentence to a DTO for four months or a YRO with an ISS requirement even though the offence for which the original YRO was imposed did not carry a custodial term in the youth court or if it did, the original offence did not cross the custody threshold.

26.10 DETENTION AND TRAINING ORDER—SS. 100–107 PCC(S)A 2000 AND PARAS. 6.50–6.53 SENTENCING CHILDREN AND YOUNG PEOPLE— DEFINITIVE GUIDELINE (2017)

A DTO is the main custodial sentence for a young offender.

The custody threshold test must be met before a DTO can be passed in that the offence or combination of offence and any associated offence must be so 'serious' that neither a fine alone nor a community sentence can be justified (s. 152 CJA 2003). In fact, there is a further additional hurdle in the case of a youth in that not only must the custody threshold test be met but the court must also give reasons as to why a YRO with intensive supervision and surveillance or a YRO with a fostering requirement (see paras. 26.9.17 and 26.9.18) cannot be justified instead (s. 174(4B) CJA 2003).

The guidance contained in the Sentencing Council's recently published *Sentencing Children and Young People—Overarching Principles—Definitive Guideline (2017)* paras. 6.50–6.53 means that custody is the sentence of last resort for young offenders. For a first-time offender who has pleaded guilty to an imprisonable offence a referral order will be the most appropriate sentence in most cases (see para. 26.4). Since any custodial term must be for the shortest term commensurate with the seriousness of the offence (s. 153 CJA 2003), and since the minimum length of a DTO is four months, unless the offence justifies a term of at least four months (taking into account any reduction for guilty plea), the sentence must be of a non-custodial nature. A pre-sentence report must be considered before a custodial sentence is imposed.

Apart from these important considerations, **a court cannot pass a DTO on an offender under the age of 12, or on an offender under the age of 15 unless the court is of the opinion that he or she is a persistent offender (see Chapter 24, para. 24.2.1 for a definition of the term 'persistent offender').**

The length of the DTO must be for one of the periods specified in the Act: 4, 6, 8, 10, 12, 18 or 24 months. (The term may not exceed the adult maximum term which a Crown Court could pass on an adult over 21, which in the case of a summary-only offence is currently six months or less if the statute so prescribes.) There is no power to suspend a DTO. The availability of a 24-month custodial term to the youth court means that its sentencing powers are considerably higher than those available to the magistrates' court sentencing an adult offender (see Chapter 21, para. 21.14.1).

Paragraph 6. 45 of the 2017 Definitive Guideline states:

'Only if the court is satisfied that the offence crosses the custody threshold, and that no other sentence is appropriate, the court may, as a preliminary consideration, consult the equivalent adult guideline in order to decide upon the appropriate length of the sentence. The guideline asks courts to bear in mind the negative effects that a short custodial sentence can have and when considering the adult guideline, the court may feel it appropriate to apply a sentence broadly within the region of half to two thirds of the adult sentence for those aged 15–17 and allow a greater reduction for those aged under 15. Furthermore, in most cases when considering the appropriate reduction from the adult sentence the emotional and developmental age and maturity of the child or young person is of at least equal importance as their chronological age.'

In establishing the length of the DTO, the young person will be entitled to a sentencing discount where he or she pleads guilty and will be given credit for periods spent on remand in custody or subject to a qualifying curfew (s. 144 CJA 2003/s. 101(8) PCC(S)A 2000). Full consideration is given to the principles underpinning reduction for guilty plea in the case of a child/young person at s. 5 of the 2017 Definitive Guideline.

Unless the young person has their eighteenth birthday in custody, a period of supervision in the community will begin halfway through the sentence, which will cease when the full term expires (s. 103 PCC(S)A 2000). Where the supervision element is breached, the court may order the offender to be detained in youth detention accommodation for three months or the remainder of the term of the order (if shorter) or a further period of supervision not exceeding three months or a fine not exceeding level 3. Under s. 6 Offender Rehabilitation Act 2014 a young person who has their eighteenth birthday in custody is subject to extended supervision for 12 months in the community irrespective of the length of their DTO.

At the present time a young person will serve the custodial element of their sentence in a young offender institution or a secure training centre. Under s. 38 Criminal Justice and Courts Act 2015 a young offender may serve their custodial term in a secure college which will focus on providing educational opportunities to young people with the aim of reducing youth reoffending. It is also intended that the provision of education and training within existing young offender institutions will also be enhanced.

 Example

Jamal, aged 14, is convicted of serious assault in the youth court. He has ten previous convictions and has previously been sentenced to a wide range of community-based disposals, many of which have not been successfully completed. As the court is satisfied that the offence is so serious that only a custodial sentence is appropriate and that Jamal is a persistent offender (PO), and that neither a YRO with an ISS requirement nor a YRO with a fostering requirement are justified, it imposes an eight-month DTO on him. Under the terms of the DTO, Jamal will serve four months in custody and four months in the community under supervision.

26.11 ENDORSEMENT OR DISQUALIFICATION OF THE YOUNG OFFENDER'S DRIVING LICENCE/RECORD

For further information on driving penalties, see the Additional Chapter 'Sentencing in Road Traffic Cases' found in the online resources. Even though a young offender may not have a driving licence, his or her driving record can still be subject to endorsement and disqualification.

26.12 COMPENSATION ORDER—SS. 130–135 PCC(S)A 2000

A convicted young offender may be ordered to pay compensation up to a maximum of £5,000 in either the youth court or the adult magistrates' court for any personal injury, loss or damage which resulted from his or her offence. The Magistrates' Court Sentencing Guidelines provide guidance as to the appropriate level of compensation. An important consideration will be the offender's ability to pay.

26.13 PARENTING ORDERS—SS. 8–10 CDA 1998 AND PARA. 3.3 SENTENCING CHILDREN AND YOUNG PEOPLE—DEFINITIVE GUIDELINE (2017)

A parenting order is directed to improving the parenting skills of the young offender's parent or guardian. Where an offender under the age of 16 is convicted of an offence and the court considers that a parenting order would be desirable in the interests of preventing further offending by the young person, it *shall* make a parenting order. The pre-sentence report should provide information relevant to this decision. A parenting order requires the parent or guardian to attend parenting guidance sessions for up to 12 months. The sessions are supervised by a member of the YOT or a probation officer or a social worker.

26.14 PARENTAL BIND OVER—S. 150(1) PCC(S)A 2000 AND PARA. 3.3 SENTENCING CHILDREN AND YOUNG PEOPLE—DEFINITIVE GUIDELINE (2017)

The young offender's parent or guardian must be bound over to prevent the juvenile under the age of 16 from committing further offences wherever the court is satisfied that it would be in the interests of justice to do so. If a court chooses not to make an order, it must give reasons in open court. A bind over may not be given where a court passes a referral order.

26.14.1 YOUTH COURT BENCH BOOK

For further information and a useful flowchart covering the various sentencing options available to the youth court: see the *Youth Court Bench Book* (2017) available through the Sentencing Council's website https://www.sentencingcouncil.org.uk/wp-content/uploads/youth-court-bench-book-august-2017.pdf and the web-link section (Youth Justice section) of our online resources.

26.15 CRIMINAL BEHAVIOUR ORDER (CBO) AND AN ANTI-SOCIAL BEHAVIOUR INJUNCTION (ASBI)

More details on the CBO can be found in Chapter 22, para. 22.20.3. The order can be applied for by the CPS when the young person has been convicted of an offence. Where the offender is under the age of 18, the local authority (or the police, if the requesting agency) must find out the view of the local YOT. The CBO aims to prevent further anti-social behaviour and is made in addition to any sentence the court may impose and requires the young offender to refrain from engaging in a specified activity or requiring them to participate in a specified activity. The minimum period for a CBO on an offender under 18 is one year. The maximum is three years, but the order should only be made for as long as the court considers necessary for the protection of the community from the individual in question. The CBO must be reviewed annually. Breaching the order is a criminal offence with the maximum penalty on conviction in the youth court is a 24 months DTO or a fine not exceeding £1,000 (£250 if under the age of 14) or both.

An Anti-Social Behaviour Injunction (ASBI) is a civil power that can be applied for against any person aged 10 and above. The ASBI is designed to offer protection to victims and communities by preventing anti-social behaviour; by preventing its continuation and/or escalation. Before applying to the court for an ASBI, all other approaches should have been considered. An ASBI is a disposal of last resort.

For offenders under 18, the application for an ASBI must be made to the youth court and can be made by several agencies including a local authority, a housing provider, and the police. The ASBI will be granted where two conditions are met: the court must be satisfied, on the balance of probabilities, that the respondent has engaged or threatened to engage in anti-social behaviour and the court considers it is just and convenient to grant the injunction to prevent the respondent from engaging in anti-social behaviour.

When granted, the injunction may prohibit the respondent from doing anything described in the injunction (a prohibition) and/or require the respondent to do anything specified in the injunction (a requirement). In the youth court, the injunction can be for no more than 12 months.

 Looking Ahead

In an attempt to stem the year-on-year increase in offences committed by juveniles involving knives, the Home Secretary announced in March 2019 that there would be an amendment to the Offensive Weapons Bill currently before parliament that will see the introduction of Knife Crime Prevention Orders which can be imposed on any person aged 12 or over to prevent young people from becoming involved in knife possession and knife crime. The order can be imposed on anyone who the police believe is carrying a knife, or is a habitual knife carrier or people previously convicted of a knife related offence. The new civil order will also restrict behaviour by placing curfews and geographical restrictions on individuals as well as limiting their social media use, preventing the rapid escalation of rival disputes. Breach of the order will be a criminal offence.

26.16 VICTIM SURCHARGE

The court must impose a surcharge on a person under the 18. The amount depends on the sentence imposed:

Conditional discharge £15

Referral order £20

Fine £20

Youth Rehabilitation Order £20

Detention and Training Order £30

26.17 SENTENCING THE YOUNG OFFENDER IN THE ADULT MAGISTRATES' COURT

The adult magistrates' court has limited sentencing powers over a young offender and will be required to apply overarching principles contained in the *Sentencing Children and Young People—Overarching Principles—Definitive Guideline (2017)*. In the few situations where the young offender is sentenced in the adult magistrates' court, the following disposals are most commonly imposed:

- fine;
- referral order;
- conditional/absolute discharge;
- disqualification from driving;
- endorsement of the young person's driving licence/record.

The young offender will usually be remitted to the youth court for sentence.

26.18 SENTENCING THE YOUNG OFFENDER IN THE CROWN COURT

While the Crown Court may pass any appropriate sentence on a young person, s. 8 PCC(S)A 2000 requires that where the young person has been convicted on indictment, para. 2.15 of the *Sentencing Children and Young People—Overarching Principles—Definitive Guideline (2017)* requires the Crown Court to remit the offender to the youth court for sentencing unless it is 'undesirable' to do so. The guideline goes on to say that in considering whether remittal is undesirable a court should balance the need for expertise in the sentencing of children and young people with the benefits of the sentence being imposed by the court which determined guilt.

With the exception of the referral order (which may be the most appropriate sentence and hence justify remittal back to the youth court), the Crown Court has the full range of sentencing disposals available to it (reparation order, YRO and DTO), with the obvious addition that it can impose a much longer custodial sentence in accordance with s. 91 PCC(S)A 2000 for a 'grave' crime where the defendant has been convicted on indictment and, upon committal for sentence, under s. 3B PCC(S)A 2000. In appropriate circumstances, it can also impose a sentence under the dangerousness provisions (see later). Where a custodial sentence is passed, the young offender will serve his or her time in a young offenders' institution or secure training centre.

Where the young person has been convicted of murder, s. 90 PCC(S)A 2000 prescribes the mandatory sentence of detention at Her Majesty's Pleasure. Guidance on setting the minimum term can be found in ss. 269–277 CJA 2003. The starting point for an offender under 18 is 12 years before taking into account any mitigating or aggravating factors.

26.19 SENTENCING A 'DANGEROUS' YOUNG OFFENDER

Sections 224–229 CJA 2003 provide the Crown Court with significant sentencing powers to deal with 'dangerous' offenders. The provisions apply to adults as well as youth offenders. The application of the dangerousness provisions in relation to adults is considered in Chapter 22, para. 22.8. We recommend you consider the provisions as they apply to adult offenders before reading further. The definition of dangerousness and other key terms can be found at Chapter 22, para. 22.8.

Only the Crown Court can sentence a young offender under the dangerousness provisions. The relevant considerations are dealt with in paras. 2.3–2.7 *Sentencing Children and Young People— Overarching Principles—Definitive Guideline (2017)*. The powers of the Crown Court may be exercised following the young person's conviction in the Crown Court (see Chapter 25, paras. 25.3.1 and 25.3.2 for an account of the circumstances in which a young person can be committed for trial in the Crown Court) or where he has been committed to the Crown Court for sentence following summary conviction in the youth court under s. 3C PCC(S)A 2000.

Schedule 15 CJA 2003 lists the categories of violent or sexual offences which come within the definition of a specified offence. A specified offence is defined under s. 224 CJA 2003 as a violent or sexual offence which carries a sentence of between two and ten years' imprisonment. A 'serious offence' is a violent or sexual offence defined in Sch. 15 which carries a sentence of at least ten or more years in the case of an adult. The sentencing powers available to the Crown Court depend on whether the young person has been convicted of a serious violent or sexual offence or a specified violent or sexual offence which carries a sentence of between two and ten years' imprisonment. If the offender falls within the first category *and* is assessed as being dangerous, he must be detained for life. If the offender falls within the second category *and* is assessed as being dangerous, the court must pass an extended sentence of imprisonment.

26.19.1 DETENTION FOR LIFE

Under s. 226(1) CJA 2003, where a person under 18 has been convicted of a serious violent or sexual offence (carrying a maximum of ten or more years' imprisonment) and the court is of the opinion that there is a significant risk to members of the public of serious harm occasioned by the commission by him of further specified offences, the court MUST impose a sentence of detention for life IF the offence he or she has been convicted of would be liable to a sentence of detention for life AND the court considers that the seriousness of the offence is such as to justify the imposition of a sentence for life (s. 226(2) CJA 2003).

If these precise circumstances apply BUT the sentence of detention for life is not available or not justified, the court MAY impose an extended sentence (see para. 26.19.2).

26.19.2 **IMPOSING AN EXTENDED CUSTODIAL SENTENCE**

When can an extended custodial sentence be imposed on a youth? Section 226B CJA 2003 (as amended by ss. 123–125 LASPO 2012) provides that a court MAY impose an extended sentence on an offender aged under 18 where:

- the offender is convicted of a specified offence (this is not limited to a serious offence); and
- the court is of the opinion that he or she is a dangerous offender (i.e. there is a significant risk to members of the public of serious harm occasioned by the commission by him of further specified offences); and
- a sentence of detention for life is not available or not justified; and
- the appropriate custodial term for the offence would be at least four years.

Where the conditions for imposing an extended custodial sentence are met, the court will set the appropriate custodial term and a further extended period of supervision which the young offender is required to serve on licence. The extended period on licence should be for such period as the court considers necessary to protect the public from serious harm occasioned by the commission of further specified offences by the young offender. Two-thirds of the term is served in custody before the young person is released on extended licence of up to five years for violent offences (s. 226B(6) CJA 2003) and up to eight years for sexual offences (s. 226B(6) CJA 2003).

26.19.3 **ASSESSING 'DANGEROUSNESS'**

In deciding whether to detain an offender under 18 for life or for public protection or to impose an extended sentence, the court must consider the seriousness of the offence and/or other offences associated with it (s. 229 CJA 2003) to determine whether the young person will constitute a danger to the public. The court will take careful note of the facts of the offence, the pre-sentence report and any other relevant report. In these kinds of cases a psychiatric report is commonly obtained.

Guidance on these complicated provisions has been given by the Court of Appeal in *R v Lang and Others* [2005] EWCA Crim 2864 (see Chapter 22) and for a recent application of 'dangerousness' in the case of a young offender, see *R v T* [2018] EWCA Crim 2464.

26.20 **CROSSING A SIGNIFICANT AGE THRESHOLD BETWEEN COMMISSION OF AN OFFENCE AND SENTENCE**

If the defendant is under the age of 18 at the time he or she enters a plea before the youth court he or she will be tried as a youth, notwithstanding the fact that the defendant reaches 18 during the currency of the proceedings.

Although the rules and the case law in relation to sentence on this point have never been absolutely clear, the position has been clarified by the 2017 guidelines, *Sentencing Children and Young People—Overarching Principles*, published by the Sentencing Guidelines Council. The approach to be taken is set out in sections 6.1–6.3 as follows:

- Where an offender crosses a relevant age threshold (12, 15, or 18 years old) between the date on which the offence was committed and the date of conviction or sentence, a court should take as its starting point the sentence likely to have been imposed on the date on which the offence was committed.

- Where an offender attains the age of 18 after committing the offence but before conviction, the adult purposes of sentencing under s. 142 CJA 2003 apply.

- When any significant age threshold is passed, it will be rare for a court to have to consider passing a sentence more severe than the maximum it would have had jurisdiction to pass at the time the offence was committed, though a sentence at or close to that maximum may be appropriate.

For further information on youth justice, consult the Youth Justice Board's website at http://www.justice.gov.uk/youth-justice.

KEY POINT SUMMARY

- Be familiar with the overarching principles stated in the *Sentencing Children and Young People— Overarching Principles—Definitive Guideline (2017)*. (The document also contains the sentencing guidelines for Sexual Offences and Robbery committed by children and young people.)

- Know the circumstances in which the youth court can impose a Detention and Training Order (DTO) and be aware that a DTO cannot be imposed upon an offender under the age of 12, and in the case of an offender under the age of 15, he or she must be a persistent offender.

- Understand that only the Crown Court can impose a lengthy custodial term (in excess of 24 months) for a 'grave' crime or under the 'dangerousness' provisions. Consequently, the only court which can pass a custodial sentence on an offender under the age of 12 or under the age of 15 and who is not a persistent offender is the Crown Court.

- Know the circumstances in which a referral order must be made and the circumstances in which a referral order might be made.

- Know the range of requirements that are available to the youth court and Crown Court when sentencing a young offender to a Youth Rehabilitation Order.

- Know the criteria that must be satisfied before a youth court or Crown Court can impose a youth rehabilitation order with intensive supervision and surveillance.

- Understand the dangerousness provisions as they apply to youths and their effect on sentencing.

SELF-TEST QUESTIONS

1. What is the main custodial sentence for a convicted young offender and when can it be passed?

2. Tracey is 15. She has been charged with an offence of arson contrary to s. 1(1) and (3) Criminal Damage Act 1971. It is alleged that she and a group of other girls set fire to a mobile classroom in the grounds of a high school, resulting in £20,000 worth of damage. The fire began at around 10.30 at night. The classroom was unoccupied. Tracey has no criminal record but comes from a family beset by social problems. She has recently been suspended from school. No one else has been charged in connection with the incident. If Tracey were to plead guilty to the offence, what sentencing options would be open to the youth court? Would your answer be different if Tracey had either (a) been found guilty of arson following a trial; or (b) having pleaded guilty, she had previous convictions for assault and criminal damage for which she has previously received a referral order and reparation order?

3. To which court would a young person appeal against conviction and/or sentence arising out of a decision taken by the youth court?

An analysis of these questions can be found in our online resources.

APPENDIX 1
ADDITIONAL CHAPTERS

Additional chapters to accompany this text can be found at the following location: www.oup.com/uk/crimlit19-20/.

ADVISING AT THE POLICE STATION—PRACTICAL STEPS

This chapter offers practical guidance for the legal representative called upon to advise a suspect at the police station. Written primarily from a defence perspective, the chapter includes advice on interviewing your client, interviewing the custody officer and the investigating officers, evaluating the evidence gathered by the police, preparing your client for the police interview as well as the tactical considerations when negotiating with the police. Information about the Police Station Representative Accreditation Scheme is also included. This chapter should be read in conjunction with the online Case Study featuring the Peter West Police Station scenario.

WHITE COLLAR CRIME—REGULATORY OFFENCES

This chapter provides an invaluable perspective on the significant area of corporate crime and regulatory offences. Written by two leading experts, the chapter takes the reader in a clear and concise way through the key substantive provisions, the role of the regulatory agencies, the professional practice and procedural steps in the prosecution of regulatory offences as well as providing a practical insight into the key strategies when representing a client in this type of case. The chapter is essential reading for those students and practitioners who have a City focus as well as those who are interested in finding out more about this specialist area of criminal practice.

SENTENCING IN ROAD TRAFFIC CASES

Representing a client in a road traffic prosecution is one of the most lucrative areas of criminal practice. This chapter is written for those students and practitioners who want to find out more about the key procedural stages and sentencing principles and practice in road traffic offences. The chapter includes a detailed explanation of the sentencing framework as it is applied to road traffic offences, guidance about mitigation including 'exceptional hardship' and 'special reasons' as well as practical advice about how to most effectively represent your client charged with a road traffic offence. The chapter should be read in conjunction with the online Case Study featuring *R v Roger Martin*.

APPENDIX 2

EXTRACTS FROM *R v LENNY WISE*

For reasons of space, we include only a selection of the documentation that forms the basis of the solicitor's file on this case study.

The complete documentation as listed overleaf, can be accessed on our online resources in the case studies section. The documents selected for inclusion in this appendix are shown in **bold type**.

CASE STUDY 1—*R v LENNY WISE*

Please note that this is a fictitious case study. All of the characters contained within it are fictitious and any resemblance to real persons, living or dead, is purely coincidental.

TIME SCALE OF EVENTS

- 20 March—Charged with an either-way offence
- 20 March—Initial appearance before Magistrates' Court (short adjournment-defendant remanded in custody)
- 27 March—Second appearance before Magistrates' Court. Plea before Venue. Not guilty plea entered followed by Allocation Hearing. Summary jurisdiction declined. Case adjourned and a date set for Plea and Trial Preparation Hearing before the Crown Court
- 29 March—Bail hearing before Crown Court-conditional bail granted
- 1 May—First appearance before Crown Court at the PTPH-date set for trial
- 30 September—Trial on indictment

INDEX TO DOCUMENTATION ON SOLICITOR'S FILE

DOCUMENT 1 Attendance upon Client and Record of First Appearance Before Magistrates' Court

DOCUMENT 2 Initial Disclosure of Prosecution Case Plus Previous Convictions Recorded Against Lenny Wise

DOCUMENT 3 CRM 1

DOCUMENT 4 Attendance Note

DOCUMENT 5 Application for Representation Order—(CRM14) *Note, this would now be submitted electronically on Crim 14 eForm*

DOCUMENT 5b Representation Order

DOCUMENT 6 Proof of Evidence of Lenny Wise

DOCUMENT 7 Consideration of Initial Disclosure of the Prosecution Case

DOCUMENT 8 Letter Requesting Copy of Custody Record

DOCUMENT 9 Client Care Letter

DOCUMENT 10 Letter to CPS Requesting Further Disclosure

DOCUMENT 11 Lymeshire Police Custody Record

DOCUMENT 12 CPS Specimen Letter

DOCUMENT 13 Record of Initial Description

DOCUMENT 14 Antecedents of Lenny Wise-Restricted Access to CPS Only

DOCUMENT 15 Record of Attendance at Allocation Hearing

DOCUMENT 16 Standard Case Sent Directions

DOCUMENT 16b Contribution Notice

DOCUMENT 17 Transcript of Bail Hearing-Submissions of Prosecution and Defence

DOCUMENT 18 Record of Decision to Withhold Bail

DOCUMENT 19 Notice of Application Relating to Bail to be Made to the Crown Court

DOCUMENT 20 Record of Crown Court Bail Hearing

DOCUMENT 21 File Note to Trainee Solicitor-Enquiry Re: Possible Alibi

DOCUMENT 22 CRM 4—Application for Prior Authority to Incur Disbursement (*Note, this now has to be submitted electronically*)

DOCUMENT 23 Letter Requesting Expert Report for the Defence

DOCUMENT 24 Letter to Client

DOCUMENT 25 CPS Letter Regarding Service of Case Sent Bundle (Specimen Letter)

DOCUMENT 25A: Record of Attendance at PTPH

DOCUMENT 25B: Plea Trial Preparation Hearing Form

DOCUMENT 26 A-J: Case Sent Bundle

DOCUMENT 26a CPS Letter

DOCUMENT 27 CPS Letter Regarding CPIA 1996 Disclosure—Specimen Letter

DOCUMENT 27A Police Schedule of Non-sensitive Unused Material

DOCUMENT 27B Police Schedule of Non-sensitive Unused Material

DOCUMENT 28 Prosecution Notice of Intention to Admit Evidence of Defendant's Bad Character under Criminal Justice Act 2003

DOCUMENT 29 File Note-Attendance upon Client

DOCUMENT 30 Additional Statement of Lenny Wise—Comments on Evidence Disclosed in the Case Sent Bundle

DOCUMENT 31 Letter to CPS Dealing With CPIA 1996 Matters

DOCUMENT 32(A) Defence Statement

DOCUMENT 32(B) Notification of Witness Requirements

DOCUMENT 33 Defence Notice Objecting to the Admissibility of Defendant's Past Criminal Convictions

DOCUMENT 34 CPS Specimen Letter Dealing with Further Disclosure

DOCUMENT 35 Further Disclosure—Police Interview with Other Suspect

DOCUMENT 36 Further Disclosure—Letter from Forensic Science Service

DOCUMENT 37 Psychiatric Medical Report

DOCUMENT 38(A) Witness Statement Accompanying Psychiatric Medical Report

DOCUMENT 38(B) Notification of Expert Evidence

DOCUMENT 39 Brief to Counsel to Attend Pre-Trial Hearing—Further Case Management Hearing

DOCUMENT 40 File Notes Based on Telephone Call with CPS

DOCUMENT 41 Trial Brief to Counsel

DOCUMENT 42 Transcript of Shirley Lewis Giving Her Evidence in Chief and Being Cross-Examined

DOCUMENT 43 Defence Submission

DOCUMENT 44 File Note Based on Trial

DOCUMENT 1 ATTENDANCE UPON CLIENT AND RECORD OF FIRST APPEARANCE BEFORE MAGISTRATES' COURT

DATE 20/3/–

Attending Lenny Wise at Lyme Magistrates' Court in my capacity as Duty Solicitor. Lenny Wise is charged with a domestic dwelling house burglary. In the course of the interview, Lenny was less than coherent and kept asking me for a cigarette. He looked rough, dishevelled and appeared incapable of concentrating during the interview. It would appear that Lenny has depression for which he receives medication, although he admitted to me that he had not been taking his medication properly. He told me that his sister was present in the court precinct somewhere and I should try and speak to her, I tried to take him through the Streamlined IDPC that the CPS had provided me with but Lenny was unable to concentrate. Lenny was able to tell me that he was not represented at the police station and that he did not commit the burglary and would fight it. He insisted that he never burgled any pensioner's home. At this point, Lenny said he felt sick and proceeded to vomit. I explained to Lenny that I would be seeking a short adjournment to enable me to properly take his instruction and that I could not guarantee his release from custody today and I expected bail to be opposed. I got Lenny to sign CRM 14. He said his sister would know what his National Insurance Number was.

Based on my brief perusal of the Initial Disclosure of the Prosecution's Case, the evidence linking Lenny to the burglary would appear to be based on admissions in interview and eye-witness evidence. A second person is suspected of being involved in the burglary but no charges have been brought against this individual. I managed to speak briefly with Lenny's sister who waiting outside the courtroom. She was concerned for her brother. She informed me he had a mental health condition for which he needed to take regular medication. She said he had been out of trouble for a while and thought he was doing OK. He had a flat of his own and she kept in contact with him. I informed the CPS lawyer that Lenny would be denying the offence and that I would be seeking a brief adjournment as my client was too unwell to provide me with firm instructions. The CPS lawyer indicated that he would not oppose my application for an adjournment but that bail would be opposed.

Attending before Lyme Magistrates and requesting a 7 day brief adjournment as my client was appearing in custody having been unrepresented at the police station and was clearly unwell. I confirmed that my client had mental health problems and that I needed to take his full instructions before being in a position to advise on plea. The application was not opposed by the CPS. Some pressure was placed on me as regards TSJ but I stood my ground and said given the serious nature of the accusation and in the interests of fairness, I needed to take clear and firm instructions. The adjournment was granted. The CPS then opposed bail. An application for bail was made by me. I explained that I had reservations about the strength of the evidence based on what had been disclosed to me and limited instructions. I asked the Bench to look carefully at Lenny's record and confirmed a fixed address and the fact that his sister was in court. Bail refused on the grounds of risk of absconding and commission of further offences. The case was adjourned for one week. Mr Wise was remanded to HMP Shawbury. **Date of next hearing is 27 March.**

I spoke to Lenny afterwards—he was clearly agitated and somewhat bewildered. I explained he could apply for bail to the Crown Court but that I would be able to reapply for bail before the Magistrates' Court in one week's time. If bail was refused on that occasion we could apply to the Crown Court. He agreed to this course of action. I explained that I or a member of my firm would be visiting him on remand in the next couple of days to take his full instructions.

Time engaged:
Considering IDPC: 10 minutes
Attending client: 20 minutes
Attending client's sister: 10 minutes
Advocacy: 30 minutes

DOCUMENT 2 INITIAL DISCLOSURE OF PROSECUTION CASE PLUS PREVIOUS CONVICTIONS RECORDED AGAINST LENNY WISE

DEFENCE COPY

INITIAL DISCLOSURE OF PROSECUTION CASE

One copy per defendant

R v Lenny WISE

LC\2928449T

Lyme Magistrates Court

Date: 20th March

ANTICPATED PLEA –GUILTY

Every file requires **(Tick if attached)**

x	MG5 Case Summary
x	All Key Witness MG11's **(no backs)**

Where Applicable (Tick if attached)

x	MG4 Charge sheet
	MG8 Breach of bail form
	MG15 Summary of interview (if not on MG5)
	MG 18 T.I.C. forms
	MGDDA/B
x	Defendant's pre-cons (Court/Defence print)
	CCTV (1 working copy per defendant)
	Copy of any order e.g. restraining/football banning

POLICE REPORT (MG 5)

| | URN | 21 | TL | 4256 | 12 |

Defendant 1: Lenny Wise	Anticipated plea: Guilty
Defendant 2:	Anticipated plea: - select -

1. **Summary of the Key Evidence**—'Key evidence' establishes every element of the offence and that the defendant committed the offence with the necessary criminal intent.

   - Set out the facts in chronological order, telling the story and covering the 'points to prove'
   - The summary must be balanced and fair
   - Record address and contact details of civilian witnesses on MG9 (and *all dates to avoid on MG10*).

Key evidence: The offence alleged is domestic dwelling-house burglary at 19 Sunrise Road, Lyme on the 17th March between 11.15am-12.15pm.

Key witness(es) and their role (e.g. eye witness, person providing identity):

Lillian KENNEDY: (victim of the burglary). When returning home from collecting her pension she was approached by a black male who offered to help her carry her shopping. She declined help. She describes this male as being tall and thin with black, straggling hair and wearing a black top and white training shoes. Approximately 20 or 30 minutes later, KENNEDY answers her front door to another male individual who engages her in conversation and asks to use her telephone. During this time, a second male who KENNEDY does not see enters her bungalow via the back door and steals her handbag containing her purse and £75. KENNEDY only discovers the theft when she is alerted by her neighbour LEWIS. KENNEDY identified the defendant as being the black male who had approached her earlier whilst being taken on a tour of the immediate area by police. KENNEDY was unable to identify the defendant from a VIPER later that day.

Shirley LEWIS: (eye-witness). At midday approximately on the 17 March, LEWIS is pegging out some washing in her back garden when she observes a male in the back garden of KENNEDY'S bungalow. Witness describes the male as being Afro-Caribbean, 5 ft 8 inches tall, wearing a black hooded sweatshirt and white training shoes. LEWIS has previously seen this individual in the local area on other occasions. LEWIS identified the defendant at a VIPER later that day.

Harold FINNEY: (neighbour). Unable to identify the defendant. Will say that he observed a black car (registration number taken—car is registered to Lloyd Green) in Sunrise Road at around midday on the 17th March and witnessed a black male approach the car, wearing a black top and a pair of white trainers. The male is described as being in his twenties with long, dark hair.

Steven FARRINGTON: (arresting officer). Will say that he attended the scene of the burglary and took a statement from KENNEDY. Took KENNEDY on a tour of the immediate area whereupon KENNEDY identified an Afro-Caribbean black male (WISE) as being the male who had approached her near her property earlier that day. The male was identified by DC SHAW as being Lenny WISE. He was observed as being of Afro-Caribbean decent, 5' 10" with shoulder-length dreadlock hair and a slight beard, wearing brown training shoes and black hooded sweatshirt. WISE not arrested until the following day 18th March at 4a Lymewood Court. Will state that a s.32 PACE 1984 search of defendant's address was undertaken and a pair of white Nike training shoes and a black hooded sweatshirt were seized. A small quantity of cannabis resin was found in WISE's trouser pocket.

Officer also arrested and interviewed Lloyd GREEN (suspected accomplice) on the 18th March. GREEN was later released on police bail. He has not been charged.

State value of property stolen or damaged (or recovered). (See Sec 9 for recording compensation details): Theft of handbag and purse-pension money £75.

2. **Defendant Interview**

   - Set out the explanation given by defendant as to **how/why offence happened**: include any **mitigation/remorse** put forward.
   - Note any **Special Warnings** given.

- State if no comment made.
- Attach copy of CCTV if shown in the interview **(to file).**

Defendant: **Lenny Wise**

Date of interview: 20/3

Interviewing officer(s): DS 4291 Farrington/ DC 2890 Sarah Shaw

Other person(s) present: None

Summary of defendant explanation: Questions put to WISE as to his whereabouts on the morning of the 17 March. Largely incoherent replies. Unable to offer alibi. Denied white training shoes seized from his flat belonged to him. Admits to knowing Lloyd GREEN.

Defendant's response/reaction to CCTV (if 'key evidence' and shown in I/V): N/A

Relevant admissions and their start/finish counter reference times:

Admission of involvement in the burglary at 44 minutes and 6 seconds. 'I stole it from the old lady, I needed the money . . .'. Refuses to identify accomplice.

---

3. **Non Key Evidence**—list witnesses present but not 'key'. State what evidence they contribute e.g. additional eye witness, arresting officer, charging officer; officer seizing CCTV. Record contact details of civilian witnesses on MG9 and dates to avoid on MG10.

Name of non-key witness(es) and their role:

Carol Jayne Lawton (SOCO)—processed crime scene and recovered several shoe marks. Confirms secure packaging and continuity of search/forensic samples.

DC 2890 Sarah Shaw—able to identify male pointed out by KENNEDY as being WISE based on previous dealings with this individual. Present during the interviews.

---

4. **Visually Recorded Evidence**—CCTV, photos, mobile phone(s). Attach a copy (*identify playback format*). Custody suite CCTV should be included as unused material unless 'key evidence'.

Is there VRE? No   If 'Yes', does it provide 'key evidence? - select -

Give details of what it shows (whether 'key' or not) and include tape counter reference times for relevant key sections (*i.e. defendant punching victim/kicking window*).

---

5. **Injuries**—a medical statement is **NOT** required unless needed to interpret x-rays or describe injuries not visible to the naked eye. Victim(s)/eye witness/police officer should **describe any visible injuries,** photos should be taken and attached (if not taken/attached, state why).

Description of injuries: Not applicable

---

6. **Forensic Evidence**—fingerprints, drugs evidence (weight, number of wraps, etc.). Include details such as street value and purity as this is essential for sentencing information. State if drugs field tested and by whom. State timescales for a full forensic statement (if required).

White training shoes recovered from WISE's flat have been sent for forensic comparison with shoe marks recovered from crime scene. Full report expected within 7 days.

---

7. **DIP testing**—attach DT2 for prosecutor.

Def. 1: Tested? ☐   Trigger off.: ☐   Result: (pos/neg) - select -   Drug: - select -

Def. 2: Tested? ☐   Trigger off.: ☐   Result: (pos/neg) - select -   Drug: - select -

---

8. **Application for Order(s) on Conviction**—consider applying for an order on conviction, e.g. compensation, forfeiture/destruction (see order list).

Defendant:

Order(s) applied for: - select -

9. **Application for Compensation**—state if an estimate. Attach quotes/receipts if available. An address for compensation must be provided on MG6. (*If more than one victim/defendant, list one after the other and give details in the description box*).

Defendant: Lenny Wise   Victim: Lillian Kennedy

Description of injury/loss and or damage:

Amount of compensation applied for: £120   Has an MG19 been sent to victim?: Yes

10.   Other: MG18 (TICs)? ☐   **Pre-cons/cautions attached ?** Y☐   MG6? ☐

11. **Officer's certification:** I certify that to the best of my knowledge and belief, I have not withheld any material that might reasonably be expected to undermine the prosecution or might reasonably assist the defence in early preparation of their case, including the making of a bail application. I further certify that relevant material has been recorded and retained in accordance with the CPIA 1996, Code of Practice, as amended.

Name & rank/job title: DS 4291 Steven Farrington

Date:

12. **Supervisor's certification:** The information in parts 1–9 is an accurate summary of the available evidence and complies with the DPP's guidance for a Streamlined Process. The file has been built to the required standard.

Name & rank/job title: DI 4565 TAPP

Signature: D. Tapp   Date: 20/3/

DOCUMENT 2 WITNESS STATEMENT (LILLIAN KENNEDY)

Form MG11

RESTRICTED (when complete)

WITNESS STATEMENT

(CJ Act 1967, s. 9; MC Act 1980, s. 5A(3)(a) and s. 5B; Criminal Procedure Rules 2011, Rule 27.1)

URN				

Statement of: *Lillian Kennedy*

Age if under 18 (if over 18 insert 'over 18'): *Over 18* Occupation: *Retired*

Title: *Mrs* (Mr/Mrs etc...)   Collar/ID Number: ....

This statement (consisting of ...3... page(s) signed each by me) is true to the best of my knowledge and belief and I make it knowing that if it is tendered in evidence I shall be liable to prosecution if I have wilfully stated in it anything which I know to be false or do not believe to be true.

Signature: *L Kennedy*   Date: *18/3/—*

Tick if witness evidence is visually recorded ☐

I live at number 19 Sunrise Road, Lyme. I
am 85 years old. On Tuesday 17th March, I
went to fetch my pension from Lyme High Street
I drew £95. Once I had paid my weekly sums
for gas and electricity I was left with around
£75. I returned home at around 11am. As I
was walking up the road, a man approached me
and asked me if I wanted any help with my
shopping. I told him, no thank you. I would describe
him as being quite tall and thin. He had a gaunt
face, was black and had long, black straggling
hair and a small beard on his chin. I think
he was wearing a short, dark coloured top
and a pair of white sports shoes. I saw

Signature: *L Kennedy*   Signature Witnessed by: *S/...*

RESTRICTED (when complete)

Form MG11 cont

Continuation of Statement of: Lillian Kennedy

him walk off into the fields near the back of my house.

I know I had my purse with me when I went into my house, because a friend of mine called in for ten minutes shortly after I got back from the Post Office. She had her grandchild with her and I gave her a pound from my purse. A short time after this I was putting some rubbish out when I thought I heard the telephone ringing. When I come in, I realised it was my front door bell I answered the door. There was a man standing there. I have never seen this man before. He was white but had a tanned complexion. He was dressed smartly, wearing a suit and tie. He was quite bald. He was not very tall. I recall he was wearing dark glasses. He told me his car had broken down and asked

Signature: L Kennedy   Signature witnessed by: ...

RESTRICTED (when complete)

Form MG11 cont

Page No: 3 of 3

Continuation of Statement of: Lillian Kennedy

if he could use the telephone. I told him he could not as I did not have a phone. Not long after this, a friend of my neighbour came round. She told me she had seen a man in my back garden and that my back door was open. I immediately checked my handbag and saw that my purse was missing. She telephoned the police. I realised that I had left my back door open when I came to answer the front door. It was silly of me. The only money I get is my pension. The theft has left me shaken and frightened. Later in the afternoon of 14th March, the police took me around the local area in one of their cars. They asked me if I could see the man who had knocked on my front door. I could not see the man who had called, but I did see the man who had offered to help me with my shopping earlier that morning. The police car stopped outside the Co-op on the High Street. I had a good look at the man and I am sure it was him.

Signature: E Kennedy   Signature witnessed by:

DOCUMENT 2 WITNESS STATEMENT (SHIRLEY LEWIS)

Form MG11

RESTRICTED (when complete)

WITNESS STATEMENT

(CJ Act 1967, s. 9; MC Act 1980, s. 5A(3)(a) and s. 5B; Criminal Procedure Rules 2011, Rule 27.1)

URN [ ] [ ] [ ]

Statement of: *Shirley Lewis*

Age if under 18 (if over 18 insert 'over 18'): *Over 18*   Occupation: *Retired Teacher*

Title: *Mrs* (Mr/Mrs etc...)   Collar/ID Number: ....

This statement (consisting of..*3*... page(s) signed each by me) is true to the best of my knowledge and belief and I make it knowing that if it is tendered in evidence I shall be liable to prosecution if I have wilfully stated in it anything which I know to be false or do not believe to be true.

Signature: *Shirley Lewis*   Date: *18/3*

Tick if witness evidence is visually recorded [ ]

On Tuesday the 17th March, I was visiting my elderly aunt at 19 Sunrise Road, Lyme. She lives next door to Lillian Kennedy at number 17. At around midday on 17th March, I went out the back of my aunt's property to bring some washing in that was pegged up on the washing line. The time was around midday.

I was facing Lillian's back garden. A low wall divides the gardens, it being largely open plan. I saw a man in her garden. I watched him for a good few seconds.

Signature: *Shirley Lewis*   Signature Witnessed by: *[signature]*

RESTRICTED (when complete)

Form MG11 cont

Page No:..2..of.....3

Continuation of Statement of:...

In fact, I nearly called out to him, to ask what he thought he was doing, but something stopped me. He didn't see me because I was behind a large sheet pegged on the line. I do not know where he came from but I watched him wander out of Lillian's garden and off down the back lane. At this point, I noticed the back door to Mrs Kennedy's house was wide open.

I would describe the man as being of Afro-Caribbean origin. He was about 5" 8/9 inches tall. He was of slim build and was wearing a black hooded sweat shirt with the hood up, so I could not see his hair. The man I saw was wearing a pair

Signature:.................................Signature witnessed by:.......................

RESTRICTED (when complete)

Form MG11 cont

Page No: 3 of 3

Continuation of Statement of:...

of white training shoes. I
went round to see Lillian
almost straightaway and she
told me that her purse was
missing. I am certain I would be
able to recognise the man again.
I had the distinct feeling I had
seen the man before. In fact I
have seen him walking his dog,
a brown and white terrier, in the
grassy area nearby on more than
one occasion.

Signature: .... Signature witnessed by: ....

DOCUMENT 2 PRINT OF PNC RECORD-PNCID: 005/6593V

Print For: WISE, LENNY

Date of Birth: 27/6/-

Date	Court	Offence/s	Sentence
10 years previous	Lyme Youth Court	Burglary (non-domestic dwelling)	Supervision Order (12 months)
7 years previous	Lyme Magistrates	Theft	Conditional Discharge (12 months)
5 years previous (February)	Blurton Magistrates	Theft Possession of amphetamine Driving without insurance	Community Order with supervision (15 months)/Licence endorsed
5 years previous (December)	Lyme Magistrates	Burglary (non-domestic dwelling) Possession of class B drug/Resisting constable/Failure to surrender/Breach community order 'Offences committed on bail'	Custody 5 months concurrent
4 years previous	Chorley Magistrates	Possession of class B drug/Theft Obtaining property by deception	Community Rehabilitation Order with supervision (12 months)
3 years previous (August)	Lyme Crown Court	Burglary (domestic dwelling) Possession of class A drug/Failure to surrender	Custody 12 months concurrent
2 years previous (April)	Blurton Magistrates	Theft/Possession of class B drug 'Offences committed on bail'	Custody 4 months concurrent + unexpired term 108 days
18 months previous	Lyme Magistrates	s. 4 Public Order Act 1986 Common Assault	Community Order with supervision (24 months)

DOCUMENT 4 ATTENDANCE NOTE

Date: 24th March

Attending Lenny in an interview room at Shawbury Remand Centre. I took him through the Initial Disclosure of the Prosecution's Case I had been served with. I took a detailed statement from him and obtained written authorisation to contact his consultant psychiatrist. I explained the prosecution's case against him and what would happen at his next appearance. I explained the credit available for a guilty plea. Based on his instructions, I advised Lenny to plead not guilty. I discussed venue for trial and his chances of securing bail at his second appearance and possible appeal to a Crown Court judge in chambers if it was further refused. I explained that I would be seeking further disclosure of evidence from the CPS (including the taped interview and custody record plus a DVD copy of the parade) and that I would be sending him a client care letter and his proof of evidence which I needed him to read through and sign. I explained I would go through it all again with him at court on the 27th March.

Time engaged:
Travel: 70 minutes
Waiting: 15 minutes
Attendance: 1 hour

DOCUMENT 5 APPLICATION FOR REPRESENTATION ORDER—CRM14

Form © Legal Services Commission 2018. Reproduced with kind permission of the Legal Aid Agency. The most recent versions of all such forms are held on the LAA's website.

Application for Legal Aid in Criminal Proceedings

Form **CRM14**

Legal Aid Agency

ⓘ Please use the Guidance
If you do not complete the form correctly, we will return it.
You will find Guidance to help you fill in the form correctly, at: www.justice.gov.uk/forms/legal-aid-agency/criminal-forms/applications
If you need more help or advice, please contact a solicitor.

Protect - Personal
(see question 32)

MAAT Reference
(for official use)

For the Legal Representative's use

If the case is an **Appeal to the Crown Court** and there is no change in circumstances, answer **1** and then go to question **23**.

Case type
- [ ] Summary
- [x] Either way
- [ ] Indictable
- [ ] Appeal to Crown Court and no changes
- [ ] Committal for sentence
- [ ] Appeal to Crown Court
- [ ] Trial now in Crown Court

The court hearing the case
Lyme Magistrates Court

Priority case
- [x] Custody
- [ ] Vulnerable
- [ ] Youth
- [ ] Late application in the Crown Court for trial
Date of trial

About you: 1

1
ⓘ GUIDANCE

Mr Mrs Miss Ms Other title — [x]
Your forenames or other names (in BLOCK LETTERS): LENNY

Your surname or family name (in BLOCK LETTERS): WISE
Your date of birth: 27 / 6 /

National Insurance Number: F R 8 2 8 5 3 1 Y
Application Registration Card (ARC) Number:

National Insurance Number and ARC Number: give one of these only.

- [x] This is a new application.
- [ ] This application relates to a change of financial circumstances.

Contacting you

2
Do you have a usual home address?
- [ ] No
- [x] Yes ⟶ Your usual home address
4al Lymewood Court, Parkdale, Lyme, Lymeshire, LY4 97Y
Postcode

3
✓ 'Your solicitor's address only, if you are of 'No Fixed Abode', or not at your usual address because you are on bail or remand.

To what address should we write to you?
- [ ] Your usual home address (the address in 2)
- [x] Your solicitor's address (see the side note)
- [ ] This address
Postcode

4
Your email address

5 _____ Your telephone number (landline)

Mobile phone number
050069734

Work phone number

About you: 2

6 _____
✓ one box and if it is 'someone else's home', give your relationship to that person

Your usual home address is:

☑ a Tenancy (rented)　☐ Temporary　☐ Your parent's home (you live with them)

☐ Someone else's home ⟶ Your relationship

Owned by:　☐ You　☐ Your partner　☐ You and your partner, jointly

7 _____

Are you under 18 years old?

☑ No　☐ Yes ⟶ Are you charged with an adult?

☐ No: Go to **23**　☐ Yes: Go to **23**

8 _____
①GUIDANCE

Do you have a partner?

☑ No: Go to **9**　☐ Yes: Go to **10**

9 _____
✓ one box

①GUIDANCE

You are:　☑ Single: Go to **14**　☐ Widowed: Go to **14**

☐ Divorced or have dissolved a civil partnership: Go to **14**

☐ Separated ⟶ Date of separation?

Go to **14**

10 _____
✓ one box

You and your partner are:

☐ Married or in a Civil Partnership　☐ Cohabiting or living together

About your partner

11 _____

①GUIDANCE

Your partner's details

Mr Mrs Miss Ms Other title　Your forenames or other names (in BLOCK LETTERS)

☐ ☐ ☐ ☐

Surname or family name (in BLOCK LETTERS)　Date of birth

National Insurance Number and ARC Number: give one of these only.

National Insurance Number　Application Registration Card (ARC) Number

12 _____
If you ✓ **Yes**, and your partner is a victim, prosecution witness, or co-defendant with a conflict of interest, do not give your partner's details for questions **13** to **22**.

Is your partner a victim, prosecution witness or a co-defendant in the case for which you require legal aid?

☐ No　☐ Yes ⟶ ☐ Victim: Go to **14**

☐ Prosecution witness: Go to **14**

☐ Co-defendant ⟶ Does your partner have a conflict of interest?

☐ No: Go to **13**　☐ Yes: Go to **14**

13 Is your partner's usual home address different from yours (the address at question 2)?

☐ No ☐ Yes ⟶ Your partner's usual home address

Postcode

Your income and your partner's income

14 Do you or your partner receive any of the benefits listed here?

GUIDANCE

In this form, if you answer Yes to any question which asks about you or your partner, and you can answer Yes for both of you, give details for you and your partner, not for one of you only.

☐ No ☑ Yes ⟶ **You**   **Your Partner**

Income Support ☐ Go to **23**   ☐ Go to **23**

Income-Related Employment and Support Allowance (ESA) ☐ Go to **23**   ☐ Go to **23**

Income-Based Jobseeker's Allowance (JSA) ☑ When did you last sign on?   ☐ When did you last sign on?

13 / 3 /

Go to **23**   Go to **23**

Guarantee State Pension Credit ☐ Go to **23**   ☐ Go to **23**

15 Do you or your partner, together, in a year have a total income from all sources before tax or any other deduction, of more than £12, 475 (£239.90 a week)?

GUIDANCE

☑ No: Go to **16** ☐ Yes ⟶ You will need to **complete form CRM15**: Go to **23**

16 Sources of income for you and your partner. Please give details in the table:

EVIDENCE

GUIDANCE
about:
- Employment
- Total of other benefits
- Other source of income

For all parts of this question:
- If you do not receive income from a source, put **NIL** after the '£'.
- After '**every**' put either:
  week,
  2 weeks,
  4 weeks,
  month,
  or year.

	You	Your Partner
Employment (wage or salary)	£　　　every ☐ Before tax ☐ After tax	£　　　every ☐ Before tax ☐ After tax
Child Benefit	£　　　every	£　　　every
Working Tax Credits and Child Tax credits	£　　　every	£　　　every
Universal Credit	£　　　every	£　　　every
Total of other benefits	£　　　every	£　　　every
Maintenance income	£　　　every	£　　　every
Pensions	£　　　every	£　　　every
Any other source of income such as: - a student grant or loan - board or rent from a family member, lodger or tenant, or rent from a property - financial support from friends and family	£　　　every Source:	£　　　every Source:

17   Are you or your partner self-employed, in a business partnership, or
either a company director or a shareholder in a private company?

(!) GUIDANCE   ☐ No   ☐ Yes ⟶ You will need to **complete form CRM15**: Go to **23**

18   Do you or your partner have any income, savings or assets which
are under a restraint order or a freezing order?

☐ No   ☐ Yes ⟶ You will need to **complete form CRM15**: Go to **23**

19   Are you charged with a Summary offence, only?

(!) GUIDANCE   ☐ No   ☐ Yes: Go to **22**

20   Do you or your partner own or part-own any land or property of any kind,
including **your own home**, in the United Kingdom or overseas?

☐ No   ☐ Yes ⟶ You will need to **complete form CRM15**: Go to **23**

21   Do you or your partner have any savings or investments,
in the United Kingdom or overseas?

(!) GUIDANCE   ☐ No   ☐ Yes ⟶ You will need to **complete form CRM15**: Go to **23**

22   Do your answers to the previous questions tell us that you have no income from any of
the sources which we have asked about?

☐ No   ☐ Yes ⟶ How do you and your partner pay your bills and daily expenses?

```



```

Information for the Interests of Justice test

23   What charges have been brought against you?

(!) GUIDANCE

Describe the
charge briefly:
for instance,
'Assault on a
neighbour'.

Charge	Date of offence
1 DOMESTIC DWELLING HOUSE BURGLARY	17 / 3 /
2	
3	
4	

24   The type of offence with which you are charged

(!) GUIDANCE
✓ one box only.
If you are charged
with two or more
offences, ✓ the
most serious.

☐ Class A: Homicide and related grave offences

☐ Class B: Offences involving serious violence or damage, and serious drugs offences

☐ Class C: Lesser offences involving violence or damage, and less serious drugs offences

☐ Class D: Sexual offences and offences against children ⟶

☑ Class E: Burglary etc

☐ Class F: Other offences of dishonesty (specified offences and offences where
the value is £30,000 or less)

☐ Class G: Other offences of dishonesty (specified offences and offences where
the value involved exceeds £30,000 but does not exceed £100,000)

☐ Class H: Miscellaneous other offences

☐ Class I: Offences against public justice and similar offences

☐ Class J: Serious sexual offences

☐ Class K: Other offences of dishonesty (high value: if the value involved exceeds £100,000)

25   **Do you have any co-defendants in this case?**

☑ No: Go to **27**   ☐ Yes ⟶ Their names

26   **Is there any reason why you and your co-defendants cannot be represented by
the same solicitor?**

☐ No   ☐ Yes ⟶ The reason(s)

27   **Are there any other criminal cases or charges against you or your partner which
are still in progress?**

☑ No   ☐ Yes ⟶ You   Your Partner

The charges

The Court hearing the case

Date of the next hearing

28   **Which Court is hearing the case for which you need legal aid?**

The Court hearing the case	Date of the hearing
LYME MAGISTRATES COURT	20 / 3 /

29

ⓘGUIDANCE

1 to **9** are possible reasons.

We suggest you choose one or more reasons with the help of a solicitor.

For each reason you choose, say why you have chosen it.

Mention any evidence that supports your choice of a reason.

If you need more space to answer, please use a separate sheet of paper and put your full name, date of birth and 'Question 29' at the top of the sheet. Please make sure you show which part of the question (**1** to **10**) your writing refers to.

Why do you want legal aid?

1 It is likely that I will lose my liberty if any matter in the proceedings is decided against me.

> SEE SEPARATE SHEET

2 I have been given a sentence that is suspended or non-custodial. If I break this, the court may be able to deal with me for the original offence.

> SEE SEPARATE SHEET

3 It is likely that I will lose my livelihood.

4 It is likely that I will suffer serious damage to my reputation.

5 A substantial question of law may be involved (whether arising from legislation, judicial authority or other source of law).

> SEE SEPARATE SHEET

6 I may not be able to understand the court proceedings or present my own case.

> SEE SEPARATE SHEET

7 Witnesses may need to be traced or interviewed on my behalf.

> SEE SEPARATE SHEET

8 The proceedings may involve expert cross-examination of a prosecution witness (whether an expert or not).

> SEE SEPARATE SHEET

9 It is in the interests of another person (such as the person making a complaint or other witness) that I am represented.

> SEE SEPARATE SHEET

10 Any other reason

Legal representation

30

ⓘ GUIDANCE

You must tell the solicitor that you have said in this form that you want them to act for you.

The solicitor who you want to act for you

Mr Mrs Miss Ms Other title ☐ ☐ ☐ ☑ ☐ Solicitor's initials, surname or family name (IN BLOCK LETTERS)

RACHEL JAMES

Name and address of the solicitor's firm

HANNIBAL AND MOUNTFORD
20 HIGH STREET
LYME BANK
LYME
LY 82 P

Postcode

Telephone (land line)	Mobile phone
01342220555	065009788

Document Exchange (DX)	Fax
DX 56499	

email address

31

✓ **1** or **2**
If you choose **2**, ✓ one of the two other options to show whether you have been instructed by a firm with an LAA contract, or by a solicitor employed by the LAA. Examples of an LAA contract are the 2010 Standard Crime Contract or an Individual Case Contract.

Declaration by the legal representative

1 ☑ I represent the applicant. I confirm that I am authorised to provide representation under a contract issued by the Legal Aid Agency (LAA).

2 ☐ I represent the applicant. I confirm that I have been instructed to provide representation by:

☑ a firm which holds a contract issued by the Legal Aid Agency (LAA).

☐ a solicitor employed by the Legal Aid Agency (LAA) in the Public Defender Service who is authorised to provide representation.

Signed	Date	Provider's LAA Account Number
	20 / 3 / —	Y 5 6 8 8 D

Full name (in BLOCK LETTERS)

RACHEL JAMES

About the information which you have provided and its protection

32

ⓘ GUIDANCE
The guidance explains how we protect and use the information which you provide in our forms or in other ways.

- The information which you give when you answer this question (which continues on page 8), will be treated in the strictest confidence and will not affect our decision on this application.

- We, or HM Courts and Tribunals Service, may use the information on this form and on forms CRM15 and CRM15C, for statistical monitoring or research. The information we publish will not identify you or anyone else. We will process the information according to the Data Protection Act 1998 and other legal requirements.

1 Are you male or female?

☑ Male ☐ Female ☐ I prefer not to say

2

✓ one box in the table to show the best definition of your disability.

The Equality Act 2010 defines disability as: 'A physical or mental impairment which has a substantial and long-term adverse effect on a person's ability to carry out normal day-to-day activities'.

3

✓ one box in the table of ethnic groups.

2 Do you consider that you have a disability?

☐ No ☑ Yes ⟶ The best definition is:

☑ Mental health condition   ☐ Mobility impairment   ☐ Other

☐ Learning disability or difficulty   ☐ Long-standing physical illness or health condition   ☐ I prefer not to say

☐ Hearing impaired   ☐ Visually impaired

☐ Deaf   ☐ Blind

3 Which of the options in the table best describes you?

White	Mixed	Asian or Asian British	Black or Black British	
☐ British	☑ White and Black Caribbean	☐ Indian	☐ Black Caribbean	☐ Chinese
☐ Irish	☐ White and Black African	☐ Pakistani	☐ Black African	☐ Gypsy or Traveller
☐ White other	☐ White and Asian	☐ Bangladeshi	☐ Black other	☐ Other
	☐ Mixed other	☐ Asian other		☐ I prefer not to say

Evidence to support the information which you have given

33

Have you been directed to complete a form CRM15 (see questions 15, 17, 18, 20 and 21)?

☑ No   ☐ Yes ⟶ If you have a partner, now go to **38**. If not, go to **39**.

34

Has a court remanded you in custody?

☐ No: Go to **36**   ☑ Yes: Go to **35**

35

Will your case be heard in a magistrates' court?

☑ No   ☐ Yes ⟶ If you have a partner, now go to **38**. If not, go to **39**.

36

ⓘ EVIDENCE

ⓘ EVIDENCE

Are you employed?

☑ No   ☐ Yes ⟶ ▪ **If your case will be heard in a magistrates' court, or it is a committal for sentence or appeal to the Crown Court**
We need a copy of your wage slip or salary advice. You must provide it with this form: see the guidance about evidence.

▪ **If your case will be heard in the Crown Court**
We need a copy of your wage slip or salary advice. You must provide it with this form or within 14 days of the date of your application: see the guidance about evidence.

37

If you have a partner, now go to **38**. If you do not have a partner, go to **39**.

Declaration by your partner

38

⚠ GUIDANCE
If your partner is not able to sign this declaration, you must give the reason at the end of question **39**.

I declare that this form and any form CRM15 and CRM15C is a true statement of all my financial circumstances to the best of my knowledge and belief. I agree to the Legal Aid Agency and HM Courts & Tribunals Service, or my partner's solicitor, checking the information I have given, with the Department for Work and Pensions, HM Revenue and Customs or other people and organisations. I authorise those people and organisations to provide the information for which the Legal Aid Agency, HM Courts and Tribunals Service or my partner's solicitor may ask.

I have read the **Notice of Fraud** at the end of question **39**.

Signed	Date

Full name (in BLOCK LETTERS)

Declaration by you

39

When you read this declaration, keep in mind that some parts of it may not apply to you because the declaration is designed to cover several types of court case.

I apply for the right to representation for the purposes of criminal proceedings under the Legal Aid, Sentencing and Punishment of Offenders Act 2012.

I declare that this form and any form CRM15 and CRM15C is a true statement of my financial circumstances and those of my partner to the best of my knowledge and belief. I understand that this form must be fully completed before a Representation Order can be issued. I understand that if I tell you anything that is not true on this form or the documents I send with it, or leave anything out:

- I may be prosecuted for fraud. I understand that if I am convicted, I may be sent to prison or pay a fine.
- My legal aid may be stopped and I may be asked to pay back my costs in full to the Legal Aid Agency.
- If my case is in the Crown Court, the Legal Aid Agency may change the amount of the contribution which I must pay.

Crown Court I understand that in Crown Court proceedings the information I have given in this form will be used to determine whether I am eligible for legal aid and, if so, whether I am liable to contribute to the costs of my defence under an Income Contribution Order during my case, or if I am convicted, under a Final Contribution Order at the end of my case, or both.

I understand that if I am ordered to pay towards my legal aid under an Income Contribution Order, or if I am convicted and ordered to pay under a Final Contribution Order, but fail to pay as an Order instructs me, interest may be charged or enforcement proceedings may be brought against me, or both.

I understand that I may have to pay the costs of the enforcement proceedings in addition to the payments required under the Contribution Order, and that the enforcement proceedings could result in a charge being placed on my home.

Evidence I agree to provide, when asked, further details and evidence of my finances and those of my partner, to the Legal Aid Agency, its agents, or HM Courts & Tribunals Service to help them decide whether an Order should be made and its terms.

Changes I agree to tell the Legal Aid Agency or HM Courts & Tribunals Service if my income or capital or those of my partner, change. These changes include the sale of property, change of address, change in employment and change in capital. ⟶

It is important that you understand that by signing this declaration you agree to the Legal Aid Agency, the courts, or your solicitor, contacting your partner to check the information that you have given in this form, and in forms CRM15 and CRM15C, if you complete them.	**Enquiries**	I authorise such enquiries as are considered necessary to enable the Legal Aid Agency, its agents, HM Courts & Tribunals Service, or my solicitor to find out my income and capital, and those of my partner. This includes my consent for parties such as my bank, building society, the Department for Work and Pensions, the Driver and Vehicle Licensing Agency or HM Revenue and Customs to provide information to assist the Legal Aid Agency, it's agents or HM Courts & Tribunals Service with their enquiries.

I consent to the Legal Aid Agency or my solicitor contacting my partner for information and evidence about my partner's means. This includes circumstances where my partner is unable to sign or complete the form.

I understand that if the information which my partner provides is incorrect, or if my partner refuses to provide information, then: if my case is in the magistrates' court, my legal aid may be withdrawn or, if my case is in the Crown Court, I may be liable to sanctions. I understand that the sanctions may result in me paying towards the cost of my legal aid or, if I already pay, paying more towards the cost of my legal aid, or paying my legal aid costs in full.

Ending legal aid I understand that I must tell my solicitor and write to the court if I no longer want public representation. I understand that if I decline representation I may be liable for costs incurred to the date when my solicitor and the court receive my letter.

Data sharing I agree that, if I am convicted, the information in this form will be used by HMCTS or designated officer to determine the appropriate level of any financial penalty ordered against me, and for its collection and enforcement.

Notice on fraud If false or inaccurate information is provided and fraud is identified, details will be passed to fraud prevention agencies to prevent fraud and money laundering.

Further details explaining how the information held by fraud prevention agencies may be used can be found in the 'Fair Processing Notice', available on the Legal Aid Agency website at: www.justice.gov.uk/legal-aid/make-an-application

Signed	Date
L Wise	20.3 —

Full name (in BLOCK LETTERS)

LENNY WISE

If your partner has not signed the declaration at **38**, please explain:

Official use

Interests of Justice test

Consider all the available details of all the charges, against the Interests of Justice criteria.

Mention issues here which you considered when you decided the application. Include information given orally.

I have performed the Interests of Justice test for case number: 4 2 9 5 1 0 0 R J M H 4 9 3 0

☑ The application is **passed**   ☐ The application is **refused.** My reason(s):

Signed	Name of the appropriate officer	Date
[signature]	JOHN GOODWIN	20/3/—

Financial eligibility for

Magistrates' Court ☑ Passed   ☐ Refused

Crown Court ☐ Refused: Ineligible

☑ Granted: No income contribution

☐ Granted: Contribution of £ [   ]

Signed	Name of the appropriate officer	Date
[signature]	JOHN GOODWIN	20 / 3 / —

CRM 14 application: LENNY WISE: DOB: 27/6/-

Question 29-additional amplification

Reason 1

I am charged with domestic dwelling house burglary. Aggravating features of the offence include the fact that the victim is an 84 year old vulnerable woman who was tricked into giving access to her home. I have previous convictions of a similar nature. Based on the magistrates' court sentencing guidelines I am likely to be committed for sentence to the Crown Court where I am at risk of a custodial term in excess of twelve months.

Reason 2

I am subject to a community order for an offence of common assault. It was imposed eighteen months ago and has six months left to run for which I stand to be re-sentenced if convicted of the burglary charge.

Reason 5

I intend to challenge the admissibility of statements I made during interview at the police station under sections 76 and 78 PACE 1984. I was unrepresented at the police station and have a diagnosed mental illness. I felt unwell during my police interview and do not believe it was conducted in accordance with my rights.

Reason 6

I have diagnosed bipolar depression for which I take prescribed medication. I am subject to mood swings and cannot concentrate for long periods of time.

Reason 7

I believe I was at a betting shop when the offence occurred. My solicitors need to make enquiries of the staff in the shop to see if my presence at somewhere other than the crime scene at the relevant time can be established.

Reason 8

I intend to plead not guilty. There are several elderly eye-witnesses who identify me as being involved. They are all mistaken and need to be carefully cross-examined. The case against me also involves forensic expert evidence which I intend to challenge. The custody officers and investigating officers need to be cross-examined to enable me to challenge the admissibility of evidence obtained at the police station.

Reason 9

The eye-witnesses and the victim of the burglary are all elderly and therefore vulnerable. Each needs to be cross-examined.

Reason 10

The case is likely to be heard in the Crown Court due to the serious nature of the offence. I need to obtain an expert psychiatric report to assist my defence at trial.

DOCUMENT 6 PROOF OF EVIDENCE OF LENNY WISE

Lenny Wise of Flat 4a, Lymewood Court, Parkdale, Lyme, will state:

1. I am 27 years old and of mixed race origin. My father is from the Caribbean and my mother (who is deceased) was white. My date of birth is the 26/7/- I have been charged in connection with a burglary at the home of an 84-year-old woman in Sunrise Road, Lyme which occurred on the 17th March at around midday. I will plead not guilty and am innocent of the charge. I was not represented at the police station prior to being charged and have been refused police bail. I am also charged with possession of a small quantity of cannabis. I intend to plead guilty to this.

2. I was arrested at home on the 19th March as I was leaving my flat. I could not believe it. The next thing I knew they were searching my flat. They seized some of my clothing and a pair of training shoes. I was taken to a police car and shoved in the back and taken to the police station.

3. I was taken to Lyme Street Police Station, and had to stay there overnight. I cannot remember if my rights were explained. The police told me I would be detained overnight because they wanted me to participate in an identification procedure and it would take time to organise. I have been in this situation before. I recall asking for an identification parade but was told I would have a video parade. I was photographed not long after arriving at the police station. I watched the officer put together a video parade but I did not have a clue what was going on. I understand that several witnesses have been shown the video and one of them has picked me out.

4. It was a difficult night in detention. I did not get much sleep and I was really worried about my dog Butch. I live on my own and there is no one to see to him. The police did try to ring my sister but she could not be reached. I was also craving a cigarette as I am a chain smoker. Additionally, I am a diagnosed manic depressive. I am prone to erratic behaviour and mood swings. Sometimes I get very depressed. My medication helps but it has side effects and I do not take it as regularly as I should. I cannot recall whether I was asked about this when I arrived at the police station as it is all a bit of a blur. I told the police the following morning that I needed my medication and that I felt unwell. When I told the officer that I needed my medication for depression, a police doctor was called. Somebody must have gone to my flat to get my pills. I was checked over by the police doctor who gave me my tablets. He said I was fit to be interviewed which I was happy about. I thought that once I was interviewed I would be able to get out and see to things.

5. I believe it was explained to me that I could see a solicitor if I wanted to. To be honest I did not think there was much point as the police were going to charge me whatever I said. When the police said they were going to interview me at last, I did not want to delay matters further by requesting a solicitor. I regret the decision now. I kept telling the officers that I needed a smoke. I was told that it was up to me. In the circumstances, I just told the police what they wanted to hear. I wish to retract my confession. It is untrue.

6. I understand that another man is alleged to have been involved in the burglary. His name is Lloyd Green. I know of Lloyd Green. He is a drug dealer and has supplied drugs to me in the past. He is no longer my supplier. Green has got rough with me in the past when I owed him money.

7. I have been trying to recollect my whereabouts on Tuesday the 17th between 11.30am–12.30pm. My daily routine is to get up at about 10am. I usually leave my flat at around 10.30am and walk my dog. Pretty much every day, I go down the High Street to place a bet or visit my girlfriend who lives just off the High Street. I think I may have been in my bookmakers—Gladbrookes in the High Street at around 11.30am—and there might be someone there who could verify the fact. I place a small bet most days just before lunch time and I am fairly certain that that was where I was.

8. I do know the area around Sunrise Road. It is quite close to where I live. I often walk my dog on fields near to the back of Sunrise Road. I know one or two of the residents in the street. Most residents are friendly, but one or two of them are a little suspicious of me. The rear gardens of the houses in Sunrise Road which back onto the fields are not fenced off so it is possible for a person to wander onto the lawns at the back of the houses.

9. I do not understand how I have come to be identified as the man seen running away from the back of the burgled property. It was not me. I can only assume it must have been someone else who maybe looks similar in appearance to me. In actuality, I am 5'10". I am of slim build. I have medium length dreadlocked hair and a slight beard. The police mentioned something about the white training shoes being worn by the burglar. I do not own a pair of white trainers. The trainers recovered from my flat were left there by a friend. I have never worn them.

10. So far as my personal circumstances are concerned, I live on my own in a housing association flat. I have a girlfriend. Her name is Sonia. We have been seeing each other on and off for six months, although we have not been living together. Sonia is four months pregnant with my child. The pregnancy was not

planned. Sonia already has a child of her own. She is hoping to move to better accommodation as her present flat only has one bedroom. I am anxious to see Sonia. I need to know if she and the baby are okay.

11. I do not work. I am in receipt of income support. With my criminal record and my medical condition, it is difficult for me to get work. Having said that, I have a job interview next week—something my probation officer has organised. It is with a floor laying company. The owner has taken on ex-offenders in the past and is prepared to give me an interview. This could offer me the first real prospect of a job leading to full-time employment.

12. I get on very well with my sister, Tessa. She is my half-sister. She is a single mother. I see my sister once or twice a week. She makes sure my flat is clean and that I have food in. My mother died when I was 14 and my father left us when I was three. I don't know where he lives. Tessa, who is six years my senior, looked after me when our mother died.

13. I have been smoking cannabis since the age of 15. I became addicted to hard drugs, including crack, in my early twenties. At this time I was mixing with a lot of low-life individuals and having to commit crimes in order to pay off debts and fund my drug habit. Prison was really hard. Drugs were available but I stayed off hard drugs. When I finished my prison sentence I got myself a girlfriend and some stability. However, it was at this time that I began suffering with mental problems which I assumed were due to my drug addiction. I wish to make it clear that I am no longer addicted to drugs and only smoke cannabis very occasionally when I am feeling really depressed and weird. I must get bail. I cannot face going back to prison. I had not smoked any cannabis in the 24 hours before my arrest.

14. My GP is Dr Shaw at the Havelock Medical Centre, Willow Lane, Lyme. I do see a consultant psychiatrist at the Royal Lyme Hospital but I cannot recall his name. I am happy for my medical notes to be released.

15. I am currently subject to supervision by the Probation Service as part of a community order I received for an offence of assault. As part of the order, I was ordered to undergo psychiatric treatment. It was as a consequence of this that doctors diagnosed my mental illness. I have a really supportive probation officer, Maxine, with whom I get on really well. She understands my problems and is the one who has secured me a job interview.

16. I do have previous convictions but I cannot recall them all. I have previous convictions for burglary, drug use and assault. My most recent offence of assault was committed 18 months ago. It was very much out of character for me. I am not a violent man. The assault stemmed from a breakdown of a relationship and was committed shortly before my illness was diagnosed and treatment for it began. Aggressive tendencies are not uncommon in sufferers of manic depression and this may have been a contributing factor in the commission of this offence.

17. I have convictions for possession of amphetamine and cocaine and convictions for theft. Most of the theft offences relate to shoplifting committed in order to obtain drugs. As far as I can remember the burglary offences were drug related. I have previous convictions for failing bail. I have no excuse. I simply did not turn up at court. I suspect I was so out of it while on drugs that I simply forgot. To the best of my recollection, I have always pleaded guilty.

Lenny Wise
27th March

DOCUMENT 7 CONSIDERATION OF INITIAL DISCLOSURE OF PROSECUTION CASE

26th March
Engaged considering the IDPC and drafting proof of evidence.

Having considered the evidence, I am of the view that Lenny should indicate a not guilty plea at the plea before venue. It is unlikely (given the seriousness of the offence and the likely sentence in the event of conviction) that the Magistrates' Court would accept jurisdiction to try this matter. In the unlikely event of Lenny being presented with a choice, my considered opinion is that he would, in any event, be best advised to elect a Crown Court trial for the following reasons:

• He stands a better chance of being acquitted.

• There are areas of disputed evidence which are best dealt with in the absence of the jury.

• A qualified judge would be more confident about excluding evidence.

Against is:

• The risk of a higher sentence (although I strongly suspect that the Magistrates' Court would commit for sentence in any event).

• It will take longer to come to trial and if remanded in custody throughout, this would be an important consideration for Lenny.

• Defence statement is mandatory—but if the case is sent to the Crown Court we stand a better chance of flushing out further disclosure.

The advantages of the Crown Court outweigh those in favour of the Magistrates' Court in Lenny's case. In any event the exercise is likely to be academic since the magistrates will almost certainly decline jurisdiction and send for trial in the Crown Court.

Time engaged: 20 minutes

DOCUMENT 11 LYMESHIRE POLICE CUSTODY RECORD

Station: **Lyme Street**

Reasons for Arrest
Burglary of dwelling house

Comments made by person, if present when facts of arrest
were explained. Y/N [N]. If Yes, comments on log.

Video Tape Ref. No. LT/369

DETAINED PERSON'S RIGHTS
An extract from a notice setting out my rights has been
read to me and I have been given a copy. I have also
been provided with a written notice setting out my
entitlements while in custody.

Signature: **Lenny Wise**
Date: 19/3/-   Time: 16.15

LEGAL ADVICE REQUESTED
DETAILS:
I want to speak to a solicitor as soon as practicable

Signature:
Time: Date:

LEGAL ADVICE DECLINED
I have been informed that I may speak to a solicitor
IN PERSON OR ON THE TELEPHONE:

I do not want to speak to a solicitor at this time.
Signature: **Lenny Wise**
Time: 19/3   Date: 15.45

Reasons given, for not wanting legal advice
None given

NOTIFICATION OF A NAMED PERSON
REQUESTED Y/N [Y]
Details of nominated person
Theresa Wise (Sister)

APPROPRIATE ADULT Y/N [N]

INTERPRETER Y/N [N]
Notices served & grounds for detention explained in the
presence of Appropriate Adult/Interpreter

Signature of A/Adult

Time: Date:

Surname: **WISE**

Previous Name:

Forenames: **LENNY**

Address: **4A**
LYMEWOOD COURT
PARKDALE
LYME

Telephone

Occupation: **NONE**
Age: **27**   Date of Birth: **27/6/-**

Place of Birth: **LONDON**

Height: **5** Feet: **11** Inches: Sex: **M**

Arrested by:
Name: DS S Farrington
ID. No: 4291
Station: Lyme Street
Place of Arrest: 4a Lymewood Court, Lyme

	Time	Date
Arrested at:	15.30	19/3/-
Arrived at Station	16.10	19/3/-

Officer In Case:
Id. No: 4291
Name: DS Farrington

Officer Opening Custody Record

Signature: Mike Williams

Id No: 4231
Name: Sgt M Williams

CHARGES(S)

Custody No. 2305/05

Surname **WISE**	
	Station: Lyme
Forename (s) **LENNY**	Sex M/F (M)
	D.O.B 27/6/-
Address **4A Lymewood Court**	
Parkdale	ID Code: 1
Lyme	
Postcode	Language: None

You are charged with the offence(s) shown below. You do not have to say anything. But it may harm your defence if you do not mention now something which you later rely on in court. Anything you do say may be given in evidence.

Consec. No.	Charge(s)
1.	That on the 17th March having entered as a trespasser a building, being a dwelling known as 19 Sunrise Road, Lyme you stole £75 in money property belonging to Lillian Kennedy contrary to s. 9(1)(a) Theft Act 1968
2.	That on the 19th March you unlawfully had in your possession a controlled drug of Class B namely cannabis, contrary to section 5(2) Misuse of Drugs Act 1971

Time and Date of Charge: 20th March 12.45hrs
Reply (if any): "you are racist pigs you lot are."

Signed (person charged)   Signed (appropriate adult)
Officer charging Surname Farrington   Rank DS   No.4291   Station: Lyme St
Officer in case   Surname   Rank   No.   Station
Charge accepted   Surname   Rank   No.   Station

Appearing at LYME REMAND COURT at LYME SQUARE, LYME on the 20/3/ at 1400 hours

LYMESHIRE POLICE
DETAINED PERSONS MEDICAL FORM

Custody Ref: 2305/05

| Name: Lenny Wise | DOB: 27/6/- | Time/Date: 20/3/- |

Reason Doctor requested:
Detainee telling me he felt claustrophobic and needed to take medication for depression

VISUAL ASSESSMENT BY CUSTODY SERGEANT

Cut-   Bruising *   Other Suspected Injury +

Front   Back

ADMINISTRATION AND MOVEMENT TIMES

	Time	Date
Doctor called	0700	20/3/-
Doctor replied		
Agreed Arrival Time		
Doctor Arrived	0745	20/3/-
Departure/Conclusion		
Ambulance Called		
Ambulance Arrived		
Detainee taken to Hospital		Time/Date

Police-Signs/symptoms & First Aid given:
Observed detainee seemed very fidgety

By whom:

DOCTORS OPINION OR TELEPHONE ADVICE (NON-CONFIDENTIAL)

Name of Doctor: Dr A Ghulam

Time/Date of Examination: 20/3/- 0800 hrs

Opinion: Anxious but lucid in thought. Orientated in time and space. Takes regular medication for manic depression

Medical Advice: Medicate per prescription

Examination/Observation: Completed /Refused   Risk of Self Harm: High/Medium /Standard

Location of Examination: Medical room /Cell/Other   Station: Lyme Street

RECOMMENDATIONS

	Yes	No		Yes	No
Recommended appropriate adult:		*	Medical review Required		*
Fit to be detained:	*		Time/Date required: Time/Date carried Out:		
	Yes	No			
Fit for interview:	*				
Fit for transfer					
Fit for charge:					

Doctors Signature:
Ghulam

LYMESHIRE POLICE

Station: **LYME STREET**	Detained Person Serial No: **2305/357**

Surname: **WISE**
Forenames: **LENNY**

Last review of detention conducted at:

Date	Time	Details of Action/Occurrence	
19/3/-	1610	DP arrived.	MW
	1615	DP searched—property removed. Rights explained. Detention authorised to secure and preserve evidence and to obtain evidence by questioning. DP taken to cell by officers—Cell F4.	MW
	1630	Phone call to DP's sister 821249 (no contact made no answering machine). DP informed.	MW
	1700	DP accepted hot drink.	MW
	1730	DP taken meal—refused.	MW
	1800	DP seen in cell—in order.	MW
	1815	DP consents to taking saliva swab—non-intimate.	MW
	1816	'I consent to providing a sample of my saliva.' Lenny Wise	
	1830	DP taken to Identification suite for photographing and parade compilation.	MW
	1930	DP returned to my custody—placed in Cell F4.	MW
	1935	DP given a cup of tea—asking for cigarette.	MW
	1955	DP uses toilet.	MW
	2015	In cell awake and pacing.	MW
	2030	In cell awake—muttering.	MW

LYMESHIRE POLICE

Station: **LYME STREET**	Detained Person Serial No: **2305/357**

Surname: **WISE**
Forenames: **LENNY**

Last review of detention conducted at: **2200 hours 19/3/**

Date	Time	Details of Action/Occurrence	
	2100	Banging on cell—uses toilet.	MW
	2130	In cell—pacing—requests cigarette—refused.	MW
	2200	In cell—in order. Custody transferred to Sgt Tom Slater. Detention reviewed. DP informed.	TS
	2230	In cell—sitting on bed wringing hands.	TS
	2300	In cell—in order.	TS
	2330	In cell—pacing.	TS
	2345	Given refreshment.	TS
	2359	DP—on bed awake.	TS
20/3/-	0015	DP in cell pacing. Requests cigarette.	TS
	0045	On bed—suspect rocking back and forwards. Asked if okay. Requested more blankets supplied. DP informed me he wanted to sleep.	TS
	0115	DP in cell—awake. In order.	TS
	0145	DP in cell—uses toilet.	TS
	0215	DP in cell—asleep.	TS
	0245	DP—awake lying on bed.	TS
	0315	DP seen pacing in cell.	TS

LYMESHIRE POLICE

| Station: **LYME STREET** | Detained Person Serial No: **2305/357** |

| Surname: **WISE** |
| Forenames: **LENNY** |

| Last review of detention conducted at: **0700 hours 20/3/** |

Date	Time	Details of Action/Occurrence	
20/3/	0345	DP awake—humming to himself.	TS
	0415	DP lying on bed—in order.	TS
	0445	DP awake—sitting on bed.	TS
	0515	DP taken to toilet.	TS
	0545	DP in cell pacing.	TS
	0603	DP complains of feeling unwell. Requests doctor.	TS
	0610	Transferred into custody of Sgt Brough.	DB
	0630	DP offered breakfast. Informed by DP that his regular medication for depression is at home. FME requested. Officer dispatched to DP's house to locate medication.	DB
	0645	DP uses toilet. Informed GP requested to attend.	DB
	0700	Review of detention. DP informed.	DB
	0740	DP taken to medical room for examination by Dr Ghulam.	DB
	0800	Dr Ghulam completes report—medication administered to DP who is fit to be interviewed. DP taken back to cell F4.	DB
	0815	DP in cell. In order.	DB
	0900	DP offered refreshment. Requests cigarette.	DB

LYMESHIRE POLICE

Station: **LYME STREET**	Detained Person Serial No: **2305/357**

Surname: **WISE** Forenames: **LENNY**

Last review of detention conducted at: **0700 hours 20/3/**

Date	Time	Details of Action/Occurrence	
20/3/-	0915	DP informed of intention to interview—asked if requires solicitor—refuses one.	DB
	0930	DP in cell. In order.	DB
	1000	DP asking when interview will be.	DB
	1030	DP in cell—agitated—pacing.	DB
	1045	DP in cell—allowed to use toilet.	DB
	1100	DP in cell pacing.	DB
	1115	DP given to the custody of DS Farrington and taken to interview room 2.	DB
	1230	Returned to my custody.	DB
	1245	DP charged and documented. Bail refused on grounds of risk of absconding and commission of further offences. DP's sister contacted and informed. DP allowed to speak with sister.	DB
	1300	Into custody of Premier for transport to Lyme MC.	DB

DOCUMENT 15 RECORD OF ATTENDANCE AT ALLOCATION HEARING

27 March

Attending Lyme Magistrates' Court. I explained to Lenny and his sister that I did not feel that the magistrates would accept jurisdiction on the burglary matter but that if they did he should elect trial by jury on the burglary charge in any event. I advised him that he had no choice but to plead guilty to the possession of cannabis charge.

A guilty plea was entered to the possession of cannabis charge and a not guilty plea was entered in relation to the burglary matter. An allocation hearing was held with the CPS inviting the magistrates to decline jurisdiction. No representations from us in relation to allocation. Jurisdiction declined—case sent to the Crown Court and adjourned to 1 May for a PTPH (Plea and Trial Preparation Hearing) before the Crown Court.

The magistrates indicated a willingness to sentence Lenny on the possession of cannabis matter. Consequently I briefly addressed the Bench in terms of sentence and a 12-month conditional discharge was imposed.

I made a second full application for bail on Lenny's behalf. Bail was once more refused on the grounds of the risk of absconding and commission of further offences.

Spoke to Lenny after the hearing and we agreed I would appeal the refusal of bail to the Crown Court.

Time engaged:
Advocacy 40 minutes
Waiting 10 minutes
Attending client 30 minutes
Travel to and from court 15 minutes
Preparing Notice of Appeal 15 minutes.

You can see the plea before venue followed by the allocation on the burglary charge in the Lenny Wise video which your lecturer can download from the online resources. It precedes Lenny's contested application for bail. A transcript, broadly based on the bail hearing, appears at Document 17. We would ask you to note that the prosecutor's reference to sentencing guidelines on burglary in the Magistrates' Court Sentencing Guidelines have now been superseded by revised burglary guidelines issued by the Sentencing Council for England and Wales in January 2012. **Please note that this courtroom scene was filmed when the now obsolete mode of trial (pre schedule 3 CJA 2003) procedure was in use.** Under the new allocation procedure, the prosecutor would have disclosed Lenny's previous convictions as part of the allocation hearing further confirming the magistrates' court's decision in this case to decline summary jurisdiction to try Lenny.

DOCUMENT 16 STANDARD CASE SENT DIRECTIONS

Crown Court- Cases sent for trial on or after the 5th January 2016
In multi- handed cases please complete part one for each defendant.
However the court may complete part two on one form only to
represent all defendants in the case.

HM Courts & Tribunals Service

Part 1 - To be completed by the parties before the hearing

Name of defendant: LENNY WISE	Date of Birth: 27/6/-	URN: 201693022/TMG

Solicitors firm representing (if any) :   Mountford and Hannibal Cjsm Email address: Hannibal@solicitors.Cjsm.org. uk

Legal Aid Status: X☐ Granted ☐ Applied for ☐ Will apply ☐ Private ☐ N/A	Has the defendant been advised about credit for guilty pleas? ☐ Yes ☐ No

Charges 1 BURGLARY (DOMESTIC DWELLING) 2 3	Pleas (either way) or indicated pleas (indictable only) or alternatives offered 1 NG 2 3

Details of any other cases linked to this defendant:

Part 2 - To be completed by the court

In so far as known **Real issues in the case (concise details will be sufficient):**
Disputes identification evidence. Disputes forensic evidence. Will challenge the admissibility of interviews at police station which may form part of the prosecution's case on the basis that he was unrepresented and was unwell and they are inadmissible in accordance with PACE 1984 and Code C.

What other areas of evidence do the prosecution anticipate serving before the PTPH?	Case sent bundle and draft indictment 7 days before
What other areas of evidence do the prosecution anticipate serving after the PTPH?	Bad character and full forensic reports if disputed
Other evidence defence say they need prior to PTPH to make PTPH effective	Review DVD of identification procedure

☐ **Child Witness Protocol- Witness under 10?**   PTPH 14 days
☐ **s.28 protocol case (pilot sites only)**   PTPH 14 days

If a G Plea- has a PSR been ordered? ☐ Yes ☐ No
NB: The type of report will be determined by the National Probation Service

If yes, ☐ long (SDR) or ☐ short (FDR)

If short (FDR), ☐ oral or ☐ written

Does the defendant require an interpreter? ☐ Yes x☐ No
Language/dialect:

Any other information that would assist the management of the case (including reporting restrictions and likely press coverage):

Date of hearing in Crown Court: 1st May   ☐ Bail or x☐ Custody – CTL expiry:16 July

The magistrates' court must remind the parties and the Defendant(s) that the Crown Court will expect, before the PTPH:
  ➤ the defendant(s) to have a conference with their legal representative;
  ➤ the parties to discuss pleas and outstanding issues (as necessary).

Name of DJ(MC)/ LA Completing the Form: Pete Morris
Date: 27th March-

DOCUMENT 20 RECORD OF CROWN COURT BAIL HEARING

File Note—29th March

Attending Lyme Crown Court. Appearing before Mr Recorder Jay. Making a further application for bail on behalf of Lenny Wise. Bail was opposed by the CPS. Lenny was granted conditional bail as follows:

1. He resides at 4A Lymewood Court.

2. He reports to Lyme Street Police Station Mon/Wed/Friday 2–3pm.

3. He does not attempt to contact in any way Lillian Kennedy, Shirley Lewis or Harold Finney.

4. He does not go in to Sunrise Road or on the fields at the back of Sunrise Road.

Telephoning Lenny's sister to relay the good news. Explained he would be released and that I would be writing to him to stress the importance of abiding by bail conditions. Reminded her that Lenny was due to appear before Lyme Crown Court on 1 May.

Time engaged:
Advocacy: 30 minutes
Waiting: 5 minutes
Travel to and from court: 15 minutes.

NB: Solicitor would need to write to Lenny advising him of his change in bail status and the importance of abiding by the conditions of his bail.

DOCUMENT 25 CPS LETTER REGARDING SERVICE OF CASE SENT BUNDLE

Important note: The letter below is the authors' interpretation of the type of letter that a solicitor might receive from the Crown Prosecution Service. The letter is not representative of any communication sent by the Crown Prosecution Service and should not be seen as representative of how the Crown Prosecution Service would respond in this scenario.

CROWN PROSECUTION SERVICE

Queen's Chambers
Blackburn Street
Lyme
LY3 2BE
Date: 15/5/-
Ref: AH/IW
Your ref: RJ/SAW

Hannibal and Mountford Solicitors
20 High Street
Lyme Bank
Lyme
LY10 34 T

Dear Sir

REGINA v LENNY WISE

PTPH: 1 MAY

SECTION 51, CRIME AND DISORDER ACT 1998

NOTICE OF SERVICE OF CASE AND WITNESS REQUIREMENTS

Notice of Service of the case

The copy statements [and depositions] that accompany this notice constitute the copies of the documents containing the evidence on which the current charge or charges are based.

These documents are served in accordance with Paragraph 1 of Schedule 3 of the Crime and Disorder Act 1998 ("the 1998 Act") and the Crime and Disorder Act 1998 (Service of Prosecution Evidence) Regulations 2000.

You are reminded that by virtue of paragraph 5 of Schedule 8 of the 1998 Act, the bill of indictment in the Crown Court may include – either in substitution for or in addition to any count you are currently charged with – any counts founded on the evidence hereby served on you (being counts which can be lawfully joined in the same indictment).

Request for information concerning defence witness requirements

The written statements [and depositions] referred to above have been made by the witnesses named below. Application may be made to the court by the prosecution for each of these statements [and depositions] to be read out at the trial without oral evidence being given by the witness who has made the statement or deposition, unless I hear from you to the contrary.

If you want a witness to attend and give oral evidence, and to be cross examined if necessary, you should inform the Crown Court and me in writing as soon as possible, and in any case, at least two weeks before the date of the Plea and Case Management Hearing set by the Court. This will enable the police to check on a witness' availability to attend court and avoid the costs and delay associated with any further adjournments for this purpose.

Failure to let me know which witnesses you wish to be called may result in the court allowing a witness' statement [or deposition] to be read, and therefore in your being unable to cross examine that witness.

You should however be aware that the prosecutor may, at his or her discretion, require the attendance of a witness to give oral evidence, even if you have indicated that you do not wish that witness to attend to give oral evidence at the trial.

Request for additional information: pleas and admissions

Additionally, you are requested to inform me as soon as possible:

- whether you intend to admit all or some of the current charges. If so, which ones?

- whether you are prepared to make any admissions under Section 10 Criminal Justice Act 1967, which may avoid the attendance of witnesses. If so, please give details.

If you have a solicitor acting for you in this case, you should take immediate steps to bring this notice and statements [and depositions] to his or her attention as soon as possible.

Additional evidence

Other evidence, if any and if relevant, may be served in response to any notice served by virtue of the Crime and Disorder Act 1998 (Dismissal of Charges Sent) Rules 1998, or under a notice of further evidence at a later stage.

Name of witnesses whose statements (and depositions) are enclosed:

See attached list.

A copy of this Notice is being served on the court for their information.

Please send any reply quoting the case name and URN number to the address given above.

Yours faithfully,

For Chief Crown Prosecutor

For Graduated Fee Scheme purposes – the updated page count is now:		
Statements	**Exhibits**	**Photographs etc**

DOCUMENT 25A RECORD OF ATTENDANCE AT PTPH

Attending Lyme Crown Court for the PTPH of Lenny Wise.

I explained to Lenny that this would be a brief hearing and that the judge and the lawyers would be working to set a firm date for his trial. He was further advised as to credit for guilty plea but confirmed he still wanted to plead not guilty. I explained that the charge would be read to him and that he should indicate a not guilty plea. I explained that steps had been taken to obtain a report from his consultant.

I was served with a copy of the PTPH form by the CPS which I proceeded to complete on behalf of the defence. The judge (HHJ Thomas Shand) went through the PTPH form. It was explained to HH that the defence would be seeking to have the defendant's interview deemed inadmissible at trial and that we were in the process of obtaining a psychiatric report from our client's consultant. We would therefore want to cross-examine the custody officer on duty and the medical doctor that saw the defendant and reviewed his medication. After some discussion, the judge agreed to list the matter for a one-day Further Case Management Hearing on 13 September, making directions for the service of skeletal arguments. A two day trial has been fixed starting 30 September. Standard orders made as per the PTPH is attached.

Time engaged
Advocacy 20 minutes
Waiting 40 minutes
Attending client 10 minutes
Travel 20 minutes

DOCUMENT 26 CPS LETTER REGARDING SERVICE OF CASE SENT BUNDLE

Important note: The letter below is the authors' interpretation of the type of letter that a solicitor might receive from the Crown Prosecution Service. The letter is not representative of any communication sent by the Crown Prosecution Service and should not be seen as representative of how the Crown Prosecution Service would respond in this scenario.

CROWN PROSECUTION SERVICE

Queen's Chamb
Blackburn Street
Lyme
LY3 2BE
Date: 21/5
Ref: AH/IW
Your ref: RJ/SAW

Hannibal and Mountford Solicitors
20 High Street
Lyme Bank
Lyme
LY10 34 T

Dear Sir

REGINA v LENNY WISE

TRIAL DATE: 30 SEPTEMBER

SECTION 51, CRIME AND DISORDER ACT 1998

NOTICE OF SERVICE OF CASE AND WITNESS REQUIREMENTS

Notice of Service of the case

The copy statements [and depositions] that accompany this notice constitute the copies of the documents containing the evidence on which the current charge or charges are based.

These documents are served in accordance with Paragraph 1 of Schedule 3 of the Crime and Disorder Act 1998 ("the 1998 Act") and the Crime and Disorder Act 1998 (Service of Prosecution Evidence) Regulations 2000.

You are reminded that by virtue of paragraph 5 of Schedule 8 of the 1998 Act, the bill of indictment in the Crown Court may include – either in substitution for or in addition to any count you are currently charged with – any counts founded on the evidence hereby served on you (being counts which can be lawfully joined in the same indictment).

<u>Request for information concerning defence witness requirements</u>

The written statements [and depositions] referred to above have been made by the witnesses named below. Application may be made to the court by the prosecution for each of these statements [and depositions] to be read out at the trial without oral evidence being given by the witness who has made the statement or deposition, unless I hear from you to the contrary.

If you want a witness to attend and give oral evidence, and to be cross examined if necessary, you should inform the Crown Court and me in writing as soon as possible, and in any case, no later than the 8 September as per the PTPH. This will enable the police to check on a witness' availability to attend court and avoid the costs and delay associated with any further adjournments for this purpose.

Failure to let me know which witnesses you wish to be called may result in the court allowing a witness' statement [or deposition] to be read, and therefore in your being unable to cross examine that witness.

You should however be aware that the prosecutor may, at his or her discretion, require the attendance of a witness to give oral evidence, even if you have indicated that you do not wish that witness to attend to give oral evidence at the trial.

<u>Request for additional information: pleas and admissions</u>

Additionally, you are requested to inform me as soon as possible:

- whether you intend to admit all or some of the current charges. If so, which ones?

- whether you are prepared to make any admissions under Section 10 Criminal Justice Act 1967, which may avoid the attendance of witnesses. If so, please give details.

If you have a solicitor acting for you in this case, you should take immediate steps to bring this notice and statements [and depositions] to his or her attention as soon as possible.

<u>Additional evidence</u>

Other evidence, if any and if relevant, may be served in response to any notice served by virtue of the Crime and Disorder Act 1998 (Dismissal of Charges Sent) Rules 1998, or under a notice of further evidence at a later stage.

<u>Name of witnesses whose statements (and depositions) are enclosed:</u>

See attached list

A copy of this Notice is being served on the court for their information.

Please send any reply quoting the case name and URN number to the address given above.

Yours faithfully,

For Chief Crown Prosecutor

For Graduated Fee Scheme purposes – the updated page count is now:		
Statements	**Exhibits**	**Photographs etc**

DOCUMENT 26A EXTRACTS FROM THE CASE SENT BUNDLE

NOTE TO THE READER
We have included the front sheets of a typical case sent bundle. In addition to the extracts we have included here, you would also receive typed versions of the prosecution's witness statements (comprising used material) as well as a full transcript of interview.

The charge(s) set out on the Schedule(s) attached to the accompanying papers has/have been prepared in indictment form in consequence of the responsibility which the Crown Prosecution Service has in relation to the form and content of indictments.

Schedules also serve as draft indictments following a sending of a case to the Crown Court but may be subject to amendments, or replaced by a new draft settled by Counsel, before being preferred for signature by the appropriate officer of the Crown Court. A copy of the indictment as signed will be supplied in the usual way.

<u>**DRAFT INDICTMENT**</u>

INDICTMENT (No........)

CROWN COURT AT LYME

THE QUEEN -V- LENNY WISE

LENNY WISE is charged as follows:

Count 1: <u>**STATEMENT OF OFFENCE**</u>

BURGLARY, contrary to section 9(1)(b) of the Theft Act 1968.

PARTICULARS OF OFFENCE

LENNY WISE on the 17th day of March having entered as a trespasser a building, being a dwelling known as 19 Sunrise Road Lyme, stole therein £75 in money.

Lillian Kennedy

Officer of the Court

REGINA

-V-

LENNY WISE

Statements

No.	Name of Witness	Date of Statement	Page No (s)
1.	L Kennedy	18/3/-	
2.	L Kennedy	20/3/-	
3.	S Lewis	18/3/-	
4.	S Lewis	20/3/-	
5.	H Finney	18/3/-	
6.	H Finney	20/3/-	
7.	S Farrington	20/3/-	
8.	S Shaw	20/3/-	
9.	A Khan	20/3/-	
10.	E Mason	20/3/-	
11.	C Sutton	20/3/-	
12.	J Bradbury	20/3/-	
13.	P Reynolds (x2)	19/3/-	
14.	C Lawton	20/3/-	
15.	S Hardacker	25/3/-	

REGINA

-V-

LENNY WISE

Exhibit List

No	Reference	Item
1.	SF2	Left size 9 Nike training shoe
2.	SF3	Right size 9 Nike training shoe
3.	SF6/a	Tape recorded interview/Wise
		Tape Reference 21/SF/59217/03–*
4.	SF6/b	Transcript of interview/Wise*
5.	CJL1	Album of photographs of shoeprints in situ
6.	CJL2	Shoe print lift
7.	CJL3	Shoe print lift
8.	SF5	Black hooded sweatshirt
9.	PR1	DVD Compilation of Video Images Ref 05/01166/20A
10.	CS2	Video of Video Identification viewing process-film ref. no. 277/05

N.B. Exhibits marked * are served with the committal papers, other exhibits may be examined on suitable appointment.

DOCUMENT 26 WITNESS STATEMENT: LILLIAN KENNEDY

WITNESS STATEMENT

(CJ Act 1967, s. 9; MC Act 1980, s. 5A(3)(a) and s. 5B; Crim PR Part 16)

Name	Lillian Kennedy
Address	Supplied
Age/Date of Birth	Over 18
Occupation	Retired

....

Who states:

This statement, consisting of one page signed by me, is true to the best of my knowledge and belief and I make it knowing that if it is tendered in evidence I shall be liable to prosecution if I have wilfully stated in it anything which I know to be false or do not believe to be true.

Dated: 18th March   Signed: L Kennedy

....

I live at number 19 Sunrise Road, Lyme. I am 85 years old. On Tuesday the 17th March, I went to fetch my pension from Lyme High Street. I drew £95.00. Once I had paid my weekly sums for gas and electricity I was left with around £75. I got home at around 11 am. As I was walking up the road, a man approached me and asked me if I wanted any help with my shopping. I told him, no thank you. I would describe him as being quite tall and thin. He had a gaunt face, was black and had long, black, straggling hair and a small beard on his chin. I think he was wearing a short, dark coloured top and a pair of white sports shoes. I saw him walk off into the fields near the back of my house.

I know I had my purse with me when I went into my house, because a friend of mine called in for 10 minutes, shortly after I got back from the Post Office. She had her grandchild with her and I gave her a pound from my purse. A short time after this I was putting some rubbish out when I thought I heard the telephone ringing. When I came in, I realised it was my front door bell. I answered the door. There was a man standing there. I have never seen this man before. He was white but had a tanned complexion. He was dressed smartly, wearing a suit and tie. He was quite bald. He was not very tall. I recall he was wearing dark glasses. He told me his car had broken down and asked if he could use the telephone. I told him he could not as I did not have a phone. Not long after this, a friend of my neighbour came round. She told me she had seen a man in my back garden and that my back door was open. I immediately checked my handbag and saw that my purse was missing. She telephoned the police. I realised that I had left the back door open when I came to answer the front door. It was silly of me. The only money I get is my pension. The break in has left me shaken and frightened.

Later in the afternoon of the 17th March, the police took me around the local area in one of their cars. They asked me if I could see the man who had knocked on my front door. I could not see the man who had called but I did see the man who had offered to help me with my shopping earlier that morning. The police car stopped outside the Co-op on the High Street. I had a good look at the man and I am sure it was him.

Signed: Lillian Kennedy

DOCUMENT 26A WITNESS STATEMENT: SHIRLEY LEWIS

<u>WITNESS STATEMENT</u>

(CJ Act 1967, s. 9; MC Act 1980, s. 5A(3)(a) and s. 5B;Crim PR Part 16)

Name	Shirley Lewis
Address	Supplied
Age/Date of Birth	Over 18
Occupation	Retired Teacher

....

Who states:

This statement, consisting of one page signed by me, is true to the best of my knowledge and belief, and I make it knowing that if it is tendered in evidence I shall be liable to prosecution if I have wilfully stated in it anything which I know to be false or do not believe to be true.

Dated: 18th March   Signed: S Lewis

....

On Tuesday the 17th March, I was visiting my elderly aunt at 19 Sunrise Road, Lyme. She lives next door to Lillian Kennedy at number 17. At around midday on Tuesday 17th March, I went out the back of my aunt's property to bring some washing in that was pegged up on the washing line. The time was around midday.

I was facing Lillian's back garden. A low wall divides the gardens, it being largely open plan. I saw a man in her garden. I watched him for a good few seconds. In fact I nearly called out to him, to ask what he thought he was doing, but something stopped me. He didn't see me because I was behind a large sheet pegged on the line. I don't know where he came from but I watched him wander out of Lillian's garden and off down the back lane. At this point I noticed the back door to Mrs Kennedy's house was wide open.

I would describe the man as being of Afro-Caribbean origin. He was about 5 ft 8/9 inches tall. He was of slim build and was wearing a black hooded sweatshirt with the hood up, so I could not see his hair. The man I saw was wearing a pair of white training shoes. I went round to see Lillian almost straight away and she told me that her purse was missing. I am certain I would be able to recognise the man again. I had the distinct feeling I had seen the man before. In fact I have seen him walking his dog, a brown and white terrier, in the grassy area nearby, on more than one occasion.

Signed: Shirley Lewis

DOCUMENT 26B WITNESS STATEMENT: HAROLD FINNEY

<u>WITNESS STATEMENT</u>

(CJ Act 1967, s. 9; MC Act 1980, s. 5A(3)(a) and s. 5B;Crim PR Part 16)

Name	Harold Finney
Address	Withheld
Age/Date of Birth	Over 18
Occupation	Retired Engineer

Who states:

This statement, consisting of one page signed by me, is true to the best of my knowledge, and belief and I make it knowing that if it is tendered in evidence I shall be liable to prosecution if I have wilfully stated in it anything which I know to be false or do not believe to be true.

Dated: 18th March   Signed: H Finney

I have lived in Sunrise Road for the past five years. I am a member of the local area neighbourhood watch scheme. On Tuesday the 17th March, at around 11.30am, I observed a black car drive into Sunrise Road, Lyme, and park. I could not see anyone in the car because the windows were dark. The car remained parked in the road for 15 minutes or so. I started to get suspicious and took a note of the registration number. It was DY 01 5JT. About five minutes after I first noticed the car I saw a man walking past my window. I watched him go over to the car and get in the passenger side. The telephone rang at this point and I did not see the man again. I was on the telephone for some time. When I went to look out of my window at around midday, I saw the black car been driven off.

I would describe the man I saw getting into the car as being black and in his twenties. He was tall and thin. He was black and had long, dark hair. He was wearing a short black top and a pair of white training shoes.

Signed: H Finney

DOCUMENT 26C WITNESS STATEMENT SGT S FARRINGTON

<u>WITNESS STATEMENT</u>

(CJ Act 1967, s. 9; MC Act 1980, s. 5A(3)(a) and s. 5B;Crim PR Part 16)

Name	Steven Farrington
Address	Lyme Street Police Station
Age/Date of Birth	Over 18
Occupation	Detective Sergeant

....

Who states:

This statement, consisting of two pages signed by me, is true to the best of my knowledge and belief, and I make it knowing that if it is tendered in evidence I shall be liable to prosecution if I have wilfully stated in it anything which I know to be false or do not believe to be true.

Dated: 20th March   Signed: S Farrington

....

On the 17th March I, in the company of Detective Constable 2890 Sarah Shaw attended the home of Lillian Kennedy at 19 Sunrise Road, Lyme. Mrs Kennedy is an 85-year-old widow. From our enquiries it was ascertained that Mrs Kennedy's purse had been stolen, containing her pension money of £75.00 in cash.

As a result of our enquires, during the afternoon of March 17th, we took Lillian Kennedy on a tour of the locality in an unmarked police car, to see if she could possibly spot the person or persons suspected of carrying out the burglary. In the course of the tour of the local area, Mrs Kennedy drew our attention to a man of Afro-Caribbean origin. The man was 5 ft 10 in and of slim build. He had shoulder-length, dreadlocked hair and a slight goatee beard. He was wearing a black hooded sweatshirt and black jogging bottoms. He was wearing a pair of brown training shoes. My colleague Detective Constable Shaw recognised the man as Lenny Wise. Mrs Kennedy was quite adamant that Lenny Wise was the man who had approached her in her street a short time before the burglary and who had offered to help her with her shopping before disappearing behind the back of Sunrise Road. Mrs Kennedy observed Lenny Wise in good light for a minute or two before confirming his identification.

A decision was taken not to arrest Lenny Wise at this time as further enquires were being pursued in connection with a possible accomplice.

At 09.30 hours on the 18th March, Lloyd Green was arrested in connection with the burglary. He was taken to Lyme Street Police Station where his detention was authorised. A video identification was convened but Mrs Kennedy failed to identify Lloyd Green. Mr Green was released on police bail at 15.30 hours on the 19th March.

At 15.15 hours on the 19th March, Lenny Wise was approached by me and Detective Constable Shaw just outside his flat at 4a Lymewood Court. Mr Wise was arrested and cautioned. A search of his flat was conducted pursuant to s. 32 PACE. In his presence, I seized a black hooded sweatshirt (Exhibit SF1) and a pair of size 9 white Nike training shoes were also seized (right shoe exhibit number SF2 and left shoe exhibit number SF3). In the course of searching Lenny Wise, a quantity of cannabis resin was found (exhibit SF4) in his trouser pocket. Also seized from Lenny Wise was his mobile phone.

Lenny Wise became obstructive at which point he was handcuffed and placed in the back of a police car. He was then taken to Lyme Police Station where his detention was authorised in accordance with the Police and Criminal Evidence Act 1984. A sample of saliva was taken from Mr Wise (Exhibit SF5).

Lenny Wise was detained overnight. On the 20th March, Lenny Wise was identified in the course of a video parade by a neighbour who lives near to the victim's burgled property, as the man she had seen in Lillian Kennedy's back garden around midday on the 17th March.

Wise was certified fit to be interviewed by a police doctor. Declining the services of the solicitor, Wise was interviewed the following day. The interview lasted 46 minutes. One tape was used during the interview and a copy of the sealed tape is available (Exhibit SF6).

In the course of the interview Wise admitted he had entered Mrs Kennedy's house and stole £75. At the conclusion of the interview Lenny Wise was charged with burglary and cautioned.

Mr Wise was denied police bail and was escorted to Lyme Magistrates' Court.

Signed: Sgt S Farrington 4291

DOCUMENT 26D

RECORD OF INTERVIEW

Policy Exhibit No:

No of pages: (3, as reproduced)

Signature of interviewing officer producing exhibit DSS Farrington

Person interviewed: LENNY WISE

Place of interview: LYME STREET

Date of interview: 20/3/-

Time commenced: 1130 HRS

Time concluded: 1216 HRS

Duration of interview: 46 MINUTES

Interviewing officer(s): DS 4291 FARRINGTON/DC 2890 SARAH SHAW

Other persons present: NONE

Tape reference number: 21/SF/59217/03/-

Exhibit Number: SF6

Tape counter Times(s)	Person speaking	Text
0000		Normal introductions were made and the interviewee was reminded of his legal rights and cautioned.
		The officer said WISE was under arrest in relation to a burglary at 19 Sunrise Road in Lyme.
0148	Sgt Farr.	Before we begin, Lenny, I just want to check you feel well enough to be interviewed. Do you feel OK?
0159	R	Just tired, okay okay.
0210	Sgt Farr.	Are you happy to be interviewed without a solicitor?
0218	R	Yeah.
0245	Sgt Farr.	I want to ask you about your whereabouts between 11 and 1pm on Tuesday the 17th March. Can you remember where you were and what you were doing?
0300	R	The usual routine. You know what I mean man?
	Sgt Farr.	What is your usual routine Lenny?
	R	(Suspect sits in silence)
0345	Sgt Farr.	I think lad, you'd better take the situation you're in a bit more seriously don't you?
0400	R	Yeah, yeah—you lot got it in for me.
0430	Sgt Farr.	You understand that you have been arrested in connection with a burglary at 19 Sunrise Road. The victim is an elderly woman and someone has stolen her pension.
0500	R	Yeah, yeah. (Suspect starts shaking his head.) Can I have a cigarette? I need a smoke. This needs sorting, right—got things that need sorting, right.
0525	Sgt Farr.	As soon as this interview is over and you start to answer my questions the sooner you can have a cigarette. Do you know the area around Sunrise Road?
0600	R	Yeah.
0624	Sgt Farr.	Did you go into Sunrise Road on the 17th March?
0635	R	No.

0702	Sgt Farr.	The old lady who was burgled has pointed you out as the man who approached her in Sunrise Road at around 11.30am and offered her help with her shopping. Was that you Lenny because she says it was?
0745	R	What day is it today?
0800	Sgt Farr.	It's Thursday—now just answer the question Lenny—the sooner we get your account the sooner this process will be over.
1100		Are we just going to sit here in silence Lenny?
1110		(Suspect stands up and starts pacing.) Sit down Lenny. The old lady describes the man who approached her in her street at around 11 or so as being a black youth, quite tall, with dreadlocks, wearing a short dark top and wearing white trainers. Would you accept that that description matches you?
1204	R	Don't know what you're getting at—don't know.
1227	Sgt Farr.	The old lady was taken on a tour of the High Street to see if she could see the man who had approached her earlier that morning. She pointed you out to us. You were seen wearing a dark hooded top. I will ask you again were you in Sunrise Road at anytime on the morning of 17th March? (Suspect starts pacing.) Sit down Lenny and answer the question. (Reply inaudible.)
1312		We have another eye-witness, Lenny, who has identified you near the back door of the old lady's house at just after midday on the 17th March. She has given us a clear description of the person she saw. She states she saw a man of Afro-Caribbean origin in the old lady's garden near the open back door. She describes the man has having pointy features, wearing a black hooded top with the hood up. Her description matches your appearance. She has subsequently identified you at a video identification parade. I am going to ask you again, can you tell me where you were between 11 and 1pm on Tuesday the 17th March?
1506	R	(Suspect makes no reply. Refuses to look at me.)
1724	Sgt Farr.	Are these your trainers Lenny? (Suspect shown a pair of white Nike training shoes.) Stop tapping the table Lenny.
1806	R	Not mine, no way.
1815	Sgt Farr.	Well they were found in your flat, amongst your other footwear. You see, all the eye-witnesses describe seeing a man matching your appearance, wearing a pair of white trainers. They are all very clear about this. It so happens that you have a pair of white trainers in your flat. Were you wearing these trainers on the morning of the 17th March?
1950	R	(Inaudible reply.)
2000	Sgt Farr.	You take a shoe size 9 don't you Lenny? These are a size 9. Are these your shoes?
2030	R	They ain't mine. Someone must have left them at my place.
2057	Sgt Farr.	Has anyone stayed at your flat recently?
2103	R	Come on, let's get this sorted. I've got big things to do.
2218	Sgt Farr.	When you were arrested you were found in possession of a quantity of cannabis. Are you using drugs at the moment Lenny?
2228	R	(No reply.) (Suspect rocking the table, asked to desist.)
2330	Sgt Farr.	Do you know a man by the name of Lloyd Green?
2400	R	I know who you are talking about right—he ain't no mate of mine.

2459	Sgt Farr.	Would it surprise you to learn that a car registered to him was seen in Sunrise Road at around 11.30am on Tuesday the 17th March?
2502	R	(No reply)
2613	Sgt Farr.	We have an eye-witness who describes a man just like you approaching Lloyd Green's car in Sunrise Road sometime before midday. I suggest that man was you. What do you have to say?
2640	R	Look—fuck you. I need a cigarette. I ain't into robbing no old woman right. I don't understand this. I don't understand all this.
2705	Sgt Farr.	Why did you need to speak with Lloyd Green, Lenny?
2804	R	(No reply.)
2905	Sgt Farr.	I will ask you again Lenny—was it you seen talking to Lloyd Green?
3000	R	(No reply.)
3104	Sgt Farr.	Is Lloyd Green putting pressure on you Lenny? Do you owe him money?
3219	R	(Suspect makes no reply.)
3315	Sgt Farr.	Look at me, Lenny. This is your chance to offer an explanation. Is there anything you wish to tell me?
3510	R	How much longer are you keeping me here? I've gotta go. I've got things to do—important things. You're fitting me up anyway like you always do.
3609	Sgt Farr.	I can't say how much longer you will be here Lenny. That's up to you.
3720	R	Don't know nothing right about Lloyd Green.
4010	Sgt Farr	Shall I tell you what I think? I think you owe Lloyd Green money. He wants it and wants it now. He tells you to get it or else. You don't have any so either you or he decides you should steal it. You know the area. You agree he will knock on the door of the old lady you saw earlier. When she is distracted, you will break in and see what you can get your hands on. Nice and easy. Is that how it happened?
4202	R	(No reply.)
4230	Sgt Farr.	Look Lenny—this is a serious matter. How do you explain the evidence against you? The eye-witness who has identified you, the white training shoes found in your flat which all the eye-witnesses make reference to and the fact that you have admitted knowing Lloyd Green. Is it all coincidence Lenny?
4406	R	Alright, I stole it from the old lady yeah. I needed the money right. Now fucking charge me and let me get out of here.
4440	Sgt Farr.	Calm down Lenny and sit down. There is no need to get uptight. Who was your accomplice Lenny? Who distracted the lady at her front door?
4500	R	I am not saying anything more. Charge me if you are going to and let me out of here. I ain't saying nothing more.
4530	Sgt Farr.	Did someone put you under pressure to commit this burglary? Was it Lloyd Green? Is he your supplier?
4600	R	(No reply.)

Suspect continues to be un-cooperative and verbally abusive. Interview terminated at 46 minutes.

DOCUMENT 26E WITNESS STATEMENT DC S SHAW

<u>WITNESS STATEMENT</u>

(CJ Act 1967, s. 9; MC Act 1980, s. 5A(3)(a) and s. 5B; Crim PR Part 16)

Name	Sarah Louise Shaw
Address	Lyme Street Police Station
Age/Date of Birth	Over 18
Occupation	Detective Constable 2890

....

Who states:

This statement, consisting of two pages signed by me, is true to the best of my knowledge and belief, and I make it knowing that if it is tendered in evidence I shall be liable to prosecution if I have wilfully stated in it anything which I know to be false or do not believe to be true.

Dated: 20th March   Signed: S Shaw

....

On the 17th March and in the company of Detective Sergeant Steven Farrington, I attended the home of Lillian Kennedy at 19 Sunrise Road, Lyme in response to a burglary.

As a result of our enquires, during the afternoon of March 17th, DS Farrington and I took Lillian Kennedy on a tour of the locality in an unmarked police car, to see if she could see the person or persons suspected of carrying out the burglary. In the course of the tour of the local area, Lillian Kennedy drew our attention to a male of Afro-Caribbean origin. The male was 5 ft 10 in and of slim build. He had shoulder-length, dreadlocked hair and a slight goatee beard. He was wearing a black hooded sweatshirt and black jogging bottoms. He was wearing a pair of brown training shoes. I recognised this male as being Lenny Wise, an individual who I have had dealings with on a previous occasion. For operational reasons, a decision was taken not to arrest Lenny Wise at this time as further enquires were being pursued in connection with a possible accomplice.

At 15.15 hours on the 19th March, Lenny Wise was approached by Sergeant Farrington and me outside his flat at 4a Lymewood Court. Lenny Wise was arrested and cautioned by Sgt Farrington. He made no comment upon arrest. A search of his flat was conducted pursuant to s. 32 PACE. In his presence, DS Farrington seized a black hooded sweatshirt (Exhibit SF1) and a pair of size 9 white Nike training shoes were also seized (right shoe exhibit number SF2 and left shoe exhibit number SF3). In the course of searching Lenny Wise, DS Farrington found a quantity of cannabis resin in his trouser pocket.

Wise was interviewed by DS Farrington in my presence at Lyme Street Police Station on the 20th March. The interview concluded after 46 minutes. One tape was used during the interview and a copy of the sealed tape is available (exhibit SF6).

At the conclusion of the interview Lenny Wise was charged with burglary and cautioned.

Mr Wise was denied police bail and was escorted to Lyme Magistrates' Court.

Signed: DC S Shaw 4890

DOCUMENT 26F FURTHER WITNESS STATEMENT OF SHIRLEY LEWIS

WITNESS STATEMENT

(CJ Act 1967, s. 9; MC Act 1980, s. 5A(3)(a) and s. 5B;Crim PR Part 16)

Name	Shirley Lewis
Address Supplied	
Age/Date of Birth	Over 18
Occupation	Retired Teacher

Who states:

This statement (consisting of one page signed each by me) is true to the best of my knowledge and belief and I make it knowing that if it is tendered in evidence I shall be liable to prosecution if I have wilfully stated in it anything which I know to be false or do not believe to be true.

Dated: 20th March

Signature: S Lewis

I reside at the address shown overleaf. I have been asked to view a video identification parade as a result of an incident that I witnessed on the 17th March, when at the home of my aunt at 19 Sunrise Road, Lyme. The incident occurred at around midday on the 17th March.

On the 20th March, I was at the Identification Suite at Lyme Police Station when I was shown a Video Identification Parade.

- After viewing the Video Parade, I identified the person at position No 2 on the Video

I can confirm that before viewing the Video Parade I was supervised by WPC Khan who informed me that I was not allowed to discuss the incident with any other person, including any other witness, and that no such conversation took place. I have not seen any broadcast or published films or photographs, or any descriptions relating to the offence for which I am a witness.

Signature: S Lewis

DOCUMENT 26G FURTHER WITNESS STATEMENT OF HAROLD FINNEY

<u>WITNESS STATEMENT</u>

(CJ Act 1967, s. 9; MC Act 1980, s. 5A(3)(a) and s. 5B;Crim PR Part 16)

Name	Harold Finney
Address	Withheld
Age/Date of Birth	Over 18
Occupation	Retired Engineer

Who states:

This statement, consisting of one page signed by me, is true to the best of my knowledge and belief, and I make it knowing that if it is tendered in evidence I shall be liable to prosecution if I have wilfully stated in it anything which I know to be false or do not believe to be true.

Dated: 20th March   Signature: H Finney

I reside at the address shown overleaf.

As a result of an incident that I witnessed on the 17th March when I saw a black man approach a car in Sunrise Road at around 11.50 am. On the 20th March I was at the Identification Suite at Lyme Police Station when I was shown a Video Identification Parade.

> • After viewing the Video Parade, I identified the person at position No 4 on the Video

I can confirm that before viewing the Video Parade I was supervised by WPC Khan who informed me that I was not allowed to discuss the incident with any other person, including any other witness, and that no such conversation took place. I have not seen any broadcast or published films or photographs, or any descriptions relating to the offence for which I am a witness.

Signature: H Finney

DOCUMENT 26H WITNESS STATEMENT OF LILLIAN KENNEDY

<u>WITNESS STATEMENT</u>

(CJ Act 1967, s. 9; MC Act 1980, s. 5A(3)(a) and s. 5B;Crim PR Part 16)

Name	Lillian Kennedy
Address	Supplied
Age/Date of Birth	Over 18
Occupation	Retired

Who states:

This statement, consisting of one page signed by me, is true to the best of my knowledge and belief, and I make it knowing that if it is tendered in evidence I shall be liable to prosecution if I have wilfully stated in it anything which I know to be false or do not believe to be true.

Dated: 20th March   Signature: L Kennedy

I reside at the address shown overleaf.

As a result of an incident that I witnessed on the 17th March when I was approached by a black man in the street where I live in Sunrise Road, I was at the Identification Suite at Lyme Police Station when I was shown a Video Identification Parade.

- After viewing the Video Parade, I was unable to identify any person

I can confirm that before viewing the Video Parade I was supervised by WPC Khan who informed me that I was not allowed to discuss the incident with any other person, including any other witness, and that no such conversation took place. I have not seen any broadcast or published films or photographs, or any descriptions relating to the offence for which I am a witness.

Signature: L Kennedy

DOCUMENT 261 WITNESS STATEMENT OF SCIENTIFIC SUPPORT OFFICER

<u>WITNESS STATEMENT</u>

(CJ Act 1967, s. 9; MC Act 1980, s. 5A(3)(a) and s. 5B;Crim PR Part 16)

Statement of: Carol Jayne Lawton   Title

Age if under 18: Over 18   Occupation: Scenes of Crime Officer

This statement (consisting of 2 pages signed each by me) is true to the best of my knowledge and belief and I make it knowing that if it is tendered in evidence I shall be liable to prosecution if I have wilfully stated in it anything which I know to be false or do not believe to be true.

Dated: 20th March

Signature: Carol Lawton

I am a Scientific Support Officer employed by Lymeshire Police based at Lyme Street Police Station. At 1430 hours on the 17th March, as a result of a message received, I attended 19 Sunrise Road, Lyme. The property is a house in a residential area and is occupied by an elderly female who lives alone. At the side of the house there is a concrete porch area which is covered from the elements by an enclosed carport. Access to the carport can be gained from the front of the property and from the rear. Access from the rear of the property involves walking through a garden which contains soil beds. The soil beds were wet from a heavy downpour of rain during the night and the preceding days. While I was in the garden area I noticed several footprints on soil beds. I conducted a visual examination of the concrete porch area leading up to the back door of the property and discovered several shoeprints bearing slight soil deposits.

While I was there I took certain photographs, some of which were duplicated, from which an album of prints has been produced marked CJL1, which I would describe as follows:

CJL1 (Shoe marks) Album of Prints (Exhibit No)

Photo 1 View of the back door of 19 Sunrise Road, Lyme

Photo 2 View of the car port from the garden gate of 19 Sunrise Road, Lyme

Photo 3 View of concrete porch

Photo 4 View of shoe mark on concrete

Photo 5 View of shoe mark on concrete

Photo 6 View of shoe mark on concrete

Photo 7 View of shoe mark on concrete

Photo 8 View of CJL2 and CJL3 (Exhibit No) in place before being lifted.

All negatives are filed at the Chief Constables office bearing reference number LP-200510965-0971.

During the course of my examination, I retained the following items, and packaged and labelled them as follows:
CJL 2 Shoe mark 16 cm from backdoor of property electrostatically lifted

CJL 3 Shoe mark 8 cm from backdoor of property electrostatically lifted

The above items were retained in my possession until I returned to the Scenes of Crime store. I placed items CJL2 and CJL3 into a laboratory sack and sealed it with a tag number B8760456. I placed the sack in the secure Scenes of Crime Store.

At 1700 hours on the 19th March, while on duty at Lyme Street police station, I attended the property store. There I took possession of the following items from reference number 256/789432:

SF2 Left white Nike training shoe (Exhibit No ....)

SF3 Right white Nike training shoe (Exhibit No ....)

I placed SF2 into a laboratory sack and sealed it with tag number B49304667. I placed the sack into the secure Scenes of Crime store. I placed SF3 into a laboratory sack and sealed it with tag number B49304668. I placed both sacks into the secure Scenes of Crime store.

At 1845 on the 19th March, I attended Lyme Street Custody Suite from where I collected the following item, labelled as:

SF5 (Exhibit no) DNA mouth swab (x2).

I placed this item into a transit sack which I then sealed with tag no B986740.

All the transit sacks collected in conjunction with this investigation were left in secure and appropriate storage within Lyme Street Scenes of Crime Department for collection and then onward delivery to the Forensic Science Laboratory.

Signature CJ Lawton SOCO 6512

DOCUMENT 26J WITNESS STATEMENT OF FORENSIC SCIENTIST

Laboratory Reference: 500 679 4033
Order Reference: 400 593 1297
The Forensic Science Service

DS Steve Farrington
Lyme Street Policing Unit
Lymeshire Police

Client Reference: URN 05/2218

<u>WITNESS STATEMENT</u>
(CJ Act 1967, s. 9; MC Act 1980, s. 5A(3)(a) and s. 5B;Crim PR Part 19)
Statement of: Sarah Hardacker BSc (Hons)
Age of Witness: Over 18
Occupation of Witness: Forensic Scientist for Forensic Science Service
Address of witness: Morley Laboratory, Forensic Science Service, Belfield House, Nile Street, Birmingham.

I declare that:
This statement (consisting of 4 pages signed each by me) is true to the best of my knowledge and belief and I make it knowing that if it is tendered in evidence I shall be liable to prosecution if I have wilfully stated in it anything which I know to be false or do not believe to be true.

Also that:
I am an expert in the field of forensic science. I hold the degree of Bachelor of Science with an Honours Degree in Applied Biochemistry and have worked as a Forensic Scientist since 1995. During this time I have dealt with many investigations involving footwear.

I have been asked to provide a statement. I confirm that I have read the guidance in a booklet known as Disclosure Expert's evidence and unused material which details my role and documents my responsibilities, in relation to revelation as an expert witness. I have the followed the guidance and recognise the continuing nature of my responsibilities of revelation. In accordance with my duties of revelation, as documented in the guidance booklet, I:

a. confirm that I have complied with my duties to record, retain and reveal material in accordance with the Criminal Procedure and Investigations Act 1996, as amended:

b. have compiled an Index of all material. I will ensure that the Index is updated in the event I am provided with or generate additional material;

c. understand that in the event my opinion changes on any material issue, I will inform the investigating officer, as soon as reasonably practicable and give reasons:

Date: 25th March
SIGNATURE: S HARDACKER

FSS Reference: 203840/YTT34
DEFENDANT: LENNY WISE

RECEIPT OF ITEMS
Records show that on the 20th March amongst other items, the 4 items described below relating to an investigation of a burglary at domestic premises in Lyme were received at the Morely laboratory of the Forensic Science Service from Lymeshire Police.

<u>From 19 Sunrise Road, Lyme</u>
CJL2 Electrostatic shoeprint lift
CJL3 Electrostatic shoeprint lift

<u>From Lenny Wise</u>
SF2 Left white training shoe
SF3 Right white training shoe.

BACKGROUND INFORMATION

From the information provided by the Police, I understand the following:

On the 17th March a burglary occurred at 19 Sunrise Road, Lyme. Entry to the property was gained through an unlocked backdoor while the sole occupant of the property was distracted by a caller at the front door.

A subsequent Scene of Crime examination recovered footwear marks on a concrete surface near to the backdoor of the property. The shoeprints are believed to belong to the offender.

Lenny WISE was arrested on the 20th March and following a search of his home address 4A Lymewood Court, Lyme a pair of white size 9 white Nike trainers were recovered.

This is the information on which I have based my examination and have used in the interpretation of the findings.

PURPOSE OF EXAMINATION

To determine whether or not the recovered training shoes relating to Lenny WISE have made the footwear marks recovered from 19 Sunrise Road, Lyme.

LABORATORY EXAMINATION

With this aim in mind, the following items have been examined:-

Re: 4A Lymewood Court, Lyme (relating to Lenny WISE)

FS2 and FS3—Pair of Nike white training shoes

Re: 19 Sunrise Road, Lyme

CJL 2—Footwear lifts from concrete porch

CJL 3—Footwear lifts from concrete porch

These items have been examined with the help of scientific assistants, details of which are noted on the Forensic Examination Record, SH/FER/1 that accompanies this statement. Details of the examination are documented in the case notes which can be inspected at the laboratory under order number 400 593 1297.

TECHNICAL ISSUES

When a person steps onto a surface, a mark may be left of the under-surface of their footwear. This footwear impression will persist for a long time if left undisturbed. It may be preserved, recovered and enhanced in order to facilitate a detailed comparison, at the Forensic Science Laboratory, between it and test impressions taken from the suspect's shoes. Details such as pattern, general size and degree of wear can be compared. Additionally, any marks in the scene impression that correspond to damage features on the under-sole of the shoe can provide conclusive evidence to connect that particular shoe to the scene. Any such footwear marks can be compared with any recovered items of footwear.

RESULTS OF EXAMINATION

Re: Lenny WISE

The training shoes (SF2 and SF3) are a pair of size 9 Nike with a sole pattern of zigzag fine bars and blocks. The soles of the training shoes are worn, with damage evident on both of the soles. The sole pattern of these boots is only one of a vast range of sole patterns available on sports/casual footwear and is one of the more frequently encountered patterns at the laboratory. On the right shoe there is a cut measuring 3 mm.

Re: CJL 2 and CJL 3

Items are two photographs of electrostatically dust print lifted footwear marks. The clearest mark, depicted on photograph CJL2 corresponds in pattern, size/configuration and wear to the submitted right training shoe (SF3). In addition there are features in the mark that correspond to features of random damage on the sole of the same right shoe. There was one mark in the impression taken from the right shoe and while not clearly defined nonetheless corresponded to the feature of damage on the right training shoe.

There is a poor quality and poorly defined footwear mark depicted on the lift CJL3 that corresponds in pattern and is appropriate in terms of size and configuration and wear to the submitted left training shoe SF2. However, given the quality of the mark and detail obtained from the footwear mark on the other lift (CJL2) this footwear mark has not been examined in any further detail.

INTERPRETATION

In my opinion, the degree of correspondence observed between the footwear mark on the concrete floor of the backdoor porch and the submitted right training shoe is of the utmost significance. Indeed, I consider the likelihood of the observed degree of correspondence occurring by sheer coincidence, if the training shoe did not make the respective mark on the concrete floor, to be so remote as to be discounted on a practical basis. There was one mark in one of the impressions that corresponds to damage features on the under-sole of Mr Wise's right training shoe. Damage features are acquired randomly on footwear and so

I therefore consider this finding enhances the significance of the pattern match and in my opinion the overall degree of correspondence is much more likely if this shoe made the impression rather than some other footwear taken from the random population.

CONCLUSION

In my opinion, the results of this examination provide very strong evidence that the right training shoe relating to Lenny WISE has made a mark on the concrete floor close to the backdoor of 19 Sunrise Road, Lyme.

(Scale of Evidential Support:—no, limited, moderate, moderately strong, strong, very strong, extremely strong, conclusive.)

Signed: S Hardacker

DOCUMENT 27 CPS LETTER REGARDING CPIA 1996 DISCLOSURE (SPECIMEN LETTER)

Important note: The letter below is the authors' interpretation of the type of letter that a solicitor might receive from the Crown Prosecution Service. The letter is not representative of any communication sent by the Crown Prosecution Service and should not be seen as representative of how the Crown Prosecution Service would respond in this scenario.

CROWN PROSECUTION SERVICE
Blackburn Street,
Lyme
LY3 2BE
21/5/-

Hannibal and Mountford Solicitors
20 High Street,
Lyme
LY10 34T

Dear Sirs,
Re: Lenny Wise
Date of Next Hearing: PTPH 13th September
Disclosure of Prosecution Material under section 3, Criminal Procedure and
Investigations Act 1996 (CPIA).
Notice of intention to adduce evidence of your client's character under s 101 Criminal
Justice Act 2003
I am required by section 3 of the above Act, to disclose to you any prosecution material, which has not previously been disclosed, which might reasonably be considered capable of undermining the case for the prosecution or of assisting the case for the accused.

Attached to this letter is a copy of a schedule of non-sensitive material prepared by the police in compliance with their duty under Part II CPIA and the provisions of the Code of Practice. The schedule has been prepared by the Police Disclosure Officer, who in this case is DS Hague.

Where the word 'evidence' appears alongside any item, all the items listed on the schedule are intended to be part of the prosecution case. You will receive a written notice should the position change.

Where indicated, copies of the items listed are attached. Material marked as available for inspection can be viewed by arrangement with myself.

This material is disclosed to you in accordance with the provisions of the CPIA, and you must not use or disclose it, or any information recorded in it, for any purpose other than in connection with these criminal proceedings. If you do so without the permission of the court, you may commit an offence.

If you supply a written defence statement to me and to the court within 28 days of the date of the receipt of this letter, material which has not been disclosed at this stage will be further reviewed in the light of that statement.

A defence statement is required in Crown Court cases. In magistrates' court cases, a defence statement is optional. In accordance with my continuing duty to consider disclosure, I will review the information you provide in the statement to identify any remaining material which has not already been disclosed. The statement will also be relied on by the court if you later make an application under section 8 CPIA. If you do not make a CPIA-compliant defence statement where one is required or provided, or do so late, the court may hear comment and/or draw an adverse inference.

It is essential that you preserve this schedule in its present form, as access to any material will only be granted upon its production to the disclosure officer.

I am also enclosing notice of my intention to adduce evidence of your client's bad character under s 101 Criminal Justice Act 2003.

If you have a query in connection with this letter, please contact myself.

Yours faithfully,
Lewis Rowe
Crown Prosecution Service

DOCUMENT 27A POLICE SCHEDULE OF NON-SENSITIVE UNUSED MATERIAL

RESTRICTED (when complete)

MG6C

POLICE SCHEDULE OF RELEVANT NON-SENSITIVE UNUSED MATERIAL

R v LENNY WISE

| | | | URN | 74 | 95 | 21 | 9 | L |

The Disclosure Officer believes the following RELEVANT MATERIAL which does not form part of the prosecution case is NOT SENSITIVE. For further detailed guidance refer to the Disclosure Manual and Attorney General's Guidelines.

FOR CPS USE:
* Enter D = Disclose to defence
  I = Item disclosable and defence may inspect
  CND = Clearly not disclosable (by description)

Item No.	Record below MATERIAL of any kind, including information and objects, which is obtained in the course of a criminal investigation and which may be relevant to the investigation; and RELEVANCE is that it has some bearing on any offence under investigation or any person being investigated or on the surrounding circumstances of the case, unless it is incapable of having any impact on the case. **Do not speculate if it is not considered relevant do not record it on the schedule.** Give a sufficiently detailed DESCRIPTION of the relevant material for the prosecutor to make a decision on whether or not it should be examined.	LOCATION State precisely where the item can be found/located	*	REASON FOR DECISION
1	The relevant material is: Tape recording of 999 call 17/3/-from witness S Lewis-description of suspect	Lyme Street Police Station control room	D	Shoe colour different when seen later in street
2	The relevant material is: Incident (CAD) Log no. 3569/0/-(17/3/-details of witness S Lewis and description of suspects	Lyme Street Police Station control room	D	Shoe colour different when seen later in street
3	Pocket note-book entry-DC 2198 Shaw re details of crime report contains details of first description of suspects	With DC 2198 Shaw	D	Shoe colour different when seen later in street
4	Pocket note-book entry DS 4291 Farrington re: arrests and interview of GREEN and WISE	With DS 4201 Farrington	CND	
5	Pocket note-book details search of premises –DC 2198 Shaw, Flat 4a Lymewood Court, Parkdale, Lyme-home address of WISE	With DC 2198 Shaw	CND	
6	The relevant material is: Custody record no. 2346/12/-GREEN	Lyme PS	CND	
7	The relevant material is: Custody record no: 2305/12/-WISE	Lyme PS	D	Disclosable under PACE 1984
8	The relevant material is: PNC printout of previous convictions of GREEN	Lyme PS	CND	
9	The relevant material is: Record of interview with GREEN	Lyme PS	CND	
10	The relevant material is: Submission forms to FSS dated	Lyme PS	CND	

Signature: Date: 28/4/

Name: DC 2486 David Hague

Reviewing lawyer signature:
Print Name: Lewis Rowe
Date 14/5

RESTRICTED (when complete)

2010/11

Page 1 of 1

DOCUMENT 27A POLICE SCHEDULE OF NON-SENSITIVE UNUSED MATERIAL

RESTRICTED (when complete)

MG6C

POLICE SCHEDULE OF RELEVANT NON-SENSITIVE UNUSED MATERIAL

R v LENNY WISE

URN | T 4 | 95 | 21 | 9 L

The Disclosure Officer believes the following RELEVANT MATERIAL which does not form part of the prosecution case is NOT SENSITIVE. For further detailed guidance refer to the Disclosure Manual and Attorney General's Guidelines.

FOR CPS USE:
* Enter D = Disclose to defence
I = Item disclosable and defence may inspect
CND = Clearly not disclosable (by description)

Item No.	Record below MATERIAL of any kind... (see guidance)	LOCATION State precisely where the item can be found/located	*	REASON FOR DECISION
11	The relevant material is: Letter from FSS dated	On file	CND	
12	The relevant material is: DNA swab sample taken from WISE	On file	CND	
13	Inspector C Sutton –contemporaneous hand written notes of Video Identification procedure (Form 116/2)	On file	CND	
14	The relevant material is: Mobile phone records GREEN	On file	CND	
15	The relevant material is: Mobile phone records WISE	On file	CND	
	The relevant material is:			
	The relevant material is:			
	The relevant material is:			
	The relevant material is:			
	The relevant material is:			

Signature:
Date: 2 8 4

Name: David Hague DC 2486

Reviewing lawyer signature
Print Name: LEWIS ROWE
Date 14 5

RESTRICTED (when complete)

2010/11

Page 1 of 1

DOCUMENT 30 ADDITIONAL STATEMENT OF LENNY WISE—COMMENTS ON EVIDENCE DISCLOSED IN THE CASE SENT BUNDLE

I have read the witness statements served by the prosecution and make the following observations.

Lillian Kennedy

I think I know this lady. I have seen her before when I have walked my dog Butch. If she says it was me who approached her on the day in question then she is mistaken. I do not recollect going into Sunrise Road on the 17th March.

Shirley Lewis

This witness is mistaken. There is no way she could have seen me at the back of the old lady's house. I was not there. She says the man she saw was wearing white training shoes. I do not wear white training shoes. She may have seen me in the area on one or two occasions. As I already said I walk my dog Butch (a terrier) in fields near to Sunrise Road. I am not the only black man who lives in the area. She is confusing me with someone else.

Harold Finney

I did not see or approach any black car in Sunrise Road.

DS Steve Farrington

I dislike this police officer. On the way back from the interview room he said that I deserved everything the court would throw at me. Nobody explained to me why I could not have an identification parade. The police let me make a phone call to my sister, but she wasn't in when I rang. I was offered a solicitor but I honestly didn't think there was much point in one being there. The police were going to fit me up whatever. I was really desperate to get out of the police station. I seemed to have been there forever. I wanted a cigarette and I was worried about Butch my dog and about Sonia. I didn't feel very well during the interview and cannot honestly remember what I said. Looking back I should have had a solicitor present. All I wanted was for the interview to be over and done with, so that I could be charged and released on bail. The police got me to say what they wanted to hear. What I said to them in interview about my involvement is untrue. I wish to retract my statement.

I told the custody sergeant the following morning that I was on medication. He asked me why I hadn't mentioned it before. I cannot remember whether I was asked at the outset whether I was on medication. I just felt totally out of it. He called the police doctor who examined me. I believe an officer went back to my flat to collect my medication.

I was examined by a GP. He didn't seem much interested in me. He gave me my medication and told me I was fine.

I swear that I have never worn the white trainers. They were given to me by a friend. I cannot remember who because I often have friends come to see me and sometimes they stay over. I have not worn the shoes.

Lloyd Green

I believe Lloyd Green has not said anything against me. I do know Lloyd Green. He is a drug dealer and loan shark. I have owed him money in the past. He can get a bit rough with you when you don't 'come up with the goods'. I cannot say whether Lloyd Green was involved in this burglary or not as I wasn't there.

Dated : 22/7

DOCUMENT 31 - LETTER TO CPS DEALING WITH CPIA 1996 MATTERS AND BAD CHARACTER NOTICE UNDER S. 101 CRIMINAL JUSTICE ACT 2003

HANNIBAL AND MOUNTFORD SOLICITORS

20 High Street,
Lyme Bank, Lyme
LY10 34T
Telephone: 01576–455971
Fax: 01576–200345
Email: Hannibal@solicitors.co.uk

Crown Prosecution Service
Queen's Chambers
Blackburn Street
Lyme
LY3 2BE

Date: 7/8
Ref: LR/JW
Our ref: RJ/SW

Dear Sirs,
R v Lenny Wise
Date of Next Hearing—Pre-Trial Hearing—Lyme Crown Court 13 September: Trial Date: 30 September

We enclose our client's defence statement under s. 5, Criminal Procedure and Investigations Act 1996. With further reference to s. 6C CPIA 1996, our client does not propose to call any defence witnesses at this time. We shortly intend to take counsel's opinion in this matter and if we are in a position to agree prosecution witness evidence we will notify you accordingly.

We look forward to receiving further prosecution disclosure. In particular, we would like disclosure of Lloyd Green's interview. We note that you do not propose to disclose the telephone records pertaining to the mobile phones seized respectively from Lenny Wise and Lloyd Green. We assume this is on the basis that the records do not establish a connection between the phones? We would like to have this agreed as a formal admission under s. 10 CJA 1967 if this is the case.

We intend to dispute the admissibility of our client's interview with the police in connection with this matter. We have instructed our client's consultant psychiatrist, Dr Oliver A Mayhew to provide us with an expert opinion as to our client's state of mind at the time of his interview. Consequently we will want to cross-examine the custody officers who were responsible for compiling the custody record in relation to our client. We will also want to cross-examine the police doctor who examined our client and Inspector Rushton who reviewed our client's detention. Please confirm that you will ensure the attendance of these witnesses. We will of course require our client's custody record and the transcript of interview to be admitted into evidence. For these reasons we will require tape-playing facilities in court. We anticipate that the point of law which arises in connection with the interview in this case will be resolved at the pre-trial hearing of the matter on the 13 September.

We also enclose notice of our intention to oppose the admission of our client's past bad character at his forthcoming trial.

We look forward to hearing from you accordingly.

Yours faithfully
R James
Hannibal and Mountford

Anthony Hannibal (BA Partner), Louise Mountford (LL.B Partner), Denis Davies
(LL.B Partner) Tim Howard (LL.B Associate Solicitor), David Temple (LL.B Associate Solicitor),
Rachel James (LL.B Associate Solicitor), Mike Tamworth (Fellow of the
Institute of Legal Executives), Lisa Hardy (Accredited Police Station Clerk),
Ali Khan (Accredited Police Station Clerk)
Regulated by the Solicitors Regulation Authority

Note: A copy of this letter and its enclosures will also be sent to the Crown Court.

DOCUMENT 32(A) DEFENCE STATEMENT

Sections 5 and 6, Criminal Procedure and Investigation Act 1996

REGINA v LENNY WISE

1. I, Lenny Wise deny that I was the person responsible for committing a burglary at 19 Sunrise Road, Lyme between 11.45am–12.30pm on the 17 March this year.

2. I take issue with those prosecution witnesses who suggest that I was one of the two men involved in the burglary.

I deny that I was in the vicinity of Sunrise Road at any time between 11am and 12.30pm on the 17 March this year. I was not in the area at the relevant time. I cannot specifically recall my precise whereabouts during these times. My daily routine is to get up at around 10am and take my dog for a walk. I believe I was in Lyme High Street between 11am–12.30pm. Consequently, Lillian Kennedy is mistaken when she identified me on the street to the police on the afternoon of the 17 March as being the male who had offered to help her with her in Sunrise Road earlier that day. I take issue with Shirley Lewis's identification of me as the male she saw leaving the back garden of the burgled property. She is mistaken. Her identification of me is based on mistaken recognition. I accept that I have walked my dog on occasions in the area near Sunrise Road and that my appearance is somewhat distinctive. However, I was not in or near Sunrise Road on the 17 March. I do not take issue with Harold Finney's statement. He does not identify me as being the male he saw approaching a black car parked in Sunrise Road.

I do not take issue with the composition or conduct of the VIPER procedure. I contend however that Shirley Lewis and Lillian Kennedy are mistaken in their identification of me.

3. I wish to retract what I said in interview on the 20 March regarding the circumstances of this offence. What I said at the end of my interview is untrue. I intend to dispute the admissibility of my interview with the police. At the time of my interview I was and still am afflicted by bipolar depression. I did not have the services of a solicitor or an appropriate adult. I will contend, as a matter of law, that my interview should be excluded under ss. 76 (2)(b) and 78 PACE 1984 for breaches of the Police and Criminal Evidence Act 1984 and Code C of the PACE Codes of Practice.

4. I deny that the white training shoes recovered from my flat belong to me. I have never worn them.

5. I do not propose to call any witnesses in my defence other than a Consultant psychiatrist who will tender an expert opinion as to the reliability of the statements I made during the interview process.

6. In compliance with my obligations under s. 6C CPIA 1996, I do not propose to call any defence witnesses at this time.

Signed: Lenny Wise   Date: 15 June

To:
Crown Prosecution Service
Lyme Crown Court

DOCUMENT 32(A)
DEFENCE STATEMENT

(Criminal Procedure and Investigations Act 1996, section 5 & 6; Criminal
Procedure and Investigations Act 1996 (Defence Disclosure Time Limits)
Regulations 2011; Criminal Procedure Rules, rule 15.4)

Case details
Name of defendant: LENNY
WISE Court: LYME CROWN
COURT
Case reference number: LC\2928449T
Charge(s): BURGLARY

<u>When to use this form</u>
If you are a defendant pleading not guilty:

(a) in a Crown Court case, you **must** give the information listed in Part 2 of this form;

(b) in a magistrates' court case, you **may** give that information but you do not have to do so.

The time limit for giving the information is:

14 days (in a magistrates' court case)

28 days (in a Crown Court case)

after initial prosecution disclosure (or notice from the prosecutor that there is no material to
disclose).

<u>How to use this form</u>

1. Complete the case details box above, and Part 1 below.

2. Attach as many sheets as you need to give the information listed in Part 2.

3. Sign and date the completed form.

4. Send a copy of the completed form to:

   (a) the court, and

   (b) the prosecutor

<u>before the time limit expires.</u>
If you need more time, you **must** apply to the court **before** the time limit expires. You should apply in
writing, but no special form is needed.

Part 1: Plea
I confirm that I intend to plead not guilty to [the charge] against me.

Part 2: Nature of the defence
Attach as many sheets as you need to give the information required.

Under section 6A of the Criminal Procedure and Investigations Act 1996, you must:

(a) set out the nature of your defence, including any particular defences on which you intend to rely;

(b) indicate the matters of fact on which you take issue with the prosecutor, and in respect of each explain why;

(c) set out particulars of the matters of fact on which you intend to rely for the purposes of your defence;

(d) indicate any point of law that you wish to take, including any point about the admissibility of evidence or about abuse of process, and any authority relied on; and

(e) if your defence statement includes an alibi (i.e. an assertion that you were in a place, at a time, inconsistent with you having committed the offence), give particulars, including:

(i) the name, address and date of birth of any witness who you believe can give evidence in support of that alibi,

(ii) if you do not know all of those details, any information that might help identify or find that witness.

Signed: R James.......................Defendant's solicitor

Date: 5 August

WARNING: Under section 11 of the Criminal Procedure and Investigations Act 1996, **if you (a) do not disclose what the Act requires; (b) do not give a defence statement before the time limit expires; (c) at trial, rely on a defence, or facts, that you have not disclosed; or (d) at trial, call an alibi witness whom you have not identified in advance, then the court, the prosecutor or another defendant may comment on that, and the court may draw such inferences as it thinks proper in deciding whether you are guilty.**

DOCUMENT 39 BRIEF TO COUNSEL TO ATTEND A PRE-TRIAL HEARING IN LYME CROWN COURT

LYME CROWN COURT   **LISTING NO.**

REGINA

-v-

LENNY WISE

BRIEF ON BEHALF OF THE DEFENDANT TO APPEAR AT FCMH – 13 SEPTEMBER AT 10 am AND AT THE SUBSEQUENT TRIAL ON 30 SEPTEMBER

Counsel receives herewith copies of the following:

1. Proof of evidence of Lenny Wise dated 20 March

2. Draft Indictment

3. Case sent bundle including:

    a) Statement of Lillian Kennedy (x2)

    b) Statement of Shirley Lewis (x2)

    c) Statement of Harold Finney (x2)

    d) Statement of DS Farrington

    e) Statement of DC Shaw

    f) Statement of WPC Anjuna Khan

    g) Statement of WPC Emma Mason

    h) Statement of Inspector Christopher Sutton

    i) Statement of WPC Josie Bradbury

    j) Statement of PC Peter Reynolds

    k) Statement of Carol Lawton SOCO

    l) Statement of Sarah Hardacker

    m) Transcript of interview: Lenny Wise

    n) Previous convictions of Lenny Wise

    o) Exhibit list

4. Statement of Lenny Wise with comments on the prosecution evidence dated 22 May

5. Defence Psychiatric Report

6. Custody Record

7. Tapes of interview

8. Initial Prosecution Disclosure (unused)

9. Defence Statement

10. Notice of intention to adduce evidence of Lenny Wise's previous convictions

11. Defence notice objecting to the admissibility of Mr Wise's previous criminal convictions.

12. Further Prosecution Disclosure

    a) Record of interview with Lloyd Green

    b) Letter from Forensic Science Service

13. Copy letter to the CPS dated 30 May including witness requirements

14. Representation order

15. Plea and Trial Preparation Form

Introduction

Counsel's instructing solicitors act on behalf of Lenny Wise. As Counsel will see from the enclosed draft indictment, Mr Wise is charged with burglary. It is alleged he broke into 19 Sunrise Road on the 17 March this year and stole £75. Mr Wise intends to plead not guilty to the burglary allegation. Upon his arrest, Mr Wise was found to be in possession of a small quantity of cannabis. He pleaded guilty to simple possession and was sentenced to a conditional discharge for 12 months by Lyme Magistrates on the 27 March.

Chronology

Mr Wise was arrested on the 19 March. He appeared before Lyme Magistrates on the 20 March when bail was refused. He subsequently appeared again on the 27 March when bail was refused for a second time and jurisdiction to try the matter was refused and the case was sent to the Crown Court. On the 29 March our client appeared before a Crown Court Judge in chambers at Lyme Crown Court and was granted bail subject to a number of conditions.

The Plea and Trial Preparation Hearing in this case was held on the 1 May. As a result of that the PTPH judge determined that a pre-trial hearing should be held to determine the admissibility of incriminating admissions made by our client whilst he was unrepresented at the police station. Counsel is instructed to attend the PTH. It is also our intention to instruct counsel to represent Mr Wise at trial on the 30 September.

Prosecution Case and Evidential Matters

On the 17 March a burglary occurred at 19 Sunrise Road, Lyme (the home of 84-year-old Lillian Kennedy) sometime between 1145 hours and midday. The prosecution contend that this was a distraction burglary. It is alleged that a man knocked on the door of 19 Sunrise Road on the pretence of having to use the telephone and whilst the occupier was distracted, the burglar gained entry to the property via an unlocked back door and proceeded to steal £75 from the victim's purse. The prosecution contend that the person entering the property was Mr Wise. It is believed that the man responsible for distracting Mrs Kennedy at her front door is Lloyd Green. Although Green was arrested and interviewed he has not been charged with any offence arising out of this incident. In his interview with the police he denied any involvement in the burglary and did not implicate Lenny Wise. Instructing solicitors do not act for Lloyd Green and did not represent him at the police station.

The principal evidence against Mr Wise comprises eye-witness identification; confession evidence and forensic circumstantial evidence. We will deal with each in turn.

Counsel will see the statements of Lillian Kennedy contained in the case sent bundle that she did not see the man who entered her property. She states however that she was stopped by a man in her street who offered to help her with her shopping. This was approximately 30–40 minutes before the burglary. On a subsequent tour of the local area the afternoon of the burglary she identified Lenny Wise as being that person. The police did not immediately arrest Mr Wise. At a subsequent VIPER identification procedure however Mrs Kennedy failed to identify Mr Wise which rather casts her earlier street identification into doubt. Mrs Kennedy does however provide a description of the man who approached her which accords for the most part with the description of a man seen leaving the backdoor of the burgled property by another eye-witness. When Mrs Kennedy pointed Mr Wise out to the police he was wearing the same attire save in one significant respect-he was not observed to be wearing white training shoes. In the circumstances it is difficult to see what Mrs Kennedy's evidence contributes to the prosecution's case. Counsel is asked to advise on this point and consider whether her evidence may be challenged on the basis of its relevance. Counsel will note that Mrs Kennedy spoke with the man who knocked on her front door. She was however unable to identify Lloyd Green at a VIPER identification procedure.

Of central importance to the prosecution's case is the evidence of Shirley Lewis. Counsel will see from her statement that she was in the back garden of a neighbouring property at midday when she saw a man behaving suspiciously near the back door of 19 Sunrise Road. She was hanging out some sheets on the washing line. She observed the man for a few seconds and was able to provide the police with a description of the man and his clothing. Her description accords with Mr Wise's actual appearance. She observed the man was wearing white training shoes. At a subsequent VIPER identification procedure, Mrs Lewis identified Lenny Wise as being that man. Her identification is based in part on recognition. She states she has seen Mr Wise before in the area. Mr Wise does not dispute this possibility as he lives near the victim and has, on occasion, walked his dog in fields near the burgled property. Mr Wise is adamant however that this witness is mistaken and that it was not the man she saw.

A link in the chain of evidence is provided by the account of Harold Finney. Mr Finney lives in a property across the road from the burgled house. At 11.30am he observed a car drive along Sunrise Road and park. He was suspicious of the car and noted the registration number. The car is registered to Lloyd Green. Mr Finney states he observed a black man on foot approach the car. He describes a man whose appearance is similar to that of Lenny Wise. He also describes the clothing the individual was wearing which included a dark sweatshirt and white training shoes. At this point Mr Finney was diverted by a telephone call. He saw nothing more of any relevance. At a subsequent VIPER identification parade, he picked out someone other than Lenny Wise. He never saw the driver of the car.

Counsel is asked to note that Mr Wise was unrepresented at the police station. Consequently the identification procedure was conducted in the absence of legal advice. Having reviewed the DVD compilation and the video of the viewing process, instructing solicitors are satisfied that the procedure was conducted fairly in accordance with Code D. The DVD compilation is included should counsel wish to consider it.

Upon arrest and pursuant to a s. 32 PACE 1984, a search of Mr Wise's flat was carried out. The police recovered a dark hooded sweatshirt and a pair of white size 9 Nike trainers. Counsel will note that in the course of the investigation shoeprint evidence was gathered from just outside the backdoor of the burgled property. Subsequent forensic comparison of the shoeprint lifts and the soles of the shoes recovered from Mr Wise's flat strongly suggest these training shoes were responsible for leaving the shoe prints. Mr Wise cannot offer an explanation for this other than to state the shoes were left at his flat by a friend, whose name he cannot recall. In interview he stated he had not worn the shoes. Document 12 b disclosed by way of further disclosure is useful in this respect. Counsel is asked to see whether this statement can be agreed under s. 9 CJA 1967.

The prosecution will seek to rely on the account given by Mr Wise in his interview with the police. It amounts to a confession. Counsel is referred to the transcript of interview in this regard. Mr Wise wishes to retract his confession for reasons considered in detail below.

The prosecution have served notice of their intention to adduce evidence of Mr Wise's previous criminal convictions.

Defence Case and Evidential Matters

Counsel will see Mr Wise's comments on the prosecution evidence in document 4. Counsel will see that a defence statement has been filed in this case. Mr Wise intends to plead not guilty. He wishes to strongly challenge the admissibility of his confession. He maintains that he is not the man responsible for the burglary. Despite our best efforts, Mr Wise is unable to substantiate his precise whereabouts at the relevant time with an alibi.

Instructing solicitors feel there are strong grounds for seeking the exclusion of Mr Wise's confession under ss. 76 (2)(b) and 78 PACE 1984. Counsel is referred at this juncture to Mr Wise's statement and to the custody record. Mr Wise was unrepresented at the police station, although on the face of it, it would appear that the police acted within the law of s. 58 PACE, albeit not the spirit. An attempt was made by the custody sergeant to contact Mr Wise's sister once during our client's detention but no contact was in fact established. Counsel will note that Mr Wise suffers from a diagnosed psychiatric condition for which he receives psychiatric care and medication. It is not altogether clear why this fact was not ascertained by the custody sergeant who should have undertaken a risk assessment having authorised the continued detention of our client. Our client is not always inclined to help himself and upon his arrest he was not found to be in possession of any medication. Our client states that he cannot recall being asked whether he suffered from a medical condition requiring medication. Our client states he was not suffering drug withdrawal symptoms at the time but is chronically addicted to nicotine. Counsel will see that he was detained overnight. The custody record suggests that Mr Wise did not have much to eat and had little sleep.

It is evident from the custody record that some 14 or so hours after having first been detained, Mr Wise mentioned the fact that he felt unwell and needed his usual medication. A police surgeon was called. Dr Ghulam examined our client and having administered his medication pronounced him fit to be interviewed. Crucially, Mr Wise was not provided with an appropriate adult, contrary to Code C. As such he went into the interview completely unrepresented, craving a cigarette, desperate to relieve the pressure of the situation and suffering from a diagnosed psychiatric condition. In the circumstances, it is difficult to see how a court could regard Mr Wise's confession as being admissible. Counsel is referred to the decision in *R v Aspinall* [1999] 2 Cr App R 115 as being a decision of the Court of Appeal which supports our contention that the confession is both unreliable and unfair to admit. The admission of a confession obtained in these circumstances would in our view represent a violation of Art. 6.

Counsel will see that we have obtained a report from Mr Wise's consultant psychiatrist. The report is extremely helpful and we intend to place reliance upon it. The report has been disclosed to the CPS in accordance with the requirements of s. 30 CJA 1988. Dr Mayhew would be prepared to attend court to give evidence if necessary on the 13 September.

Clearly if the confession can be excluded in this case, a major component of the prosecution's case is lost and counsel may wish to consider whether a submission of no case to answer might be mounted in these circumstances.

Instructing solicitors have notified the CPS of its intention to challenge the admissibility of the confession in this case. Unless the CPS decides to concede the point at the PTH, we anticipate the issue will be the subject of a binding ruling on its admissibility. We would welcome Counsel's views on this point.

Instructing solicitors have served the appropriate notice on the prosecution objecting to the admissibility of Mr Wise's criminal convictions. Counsel is asked to use her best endeavours to ensure that this prejudicial evidence is excluded before the trial commences.

Counsel is requested to advise on all issues likely to arise at the PTH and generally on the evidence and on preparation for trial. At present we are of the view that the defence will require the attendance of all the prosecution eye-witnesses; the interviewing officer, custody officer and the police forensic medical practitioner. We think the other witnesses can be agreed. We would ask counsel to specifically consider this point so that we may write to the CPS. Should Counsel require a conference we would ask her clerk to contact us.

Counsel is instructed to appear on behalf of the defendant at the pre-trial hearing on the 13 September at 10am. The hearing will be attended by our client.

Rachel James-Hannibal and Mountford Solicitors

Date: 29 July

DOCUMENT 40 FILE NOTE BASED ON TELEPHONE CALL WITH CPS

4 September

I was contacted by Sheila Steel Senior CPS lawyer in connection with the FCMH listed for 13 September. She said the CPS conceded breaches of Code C and indicated that the CPS would not be placing reliance upon Mr Wise's confession which is extremely good news. She agreed to contact Lyme Crown Court to vacate the date and that the CPS would continue to work towards the trial date of the 30 September.

Phone call made to Dr Mayhew's office telling him he was not required to attend for trial on 13 September.

Phone call to Lenny to explain the development and reminding him to attend on the 30 September.

Phone call to Ms Stockley of counsel confirming pre-trial hearing had been vacated as the prosecution would not be relying on our client's interview but that the trial would go ahead on the 30 September.

Speaking with

Time engaged:
Travel: 20 minutes
Waiting: 60 minutes
Conference: 40 minutes
Hearing: 30 minutes
BW

DOCUMENT 44 FILE NOTE BASED ON TRIAL

30 September

Attending Lyme Crown Court for Lenny Wise's trial. Ms Stockley for Lenny Wise and Mr Jaswinder Singh for the prosecution. His Honour Thomas Shand presiding. Before the trial began, Ms Stockley asked the judge to rule on the prosecution's bad character application. Argument was heard in relation to s. 101 (1) (d) CJA 2003. HH Judge Shand ruled in favour of the prosecution. The prosecution opened the case and called Shirley Lewis who was extensively cross-examined with Mrs Lewis conceding that she could have been mistaken. CPS called Lillian Kennedy and Harold Finney. Before the investigating officer was called, Ms Stockley asked for confirmation that the officer would not be asked questions regarding the defendant's previous convictions as she was minded to make a submission of no case to answer and would be asking HH to re-consider his earlier ruling on admission under s. 101 (1) (d) CJA 2003. After some argument, HH agreed with Ms Stockley's submission. Prosecution read out a number of s. 9 statements which included the forensic evidence and closed the prosecution's case. Ms Stockley then made a submission of no case to answer. She explained that the most important eye-witness linking Mr Wise to the crime scene was Shirley Lewis and her evidence had been discredited. There was no concrete forensic evidence to link the defendant to the crime scene. The only remaining 'evidence' was the fact of his previous convictions and that it was clearly contrary to the defendant's right to a fair trial that a conviction could be based on this fact alone. Contrary representations were made by the prosecution. The submission of no case to answer was however upheld by the judge. The jury were directed to acquit on the burglary charge. Mr Wise and his sister were immensely relieved and pleased.

Time engaged:
Travel 30 minutes
Waiting 40 minutes
Conference 30 minutes
Hearing 4 hours
BW

> *The case having now concluded the defence solicitor can submit her final claim for costs from the Legal Aid Agency via the Crown Court.*

APPENDIX 3

EXTRACTS FROM MAGISTRATES' COURT SENTENCING GUIDELINES

At the point of publication, the extracted guidelines are current. The complete and most up-to-date version of SC sentencing guidelines and the Magistrates' Court Sentencing Guidelines (MCSGs) are accessible via the Sentencing Council's (SC) website.

- Allocation guideline

- Using Sentencing Council Guidelines

- List of aggravating and mitigating factors

The following 'offence-specific' guidelines are reproduced in this appendix:

- Assault occasioning actual bodily harm
- Burglary in a dwelling (domestic dwelling)
- Theft Offences—Definitive guideline (General theft and shoplifting). Affray-Public Order Act 1986-'old-style' MCSG

Allocation Definitive Guideline

ALLOCATION

Allocation guideline

Determining whether cases should be dealt with by a magistrates' court or the Crown Court

Applicability of guideline

In accordance with section 122(2) of the Coroners and Justice Act 2009, the Sentencing Council issues this definitive guideline. It applies to all defendants in the magistrates' court (including youths jointly charged with adults) whose cases are dealt with on or after 1 March 2016.

It also applies to allocation decisions made in the Crown Court pursuant to Schedule 3 of the Crime and Disorder Act 1998. It will not be applicable in the youth court where a separate statutory procedure applies.

Venue for trial

It is important to ensure that all cases are tried at the appropriate level.

1. In general, either way offences should be tried summarily unless:

- the outcome would clearly be a sentence in excess of the court's powers for the offence(s) concerned after taking into account personal mitigation and any potential reduction for a guilty plea; or

- for reasons of unusual legal, procedural or factual complexity, the case should be tried in the Crown Court. This exception may apply in cases where a very substantial fine is the likely sentence. Other circumstances where this exception will apply are likely to be rare and case specific; the court will rely on the submissions of the parties to identify relevant cases.

2. In cases with no factual or legal complications the court should bear in mind its **power to commit for sentence after a trial** and may **retain jurisdiction** notwithstanding that the likely sentence might exceed its powers.

3. Cases may be tried summarily even where the defendant is subject to a Crown Court Suspended Sentence Order or Community Order.[1]

4. All parties should be asked by the court to make representations as to whether the case is suitable for summary trial. The court should refer to definitive guidelines (if any) to assess the likely sentence for the offence in the light of the facts alleged by the prosecution case, taking into account all aspects of the case including those advanced by the defence, including any personal mitigation to which the defence wish to refer.

Where the court decides that the case is suitable to be dealt with in the magistrates' court, it must warn the defendant that all sentencing options remain open and, if the defendant consents to summary trial and is convicted by the court or pleads guilty, the defendant may be committed to the Crown Court for sentence.

---

1. The power to commit the case to the Crown Court to be dealt with under para 11(1) of Schedule 12 or para 22 of Schedule 8 to the Criminal Justice Act 2003 can be exercised if the defendant is convicted.

Effective from 1 March 2016

Allocation Definitive Guideline

Committal for sentence

There is ordinarily no statutory restriction on committing an either way case for sentence following conviction. The general power of the magistrates' court to commit to the Crown Court for sentence after a finding that a case is suitable for summary trial and/or conviction continues to be available where the court is of the opinion 'that the offence or the combination of the offence and one or more offences associated with it was so serious that the Crown Court should, in the court's opinion, have the power to deal with the offender in any way it could deal with him if he had been convicted on indictment'.[2]

However, where the court proceeds to the summary trial of certain offences relating to criminal damage, upon conviction there is no power to commit to the Crown Court for sentence.[3]

The court should refer to any definitive guideline to arrive at the appropriate sentence taking into account all of the circumstances of the case including personal mitigation and the appropriate guilty plea reduction.

In borderline cases the court should consider obtaining a pre-sentence report before deciding whether to commit to the Crown Court for sentence.

Where the offending is so serious that the court is of the opinion that the Crown Court should have the power to deal with the offender, the case should be committed to the Crown Court for sentence even if a community order may be the appropriate sentence (this will allow the Crown Court to deal with any breach of a community order, if that is the sentence passed).

Youths jointly charged with adults – interests of justice test

The proper venue for the trial of any youth is normally the youth court. Subject to statutory restrictions, that remains the case where a youth is charged jointly with an adult.

This guideline does not provide information on the complex statutory framework for dealing with a youth jointly charged with an adult: consult your legal adviser for advice.

The following guidance must be applied in those cases where the interests of justice test falls to be considered:

1. If the adult is sent for trial to the Crown Court, the court should conclude that the youth must be tried separately in the youth court unless it is in the interests of justice for the youth and the adult to be tried jointly.

2. Examples of factors that should be considered when deciding whether it is in the interests of justice to send the youth to the Crown Court (rather than having a trial in the youth court) include:

- whether separate trials will cause injustice to witnesses or to the case as a whole (consideration should be given to the provisions of sections 27 and 28 of the Youth Justice and Criminal Evidence Act 1999);

- the age of the youth: the younger the youth, the greater the desirability that the youth be tried in the youth court;

- the age gap between the youth and the adult: a substantial gap in age militates in favour of the youth being tried in the youth court;

- the lack of maturity of the youth;

- the relative culpability of the youth compared with the adult and whether the alleged role played by the youth was minor;

- the lack of previous convictions on the part of the youth.

---

2. Powers of Criminal Courts (Sentencing) Act 2000, s.3.
3. Magistrates' Courts Act 1980, s.3(4) and s.22.

Effective from 1 March 2016

ALLOCATION

3. The court should bear in mind that the youth court now has a general power to commit for sentence following conviction pursuant to Section 3B of the Powers of Criminal Courts (Sentencing) Act 2000 (as amended). In appropriate cases this will permit the same court to sentence adults and youths who have been tried separately.

Statutory Framework

Section 19 of the Magistrates' Courts Act 1980 provides that:

"(1) The court shall decide whether the offence appears to it more suitable for summary trial or for trial on indictment.

(2) Before making a decision under this section, the court –

    (a) shall give the prosecution an opportunity to inform the court of the accused's previous convictions (if any); and

    (b) shall give the prosecution and the accused an opportunity to make representations as to whether summary trial or trial on indictment would be more suitable.

(3) In making a decision under this section, the court shall consider –

    (a) whether the sentence which a magistrates' court would have power to impose for the offence would be adequate; and

    (b) any representations made by the prosecution or the accused under subsection (2)(b) above,

and shall have regard to any allocation guidelines (or revised allocation guidelines) issued as definitive guidelines under section 122 of the Coroners and Justice Act 2009.

(4) Where –

    (a) the accused is charged with two or more offences; and

    (b) it appears to the court that the charges for the offences could be joined in the same indictment or that the offences arise out of the same or connected circumstances,

subsection (3)(a) above shall have effect as if references to the sentence which a magistrates' court would have power to impose for the offence were a reference to the maximum aggregate sentence which a magistrates' court would have power to impose for all of the offences taken together."

Section 125(1) of the Coroners and Justice Act 2009 provides that when sentencing offences committed after 6 April 2010:

"Every court –

    (a) must, in sentencing an offender, follow any sentencing guideline which is relevant to the offender's case, and

    (b) must, in exercising any other function relating to the sentencing of offenders, follow any sentencing guidelines which are relevant to the exercise of the function,

unless the court is satisfied that it would be contrary to the interests of justice to do so."

Using Sentencing Council guidelines

STEP ONE: Determining the offence category

The decision making process includes a two-step approach to assessing seriousness. The first step is to determine the offence category by means of an assessment of the offender's culpability and the harm caused, or intended, by reference only to the factors set out at step one in each guideline. The contents are tailored for each offence and comprise the principal factual elements of the offence.

STEP TWO: Starting point and category range

The guidelines provide a starting point which applies to all offenders irrespective of plea or previous convictions. The guidelines also specify a category range for each offence category. The guidelines provide non-exhaustive lists of aggravating and mitigating factors relating to the context of the offence and to the offender. Sentencers should identify whether any combination of these, or other relevant factors, should result in an upward or downward adjustment from the starting point. In some cases, it may be appropriate to move outside the identified category range when reaching a provisional sentence.

FURTHER STEPS

Having reached a provisional sentence, there are a number of further steps within the guidelines. These steps are clearly set out within each guideline and are tailored specifically for each offence in order to ensure that only the most appropriate guidance is included within each offence specific guideline. The further steps include:

- reduction for assistance to the prosecution;

- reduction for guilty pleas (courts should refer to the Guilty Plea guideline);

- where an offender is being sentenced for multiple offences – the court's assessment of the totality of the offending may result in a sentence above the range indicated for the individual offences, including a sentence of a different type (for more information, refer to the Offences Taken into Consideration and Totality guideline);

- compensation orders and/or ancillary orders appropriate to the case; and

- reasons for, and explain the effect of, the sentence.

Where there is no guideline for an offence, it may assist in determining sentence to consider the starting points and ranges indicated for offences that are of a similar level of seriousness.

Taken from Sentencing Guidelines Council Guideline **Overarching Principles: Seriousness**

The lists below bring together the most important aggravating and mitigating features with potential application to more than one offence or class of offences. They include some factors which are integral features of certain offences; in such cases, the presence of the aggravating factor is already reflected in the penalty for the offence and cannot be used as justification for increasing the sentence further. The lists are not intended to be comprehensive and the factors are not listed in any particular order of priority. If two or more of the factors listed describe the same feature care needs to be taken to avoid "double counting".

Aggravating factors

Factors indicating higher culpability:

- offence committed whilst on bail for other offences;

- failure to respond to previous sentences;

- offence was racially or religiously aggravated;

- offence motivated by, or demonstrating, hostility to the victim based on his or her sexual orientation (or presumed sexual orientation);

- offence motivated by, or demonstrating, hostility based on the victim's disability (or presumed disability);

- previous conviction(s), particularly where a pattern of repeat offending is disclosed;

- planning of an offence;

- an intention to commit more serious harm than actually resulted from the offence;

- offenders operating in groups or gangs;

- 'professional' offending;

- commission of the offence for financial gain (where this is not inherent in the offence itself);

- high level of profit from the offence;

- an attempt to conceal or dispose of evidence;

- failure to respond to warnings or concerns expressed by others about the offender's behaviour;

- offence committed whilst on licence;

- offence motivated by hostility towards a minority group, or a member or members of it;

- deliberate targeting of vulnerable victim(s);

- commission of an offence while under the influence of alcohol or drugs;

- use of a weapon to frighten or injure victim;

- deliberate and gratuitous violence or damage to property, over and above what is needed to carry out the offence;

- abuse of power;

- abuse of a position of trust.

Factors indicating a more than usually serious degree of harm:

- multiple victims;

- an especially serious physical or psychological effect on the victim, even if unintended;

- a sustained assault or repeated assaults on the same victim;

- victim is particularly vulnerable;

- location of the offence (for example, in an isolated place);

- offence is committed against those working in the public sector or providing a service to the public;

- presence of others for example, relatives, especially children or partner of the victim;

- additional degradation of the victim (for example, taking photographs of a victim as part of a sexual offence);

- in property offences, high value (including sentimental value) of property to the victim, or substantial consequential loss (for example, where the theft of equipment causes serious disruption to a victim's life or business).

Mitigating factors

Factors indicating lower culpability:

- a greater degree of provocation than normally expected;

- mental illness or disability;

- youth or age, where it affects the responsibility of the individual defendant;

- the fact that the offender played only a minor role in the offence.

Offender mitigation

- genuine remorse;

- admissions to police in interview;

- ready co-operation with authorities.

Assault occasioning actual bodily harm
Offences against the Person Act 1861 (section 47)

Racially/religiously aggravated ABH
Crime and Disorder Act 1998 (section 29)

These are specified offences for the purposes of section 224 of the Criminal Justice Act 2003

Triable either way

Section 47
Maximum when tried summarily: Level 5 fine and/or 26 weeks' custody
Maximum when tried on indictment: 5 years' custody

Section 29
Maximum when tried summarily: Level 5 fine and/or 26 weeks' custody
Maximum when tried on indictment: 7 years' custody

Offence range: Fine – 3 years' custody

This guideline applies to all offenders aged 18 and older, who are sentenced on or after 13 June 2011. The definitions at page 145 of 'starting point' and 'first time offender' do not apply for this guideline. Starting point and category ranges apply to all offenders in all cases, irrespective of plea or previous convictions.

STEP ONE
Determining the offence category

The court should determine the offence category using the table below.

Category 1	Greater harm (serious injury must normally be present) **and** higher culpability
Category 2	Greater harm (serious injury must normally be present) **and** lower culpability; **or** lesser harm **and** higher culpability
Category 3	Lesser harm **and** lower culpability

The court should determine the offender's culpability and the harm caused, or intended, by reference **only** to the factors identified in the table below (as demonstrated by the presence of one or more). These factors comprise the principal factual elements of the offence and should determine the category.

Factors indicating greater harm	Use of weapon or weapon equivalent (for example, shod foot, headbutting, use of acid, use of animal)
Injury (which includes disease transmission and/or psychological harm) which is serious in the context of the offence (must normally be present)	Intention to commit more serious harm than actually resulted from the offence
Victim is particularly vulnerable because of personal circumstances	Deliberately causes more harm than is necessary for commission of offence
Sustained or repeated assault on the same victim	Deliberate targeting of vulnerable victim
Factors indicating lesser harm	Leading role in group or gang
Injury which is less serious in the context of the offence	Offence motivated by, or demonstrating, hostility based on the victim's age, sex, gender identity (or presumed gender identity)
Factors indicating higher culpability	**Factors indicating lower culpability**
Statutory aggravating factors:	Subordinate role in group or gang
Offence motivated by, or demonstrating, hostility to the victim based on his or her sexual orientation (or presumed sexual orientation)	A greater degree of provocation than normally expected
Offence motivated by, or demonstrating, hostility to the victim based on the victim's disability (or presumed disability)	Lack of premeditation
	Mental disorder or learning disability, where linked to commission of the offence
Other aggravating factors:	Excessive self defence
A significant degree of premeditation	

STEP TWO
Starting point and category range

Having determined the category, the court should use the corresponding starting points to reach a sentence within the category range below. The starting point applies to all offenders irrespective of plea or previous convictions. A case of particular gravity, reflected by multiple features of culpability in step one, could merit upward adjustment from the starting point before further adjustment for aggravating or mitigating features, set out below.

Offence Category	Starting Point *(Applicable to all offenders)*	Category Range *(Applicable to all offenders)*
Category 1	Crown Court	Crown Court
Category 2	26 weeks' custody	Low level community order – Crown Court (51 weeks' custody)
Category 3	Medium level community order	Band A fine – High level community order

The table below contains a **non-exhaustive** list of additional factual elements providing the context of the offence and factors relating to the offender. Identify whether any combination of these, or other relevant factors, should result in an upward or downward adjustment from the starting point. In some cases, having considered these factors, it may be appropriate to move outside the identified category range.

When sentencing **category 2** offences, the court should also consider the custody threshold as follows:
- has the custody threshold been passed?
- if so, is it unavoidable that a custodial sentence be imposed?
- if so, can that sentence be suspended?

When sentencing **category 3** offences, the court should also consider the community order threshold as follows:
- has the community order threshold been passed?

Factors increasing seriousness
Statutory aggravating factors:
Previous convictions, having regard to a) the nature of the offence to which the conviction relates and its relevance to the current offence; and b) the time that has elapsed since the conviction
Offence committed whilst on bail
Other aggravating factors include:
Location of the offence
Timing of the offence
Ongoing effect upon the victim
Offence committed against those working in the public sector or providing a service to the public
Presence of others including relatives, especially children or partner of the victim
Gratuitous degradation of victim
In domestic violence cases, victim forced to leave their home
Failure to comply with current court orders
Offence committed whilst on licence
An attempt to conceal or dispose of evidence
Failure to respond to warnings or concerns expressed by others about the offender's behaviour
Commission of offence whilst under the influence of alcohol or drugs
Abuse of power and/or position of trust

Exploiting contact arrangements with a child to commit an offence
Established evidence of community impact
Any steps taken to prevent the victim reporting an incident, obtaining assistance and/or from assisting or supporting the prosecution
Offences taken into consideration (TICs)
Factors reducing seriousness or reflecting personal mitigation
No previous convictions **or** no relevant/recent convictions
Single blow
Remorse
Good character and/or exemplary conduct
Determination and/or demonstration of steps taken to address addiction or offending behaviour
Serious medical conditions requiring urgent, intensive or long-term treatment
Isolated incident
Age and/or lack of maturity where it affects the responsibility of the offender
Lapse of time since the offence where this is not the fault of the offender
Mental disorder or learning disability, where **not** linked to the commission of the offence
Sole or primary carer for dependent relatives

Section 29 offences only: The court should determine the appropriate sentence for the offence without taking account of the element of aggravation and then make an addition to the sentence, considering the level of aggravation involved. It may be appropriate to move outside the identified category range, taking into account the increased statutory maximum.

STEP THREE
Consider any other factors which indicate a reduction, such as assistance to the prosecution
The court should take into account any rule of law by virtue of which an offender may receive a discounted sentence in consequence of assistance given (or offered) to the prosecutor or investigator.

STEP FOUR
Reduction for guilty pleas
The court should take account of any potential reduction for a guilty plea in accordance with section 144 of the Criminal Justice Act 2003 and the *Guilty Plea* guideline.

STEP FIVE
Dangerousness
Assault occasioning actual bodily harm and racially/religiously aggravated ABH are specified offences within the meaning of Chapter 5 of the Criminal Justice Act 2003 and at this stage the court should consider whether having regard to the criteria contained in that Chapter it would be appropriate to award an extended sentence.

STEP SIX
Totality principle
If sentencing an offender for more than one offence, or where the offender is already serving a sentence, consider whether the total sentence is just and proportionate to the offending behaviour.

STEP SEVEN
Compensation and ancillary orders
In all cases, the court should consider whether to make compensation and/or other ancillary orders.

STEP EIGHT
Reasons
Section 174 of the Criminal Justice Act 2003 imposes a duty to give reasons for, and explain the effect of, the sentence.

STEP NINE
Consideration for remand time
Sentencers should take into consideration any remand time served in relation to the final sentence. The court should consider whether to give credit for time spent on remand in custody or on bail in accordance with sections 240 and 240A of the Criminal Justice Act 2003.

Domestic burglary
Theft Act 1968 (section 9)

This is a serious specified offence for the purposes of section 224 Criminal Justice Act 2003 if it was committed with intent to:

(a) inflict grievous bodily harm on a person, or
(b) do unlawful damage to a building or anything in it.

Triable either way

Maximum when tried summarily: Level 5 fine and/or 26 weeks' custody

Maximum when tried on indictment: 14 years' custody

Offence range: Community order – 6 years' custody

Where sentencing an offender for a qualifying **third domestic burglary**, the Court must apply Section 111 of the Powers of the Criminal Courts (Sentencing) Act 2000 and impose a custodial term of at least three years, unless it is satisfied that there are particular circumstances which relate to any of the offences or to the offender which would make it unjust to do so.

STEP ONE
Determining the offence category

The court should determine the offence category using the table below.

Category 1	Greater harm **and** higher culpability
Category 2	Greater harm **and** lower culpability **or** lesser harm **and** higher culpability
Category 3	Lesser harm **and** lower culpability

The court should determine culpability and harm caused or intended, by reference **only** to the factors below, which comprise the principal factual elements of the offence. Where an offence does not fall squarely into a category, individual factors may require a degree of weighting before making an overall assessment and determining the appropriate offence category.

Factors indicating greater harm
Theft of/damage to property causing a significant degree of loss to the victim (whether economic, sentimental or personal value)
Soiling, ransacking or vandalism of property
Occupier at home (or returns home) while offender present
Trauma to the victim, beyond the normal inevitable consequence of intrusion and theft
Violence used or threatened against victim
Context of general public disorder

Factors indicating lesser harm
Nothing stolen or only property of very low value to the victim (whether economic, sentimental or personal)
Limited damage or disturbance to property

Factors indicating higher culpability
Victim or premises deliberately targeted (for example, due to vulnerability or hostility based on disability, race, sexual orientation)
A significant degree of planning or organisation
Knife or other weapon carried (where not charged separately)
Equipped for burglary (for example, implements carried and/or use of vehicle)
Member of a group or gang

Factors indicating lower culpability
Offence committed on impulse, with limited intrusion into property
Offender exploited by others
Mental disorder or learning disability, where linked to the commission of the offence

STEP TWO
Starting point and category range

Having determined the category, the court should use the corresponding starting points to reach a sentence within the category range below. The starting point applies to all offenders irrespective of plea or previous convictions.

Where the defendant is dependant on or has a propensity to misuse drugs and there is sufficient prospect of success, a community order with a drug rehabilitation requirement under section 209 of the Criminal Justice Act 2003 may be a proper alternative to a short or moderate custodial sentence.

A case of particular gravity, reflected by multiple features of culpability or harm in step 1, could merit upward adjustment from the starting point before further adjustment for aggravating or mitigating features, set out on the next page.

Offence Category	Starting Point (*Applicable to all offenders*)	Category Range (*Applicable to all offenders*)
Category 1	3 years' custody	2 – 6 years' custody
Category 2	1 year's custody	High level community order – 2 years' custody
Category 3	High Level Community Order	Low level community order – 26 weeks' custody

The table below contains a **non-exhaustive** list of additional factual elements providing the context of the offence and factors relating to the offender. Identify whether any combination of these, or other relevant factors, should result in an upward or downward adjustment from the starting point. **In particular, relevant recent convictions are likely to result in an upward adjustment.** In some cases, having considered these factors, it may be appropriate to move outside the identified category range.

When sentencing **category 2 or 3** offences, the court should also consider the custody threshold as follows:
* has the custody threshold been passed?
* if so, is it unavoidable that a custodial sentence be imposed?

Factors increasing seriousness	Factors reducing seriousness or reflecting personal mitigation
Statutory aggravating factors:	Offender has made voluntary reparation to the victim
Previous convictions, having regard to a) the nature of the offence to which the conviction relates and its relevance to the current offence; and b) the time that has elapsed since the conviction*	Subordinate role in a group or gang
	No previous convictions **or** no relevant/recent convictions
Offence committed whilst on bail	Remorse
Other aggravating factors include:	Good character and/or exemplary conduct
Child at home (or returns home) when offence committed	Determination, and/or demonstration of steps taken to address addiction or offending behaviour
Offence committed at night	Serious medical conditions requiring urgent, intensive or long-term treatment
Gratuitous degradation of the victim	
Any steps taken to prevent the victim reporting the incident or obtaining assistance and/or from assisting or supporting the prosecution	Age and/or lack of maturity where it affects the responsibility of the offender
	Lapse of time since the offence where this is not the fault of the offender
Victim compelled to leave their home (in particular victims of domestic violence)	Mental disorder or learning disability, where not linked to the commission of the offence
Established evidence of community impact	Sole or primary carer for dependent relatives
Commission of offence whilst under the influence of alcohol or drugs	
Failure to comply with current court orders	
Offence committed whilst on licence	
Offences Taken Into Consideration (TICs)	

* Where sentencing an offender for a qualifying **third domestic burglary**, the Court must apply Section 111 of the Powers of the Criminal Courts (Sentencing) Act 2000 and impose a custodial term of at least three years, unless it is satisfied that there are particular circumstances which relate to any of the offences or to the offender which would make it unjust to do so.

 Effective from 16 January 2012

STEP THREE
Consider any factors which indicate a reduction, such as assistance to the prosecution
The court should take into account sections 73 and 74 of the Serious Organised Crime and Police Act 2005 (assistance by defendants: reduction or review of sentence) and any other rule of law by virtue of which an offender may receive a discounted sentence in consequence of assistance given (or offered) to the prosecutor or investigator.

STEP FOUR
Reduction for guilty pleas
The court should take account of any potential reduction for a guilty plea in accordance with section 144 of the Criminal Justice Act 2003 and the *Guilty Plea* guideline.

Where a minimum mandatory sentence is imposed under section 111 Powers of Criminal Courts (Sentencing) Act, the discount for an early guilty plea must not exceed 20 per cent.

STEP FIVE
Dangerousness
A burglary offence under section 9 Theft Act 1986 is a serious specified offence within the meaning of chapter 5 of the Criminal Justice Act 2003 if it was committed with the intent to (a) inflict grievous bodily harm on a person, or (b) do unlawful damage to a building or anything in it. The court should consider whether having regard to the criteria contained in that chapter it would be appropriate to award imprisonment for public protection or an extended sentence. Where offenders meet the dangerousness criteria, the notional determinate sentence should be used as the basis for the setting of a minimum term.

STEP SIX
Totality principle
If sentencing an offender for more than one offence, or where the offender is already serving a sentence, consider whether the total sentence is just and proportionate to the offending behaviour.

STEP SEVEN
Compensation and ancillary orders
In all cases, courts should consider whether to make compensation and/or other ancillary orders.

STEP EIGHT
Reasons
Section 174 of the Criminal Justice Act 2003 imposes a duty to give reasons for, and explain the effect of, the sentence.

STEP NINE
Consideration for remand time
Sentencers should take into consideration any remand time served in relation to the final sentence at this final step. The court should consider whether to give credit for time spent on remand in custody or on bail in accordance with sections 240 and 240A of the Criminal Justice Act 2003.

General Theft
Theft Act 1968 (section 1)

Including:

Theft from the person
Theft in a dwelling
Theft in breach of trust
Theft from a motor vehicle
Theft of a motor vehicle
Theft of a pedal bicycle
and all other section 1 Theft Act 1968 offences,
excluding theft from a shop or stall

Triable either way
Maximum: 7 years' custody

Offence range: Discharge – 6 years' custody

Effective from 1 February 2016

4 Theft Offences Definitive Guideline

GENERAL THEFT

STEP ONE
Determining the offence category

The court should determine the offence category with reference **only** to the factors identified in the following tables. In order to determine the category the court should assess **culpability** and **harm**.

The level of culpability is determined by weighing up all the factors of the case to determine the offender's role and the extent to which the offending was **planned** and the **sophistication** with which it was carried out.

CULPABILITY demonstrated by one or more of the following:
A – High culpability
A leading role where offending is part of a group activity
Involvement of others through coercion, intimidation or exploitation
Breach of a high degree of trust or responsibility
Sophisticated nature of offence/significant planning
Theft involving intimidation or the use or threat of force
Deliberately targeting victim on basis of vulnerability
B – Medium culpability
A significant role where offending is part of a group activity
Some degree of planning involved
Breach of some degree of trust or responsibility
All other cases where characteristics for categories A or C are not present
C – Lesser culpability
Performed limited function under direction
Involved through coercion, intimidation or exploitation
Little or no planning
Limited awareness or understanding of offence

Where there are characteristics present which fall under different levels of culpability, the court should balance these characteristics to reach a fair assessment of the offender's culpability.

Effective from 1 February 2016

GENERAL THEFT

HARM

Harm is assessed by reference to the **financial loss** that results from the theft **and any significant additional harm** suffered by the victim or others – examples of significant additional harm may include **but are not limited to**:

Items stolen were of substantial value to the loser – regardless of monetary worth
High level of inconvenience caused to the victim or others
Consequential financial harm to victim or others
Emotional distress
Fear/loss of confidence caused by the crime
Risk of or actual injury to persons or damage to property
Impact of theft on a business
Damage to heritage assets
Disruption caused to infrastructure

Intended loss should be used where actual loss has been prevented.

Category 1	Very high value goods stolen (above £100,000) **or**
	High value with significant additional harm to the victim or others
Category 2	High value goods stolen (£10,000 to £100,000) **and** no significant additional harm **or**
	Medium value with significant additional harm to the victim or others
Category 3	Medium value goods stolen (£500 to £10,000) **and** no significant additional harm **or**
	Low value with significant additional harm to the victim or others
Category 4	Low value goods stolen (up to £500) **and**
	Little or no significant additional harm to the victim or others

See page 6.

Effective from 1 February 2016

6 Theft Offences Definitive Guideline

> **STEP TWO**
> **Starting point and category range**

Having determined the category at step one, the court should use the starting point to reach a sentence within the appropriate category range in the table below.

The starting point applies to all offenders irrespective of plea or previous convictions.

Harm	Culpability		
	A	**B**	**C**
Category 1 Adjustment should be made for any significant additional harm factors where very high value goods are stolen.	**Starting point** 3 years 6 months' custody	**Starting point** 2 years' custody	**Starting point** 1 year's custody
	Category range 2 years 6 months' – 6 years' custody	**Category range** 1 – 3 years 6 months' custody	**Category range** 26 weeks' – 2 years' custody
Category 2	**Starting point** 2 years' custody	**Starting point** 1 year's custody	**Starting point** High level community order
	Category range 1 – 3 years 6 months' custody	**Category range** 26 weeks' – 2 years' custody	**Category range** Low level community order – 36 weeks' custody
Category 3	**Starting point** 1 year's custody	**Starting point** High level community order	**Starting point** Band C fine
	Category range 26 weeks' – 2 years' custody	**Category range** Low level community order – 36 weeks' custody	**Category range** Band B fine – Low level community order
Category 4	**Starting point** High level community order	**Starting point** Low level community order	**Starting point** Band B fine
	Category range Medium level community order – 36 weeks' custody	**Category range** Band C fine – Medium level community order	**Category range** Discharge – Band C fine

The table above refers to single offences. Where there are multiple offences, consecutive sentences may be appropriate: please refer to the *Offences Taken Into Consideration and Totality* guideline. Where multiple offences are committed in circumstances which justify consecutive sentences, and the total amount stolen is in excess of £1 million, then an aggregate sentence in excess of 7 years may be appropriate.

> Where the offender is dependent on or has a propensity to misuse drugs or alcohol and there is sufficient prospect of success, a community order with a drug rehabilitation requirement under section 209, or an alcohol treatment requirement under section 212 of the Criminal Justice Act 2003 may be a proper alternative to a short or moderate custodial sentence.
>
> Where the offender suffers from a medical condition that is susceptible to treatment but does not warrant detention under a hospital order, a community order with a mental health treatment requirement under section 207 of the Criminal Justice Act 2003 may be a proper alternative to a short or moderate custodial sentence.

Effective from 1 February 2016

GENERAL THEFT

The court should then consider further adjustment for any aggravating or mitigating factors. The following is a **non-exhaustive** list of additional factual elements providing the context of the offence and factors relating to the offender. Identify whether any combination of these, or other relevant factors, should result in an upward or downward adjustment from the sentence arrived at so far.

GENERAL THEFT

Factors increasing seriousness	Factors reducing seriousness or reflecting personal mitigation
Statutory aggravating factors	No previous convictions **or** no relevant/recent convictions
Previous convictions, having regard to a) the **nature** of the offence to which the conviction relates and its **relevance** to the current offence; and b) the **time** that has elapsed since the conviction	Remorse, particularly where evidenced by voluntary reparation to the victim
Offence committed whilst on bail	Good character and/or exemplary conduct
Offence motivated by, or demonstrating hostility based on any of the following characteristics or presumed characteristics of the victim: religion, race, disability, sexual orientation or transgender identity	Serious medical condition requiring urgent, intensive or long-term treatment
	Age and/or lack of maturity where it affects the responsibility of the offender
Other aggravating factors	Mental disorder or learning disability
Stealing goods to order	Sole or primary carer for dependent relatives
Steps taken to prevent the victim reporting or obtaining assistance and/or from assisting or supporting the prosecution	Determination and/or demonstration of steps having been taken to address addiction or offending behaviour
Offender motivated by intention to cause harm or out of revenge	Inappropriate degree of trust or responsibility
Offence committed over sustained period of time	
Attempts to conceal/dispose of evidence	
Failure to comply with current court orders	
Offence committed on licence	
Offences taken into consideration	
Blame wrongly placed on others	
Established evidence of community/wider impact (for issues other than prevalence)	
Prevalence – see below	

Prevalence

There may be exceptional local circumstances that arise which may lead a court to decide that prevalence should influence sentencing levels. The pivotal issue in such cases will be the harm caused to the community.

It is essential that the court before taking account of prevalence:

- has supporting evidence from an external source, for example, Community Impact Statements, to justify claims that a particular crime is prevalent in their area, **and** is causing particular harm in that community, **and**
- is satisfied that there is a compelling need to treat the offence more seriously than elsewhere.

Effective from 1 February 2016

GENERAL THEFT

STEP THREE

Consider any factors which indicate a reduction, such as assistance to the prosecution
The court should take into account sections 73 and 74 of the Serious Organised Crime and Police Act 2005 (assistance by defendants: reduction or review of sentence) and any other rule of law by virtue of which an offender may receive a discounted sentence in consequence of assistance given (or offered) to the prosecutor or investigator.

STEP FOUR

Reduction for guilty pleas
The court should take account of any potential reduction for a guilty plea in accordance with section 144 of the Criminal Justice Act 2003 and the *Guilty Plea* guideline.

STEP FIVE

Totality principle
If sentencing an offender for more than one offence, or where the offender is already serving a sentence, consider whether the total sentence is just and proportionate to the overall offending behaviour in accordance with the *Offences Taken into Consideration and Totality* guideline.

STEP SIX

Confiscation, compensation and ancillary orders
The court must proceed with a view to making a confiscation order if it is asked to do so by the prosecutor or if the court believes it is appropriate for it to do so.

Where the offence has resulted in loss or damage the court must consider whether to make a compensation order.

If the court makes both a confiscation order and an order for compensation and the court believes the offender will not have sufficient means to satisfy both orders in full, the court must direct that the compensation be paid out of sums recovered under the confiscation order (section 13 of the Proceeds of Crime Act 2002).

The court may also consider whether to make ancillary orders. These may include a deprivation order, or a restitution order.

STEP SEVEN

Reasons
Section 174 of the Criminal Justice Act 2003 imposes a duty to give reasons for, and explain the effect of, the sentence.

STEP EIGHT

Consideration for time spent on bail
The court must consider whether to give credit for time spent on bail in accordance with section 240A of the Criminal Justice Act 2003.

Theft from a shop or stall
Theft Act 1968 (section 1)

Triable either way
Maximum: 7 years' custody

(except for an offence of low-value shoplifting which is treated as a summary only offence in accordance with section 22A of the Magistrates' Courts Act 1980 where the maximum is 6 months' custody).

Offence range: Discharge – 3 years' custody

10 Theft Offences Definitive Guideline

THEFT FROM A SHOP OR STALL

STEP ONE
Determining the offence category

The court should determine the offence category with reference **only** to the factors identified in the following tables. In order to determine the category the court should assess **culpability** and **harm**.

The level of culpability is determined by weighing up all the factors of the case to determine the offender's role and the extent to which the offending was **planned** and the **sophistication** with which it was carried out.

CULPABILITY demonstrated by one or more of the following:
A – High culpability
A leading role where offending is part of a group activity
Involvement of others through coercion, intimidation or exploitation
Sophisticated nature of offence/significant planning
Significant use or threat of force
Offender subject to a banning order from the relevant store
Child accompanying offender is actively used to **facilitate** the offence (not merely present when offence is committed)
B – Medium culpability
A significant role where offending is part of a group activity
Some degree of planning involved
Limited use or threat of force
All other cases where characteristics for categories A or C are not present
C – Lesser culpability
Performed limited function under direction
Involved through coercion, intimidation or exploitation
Little or no planning
Mental disorder/learning disability where linked to commission of the offence

Where there are characteristics present which fall under different levels of culpability, the court should balance these characteristics to reach a fair assessment of the offender's culpability.

Effective from 1 February 2016

HARM

Harm is assessed by reference to the **financial loss** that results from the theft **and any significant additional harm** suffered by the victim – examples of significant additional harm may include **but are not limited to**:

Emotional distress
Damage to property
Effect on business
A greater impact on the victim due to the size or type of their business
A particularly vulnerable victim

Intended loss should be used where actual loss has been prevented.

Category 1	High value goods stolen (above £1,000) **or**
	Medium value with significant additional harm to the victim
Category 2	Medium value goods stolen (£200 to £1,000) **and** no significant additional harm **or**
	Low value with significant additional harm to the victim
Category 3	Low value goods stolen (up to £200) **and**
	Little or no significant additional harm to the victim

See page 12.

Effective from 1 February 2016

THEFT FROM A SHOP OR STALL

12 Theft Offences Definitive Guideline

STEP TWO
Starting point and category range

Having determined the category at step one, the court should use the starting point to reach a sentence within the appropriate category range in the table below.

The starting point applies to all offenders irrespective of plea or previous convictions.

Harm	Culpability		
	A	B	C
Category 1 Where the value greatly exceeds £1,000 it may be appropriate to move outside the identified range. Adjustment should be made for any significant additional harm where high value goods are stolen.	**Starting point** 26 weeks' custody	**Starting point** Medium level community order	**Starting point** Band C fine
	Category range 12 weeks' – 3 years' custody	**Category range** Low level community order – 26 weeks' custody	**Category range** Band B fine – Low level community order
Category 2	**Starting point** 12 weeks' custody	**Starting point** Low level community order	**Starting point** Band B fine
	Category range High level community order – 26 weeks' custody	**Category range** Band C fine – Medium level community order	**Category range** Band A fine – Band C fine
Category 3	**Starting point** High level community order	**Starting point** Band C fine	**Starting point** Band A fine
	Category range Low level community order – 12 weeks' custody	**Category range** Band B fine – Low level community order	**Category range** Discharge – Band B fine

Consecutive sentences for multiple offences may be appropriate – please refer to the *Offences Taken Into Consideration and Totality* guideline.

Previous diversionary work with an offender does not preclude the court from considering this type of sentencing option again if appropriate.

Where the offender is dependent on or has a propensity to misuse drugs or alcohol and there is sufficient prospect of success, a community order with a drug rehabilitation requirement under section 209, or an alcohol treatment requirement under section 212 of the Criminal Justice Act 2003 may be a proper alternative to a short or moderate custodial sentence.

Where the offender suffers from a medical condition that is susceptible to treatment but does not warrant detention under a hospital order, a community order with a mental health treatment requirement under section 207 of the Criminal Justice Act 2003 may be a proper alternative to a short or moderate custodial sentence.

Effective from 1 February 2016

The court should then consider further adjustment for any aggravating or mitigating factors. The following is a **non-exhaustive** list of additional factual elements providing the context of the offence and factors relating to the offender. Identify whether any combination of these, or other relevant factors, should result in an upward or downward adjustment from the sentence arrived at so far.

<table>
<tr><td>Factors increasing seriousness</td><td>Factors reducing seriousness or reflecting personal mitigation</td></tr>
<tr><td>Statutory aggravating factors</td><td>No previous convictions or no relevant/recent convictions</td></tr>
<tr><td>Previous convictions, having regard to a) the nature of the offence to which the conviction relates and its relevance to the current offence; and b) the time that has elapsed since the conviction</td><td>Remorse, particularly where evidenced by voluntary reparation to the victim</td></tr>
<tr><td>Relevant recent convictions may justify an upward adjustment, including outside the category range. In cases involving significant persistent offending, the community and custodial thresholds may be crossed even though the offence otherwise warrants a lesser sentence. Any custodial sentence must be kept to the necessary minimum</td><td>Good character and/or exemplary conduct

Serious medical condition requiring urgent, intensive or long-term treatment</td></tr>
<tr><td>Offence committed whilst on bail</td><td>Age and/or lack of maturity where it affects the responsibility of the offender</td></tr>
<tr><td>Offence motivated by, or demonstrating hostility based on any of the following characteristics or presumed characteristics of the victim: religion, race, disability, sexual orientation or transgender identity</td><td>Mental disorder or learning disability (where not linked to the commission of the offence)

Sole or primary carer for dependent relatives</td></tr>
<tr><td>Other aggravating factors</td><td>Determination and/or demonstration of steps having been taken to address addiction or offending behaviour</td></tr>
<tr><td>Stealing goods to order</td><td>Offender experiencing exceptional financial hardship</td></tr>
<tr><td>Steps taken to prevent the victim reporting or obtaining assistance and/or from assisting or supporting the prosecution</td><td></td></tr>
<tr><td>Attempts to conceal/dispose of evidence</td><td></td></tr>
<tr><td>Offender motivated by intention to cause harm or out of revenge</td><td></td></tr>
<tr><td>Failure to comply with current court orders</td><td></td></tr>
<tr><td>Offence committed on licence</td><td></td></tr>
<tr><td>Offences taken into consideration</td><td></td></tr>
<tr><td>Established evidence of community/wider impact (for issues other than prevalence)</td><td></td></tr>
<tr><td>Prevalence – see below</td><td></td></tr>
</table>

THEFT FROM A SHOP OR STALL

Prevalence

There may be exceptional local circumstances that arise which may lead a court to decide that prevalence should influence sentencing levels. The pivotal issue in such cases will be the harm caused to the community.

It is essential that the court before taking account of prevalence:

- has supporting evidence from an external source, for example, Community Impact Statements, to justify claims that a particular crime is prevalent in their area, **and** is causing particular harm in that community, **and**
- is satisfied that there is a compelling need to treat the offence more seriously than elsewhere.

14   Theft Offences Definitive Guideline

STEP THREE

Consider any factors which indicate a reduction, such as assistance to the prosecution

The court should take into account sections 73 and 74 of the Serious Organised Crime and Police Act 2005 (assistance by defendants: reduction or review of sentence) and any other rule of law by virtue of which an offender may receive a discounted sentence in consequence of assistance given (or offered) to the prosecutor or investigator.

STEP FOUR

Reduction for guilty pleas

The court should take account of any potential reduction for a guilty plea in accordance with section 144 of the Criminal Justice Act 2003 and the *Guilty Plea* guideline.

STEP FIVE

Totality principle

If sentencing an offender for more than one offence, or where the offender is already serving a sentence, consider whether the total sentence is just and proportionate to the overall offending behaviour in accordance with the *Offences Taken into Consideration and Totality* guideline.

STEP SIX

Confiscation, compensation and ancillary orders

The court must proceed with a view to making a confiscation order if it is asked to do so by the prosecutor or if the court believes it is appropriate for it to do so.

Where the offence has resulted in loss or damage the court must consider whether to make a compensation order.

If the court makes both a confiscation order and an order for compensation and the court believes the offender will not have sufficient means to satisfy both orders in full, the court must direct that the compensation be paid out of sums recovered under the confiscation order (section 13 of the Proceeds of Crime Act 2002).

The court may also consider whether to make ancillary orders. These may include a deprivation order, or a restitution order.

STEP SEVEN

Reasons

Section 174 of the Criminal Justice Act 2003 imposes a duty to give reasons for, and explain the effect of, the sentence.

STEP EIGHT

Consideration for time spent on bail

The court must consider whether to give credit for time spent on bail in accordance with section 240A of the Criminal Justice Act 2003.

Effective from 1 February 2016

Public Order Act 1986, s.3

Public Order Act, s.3 – affray

Triable either way:
Maximum when tried summarily: Level 5 fine and/or 6 months
Maximum when tried on indictment: 3 years

Offence seriousness (culpability and harm) A. Identify the appropriate starting point Starting points based on first time offender pleading not guilty		
Examples of nature of activity	Starting point	Range
Brief offence involving low-level violence, no substantial fear created	Low level community order	Band C fine to medium level community order
Degree of fighting or violence that causes substantial fear	High level community order	Medium level community order to 12 weeks custody
Fight involving a weapon/throwing objects, or conduct causing risk of serious injury	18 weeks custody	12 weeks custody to Crown Court

Offence seriousness (culpability and harm)
B. Consider the effect of aggravating and mitigating factors
(other than those within examples above)
Common aggravating and mitigating factors are identified in the pullout card –
the following may be particularly relevant but **these lists are not exhaustive**

Factors indicating higher culpability	Factors indicating lower culpability
Factors indicating higher culpability 1. Group action 2. Threats 3. Lengthy incident **Factors indicating greater degree of harm** 1. Vulnerable person(s) present 2. Injuries caused 3. Damage to property	**Factors indicating lower culpability** 1. Did not start the trouble 2. Provocation 3. Stopped as soon as police arrived

Form a preliminary view of the appropriate sentence,
then consider offender mitigation
Common factors are identified in the pullout card

Consider a reduction for a guilty plea

Consider ancillary orders, including compensation and football
banning order (where appropriate)
Refer to pages 168-174 for guidance on available ancillary orders

Decide sentence
Give reasons

Effective from 4 August 2008

INDEX

A

Absconding whilst on bail 10.6, 10.7, 10.8, 10.9, 10.10, 10.11, 10.19
Absence of defendant
Crown Court 14.8.6
magistrates' court 12.4, 12.10
Absolute discharges
sentencing options 22.18
young offenders 26.7
Abuse of process 6.12
Accused *see* **Defendants; Suspects**
Acquitted persons
costs 14.17
public funding 9.13
Activity requirements 26.9.1
Administrative Court 1.7.6
Admissibility
bad character evidence 19.7–19.12
challenging unlawful and unfairly obtained evidence
challenging 'other' evidence 6.9
common law discretion 6.10
oppression 6.5.1
procedure 6.6
statutory discretion 6.11
unfairness 6.5.3
unreliability 6.5.2
co-accused's bad character 19.8
consequences of failure to comply with PACE Code on identification 7.8
core concept 2.4.2
defendant's bad character
admissible evidence 19.6, 19.7
attacks on others 19.10
by agreement 19.7.2
correction of false impressions 19.9
explanatory evidence 19.7.4
important issue 19.7.5
judicial discretion 19.7.1, 19.7.5, 19.10.2
miscellaneous matters 19.13
procedure for admission 19.11
propensity to commit similar offences 19.7.5
relevance 19.12
statutory provisions 19.7
voluntary disclosure 19.7.3
eye-witness identification Fig. 7.1
hearsay evidence
business documents 18.7
by agreement 18.9
confessions 18.8.3
judicial discretion 18.10
procedure 18.13
res gestae statements 18.8.1
unavailable witnesses 18.6
identification evidence, failure to comply with PACE Code on 7.8

procedure for determination 2.5
Admissions
effect 15.8
previous consistent statements 16.8.3
Adverse inferences
conditions for Drawing 5.2.1
defence statements 13.9.5
evidential effect 5.3.1
from silence
advice on whether to testify 19.4.1
statutory provisions 19.4
meaning 5.2.2
overview Fig. 5.1
practical aspects 5.4
statutory provisions 5.3
Advocacy
art of communication 2.11
basic requirements
checklist for oral presentation 2.11.2
preparation and persuasion 2.11.1
Crown Court trials
closing speeches 14.13
conferences with counsel 14.5.1
defence case 14.12
prosecution case 14.10
support for advocate at trial 14.3, 14.8
mitigating pleas 22.21.1, 22.23
professional duties
general duties to court 1.10.2
specific obligations 1.10.3
Affirmations 16.7
Alcohol treatment requirements 22.11.10, 26.9.15
Allocation hearings
ancillary matters 11.8
applications for dismissal 11.9
change of decision 11.10
co-accused 11.7.2–11.7.3
decisions 11.3, 11.3.5
defence submissions 11.3.4
election for trial 11.4
guidelines 11.3.1
introduction 11.1
linked offences 11.7.1
magistrates' court accepts jurisdiction 11.3.5
magistrates' court declines jurisdiction 11.3.5
outcomes 11.3.5
particular offences 11.6
prosecution submissions 11.3.4
sending to Crown Court 11.3.5, 11.7
special procedure for criminal damage 11.5
statutory factors 11.3.2
trial venue 11.3.2
young offenders 25.3.2

Ancillary orders
confiscation and forfeiture 22.20.2
Criminal Behaviour Orders (CBOs) 22.20.3
overview Fig. 22.2
prosecution costs 22.20.1
restraining orders 22.20.4
Anonymity
special measures directions 16.5.9
Anti-Social Behaviour Injunctions (ASBIs)
young offenders 26.15
Appeals
Attorney General's references 23.9
bail
by defendant 10.15
by prosecutor 10.16
case stated 23.4
Court of Appeal
from Crown Court 23.6
to Supreme Court 23.8
Criminal Cases Review Commission 23.10
Crown Court
against conviction 23.6
against sentence 23.6, 23.7
from magistrates' court 23.3
to Court of Appeal 23.6
introduction 23.1
judicial review 23.5
magistrates' courts
cases stated to Divisional Court 23.4
re-opening by magistrates 23.2
to Crown Court 23.3
overview Fig. 23.1
prosecution rights 14.18, 23.11
representation orders 9.9.7
Appropriate adults 24.6.3, 24.8.2, 24.8.3
Arraignment in court 14.7
Arrest
arrival at police station 4.3
citizens' powers 3.7.8
common law powers 3.7.2
defined 3.7.1
flowchart Fig. 3.1
informing someone of arrest 4.7.1–4.7.2
preserved powers 3.7.9
reasonable force 3.7.7
search of suspects
at premises where arrested 3.9.3
away from police station 3.9.2
with permission 3.9.1
powers of entry and search 3.9.4
of premises 3.9.5
preserved powers of entry 3.9.7
seizure 3.9.6
statutory powers 3.7.4

Arrest (*Cont.*)
statutory requirements 3.7.6
stop and search before arrest 3.2
unlawful arrest 3.7.10
warrants
arrest with 3.7.3
arrest without 3.7.5
Assessment of evidence
Crown Prosecution Service
(CPS) 2.6
custody officers 4.4.4
defence solicitors 2.7
Full Code Test 8.2.3, 8.2.5
preparations for summary
trial 12.7.7
**Attendance centre require-
ments** 22.11.11, 26.9.5
Attorney General's references 23.9

B

Bad character evidence
admissibility 19.7–19.12
co-accused 19.8
cross-examination of non-
defendants 16.9.4
defendants
admissible evidence 19.6, 19.7
attacks on others 19.10
by agreement 19.7.2
correction of false impressions 19.9
defined 19.6.1
explanatory evidence 19.7.4
important issue 19.7.5
judicial discretion 19.7.1,
19.7.5, 19.10.2
procedure for admission 19.11
propensity to commit similar
offences 19.7.5
relevance 19.12
statutory provisions 19.7
voluntary disclosure 19.7.3
miscellaneous matters 19.13
overview Fig. 19.1
Bail
appeals Fig. 10.1
by defendant 10.15
by prosecutor 10.16
to CA 23.6.4
to Crown Court 10.15, 10.16,
10.18
to High Court 10.16
Applicable Bail Period 4.14.2
conditions Fig. 10.1
common provisions 10.10
failure to comply 10.10.2
sureties 10.10.1
variation 4.14.1, 10.18
contested bail hearings 10.12
Crown Court jurisdiction 10.15,
10.16, 10.20, 13.6
custodial sentence, where no real
prospect of 10.6, 10.8
exceptions to right Fig. 10.1
failure to comply with conditions 10.10.2
failure to surrender 10.19
full argument certificates 10.15
grounds for denying bail
indictable imprisonable
offences 10.6

non-imprisonable offences 10.9
overview 10.5–10.9
statutory factors for consideration 10.7
substantial grounds 10.11
summary-only imprisonable
offences 10.8
High Court jurisdiction 10.21
introduction 10.1
murder 10.4, 10.6
overview 10.2, Fig. 10.1
police bail
after charge 4.14.4
pending investigation 4.6.2
positive drug testing 10.6
practical considerations 10.23
pre-charge bail
Applicable Bail Period 4.14.2
pending CPS decision 4.14.1
'released under investigation' 4.14.2
preliminary hearings before
Crown Court 13.6
presumption of release without 4.14.2
reasons for decisions 10.12.1
reconsideration 10.17
record of hearings in Crown
Court App 2
reform 10.6
refusal of 10.15
'released under investigation' 4.14.2
remand periods 10.13
repeat applications 10.14
reversal of presumption in favour 10.4, Fig. 10.1
right to liberty and security (Art
5) 10.22
sendings to Crown Court 11.8.1
statutory right 10.3
street bail 3.8
sureties 10.10.1
young offenders
conditional bail 25.2.3
court bail 25.2.1
**Better Case Management
(BCM)** 13.4
Binding overs 22.19
Briefing counsel 13.12.3
Burden of proof
evidential burden of proof 15.5
example 15.6
fair trial, right to 15.7
formal admissions 15.8
legal burden of proof
general rule 15.2
reverse burden rules 15.3
overview Fig. 15.1
practical considerations 15.9
reverse burden
legal burden 15.3
right to a fair trial (Art 6) 15.7
Business documents 18.7,
Fig. 18.1

C

Case management
first appearances before
magistrates 9.15.1
pre-trial disclosure

CPS obligations 8.11–8.12
flowchart Fig. 8.3
introduction 8.8
obligations on police 8.10
overview Fig. 8.2
public interest immunity 8.14
third parties 8.13
used and unused material dis-
tinguished 8.9
role of Crim PR 1.9
summary proceedings 12.6.2
Cautions
alternatives to prosecution 4.14
conditional cautions
8.6.2–8.6.4
overview Fig. 8.1
simple cautions 8.6.1
conditions for drawing adverse
inferences 5.2.1
guidance 8.6.2
proportionality 8.6.2
suspects 4.11
volunteers at police station 4.2.1
young offenders 8.6, 24.8.2–24.8.3
CCTV
identification by police officers 7.9
identification procedures 7.1
Character evidence
co-accused 19.8
defendant's bad character
admissible evidence 19.6, 19.7
attacks on others 19.10
by agreement 19.7.2
correction of false impressions 19.9
explanatory evidence 19.7.4
important issue 19.7.5
judicial discretion 19.7.1,
19.7.5, 19.10.2
procedure for admission 19.11
propensity to commit similar
offences 19.7.5
relevance 19.12
statutory provisions 19.7
voluntary disclosure 19.7.3
defendant's good character 19.5
miscellaneous matters 19.13
mitigating pleas 22.21.4
overview Fig. 19.1
statutory definition 19.6.1
Charges
alternatives to 4.14
amending 12.5.1
applications to dismiss 13.10
CPS powers
Full Code Test 8.2.3, 8.2.5
introduction 8.1
policies 8.3
responsibility to charge 8.2.2
threshold test 8.4
defence solicitor's role 8.7
detention without charge
following arrest
beyond 24 hours 4.5.3
beyond 36 hours 4.5.4
initial 24 hours 4.5.2
time limits 4.5.1, Fig. 4.1
police bail after 4.14.4
police powers
Full Code Test 8.2.3

procedure 8.2.3
  'specified proceedings' 8.2.3
  statutory provisions 8.2.1, 8.2.3
pre-charge bail
  Applicable Bail Period 4.14.2
  pending CPS decision 4.14.1
questioning after charge 4.14.3
selection of charges 8.5
young offenders 24.10
Circumstantial evidence 2.8.5
Citizens' arrests 3.7.8
CJ-Triple S *see* **Simple, Speedy, Summary Criminal Justice (CJ-SSS)**
Classification of offences 1.5
Client care 1.10.3
Closing speeches 14.13
Co-accused
  allocation hearings 11.7.2–11.7.3
  bad character evidence 19.8
  sendings to Crown Court 13.3.2
Committal proceedings
  for sentencing
    either-way offences 21.14.3
    summary offences 21.14.2
Communication aids 16.5.8
Community sentences
  alcohol treatment requirements 22.11.10
  attendance centre requirements 22.11.11
  curfews 22.11.5
  determination 22.10.1
  drug rehabilitation requirement 22.11.9
  enforcement 22.13
  exclusion requirement 22.11.6
  guilty pleas 22.12
  meaning 22.9
  mental health treatment requirements 22.11.8
  overview 22.10, Fig. 22.2
  programme requirements 22.11.3
  prohibited activity requirements 22.11.4
  rehabilitation activity requirements 22.11.2
  requirements 22.11
  residence requirement 22.11.7
  serious offences 22.9.2
  threshold 22.9.1
  unpaid work 22.11.1
Compellability of witnesses
  defendants Fig. 19.1
  general principles 16.3.3
  overview Fig. 16.1
Compensation orders
  overview Fig. 22.2
  sentencing options 22.16
  young offenders 26.12
Competence of witnesses
  challenges 16.3.2
  defendants
    general principles 19.2
    overview Fig. 19.1
    prosecution witness 19.2.1
  experts 17.9.1
  general principles 16.3.1
  overview Fig. 16.1
Computer generated documents 18.3.4

Conditional bail 25.2.3
Conditional cautions
  alternatives to prosecution 8.6.2, Fig. 8.1
  enforcement 8.6.4
  failure to comply 8.6.4
  possible conditions 8.6.3
Conditional discharges
  sentencing options 22.17
  young offenders 26.6
Conferences with counsel 14.5.1
Confessions
  challenging admissibility
    oppression 6.5.1
    procedure 6.6
    unfairness 6.5.3
    unreliability 6.5.2
  defined 6.3
  editing 6.7
  evidence obtained by inadmissible confessions 6.8
  hearsay exceptions 18.8.3
  inducements to confess 4.12.2
    oppression 6.5.1
  overview Fig. 6.2
  suspect's rights 6.4
  unlawfully obtained evidence 6.2
  voir dire 6.6
Confidentiality 1.10.1, 1.10.4
Confiscation orders 22.20.2
Conflicts of interest 1.10.4
Confrontation by witnesses 7.5.1
Corroboration
  introduction 17.1
  judicial discretion
    general principles 17.4
    need for jury warnings 17.4
  meaning 17.2
  overview Fig. 17.1
  qualifying requirements 17.5
  requirement for
    generally 17.2.1
    statutory provisions 17.3
  Turnbull guidelines
    excluded cases 17.6.5
    eye-witness identification in good conditions 17.6.1
    eye-witness identification in poor conditions 17.6.2
    failure to give warning 17.6.4
    overview 17.6, Fig. 17.1
    practical considerations 17.6.6
    summary proceedings 17.6.3
Costs
  fair trial, right to 9.2
  legal advice at police station 4.7.4
  professional duty 1.10.3
  prosecution costs orders 22.20.1
  public funding
    acquitted persons 9.13, 14.17
    court representation 9.5
    Defendants' Costs Order 9.13
    disbursements 9.12
    pre-charge advice and assistance 9.4
    recovery of costs 9.13
    representation orders 9.6–9.11
    right to a fair trial (Art 6) 9.2
    wasted costs 9.14
Counsel
  conferences with counsel 14.5.1

preparations for trial 13.12.3
Court of Appeal
  appeals
    from Crown Court
      conviction 23.6
      sentence 23.6, 23.7
    to Supreme Court 23.8
  overview 1.7.7
Courts
  Administrative Court 1.7.6
  Court of Appeal
    appeals 23.6–23.8
    overview 1.7.7
  Crown Court
    appeals 23.3, 23.6, 23.7, Fig. 23.1
    bail applications 10.16, 10.18, 10.19, 10.20, 13.6
    Better Case Management 13.4
    determination of admissibility 2.5
    Digital Case System 13.2
    overview 1.7.5
    preliminary hearings *see* **Crown Court**, preliminary hearings
    sendings to Crown Court 13.1
    sentencing 21.9, 21.15, 26.18
    trials 14.1–14.16
    young offenders 25.3–25.4
  first appearances before magistrates
    case management 9.15.1
    preparations 9.16
  High Court (QBD) 1.7.6
    appeals by case stated 23.4
    bail applications 10.21
    judicial reviews 23.5
    overview 1.7.6
  magistrates' courts
    appeals 23.2–23.4, Fig. 23.1
    first appearances 9.16
    judiciary 1.7.2
    Legal Adviser 1.7.3
    overview 1.7.1
    sending to Crown Court 13.1
    sentencing 11.3.3, 21.11, 21.14.2, 21.14.3, App 3
    summary proceedings 12.1–12.11, Fig. 12.1
    Turnbull guidelines 17.6.3
    young offenders 25.5
  Supreme Court
    appeal jurisdiction 23.8
    overview 1.7.8
  Youth Courts
    absolute discharges 26.7
    age thresholds 26.20
    Anti-Social Behaviour Injunctions (ASBIs) 26.15
    compensation orders 26.12
    conditional discharges 26.6
    Criminal Behaviour Orders (CBOs) 26.15
    dangerous offenders 26.19
    deferred sentences 26.3
    detention and training orders 24.2.1, 26.10
    fines 26.5
    first appearances 25.2
    knife crime prevention orders 26.15

Courts (*Cont.*)
overview 1.7.4
parental bind overs 26.14
parenting orders 26.13
procedure 25.6
referral orders 26.4
reparation orders 26.8
road traffic cases 26.11
sentencing procedure 26.2
trial of young offenders 25.3
victim surcharge 26.16
youth rehabilitation or-
ders 24.2.1, 26.9
Covert images 7.4.5
Credibility
cross-examination 16.9.2
hearsay evidence 18.12.3
unlawfully obtained confessions 6.5.2, Fig. 6.2
Criminal Behaviour Orders (CBOs)
ancillary orders 22.20.3
young offenders 26.15
**Criminal Cases Review Commis-
sion (CCRC)** 23.10
Criminal Justice Boards 24.3
Criminal Procedure Rules
flowchart of procedure Fig. 1.4
human rights 1.8.3
overriding objectives 1.9
professional duties 1.10.6
Cross-examination
attacking credibility 16.9.2
bad character evidence 16.9.4
challenging factual evi-
dence 16.9.1
defence witnesses 14.12
disabilities 16.10
general principles 16.9
overview Fig. 16.2
previous inconsistent
statements 16.9.3
prosecution witnesses 14.10.2
representation orders, need
for 9.7.8
sexual offences 16.12
special measures directions 16.5.6
Crown Court
appeals
against sentence 23.6, 23.7
bail decisions 10.15, 10.16,
10.18
from magistrates' court 23.3
overview Fig. 23.1
to Court of Appeal 23.6
bail 10.16, 10.18, 10.19, 10.20,
13.6
Better Case Management 13.4
determination of admissibility 2.5
Digital Case System 13.2
means testing 9.10
overview 1.7.5
preliminary hearings
applications for dismissal 13.10
disclosure of unused
material 13.9
disclosure of used material 13.8
flowchart of procedure
Fig. 13.1
Further Case Management
Hearing 13.5.3, 13.5.6

Plea and Trial Preparation
Hearing 13.5
preparatory hearings 13.11
preparatory steps 13.7
rulings 13.11.1
sendings to Crown Court
first appearances 13.3, 13.4.1
introduction 13.1
linked co-defendants 13.3.2
related offences 13.3.1
young offenders 13.3.3
sentencing
56-day slip rule 21.15.1
general powers 21.15
guidelines 21.9
mandatory sentences 21.15.2
young offenders 26.18
trials
absence of defendant 14.8.6
arraignment and pleas 14.7
closing speeches 14.13
costs for acquitted defendants 14.17
defence case 14.12
directions to juries 14.14
first day of trial 14.5
indictments 14.2
introduction 14.1
judge-only trials on
indictment 14.19
last-minute checklist 14.4
no case submissions 14.11
plea bargaining 14.6
preliminaries 14.7, 14.8
preparations for 13.12
presentation of evidence 14.10
procedure after verdict 14.16
prosecution appeals 14.18
prosecution case 14.9
summing up 14.14
support for advocate at
trial 14.3, 14.8
verdicts 14.15
young offenders
dangerous offenders 25.3.4–
25.3.5
grave crimes 25.3.1, 25.3.3
jurisdiction over dangerousness 25.3.5
overview 25.3.1
trial 25.3–25.4
Crown Prosecution Service (CPS)
allocation hearing
submission 11.3.4
appeals 14.18, 23.11
assessment of evidence 2.6
bail appeals 10.16
burden of proof
evidential burden of
proof 15.5.1
practical considerations 15.9
Crown Court trials
last-minute checklist 14.4
prosecution case 14.9
rights of appeal 14.18
support for advocate at
trial 14.3, 14.8
decision to charge 8.2.2, Fig. 8.1
procedure 8.2.4
Full Code Test 8.2.3, 8.2.5
introduction 8.1

policies 8.3
pre-trial disclosure
compliance with Crim
PR 8.11.1
unused material 8.12, 13.9
used material 8.11, 13.8
preparations for summary
trial 12.8
preparations for trial
briefing counsel 13.12.3
witnesses 13.12.1
responsibilities 1.6.1, 8.2.2
selection of charges 8.5
sentencing role 21.3
service of case sent bundle App 2
statutory obligations 8.2
threshold test 8.4
unlawfully obtained evi-
dence 6.13.1
witnesses, preliminary duties
towards 16.2
Curfews
bail conditions 10.10
community sentences 22.11.5
young offenders 26.9.7
Custodial sentences
credit for guilty pleas 22.4.3
custody threshold test 22.2.1–
22.2.2
dangerous offenders 22.8
discretionary sentences 22.2–22.6
fixed length sentences 22.7
length 22.4
overview Fig. 22.1
release on licence 22.4.2
suspended sentences 22.5
time spent on remand 22.4.4,
22.12
totality principle 22.4.1
young offenders 22.3, 26.18–
26.19
see also **Detention**
Custody officers
assessment of evidence 4.4.4
detention of young of-
fenders 24.6.2
example record App 2
informing suspects of rights 4.4.2
record keeping 4.4.1
role 4.4
search on arrival 4.4.3
Custody time limits 10.13.1

D

Dangerous offenders
deciding dangerousness 22.8,
25.3.5, 26.19.3
declining jurisdiction over young
persons 25.3.4
sentencing 22.8
statutory powers 22.8
young offenders 25.3.4, 25.3.5,
26.18, 26.19
Deception
statutory discretion to exclude
evidence 6.11.1
unlawfully obtained evidence 6.2
Defence solicitors
allocation hearing submission 11.3.4

assessment of evidence 2.7
attendance notes App 2
burden of proof
  evidential burden of
    proof 15.5.2
  practical considerations 15.9
Crown Court trials
  last-minute checklist 14.4
  support for advocate at
    trial 14.3, 14.8
decision to charge 8.7
disclosure obligations 8.12.4
expert evidence 12.7.3
pre-trial disclosure 8.12.4, 13.9.2
preparations for summary trial 12.7
  assessment of evidence 12.7.7
  attendance of witnesses 12.7.8
  disputed evidence 12.7.9
  expert evidence 12.7.3
  mitigating pleas 12.7.10
  pre-trial disclosure 12.7.4
  statements 12.7.5, 12.7.6
  unused material 12.7.5
  visiting scene 12.7.1
  witnesses 12.7.2
preparations for trial
  briefing counsel 13.12.3
  witnesses 13.12.1
sentencing assessments 21.10
unlawfully obtained
  evidence 6.13.2
witnesses, preliminary duties
  towards 16.2
young offenders 24.7
Defendants
absence
  Crown Court 14.8.6
  magistrates' court 12.4, 12.10
acquittal after trial 14.17
adverse inferences from silence
  advice on whether to
    testify 19.4.1
  statutory provisions 19.4
arraignment in court 14.7
bad character evidence
  attacks on others 19.10
  by agreement 19.7.2
  correction of false impres-
    sions 19.9
  defined 19.6.1
  explanatory evidence 19.7.4
  gateways to admission 19.7
  important issue 19.7.5
  judicial discretion 19.7.1,
    19.7.5, 19.10.2
  miscellaneous matters 19.13
  overview Fig. 19.1
  procedure for admission 19.11
  propensity to commit similar
    offences 19.7.5
  relevance 19.12
  statutory provisions 19.7
  voluntary disclosure 19.7.3
compellability Fig. 19.1
competence
  general principles 19.2
  overview Fig. 19.1
  prosecution witness 19.2.1
Crown Court trials
  no case submissions 14.11
  witnesses 14.12

defence statements App 2
double jeopardy rule 14.17.1
good character 19.5
joinder 12.5, 14.2.4
order of appearance 19.3
proof of evidence App 2
record of interview App 2
special measures directions
  19.3.1
unaware of proceedings 12.4
see also **Suspects**
Defendants' Costs Order 9.13
Deferred sentences 22.14, 26.3
Detention
advising at the police station
  App 1
appropriate adult 4.9
arrival at police station 4.3
custody time limits 10.13.1
review 4.6
  time limits 4.6.1
role of custody officers 4.4
  assessment of evidence 4.4.4
  informing suspects of
    rights 4.4.2
  record keeping 4.4.1
  search on arrival 4.4.3
suspect's rights
  informing someone of
    arrest 4.7.1–4.7.2
  legal advice 4.7.3–4.7.6
time limits 10.13.1
vulnerable persons 4.9
without charge
  beyond 24 hours 4.5.3
  beyond 36 hours 4.5.4
  initial 24 hours 4.5.2
  time limits 4.5.1, Fig. 4.1
young offenders
  appropriate adults 24.6.3
  custody officers 24.6.2
  determining age 24.6.1
  other rights 24.6.4
see also **Custodial sentences**
**Detention and training
  orders** 26.10
Deter Young Offenders Scheme
  24.3
Digital Case System (DCS) 13.2
Direct evidence 2.8.5
Directions
for loss of time 23.6.3
sendings to Crown Court 11.8.3,
  App 2
summary proceedings 12.6.2
to juries 14.14
Discharges
absolute discharge 22.18
conditional discharge 22.17
overview Fig. 22.2
young offenders
  absolute discharge 26.7
  conditional discharge 26.6
Disclosure
advance information App 2
declaration on MG5/Digital Case
  File Form 8.1
defence obligations 8.12.4
either-way offences, application
  for further 13.9.8
expert evidence 17.9.3

extracts from case sent
  bundle App 2
indictable-only offences
  unused material 13.9
  used material 13.8
pre-trial disclosure
  CPS obligations 8.11–8.12
  expert evidence 17.9.3
  flowchart of procedure
    Fig. 8.3
  initial details of prosecution
    case 8.11
  introduction 8.8
  obligations on police 8.10
  overview Fig. 8.2
  public interest immunity 8.14
  Streamlined Disclosure
    Code 8.8
  third parties 8.13
  used and unused material
    distinguished 8.9
preparations for first appearance
  before magistrates 9.16
preparations for summary
  trial 12.7.4
professional conduct 1.10.1,
  1.10.4
prosecutor's continuing
  duty 8.12.5, 13.9.7
public interest immunity 8.14
sendings to Crown Court 11.8.3
Streamlined Disclosure Certificate Form 8.1, 9.15
Streamlined Disclosure Code 8.8
Dismissal of charges 13.10
related charges 13.10.2
Disqualification from driving
young offenders 26.11
District Judges
magistrates' courts 1.7.2
youth courts 1.7.4
DNA evidence
identification evidence 7.13
procedure and presentation 7.13
retention of samples 7.13.1
Dock identifications 7.11
Documentary evidence
defined 2.8.3
hearsay exceptions
  business documents 18.7,
    Fig. 18.1
  computer generated docu-
    ments 18.3.4
  public documents 18.8.2
  memory refreshing 16.8.2,
    Fig. 16.2
Domestic violence 22.20.4
Double jeopardy rule 14.17.1
Drugs
drug rehabilitation requirements 22.11.9
testing at police station 4.14.5
bail 10.6
youth rehabilitation orders
  drug testing 26.9.14
  drug treatment 26.9.13
Duplicity 14.2.2
Duty Solicitor Scheme 9.5.1

E

Education requirements 26.9.16

Either-way offences
allocation guidelines 11.3.1
allocation hearings
ancillary matters 11.8
applications for dismissal 11.9
change of decision 11.10
co-accused 11.7.2–11.7.3
decisions 11.3, 11.3.5, 11.10
defence submission 11.3.4
election for trial 11.4
introduction 11.1
linked offences 11.7.1
particular offences 11.6
prosecution submission 11.3.4
sending to Crown Court 11.7
special procedure for criminal
damage 11.5
statutory factors 11.3.2
bail 11.8.1
classification 1.5, 1.5.2
co-accused 11.7.2–11.7.3
committal for sentencing 21.14.3
directions 11.8.3
disclosure 11.8.3
introduction 11.1
magistrates' court accepts
jurisdiction 11.3.5
magistrates' court declines
jurisdiction 11.3.5
plea before venue 11.2
pre-trial disclosure 11.2
flowchart of procedure Fig. 8.3
overview Fig. 8.2
procedural flowchart Fig. 1.2
representation orders 9.10.1,
11.8.2
sentencing powers 11.3.3
standard case progression
directions 11.8.3
summary trial merits 11.4.2
trial on indictment merits 11.4.1
Election for trial
allocation proceedings 11.4
Electronic monitoring 26.9.11
Entrapment
admissibility of evidence 6.11.3
private entrapment 6.11.3
unlawfully obtained evidence 6.2
Entry powers
powers of entry and search 3.9.4
preserved powers 3.9.7
Environment Agency 1.6.1
Evidence
abuse of process 6.12
assessment
defence solicitors 2.7
role of CPS 2.6
challenging unlawfully and unfairly obtained evidence
abuse of process 6.12
challenging 'other' evidence 6.9
common law discretion 6.10
introduction 6.1
meaning and scope 6.2
oppression 6.5.1
overview Fig. 6.1
practical considerations 6.13
procedure 6.6
statutory discretion 6.11
statutory provisions 6.5
suspect's rights 6.4

unfairness 6.5.3
unreliability 6.5.2
circumstantial evidence 2.8.5
core concepts
admissibility 2.4.2
conclusions 2.10
relevance 2.4.1
weight 2.4.3
Crown Court trial 14.10
determining admissibility 2.5
direct evidence 2.8.5
documentary evidence 2.8.3
importance of 'big picture' 2.9
importance of rules 2.1
opinion evidence 2.8.2
oral testimony 2.8.1
overview Fig. 2.1
facts in issue 2.3
purpose of rules 2.2
police 8.10
preparations for summary trial
Crown Prosecution Service
(CPS) 12.8
defence solicitors 12.7.7
public interest immunity 8.14
real evidence 2.8.4
summing up 14.14
types 2.8
weight of evidence 2.4.3
withholding 8.14
see also **Burden of proof;**
Character evidence;
Confessions; Disclo-
sure; Hearsay evidence;
Identification; Witnesses
Evidential burden of proof
defendants 15.5.2
example 15.6
overview Fig. 15.1
prosecution 15.5.1
Examination-in-chief
defence witnesses 14.12
general principles 16.8
leading questions 16.8.1
overview Fig. 16.2
prosecution witnesses 14.10.1
special measures directions 16.5.5
Exclusion requirements 22.11.6,
26.9.8
Expert witnesses
competence 17.9.1
DNA profiling 7.13
duties to court 17.9.2
facial mapping 7.14
identification evidence 7.13–7.14
meaning 17.9.1
practical considerations 17.10
pre-trial disclosure 17.9.3
preparations for summary
trial 12.7.3
reports 17.9.4
scope 17.9
Eye-witness identification
dangers 7.2
how obtained 7.3
Turnbull guidelines
in good conditions 17.6.1
in poor conditions 17.6.2

F

Facial mapping 7.14

Facts in issue 2.3, Fig. 2.1
Fair trial *see* **Right to a fair trial**
(Art 6)
Family life, right to respect for
see **Right to respect for**
private and family life
(Art 8)
Fines
general powers 22.15
overview Fig. 22.2
victim surcharges 22.15.1, 26.16
young offenders 26.5
Fingerprints
following arrest 4.1
identification evidence 7.12.2
Footwear identification 7.12.2
Forensic evidence
identification procedures
DNA evidence 7.13
fingerprints and foot-
wear 7.12.2
importance 7.12.1
intimate samples 7.12.4
non-intimate samples 7.12.3
Forfeiture orders 22.20.2
Formal admissions 15.8
Fostering requirement 26.9.18
Full Code Test 8.2.5
Funding *see* **Public funding**
Further Case Management
Hearings 13.5.3, 13.5.6

G

GAP *see* **Guilty Anticipated Plea**
Hearings
Good character evidence
defendants 19.5
overview Fig. 19.1
Group identification
formal procedures 7.7.3
types of procedure 7.5.1
Guilty Anticipated Plea
Hearings 9.15
disclosure Form 8.1, 9.15
Guilty pleas
at Plea and Trial Preparation
Hearing 13.4.1, 13.5.3
basis of plea 21.4.3
before Plea and Trial Preparation
Hearing 13.5.2
change of plea 14.7.3
community sentences 22.12
Crown Court procedure
changes of plea 14.7.3
procedure following 14.7.2
unambiguous and volun-
tary 14.7.1
custodial sentences, effect
on 22.4.3
legal advice 12.6
online conviction procedure 12.2
plea before venue 11.2.2
post, by 12.3
professional duties 1.10.3
sentencing
custodial sentences, effect
on 22.4.3
discount 21.13
overview Fig. 21.1
procedure 21.4.2, Fig. 21.1
summary offences